ISLAM AND THE WEST

ناقل الكفـــر ليس بكافـــر

———

nulla falsa doctrina est
quae aliquid veritatis non immisceat

ISLAM
AND
THE
WEST

The Making of an Image

NORMAN
DANIEL

at the University Press
EDINBURGH

© Norman Daniel 1960, 1962, 1966
EDINBURGH UNIVERSITY PRESS
George Square Edinburgh 8
North America
Aldine Publishing Company
320 West Adams Street, Chicago
Australia & New Zealand
Hodder & Stoughton Ltd
Africa, P. C. Manaktala & Sons Private Ltd
Far East, M. Graham Brash & Son

First published 1960
Reprinted 1962, 1966

Printed in Great Britain by
Robert Cunningham and Sons Ltd
Alva, Scotland

Foreword

I HOPE that Muslim readers will not be scandalised by some of the things in this book, or consider that I have been wrong to revive the memory of, among other things, certain silly and unpleasant libels of their religion and their Prophet. My primary purpose has been the scientific one of establishing a series of facts, and this I believe to need no justification. My secondary purpose has been (in chapters VIII and IX) to see what is implied by this unpleasantness and ignorance in men's attitudes towards those they suppose to be their enemies. Both these aims involve asking Europeans to recognise how many erroneous ideas their civilisation has in the past accepted; but Muslims, on their side, may suspect that they themselves have done (*mutatis mutandis*) very much the same, although this is not my subject. My final chapter is concerned, not to bring up to date the whole history of the European attitude to Islam since 1350, but to bring out particular aspects of post-mediaeval development which may help Europeans and Muslims alike to identify prejudices which still, after so many centuries, affect European attitudes; and which do so, despite the great contemporary improvement in understanding, on which many Muslims – recently, for example, the editor of the *Islamic Review* – have remarked.

I should like to use this opportunity to acknowledge my debt to those who were my teachers: before the war, my tutor, Mr John Prestwich, of the Queen's College, Oxford; after the war, the Rev Dr W. Montgomery Watt, of the University of Edinburgh, the supervisor of my doctoral thesis; and, over many years, my friend, the Rev Gervase Mathew, o.p. To Dr Hugo Buchthal I owe it that I was first interested in my subject, and from Archbishop David Mathew I have received valuable insights into the issues involved. It will be clear to the reader how much my work has benefited from that of Mademoiselle M. Th. d'Alverny, and I should like to thank her for many kindnesses, and especially for her guidance among the manuscripts that are in her care. I have been fortunate to have opportunities to discuss particular points of history or theology with the Very Rev Dr Daniel Callus, o.p., the R.P. Raymond Charbonnier, o.c.d., Dr Abdul Aziz al-Duri, Dr Umar Farukh, Monsieur Louis Gardet, Professor Denys Hay,

Mr R. W. Highwood, the Revd Dr R. J. McCarthy, s.j., Dr N. A. R. MacKay, Dr Selim al-Nuaimi, Mr W. A. Pantin, Dr Muhammad Badi Sharif and Sayid Tawfik Wahbi; also Dr Saleh Shamma, to whom I am grateful moreover for his help in the revision of certain passages, and the Revd Professor Norman Porteous, to whom I am additionally indebted for his help and encouragement over publication. I have received valuable advice and information on particular points from Dr P. Cachia, Dr L. P. Harvey, Dr P. M. Holt, Dr Georg Krotkoff, Dr Shamoon Lokhand-walla, Mr J. R. Walsh and my wife. None of the people whom I have mentioned bears the slightest responsibility for any faults in my work or for any opinions I express or imply. I am very grateful for the practical help I have received from my wife, from my former colleagues in the British Council in Edinburgh, and from friends in France and Britain. I am under a great obligation to the Convener and Committee of the Edinburgh University Press, and in particular to the Secretary and his staff. I should like also to thank the staff of Edinburgh University Library, the National Library of Scotland, the Bodleian Library, the Cambridge University Library, the British Museum, the Bibliothèque Nationale and the London Library for their help on many occasions; and the authorities of those same libraries, and also of the Austrian National Library, the Bavarian State Library, Tübingen University Library (in charge of Berlin manuscripts), the National Library, Madrid, and the Vatican Library for providing microfilm of books or manuscripts. Finally, I am grateful for permission to reproduce illustrations from books or manuscripts in Edinburgh University Library, the National Library of Scotland, the Bibliothèque Nationale and the Bibliothèque de l'Arsenal.

NOTE TO THE 1966 EDITION

Since this book was completed in its present form, R. Southern's lectures, *Western Views of Islam in the Middle Ages*, have appeared, and supplement it chiefly for the earlier and later Middle Ages. His treatment of Wycliffe and Luther is particularly interesting. M. Th. d'Alverny's *La Connaissance de l'Islam en Occident du IXe au milieu du XIIe siècle* is the best guide to her period, and as full as is possible in a single lecture, with detailed bibliographical notes. M. C. Diaz y Diaz of Salamanca has announced a manu-script containing a Visigothic text, and Mademoiselle d'Alverny thinks that this is likely to shed light on the sources of the *Liber Nicholay*; she hopes shortly to publish the text of the latter. The whole of Peter the Venerable's personal contribution to the Cluniac corpus has been published by J. Kritzeck (*Peter the Venerable and Islam*), with introductory matter to interest the general reader as well as the specialist. A. Cutler's article, *Who was the 'Monk of France' and when did he write?* argues that the author of the Christian Letter published by D. M. Dunlop in his *Christian Mission to Spain in the 11th Century* was Abbot Hugh of Cluny. His interesting suggestion that there was a considerable school of Islamic studies in Cluny in the eleventh century must remain unconfirmed unless further evidence is found; the character of the Cluniac activity of the century following implies that at that date there were no materials in Cluny itself for such studies.

Contents

LIST OF PLATES

Introduction

THE earliest Christian reactions to Islam were something like those of much more recent date. The tradition has been continuous and it is still alive. There has been a natural variety within the wider unity of that tradition, and the European West has long had its own characteristic view, which was formed in the two centuries or so after 1100, and which has been modified only slowly since. One chief reason for continuity has been, not only the normal passage of ideas from one author to the next, but the constant nature of the problem. The points in which Islam and Christianity differ have not changed, so that Christians have always tended to make the same criticisms; and even when, in relatively modern times, some authors have self-consciously tried to emancipate themselves from Christian attitudes, they have not generally been as successful as they thought themselves. My book describes the formation of the Western Christian attitude and ends with a brief survey of its later development.

Islam and Christianity are concerned apparently with much the same themes; fundamentally, they differ about the means that God has used to reveal Himself. They differ about the nature of revelation itself; about the nature of the revelation which they agree was made by Christ; and about the nature of the revelation which only Muslims believe was made through Muhammad. The field of disagreement involves such questions as the character of prophethood, of the Trinity of Persons in the Godhead, and of the Incarnation. Finally, there are questions deriving from the prophethood of Muhammad. What was the character of the Law revealed to him? Was it a fiction composed to suit the immediate needs and desires of Muhammad, of his Companions and of the Arabs generally? Many Christians, and many non-Christians, have thought so. Did it take the shape it did because it was calculated as a demonstration of force, to achieve the astonishing political and military success which within one generation Islam did achieve? Was it, similarly, calculated to indulge its followers, allowing in personal morality what Christianity forbade? It was inevitable that Christians would ask these questions.

1

They did not ask them disinterestedly or with detachment. After the first conquests, Christians were cut off from Muslims by the frontiers of the Byzantine Empire and the Cordova Caliphate. Even when the two religions shared territory or when Christians lived under Islamic rule, in Spain, Egypt, Syria and Iraq especially, they lived separately, and never intermingled as different denominations intermingle in Europe to-day. Men seem to take it for granted that an alien society is dangerous, if not hostile, and the spasmodic outbreak of warfare between Islam and Christendom throughout their history has been one manifestation of this. Apparently, under the pressure of their sense of danger, whether real or imagined, a deformed image of their enemy's beliefs takes shape in men's minds. By misapprehension and misrepresentation an idea of the beliefs and practices of one society can pass into the accepted myths of another society in a form so distorted that its relation to the original facts is sometimes barely discernible. Doctrines that are the expression of the spiritual outlook of an enemy are interpreted ungenerously and with prejudice, and even facts are modified – and in good faith – to suit the interpretation. In this way is constituted a body of belief about what another group of people believes. A 'real truth' is identified; this is something that contrasts with what the enemy say they believe; they must not be allowed to speak for themselves. This doctrine about doctrine is widely repeated, and confirmed by repetition in slightly varying forms. The experts, perhaps because their proximity to the facts is a constant stimulus to their zeal, contribute most to the process, and they are themselves wholly convinced by it.

This process began among the Greeks whom the Arab armies conquered when they occupied Syria, permanently as it proved, but probably not as the first generations of Greek-speaking Syrians under the Umayyads expected. The Oriental polemic tradition gradually divided; among the Christians living under Islamic rule there grew up an Arabic literature, which enjoyed periods of greater and less freedom and prosperity, and which was inclined to apocalyptic vision; and a Byzantine polemic developed which was freer to express its open hostility, but, at the same time, more academic. The 'war psychosis' of Christian writers was not, however, less among Christians who were living under Islamic rule; who were tolerated, but as inferior citizens; who were often excluded from the confidence of their rulers, and who were always at some disadvantage, if only through their perpetual uncertainty about the future. In a world in which every man was dependent on the favour of his rulers, such as was the urban society of Iraq and Syria under the Umayyads and 'Abbāsids, and such as had been that same urban society under the Seleucids and the

Romans, there was nothing desperate, or even unusual in the situation of Christians – and Jews – as clients; but, as the years passed, there was undoubtedly an increasing bitterness. The ideas of Islam which Christians first formed under these conditions were absorbed and adapted by the Latin West; and it is the creation of a canon of what (according to the Latins) Muslims believe and do that is the subject of the present study. The integrated view thus created was purely European; but it had come to the Latins through their capacity to make the traditions of Greeks, of Arab Christians and, in Spain, of Mozarabs, their own.

Christian reactions to Islam are documented from an early date. A formula for its abjuration by converts to Christianity has reasonably been thought to date from the first generations after the rise of Islam, and is related to the work of St John of Damascus, himself born about fifty years after the Hijrah.[1] The formula takes an unusually severe attitude in condemning whatever a Muslim believes, including the whole of what he believes about God and about Christ, although some of that is true according to the Christian faith. This may well be due to its special purpose. It also requires what is apparently abjuration of pagan beliefs held by Arabs before they became Muslims; Cumont points out that it is not necessary to suppose that these pagan beliefs were thought still to be actually part of Islamic doctrine, and it is true that Islam at that date may have seemed to overcivilised Syrian-Greek ecclesiastics to be only a temporary manifestation by simple desert-dwellers apt to revert to ancient superstition. The formula, however, definitely confused Islam itself with pre-Islamic paganism, and associated an idol of 'Aphrodite' with the Ka'bah; there is no suggestion that such an idol had been removed.[2] The formula's editor, Montet, describes it well when he calls it 'at once exact and mistaken'. It reveals a detailed knowledge of some of the Qur'ān and of early Islamic history; Cumont supposes that it shared a common source with St John of Damascus; if so, the original document would date almost from the first years of the conquest.

St John was the real founder of the Christian tradition. He saw some significance – what significance is not clear – in the idolatrous worship practised by the Arabs before the 'false prophecy' of Muhammad, but he concentrated his attention on other points, which after him were taken up and developed further; his were attitudes which were to become customary, but which he set on their way. He stated the Islamic doctrine of Christ neatly, at the beginning of the relevant section of his *de haeresibus*.[3] Most important, he began the long tradition of arguing about the Persons of the Godhead in the context of Qur'anic Christology, especially in his *Dialexis*, which appears to be a guide to disputation with Muslims; he seems to have conceived a situation where the Christian is basically defensive, but where he is recommended to retaliate vigorously; does the Muslim, for example, suppose the Word and Spirit of God to be created or uncreated? Does he suppose that there was a time when God was wordless and spiritless? This technique of argument set the tradition of dialectic treatment of the theme; it was really the application to Muslims of the technique used among Christians themselves; it had established heresy and orthodoxy with the finest of definitions, but it was too alien from Islam to fulfil this new function effectively. Sometimes St John's attitude was realistic; in the case of the argument I have just quoted he expected the Muslim to return to the attack by asking if all God's words were uncreated; he also expected that it would be necessary to explain such words, characteristic of Christian Scriptural exegesis, as *tropological*. Yet he was also unrealistic or inexperienced enough to imagine that a Muslim might argue on the basis of the Christian Scriptural canon, and might even quote Jeremias. This delusion remained with Christians across the centuries. St John also introduced other elements that would long survive: he descended to ridicule, for example, of what he mistakenly took to be Qur'anic belief, the *camel of God*, in a petty way; and he began the long tradition o attacking Muhammad for bringing in God – simulating revelation – in order to justify his own sexual indulgence, instancing the story of Zayd and Zaynab, which would become a classic Christian theme.[4] He also asserted that Muhammad made up his doctrine from the Old and New Testaments on the advice of an Arian monk who instructed him. All these ideas were to be important in later Christian polemic.

St John probably never imagined that Islam would last for long; just as there are elderly men of religion alive to-day who do not believe that in Communism they observe any but a temporary phenomenon. They may be right or wrong; we now know that the Greeks were wrong about Islam. As Islam became more firmly established and the Christians increasingly a minority, as Islamic beliefs became better known and were more clearly defined and integrated for an outsider to see, the polemic against Islam became more specialised. The tradition of Trinitarian argument is well exemplified in Yaḥyā ibn 'Adi, who wrote in Arabic in the tenth century, and who in many ways seems to be an oriental Ramon Lull, anxious to prove the Trinity by natural reasons alone; he at least avoided the contrary mistake of citing Scripture to Muslims who consider the canonical text corrupt.[5] There was a body of literature which arose out of the story of Baḥīrā, who in the earliest

Muslim legend recognised the young Muhammad and foretold his destiny.[6] Baḥīrā is presumably the source of the 'Arian monk' spoken of by St John Damascene, who later became the *Sergius* (generally a Nestorian) of Byzantine and Western legend, the mysterious teacher of Muhammad (who appears to be referred to in Q.xvi.105).[7] Among Arabic-speaking Christians a whole literature on this theme developed; it was apocalyptic, because it was concerned with prophecies of the end of the reign of the Arabs; it was also polemic and retrospective, describing how Baḥīrā was forced to reveal the Christian mysteries to Muhammad, how the people were deceived by a cow that was supposed to have come from Heaven, bearing the Qur'ān on her horns; it was a literature that attacked the person, history and character of the Prophet.[8] In the Byzantine polemic of Nicetas of Byzantium, in the ninth century, we meet a different tradition, less febrile but inclined to a niggling pettiness, and a dialectical subtlety that one would suppose could convince nobody, and least of all a Muslim; this sort of polemic was written as a philosophical exercise and sport. The greatest part of his *Anatrope* is devoted to picking piecemeal at the Qur'ān; it does not even try to understand the Qur'ān before refuting it. Nicetas seems to argue in one chapter that Muhammad's 'admission' of some things out of Scripture implies acceptance of Scripture, and that since he also asserts different things of his own invention of the same God, he makes God either not to exist or to be changeable; the God he speaks of does not accept the Christian Law, and so cannot be the true God; it follows that the God of Muhammad is really a devil. It is difficult to be patient with much of this. The same author's *Ekthesis Kataskeuastike* is less disagreeable; it is defensive in form, but once again far too abstract and subtle to interest any reader but a Greek ecclesiastic of that age.[9] The *Anatrope*, at least, compares ill with so late a writer as Euthemius Zigabenus, in the Comnenan period, whose Trinitarian argument, in his *Panoplia Dogmatike*, though doubtless unimpressive to a Muslim with a wholly different background, is dignified, and as calm and charitable in tone as the work of St John of Damascus, by which he was influenced.[10]

Meanwhile, the Islamic victories in the West had not produced a Christian literature comparable to that of the Christian Arabs. Mozarabs were silent and untheological, except for the episode of the Martyrs' Movement, when the former epithet at least was not deserved. The brief literature of the Movement is not impressive and it is important only as illustrating the idea of Christians then current; the story of Muhammad recounted by St Eulogius in his *Liber Apologeticus Martyrum* is couched in savage language, and varies between the ridiculously inaccurate and the unpleasantly absurd. Nevertheless, it is told with economy and, in comparison with some Christian anti-Islamic polemic, its allegations are even – in places – sober. One of its several nastier absurdities is the notion that Muhammad expected to rise again on the third day after his death; in the Middle Ages this reappeared in the very slightly more reasonable version that he expected his body to be carried to Heaven by angels.[11] On the whole, the Martyrs' Movement has no close literary ties with later Western writers.

All these strands were brought together when the West began to form its own canon of what Islam is and what Muhammad had been. The most important sources of information reached Latin Europe by way of Spain. One of the most influential was the Arabic *Risālah*, or *Apology*, attributed to 'Abd al-Masīḥ ibn Isḥāq al-Kindi, a work of which the authorship (which is pseudonymous) and dating are still in dispute, but which is certainly earlier than the eleventh century.[12] The apparent polemic utility and the authenticity of the information of this work are so great that it was republished in the nineteenth century in London, for the use of Missions, and Muir himself shortly after brought out a summarised translation. Its reputation was not less in the Middle Ages, and it was translated by Peter of Toledo, as part of the Cluniac corpus of translations commissioned by Peter the Venerable, and very long extracts were given still wider publicity by their inclusion in Vincent de Beauvais' *Speculum Historiale*. The chief characteristics of this work are its tendency to Scriptural and Trinitarian discussion (aspects neglected both by Vincent and by Muir) and its detailed stress on those events in the Prophet's life which reveal him as sexually self-indulgent and as a murderer, if presented in the way this author presents them; it also criticises the religious practice of Islam, attacks the doctrine of the Qur'ān, especially the teaching of the holy war, jihād, and defends the integrity of the Scriptural text. Another important work, because it was the greatest single influence upon Ricoldo da Monte Croce, himself extremely influential in the subsequent history of anti-Islamic polemic, not because of its own wide distribution, was the *Contrarietas elfolica*. This work is known to us only in a poor manuscript of the late sixteenth century, and in its Latin translation by Mark of Toledo, not in any Arabic original; I suggest that it may be, not what it claims to be, the work of a Muslim convert to Christianity, but an exercise by a Mozarab polemist. This, and the translations of the Qur'ān by Robert of Ketton and Mark of Toledo, of which the former belongs to the Cluniac corpus; and also the other Cluniac translations, of which the most influential was the *de doctrina Machometi*, together with the often erudite marginal annotations to Ketton's Qur'ān: all these, which are dis-

cussed by M. T. d'Alverny in her very important articles to which
I refer below, constitute a large body of material that was made
available to the West in a relatively short period.[13] Mark of
Toledo's translation of ibn Tūmart was perhaps not influential;
much more so was the earlier work of the converted Jew Pedro de
Alfonso, to whom the Middle Ages owed much of their knowledge
of Islam. His *Dialogi*, written after his conversion in 1106 and
before his death in 1110, devote one entire dialogue to polemic
against Islam which is careful to separate the factual element from
the critical; it is precisely this that the Risālah failed to do. The
material translated by Alfonso Buenhombre, which purports to be
written by a converted Jewish rabbi, reached the Latin West only
in the mid-fourteenth century, by which time the main canon had
been established. This is not a complete list of the sources that
contributed to the Western literature of this subject. The kitāb
al-mi'raj[14] influenced, not only ideas of religion, but literary forms.
The Cluniac *summula* acknowledges its debt to the translation of
the *Chronographica* of Theophanes by Anastasius the Roman
Librarian, and the circulation of legends of an infinite variety
testify to our failure to identify a large number of sources. In the
course of the thirteenth century Arabic sources became directly
available to a few writers, to the Dominican schools associated
with Ramón Martí, to San Pedro Pascual and to Ramón Lull. As
we consider the literature of the West we shall see the recurrence
of all the traditional Christian themes.

2. THE LIMITS SET TO THE PRESENT WORK

To sum up the period with which I am concerned, we may say
that at the beginning of the twelfth century Islam began to be
treated seriously in works written in the West. Some of these
were treatises wholly or largely concerned with Islam, and some
dealt with the subject only incidentally. By the end of the thirteenth
century there was a considerable literature, and by the middle of
the fourteenth the ideas that it expressed were widespread. In
Britain, for example, Matthew Paris made use of important
material in the thirteenth century, but in the fourteenth Higden
and Mandeville gave material of similar importance a still greater
circulation. In the East, this period covers the whole history of
the Latin States, together with that of practical re-adjustment to
their loss, which may be said to be marked by the establishment
of the Franciscan guardianship of Terra Santa and by the resump-
tion of trade with the Islamic powers, under licence. In Spain, the
period includes the greater part of Murābit, and the whole of
Muwaḥḥid rule, as well as the chief effort of actual Reconquest,
and also a period of assimilation of the conquered areas. The

middle of the fourteenth century is an arbitrary but convenient date to stop detailed investigation; it allows time for the consequences of the military events of the thirteenth to appear.

This, then, is the period with which I am concerned, and my subject is the absorption of Christian traditions of Islam already existing, and their development into a new body of opinion. At a time when the Byzantine Empire was politically and militarily infirm, and was itself the object of Western aggression and Western polemic, when the Muslims were at many points upon the frontiers of Latin Christendom, and shared with Christendom the inland sea, the deformed image of Islam was established in the conscious European mind. It is this deformed image that I hope to delineate, in the process of becoming one of the dogmas of Christian society; not, of course, of the Christian Church as such, but (in variant forms) of most of its members. I wish also to examine some of the reasons that caused this image of Islam to be deformed, rather than reasonably accurate, as it might equally well have been; that led men to prefer, sometimes nonsensical, and often unpleasant and untrue versions of the history of Muhammad and of the tenets and practices of Islam; and that did so even when sound information was available and when better might easily have been obtained. I wish also to try to discover what purpose and motives formed the communal opinion thus established; and to clarify the function served by such communal opinion. Finally I wish to survey briefly the subsequent history of the now firmly established canon of opinion, which survived long unshaken, which did not fail to influence the very people who ultimately succeeded in shaking it, and which is still alive to-day. In a very few concluding notes I hope to suggest the changes in the Christian position that have come about very recently, so that a scientific-atheist in the U.S.S.R. now adopts much of the mediaeval attitude, while Christians at last find themselves freed to develop something new; not, I suggest, something wholly new, but something that builds upon the work done in the Middle Ages and after, while giving up the old pejorative tone; that aims to illuminate and to fructify the relations of Christians with Muslims, and not to destroy understanding through hatred or malice or fear.

I have limited my theme in the body of my book to the representation – and misrepresentation – of Islam in the period I have chosen; I have been concerned with the attitudes and the opinions of Latin Christians, and not primarily with the data available to them. On the other hand, the use that they made of their data has been treated as a valuable indication of their attitudes. What an author omits or asserts sometimes allows us to recognise that he has made a deliberate choice between alternative data, perhaps that he has positively rejected accurate knowledge, or shown a preference for the absurd. Fantasies to which ignorance, or part-ignorance, of Islam gave rise are interesting, but the use to which authentic information was put is more so. Broadly, the same attitude underlay both, but the detailed study of real facts at that time seemed to produce convincing and circumstantial evidence highly suitable to serve polemic ends. The general attitude of educated men was informed and supported by the Islamic experts of the day.

My subject is as strictly confined to matters of religion as I can make it. I have tried wholly to exclude philosophical questions, such as those that derive from Averroism, because the inter-relation of what is specifically Islamic and what is specifically Christian in the transmission of philosophical thought from the one society to the other is an immense, and immensely difficult, subject needing special and separate attention. Equally I have not attempted to consider the cultural relations of the two societies, for example in the field of scientific translations, or in that of art and architecture, or in any other aspect than religion; still less have I attempted to survey their cultural relations as a whole. I have taken religion in a narrow and strict sense to mean both revelation and the duties laid upon men by revelation, and even within the field of religion I have had to confine myself inside these limits. I have excluded all consideration of mysticism and of that speculative theology which is on the borders of philosophy. I have not been concerned with such men as al-Ghazālī or ibn al-ʿArabi. On the other hand, I have dealt with sources of information that I could identify and that were relevant to my purpose. I have indi-cated indebtedness by Latin authors to authentic Arab and Muslim documents, such as ibn Isḥāq or al-Bukhārī, wherever I could; and also to the less authoritative sources that I have mentioned above. This I have done in order to try to determine the attitude of a Latin writer to his material; but in doing so I have not attempted to write a literary history, nor have I given any account of the relationships between writers, except in instances where it illu-mines their treatment of their data to do so.

I am aware that the subject, even within the limits indicated, is not as simple as I may have seemed to suggest. The issue was not a straightforward one between orthodox Christianity and orthodox Islam. There were important Jewish communities in Spain, and Jewish information from this source may have reached Christians at different points in Europe which Jewish travellers visited. There were heretical communities both in Islam and in Christendom. Again, in Spain and in Syria alike Christians acquired ideas at a popular level from oral Islamic sources which may sometimes have been orthodox and misunderstood; which may have been heretical, and either understood more or less correctly, or, more probably, again completely misunderstood; or which may simply have been ignorant of orthodox doctrine. Our literary sources habitually prefer literary authority for what they say, but we find in them some evidence of ideas of Islam derived from the superstitious Muslim proletariat, rather than from men of education; and such ideas may have been interchanged orally on a much larger scale. Only some of this material is likely to have reached written expression quickly, and much may never have done so at all. To evaluate these broad influences and confused cross-currents may not be possible with the material known to us, and it is certainly outside my present capacity and purpose.

I have confined myself to a large but definable body of written sources. I have avoided speculation about the popular thought of uninformed Europe. The masses tend always to be aggressive and xenophobe in their social attitudes; they have a sense of solidarity which is based upon suspicion of the 'enemies of the people'. The identification of these enemies is not always rational, and revolutionary leadership to-day seeks to guide it. The *Tafurs* of the First Crusade, and the mobs of Pastoureaux who slaughtered Jews, clergy and wealthy men, although they had originally set out on a Crusade against Islam, lacked discriminating leadership.[15] The differences between the attitudes of the ruling classes and the ruled at that date could easily be exaggerated; the association of Jew with Muslim as enemy of Christ, for example, was both popular and canonical. Nevertheless, the law was rational; and some feudal lords were more civilised, some clerics more reflective, so that they had knowledge and a degree of tolerance. It is literate opinion that provides the material of this book; it is not a study of the psychology of the crowd, although it studies group consciousness in an intellectual élite.

3. SOME BIBLIOGRAPHICAL NOTES

The recent revival of interest in this field of study seems to date from the publication of Ugo Monneret de Villard's *Studio dell' Islam in Europa* in 1944. This scholar's work ranged widely in search of material and it is an invaluable guide. He was not greatly interested in the opinions expressed by mediaeval writers and was more concerned with historical, geographical and linguistic aspects. Miss d'Alverny thereupon published two works of crucial importance. In the first she closely examined a key subject – the Toletano-Cluniac corpus – and she also announced her discovery of a later Toledan school. In the second she carried the latter question very much further and widened the scope of her enquiries.

The material to which she has drawn attention profoundly affects our knowledge of the sources of Western literature about Islam. It is not only that the translations of Mark of Toledo's which she has identified, publishing some, are inherently both interesting and important, but that the light she has shed upon Ricoldo's sources wholly changes our estimate of that crucial figure.

Her work was revolutionary, and Monneret de Villard was unfortunate enough to publish his books too early to benefit from it. Much that he says, not only in the book to which I have referred, but also in his study devoted to Ricoldo, is in consequence outdated. Miss d'Alverny incidentally cleared away a number of accumulated misconceptions, which dated from Père Mandonnet's pioneer work upon the subject, and which Monneret de Villard did not tackle, helping, indeed, to perpetuate them. The idea that the *summula* (part of the Cluniac corpus) could be a translation from an Arabic original was natural in a scholar who was in no sense an orientalist, as was the case with Mandonnet; but no one could have maintained it who had any knowledge of the East and gave it any attention at all. This one example will suffice. It is not now possible to work in this field except on a basis of what Miss d'Alverny has established. Sweetman in England has recently paraphrased much of Monneret de Villard's book of 1944, but unfortunately he does not seem to have made use of later work done on the subject, and he ignores Miss d'Alverny's. This invalidates much that he has to say on Latin treatment of Islam; he repeats a number of mistakes that had already been passed from one writer to another, and he initiates some of his own. In fairness it should be said that his intention is rather oecumenical than scholarly, and that my criticisms do not affect one way or another the value of his work from the point of view of the relation between Christian and Islamic theology which is his primary interest.

In the meantime E. Cerulli and J. M. Munoz published their editions of the *Liber Scalae Machometi*, the translations of the kitāb al-mi'raj, or account of Muhammad's Night Journey to Heaven, which Asin identified as a principal source of the *Divine Comedy*. Although it was to shed light upon Dante's sources that both these scholars undertook their work, both published a considerable quantity of other material, chiefly relating to Islamic concepts of Heaven.

It remains true, in spite of all this work already done, that a great deal of doubt still attaches to the authorship of most of the written sources of Latin knowledge of Islam in the period. This is true even of the most influential of all, the Risālah, to which I have already referred; but it is not in question that its author was an oriental Christian. Godfrey of Viterbo and the *scriptum Gregorio nono missum* (which was incorporated into the St Albans Chronicle by Matthew Paris, and to which I refer for convenience as the Gregorian Report) copy some common source, on which Jacques de Vitry also depends, often closely; but what this was is quite uncertain. It does closely resemble the Risālah, and may even have been a portion of that work, or a version of a part of it; but the failure of those who used it to make use of much Risālah material that would certainly have interested them makes it highly improbable that they knew a complete version. There are, moreover, discrepancies of detail. The missing source may only have been a work generally inspired by, or just similar to, the Risālah.

There is very little to be said upon the *Contrarietas* apart from what Miss d'Alverny has already said; but I should like to add a few tentative suggestions. Its case may be similar to that of the Risālah and other examples of Oriental Christian polemic. The Risālah's arguments appear and reappear in different forms in different Christian works, so that it seems safe only to speak of a living tradition of Oriental Christian polemic in which many authors (including Latin authors) drew, to which they in turn contributed, and of which the Risālah is itself perhaps only one important example. In the same way the *Contrarietas* may have drawn upon a living and oral tradition among the Mozarabs, whose contribution to anti-Islamic polemic, as I have already remarked, is unexpectedly small. The *Contrarietas* claims to be written by a convert from Islam, but it seems to me to be possible that it is really by a Christian who wished to give it greater authority by such a fictional claim. It is often difficult to imagine that a convert, however much he hated his old religion, could take just the line that the author of this work takes; and the Mecca pilgrimage that he claims to have made is particularly unconvincing. Pedro de Alfonso again and again reminds us by something that he says that he was once a Jew; there is nothing comparable in this other case. On the other hand, this author's knowledge of the Qur'ān was sound and we must suppose him at least to have lived for many years among Muslims on reasonable terms of intimacy.

Pedro de Alfonso's own sources are not in doubt. We may assume that it was normal for well-informed Jewish circles in Spain to know a good deal about Islam. Written sources for his statements are not known. In contrast to this, much doubt attaches to the origin of what I have called the 'Corozan' story. This is the very popular legend by which Muhammad married the 'lady' of a 'province' called Corozan; in this story he was a skilled magician. The earliest version of this known to me is that of Hugh of Fleury. There is no reason to doubt the origin of the account that claims to have been sent to Innocent III by the Latin Patriarch of Jerusalem, Haymar; see my bibliography under *Scripta domino Pp. Innocento . . . missa.* The account called the *libellus in partibus trans-marinis de Machometi fallaciis* by Vincent de Beauvais is connected with the account that begins *Bonifacii papae temporibus*; there is no reason not to think that this statement, which relates the false miracles of the ox with the Qur'ān in its horns, and the dove that whispers, as messenger from God, in Muhammad's ear, originates as Vincent says in Syria, among Christian Arabs. The present writer has heard equally strange stories on the same subject from the same source.

I have used the name *quadruplex reprobatio* to describe the work printed in 1550 as the work of John of Wales; Monneret de Villard did not question this attribution which is made on two Berlin manuscripts. There is, however, no doubt that this work is Spanish in origin. *Axa* transliterates '*Ā'ishah*. Miss d'Alverny has pointed out that parts of it are identical with parts of Ramón Martí's *explanatio simboli* and she has suggested that Martí may be its author. If he is not the author (and it is not possible to be positive yet) it at least seems highly likely that the two works sprang from the same milieu. The *reprobatio* consists of two parts, the fourfold refutation proper (which I will call *F*) and a shorter group of arguments (which I will call *V*) calculated to validate Scripture on general and special grounds, and so enable the author to quote it henceforward even to Muslims. Most of *V* also forms the introduction to Martí's *explanatio*, where in fact it fits better, since it should obviously always come at the beginning of a work. In style and method *F* and *V* are unlike each other, except in one section. The difficulty in regarding *V* as wholly detachable from *F* (or from both *F* and the *explanatio*) is that this one section of *V*, which deals with Qur'anic validation of Scripture, uses the method of *F*. It is possible that the author of the *reprobatio* was a member of the Dominican school associated with Martí and that he contributed one section to the total passage of Scriptural validation.

Finally, E. Cerulli has questioned the attribution of the works against Islam which are traditionally San Pedro Pascual's, but he does not come to any very definite conclusion, and he proposes to await the definitive edition of the saint's works now in course of preparation. I feel that I cannot do better than do likewise. I have not been concerned with the relation between these works and their author's life, and should have to alter only a name if they proved not to be San Pedro's. At the same time, I am convinced that the author was a Latin Christian priest, born in Christian territory (probably Aragonese) and working often in Islamic territory (possibly therefore a Mercedarian); all the internal evidence, the author's preoccupations, interests and prejudices, indicates as much. I am content for the time being to suppose him to be San Pedro Pascual.

Other bibliographical indications are given in the course of the notes, and I have supplied as full a bibliography as I am able. I should like to draw attention to J. Kritzeck's work, because much of it, together with that of A. Malvezzi, I unhappily missed when I was writing.

A NOTE ON TRANSLATIONS FROM THE BIBLE AND THE QUR'ĀN

The Bible is always quoted by mediaeval authors in the Vulgate, and to avoid inconsistency I have therefore used the English translation of the Vulgate throughout. Also for the sake of consistency I have therefore used the Vulgate form of proper names in my own text.

Most of the quotations from the Qur'ān are explicitly quotations from one or another mediaeval or later Latin version, and my English is meant to render these particular versions. Where it is a case of quoting the Qur'ān itself, and not a particular Latin version, I have used Sale's translation, as best expressing in English the meaning traditionally understood in Islam.

As far as transliteration from Arabic is concerned, I have meant to neglect consistency only with often used words, and with these to be only as scientific as will help the reader who does not speak Arabic (thus *Qur'ān*, but *Muhammad*, not *Muḥammad*); the reader who does speak Arabic will make his own correction as he reads.

A NOTE ON TERMS

I have almost always translated the word *Saracenus* as Muslim; the word *Muslim* in a translated passage must represent *Saracenus* or one of its equivalents, *Maurus*, *Ismaelitus* and *Agarenus*. (Occasionally *Saracenus* has another meaning, for example, when it is applied to pre-Islamic Arabs.) In mediaeval usage it was possible to become a Saracen or a Moor, just as later men were said to 'turn Turk'. *Saracen* means *a man who holds the same religion as Muhammad*, that is, a *Muslim*. I prefer to avoid its use in modern English because of its quaint and romantic associations.

Lex I have sometimes translated *law* (as in 'Mosaic Law') and sometimes *religion* (in the sense in which we say, 'the great religions of the world', or 'what is your religion?'). My practice varies according to the context.

The word *Latin* is often used (as a noun) in the sense usual in the East to-day, that is, to mean a man whose rite is Latin (not Greek, Arabic or Syriac). *Western European* is an alternative, but less exact, term. *Frank* also has the same meaning; *frangi*, though more common later, was used by Muslims in the Middle Ages. It was not, however, used in Spain, and the more technical expression seems more apt.

ISLAM AND THE WEST

✥ I ✥

Revelation: Christian understanding of Islamic belief

THE essential differences that separate Christianity and Islam are about Revelation. For Christians the prophetic preparation of the Jews leads to a single event, the Incarnation, which is the inauguration of the Messianic Kingdom; for Catholics this Kingdom is the sacramental life of the Church. Any other scheme must seem a composite affair denying some and asserting other aspects of the single truth. For Muslims too there is just one Revelation, of the only religion, Islam, or submission to God; but it was made again and again through successive prophets. Muhammad's was the final prophecy, but his was not more 'Muslim' than that of Jesus, or Moses, or Abraham, 'who was neither a Jew nor a Christian'.[1] For the Latin, it was an impossible imaginative effort so to suspend belief that this association of sacred names, which includes the most sacred of all, could seem anything but grotesque; yet it would be a mistake to imagine that mediaeval writers were ill-informed. There is evidence that they believed as much as they were willing to believe, and all who knew the Islamic reassessment of the familiar sequence of God's servants found it intolerable. As a result, Islam was often deformed when it was presented by Christians. In spite of this, the basic tenets of Islam were well understood by a great number of writers.

1. MUHAMMAD AS PROPHET

Early in the history of Western polemic, Peter the Venerable stated clearly the Islamic attitude to Revelation. His work in this context reveals some preoccupation with the prophetic aspect. Addressing an imaginary Muslim public, he was compelled to conceive their replies on their behalf. He very fairly allowed them to rebut the charge that they were deluded about God and the worship that He requires:

We have imagined nothing about God, and invented absolutely nothing. What we understand about Him, and publicly confess about Him, is not according to the figments of our hearts, but according to

IW C

17

what our Prophet, who was sent by Him, transmitted to us. As he was
the last of all the prophets in order, and like a seal of all the prophets;
as he was not the author, but the bearer of the divine law; not the Lord,
but the messenger: he received the heavenly commands which were sent
to him by God through Gabriel, and nothing more nor less. What he had
received he transmitted to our fathers and to us, to be observed . . .[2]

There was an uncommon appreciation here of a view opposed to
the Christian view and still not presented as absurd; but throughout the Middle Ages there was a wide awareness of the Islamic
conception of Muhammad, as nothing more than a prophet.

It is obvious that Peter the Venerable's mind was here well-
informed as well as clear. In the Cluniac translation of the Qur'ān
which he had commissioned from Robert of Ketton, the function of
Muhammad was allowed to appear unambiguously. 'Believe in the
envoy sent to you with the divine truth.'[3] Without the help of any
Qur'anic text, Guibert of Nogent had already insisted that Muslims
thought Muhammad one 'through whom the divine laws are transmitted'. The sentence which we have just quoted from Ketton's
version of the Qur'ān was rendered, 'Ye men, now an envoy has
come to you with the truth of your Creator' by Mark of Toledo,[4]
who, when he came to summarise the doctrine of the Qur'ān in the
preface to his translation, began, 'As often as he preached he said
to them, "I am the envoy of God; I expound to you the words which
the angel puts in my mouth . . ." ' Mark thought he saw inconsistency in that Muhammad 'sometimes called himself envoy of God
(legatus), sometimes, however, prophet of God (propheta)'; but
there was in either case a purely prophetic message. Muhammad's
claim to be no more than the messenger of God is implicit in the
words used by a wide variety of authors. Propheta (with pseudo-
propheta) was the word most often used, but words which more
nearly translated rasul than nabī were also used – messenger or envoy (nuntius) and apostle (apostolus). Combined phrases are
found, propheta vel nuntius or propheta Dei et nuntius.[5] Sometimes
the participle missus was used with propheta[6]; and William of
Auvergne showed a clear comprehension, which he presumably derived from Cluny, in his phrase hic ergo legis Abrahae latorem se
dixit.[7]

San Pedro Pascual spoke of the Prophet's religion as having
been 'transmitted by the command of God'. This use of the word
trado was common; ab angelo traditam said Humbert of Romans.
Richard Fitzralph described the Prophet's function as Dei precepta
dare.[8] This point appeared most clearly in San Pedro's Latin
version of ibn Isḥāq's account of the death of the Prophet. When
'Umar could not believe him dead, abū Bakr addressed and
quietened the murmuring crowd:

. . . and if ye believe thus in Muhammad, know now that he is dead; and if ye believe in God, know that God lives and shall never die; and that it is true indeed that Muhammad was nothing but the messenger of God, and therefore he is dead like this, like the other messengers of God, as they killed him. If ye desert your faith in God it will harm, not God, but you.[9]

Roger Bacon, arguing a related point, clearly understood that Muhammad claimed only to have received a Revelation which God had sent.[10]

At a less rarefied intellectual level, it is not clear that there was the same good understanding of the position. The most popular life of Muhammad referred to a 'concealed divinity' in him which Khadījah was supposed to have recognised, though it does not say that the Arabs generally did so.[11] Even in writings of this kind, Muhammad was not usually thought to have claimed divinity, rather than divine inspiration. It was only implied, what the Pisan text specifically asserted, that he was claimed to have been specially filled with grace.[12] The popular writers tended to be indifferent; they were certainly more concerned to attract and amuse than to be academic.

In this connection the Islamic presentation of the prophetic sequence was often referred to, though less often defined. Robert of Ketton's Qur'ān, which lay before Peter the Venerable, was widely distributed among the libraries of Europe,[13] and it rendered the classic verses which deal with this subject, not accurately, but without misrepresenting Islamic belief: 'Certainly we have made a revelation to you, as to Noe and the Prophets succeeding him.'[14] There was mistranslation, but no deliberate misrepresentation.

Therefore thou shalt preach faith in the Creator, utterly persuading men, so that they may hold a firm faith in the books sent down from Heaven to thee and to Abraham and Ismael and Isaac and Jacob and the tribes, and in the laws of Moses and of Christ and of the other prophets, among whom thou shalt not make distinctions; and they shall adore the Creator.[15]

The phrase here, 'the books sent down', is a paraphrase, and can only be intended to clear up ambiguity or obscurity. Mark of Toledo in the same passage is much closer to the original, but his 'what was given to Moses and Jesus' must obviously have been much less informative to the ignorant reader than Ketton's 'laws of Moses and of Christ'. The three other Cluniac translations of Arabic works that were made at the same time, and which are rarely found separated from the Qur'ān, all contained statements of the prophetic sequence in an exaggerated and unorthodox form.[16]

It was common to speak of Islam as appropriating distinct

functions to the greater prophets. 'Among the Muslims there is an important article of belief', said William of Tripoli, 'that Abraham is the friend of God, Moses again the spokesman of God, Jesus, son of Mary, the word and spirit of God, and Muhammad messenger of God.' These descriptions are taken from the Qur'ān, and were adopted by Mandeville. Tripoli pointed out that the Qur'ān praises Jesus and Mary and the 'holy fathers of the Old Testament' and added that it claims to be the fifth Book sent down from Heaven.[17] James of Acqui later noted Islamic belief in Moses, as one to whom God said many good things, in Aaron, as one who received grace, and in Christ, as a greater prophet than Moses and as enjoying greater grace than Aaron.

The verse of the Qur'ān which we have already quoted was cited by Fitzralph also, and summarised by the *quadruplex reprobatio*: the Muslims are commanded to believe in God and the Law and the Prophets and the Gospel of Jesus Christ and not to make any difference between them. San Pedro was familiar with the Qur'ānic expression of the sequence of revelations: 'O ye of the Book, ye shall understand nothing until ye fulfil the Law and the Gospel and what descended to you from my God.'[18] Lull's references to this subject are oblique and contributed little that was new. He caused a fictional pagan to argue that if God had improved the prophetic sequence in Muhammad, he might equally improve it again; but this had little relevance to Islamic belief. Elsewhere he imagined a Muslim who argued that if Islam possessed the place which the prophets of old possessed, Jerusalem, the Islamic religion must be 'given by God through Muhammad his Prophet', whom he best loved, and allowed to rule there. Another of his characters stressed Muhammad's pre-eminence among the other prophets at the Last Day. These are examples only of passing references to the Muslim doctrine.[19]

There are more definite statements than these. Peter the Venerable's 'last of the Prophets in order and like a seal of all' made the culmination of the series in Muhammad very obvious. 'They mendaciously affirm', said James of Vitry, 'that (Muhammad) had the spirit of prophecy above all other prophets.' Another statement from a later generation in Syria was more exact: 'The Muslims say of Muhammad that he is the seal of all the prophets, because, they say, he is the greatest of them, and because prophecy is sealed in that after Muhammad no other Prophet will arise.'[20] There were other references to Muhammad as 'greatest prophet' or as 'over all the prophets'.[21] Ricoldo da Monte Croce said that Muhammad claimed to be 'the end and the seal and the silence of all the prophets'; never, Ricoldo protested, could the hand of God be so shortened as to cease to give the prophetic spirit.[22]

Where there was less knowledge the picture was more confused. Peter of Poitiers, when he was sending his Abbot, Peter the Venerable, the headings which would guide him in preparing his polemic and missionary work against Islam, ridiculed the idea of a light in the side of Adam (*nūr muḥammadī*) which passed from Prophet to Prophet till Muhammad; he did not distinguish the doctrine as peculiar (ṣūfī or Nūṣairī), except that it was *omnium risu dignissima*.[23] Joinville, in very different circumstances, recognised an incomplete version of the *nūr muḥammadī* as heretical.[24] These ideas yet retain the basic prophetic notion clearly. In other accounts the Islamic belief in one religion of all ages and nations was obscured by the idea of nations, each prophet, Moses or Jesus, speaking to his 'own' people.[25] Another false idea represented the Islamic belief as a superseding of different revelations in turn, Islam taking the place of Christianity, as the latter had taken that of Judaism. The erratic second account of Islam which Matthew Paris published added, to a crude limitation of the number of prophets to three, a subtler explanation of the one Revelation; Muhammad preached

. . . that there were only three Prophets, and there would not be any more to come . . . Moses instituted those things which agreed with his own time, by means of the Law which was given him by God; Jesus, again, preached and transmitted by the Gospel the things that were to be done in his time; and in the same way Muhammad himself established the things that were fitting in his.[26]

Thus were God's revelations explained and illumined: 'when the time of the Law of Moses was exhausted, the Gospel succeeded; when the time of the Gospel was exhausted, the Law of Muhammad succeeded, as though to supply a defect in the previous and bygone Laws.' A longer passage of William of Tripoli's presented the failure of both Jews and Christians to preserve in a pure state the revelations made to Moses and to Jesus, and contrasted the absence of any revelation to the great nation of the Arabs. 'Now the decree went out from the fountain and court of divine justice that they should be sent a prophet of their own language and nation.' This was to put the national interpretation, and to ignore the claim of Islam to be universal. At the same time it was asserted 'that the Jews have broken the Law and the Christians the Gospel and that (the Muslims) have served their own divine Law, the Qur'ān, in its excellence and purity'. Tripoli was disinclined to recognise the whole extent of Islamic claims; writing in 'Akka immediately before the final fall of the Latin Kingdom, he yet contended that Islam approached its end and that already Muslims began to be converted in numbers. He was extraordinarily sensitive in some aspects to shades of Islamic opinion, but he was blind to its aggressive and triumphant aspects. Substantially the same passage about the Prophets was reproduced by Higden, who attributed this belief not, as Tripoli with greater verisimilitude had done, to the 'ulamā', but to the Qur'ān. He also said that the latter praised the 'ancient fathers' and also Muhammad, assuming that the Qur'ān 'praises' Muhammad, a common-sense, but quite mistaken, correction of Tripoli's statements. Yet in so popular a work as Higden's Polychronicon the authenticity of this passage stands noticeably out of a generally legendary account of Islam.[27]

2. THE RELIGION OF ABRAHAM

It seems established that writers with any claim to be taken seriously recognised the existence of a prophetic sequence in Islamic belief. This was not necessarily to recognise what relation the Qur'ān claimed to bear to the previous revelations. It did come to be realised by several writers that, according to Islam, Muhammad's prophethood 'corrected' the earlier revelations. Here Ketton's paraphrase of the Qur'ān, again intended to explain or illuminate the original text, allowed this point to appear:

. . . (the Jews) have the Testament that teaches the judgement of God' and shows the right way, and light and wisdom . . . Then for the com⁻ pletion of your Law We sent Christ, son of Mary, to whom We entrusted the Gospel, which is a light and confirmation of the Testament, and a cleansing and a right way for those that fear God . . . To thee also We sent the Book of truth, the confirmer of the commands to the others, with which it is thy office to judge . . .

Once again, Mark of Toledo's translation, which aimed to be literal, could not have given the uninformed reader so clear an idea of what the Qur'ān was actually saying.[28] Ṣalāḥ ad Dīn's letter to the Emperor, often quoted by his Latin contemporaries, enshrined the succinct formula, 'Our instructor and God's Apostle, Muhammad, whom He sent for the correction of the right religion: may He make it appear above all religions.' James of Vitry realised that Muhammad's mission was to 'expound to the world and declare' the revelations given to Moses and Christ, and to 'correct and instruct those who ill understood the commands of religion'.[29] All these statements had a wide circulation.

Humbert of Romans, in sermon material for the preaching of the Crusade, said that Christ was supposed to be greater than Moses, and Muhammad than Christ, each for the correction and setting forth of the former religion. In a later work, intended to influence, not the general Crusading public, but the Fathers of the Council of Lyons, he spoke still more clearly. Muhammad gave his religion 'especially for the destruction of Christianity', in that 'he said that he was sent as a prophet of God to explain and correct the religion of the Christians and the religion of the Jews'. Ricoldo made a neat statement on this aspect of prophecy. 'Therefore they say that the Qur'ān succeeds, so to say, in the place of the Gospel, and that the whole of whatever was good in the Gospel is in the Qur'ān, and that there is no further work for the Gospel (to do).'[30]

The accuracy of the impression given by Ketton's paraphrase of the Qur'ān was tested when, two centuries after it was made, Richard Fitzralph, in very different circumstances, used it in defence of the Scriptures in his *Summa de questionibus Armenorum*. His knowledge seems to have derived from this solitary source, which he studied minutely. He quoted Ketton where his text was unambiguous: the Qur'ān claimed to be the same revelation as was delivered by God to 'Moses and Christ and the other Prophets of God'. Fitzralph repeated one phrase insistently: 'that religion (Islam) expressly says that it is given to the Jews as a prop of their religion'. The passages from Ketton which we have quoted above he also quoted, as well as other similar ones. Of the opening of the third sūrah he said, 'What could be said more explicitly than that God delivered right ways to men, first the Testament, that is, the Old one, and then the Gospel; or how could either Testament be more explicitly approved?' These extracts from the Qur'ān interested him because he thought that they guaranteed the existing canon of Scripture; but while he was mistaken about that, he must certainly have realised that Islam claimed to be one continuous religion in the many revelations. He knew that it claimed to 'announce nothing contrary to the past Prophets'. He even found wearisome the phrases which seemed most applicable to his own thesis. The verse which, according to Ketton, read, 'We now teach the commands and rules of the Laws, as We revealed them to Noe and to thee and to Christ and to the children of Israel' provoked from him the comment, *istud sepissime repetit*. Without setting out to illustrate Islamic themes of prophecy, the loving attention he devoted to the written word of his text compelled him lucidly to establish the Qur'ānic claim to be the culmination of past revelations. 'His Law, that is, the Qur'ān, he affirms to be nothing but a completing of those (Old and New) Testaments . . .' If every reader had read Ketton's text as carefully, there would have been no delusion on this point, at least among the scholarly and discriminating public.[31]

We shall see later that in spite of this there was almost universal reluctance to realise that the Qur'ān did not accept any Scriptural text used by Christian writers as valid for polemic purposes. Both Ricoldo and Fitzralph, among others, wished to 'prove' that the

Qur'ān guaranteed the Christian Bible.[32] Probably the reason for this hopeless attempt was the general dislike of the claim of Islam to be the religion of Abraham and all the Prophets. The more clearly this was understood, the more it was resented. In this connection it is important that Ketton failed to translate the word 'Muslim' and its related forms.[33] In consequence, his translation tended to obscure passages which define the religion of Islam and to thin the more specifically Islamic content of the Qur'ān. Words like 'surrendered' or 'resigned' or 'submitted', which convey the sense understood by Muslims, were never used; the word 'Muslim' was itself avoided, and there was always some circumlocution, often based on the word *credere*. In the very clear passage in sūrah II which describes the religion of Abraham and Ismael and Jacob, of which part has already been quoted, *credere* is used three times; the latter part of Ketton's wording, 'hold a firm faith, adoring the Creator', seems to be particularly related to the word *muslimūn*; what Sale translates 'die not, unless ye also be resigned' becomes, obscurely enough, *ante mortem ne mutetis*. In sūrah III the phrase 'the true religion in the sight of God is Islam' was completely lost, and almost immediately after, 'If they dispute with thee, say, I have resigned myself unto God, and he who followeth me doth the same: and say unto them who have received the Scriptures, and to the ignorant, Do ye profess the religion of Islam? Now if they embrace Islam they are surely directed . . .' became 'Say that you have turned your face to God, and so have his followers.[34] In doing this those who are learned in religion as well as the uneducated follow the good religion.' In the passage a little later about the religion of Abraham, *credere* was again used, although the argument that Abraham preceded both Jews and Christians was presented clearly enough.

. . . the Testament and the Evangel were delivered after him; you assert what you do not know. He certainly was not a Jew or a Christian, but a faithful man of God, and he did not live an unbeliever.

Vir Dei fidelis et non incredulus vixit here represents *hanīfan musliman wa mā kāna mina'l-mushrikīn*, Sale, 'of the true religion, one resigned unto God, and was not of the number of the idolators'. In a very different revelation, we read, 'Men or women *vowing themselves wholly to God*, believing, praying . . .'[35] In this case it was not possible to use *credere* for 'Muslim', because in the Arabic *al-mu'minīn* (believers) immediately follows *al-muslimīn*. In the few examples quoted here, *se faciem ad Deum convertere*, *Creatorem adorantes, bonam legem sequi* and *se Deo penitus vovens* were used for 'Muslim', as well as the different forms based on *credere* and the complete omissions. This was deliberately to ignore the claim of Islam to be and to have been the religion of all the Prophets, while accepting that Muhammad pretended that his prophethood belonged in the grand tradition.

These points will become more obvious if we compare Mark of Toledo's practice in the same passages. In the first group quoted, he used *oblatus* for 'Muslim' – *et nos sumus ei oblati*; this, of course, is a very reasonable attempt at translation of exactly the sort so conspicuously absent in Ketton. In the second group of passages, those from sūrah III, he used a variety of phrases which still constitute an unmistakable struggle for exactitude. 'There is no light with God, except that of the Muslims' (*Saracenorum*), he said in the phrase that Ketton omitted. In verse 18/19 his version and Ketton's approximate: *Dic, Contuli faciem meam Deo* compared to *Dic te faciem tuam ad Deum . . . convertisse . . .* He continues, however, 'And say to those to whom the Book is given and to the simple people, Be joined to the Muslims (*ysmahelitas*); and if they are turned, then they are guided aright . . .' The later passage was rendered:

O ye who received the Book, why do ye dispute about Abraham, when the Decalogue and the Gospels were not given until after him? Do ye not understand? Do ye not dispute about what ye know – why then do ye dispute about what ye are ignorant of? And God knows, and ye do not know. Abraham was not a Jew, nor was he a Christian, but he was a Muslim and not an idolator.

The word that I have here rendered 'Muslim' was again 'Ismael-ite'.[36] Thus we see that in Mark's case mistranslation and the omission of phrases show every sign of being simple mistakes, either of translation or of copying. There is no deliberate telescoping of dull or difficult verses, and the text proceeds phrase by phrase, free of the translator's interpretation, and of his personality. No doubt there is a real difficulty in translating the different forms of 'Muslim'; in each separate context it is necessary to decide between a rendering like 'we are Muslims', which uses the proper name, and one such as 'we are resigned' which represents the traditional sense of the verb. Mark made his choice of words in each context, and he did not avoid any specific or identifiable word as Ketton had. Yet it was Ketton's and not Mark's translation which achieved wide distribution in Europe, both in the Middle Ages and, thanks to Bibliander, at the Reformation.[37] Unlike Mark's, Ketton's obscured the identification of all the Prophets as Muslim. This seems deliberate, because elsewhere the paraphrase made the Qur'anic conception of the Prophetic sequence clearer.

'The religion of Abraham' was only clear to some writers. The experienced Annotator of Ketton's text, introducing the Qur'ān, wrote that it 'says openly that the Prophets were supporters and helpers of the followers of his religion'; and in the marginal comment on the main text he said that the Qur'ān intended what the Muslims claim, that they hold the faith of Abraham, as Muhammad restored it.[38] William of Auvergne, with no direct knowledge of the subject, explained the situation admirably: 'He then called himself the bearer of the religion of Abraham, and in his religion he clearly claimed that Abraham himself was a Muslim.'[39] The Islamic view was never more neatly put than by the Syrian Apology, cited by Godfrey of Viterbo and by the report to Pope Gregory which Matthew Paris published: 'They also witness', this said, 'that from the time of Noe all the Patriarchs and Prophets and Jesus Christ himself held the same religion which they themselves hold, and were saved by it.'[40] Finally, San Pedro borrowed from ibn Isḥāq a story which really illuminates the attitude of the Qur'ān and of the Prophet. Abū Ṭālib, Muhammad's uncle and protector, found his own son, 'Alī, the Prophet's protégé, being taught to pray; he asked what religion this was, and Muhammad replied, 'This is the religion of God, of the angels, of the Apostles, of our father Abraham.' This aspect of Islam was overcast in San Pedro's mind by the dominant thought that the Qur'anic version of the Prophets was inaccurate.[41] He was too concerned to correct the Qur'ān to pay attention to its own claim to be the corrector.

The *quadruplex reprobatio* drily numbered among the few true statements of the Qur'ān that the Apostles were 'helpers of God'; it was untrue, Ricoldo said, that they were 'Muslims and imitators of the envoy and messenger, that is, of Muhammad'.[42] In his indignation that Apostles or Prophets should be called Muslim (Saracen) he was representative of the feelings of Latins who saw the polemic dangers of the claim. In the case of the old Patriarchs, he argued,

(Muhammad) himself said that Noe, Abraham, Isaac and Jacob and his sons were Muslims. Then he himself said that it was enjoined upon him that he was to be the first Muslim. How then were they Muslims, if Muhammad was the first?

This rationalist type of argument had a strong appeal, particularly for a certain type of school-trained mind.

And, again, he says the same about Noe: that he was a Muslim, and that the reason why the Flood came to the Earth was because he preached to men that they should become Muslims, and they refused. This, indeed, is undisguisedly false; for how could Noe, who preceded Muhammad by two thousand five hundred years, be a Muslim?

Ricoldo seems to have understood the Qur'anic position, although he subjected it to petty and pedantic arguments:

Neither can the Muslims say that Abraham and Noe are Muslims because Muslims are descended from them; for this interpretation is contrary to the Qur'ān, where it says that Abraham was not a Christian and was not a Jew, but a pure Muslim.

For the most part the idea that Islam is one single Revelation made to all Prophets was not known, or else misunderstood, or else understood and neglected. Yet Gregory VII had so much earlier told a Muslim king that he prayed that 'God bring you to the bosom of blessedness of the most holy patriarch Abraham'; was this a conscious effort to communicate with Islam at that point where the two religions most naturally meet?[43] The subject offered limited scope for controversial writing.

3. THE REVELATIONS MADE TO MUHAMMAD

To the idea of a repeated revelation which reached its final form in that made to Muhammad Christians opposed the notion of the audacity of Muhammad's pretence. 'He broke out into such madness', said William of Tyre, 'that he dared to lie that he was a prophet, to say that he was sent by God . . .'[44] Quite so bald a statement was rare; it is to be presumed that William elaborated it in his lost work on Islamic history. It was usually realised that Muhammad claimed to have been *sent* by God, and that there must have been something remarkable about his inspiration, to explain the otherwise incredible credulity of the Muslims. At the most fabulous end of the spectrum the explanation was said to lie in the fabrication of false miracles; at the other extreme, it was recognised that traditional Christian attitudes must take the Muslim version into account. The manner of revelation was almost always thought to be important.

The commonest fairy-tale, in the often repeated 'Corozan' version of the Prophet's life, had immense popularity.

. . . he began to fall down often in epileptic fits. Khadījah perceived this and grew exceedingly sad at having married a very impure epileptic. Wanting to propitiate her, he soothed her with these words: I gaze upon Gabriel the Archangel, who speaks with me; and not being able, as fleshly man, to bear the splendour of his face, I fail and fall down.[45]

This legend has shown extraordinary vitality among both Latin and oriental Christians. In some versions Muhammad had already convinced Khadījah of his 'latent divinity' by magic arts; in others he only claimed revelation after (and in order to explain away) his first epileptic stroke, which the judgement of God meted out to him.[46] At its simplest, the story omitted Khadījah's part; they were just epileptic fits explained as angelic visitations.[47] Serious writers were doubtful of the whole story, sometimes regretfully. Ricoldo preferred it deliberately to authentic versions; but although he was always disposed to drag in every known argument and to utilise the nastiest, he even so gave it little prominence.[48] Mark of Toledo had spoken more cannily of Muhammad's acting *as though* he suffered from epilepsy, *quasi morbum caducum patiens*; equally, he spoke of his rising from his fits, and rolling his eyes, *quasi a demonio arreptus*. Whatever Mark owed to the epileptic theory, he refused to commit himself either to it or to that of demoniac possession.[49] On the whole, epilepsy was the explanation of those who sought to amuse rather than to instruct.

The manner of the revelation was inherently of interest, but it is not always obvious what its polemic significance was thought to be. Mark of Toledo related the violence of the seizures ('like' epilepsy and 'like' demoniac possession) to the 'confused style' of the Qur'ān which he thought an important defect. He pictured Muhammad himself as having stressed the angelic violence: *cogit me angelus*.[50] The *quadruplex reprobatio* ostensibly set out to show on Arabic and Muslim authority that Muhammad gave himself out to be a prophet; one would have thought proof superfluous. The author, with sound historical judgement, rejected the wealth of legendary material available to him.

. . . that he said he was a prophet can be gathered from the words of his wife 'Ā'ishah placed in the book called Muslim. These are the words of this 'Ā'ishah: It was given to Muhammad to love solitude, and he went away and was solitary in a certain cave of Ḥirā', and there for many nights he gave himself to worship; and, returning to his wife Khadījah, he carried food thence to that place, and there he lived. When he was coming out of it, an angel came to him and said to him, Read. He answered, I do not know how to read. The angel took him and crushed him, by hugging him violently, and let him go. Again he said to him, Read, and he answered, I do not know how to read; and in the same way he crushed him. A third time he said to him, Read, and he answered in the same way, and a third time he crushed him. Then he said, *Read in the name of the Lord thy God, Who created man from congealed blood. Read, and the Lord thy God, He shall be honoured, Who taught man with a pen what he did not know.* When he heard this, he went back to his wife Khadījah, of whom we have spoken, and said to her, Cover me, and they covered him until the trembling went away from him.

Also it says in the book which is called *Bukhari* – this also concerns the same 'Ā'ishah – that a certain man asked him how that inspiration came to him. He said, It was just like the sound of bells; and that was the more violent way for me. That sound receded from me when I yet retained what was said And sometimes an angel came to me in the form of a man and I remembered what he said. Again, the same 'Ā'ishah said, I saw that inspiration descended on Muhammad, and on a day of great cold it went away from him, and abandoned him in a perspiration.[51]

This account could not more closely or faithfully record the Muslim idea of how Muhammad received the revelations. The author's intention is likely to have been to provide information, and so to assist Christian controversialists to prepare polemic which would be based on authentic and Muslim sources. The purpose of this is discussed below.[52] There may have been some idea that the falsity of the inspiration was self-evident.

Certainly these Muslim accounts of Muhammad's revelations did circulate in Spain and were used to support some Christian theories. San Pedro thought that the same tradition from 'Ā'ishah about the Prophet's perspiring while he received a revelation showed that he was exactly what the Quraysh, his enemies among his own people in Mecca, accused him of being, a soothsayer. His choice of authorities was only a little less discriminating than his predecessor's.

When Muhammad reached the age of forty he discontinued the adoration of idols, and said that he was a prophet, and began to wander alone through the mountains, valleys and hills, as if possessed by a demon; sometimes also for a month or longer he stayed alone in the mountain near Mecca which is called Hirā'. Muhammad asserted that the angel Gabriel first appeared to him in the same mountain; and he first told it to his wife Khadījah . . .

The story continued: 'the Muslims make Muhammad describe how he returned home to his wife after he had seen the angel Gabriel in the mountain, and sat in her lap and lay down over her . . .' She asked him whence his 'companion' came; this, pointed out San Pedro, was the form used to test diabolical possession. As she did so the angel appeared to Muhammad again; or, added San Pedro, so Muhammad said; but he, Pedro, certainly did not believe it. Muhammad told Khadījah that he saw 'our companion Gabriel'; she then made him sit, first on her left and then on her right knee, asking each time, 'O son of my uncle, dost thou see thy friend?' and receiving the answer *yes*. Then she covered her husband with a veil, or, as some say, hid him between her shirt and her flesh, and this time he replied that he did not see the angel. Then she said, 'Be comforted, O son of my uncle, for it is certain that this friend who appears to thee is not the demon, but, as I suppose, the angel of God; wherefore I hope that thou art the Prophet to be of this Nation.' Thus it was that Khadījah became the first Muslim.

- But I say to you, cursed Khadījah: you do not affirm that you saw that angel or demon; and if indeed you did not see him, why did you believe the futility that Muhammad told you? Did you not know that he was a man, and therefore that he could lie? But you and your husband seem extremely low and unclean in the experiments you made, beside the fact that experiments of this sort merit no faith; nor do they produce any certainty.

Thus two distinct accounts by Latin writers described Muhammad's withdrawal into solitary life and the sudden eruption of an abnormal event which had the appearance of divine inspiration. This was to investigate the Prophet's claim with care and solicitude, not with easy dismissal.

San Pedro also objected to this account of the first revelation because it seemed contrary to other accounts, also of Muslim origin, according to which Muhammad fell down at the appearance of the angel; so that they treated him like someone possessed by a devil: 'they covered his head with a sweat-cloth and the rest of his body with a fine cloth, and he remained altogether soaked with sweat; but when he regained possession of his spirit, he rose up and prophesied'. In the same place, this author mentioned that Muhammad attributed his infirmity to Gabriel's overbearing him; this looks like an intrusion of the epileptic theory, but it is not made so explicitly. San Pedro pointed out that really Muhammad was taught by a false monk, but himself always claimed that Gabriel appeared to him, and flattered Khadījah by telling her that Gabriel ordered him to assure her of salvation. In several places San Pedro referred incidentally to Muhammad as one possessed, and he let no opportunity go of drawing attention to a demoniac element, or suggestion, in any Arabic account. He described, also, how 'Ā'ishah, when she was slandered, appealed to test her truthfulness by a revelation; 'and on the spot he fell down to the ground, pretending that the spirit had entered into him, as he used to do; and they covered him with a fine cloth, and covered his head with a sweat-cloth, as was the custom, and after a little he got up . . .' San Pedro drew out still more fully the significance that he saw in what he thought of as self-induced fits, when he went on to describe the magic which Islam permitted. He spoke of the fits thrown by professional diviners in his own time. They told fortunes for a penny:

> Indeed I say to you, Muhammad, that you did not prophesy, but you said certain things, as to-day the diviners are accustomed to say them, by conjuration of demons, or some other way. Nor is this surprising, because there were and are and will be many diviners in the world, who say few truths and many lies.

For San Pedro, this case, familiar in his own world, was precisely the case of Muhammad. When he summed up the Prophet's career he called him *demoniacus*. This was as near as he came to committing himself to a definite theory; it was enough to show with certainty that his apparent visions could be induced at will.[53]

Roger Bacon pointed out that in all religions, even paganism, the faithful believe that the god has revealed himself. Muslims certainly believed that Muhammad received a revelation, he said, and that was what Muhammad himself pretended; 'and if he did not have God making a revelation, yet the demons made one to him'. Bacon was not very close to Islam, nor particularly fully informed, but he had thought more than San Pedro about the general problems of comparative religion. It is interesting that both should have fallen back upon demoniac possession as the final explanation of a prophethood partly, but not wholly, explicable as feigned. At a vastly more popular level of quasi-pornographical abuse, the Pisan text asserted that Muhammad would pretend to be going to speak with God in Heaven, and would actually go off to spend some time, from a few days to a fortnight, in debauchery. Then he would return, call the people to his palace, and, 'seized by the demon', would simulate prophecy. Here again it was assumed that possession can be induced, and perhaps that this is a normal phenomenon; certainly that Muhammad induced it habitually in himself: 'thus he spent his days in evil'.[54]

The classic point of reference for the 'self-induced' revelation was the story of Zayd and his wife Zaynab, whom he divorced, and whom the Prophet married by divine command. The details are considered elsewhere; the point so eagerly exploited was that the Prophet justified his personal desires by revelations.[55] The *reprobatio* quoted a tradition from 'Ā'ishah which is still popular with those who doubt the Prophet's sincerity; according to this she said, 'I see that the Lord thy God hastens to fulfil thy desire.' Ricoldo quoted the same incident in much more elaborate form, and said that to justify adultery in the name of God was to hide the lesser sin by a greater. San Pedro was astonished that the earth did not devour Muhammad for simulating these fits to obtain other men's wives.[56] Adultery apart, the Latins were genuinely scandalised by the Islamic conception of *ad hoc* revelations given in response to political or social problems of the moment. For the Muslim, a revelation that responded to the circumstances of a particular moment was normal, whereas to the Christian mind such a thing seemed to be its own condemnation. This point was clearly raised by San Pedro when he said that Muhammad pretended that the Qur'ān was sent from Heaven, when it was actually written down twenty years after he began to preach. This seems to imply that a 'sent' text conflicted with gradual or progressive revelation, and recalls the idea that Muslims claimed a 'carta' that was sent from Heaven. He similarly objected that over twenty-three years the Prophet 'introduced many things that happened to him and his companions over those years', and yet 'afterwards' asserted that he received them from God. San Pedro added that it was well known that many things were written on the advice of 'Umar. There is Islamic authority for this, in so far as revelations were said to be given in response to suggestions from 'Umar.[57]

The vast majority of accounts of the prophetic career of Muhammad explain that its medium was the angel; this was a simplification, but not far from the actual belief of Muslims. In a sound statement by Peter the Venerable, the Qur'ān was described (to Muslim readers) as supposed by them to be 'what was sent down from Heaven by God and delivered by Gabriel to your Prophet, not all at once, but bit by bit, through the parts of the month that among you is called Ramaḍān'.[58] In the fourteenth century the Franciscan Simon referred to the same fact. Vaguer, less accurate, more typical of the average Christian authors, is such a phrase as 'he lied that a Book was sent to him by the angels'.[59] It would be tedious to quote every reference to Gabriel as the medium of revelation, when there were so many; references to Muhammad's revelations which ignored the angelic vehicle were in fact rare.[60]

There is one important group of stories that excluded Gabriel. These are all fantasies. They are stories that told of a dove whom Muhammad, or a wicked teacher of Muhammad, trained to eat a grain of corn from the Prophet's ear, to simulate the Holy Ghost; or of a bull, or calf, or camel, similarly trained to come at his call, bearing the Book of the Law bound to its horns. These were prodigies which it was sometimes believed had been confirmed by further bogus miracles, by secreted milk and honey made at the appropriate moment to flow like fountains.[61] The narrators cannot have given much thought to the difficulties of rigging such tricks up, but they did see that it was necessary to stress the folly and simplicity of the Arabs, who were deceived by such devices. These were romantic tales that appealed to the story lover, but they must have seemed to some people really to explain the acceptance by so many infidels of apparently outrageous claims. Such tales were always associated with some of those stories which showed Muhammad to have been misled by a malicious Christian, often a Roman apostate[62]; they have not the remotest basis in historical reality, or in anything that related to the actual Islamic world. Yet common to these absurd tales, and to accurate renderings of Muslim sources, is the conviction that something out of the ordinary did actually happen to Muhammad, something that needed explaining. There was an intense interest in his revelations, a sense that they were crucial to the controversy between the two religions.

4. THE NATURE OF THE QUR'ĀN

The Qur'ān has no parallel outside Islam. Christians have some-times seen it as equivalent to the Bible. They have not always realised that the Qur'ān describes itself (and previous revelations also, though not word for word) as copied from a heavenly proto-type, so that it is really unlike anything known to Christianity. Still less have they understood that it is believed to be the un-created Word of God. This doctrine, which was arrived at compara-tively late in the development of the consensus of Islamic opinion, was yet generally accepted two centuries before the period that concerns us. The Qur'ān in Islam is very nearly what Christ is in Christianity: the Word of God, the whole expression of revelation. For the most Bible-loving, Protestant or Catholic, the Bible derives its significance from Christ; but Muhammad derives his from the Qur'ān. In their failure to realise this, Latins persistently contrasted Christ and Muhammad, and nothing marks more clearly the distance between Islamic and European thought.

What was generally understood was the importance of attacking the high authority of the Qur'ān, even when it was not understood precisely how high that authority was claimed to be. Christians realised that the Law and faith which the Qur'ān contains revealed alien patterns of thought and behaviour which interested them, but there was a failure to perceive the springs of the life of that society, so long as the Qur'ān was not treated as the spiritual source of Islam. Sometimes, as the 'Law' of the Muslims, it was not distinguished from the whole system of jurisprudence that derives from it.

It was common to speak of the Qur'ān as a 'collection of commandments'; the phrase is Cluniac, *collectio preceptorum*; it was adopted by Fitzralph, who depended closely upon Cluny, and even by Ricoldo.[63] The ideas of *religion* and *law* were closely related in the mediaeval concept, as is probably implicit in the phrases *lex Saracenorum*, *lex Christianorum*, which may mean equally the religions generally, or the Revealed Books.[64] The heading of Ketton's Qur'ān associates the two: *liber legis*, not an uncommon definition of the Qur'ān; *lex seu liber* was the phrase with which Tripoli introduced the subject. Matthew Paris took the trouble to delete a passage from the St Albans Chronicle in the entry for 622, and to substitute after *Alcoranus* 'or *Althoranus*: *al* in Arabic is the same as *the whole*, and *thoran* means *Law*'. The linguistics of this are nonsense, but the theological implications are obvious. Ramon Lull was exceptional when he spoke of the Qur'ān as containing the law.[65]

Law and *revelation* were very close in the mediaeval idea. A *praeceptum* was not an aphorism, but a divine command. This

IWD

comes out clearly in the explanation, by the Annotator of Ketton, of the alif, lām and mīm placed initially at the second surah.

. . . *elif* is the first of the letters with them, both in order of letters, and in the name of God; by *lem* in fact the majesty of God is meant, and by *mim* authority; so that they insinuate, Almighty God, to whom belong this messenger and these commandments.

The same author used *azoara* (sūrah), *preceptum* and *oraculum* as synonymous and as meaning a revelation.[66] In Spanish, *mandamiento* might be used for sūrah; and *preceptum* seems generally to have been used for a divine command.[67] The notions of law and revelation were so closely intertwined that it is impossible to say what sense is implied by the words chosen to describe or to refer to the Qur'ān.

It is also impossible to be sure exactly what relation the Qur'ān was thought to be supposed to bear to the actual revelations brought by the angel. The actual writing down of the Qur'ān and the preparation of the existing text were known to have been quite distinct from the originals they record. Pedro de Alfonso said that the Qur'ān was not written by the hand of the Prophet, but that his companions composed it after his death, each one surrendering his own individual reading to form the combined whole. The difficulties experienced by the early Caliphs in securing an acceptable text were utilised polemically by the Arab author of the Risālah, and this theme was thought by William of Auvergne, and after him by Vincent de Beauvais, to constitute the special value of this work: 'it speaks of the Book of his Law, which is called the Qur'ān, how it was composed and how torn apart and disordered'. Paris thought that bits of the Bible were added to the Qur'ān, after Muhammad's death, to satisfy popular demand. Tripoli contrasted with the simple idea of the Muslims, that Muhammad's revelations were put into a book after his death, the Catholic 'truth' – that fifteen years after his death his companions met to discuss the compilation of a book, which they committed to 'Uthmān. He proved unequal to it, and he was given the forced assistance of Christians and Jews, who found no material in the Prophet's life and doctrine, and invented their own book. San Pedro, although he referred to the penning of the Qur'ān twenty years after the Prophet began to preach, and also to the gradual accumulation of revelations over years, did not refer particularly to the process of compilation. All these writers thought that the existing Qur'ān does not really represent what the Prophet originally proclaimed, Pedro de Alfonso only implying that the text was inaccurate, others that it had very little to do with Muhammad indeed.[68]

Finally, Ricoldo, from his different sources, and particularly the *Contrarietas*, inherited a complex version of the different recensions of the Qur'ān. He described the protagonists of the different readings as 'fighting each other to death'; this extraordinary assertion he owed to the *Contrarietas*. The account is most confused when, after reaching the burning of all versions of the Qur'ān but one by 'Uthmān, it suddenly reverts to consider abū Bakr's collection of the texts existing in his time. There is also a statement that there was no Qur'ān at Muhammad's death. The Muslims agreed together to pretend that this disorderly collection should be accepted as of God, and abū Bakr burned the rest. The most disorderly thing here is Ricoldo's own story.[69] The purpose of all these arguments was to show that the Qur'ān was a haphazard collection of human documents prepared under highly disedifying circumstances. Evidently it was thought important to discredit, not only the actual revelations that Muhammad claimed to have received, but the written text of the Qur'ān as well. This attack at least implies some recognition of the unique importance of the Qur'ān to Muslims.

In spite of this, it is difficult to be precise about how Christians supposed Muslims to regard the Qur'ān. Much that was said of the Qur'ān implied that it contains, rather than consists in, revelations. Because writers wished to insist that the 'pseudoprophet' manufactured *his* Qur'ān, they very generally used such phrases as *dicit in alchorano suo*. Where God was named as the speaker of a revelation, the word most often used was 'introduced', and readers must often have thought that Muhammad only sometimes 'introduced' God as speaker into his Book. Peter the Venerable used some phrases that are of interest: he spoke of Muhammad's 'pretending that God was speaking to him' and of 'that evil and lying man, introducing God speaking to him, like a poetic figment'. The words 'poetic figment' seem barely appropriate, and were no doubt called forth by the sense of theological irritation.[70] There is an interlinear gloss on the opening of sūrah II in Ketton's text, *vox Dei ad Mahumet*. The words glossed are, *liber hic absque falsitatis vel erroris annexu*. The same explanation recurs marginally in places appropriate in the view of the Annotator, who had a clearer grasp of the problem than most writers, but the effect of identifying any part of the text as God's must have been to make the whole appear a hodge-podge attributable to Him only in part.[71] Most of the more serious writers customarily distinguished particular passages of the Qur'ān; such as San Pedro's phrase *loquens in persona Dei* and Fitzralph's *facit Deum sic alloqui*. Lull spoke of Gabriel as supposed to bring 'words of God that are now *in* the Qur'.[72]

The crux was that Christians could not distinguish between God speaking (in the Qur'ān) and Muhammad speaking (as reported in the Lives of him and in the Traditions). They would not even distinguish in purely Christian terms between Muhammad speaking *in propria persona* in the Traditions and *in persona Dei* in the Qur'ān. It is very remarkable that Europeans who knew enough to distinguish between Qur'ān and Traditions and other sources of information about Muhammad, more or less authentic, very generally failed to do so. They always argued 'Muhammad said . . .' when, in conversation with Muslims, it would surely have been more effective to say 'You believe that God said . . .' It would certainly have been more courteous. Thus Oliver of Paderborn used the phrase, 'Muhammad says in his Qur'ān', when he was supposed to be writing a friendly and encouraging letter to the Ayyūbid Sultan in Cairo. Peter the Venerable thought to disprove the truth of a prophecy, attributed to Muhammad in a weak tradition, by the supposed assertion of the Qur'ān that what did not conform to it was untrue; but he did so, not on the ground that the Qur'ān claimed to be revealed, but on the grounds that it was most authentically Muhammad's.[73] There is a similar confusion in other writers.[74] Mark of Toledo could even use the phrase: 'albeit the words of Muhammad are of greater authority among the Muslims than the sayings of ibn Tūmart, since the Qur'ān is accepted universally among them all'. This is unexpected in an able translator of the Qur'ān. To compare with it any theologian, however eminent, is to show a lamentable failure to comprehend. The author of the *reprobatio* gave equal authority to Qur'ān and Traditions as sources of historical information. His Qur'anic quotations were introduced with bare references ('it is said in the chapter such and such') and sometimes with the phrase 'Muhammad said . . .' He was careful to cite the references of his quotations, and this accuracy establishes minutely his knowledge of his sources. We may take it that his implicit attitude was deliberate. The *Liber Scalae Machometi* purported quite unambiguously to be the direct work of Muhammad and was treated, as an authority, like the Qur'ān. San Pedro did not distinguish clearly between the Qur'ān, the *Liber Scalae* and other traditional material, especially the *sīrat rasūl allāh*. His quotations from the latter two are more accurate than those from the first; to him, they were apparently all just sources of the *dichos* of Muhammad. Ricoldo would base an argument on the assumption that a doubtful phrase in the Qur'ān must bear the sense imputed to it by the Arabic commentators, who, he thought, must know what the Prophet had meant by what he chose to express secretly. Lull similarly had recourse to the *expositores*, as wholly authoritative in defining doctrines only adumbrated in the Qur'anic text. The failure to distinguish between the authority of the Qur'ān, of the Prophet's reported utterances, and of the Arabic commentators, may have been deliberate, intended to make it clear that all three were equally human artefacts; but, if so, this makes it impossible for us to tell now whether the Islamic attitude was clearly understood.[75]

On the other hand it is at least certain that the Qur'ān was very widely understood to be without equal in the eyes of Muslims. Writers who spoke of parts of the Qur'ān as sent by God might also speak, at another time, as though they knew that the whole was claimed to have been revealed. Peter the Venerable did so when he said, 'your law, which you are wont to boast was sent from Heaven'. Again, in his phrase, *falsum est ergo oraculum tuum*, he seemed to stress the divine claim which he had 'proved' to be false. The phrase was borrowed by William of Auvergne, to use less ambiguously: '. . . the Muslim people holds and adores those lunacies which we read in its Law, as divine oracles sent to it through the Prophet of God; and obeys them as commands of God'.[76]

Ketton himself made the Qur'anic claim abundantly clear. He regularly used the words *divinitus* and *celitus* in his translation: *in omnibus quidem (nisi) divinitus mihi mandatis* . . . (for 'that which hath been revealed to me'); *hunc librum meae legis a me celitus missum* (for 'the revelation which I have sent down'); . . . *et si testamenti simul et evangelii et celitus super eos missi precepta sequerentur* (for 'if they observe the Law and the Gospel and the other Scriptures which have been sent down to them from their Lord'). In this context Mark more accurately used forms of the verb *destino*, but Ketton's phraseology will have made the point clearer to a mediaeval reader lacking Islamic works of reference.[77] The word *celitus* did not pass into general usage in this connection. It was naturally familiar to Fitzralph, who actually quoted all the examples of Ketton's work which have just been quoted here.[78] He quoted, but did not remark on, another phrase of Ketton's, 'this Book is composed by God, the merciful, the wise'.[79] This word *celitus* was used independently by Guibert of Nogent and was also used by a few other authors unconnected with each other.[80]

Some statements made by the Annotator of Ketton's text were extraordinarily judicious. He was conscious that the constituent revelations of the Qur'ān are separate, and puzzled to know how the whole could be thought to be revealed from a heavenly proto-type. He explained that its separate writings (*cartae*) are called sūrahs, and that Gabriel is supposed to have brought them from God, not all at once, but bit by bit. 'For through the whole of this Book no word is ever ascribed save to God conversing with Muhammad', he pointed out.[81]

Readers of this Book should note that God Himself, so Muhammad pretended, wrote this Law with His own hand and delivered it to the aforementioned Prophet to preach to the world. He said that he had never been able to read, or to know letters, lest it should have been thought to have been composed by him. In spite of this, in speaking he assumed a variety of persons; now indeed he speaks in the person of God, now of the Prophet, now of good people invoking God and giving thanks to Him, and even, occasionally, of those who upbraid the good people: all according to the difference of places.[82]

'Note', he added with finality, 'that this Book is the height of authority among them, so that whoever says something against it is killed immediately and without further delay.' This was the most perceptive statement of the status of the Qur'ān, but not the only decisive one.

The *Liber Scalae*, although it was itself treated as excessively authoritative, represented Muhammad's receiving the Qur'ān from the hand of God.[83] According to the *Liber Nicolay*, he told the people that a Scripture fell upon him, and he received a light. According to Tripoli, Gabriel revealed and taught *divinum librum Alcoranum*, the 'doctrine and Law of God, given through Muhammad', which asserted its own divine origin, when it claimed to be the fifth Book descended from Heaven. The very praise of Christ 'Muslims believe with the heart to be true, and profess with the mouth, *as words of God written in their Qur'ān*'.[84]

San Pedro mentioned that Muhammad pretended that the Qur'ān was sent from Heaven, but was not much interested in this aspect.[85] Ricoldo treated the matter more plainly. The Muslims, he said, 'are not content to say that it is the book of Muhammad, but (say) that it is truly the Word of God'; again, they try to show it to be 'the work of God and not of man', *testamentum Dei et verbum Dei*. He noticed that Muslims laughed at the doctrine of the Trinity as 'contrary to the Qur'ān, which they most constantly take to be the Word of God'. His interest in the subject was chiefly in its polemic possibilities. The reason for his attack on the authenticity of the text of the Qur'ān, as it was compiled under the early Caliphs, was to show its claims to be false, when it made God out to say, 'We have caused the Reminder to descend and We shall be its keeper(s).' This criticism presupposes that Ricoldo understood that the revelations were conceived to be integral. Like so many writers, he would often single out individual revelations as made *tanquam ex ore Dei*, as though not all were; but he knew much better than that. The fuqahā', he said, teach that God revealed the Qur'ān to Muhammad, and that he wrote it from the mouth of God; but, he went on, the Muslims agree only that it was given by God – *totum enim est a nostro Deo* – and will never agree about its interpretation.[86] Higden, who naturally could only repeat what he read, apparently understood that Muhammad proclaimed the revelation of the whole Qur'ān: 'at the beginning of the books which he put out, he said, *the Lord has spoken to Muhammad His Prophet*', so that he might give these 'fabrications' a divine authority.

Other statements are more or less obscure. Peter de Pennis said, *quasi verbum Dei ab eis colitur*; this is a very good expression, if it is a reminiscence of John 1.14.[87] References to a book, or to volumes, as 'sent down' are vague.[88] The St Albans Chronicle spoke of Muhammad's having 'the Book containing his Law called Prothosimbolus'.[89] This might mean almost anything. In the world of the romances, the Qur'ān scarcely figures. In the fifteenth-century English Charlemagne versions it is numbered among the idols which also include Muhammad:

> He defyed Mahounde and Apolyne,
> Iubiter, Ascarot and Alcaron also.

This poem here represents a tradition older than itself. It also equates the Qur'ān with the Christian Scriptures:

> And songe the Dirige of Alkaron,
> That bibill is of here laye.[90]

We can only say that the significance of the Qur'ān found some reflection even in the most romantic works.

It is important to remember that the stories of bogus miracles definitely assert a claim to a special and direct Revelation. The dove that whispered in Muhammad's ear was supposed to represent, however absurdly, God speaking to His Prophet; the Law which a calf or bull bore upon its horns was playing the part of a text sent direct from Heaven: 'behold your Law', as one version had it, 'written not with human ink, but by the hand of the angel'.[91] Marino, who credited these stories, or at least expected hardheaded Venetian business men to find them useful, seems to stress the pretence to revelation from the Holy Ghost. Thus equally in the most learned authors and in the silliest tales the Qur'ān appears as claiming to be the direct revelation of God. If not all statements are as clear as these at the extremes of knowledge and ignorance, it is certain that no one failed to realise that Islam gave the Qur'ān a peculiar significance.

5. THE CONTENT OF REVELATION: ONE GOD

It has always been perceived, even by its enemies, that the essential message of Islam is to proclaim the unity of God. It has also been admitted at least that this was always the ostensible purpose of the Prophet's mission. Educated mediaeval writers fully understood this, although there were poets who spoke of the 'worship' of Muhammad, and of other idols, probably because they were not concerned with facts at all; there were soldiers who fed their hate by believing that their enemies were idolatrous; occasionally there were serious writers who knew better but carelessly repeated false or exaggerated statements. The supposition of idolatry in Islam was very rare among the educated, and perhaps did not exist among the learned.[92] Yet even those who knew Muhammad to have believed that he was sent primarily to call the Arabs from polytheism did not greatly stress this.

The clearest example of emphasis is found in an untypical writer, the Annotator of the Cluniac Qur'ān. This aspect of Islam would never be more clearly seen than by him. He recognised in the fātiḥah a thanksgiving to the Creator for the other revelations which it precedes in the Qur'ān. His account of the names of God, which constituted so full and so extraordinary a comment at the beginning of the Qur'ān, serves admirably to introduce the whole Book: 'God is called by many names in this Book, on account of His manifold power.' He continues, 'He is called the Compassionate (*misericors* for ar-Raḥmān) because He magnifies what is good for all good men, and He lessens the punishment of all bad men, or returns only the same evil that they did. He is called Merciful (*pius* for ar-Raḥīm) because He hears all who invoke Him, and relieves all who wish . . .' These names of God put beyond any misapprehension the Islamic concepts of His attributes and His works, and must have refined the ideas of many readers. '. . . *Abounding*, for He wants nothing, possessing all things. *Outpouring*, because He distributes both temporal and eternal good. The *Founder*, because He alone created all things, and nothing is impossible to Him. The *Examiner* or *Seer*, because nothing is hidden from Him. *Near*, because He is everywhere present. *Vast*, because He contains all things, and is by none contained . . .'[93] In such theology as this the distance between Islam and Christianity is at its least; the difference is one of tone, not of fact. It would be difficult for a mediaeval reader to take notice of these annotations and still to feel that an untrue notion of God was believed over the border of Dār al-Islām.

To quote two authors who mentioned the belief in God without revealing any special interest, 'the Muslims believe that there is one God of all', moreover, 'idols they abominate by the teaching of Muhammad'; and 'zealously he preached that there is one, true and only God, and effectually with the sword and vigorously he exterminated idolatry'.[94] Similar phrases were often used. By the second half of the thirteenth century this theme was so far taken for granted that Roger Bacon, by no means an Islamic specialist, could list the divine qualities upon which there was a consensus of opinion of all nations, and remark, 'in this description agree the Tartars and Muslims and Jews and Christians'.[95] Bacon was not always so representative of his age. Even those who believed, or repeated, what now seems ridiculous, for example, the 'dove' and 'bull' stories, had no doubt of Muhammad's monotheistic doctrine: 'they worship one God almighty, Creator of all things'.[96]

Much authentic detail was available. Where Muslims were brought into an historical narrative, their attitude was often fairly represented. Ṣalāḥ ad-Dīn wrote to Frederick 'in the name of God the Compassionate, by the grace of the one God, powerful, excellent, victorious, enduring, Whose kingdom is without end'. Muhammad an-Nāṣir of Marrakesh was given a speech in which he emphasised a point by saying, 'Almighty God, Creator of all things, from Whom nothing is hidden, knows . . . '[97] If the episode in question is a fiction, as seems likely, the choice of phrase is even more remarkable. These are not examples of a speculative approach like that of the schools, but are independent, casual, a stereotype deriving ultimately from knowledge of life in Syria, Spain or North Africa, rather than from any academic interest in Islamic theology.

Mark of Toledo, as little typical of his age, but as much a product of the Spanish Reconquest as Ketton's Annotator in an earlier generation, chose Qur'anic phrases to quote directly: 'Adore the living God . . . you should not adore gods who can do you no good and no harm.' He imagined how historically Muhammad planned to draw the nations to the worship of the one God. The Qur'ān he thought to be very inadequate as proof of the one God, but he did not doubt that this was what it intended. Some of his other translations are comparable to the Annotator's citations of the names of God; but the original is less characteristically Islamic in being more characteristically scholastic, and as such naturally attractive to a Christian brought up in the Schools. (God is the subject.)

The First, not limited by anything before; the Last, not limited by anything after; the Only, not limited by place; Sempiternal, not limited by quality; Glorious, not limited by any likeness; Whom minds do not grasp, nor the intellect conceive, nor thoughts comprehend, nor senses warm; Whom the apprehension of place does not define, nor motion, nor change and movement indicate, nor ignorance and necessity.[98]

Most scholastics were preoccupied by differences in belief, especially such as involved the Trinity, and showed nothing like Mark's interest in the unity of God as Muslims conceived it.

Muslim forms were not often allowed to stand alone; to believe

in God was rather to 'agree with the Christians'. Thus Alan of
Lille could say that the Muslims agree with the Christians in
affirming one God, Creator of all things together; and with the
Jews in denying the Trinity within the divine unity. Again, Vitry
said that Muslims, like Jews, reject pork and scaleless fish as food,
'but agree with the Christians in this, that they believe in one
only, almighty God, Creator of all things'. Fra Fidenzio was non-
committal: 'For they confess there to be one God, Creator of
Heaven and Earth, and of all things visible and invisible; and they
say that God is one, alone and true, Who is not multiplied and has
no consort.' The first part of this formula seems to derive from
the Nicene Creed, whereas Qur'anic phrases lie behind its later
phrases; but there is neither approval nor disapproval. San Pedro
was willing to appreciate the Prophet's destruction of idolatry: he
had 'taught and appointed a law that they should believe in one
God only, almighty, Maker and Creator of all things; this against
the pagans, who worship many gods, was the best thing he said'.
San Pedro also, however, enjoyed the memory of how 'once, a
little, he praised the gods of the pagans' – a reference to the false
revelation in praise of Al-lāt, Al-'Uzzā and Manāt. Tripoli, while
remaining critical, admitted that the Qur'ān praises the Creator,
'His power, knowledge, goodness, mercy, justice and equity'. All
these writers tend to express Muhammad's doctrine of God in
Christian terms, and all are very moderate in their appreciation of
it, although they do not doubt that, expressed in their own terms,
it is true.[99]

While there was no question about what Islam believed itself to
believe, there was some attack on the Islamic belief itself. Thus
Peter the Venerable, in recognising the profession of faith, the
shahādah, wished to distinguish between what Muslims believed
and what they thought they believed. 'I know that this is what you
understand and what you profess: that you truly believe in God
and the true God. But whether this is true a later and unanswerable
reason will show you, also by the Spirit of God.' In the *summula*,
he spoke of Muhammad's traducing the Arabs 'away from idolatry,
yet not to the one God, but . . . to the error of his own heresies'.
The 'unanswerable reason' has not survived; we may conjecture
by analogy from his argument about the Qur'ān that he maintained
that a partly wrong belief (one, for example, that denies the
Trinity) becomes thereby wholly wrong. Lull thought that there
could not be true unity without Trinity, but there is no single
Latin expression very close to Peter's subtle distinction.[100] It has
a Greek parallel. The form for the reception of a convert from
Islam into the Byzantine rite, parts of which are probably nearly
as old as Islam, lays stress on anathematising 'the God of Muham-

mad', i.e. He who 'neither generates nor is generated'.[101] This may also be Humbert's meaning when, although he knows very well that belief in one God is common to the two religions, he speaks of the need to expel the *superstitious* people from the Holy Land, and to *introduce* there the worship of God.[102] It was presumably to a current theological distinction that the unknown English pilgrim of the fourteenth century referred when he said, 'If they believed in God as they believe God (to be) . . .': *si in Deum crederent, sicut Deum credunt.*[103] These distinctions sometimes seem to do more credit to the heads than to the hearts of those who thought them appropriate; but it was certainly more usual to recognise the wide range of common belief, particularly about the unity of God, and to assume that even what was said in error was said of the same God. 'We who believe and confess one God, admittedly in a different manner', had written Gregory VII, that man of practical insight, to the Ḥammādid, Nāsir ibn 'Alnās. An unknown author was equally realistic when he said, 'Yet all, Christians, Jews and Muslims, adore one God, Creator of Heaven and Earth, and all believe that they will be saved without doubt.'[103]

Ricoldo attacked, not the Islamic image of God, but what he thought he could show its implications to be. He detested the shahādah, *no God but God and Muhammad His Prophet*, and thought it gave him the opportunity to reverse the Islamic accusation that Christians associate others with God. He seems to have been very satisfied with a not very convincing argument. What, he asked, did Muhammad mean when

so often – and how often! – he asserts and reasserts, writing about himself, *believe in God and the Apostle, obey God and the Apostle, follow God and the Apostle.* For we know that to God alone is owed the faithfulness of belief, the honour of worship, the working of obedience and the following of a way; for He alone is the Beginning and the End. Therefore no one has ever dared to say these things, so as to associate himself in such a way and in such matters with God, who can never have any partner or consort.

This wearied sense of confidence represents only one of Ricoldo's moods; for the Islamic doctrine he would sometimes feel a rising irritation which betrayed him into indefensible argument:

And that word is to be noted which Muhammad puts in the Qur'ān more than a hundred times, I believe: *There is no God except God.* For this proposition is true simply of everything: there is no dog except a dog; there is no horse except a horse.

Within his own experience, however, Ricoldo was impressed as he travelled by the Muslim reverence for the name of God.[104] Always conscious, and often resentful, of the Islamic expression of the doctrine of the unity of God, he does not seem to have doubted the doctrine itself. The desperate length to which he sometimes pursued his objections suggests that he felt against his wish that the religions were here in agreement.

Lull constantly presupposed, but normally treated as superfluous to assert, the Muslim belief in one God. He was aware that historically the Prophet called the Meccans away from paganism. The sum of all the controversy that he maintained against Islam through so long a life was to assert that the Christian doctrine of the Trinity and of the Incarnation is more appropriate to belief in the unity and power of God than Islamic definitions are. The point of this argument was that Muslim belief implies, although Muslims will not accept, the Christian creed. 'The Muslims believe in one God, but they do not believe that the Divine Unity has infinite and eternal Act in itself . . . The Muslim religion postulates that there is one God, but does not prove it.' According to Lull, the doctrine of the Trinity did prove it. The Muslim belief was presented by him rather as incomplete than as false. In the *Book of the Gentile*, where three religions compete for the soul of the pagan, the two items that are first in the Muslim creed were rendered as *Credere in Deum* and *Creatorem*, but were passed rapidly over as substantially the same as in the Jewish concept. This recalls Bacon's assumption that the Islamic belief belongs in the consensus of world opinion. The only addition shown by Lull as characteristic of Islam was that God's honour required that He should be Creator of good and evil alike.[105]

Some of these points are interesting to compare with an adapted Muslim creed which in the Cambridge manuscript precedes the *quadruplex reprobatio*. This is not close enough to the Creed in Lull's *Book of the Gentile* to suppose either indebted to the other, but both obviously compare with other Creeds of Spanish origin. The first item is the existence of God the Creator; the second is his being the source of evil as well as good; the third, the mission of Muhammad the Prophet to the Arabs, 'to call them from the error of idolatry and to teach them the way of salvation'.[106] All these points made in different Latin authors were variations in the general understanding of the basic doctrine of Islam.

When it came to debating about the existence of God in front of pagans, it was realised without difficulty that there was community of belief with Islam. William of Rubruck recounted how he had had to point out, 'the Saracens agree with us in that they say there is one God; they would therefore be on our side against the *tuins*'. When a pagan said that no god was omnipotent, 'all the Saracens burst into loud laughter'. These Muslims, when a Nestorian group wanted to dispute with them, refused to do so, accepting that 'whatever is said in the Gospel is true, therefore we do not wish to argue any point with you'. If the Muslim party thus glossed over their differences with the Christians, it seems like a case of tact and prudence and some real sense of natural alliance on their part; and on Rubruck's side, if not among the Nestorians, there was a practical recognition that one quarrel at a time is enough, and that over the existence of God there is none.[107]

It is certain that the essentials of Islamic belief were known to those scholastic and other educated authors who took a serious interest in the subject; much was even publicised by popular writers. There was not, of course, any very subtle appreciation of the niceties of Islamic doctrine, and there was not usually a great desire to understand what was known. We shall see that this knowledge served a polemic use, and that the data were assessed in ways which must be unacceptable to Muslims. There was more Christian propaganda than genuine attempt to communicate over the frontier. The physical frontier was not very clearly marked and was easily crossed. The frontier that divided the mental attitudes of Christians and Muslims was emphatically defined and crossed only with the greatest difficulty.

Plate 1

The monk Baḥīrā recognises the young Muhammad as the Prophet to be: the Muslim source of the Christian legend of the monk who was Muhammad's guide and teacher.

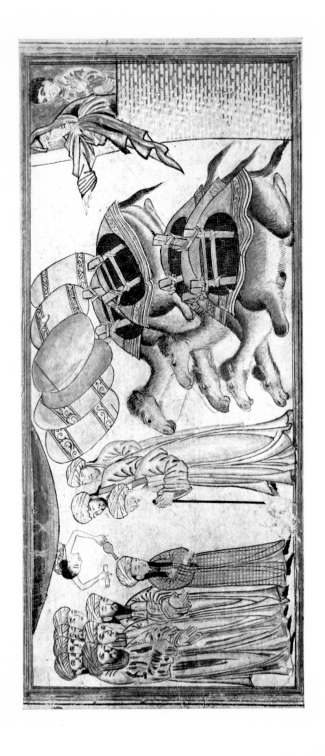

Revelation: the Christian attack upon 'Pseudoprophecy'

THE mediaeval writers challenged the Islamic Revelation at its foundation, with no apparent doubt or hesitation. They insisted constantly, in arguments that were based in general reason and in Scripture, that it was demonstrably impossible that the Qur'ān should be true or that Muhammad should have been a Prophet. Many of their arguments were founded on premises unacceptable to Muslims. Logically it seems absurd to argue from facts derived from Scripture that Scripture must be sound and the Qur'ān in error. Similarly, more general arguments, intended to show that the Islamic claim cannot stand, could have satisfied only men who already shared the writers' attitude to morals and faith, and their mental background. Such discussion went no distance to bridge the differences between Europeans and Islamic traditions. There was not much to convince the Muslim in what was said.

1. THE RELATION OF THE QUR'ĀN TO THE SCRIPTURES

The Qur'ān makes it clear that it not only confirms, but corrects, the Laws of the Gospel (Injīl) and the Pentateuch (Tawrāt). The Jews and the Christians misrepresent the Revelations entrusted to them. In so far as the Biblical text now known to us is inconsistent with the Qur'ān, Muslims believe, sometimes that the latter abrogates the earlier Revelations, sometimes that Christians and Jews understand the text perversely, and sometimes that the existing text does not faithfully represent the Revelations actually made to Jews and Christians in turn. These were committed to human care, without being verbally guaranteed as the Qur'ān was. This corruption of the written text by omitting, in particular, prophecies of the coming of Muhammad, was called taḥrīf. It was of the allegation of taḥrīf that Christian writers took greatest and most detailed notice.

Against this Islamic position there was a good deal of ingenious but sometimes misapplied Christian argument. Some authors did not realise exactly what the Muslims claimed; thus Sigebert just said that Muhammad 'confirmed his pseudoprophecy in some things from the Scriptures'. Most writers were much clearer on the subject; Peter the Venerable's technique was to state the Muslim case that he proposed to refute: '. . . one of your people would reply, *I do not deny that the Jewish and Christian Books are of God, but (only) in the form in which they were written by their first authors*'. The importance of this Islamic assertion was obvious to all who understood what it was. If the existing text of Scripture could not be vindicated, Islam would have a strong call upon the loyalty of those who loved Jesus, since it asserted a truer and purer devotion to Him. Peter of Poitiers would have had his Abbot start with this question, from which the whole great refutation of Islam which he planned would have proceeded. Neither Jews nor Christians could have falsified their Scriptures, he noted down: in many languages over all the world one and the same Gospel had been preserved. It was impossible that so many men of different languages and nations, especially the learned, could have concealed a falsification, or allowed themselves to be deceived, or mistaken false things for true. This was the sum of the Christian contention, which would be put forward with variations of detail by many writers.

Peter the Venerable simplified the Islamic case. Muslims alleged (he said) that the Jews lost their Law in the return from Babylon, when the donkey that carried it strayed from the crowd of refugees. Much rhetoric went to the ridiculing of this proposition: 'Haeccine est, o viri, fama? Haeccine est traditio . . .?' It was most improbable that the Jews should have been so careless; but if they had been, how could they have hidden it? How could a text have been kept secret and uncorrupt for a thousand years, in a form known to nobody, and then have been published in the falsified form? It was characteristic of this argument that it depended on the accuracy of historical data derived solely from the Bible. Esdras read the Law to the Jews as soon as they reached the Holy City; he could not have forged a false Law so quickly. Similar arguments defended the New Testament. Always in Peter's thought it would be impossible seriously to suspect the sacred history; one phrase summed up all: 'tunc aliquando sensus humanus obrutus?'[1]

Ramón Martí's treatment was more impersonal and discreet and orderly. One original contribution of his was to insist that the Qur'ān must be judged by the standards applied to Scripture. 'You believe the Qur'ān, and that your Book is whole and unchanged and uncorrupted, because you believe that he who delivered it to you was a seer (vates) and came speaking truth; and similarly that those who heard and received it from him, and wrote and published it, were speaking the truth.' This was what had happened in the case of Scripture. Much of Martí's argument pursued this parallel between Scripture and Qur'ān; whatever could be used to argue the validity of the latter proved equally that of the former. These points included as their climax the argument that so many men, and men of such a kind, could not have falsified a Holy Book. Martí's emphasis on the truthfulness of Christ and of the Apostles, which the Qur'ān maintains, as guarantee of the Gospel, was also original. For him, the zeal of Christians and the comparison of scattered manuscripts were equally proofs of Scripture; this was more traditional. Martí was above all anxious to establish the authority of Scripture on rational grounds, and yet he too defended Scripture with Scriptural data. He discussed at length the possibility that Nabuchodonosar burned the books of the Law and the Prophets, using historical evidence in the fourth (second) book of Kings. If Muslims believe the Qur'ān, or even a single work of grammar, to be uncorrupt, they must equally accept the text of Scripture. Finally, who would dare defy the Scriptural warnings against meddling with the text?[2]

Ricoldo was less academic, less discreet and more obviously prejudiced. Yet he had a wide experience of the Eastern world and of Eastern Christians, and he had a flair for penetrating a moral issue when he was not under the intellectual domination of one of his sources. The usual point, that there could never have been agreement throughout the world to suppress the supposed original Gospel, took with him a form which reflected conditions that he had personally known. How could Jews and Christians 'between whom there is so ancient a hatred' agree to corrupt a text? 'And how could the Latins and the Greeks agree with the Chaldeans, who are Nestorians and Jacobites, and were treated as schismatic and excommunicated by them before the time of Muhammad; and who were also opposed to each other?' Although these churches were separated before Muhammad's day, the schismatics have the same text in Chaldean and Hebrew that the Latins and Greeks have. A forgery must be secret, in which case it could not be universal, or general and open, in which case it could not be hidden, or even believed. Ricoldo challenged Muslims to produce the supposed ancient version: 'For there was a studium in Baghdad and in Mecca from ancient times, where the most ancient books of the Muslims can be found and are preserved in the archives, which they showed us; and yet they could never show any Gospel other than like the one that we have.' In his much more elaborate *Disputatio* Ricoldo added little to these arguments. He stressed the history of the writing of the Gospels and suggested that if the Christians had changed their religion it would have been to deny, not to assert, the divinity of Jesus, since this would have been the easier to believe.[3]

Fitzralph derived some ideas from the Cluniac corpus, and used other arguments which Ricoldo and the Spaniards also exemplify, and for which his sources are unidentified, and may have been oral. His thought was detailed and painstaking, careful, his method scholastic, his approach, like that of his predecessors, profoundly Scriptural. Whatever proved the integrity of the Qur'ān better proved that of the Gospel. The evangelists, separated geographically, confirmed one another. The division of the world among the Apostles made forgery impossible after their time, any more than during it. Could the manuscripts of books for which the martyrs died have been altered without its being noticed? What motive could there have been? Here Fitzralph was treading a path already well worn.[4] It is very clear that Christians felt themselves on particularly safe ground here: taḥrīf was the 'last and miserable refuge' of the Muslim position.[5]

There was another type of defence against the Qur'anic attitude to the Bible; and this was taken from the Qur'ān itself, or from what it was supposed to say. The fact that the Qur'ān recognised the earlier revelations as true induced in many Christians a curious sense of reassurance which Robert of Ketton himself best summed up. 'But although this Law is in many places very amusing, it represents, to observers and to those who take part, the greatest witness to, and the strongest foundation of, the sanctity and excellence of our Law.'[6] Here *Law* may mean either *Religion* or *Book*. A century or rather more later, the author of the *reprobatio* was able to exploit the argument from the Qur'ān more fully. He wished to show that the Qur'ān necessarily presupposed the truth of Scripture. He took three texts from sūrah v which 'introduces the Lord, saying about Jesus, *We gave Him*, that is, Jesus, *the Gospel, in which there is direction and light*'. But God, he argued, could not have said that there was guidance and light in the Gospel if it were corrupt. '*Until you establish the Law and the Gospel, you are nothing*; there God is speaking to the Christians and Jews, as the Muslims say.' To a third passage the author gave prime importance, but here he confused the Qur'ān with the commentator. He described how the Jews sent to Muhammad for a judgement, and how Muhammad sent them back, that they should judge their own people by their own Law, and warned them to judge justly. But this was to admit that the Jews then had a Law capable of containing the true judgement of God, and, therefore, incorrupt. Similarly, the command not to distinguish between the Prophets, and between the Law, the Gospel and the Qur'ān, must mean that the Law and the Gospel were incorrupt when the Qur'ān was composed. Another text of the Qur'ān, the author of the *reprobatio* happened completely to misunderstand, though not to misquote:

> In the tractate al-ḥijr, God is brought in, saying: *We have caused a reminder to go down, and We are its guardian.* Yet, so the Muslims say, he calls the Law and the Gospel the *reminder* of God, which, as God Himself guards it, is not corrupt, unless God is not Himself a faithful guardian; quod absit.

Here the interpretation was mistaken on a point essential to the argument; the *reminder* in the Qur'ān is the Qur'ān itself. Referred to the same sūrah was the verse, *there is no alteration of the Word of God.* 'But the Word of God is the Law and the Gospel.' What stands out most clearly in these passages is the author's conviction that the Qur'ān really did endorse the Scripture.[7] The different forms of this argument seem to do little more than impose a logical dilemma on Muslims, but it had a very powerful appeal for mediaeval writers. Ricoldo, here heavily indebted to the Spanish schools, copied the *Contrarietas*, and possibly borrowed from the Cluniacs.[8]

Some of these considerations were reflected by San Pedro Pascual, who seems to have reproduced much that was probably current in the Peninsula towards the end of the century. He contended that the Qur'ān, when it asserted that Christ was the Word and the Spirit of God, condemned itself, because Christ's precepts were contrary to those of Muhammad. It affirmed definitely that the Christians were in the way of salvation: 'certainly those who believed in God and who served the Law of the Jews, also the wise and the Christians, who believed in God and the Last Day, did well; they shall receive reward with God'. Again, it praised the same Prophets as Jews and Christians praised, and so the Muslims are positively 'compelled to accept the sayings of the Prophets, although contrary to themselves'; that is, Muslims must recognise the Christian canon of Scripture. Here, as in so many cases, the Christian polemists apparently knew very well what the Qur'ān says, and yet refused to consider what Muslims claim it means.[9]

Fitzralph took the Scriptural defence further than any other author, either the Spaniards of a few generations before him, or the Cluniacs of a still earlier age to whom he owed his Islamic material. He thought that Christianity was alone among religions in being able to prove its case by the authority of another religion, and in spite of the fact that superficially the Christian religion was the most repugnant to reason.[10] A few examples will illustrate his method. Commenting on sūrah II he worked his way slowly through the Cluniac text, ignoring the entire content of the passages he quoted, except in respect of the sole point that interested him. On text after text, with repetition that wearied him, he confined his comment to this unemphatic point: *hic etiam approbat testamentum et evangelium.* Occasionally he was delighted by the terms of this 'approval': 'how could it endorse either Testament more explicitly?' It is not likely that he would have thought differently, had he had a more accurate translation before him. The Qur'ān, he continued, confirmed the authority of the earlier Testaments as prior to its own, 'not only for the past, but for the present'. By guaranteeing the Scriptures, it invalidated itself, and yet, 'so far as the visions of such a man could', its confirmation of the Scripture held good.[11]

In an important chapter he summarised his findings.

There is even greater confirmation of this, in that Muhammad, wanting to invalidate the same Gospel, like Caiaphas prophesying, inserted such things into his law as would in every way make the truth of the Gospel clear. First, this is done by his affirming the Gospel of Christ to be given by God, as sūrah LXVI says, quoted above; and sūrah V adds, as quoted above, that God gave the Testament and the Gospel as right ways to men; and sūrah XII says that the Gospel is a light and confirmation of the Testament and a correction and a right way to those who fear God. It follows that the Gospel must contain the truth in all things, otherwise it would not be a light; it would not be a right way, but a wrong one; above all, it would not be given by God, who is the highest truth, to men, in order that salvation and grace should result, as it says . . . If indeed the Gospel contains the truth in all things, as this Muhammad admits in this Qur'ān, it follows that the Qur'ān contains falsity in all things which are repugnant to the Gospel; thus it is most rashly that he repeats endlessly that God has no Son, when (this) is most often affirmed in the Gospel, and in the psalter, which he himself says was given by God to David . . .[12]

In addition, the Qur'ān was committed to the praise of Christ and the Apostles; for if Christ were a just and true guide, those who adhered to Him and to His doctrine could not be evil men. The Apostles were described in the Qur'ān as *veri* and as *penitus obedientes*.[13] Thus it was very carefully re-stated that the Qur'ān validated Scripture, but that the inconsistency between them invalidated the Qur'ān. This, of course, was still to play with the Qur'anic text, while ignoring the Islamic interpretation of it. There was no wish for originality. Fitzralph had no personal contact with Islam[14]; but those who had, shared the same fault. All these arguments may be reduced to the formula, that if the Qur'ān were valid, the Scriptures must be so too, but both could not be. 'Whatever tends to confirm that religion tends also to confirm ours', said Fitzralph.[15]

It was seen as crucial that, although the Qur'ān seemed to

support the Bible, 'on the other hand, neither Testament approves, foretells or confirms the Qur'ān'. Fitzralph saw the importance of the point, without realising that this was just what Muslims claimed. 'No one indeed doubts that the Law of Muhammad would have greater authority than it has at present, if it were affirmed by statements in the Old Testament and the New, or in either.'[16] Similarly, Benedict of Alignan, who derived his ideas of Islam at third hand, thought it a strong point against Muhammad's claims that God sent no Prophet without prior verification in earlier Scripture. Roger Bacon, upon the authority of Al-Fārābi, argued that the founder of any religion must receive witness from Prophets who precede and follow him; but, apparently not realising the Muslim position, Bacon concluded without further demonstration that only Christ satisfies the conditions. Aquinas argued that, since the preceding prophets had not borne witness to Muhammad, the latter had corrupted the Scriptures, 'as is clear to anyone looking into his law'; in consequence, he had astutely forbidden his followers to read our Bible. Here too only part of the picture was understood.[17]

Muslims in fact believe that prophecies of Muhammad have been suppressed, and notably that Jesus foretold 'an Apostle who shall come after Me and his name shall be Aḥmad'.[18] This claim was attacked by those who knew of it. In the twelfth century it was stated without discussion that Christians were accused of having cut the name of Muhammad out of the Gospel, and Ketton's annotator thought that the idea had been borrowed from the Manichees.[19] The *reprobatio*, although it is a short book, treated the question three times. 'In the sūrah as-saff, that is, *of order*, he said that Christ prophesied about him, saying, *there will come an Apostle after Me whose name is Ahmad (Ahimez).*' In an argument which sounds like a polemic stereotype, he argued that there could have been no motive for Christians to remove the name, which would have been bound to be cherished, either as the announcement of a good thing to come, or as a warning of future evil. In a passage at the end of his book, the author argued the impossibility of taking the prophecy of the Paraclete for Muhammad. The former was the Holy Spirit and invisible and was to teach the Apostles all things; the latter was not a spirit, not invisible, and taught the Apostles nothing. Paraclete means *consolator*, but Muhammad, who came with the sword, was *desolator* rather. There is a note of ecclesiastical humour in this passage which appears equally in Martí's *explanatio*.[20]

San Pedro referred to a certain Jew of Medina who converted many to Islam by saying that Muhammad was the Prophet foretold by Jewish Law, in which his name was prefigured. Lull mentioned the alleged suppression of Muhammad's name from the Gospel, but did not stress this.[21] Ricoldo treated the subject very seriously. He rendered the supposed text, 'I announce to you that the Messenger of God will come after Me and his name will be Muhammad', and commented, 'But because this is not written in the Gospel, they do not receive the Gospel and say that we have corrupted it.' He urged historical arguments which echoed his forerunners: why should the name of Muhammad have been omitted if those of Herod and Annas and Caiaphas and Judas were retained?[22] His treatment was a little more elaborate, a little less accurate, than that in the *reprobatio*. The Rabbi Samuel letters, which were put into Latin only in the middle of the fourteenth century, were asserted by their translator to have long circulated in Arabic among Christians. Their originality was to interconnect the mutual verification of the Three Laws: that is to say, both Rabbinic teaching and the Qur'ān confirm the truth of the Gospel, while each of them destroys the claim of the other. Islam taught the Rabbis that Jesus Christ is the Messias, while the Jews made the Muslims understand that Muhammad was neither Messias nor Paraclete.[23]

These writers knew what they were talking about. Peter the Venerable, unusually, was ill-informed; he strangely insisted that the Qur'ān does not mention the falsification of Scripture (or, he implies, the falsification of their revelation) by Christians and Jews; his imprecision may be the source of Fitzralph's. The plain fact is that the text of Ketton's Qur'ān which Peter claimed to have searched in vain, made clear sense of verses which assert or imply taḥrīf, the corruption of Scripture. 'And dost thou therefore expect the conversion of (the Jews) to thy religion? Definitely not. For they changed the word of God, which they had heard and known, and they did not want anything from it to be effected.' Peter curiously pretended that one could search the Qur'ān in vain 'from the first word to the last' for any such statement. Most improbably, he missed even the 'Aḥmad' prophecy, which Ketton rendered quite clearly: 'Christ, the son of Mary, saying, *O children of Israel . . . I announce an Apostle to you; they claimed with a lie that the Apostle who is to come after Me, whose name is Muhammad, is a sorcerer.*' This is a muddled translation, but it is not muddled about the contention that Christ foretold Muhammad. Moreover, so far as most readers were concerned, the marginal annotations were explicit that Christians were accused of corrupting the text of Scripture and changing it as it pleased them.[24]

In considering the Christian reaction to the accusation of taḥrīf, I have stressed the part played by Scripture, which it was the all but universal practice of the age to cite, even though no Muslim in real life would accept it. The Christians – St Thomas Aquinas is the great but lonely exception – wanted to insist that they must. This was most explicit in the Cluniac approach. It was Peter of Poitiers' view that the Scriptures must be accepted or rejected whole, and his Abbot elaborated this. For him it was quite intolerable that the Muslims should make use of the names of characters in Sacred Scripture without accepting the whole canon. They should entirely reject Scriptures – *ex toto reprobandae sunt* – if they could not accept them, as they ought, in their entirety. It was their duty to accept the Jewish Prophets, because the Holy Ghost inspired them, whatever their racial origin; and also because Arabs and Jews shared the same inheritance: the descent from Ismael and Isaac; the practice of circumcision inherited from their father Abraham 'either by innate usages or by laws that have been handed down'; common race, an 'almost common' language, style and 'famous things of literature'. Within the circumambience of his second-hand knowledge, Peter would often return to his fundamental point. He exhorted Muslims, 'either abandon the Qur'ān, because of the false things which have been taken out of Books which you call false, and put into your Book; or, if you do not want to do that, acknowledge that the Christian and Hebrew Books from which these things are taken are true'.[25] Peter the Venerable's humane and enthusiastic personality, his limited power of discrimination, are reflected in this insistence on premises unacceptable to his opponents. Yet this conception had a wide influence. We have just seen how the principal Christian thinkers considered that Muslims were bound by the Qur'ān to accept the Christian canon of Scripture. Where the idea was not asserted, it was implicitly assumed. The general impression may be seen in serious writers remote from personal contact with Islam. Alan of Lille took it for granted that Muslim doctrines were based on heretical interpretation of canonical Scripture, and formed his own polemic accordingly. Alexander III wrote similarly, although it is not clear that this pontiff put his arguments forward as acceptable to any and every Muslim, rather than to a single individual, the Sultan of Konya. Much later, Guido Terrena, representative of a highly educated public, used Scriptural authorities in the same way, condemning, for example, the regulations governing the Ramadān fast, by appeal to Isaias.[26]

There were a number of attempts to determine which parts of Scripture Islam could accept. Verona said Genesis; he may have meant it to stand for the whole Pentateuch. Oliver of Paderborn realised that the New Testament needed to be proved by external authority, but, believing the Old Testament to be acceptable to

Muslims, as to Jews, he used its prophecies in great detail to prove the New. Vitry investigated carefully how much was acceptable, but mistakenly thought that the New Testament Epistles were. Tripoli thought that the Prophetic Books were, as well as Pentateuch, Psalter and Gospel. The author of the *Liber Nicolay*, realising that the Qur'ān accepts David, thought that the Psalter (as known to Christians) was adopted by Muhammad 'word for word'. Martí realised that it was necessary to 'prove' Scripture on solely rational grounds, but, in spite of knowing better, Ricoldo, followed by Peter de Pennis, could take it for granted that Muslims accepted the Gospel, which he used to 'prove' the Trinity. We have seen how San Pedro said that Muslims must logically accept the words of Christ in the Gospel, and of the Jewish Prophets. St Raymund of Peñaforte, however, first characterised Muslims as rejecting both Old and New Testament, and then remarked that one party among them accepted the Pentateuch, while rejecting the prophetical books. These people he called Samaritans, quoting John iv.9. It was widely and erroneously thought that Muslims rejected the Gospel, but accepted the Old Testament.[27]

Arguments that stressed that the form of the Scripture which Muslims must accept was that which Christians held are most fully developed by Ricoldo. Two repetitive passages of his were neatly combined by Peter de Pennis to clarify the fact that Muslims reject Scripture just because it is contrary to the Qur'ān. Ricoldo phrased the Muslim attitude well, that 'the Jews corrupted the Law of Moses and the Prophets, and the Christians the Gospel, and that nothing of the truth remains, *except in so far as it is in the Qur'ān*'. Yet almost in the same sentence he asked why Muslims do not have and read 'the Gospel and the Law which Muhammad commended, in which he said were salvation and guidance'; Ricoldo contrasted the way Christians accept and study the Jewish Law, that is, the Old Testament, in the form in which they inherit it. He stressed that Muhammad set the Jews and the Christians up as depositories of faith, with whom God Himself had preserved and would continue to preserve the truth; yet in that case, he argued, as the *reprobatio* had done, the Qur'ān refers men to a corrupt source and makes God into a false witness. Martí put the same point in a simplified form when he said that, on the subject of Christ, it was the Christians who must be consulted: 'anyone is to be believed in his own science or art rather than another; it is foolish to believe a doctor about agriculture or a farmer about medicine'.[28]

Ricoldo was even prepared to attempt to force Muslims in logic to accept Scripture, by contending perversely that in the Qur'ān the 'people of the Book' means the Muslims; actually there is no question but that it means Jews and Christians.

In the chapter *al-maydah*, which means the *Table*, it says, *the people* (familia) *of the Book are nothing, unless they fulfil the Law and the Gospel.* But the people of the Book are the Muslims; that is why it says, *unless they fulfil the Law and the Gospel and what is revealed to you.* By *what is revealed to you* is understood the Qur'ān, which has been revealed, as they themselves say, to the Muslims alone.[29]

Ricoldo was apparently satisfied that this would have a polemic value against Muslims who, if they had ever really heard it, would have ridiculed it.

The extraction of verses from their context in the Qur'ān, and their dissociation from the traditional Islamic interpretation, is typical of this class of polemic. Peter the Venerable, San Pedro and Ricoldo in particular, but in some degree all the Latins, assumed the freedom to understand a Qur'anic authority in whatever sense pleased them; they would always prefer their own reading to that which is traditional in Islam. In Martí's own phrase, the doctor was too often anxious to offer advice on agriculture, the farmer to teach medicine. Christian polemists would never allow their opponents to speak for themselves; yet their arguments, often ingenious to the point of brilliance, could never have been convincing to Muslims; and ostensibly they were not intended for Christians.

2. THE ALIEN QUALITIES OF THE QUR'ĀN

Much mediaeval argument depended on showing that the Qur'ān was incongruous with the other revelations with which it associated itself. This was more than a matter of logical inconsistency. It was held to be incompatible with Scripture in its inherent qualities, and not only with Scripture, but with philosophy and natural reason also. Its strangeness and unfamiliarity in certain ways were genuinely shocking to the Latin reader; in Western tradition it stood out as a freak, both in content and in form. The same reaction may be observed, even among the educated, in the West to-day. Ricoldo plundered his more learned sources for illustrations of this theme. Peter de Pennis rearranged the same material in a form a little more precise. In all there was a formidable quantity of attacks on the Qur'ān for its form and style and its unreasonableness.

A number of criticisms may seem frivolous now, which were first put forward with unattractive zeal. So small a point as the traditional naming of the sūrahs was made the object of carping ridicule. The annotator of Ketton's Qur'ān was at some pains to

explain its general appearance: 'separate chapters are called after
something which is specially mentioned in (them)'; the second,
for example, was named after a cow, of which it 'fabulously interwove mention'. For Ricoldo this nomenclature was more specifically a sign of irrationality. The Qur'ān, he said, has special
chapters for *the ant, the spider* and *smoke*, unsuitable subjects for
divine revelation. This was disingenuous; he must have known
that the names of the sūrahs do not claim to describe their contents.
Some of the more petty of the criticisms of the Qur'ān which he
amassed are most revealing of his approach to it. It is full, he said,
of things that are not worth saying, *nihil omnino notabile dicit* –
'just that God is great and high and wise and good, and that all
things that are in Heaven, and that are on Earth, and that are
between them, are His; and that He judges justly'. Some such
phrases, he insisted, were too often, and unnecessarily, repeated:
'may He be praised', and then, 'there is no God but God' and
'believe in God and His Apostle', *dicens se nuncium Dei antonomasite*. God was not accustomed to say, as though of someone
else, 'God is great', and so on. Moreover, the Qur'ān was obscene,
in that it used such words as *coitus*.[30]

This excessively small-minded carping sprang from a genuine
divergence of Western and Eastern traditions. The form and the
manner of the Qur'ān remained always alien to the scholastic age
which so specially honoured the systematic classification of arguments. It was supposed that its style gave a strong presumption of
its human origin; it was too badly written to be of God. In this
way the attitude of the Arab and the Muslim, and the assertion of
the Qur'ān itself, were exactly reversed. It is the Qur'ān that says
that it is its own proof, that issues the challenge to produce one
revelation equal, in matter and expression, to those that it contains. The language could naturally not be appreciated across the
barrier of translation; yet it was felt to be antipathetic. The
Cluniac *summula* mentioned various elements in the Qur'ān that
Muhammad 'interwove in his barbarous way', and Peter the
Venerable referred scornfully to a 'barbaric and unnatural way of
speaking', with which we should probably connect his hostility to
'poetic figment'. We might naturally expect the translators of the
Qur'ān to resent the difference in genius between Arabic and
Latin to the detriment of the foreign idiom. Robert of Ketton may
be inferred to have done so from the extent to which he introduced
changes into the text, by paraphrases and omission, or, as he put
it himself, 'changing nothing perceptibly, except only for the sake
of understanding'. It was Mark of Toledo, however, perhaps under
the influence of Mozarab ideas, who first voiced the full force of
this criticism:

. . . sometimes he speaks like a crazy man, sometimes however like one
who is lifeless, now inveighing against the idolators, now menacing them
with death, occasionally indeed promising eternal life to converts, but in
a confused and unconnected style. But the confusion of this style is excused by some because they make out that he was invisibly troubled in
soul and body, and tormented, by the angel . . .

There seems as little appreciation here of the language of the
Qur'ān as understanding of the Arab admiration of it. Mark knew
that Muslims argued from the style of the Qur'ān on the lips of an
illiterate prophet to its divine origin; and the whole of his prefatory
summary of Qur'anic teaching, which in précis of the Qur'ān he
put into the mouth of the Prophet, is a *tour de force* of mimicry that
makes it impossible to suppose him insensitive to Arabic style.
Yet it was not just that he felt that good Arabic made bad Latin.
For Mark, the very words of the Qur'ān were inherently and
perniciously defective. Thus he could even conceive that Ibn
Tūmart's reasoning might be invalidated, although in itself particularly sound, by the frequent citation of the 'disorderly and
extremely confused' words of the Qur'ān. The Qur'ān reproached
and threatened idolators, but not clearly, rationally or usefully.[31]

Although it was a commonplace to accept the idea that Muhammad was illiterate, in order more convincingly to impute the
composition of the Qur'ān to his supposed collaborators, it was
very rarely realised that for Muslim thinkers illiteracy was taken
as a proof of the revelation of the Qur'ān. 'He wished the eloquence
of the Qur'ān to be considered a miracle', said Ramón Martí.
Lull spoke freely about this point. In one passage a Muslim
teacher argues, for the benefit of one of Lull's mythical and ingenuous Tartars, that there is nowhere in the world such beauty
of expression as there is in the Qur'ān; 'from this it appears that
our Law is from God; for all men, as many as live, could not
discover or compose in a more beautiful style'. To this the Tartar
replied, with a precocious priggishness, that 'the whole virtue of
words lies in their truth'. So short a passage yet reveals a very
clear lack of sympathy for the Arabic spirit. Lull even felt sure
that he could write a poem on the Names of God which would be
so much more beautiful than the Qur'ān, that Muslims would be
convinced of the folly of accepting the divine inspiration of the
latter.[32]

Ricoldo's attitude, more closely related to Scripture, was based
on a similar antipathy. The text of the Qur'ān, that men and jinns
could not produce the like, he exploited fully. 'He said that
neither angels nor demons could make such a book.' This provided
an irresistible opportunity for facetiousness: angels would not
write a book filled with lies, blasphemy and obscenity, but, of

course, demons very well might. He pointed out that to the reader
of Arabic it is obvious that the Qur'ān is in verse, but that it is not
possible to preserve the verse in translation.

The Muslims and the Arabs glory in this especially, that the diction
and style of their law is rhythmical; and they say that it is clear from this
that God made that Book and revealed it word for word to Muhammad,
because Muhammad was an uneducated man, and did not know how to
contrive such style and such sentiments.

The same passage was pitched more strongly still in the rendering
of Peter de Pennis: the style constituted 'so beautiful and adorned
a way of speaking, that is, metrical' and the Muslims 'argue from
this that Muhammad was true Prophet' as well as that God made
this Book. Ricoldo, however, followed by Peter, replied that in
fact the very opposite is true: divine laws are not like this at all;
neither the Old Testament nor the New is metrical [*sic*]; of 'the
other prophets who heard the voice of God', we are told that 'none
said that God spoke in verse; which also the wise philosophers
disdained'. The Qur'ān itself admitted that the Prophet was
accused of being a dreamer and a poet, and not a prophet.[33] This
was not the only occasion when a scholastic adopted the attitude
that the Quraysh had taken up in Muhammad's own day.

To several authors the arrangement of the Qur'ān seemed disorderly. Pedro de Alfonso early pointed out that the way that it
was finally compiled made it impossible to tell what its original
order had been. Vincent de Beauvais remarked, after he had read
the description of the process of compilation in the Risālah, that
this showed how the Qur'ān was 'fabricated, torn about, disorderly'.[34] Fitzralph, we have seen, found the repetitions wearisome. It was again Ricoldo who most fully elaborated this theme,
which he did by an analysis, of scholastic type, of the supposed
lack of order. There was no order of time, by periods and kings,
as there was in the Old Testament, he complained; no narrative
order, in that, beginning properly with the praise of God, it then
slips abruptly into the middle of things; no order of subject-
matter, passing from one irrelevance to another; and no logical
order, because it proceeds from true propositions to things unrelated, as when it says that God is good and the Qur'ān the Law
of salvation. This final offence was apparently for Ricoldo the least
forgivable of all, and he brought many examples, which he owed,
like much that was most ungenerous in his work, to the *Contrarietas*:

Thus in the chapter *elmeide*, which means the *Table*, it says, *God
established for you the house elharam, that is, of prohibition*; this is the house
of the mosque; *and the month of the Muslims' fast*; *and this, that ye may*

know that God knows the things which are in Heaven, and which are on earth, and God is knowing all that is. But who is so silly as to doubt that God knows all things? But, granted that it could be doubted, by what connection do the house of the mosque and the Muslims' fast of a month make it known that God knows all things?

For Ricoldo, recollecting Muslim Baghdad when he was at peace at Santa Maria Novella in Florence, it was natural, but ungenerous, to make fun of the Qur'ān and the Prophet. 'Very often he seems to speak like a man dreaming, and especially towards the end of the Book, where there seem to be some words missing.' This refers, of course, to the early sūrahs, revealed at Mecca, and now thought of as more 'religious'.

Thus in the chapter *elkaferin*, this is word for word what he says: *O profane ones, I do not adore what you adore, nor do you adore what I adore, and I do not adore what you adore, and you do not adore what I adore. Your Law is for you and my Law is for me.* But every heretic can say as much, in order to cut short a matter of which the truth is under examination.

Confusion, thought Ricoldo, was itself confused; he could remember no book which so offended the rules of logic. The scholastic taste was for a numbered and schematised presentation; but the Qur'ān had no order at all, except the damning order of poetry 'qui Deo non competit'.[35]

It occurred to Christians that the literal sense of the Qur'ān was so plainly contrary to religion that its defenders might shelter behind some 'mystical' sense, comparable to that of Scripture which added the spiritual meaning of a text to the literal one. William of Auvergne, after a lengthy attack on the idea of a material Paradise, said that learned Muslims saw that such ideas made Muhammad ridiculous in the eyes of the whole world, and they therefore taught that such promises should not be taken to the letter. Lull, better informed, realised the importance in Islam of the verbal revelation of the Qur'ān, and in practice of literal interpretation by the orthodox; he said that those Muslims who believed the description of Paradise to be spiritual did not observe the Qur'anic law in other respects either. Ricoldo remarked of a passage which he thought came from the Qur'ān, 'the Muslims do not expound this hyperbolically or by similitude or in any other spiritual way, as we do some things which are in the Apocalypse; but they expound all their expositions to the letter . . .'[36] This situation was wholly satisfactory to the Christian polemist who anticipated saying many hard things of the letter of the Qur'ān. Moreover, it was a further example of the disparity between Qur'ān and Scripture.

Still stronger emphasis was laid upon the incongruity of the

Qur'ān, both with Scripture and with philosophy, in content. The annotator of the Cluniac Qur'ān was very free with condemnation of the fables about Old Testament characters; from a Muslim point of view this meant those stories in the Qur'ān that do not agree in detail with the stories in the Scriptures. His vocabulary of abuse was irritated and repetitive. Of sūrah VII he said, 'Here he unravels infinite fables of Adam and Eve and Beelzebub and certain unheard-of prophets; and, under the influence of an evil spirit, he does not cease from repeating the usual ravings and lunacies and most stupid words about Moses.' This is the style of much of his marginal commentary – 'ea quae sepe solet deliramenta repetit', 'nota insanias mendaces quas assidue repetit'. The rubrics at the heads of sūrahs often read 'stulta, vana et frivola', 'vana, mendax et impia' or similarly. The commentary seems to nag at the Old Testament 'fables', and emphasises the absence of Scriptural support for the Qur'ān.[37] This sense of the unreliability of the Qur'anic version of Scriptural stories was very general. Among the Cluniacs it was probably associated with Talmudic Judaism. The Annotator spoke of Christian *and Jewish* apocryphal writings, and the *summula* attributed the fabulous element in the Qur'ān to the influence of Jews; Poitiers, moreover, explicitly blames the Talmud. Peter the Venerable based much of his polemic on the contrast between the Prophets of the Old Testament and Muhammad.[38]

With Mark of Toledo there began to appear in Spain a greater precision of knowledge and a calmer tone. Mark explained the Qur'ān's name 'Alforcan, which means *distinct* in Arabic, and which is a distinction between the Old Testament and the New, or, as some interpret it, between the profanity of the pagans and the faith which he himself taught'. Mark thought it important to deny the consonance of Islam with the earlier religions from which he said it was derived.

The manner of his handling, as it is contained in the course of the book, is foreign from the others. For it does not agree with the Gospel, either in its manner of speaking or its precepts; neither does it agree with the Old Law . . .[39]

He specified a few exceptions that linked the laws of Islam and of the Jews; it was a question of contrasting a fundamental dissonance with superficial borrowings.

At the end of the century San Pedro Pascual condemned the 'many contradictions, fables, lies and heresies' in the Qur'ān and the ḥadīth; here 'fables' has again the sense of 'inaccurate versions of Old Testament stories'. San Pedro devoted a whole chapter to this theme. He felt deeply this conflict with the true Scriptures. It was the Qur'ān's dissonance that marked it as false. 'O Muhammad', said San Pedro, 'I do not at all believe that thou hast received these things from God, because thou art peculiar in thy witness, and thou dost not agree with any other Scripture whatever.' If Muhammad's was a Law of profligacy, it followed that 'this law of thine is not like the Law which Moses wrote, nor the Law which Jesus Christ our Lord taught by word and deed'. What Muhammad claimed to have received from God must be rejected 'because they are contrary to those things which were written by Moses and by the Prophets and after by the Apostles, by the inspiration and command of God . . .' Among the defences of the Christian position, this thought was prominent in San Pedro's mind.[40]

Similarly, Ricoldo contended that the Qur'ān does not agree with the authentic revelations, and contains fabulous tales. The Muslims themselves would realise this, if their learned men allowed them to see the Christian Scriptures. He exploited their inherent absurdity rather more than their conflict with Scripture. He summarised the story of Solomon in the sūrah an-naml, and, assuming the short Qur'anic text necessarily to imply the whole Islamic tradition subsequently attached to it, he related the death of Solomon and the story of Hārūt and Mārūt, in such a way as to make them seem as ridiculous as possible, and to impute all this to the Qur'ān. Here he was followed by Peter de Pennis.[41]

This treatment leads on to another great field in which the Qur'ān was thought alien to Western tradition: its inconsistency with reason, that is, both with natural philosophers in moral and scientific matters, and with itself in simple logic. This was inevitably how it would strike a mediaeval reader trained in the schools. For example, some of the material edited by Peter de Pennis was grouped under the head 'that Muhammad speaks ignorantly of the nature and properties of certain things'. This included legends from the de doctrina of the Cluniac corpus, once again a source of derision: stories of Creation and the Last Day, of Noe and the swine's flesh, of Hārūt and Mārūt.[42] In an unusually unreasonable marginal comment, the Annotator of Ketton castigated the ignorance of the physical world shown by the Prophet who claimed that birds flying in the air are upheld by the power of God. Really air supports them just as water does the fish that swim in it; God made no special miracle for birds.[43] Benedict of Alignan was most probably referring to morals when he said that 'neither Scripture nor philosophy testifies to Muhammad'. For Roger Bacon, neither Islam nor Judaism had the support of philosophy.[44] These were in three cases the conclusions of writers with no personal knowledge of Islam. Ricoldo constantly drew attention to the opposition of traditional philosophic principles to those of the Qur'ān, which should be confuted 'by the books of the philosophers and by the way of reason'. It does not agree with Aristotle, Christ or Moses; it 'says practically nothing about the virtues, but (speaks) about wars and plunder . . .' But the most important point was inherent logic; Muslims who denied Scripture and the philosophers must still accept reason.[45]

The theme of self-contradiction in the Qur'ān can be illustrated over a wide field of examples. Some were noted in the margins of Ketton's Qur'ān: 'A little before, he said that those who were rich in this world will be lost in the next; but now he says that Abraham was rich in this world and yet is to be numbered among the good.' The Annotator apostrophised the Prophet, asking why there were these contradictions, and replying for him: *sed ut mendax ubique tibimet ipsi contrarius existis*.[46] On the whole this theme, which had been developed in the Risālah and the *Contrarietas*, was not fully treated among Latin authors until San Pedro and Ricoldo.

The 'fables' and the 'contradictions' in the Qur'ān ranked with equal prominence in San Pedro's mind. If there were no other evidence than these, it would be known that what Muhammad said was not of God. The Qur'ān, he said, both asserted and denied that Islam should be enforced, that Christians might be saved, that God at the Last Day would reprobate the wicked; it both forbade and permitted augury; it asserted rightly that good is from God and sin from men, but then said that both good and evil are of God; it claimed both that God would judge the world and that good and evil are predetermined. These points reflect San Pedro's knowledge of actual Islamic theology; they may not be typical of controversy in the Peninsula. Muhammad had said that if there were contradictions in the Qur'ān it would not be from God. 'The Muslims are more to be blamed', commented San Pedro, 'because they believe the sayings of Muhammad, than because of the evil things they do, for Muhammad taught his followers more and greater evils, in example and in speech, than they perform when they try to imitate their master.'[47] This judgement is characteristic of its author.

The thought of the Qur'anic contradictions exercised a special charm for Christian writers. 'In many things he is found to be contrary to himself,' said Fitzralph wistfully, 'as, if God gave us time to write about this, would be more clearly shown . . .'[48] Ricoldo was given the time; his treatment was traditional and academic. It was in the choice of examples that individual preferences appeared.[49] Not all the inconsistencies noted by him are irreconcilable to the modern eye: for example, that Muhammad claimed to be a great prophet, and yet admitted that he had been born an orphan and an idolator. It seems a more substantial one that he claimed to be a universal prophet, and yet that God gave the Qur'ān in Arabic; an almost pointless one, that he said that God does not lead a man who wanders, and yet taught men to pray to be led from shadow to light. This does relate to the theme of predestination in which only San Pedro took a close interest; like him, Ricoldo also numbered the Qur'anic attitudes to augury, and to the People of the Book, among the contradictions. He counted the notion that the Old Testament prophets were *Muslim* as inherently self-contradictory. He distinguished certain points as obviously absurd, here following the *Contrarietas*. Among these *falsa et fatua* he classed the Qur'ān's reiterated assertion, as he called it, that God did not create the world in play; for who would be fool enough to suppose that He had? The Qur'ān, if true, would prove God Himself to be *fatuus*. The polemic weakness of this kind of ridicule is obvious enough, but it never appears more clearly than in the argument about the supposed phrase, 'God prays for Muhammad.' Instead of assuming that if this phrase is nonsense he must be mistranslating it, Ricoldo argued that it is another proof of Islamic unreason. The polemic aim was identical in Ricoldo and San Pedro. Ricoldo quoted the Qur'ān as saying, 'in the chapter an-nisā', which means *the women, if this Qur'ān were not from God, many discrepancies would certainly be found in it*', and, like San Pedro, he inevitably commented, 'It is evident that many discrepancies are found in it.' Peter de Pennis gave the same arguments even greater prominence.[50]

There was a corollary, put forward by a few well-informed writers, that there was an acute quarrel between philosophy and religion within Islam itself. Mark of Toledo seemed to take this for granted, when he said of ibn Tūmart, *cum in nullam crediderit legem, utpote philosophus Algazelis didasculus*. Vitry took it for granted that educated Muslims followed Muhammad's example but derided his doctrines. William of Auvergne was shocked that so great a philospher as ibn Sīna should expressly admit corporal delights in Paradise which the Qur'ān had promised. He could not imagine that any pretender to prophecy could have 'declared' the Qur'ān, but supposed the 'absurd and ridiculous things' to have been inserted after Muhammad's time by enemies of the truth who exploited the inexperience or negligence of his followers. Only a man obviously insane 'or in some other way bereft of sense' could have propounded such 'ridiculous ravings and such shameful tenets' himself. Learned Muslims accepted Muhammad as the faithful prophet of God, but 'believe him rather to have permitted to that people, because of their ignorance and barbarity, than to have enjoined, those things in his Law which seem to be iniquitous'.[51] William spoke in ignorance of the actual history and thought of Islam, which Martí, Tripoli, Ricoldo and Lull all understood much more clearly; yet all of them exaggerated the conflict between religion and philosophy in the Islamic world. Martí was at great pains to show that in the matter of Paradise the great Arabic philosophers condemned the Islamic position. This was taken up by Western scholastics whom it interested. Bacon cited the 'philosophers of the Muslims' against their own religion, quoting ibn Sīna and al-Fārābi on several themes, notably that of eternal beatitude: 'praised be God', he said, 'who gave the light of wisdom to philosophers'.[52] This was thought to be an open conflict. Tripoli asserted that the Muslim teachers despise the Qur'ān; 'their learned men', added Ricoldo in his *Itinerarium*, 'entertain no faith in the sayings of the Qur'ān, but deride it in secret; in public, however, they honour it on account of fear'. The Caliph, he maintained, had been compelled to prohibit the teaching of philosophy in the schools, so that in Ricoldo's time, when he lived in Baghdad, only the study of the Qur'ān had been enforced and encouraged. In consequence, he had found that learned Muslim knew very little of the truth of theology or the subtlety of philosophy. He had received a strong impression that they disbelieved the Qur'ān and that that was why they refused to dispute about it freely, or to allow it to be translated into other languages. He contrasted the Christian attitude to the Bible. Lull also said that the teaching of logic and natural philosophy was publicly forbidden among the Muslims, because it led to heresy and to a denial of the prophethood of Muhammad. In different places he spoke of Muslims as difficult, and as easy, to convert, but in either case, he maintained, they were convinced of the error of Islam. He took it for granted that learned Muslims were in a state of doubt; in one of the fictional settings in which he liked to present his controversial writings in form of debate, he imagined a Muslim led by long study alone to doubt the truth of Muhammad's claims. Buenhombre also seems to have taken it for granted that the Qur'ān and its commentators could be ignored, because Muslims did so themselves.[53]

Ricoldo's attitude seems to represent that of his contemporaries in an extreme form. From all the polemic that he inherited, both the books and the living tradition, he constructed an encyclopaedic refutation of Islam from which nothing he had ever heard was omitted, and this is specially noticeable in his treatment of the present theme. The literalism of his attack, which often he owed to the *Contrarietas*, went beyond reason; for example, over the supposed Qur'anic absurdity that God prays for Muhammad. If the Qur'ān appeared to say such a silly thing, it must really say it;

Arabs could not be allowed to explain what the Arabic meant. There was a deeper weakness in Ricoldo's approach. He was lucky not to have to refute the very arguments that he used against Islam, but brought against Christian doctrine, as many of his very rationalist arguments would in fact be brought in later ages. He would not have appreciated being told that the Old Testament is often 'metrical', poetry not to be taken literally; or that it is far too repetitive in its praise of God; that it contains words that in another context might be considered indecent, or stories that a sceptic might consider fabulous, especially in their traditional interpretation; that it deals with wars, and fails to treat continuously of the virtues as a philosophical tract does; that inconsistencies can be alleged of it, and that it offends the order of time and the order of subject-matter and of logic. All these things have been said of the Bible since Ricoldo's day; any inspired book, whether true or not, will be liable to attacks of this kind.[54] Ricoldo was too concerned with what are really only debating points. So much of what he wrote did nothing to illumine Islam for his contemporaries. San Pedro's work often seems more sober, less cocksure. If the works on Islam are indeed correctly attributed to him, they were the fruit of a long life spent in controversy and in works of mercy, not of one single incursion into the lands of Islam, and they certainly corresponded better with the actual requirements of debate. Yet in its general lines his polemic follows the same traditional pattern as Ricoldo's. The main attack on Islam was already determined in the thirteenth century. The Christian champions were convinced, not only of the truth, but of the best method to convey it, beyond any possibility of reviewing the force of their arguments. This is most apparent in their treatment of the Qur'ān. Ricoldo tells us that as often as he read it, he placed it upon the altar, and indignantly demanded of God that He read what it said.

3. THE PROPHETHOOD OF MUHAMMAD

Christian polemic ought, it seemed to those most concerned with it, to be so directed as wholly to discredit the Prophet. If he could be shown to be no prophet, the whole Islamic fabric failed. The reverse was also true. 'We concede', said Peter the Venerable, 'that a true prophet ought to be believed', and the proof that Muhammad claimed the title falsely had to be explicit.[55] This task came gratefully to Christian writers. The character and the history of the Prophet were such as genuinely shocked them; they were outraged that he should be accepted as a venerated figure. Although it was generally known that he pretended only to be a prophet, *legis divinae non auctor sed lator*,[56] the chief object of

Christian polemic would be, on the contrary, to show that he was the author of his religion, and to discredit his revelation by showing it to have arisen out of the social and political circumstances of a particular place and age.

Whatever in Islam was most repellent to the Christian seemed to him also to be most typical of it, and it was easy to set up standards against which all prophethood might be tested and Muhammad's be dismissed. Such standards were at hand. 'Indeed,' said Pedro de Alfonso, 'the signs of a true prophet are probity of life, the presentation of true miracles and the constant truth of all his sayings.' This scheme would serve as a good summary of the main argument of either the Risālah or the *Contrarietas*, although there is no indication of a direct connection. Indeed, these three points almost summarised the entire mediaeval polemic. Peter of Poitiers, when he prepared his headings, preserved Pedro's plan more clearly than his Abbot would in working them out. He intended the second book of the work to show that Muhammad could not be a prophet, because he was a robber, a murderer, a traitor and an adulterer. To disqualification on account of his 'evil life' were added Pedro's other two points: the shameful and contradictory teaching of the Qur'ān and its not being confirmed by miracles. Except to point out Muhammad's failure to foretell his own successors, the whole of the third book would have been devoted to the absence of confirmatory miracles.[57]

Peter the Venerable, when he came to put the plan into effect, was a good deal less systematic still. His thought is complex, but lacks a clear schematisation of reasons for rejecting Muhammad's claim; in that respect he was unscholastic. He sought a definition of the office of prophet which his imaginary Muslim readers would be bound to accept, and which would exclude Muhammad. To this end he elaborated Muhammad's failure actually to foretell. Thus he argued that the prophet must publish things unknown, 'either of time past, or present or future', by divine inspiration. This is to give 'prophecy' its familiar everyday sense, with good Patristic authority, and it is to ignore any claim based chiefly upon the religious leadership of the community by divine appointment. Muhammad quite simply foretold nothing that was unknown: 'while he affirms himself the prophet of God almost *ad nauseam*, and affirms it and repeats it, he says nothing about things to come, utters nothing prophetic'.[58] Yet this was a narrower interpretation of the prophetic function than the Christian view really requires; the prophecies of the Holy Saturday liturgy are a series of divine mercies which prefigure the final mercy, rather than prophecies within Peter's definition.[59]

We may compare the Christian conception of the Red Sea

Crossing, as both a mercy and a promise of God to His people, to the Qur'anic idea of His mercy to the Muslims at Badr, His endorsement thereby of the prophethood of Muhammad and promise that Islam would prevail.[60] It would be difficult to exclude Muhammad by definition, without excluding Moses, 'the greatest of the prophets',[61] by the same definition. It would be even harder to find a definition that would admit Abraham while excluding Muhammad. We may say that theophany by a human medium is prophecy. A prophet is one who acts as the interpreter of God, one through whom God speaks: *Qui locutus est per prophetas*. This primary meaning seems to subsist, whether we speak of the Old Testament prophets, or of prophets of pagan religions, or even of prophets of purely secular modern events, who reveal (or claim to reveal) the providential designs of God. In this primary sense, which has nothing to do with the truth or otherwise of any particular claim to prophethood, Muhammad could clearly not be excluded simply by definition.

It is true that a prophet must be a means of actual revelation, not a repeater of commonplaces. This was advanced to show that Muhammad could be excluded by definition, but it is difficult to defend such a train of thought. St Thomas, it is true, defined a prophet as primarily one to whom *distant things appear*,[62] and in this he certainly agreed with Peter the Venerable; but it is to take even this or any similar definition too literally to assert, as Peter and others did, that what Muhammad claimed fell outside its scope. St Thomas and any theologian would agree that the existence of God is not only known to reason, but is also the subject of Old Testament revelations; and the Last Judgement and Heaven and Hell and the duties of religion, all of which Peter knew Muhammad to have proclaimed, can only be known through revelation. They are 'distant things', 'things unknown'. Above all, the claim that Muhammad is prophet of God and head of His community, to which Peter actually refers when he is ridiculing Muhammad's claim, falls well within the definition. Pedro de Alfonso had disqualified Muhammad for reasons much sounder, at least so far as logic is concerned.

The existence of kinds of prophecy outside the framework of the Old Testament, and of evil prophets within it, was generally assumed in the Middle Ages, although the prophets of Christ were incomparably more important than the others. St Thomas referred to the *vates* of ancient paganism, citing St Isidore on the classical poets, and he justified the possibility of truthful prophecy in cases of 'demoniacs, possession and false prophecy'; that is, pseudoprophecy might utter truths.[63] We have already seen that prophecy by demoniac possession was sometimes thought possibly

to explain Muhammad's revelations. Wide credit was given to
secular prophecies of the rise and fall of Islam, as well as to other
prophecies of an historical and secular character.[64] Roger Bacon
could speak of the saints as *prophetae posteriores* who possess
discernment of the truth of past, present and future matters.[65] This
wider view of prophethood, within which it was not possible to
exclude Muhammad by definition, indicated another and more
effective direction of attack, which brought Peter the Venerable's
thought closer to that of his contemporaries and successors, and
to an argument more securely set in Christian tradition. It proceeded, he himself said, from a 'new starting-point'. This was to
classify prophets as good and bad; the good as either universal or
particular, the bad as either true or false. Universal prophets are
those who foretold Christ; their supply was now naturally dried
up. Particular or personal prophets foretell particular things, but
the Qur'ān contains no such prophecy. Bad prophets were those
whose life was reprobate, their teaching false, like the prophets of
Baal. It is obvious where Muhammad was to fit into this classification, although the author failed to develop this part of his
argument. Peter's attack on Muhammad as wicked and as false
thus represents two elements in the systematic attack put forward
by Pedro de Alfonso. A great deal of Peter's argument consisted
in setting the claims of Islam beside the story of the Hebrew
prophets, to show the two to be inconsistent; this was also in line
with the Risālah, with Pedro de Alfonso and with the wide
Christian tradition, and excluded Muhammad's claims, not by
definition, but by requiring particular qualities in the prophet and
his prophecies.[66] In all this field Peter was less systematic, and yet
more thorough, than any other writer.

The clearest schematisation of standards of prophecy that must
ensure the rejection of Muhammad's claim was that of the *reprobatio*. This began with the evangelical warning, 'Beware of false
prophets', in which it distinguished three elements, the warning,
the description of sheep in wolves' clothing, the recognition of them
by their fruits.[67] There must be four fruits or signs, and each must
be demonstrated by reason and by authority. The prophet must
speak the truth: as reason shows, because God is truth and no lie
can derive from Him; as authority does, when Holy Scripture says,
'Whatsoever that same prophet foretelleth in the name of the
Lord, and it cometh not to pass: that thing the Lord hath not
spoken, but the prophet hath forged it in the pride of his mind.'[68]
This will indicate the method, which was wholly scholastic. By
the same means it was shown that the second sign was the goodness
and virtue of the prophet (*ambulans in via immaculata* . . .)[69]; the
third was the ability to work miracles; the fourth, that the Law by

which he comes must be 'holy and good, leading the nations to the worship of the one God, and men to holiness of life and concord and peace'. Whoever exhibited fruits the contrary of these must be a false prophet.[70]

As in the other cases we have considered, it is obvious that these tests have to some extent been tailored in advance to fit Muhammad's circumstances. Essentially this is the scheme of Pedro de Alfonso, improved by the addition of the fourth head which distinguished Muhammad's religious institutions from his personal probity of life or his truthfulness. It sometimes recalls Peter the Venerable's work, but it ignores that enthusiast's stressed point that Prophecy means only a foretelling of the future in which Muhammad failed. The rejection of Muhammad's prophethood by the fourfold test constitutes the bulk of the *reprobatio*, and this gives it an admirable clarity.[71] The author was not one of those who invented details of Islamic religion or of the life of the Prophet in order to attack them. Thus his outline of the career of Muhammad from his birth to his call summarised the ḥadīth and contained little that was controversial, or even that was unfavourable to Muhammad. The lies of the Prophet which the author cited were just different erroneous aspects of Islamic belief, simply listed from the Qur'ān and the Traditions, and classified as true or untrue. The same economy of method was employed against the holiness of the Prophet and of his religion, and against his miracles: a chain of Islamic authorities. This work was presumably intended rather for the information of propagandists than for propaganda; but it was a skilled advocacy that did not overstate the case.

Humbert of Romans adopted the same scheme in his recommendations to preachers. Other religions, the preacher should say, were delivered by holy men, this one by an adulterer whose revelations justified his sins and whom no miracle confirmed. 'The vileness of his religion is clear, then, as much from the vileness of the person teaching it, as from the shameful character of the things taught, and from the defect in the divine evidence (*ostensio*) which God is accustomed to provide (*facere*) in the handing down of His Laws.'[72] Ricoldo was even more inclined to schematisation, but with him an excess of it resulted in confusion. He attacked the Qur'ān through the Prophet, thus reversing the more usual dismissal of the lawgiver because of the law, possibly because he recognised the greater significance of the Qur'ān than of the Prophet. Yet he covered all the aspects that we have been considering: the Law was irrational because unconfirmed by miracles, because of the wickedness and lewdness of its institutor, because it contradicts itself and lies and is iniquitous. There was special emphasis on sexual sin; any other sin would be more tolerable in a prophet. 'For the Spirit does not touch the hearts of prophets', he quoted, 'in the sexual act, as Jerome says; and the Philosopher says that in that act it is impossible to have understanding.' The authorities seem irrelevant; they were traditionally associated with the scholastic treatment of prophecy, but in the context of Muhammad's claims there was no question of prophecy made in the course of 'that act'; this illustrates that sexual aspect of the polemic which nearly every mediaeval writer thought to be particularly important. In one respect Ricoldo picked up Peter the Venerable's argument. He listed among Muhammad's 'lies' the claim to be the seal of the prophets, to which he objected that the prophetic gift continued to be given. This had no prominence in his scheme, which was so repetitive that we can only say that he used the traditional arguments without improving the form of their presentation.[73]

In the fourteenth century Marino Sanudo owed much of his supporting material to Pedro de Alfonso; the tests of prophethood were holiness, miracles and 'an exact observation of future things'. To these he opposed three radical sources of sin by which Muhammad might be recognised as false: concupiscence of the eyes, by reason of robbery; pride of life, by reason of usurped power; concupiscence of the flesh, by reason of lasciviousness. This second scheme would modify the first to which it does not provide neat parallels.[74]

These schematised rejections of Muhammad's claim to the character of a true prophet may have been slightly adapted to suit the particular case, but they were wholly in line with contemporary theological thought on prophecy. All the points we have seen applied to Muhammad are to be found in St Thomas' treatment of prophecy, where he does not explicitly admit that the thought of Muhammad was in his mind at all. He taught that it was a condition of true prophecy that it be always true; that passions were wholly incompatible with prophecy; and that miracles were an integral part of it, because, just as the gift of tongues and the grace of eloquence enable a prophet to convince the people, so do miracles confirm what he says. Thus the contribution of the anti-Islamic polemists was chiefly to apply existing arguments to the case in question; but this case may have stimulated the scholastics to narrow and make more precise the functions of a prophet.[75]

Fragments of the same attitude were reflected in a number of writers, whether they derived from actual polemic or from the common stock of theological perceptions of the time. It was, for example, a favourite theme of Lull's that Islam failed to teach the enjoyment of the Divine Essence in Paradise, 'and thus it is impossible that he who excites his people to sensual things rather than to spiritual ones should be a true messenger of God'. San Pedro ignored the schematic treatment; he stressed that, even in the form that Muslims themselves related the Prophet's life, Muhammad spoke of 'many things which it was proper for no man to say or do who declared himself to be the messenger of God'. The fourteenth-century English pilgrim used the phrase *simulator sanctitatis*; and it was often as characteristically the deceiver that he was mentioned: *praestigiator animarum*, said the second account of Islam quoted by Matthew Paris, and Guido Terrena, like the *reprobatio*, identified him as a false prophet in the evangelical context.[76] The whole presentation of Muhammad's life by every Latin writer was intended to demonstrate its incompatibility with a prophetic vocation.

4. THE DIVINE WITNESS OF MIRACLES

The mediaeval treatment of some of these themes, of the wickedness of life of the Prophet, and of the evil and falsity of his teaching, is discussed in more detail separately. The question of his not having worked miracles was also regarded as cardinally important, although it was not capable of as much elaboration as these other themes. It is considered here as integral to the concept of prophecy which Muhammad did not satisfy. It was an essential part of the 'disproof' and it was in itself believed to be conclusive.[77]

Pedro de Alfonso associated the necessity of miracles with law-giving prophecy. In his dialogue with his former unconverted self, *Moyses*, he referred to Muhammad:

Peter: . . . And certainly we do not know of . . . any miracle of his, such as we have heard of in the cases of Moses, Josue, Samual, Elias and Eliseus, who, we read, did many miracles.

Moses: But we do believe in many prophets of whom we read of no miracles, such as Jeremias, Abdias, Amos, Osee and others.

Peter: Miracles are not to be sought in their case, because they did not introduce any novelty of law . . .

The Latins agreed with the first Quraysh against whose unbelief the Qur'anic revelations about miracles were directed. With gratification Latins maintained that in the Qur'ān Muhammad had denied his own power to work miracles; we have seen already that they could not take seriously the Qur'ān's assertion that it is itself the true miracle.[78] Pedro said that the Qur'ān gave as its reason that men would 'speak against' the Prophet for his miracles, 'as against the other prophets', if he were given the power to work them.[79] Peter of Poitiers thought it impossible that there should be lawgiving and prophecy without miracles; Peter the Venerable ridiculed at some length the idea that God renounced miracles for

Muhammad, and that He did so because Muhammad would not have been believed, if he had had their aid. Moses and Christ, said Peter, worked miracles and were believed; multitudes believed Muhammad without miracles; was it likely that they would have disbelieved him with them?[80] This was a little disingenuous. Peter may have had no clear picture of the relations of Muhammad to the Quraysh in Mecca; but he certainly knew that Moses, and still more Christ and the Apostles, had encountered unbelief. It seemed important to him, as to so many, that Muhammad had himself denied that he had this power; this was treated as though it were a confession on Muhammad's part that he was not what he pretended.

The same theme is clearly expressed by other authors.[81] Of these, one of the earliest, the Syrian Apology, gave a full list of the false miracles alleged of Muhammad and suitable for Christian ridicule; these were the miracles, asserted by Muslims, which their own Prophet had repudiated for them in advance: the wolf by the wayside, the ox that talked, the fig-tree that prostrated itself and came at the Prophet's call, the moon that was divided and re-joined, the poisoned leg of lamb that warned Muhammad not to eat. All these, the author pointed out, had been denied in advance by the Qur'ān.[82] Alan of Lille pithily expressed an idea which penetrated far beyond the immediate circle of Islamologists: 'With them, miracles are worked by not working miracles (*fiunt miracula per antiphrasim*).'[83] This presumably refers to the notion of the Qur'ān as the true miracle.

In connection with miracles there was yet another association of ideas: the place of miracles was supplied by force of arms, said Martí; not successfully, he pointed out, at Uḥud.[84] The first spread of Islam, the conversion of the world to Christianity, were contrasted under this aspect. There was pleasure in the Prophet's wounds at Uḥud, because they disproved the claim that angels guarded him. Roger Bacon analysed the suggestion that miracles could be superfluous; they were a sign of the truth of the saints; he insisted that Muhammad's were false, miracles only in appearance. Muslims' claim that he did work miracles was an admission that they were necessary, and al-Fārābi openly admitted this.[85] Another account rubbed in the notion of conscious fraud: Muhammad was compelled to pretend that conversion to Islam must be spontaneous and uninfluenced by miracles, the more meritorious for being so, because he knew 'that his merit with God was not so great that God would do anything miraculous for him'.[86] This is ingenious, but does not reflect any Islamic ideas.

Some of these statements were remote from any real knowledge of the Qur'ān or of the historical circumstances of the Prophet's preaching in Mecca. It is interesting to compare those accounts which are better-informed, but which adopt the same attitude. Ketton's text once again rendered the general sense of the relevant passages, not of course with verbal accuracy, but unambiguously and truly.[87] San Pedro told of the Prophet's encounter with the Quraysh in an elaborate version which is substantially close to the Arabic sources. His summing up was the usual one: Muhammad had told the men of Mecca himself that he was not sent to accomplish miracles, and if his modern followers pretended otherwise, they made him a liar.[88]

The two fullest treatments were that in the *reprobatio* and that by Ricoldo. The former, even more than the work of San Pedro or Ricoldo, added convincing authority by its authentic use of sources. It gave greatest prominence to the Qur'anic text so often, but more vaguely, referred to: the Prophet's insistence that he is called to announce and warn, but not to work miracles for which 'certain Arabs' (the Quraysh) had asked: to move the mountains from round Mecca, to make the soil fertile, or to raise up their ancestor Quṣayy. The author stressed his sympathy for the Quraysh, when he reported their saying to Muhammad that God should have foreseen the quandary in which their demand had put His Prophet, and should have taught him in advance how to reply. Next in his list of authorities was sūrah xvii: 'Or thou *cause* the Heavens to fall down upon us, *as thou hast given out*, in pieces': the Meccans would not believe unless the Prophet's warnings were realised; this was rendered, *dicentes ei, ut faceret coelum cadere super eos, ut dixerat se facturum* . . . There seems to be here a slight but important distortion; Muhammad had not threatened personally to ensure that the Heavens would fall. Another authority was in fact more pertinent: 'Am I other than a man, sent as an apostle?' (*respondit quod ipse non esset nisi homo nuncius*). 'As though to say', the Spanish writer emphasised, 'that he could not do what they asked him', that is, work miracles. The same author also quoted al-Bukhārī: Muhammad said that it was not given to him to work such miracles as might make men believe him, but to receive the inspiration with which God inspired him. From all these authorities a restricted conclusion was drawn: 'It is obvious that he never worked miracles.' It was thought worth the trouble of so detailed a demonstration.[89]

It is interesting to compare what Ricoldo had to say. His summary of the Qur'anic denial of miracles reveals commoner, less authentic sources. Moses and Christ were not believed; God for that reason did not permit Muhammad miracles, but instead he came 'in the strength of arms'. Ricoldo contrasted Christianity, which converted the world by persuasion. Logically this must have been either with, or without, the help of miracles; if without, that were the greater miracle, since it is a creed of self-denial. In either alternative, it can be seen that Christianity is based on astonishing miracles, *stupendis miraculis esse fundatam*. Ricoldo treated the miracle of the divided moon, attributed by Muslims to Muhammad, with particular attention, as did also the *reprobatio*. The latter distinguished carefully between what the Qur'ān says and what the Muslims assert; the tale was, of course, absurd: *fabulose asserunt Saraceni* . . . But the Qur'ān says nothing of this tale in which Muhammad gives orders to the moon, the author warned his readers; it says only that the day is drawing near when the moon shall be divided, and this, to anyone who understands it correctly, means the Day of Judgement. 'In the authority, the phrase *when the Day of Judgement draws near* is put first, and *the moon is split* follows after.' This was a fair and reasonable use of sources. Ricoldo, in the *Itinerarium*, began with assurance that masked inaccuracy. 'Indeed Muhammad himself says in the chapter al-qamr, which means *moon*, that the moon was cut up in his time, and half fell on one mountain . . .' In the *Disputatio* he admitted that the miracle was only clearly claimed by the commentators, and by the Qur'ān itself just vaguely. In both accounts he blurred the distinction between the Islamic assertion and the Qur'anic denial, which, from the Christian point of view, is the only point of the story. Ricoldo's statement owes its unfairness and obscurity to the *Contrarietas*; it comes in a chapter devoted to proving Islam to be 'mendacissima'; Ricoldo was not the first or the last to do so, in good faith or ill, mendaciously. Both he and the author of the *reprobatio* concluded by stressing physical and historical arguments to disprove the alleged miracle; the one said that, as the moon is not a heavy body, it could not fall, the other that, as it is larger than the earth, it could not fall on a part of the earth only; both said that such a thing could not have happened unknown to all the world, and unrecorded.[90]

Fitzralph, working from Ketton's text, and evidently influenced by the traditional exegesis, considered more general aspects principally. He was specially impressed to be able to quote the authority of the Qur'ān itself – *ex ipsa lege sarracenorum apparet* – for the fact that the Gospel was confirmed by miracles – *nostra lex specialiter per miracula roboratur*; this was in contrast to the revelation claimed for Muhammad.

Again, he excuses himself from the idea of miracles, as by divine authority, as if God would not wish to occupy him in this way. From this it appears that he affirms that he was not sent to work wonders, but to bestow the precepts of God: and nevertheless he affirms that Christ taught the Book of the Gospel with many great miracles . . . From the

Law of the Muslims itself it is clear that our Law especially is strengthened by miracles, and that, he affirms, theirs is not so confirmed.

The witness even of the Apostles and disciples of Christ was fortified by miracles. How clearly this showed the superiority of Christ to Muhammad.[91]

Thus every Christian critic insisted that there was no miracle in Islam; this was an approach that took it for granted that Heaven would always endorse a genuine revelation with prodigies. This, said William of Auvergne, was the testimony that distinguished the Christian from other dispensations, pagan, Muslim or heretical. His language when he defines what he means by miracles curiously recalls what the Qur'ān itself says of Christ: ' . . . unaccustomed operations contrary to the course of nature, such as raisings from the dead, giving sight to the blind, cleansing of lepers, cures of demoniacs, throwings out and bindings of demons and such . ..'[92] These were the authentic mark of Christendom, and there was Qur'anic authority for saying so. That is why the Qur'anic admission that the Prophet did not work miracles was greeted with delight; why the denial of the necessity for them, and the idea that the Qur'ān itself was the miracle, were both ignored or derided. The faith in visible signs was based on the broad tradition of Christian and Jewish, and indeed pagan, religion, in which miracles are a normal element; the Latins felt that they stood here on self-evident data.

5. CONCLUDING REMARKS

The feeling of Latin Christians was so strongly that they were supported by the weight of world opinion and history. They believed that what they rejected was peculiar and alien to all nations, to the pagan philosophers and to the Holy Scriptures; obviously offensive to good taste and to reason. It is exactly in their conviction that they shared a universal opinion that they seem most provincial. It was natural, but polemically profitless, that they could not imagine Scriptural stories in forms other than those in which Scriptures recounted them. They could not think themselves, even for purposes of argument, into a position that was not based upon Scripture. The Qur'ān became the object of their ridicule because it was unfamiliar, and the effort to see that that kind of ridicule was applicable by an enemy to their own Scripture was beyond them. They were tied to their own tradition and unable to look outside it.

The idea of 'pseudoprophecy' was wholly Scriptural. Muhammad corresponded to such figures as the prophets of Baal and to the false prophets against whom Christ warned. It seemed necessary to push condemnation to its fullest extent. If the easy dismissal, as truisms, of the revelation to Muhammad of the unity of God, of the warnings of hell-fire, of demands for belief in and submission to God, seem uncharitable and even obtuse, it must be remembered that no historical imagination could then reconstruct the Meccan situation in the time of the Prophet. On the contrary, the contemporary professional necromancer and charlatan fitted with the Scriptural picture and with the accepted caricature of Muhammad.

The tests of prophethood were not invented for the occasion; but from the details of how they were put forward it is obvious that the intention was to show Muhammad to be a false prophet, not to establish the prophetic signs with academic impartiality. These points were the very ones where Muhammad failed. Naturally they were given prominence, as *fruits* in the Gospel sense, till they excluded all other aspects of prophethood. 'Disproof' in consequence did not relate exactly to the case that was actually made out by Muslim apologists, who would stress that Muhammad restored the purity of worship, that he led the people of God with a divine approbation that was proved by success, notably at the battle of Badr, above all that the Qur'ān which was revealed to him was almost self-evidently of God. The latter point was so ill appreciated that it could not be effectively attacked; the others were considered and rejected by Latin polemists, but not emphatically; for Christian writers their own favourite schematisation was more important. Their polemic scheme was well suited to convincing convinced Christians; hardly at all to real debate against Muslims in the flesh.

Argument taken from Scripture and argument about Scripture based upon a peculiar interpretation of the Qur'ān were unlikely to impress Muslims at all. We shall see that this was also true of much historical analysis of the Prophet's life. It is only in the field of moral philosophy that arguments were based on common ground, and the same weakness appears there, when data were defined by Christians without proof of their validity, still less of their acceptability by Muslims. We may say that it was absurd to insist on the absence of miracles in Islam, and yet to refuse to take seriously the Qur'anic argument that they were not needed, or that the Qur'ān's own inspiration was self-evident. If we say this we criticise anachronistically; our circumstances, which make this possible, are different. At that time in Europe too great an effort was required to understand the unfamiliar; and in Asia and Africa the same was true of Muslims. Common ground between Christian and Muslim, either to understand each other or to find mutually acceptable premises to justify rejection, was rarely sought, and, when sought, was sought half-heartedly and generally without success.

✍ III ✍

The life of Muhammad:
polemic biography

THE life of Muhammad was seen as an essential disproof of the
Islamic claim to Revelation. It was often treated as the most
important disproof of all. To this end writers believed and wished
to show that Muhammad was a low-born and pagan upstart, who
schemed himself into power, who maintained it by pretended
revelations, and who spread it both by violence and by permitting
to others the same lascivious practices as he indulged in himself.
Moreover, if this were Muhammad, it was necessary to show how
he ever came to be accepted at all. The Arabia into which he was
born is of crucial importance for any study of his life: this is
obvious now, and seemed equally so to mediaeval writers. A
convincing explanation of the rise of Islam required, not only that
the Prophet should have been cunning, but that the pagan Arabs
should have been ignorant, and the Arabian Jews and heretical
Christians malicious.

1. THE JĀHILĪYAH

Christian and Latin writers followed Muslim Arab practice in
emphasising the descent of Muhammad. The most popular of
mediaeval accounts began with a description of Muhammad as
prince of the Arabs, pseudoprophet, of the race of Ismael, son of
Abraham.[1] Perhaps his tree of descent seemed to reverse the tree
of Jesse; many writers were sensitive to a contrast between the
lives of Jesus and of Muhammad. Sometimes Muhammad's whole
lineage was thought worth stating, even by itself, without context.[2] With this theme was associated the argument that Saracens
were not of Sara, and should be called Agarenes, from Agar; the
term Ismaelite was similarly used.[3] It was quite wrongly supposed
that the word 'Saracen' was an Islamic term, implying a claim to
legitimate descent from Abraham. This Agarene descent, though
often stated without comment, had polemic significance. Peter the
Venerable said that it committed the Arabs to accept the Jewish
Holy Books; but more typically William of Auvergne saw in it

the fulfilment of the divine purpose: 'I will make the son also of
the bondwoman a great nation.' For William of Tripoli another
promise was fulfilled in Muhammad, who was 'wild and powerful
to pitch his tents against all men'.[4] This by implication imputed
the lawlessness of the desert nomad to the whole people of Islam.
Vitry, like Tripoli from 'Akka, but of an earlier generation,
brought forward the same theme less strongly.[5] San Pedro found
it strange that Muhammad should wish to claim descent from the
cursed and disinherited son; three hundredth in descent from
Abraham, this ancestry was a figure of the thirty pieces of silver,
because Muhammad betrayed the people of Christ. Ismael had
been cast off for idolatry; the issue of the illegitimate struggled
against the legitimate succession; it was to have been expected
that the Arabs would raise enemies to the Church.[6] There was
widespread a strong sense of this great but evil destiny that lay
behind Muhammad.

There is something in this of the distrust felt by the citizen for
the desert nomad, made to serve a polemic end. There was
sympathy for the Meccans who persecuted their Prophet, for the
merchants who disbelieved, and contempt for the foolish simplicity
of the Medinans and the desert people, the rustics who believed.
The actual differences between Mecca and Medina, and the
presence of the Jews at Medina, were known, but were usually
much confused.[7] There was some thought for the historical context. Arabia was generally understood to have traded freely with
Syria and Egypt.[8] Muhammad was often dated, following the
Greek authorities, by the reign of Heraclius and the restoration
of the True Cross in the Persian campaign; some chroniclers
quoted the year of the Visigothic King of Spain, the Papal and
other regnal years. The year of grace was often muddled.[9] The
world situation in Muhammad's day was better documented and
understood than that in the Arabian peninsula.

Yet a recognisable picture of the Ḥijāz in the Prophet's day
emerged. Pedro de Alfonso spoke of the Arabians as mostly
'soldiers and farmers', idolators except for some Jews, who were
Samaritan heretics, and some Christians who were Nestorian and
Jacobite. When Viterbo said that Muhammad's mother was a
Jewess, his father a pagan, he may have reflected confusedly this
already confused description. Mark of Toledo said that Mecca
means *adulteria* (*moecha*): 'who, leaving God, her lawful husband,
like a prostitute, and substituting many gods to herself, per-
petrated an impious adultery'. The Arabs were 'rough and untaught', but Muhammad knew about Christianity and Judaism.
More plainly, Roderick of Toledo said that at Muhammad's birth
Arabia and Africa were torn between the Catholic faith, the Arian

heresy, the Jewish perfidy and idolatry; that his father's preference fluctuated between the Catholics and the Jews. Mecca owed its importance to its many idols.[10]

A description in the *Historia Arabum* of the rebuilding of the Ka'bah in pagan times speaks of this shrine as a church; yet the account is clearly based on a Muslim source deriving ultimately from ibn Isḥāq. The sanctity of the Black Stone, the selection by chance of Muhammad to put it into position, his solution of the rival tribal claims to participate, by which four of the Quraysh lifted it in their mantle, while he himself set it in its place; the acclaim of this as a miracle; these episodes which Roderick described have authentic Arabic sources, barely comprehended. Other points were still more confused; for example, that a Meccan critic disliked Muhammad's decision and foretold trouble for the City; or that it was now that the Quraysh were taught to pray towards the Ka'bah. The Quraysh appear as a Council of City Fathers, humiliated by having to follow the lead of their junior.[11]

Muhammad's youth spent among merchant travellers was more widely recounted; in the *reprobatio* his acting as agent for Khadījah is clearly told. San Pedro's more lucid picture of Meccan society in general included abū Bakr, 'a merchant, as all the rest of the inhabitants of Mecca were merchants'; to him the others would listen, because he knew their ways. The 'citizens' took action when they heard that their 'fellow citizens' were being converted. They insisted that Muhammad should renounce his *demon*, lest it bring wars on the City; or else work miracles to prove himself, causing the mountains which circumscribed them so closely to recede: 'thou dost well know that no other people possesses a more confined territory or a more arid land than we'. They were prepared to bribe him to be silent, with riches and power. The *reprobatio*, recounting the same incident in a context less clearly expounded, had also left the reader with an impression of the poverty of the cultivable land around Mecca, waterless and narrowly enclosed among mountains, but it lacked a clear vision of the Quraysh as merchants of substance within this setting.

San Pedro told the story of the Jewish challenge to Muhammad about the Seven Sleepers of Ephesus in some detail; in this the Meccan pagans appear as prudent in their investigations, the Jews of Medina as foolish to produce so legendary a test of prophecy, although the Old Testament taught the true tests. San Pedro inclined to blame these Jews for the early success of Islam, but he liked to dwell on the incredulity of the Meccans, their suspicion that Muhammad had a secret teacher, their ridicule of the mi'rāj: 'and I certainly say to you, inhabitants of Mecca, . . . that it would

have been better if you had persevered in resisting Muhammad
. . .'[12] He was compelled to admit that the Prophet had done right
to speak against their many gods; Vitry had been similarly
reluctant to disapprove of the Meccans for wanting nothing to do
with Muhammad's empty words, although he had attacked their
idolatry. Vitry also spoke of Medina as divided between Jews and
'idolators, rough and untaught, who had never or rarely heard
the preaching of the truth'. Other works derived from the Risālah
also expanded what was only a hint in the original. The Syrian
Apology spoke of 'Arabs, *villani*, uneducated people who had
never seen a prophet'. They were 'rough, uneducated, simple men,
easy to seduce and fleshly, as in the poem: *Et nos in vitium caterva
sumus*'.[13] William of Auvergne took the ignorance and barbarity
of these people for granted. Fra Fidenzio, in an account which
shares sources with Mark's, generations earlier, spoke of Mecca
as specially given to worship of idols, and he confused it with
Medina, because he described it as divided between Jews and
idolators; he too spoke of the roughness of the people thus easily
deceived. Humbert of Romans referred to 'brutish people', and
Ludolf, with the pilgrim's experience, to 'rough men wandering
in the desert'; Aquinas combined the two phrases.[14]

Lull knew the old name, 'Yathrib', for Medina, but he had no
clear topographical notions. He told his son that 'Yathrib and
Mecca and all that province were full of people who believed in
idols and who adored the sun and the moon and the beasts and the
birds, and had no knowledge of God, and had no king, and were
people of little discretion or understanding'. The nature worship
is his own invention, implying presuppositions about the dogmatic
content of paganism; but he rightly said that the people had no
belief in immortality, and he described Muhammad's preaching of
Judgement and heavenly reward.[15] Acqui imagined a nation that
was almost lawless, composed of crude and simple mountaineers.
Another writer spoke of the grossness of the Arabians who had no
lord, no king and no law; he did not know the name of Medina,
but he knew that it was inhabited by both Jews and pagans.[16] Thus
most of those who could distinguish at all thought of Mecca as a
true city, ruled by its merchants, while Medina belonged to Jews
and illiterate pagans. The fault of the latter city was to have
accepted, the virtue of the former to have rejected, the prophethood
of Muhammad.

The paganism of Muhammad's birth was seen as an argument
against his claims; this reversed the modern view that the revelation is more impressive that comes to an idolator, the conversion
more creditable that happens in spite of circumstances. Muhammad
was also often supposed quite wrongly to be ignobly born: 'base

by birth, at first a follower of the ancient idolatry, as were all the other Arabs of his time'. The Cluniac *summula* said that he 'lived a barbarian among barbarians and an idolator among idolators'. This pagan background was so often stressed. Pedro de Alfonso and authors who followed him cited the Qur'ān to prove how the Prophet 'served the widespread idol-worship of the Arabs': 'thou wast an orphan and I received thee, thou didst remain long in the error of idolatry and I led you from it, thou wast poor and I made thee rich'. Other writers stressed the worship of idols by the young Muhammad; mentioned his father's name as 'Habedileth, that is, slave of the idol Leth'; imagined the Christian Baḥīrā's exhorting him to 'fly the worship of idols'; suspected a wish to compromise with paganism and with magic. The *reprobatio* stressed that Muhammad committed 'the sin of idolatry' until he was forty years old: the Qur'ān 'says that God found Muhammad in error – that is, in error about the laws of God – and directed him'; this seemed sufficiently important to seek corroboration in Bukhārī. The Devil, said Ricoldo in his turn, chose for his purposes an idolator; Ricoldo thought it inconsistent to claim to be a great prophet, after spending a pagan youth. With this emphasis on Muhammad's pagan upbringing went references to the fact that his relations who died before his call were heathen to the last and went to hell; this had Islamic authority. By a curious irony, when Trevisa translated Higden's phrase about Muhammad's serving the cult of idolatry in his youth, with all the Arabian people, he used the word 'mawmetrie'.[17] All the better-informed authors realised that Muhammad attacked the idolatry of his people: '. . . by preaching that one God only should be adored, he very often quarrelled with those who were of the race of the Quraysh and adored idols . . .' There was a general awareness of the paganism that surrounded Muhammad in his youth and which Islam destroyed.[18]

The fable to the contrary which imagined Islam to be an apostasy from Christianity (often from a recent conversion) was largely literary. This bizarre tale must ultimately derive, in all the ramifications of its different forms, from the idea that Islam was formulated out of Christian dogmatic elements, and from the ever-present memory of those Christian provinces in Syria, Egypt, North Africa and Spain which the Christian world had in fact lost to Islam. There were stories that associated Muhammad with the New Testament heresiarch Nicholas; others that supposed him to have been under the influence of, or actually to have been, a Roman cardinal or cleric, frustrated in his ambition, who perverted his own converts to spite the Roman Church; together with the poems of Waltherius, du Pont, and before them Hildebert, all these presuppose that Islam arose in a Christian people: 'derelicta fide catholica'.[19]

More often and more reasonably Arabia was conceived to have been on the fringe of the Christian world, a natural asylum for heretical outlaws. Islam seemed to be a compound of Christian, Jewish and pagan dogmas, and it was natural to assume that historically these three religions were present in Arabia and exerted their various influences over the Prophet. The belief that Muhammad had Jewish or Christian teachers, often that he had only a Christian one, was all but universal. There was abundant detail about this person available; he seems sometimes, particularly in his malice against Rome, a reflection of the Muhammad-cardinal story; the hermit of Waltherius, whose motive was ignoble fear of Muhammad, was less representative. A rapid conspectus of the legend of the monk Sergius will illustrate how the penetration of Arabia by Christian and Jewish missionaries was imagined to have happened. Sergius, in the typical form of the legend, was expelled from Christendom for heresy, or for crime and heresy, and fled to Arabia, where alone, or with Jewish colleagues, he corrupted the Arabs, through the agency of his protégé Muhammad. William of Auvergne's version is a good summary of this story, which convinced Christian writers almost until modern times; it is curiously confused about the Councils of the Church.

After Eutyches and Nestorius his master were condemned by the Constantinopolitan synod, actually for denying the double nature of Christ, that is, the divine and the human, this Sergius crossed into Arabia, where, simulating the eremitical life, he appeared to be of such piety and holiness that Muhammad wished to make him his teacher; and sometimes he called him 'Gabriel the Archangel' – hiding what he dared not reveal, that the lunacies which he delivered to those whom he deceived he had learned from a man.

A number of other versions add little that differentiate their concept of events from this one, in any substantial particular.[20]

Some variants distinguished Jewish influences in addition to heretical Christian ones. Pedro de Alfonso, true to his own Hebrew origin, supposed a Jew who was as heretical as the Christian. Some versions took it for granted that any Jewish influence would have been malicious. Jewish influence was sometimes supposed in order to explain Old Testament loans to the Qur'ān; sometimes it was more explicitly identified as Talmudic. This last was characteristic of the Cluniac view. Ricoldo, who shared it, presented the 'facts' which he derived from sources that were written and Spanish (not oral and Syrian, as used to be supposed) in a way so convincing that Prideaux, four centuries later, felt no need to improve on them. His intention was as polemic as Ricoldo's, and the later author seems to represent no advance in knowledge or attitude over the earlier. In all these stories there was almost every possible permutation of a few basic versions. The sudden success of heretical Christianity and Talmudic Judaism which such a picture supposed the rise of Islam to represent fitted conveniently the idea of a more or less Christian pre-Islamic Arabia, but it equally well suited that of an ignorant, undiscriminating and wholly obtuse heathenism.[21]

Thus, in the less fabulous writers a fairly consistent picture of ancient Arabia develops: wild, barbaric, a simple and illiterate population, unorganised, ungoverned, at least in Medina; exposed to outside influences from the East Roman Empire, but penetrated rather by refugees from ecclesiastical conflict than by orthodox missionaries. Such unofficial missions succeeded, not among the superior mercantile community of Mecca, but among the rustics of Medina whose Jewish neighbours had already influenced them. Muhammad was the natural product of this world, sometimes as himself one of the dupes, but usually as the prime deceiver. This is not a ridiculously unhistorical picture, as is, on the contrary, that which imagined any considerable acceptance of orthodox Christianity in the Arabia into which Muhammad was born.

2. MUHAMMAD'S EARLY LIFE

Muhammad's personal origins as *pauper et orphanus* were thought to be important, like the paganism of his upbringing. It was known that the Qur'ān itself associated his early poverty, orphanhood and idolatry.[22] The feudal West, with its strong sense of the propriety of secular lordship, added the reproach of low birth. This idea was rather less common than those of poverty and orphanhood from which it is presumably the unjustified inference. The impression of Muhammad's dereliction was very nearly universal; the simple statement that his marriage to Khadījah raised him up from being an orphan and destitute circulated very generally.[23] Mark of Toledo referred to Muhammad's royal line, and the *reprobatio*, misquoting ibn Isḥāq, to his noble family; but most writers, including some who lived as close to Islam as these two writers, took the opposite view: 'in fortune a poor man . . . base by birth and repute', said Ricoldo, and William of Tripoli, 'the boy . . . was orphaned, sick, poor and low-class, a camel-herd'.[24]

Among more legendary writers du Pont is particularly interesting in this connection. The most characteristic episode in the French poem is the fall of the well-born Khadījah from standards of gentility, rather than of morals. Her able but base-born steward Muhammad tempts her (with arguments that often belong to the tradition of mediaeval satire upon marriage) into preferring marriage with himself to every alternative. Here it was the tragedy of misalliance that was so sincerely felt. From so unseemly a union, a 'law' of heresy and sexual promiscuity sprang naturally. This particular poem is, historically, absurd, but it only exaggerates a general opinion; if Muhammad was a poor idolatrous orphan (and sometimes base-born as well) it was no credit to him to have risen from the estate into which he was born. There was no feeling for the self-made man, save disapproval. There was, however, a sense of dramatic contrast between the poor orphan of humble origin and the *princeps Saracenorum* that he became.[25]

Versions of Muhammad's upbringing contrasted more sharply. The Muslim belief that he was illiterate is traditional and has served as an argument that the revelation of the Qur'ān must be miraculous. To many Christians this same assertion seemed, not proof of his mission, but simple derogation of his standing. He was often portrayed as a cipher, instructed by some more cunning, more malicious and better educated plotters. This was the scheme of the wholly fabulous stories recounted by San Pedro (who characterised them as 'Christian'), and those before him of Guibert and, earlier still, of Hildebert of Mans. The degree of Muhammad's tutelage varied from the extreme by which he was 'brought up' by 'a certain noble Roman cleric' apostate, to that which made him the most accomplished and knowledgeable of the conspirators himself.[26]

The supposition of illiteracy fitted into the idea that he was taught religion by Christian heretical refugees; the annotator of the Cluniac Qur'ān, for example, took it for granted that he owed his knowledge of Scripture to Jewish and heretical guidance, and the *summula* spoke of him as 'almost entirely illiterate'. Mark of Toledo did not credit, but reported, the claim to illiteracy; William of Auvergne insisted that it was established that Muhammad was more than rustic, 'bovine or swinish'. Ricoldo, to whom alternative versions were certainly available, accepted the opinion that Muhammad was illiterate. San Pedro pointed out that a Muslim who did not hold Muhammad to have been uneducated was a heretic in his own religion; without persuading himself that all the details of the 'Christian' version of the monk who taught Muhammad, which he recounted, were true, he was reasonably sure that Muhammad would have needed to be taught such erudite matters as the history of the Seven Sleepers of Ephesus. Ricoldo accepted the description of the Prophet as 'homo ydiota' and Ludolph said that he was 'rough and stupid'.[27]

In contrast to these stories were those which imputed to the Prophet a vast learning that culminated in magic. Waltherius, followed by du Pont, said:

> Rethor, arismeticus, dialecticus et geometer,
> musicus, astrologus, grammaticusque fuit.

Muhammad again appeared as highly educated in the Liber Nicholay and the Pisan text. Mark of Toledo and Fra Fidenzio cited a version which spoke of him as skilled in letters and mathematics; Mark said that as *magus* he led simple people astray. Roderick believed him to have been instructed in the natural sciences, the Catholic Religion and the Jewish Perfidy, under the guidance of a Jewish astrologer and magician who had also been his father's mentor. This story derives from the *de generatione Machumet*. In the Cronica de España the magical element predominated:

> Este Mahomet era . . . muy sabidor en las artes a que llaman magicas e en aquesto tiempo era el ya uno de los mas sabias de Arabia et de Africa . . .

Some of the commentators on Dante thought the Prophet a necromancer, and writers who reproduced the Corozan story knew him as *magus perfectissimus* or *nequissimus*.[28]

With these Christian fantasies of Muhammad's childhood as illiterate, or as given to the learning of the mage, we may contrast the survival, only in the best-read writers, of genuinely Islamic legends of the Prophet's childhood. The *reprobatio* was plain and factual, recounting the deaths in turn of 'Abdallāh and Āminah, the boy's father and mother. Curiously this work stressed the story which ibn Isḥāq tells of the child's visit to the Ka'bah:

> After his mother bore him, she sent to his grandfather 'Abd al-Muṭṭalib . . . He came and took Muhammad his (grand)child, and entered his temple with him and adored his God, and gave thanks for such a blessing given to him, and returned (Muhammad) to his mother. After the death of his mother, however, he stayed with his same grandfather, 'Abd al-Muṭṭalib, and when he reached the age of eight, that grandfather died.

The reason for telling this episode is obscure; perhaps it was seen as an attempt to emulate the Purification. The contrast between Muhammad and Christ, the thought of Muhammad as a false Christ, were often present in Christian minds.

San Pedro's account derived from the same or a related source but is confused. It gives flesh to the bare bones of the stories it tells. It includes the episode of the angels who visited the child to cut out and wash his heart, and also the foster-parents' returning the

child to his mother because they saw a devil possess them. San
Pedro seems not to have realised that these two stories are really
one. The incident of the washing of the heart is also told by the
Historia Arabum, which is generally much more confused, but
which tells the actual incident well:

and they cut out his heart, and they took a blackened clot of blood from
it; and after, they washed it in a bowl of snow; and they weighed his
heart against ten hearts of his people, and after against a thousand, and
it was found to be the heavier. One angel said to the other: 'If it were put
in the scale with all the Arabs, it would outweigh them all.'[29]

As well as authentically Islamic legend, some genuine history
was recounted. The *reprobatio* ignored the part played in Muhammad's life by abū Ṭālib, who was, however, known by San Pedro
('whenever in the course of his trading he took himself off some-
where, he took with him Muhammad, for he loved him very
much'). Abū Ṭālib also appears in Roderick's work, where he
confides the child to the care of the astrologer, and William of
Tripoli, here closest to the Islamic sources, knew that it was in
abū Ṭālib's care that Muhammad first travelled. The notion that
Muhammad did travel, and often that he travelled great distances,
was general; usually he was thought to have done so as a merchant,
or as Khadījah's agent in handling her merchandise.[30] The idea of
his travels offered an alternative explanation of his knowledge of
Christianity and Judaism, to that which depended on apostate
monks and cunning Jews in Arabia.

With this must be associated the adoption by some Christians
of the authentic story of Baḥīrā as Muslims told it, in preference
to the Greek legend of Sergius to which it had given birth.
William of Tripoli is the author who did so most clearly; he
seems to have been influenced remotely by the idea that Arabia
was Christian. He had a strong impression of the spiritual con-
stellations of monks in Egypt, 'in cities and deserts like the stars
of the firmament'. The monk Baḥīrā lived a recluse in a monastery
which was a natural stopping-place at the end of a day's stage on
the road from the Ḥijāz.[31] There travelling merchants, Syrian,
Arab and Egyptian, were accustomed to meet.[32] It had been
revealed to Baḥīrā that one of these travellers would become
ruler of a great and hardy nation which would afflict the Church of
Christ. This, of course, is not the Islamic version, for which
William or his source has substituted it; but the next phrase
certainly belongs to the Islamic original: 'on account of this he
keenly desired that (the foretold visitor) should come, and daily
he expected his arrival'. Tripoli referred the account of Muhammad's arrival at the monastery explicitly to Muslim sources:

The Muslims regard this as the first miracle that God – as they say –
worked for His servant while he was still young. They say that a small
door of the courtyard of the monastery, through which they passed, when
the child wanted to go through, by the divine impulse grew so much
wider and higher, like an arch, at the presence of the boy, that it seemed
to be the gateway to an imperial court, or the entrance to a home of
royal majesty.

Tripoli did not suppose that Baḥīrā apostatised, but said that he
remained a holy man, and taught Muhammad to believe in one
God and to love Jesus Christ and His Mother. It is here that
Tripoli's version merges into the Sergius legend, while continuing
to treat Baḥīrā as personally innocent. The monks allowed
Muhammad to stay with them only for a time; Muhammad then
obtained the patronage of a rich merchant, acted faithfully as his
agent, prospered in his service and often visited Baḥīrā. When
ultimately Muhammad became rich and powerful, he sent for
Baḥīrā and kept him as his adviser until his companions murdered
him out of jealousy.[33]
San Pedro also knew the Muslim stories of Baḥīrā, which he
rendered without Christian accretions. He showed Baḥīrā as a
solitary. Muhammad was taken by his guardian abū Ṭālib on
mercantile expeditions; Baḥīrā, 'exceedingly learned, well-known
(as) a friend of God', received the party of Meccans 'kindly and
courteously'. He warned Muhammad's uncle

that they should serve him and take care of him, because he would
become a prophet and the lord of a great people, and that they should
immediately protect him from the Jews, for the time would come when
these would want to kill him, because he was going to say things contrary
to the Law of the Jews.

Although San Pedro rendered the story with so little admixture
of Christian elements, he went on to speculate whether Baḥīrā
might not prove in fact to have been the same as the monk whom
the books of the Christians reported as Muhammad's evil influence,
i.e. Sergius, or, in San Pedro's account, 'Maurus'.[34]
Muhammad's relation to Khadījah was generally realised to
have sprung from his having forwarded her interests well and
faithfully during his agency. The story appears most soberly and
accurately in the *reprobatio*, where she employs him as reputed a
true and faithful man, and he leaves for Syria in the company of
her slave Maysara. The expedition is successful, and Maysara
reports favourably to his mistress. Khadījah sends for Muhammad
and says,

'O son of my (maternal) uncle, already I have desired thee, because
of thy noble family and thy fidelity and thy good habits.' So she bestowed

herself upon him, and he finally contracted with her that she should give herself a dowry of twenty young camels. She was the first wife that Muhammad had, and he did not marry another until she was dead. He had three sons by her, who died in idolatry, and four daughters who afterwards became Muslims.

With this we may compare the cunning imputed by Vitry and the associated account in Viterbo and Paris.

. . . as now he could earn his living for himself laboriously by the exercise of his own body, after the manner of poor people, he became the employee of a certain widow woman. He looked after her ass, and he was paid, for her account, by certain travellers whom he guided on the ass to parts of Asia. Soon she committed her camels also to his care, and he was made her agent in neighbouring cities and in towns roundabout, and made a profit. He was admitted to the grace and familiarity of the widow through his service, and all this commerce; and, desiring each other libidinously, they lay together, at first in secret and fornicating union; but afterwards that woman contracted matrimony with him publicly, and handed an abundance of money over to him.

Other accounts were altogether less emphatic, or were different in emphasis. Khadījah's wealth and the importance of the marriage to Muhammad's career were generally brought out, and the general ignorance of most detail of Muhammad's Meccan career made the marriage seem almost the only important event, apart from the actual call to prophethood. Some writers thought that Muhammad was indebted for his early career to a patron, whose relict, Khadījah, it was, whom he finally married. This suggests a confused reflection of the personality of abū Ṭālib, and Lull actually did think Khadījah his widow.[35]

Thus Muhammad was always seen as a man of no importance until his marriage, and this was always seen as the great crisis of his life. It figured prominently in so short and inaccurate a summary as the Corozan story, where it was a special function of the art of the mage Muhammad to deceive the Arabs in general, but Khadījah, as the 'lady' of the 'province', in particular. Although there was a confusion even in writers still close to the Arabic sources, elements of truth obtruded in the accounts of the most ignorant. Some were absurd and none was both complete and accurate, but the general impression given by Western writers – apart from the nonsensical theme of magical learning – was not completely different from that which is given by Muslim writers about the early life of the Prophet.

3. THE EARLY MUSLIM COMMUNITY

The pretence to prophecy was thought of sometimes as arising only to explain the premise of epileptic fits; but the more typical reason was to see it as a device to obtain, or to retain, power. 'By the prestige of his heresy', said Sigebert, 'he arrived at the kingship.' Pedro de Alfonso's statement to the same effect was echoed many times down the centuries; and the *summula* put it neatly when it said that Muhammad 'attempted to become king under the veil of religion and the name of a divine prophet'. Once at least Muhammad was seen to stand close to some aspects of Old Testament religion: 'he obtained the kingship as envoy of God, and prophet, on the model of David and Solomon . . .'[36]

Sometimes his sudden elevation from poverty to riches was supposed to have turned Muhammad's head. Because his claim was presumed to be fraudulent, it was thought necessary to explain why he should ever have wanted to be a prophet. Thus Vitry said that when he was 'suddenly made great' by his marriage, he 'began to be exalted' and planned 'by every means how he could obtain the lordship'. The Syrian Apology put this more fully and rather more subtly:

When he was thus raised up, he began to vaunt himself exceedingly, and he determined to have the lordship over all the tribes and over his nation; he would have presumed to be called king if those who were more noble and more powerful than he had not resisted his usurpation. He therefore taught that he was a prophet sent by God, whose sayings every people should believe.

In many accounts Muhammad's religious deceit was presented as the implement of his secular ambition.[37]

In its public aspect Muhammad's crime was a double one; Fra Fidenzio expressed this well when he said that Muhammad, because he had few supporters, used a double contrivance, of fiction and of oppression, to gain a larger following. From the *fiction* of prophethood it was never possible to separate the *oppression* by force and violence which was always associated with the 'kingship' of Medina; but, important as this was thought to be, detailed knowledge of the Medinan period was rare.

Much of what was known derived from the Risālah. The attacks on the Medinan caravans, each in turn, and the assassinations of individual Jews, were described, and, wherever possible, the kingship and the prophethood were interrelated. For example, the disaster at Uḥud was emphasised, and especially the wounds there suffered by the Prophet himself. Muhammad (these accounts sneered), unlike the Jews of the Old Testament, experienced the usual ups and downs of warfare; he had no guard of angels, as he claimed he had. This short summary would do equally well to represent the Arabic Risālah or any of the Latin texts derived from it.[38] The same point was neatly epitomised by Ricoldo:

Machometus, autem, vincebat aliquando, et vincebatur, sicut alii tyranni. The *summula* seems to have been based upon the Risālah also:

Energetic in individual matters and greatly cunning, he was advanced from lowliness and destitution to riches and fame. As, bit by bit, this grew, he spread terror of himself, often pursuing his neighbours, and especially his blood relations, in ambushes, robberies, and forays, and killing as many as he could, either secretly or publicly.

In a way, this does describe the war with the Quraysh; but it distorts it practically beyond recognition.[39]

It is easy to see how this concept developed. The author of the Risālah, an Arab, took the facts of Muhammad's life for granted. He referred to some of them to prove his argument, and ignored such as were no use to this end. The defeat at Uḥud was discussed, the victory at Badr ignored; the latter was irrelevant to any attack on Muhammad, and Muslims, and the Qur'ān itself, considered it in fact the special sign of God's mercy. The Christian Arab polemist had no occasion to refer to it, and it happened that refutation of the Islamic attitude to it did not enter into his scheme. Yet Latin readers depended on him for their facts, and so many important events, undoubtedly known to, but not mentioned by, him, they never learned. Moreover, they were unable to check or confirm the facts that they did learn from the Risālah, since it was usually their sole source of information about them. What in the Arabic was really a critical appraisal of events had now to serve in the place of a straightforward recital of them. If the Arabic condemned the acts of the Companions as robbery, European readers understood that Muhammad literally gathered together a band of 'profane men, highwaymen, plunderers, murderers and robbers' and terrorised the countryside. The scene was reset in Western terms; this aspect is clear in Fra Fidenzio's account, not usually so indebted to the Risālah:

. . . he gathered to himself men who were fugitives, pernicious men, corruptors of manners and oppressors of others, and also as many murderers as he could; and he became their prince. He sent them to woodland by-ways, to hill-tops, to roads frequented by travellers and to every other place, to rob men, both to plunder their goods and to kill those who put up opposition; and the fear of Muhammad fell upon all the men of those parts.

This is a picture topographically suited to Palestine or Lebanon, or anywhere else in the Mediterranean, but not to the Arabian desert. Tripoli attempted geographical exactitude: 'there came to join him families of Arabs, living in the deserts of southern Arabia' (that is, Arabia south of the Syrian desert: Tripoli counted Arabia from Aleppo). He cast a Biblical flavouring over his narrative which was similar in substance to those already cited: 'there began to fear him the provinces and the kings of the provinces and all the peoples and princes and judges of all the land'. Especially after the death of Baḥīrā, the bandits spread terror and ruin. Ricoldo again summed up this aspect of Muhammad's career: *factus princeps latronum*. It was natural that banditry should be conceived in contemporary terms.[40]

All accounts related to the Risālah stressed two points particularly. The offer of the fifth part of the booty as the Prophet's share interested Western readers, for example, over the conquest of the Banū Qurayẓah: 'he brought back to Muhammad a fifth part of all the spoils, saying, "Such a part is owed to thee, Prophet of God." ' There was a shocked but gratified sense of how scandalous this was; what Muslims saw as following the law, Christians took for granted was contrary to it. The physical detail of Muhammad's wounds at the Muslim disaster at Uḥud were closely studied, because they corroborated Muhammad's ordinary humanity: the teeth on the right side knocked out, the upper lip split, the cheek gashed, these were seen to constitute a record of convincing evidence. Muhammad was protected by his companion Ṭalḥa, who lost a finger in doing so. No angel ministered to their wounds. The historical context of the battle was incredibly vague, but still these details were preserved with loving attention, and there were many references to the occasion in spite of general ignorance of its context. On the whole, the facts were left to speak for themselves, without direct theological comment. Pejorative phrases were used to describe the Medinan period as criminal; thus Vitry said of it that Muhammad 'had his neighbours, of whom he was envious, secretly and treacherously slaughtered . . .'[41]

The absence of authentic detail, except what derived from the Risālah, meant in most cases a complete ignorance of the historical sequence of Muhammad's public career. Only a very few authors were able to distinguish even the Meccan and Medinan periods in his life, and his final triumph, after the agreement at Ḥudaybiyah, seems to have been mentioned by, perhaps was known to, none. There simply did not exist in this period a straightforward chronological account of the whole of Muhammad's life which was anything like accurate. The absence of adequate information between his relatively well documented early life, to his call to Prophethood at the one end, and his death at the other, is very remarkable. Between the two there was little precise information.

It is instructive to consider how far the few works that show some realisation of time and sequence were clear and accurate. The *Historia Arabum* speaks of Muhammad's lying hidden for

three years in Mecca after deciding in his fortieth year to declare
himself prophet, of the hostility of the Meccans and his departure
'as if from humility' to Medina, and finally of his return 'resumptus
viribus' to Mecca, his humiliation of the Quraysh, who appealed
to his generosity and courtesy, his symbolic imposition of the
adhān, the call to prayer, upon the city. This might do as a simplification of the actual history, and is at any rate clear; unfortunately
it was hopelessly confused by the apocryphal story of Muhammad's
war with the Romans and his capture of Syria and Mesopotamia,
with which it was combined. A description of the Prophet's claim
to receive Revelation even follows that of the conquest of Mecca.
An account of Revelation, and also of the mir'āj, is cut off from its
proper place in the story; in the *Cronica* version, the Corozan story
is also interpolated. The *Historia*, and still more the *Cronica*, are
full of fabulous elements which overlay the sound chronological
basis with errors, the insertion of both true and fabulous events
in inappropriate places. In both these books, an episode involving
abū Ṭālib, based on his death-bed refusal to believe (which in fact
occurred before the Migration to Medina) lest the Quraysh think
he did so from fear, was recounted near the end of Muhammad's
life.[42]

The *quadruplex reprobatio* described the conversion of the first
Muslims in Mecca: Khadījah, 'Alī (the first male), Zayd, abū
Bakr; the list continued, as it did also in San Pedro's version. The
reprobatio telescoped the rest of Muhammad's public career into a
few vague phrases; Muhammad claimed that it was his office to
require men to confess no other than God and Muhammad His
messenger, and otherwise to be killed or pay tribute. The author
was more interested to analyse the reasons for which men believed
Muhammad: deceived by the Devil, out of a silly simplicity;
following their relatives into error, the blind leading the blind
into the pit; for honour and the multiplication of worldly goods.
These generalisations contrast with the accurate detail from the
best Islamic sources which the author used to describe what
interested him.[43]

San Pedro, also starting from the list of the first Muslim
converts, composed the fullest reasonably accurate mediaeval
Latin history of Muhammad. He described the Meccan period
intelligibly. A curious error was to begin by adding to the list of
early Muslims the name of the Jews of the Banū Qurayzah. It was
a feature of San Pedro's attitude to treat the Jews of Arabia as
disloyal Jews, supporters of Muhammad; their final fate was
therefore all they deserved. This may indirectly reflect Islamic
histories, but is not precisely presented. San Pedro told many
stories, direct from Arabic sources, which describe the opposition,

in Mecca, between the Quraysh and the Prophet; for example, their challenge to him to work miracles, the puzzle questions suggested by the Jews of Medina whom the Meccans consulted, the assembly of Meccans to hear the challenged revelation of the solution, the jeers when it was at first delayed.[44] The episode of the Satanic verses[45] San Pedro saw as a deliberate attempt to compromise with paganism, which the logic and honesty of the Prophet's own companions prevented. He realised something of the troubles of early Islam, describing the deaths of Khadījah and abū Ṭālib and the flight to Ethiopia. He recounted the wrestling with Rukāna, a little pointlessly.[46] He saw clearly that the Prophet 'frightened (the people) with the threat of Hell, or encouraged them with the promise of Paradise'; this was indeed the essential of the Prophet's message. Finally, 'the citizens of Mecca made a league against Muhammad, who was thrown out, and took himself off to live in the city which was then called Yathrib, where he was later buried; and henceforth it was called Almedina, the City'. This was a simplified but generally fair and true account of the Meccan period; the issue between Muhammad and the pagans was put as primarily a religious one.[47]

San Pedro's picture of the Medinan period was less adequate. He knew the Risālah, but his version bears no resemblance to it, and the 'band of robbers' concept is absent. He ignored the early expeditions against the Meccans, and leapt from mention of a Jew who recognised him as a prophet foretold in Scripture to the battle of Uḥud. There was also a Jew who wished to persuade his people to fight for the Muslims, but they refused because it was the Sabbath.[48] He made Muhammad his heir, and was killed in the battle; but Muhammad did not fall heir (said San Pedro sarcastically) to the four teeth he lost in the fighting. Next San Pedro interposed, where there should come an account of the Battle of the Ditch, what looks very like a description of the Battle of Badr, and should, if so, have preceded mention of Uḥud.

Then he heard that many merchants of Mecca were approaching that city from other parts, with a great column of laden beasts of burden; he hid in ambush with his companions, and killed seventy of the merchants and muleteers of Mecca, and took seventy more captive; and the whole caravan was plundered.

Thence the account proceeds direct to the attack on the Banū Qurayẓah, but the tale peters out in an account of war against the Meccans, remaining Jewish fortresses, and finally the East Romans; this last attack was unsuccessful, and was not repeated while Muhammad lived. This part of the story is very vague. San Pedro dealt separately with his Christian sources, and in doing so preferred the wholly fabulous to the sobriety of the Risālah; in dealing with Arabic sources, he seems carefully to have excluded information from the Risālah, and confined himself to what was Islamic. He owed his chronology to the Muslim sources, and while he was prepared to give equal credence to silly Western fables, he did not attempt to substitute any other chronology for the true one. He was chiefly indebted to ibn Isḥāq, but in the Medinan part of the story he seems to have lost the chronological thread. He contrasted, as most writers must do still, the unsuccessful preaching in Mecca and the resulting ostracism with the military strategy and worldly success in Medina. Yet by omitting the final return to Mecca he largely falsified his picture. In spite of this, San Pedro was unique in his sense of time and sequence, of cause and effect.[49]

In all the accounts of Muhammad's life which have some relation to reality, but omitting the wholly fabulous, two consistent themes dominate all that is said. Muhammad was violent; he levied war and ordered assassinations unscrupulously for private ends, for plunder, and even more for ambition. Secondly, he was subject to human frailty; he had his ups and downs, a history which revealed the ordinary fluctuations of fortune: *sicut alii tyranni*. This seemed extremely important to the mediaeval writer whose mind was filled by thoughts of the divinely guaranteed successes of the Jews of the Old Testament. Still more important was the comparison between Muhammad and Christ; although Muslims claimed no divinity for the Prophet, Christians were aware of the contrast at every moment. Muhammad was both wicked and human, and these two points seemed almost equally important.

4. THE HOUSEHOLD OF THE PROPHET

It is not possible to ignore, in the name of good taste, an aspect of the history of Muhammad which was considered particularly important by mediaeval writers. Muhammad shocked their conception of what a secular ruler, let alone a prophet, might do, and the immodesty of Muslim writers in describing sexual episodes intensified this shocked response. Although Muhammad himself may really have had no great sensual leanings, the treatment of his marriages and of some episodes in his relations with his wives by Islamic authors gave a very different impression to clerical Europe, with its strong sense of what was proper.

One extremely popular theme is a case in point; it will be convenient to cite it in its most accurate form, that taken from Bukhāri by the *reprobatio*.

Dicitur in libro Bohari III capitulo locutionis, Emus filius Elech (= Anas ibn Mālik) dixisse quod Machometus circumibat mulieres suas, iacendo cum eis in una hora noctis vel diei, et erant undecim. Et dictum fuit isti Emus, *numquid potuit facere?* Qui dixit, *nos dicebamus inter nos, quod potestas seu virtus triginta virorum data fuit Machometo in coitu.*

This is not a particularly authoritative translation, and may well be only a case of giving Muhammad all the attributes of a popular hero and pleasing his simpler followers; but it was cited by all the best-informed and most serious mediaeval writers, sometimes in a vaguer form which gives it a nastier sound, for example, 'non erubuit ut diceret datum suis renibus a Deo, XL viros in coitu potentissimus fortitudine libidinis adaequare'. It soon came to be believed that this 'boast' was in the Qur'ān: 'ipse enim gloriatur in lege sua quod data sit sibi potestas in lumbis . . .' said Humbert, completing the quotation in the usual form.[50]

Probably the favourite mediaeval story of Muhammad was that of his marriage to Zaynab bint Jaḥsh after her divorce from Zayd ibn Ḥāritha. The story has popular appeal of a police-court character, if told with the imputation of police-court motives, as it always was: the all but incestuous adultery with the wife of an adopted son; Muhammad's inability to resist fleshly temptation; the use of a special revelation to justify what he had done. The story was told so often that no attempt can be made here to trace its literary history. One example will suffice, from the version of Fra Fidenzio, who gave the story a romantic colouring, and yet allowed something of the Muslim original version to appear.

There was a certain man called Saidus, and he had a wife called Sebib, who was one of the most beautiful women who lived on the earth in her days. However, Muhammad heard of the fame of her beauty, and burned with desire of her. Wanting to see her, he came to the house of the woman in the absence of her husband, and asked for her husband. She said, 'O Messenger of God, what do you want, what are you here for? My husband has gone out on business.' This was not hidden from her husband. When he came back to his home, he said to his wife, 'Was the Messenger of God here?' she replied, 'He was.' He said, 'Did he see your face?' She replied, 'He did see it, and he watched me for a long time.' He said, 'I cannot live with you any longer.'

Here the setting, the burning with desire, the beauty of 'Sebib' are all Romance; but the conversation is basically from the Arabic. The account continues with the Revelation that required Muhammad to take Zaynab as his wife; it is likely that a passage is missing in which Muhammad promises Zayd he will not take his divorced wife. In any case, Heaven overrules him, and he marries her. 'And afterwards, she used to glory in front of Muhammad's wives, saying, You were given to the Messenger

of God as wives by your friends on earth, but God married me to
the Messenger of God from Heaven.' The point of this was to
emphasise Muhammad's hypocrisy, in using a pretended revelation
to further seduction and adultery. Lull told the story in a similarly
romantic way, in which Muhammad generously insists that Zayd
shall retain his wife, and is then reproved by Gabriel for not
taking the wife he desired. He uses a romantic psychology: Zayd
cunningly (cautelose) offers Muhammad his wife, who refuses (at
first) what has been courteously (curialiter) offered.[51]

I cannot stress too much the popularity of this story which I
have cited in only two examples. In accounts dependent on the
Risālah the Revelation with which Muhammad justified himself
amounted to the promulgation of a general law that he who
received another man's repudiated wife might always marry her.
In Christian terms, this was very shocking; and Christians also
understood that the Arabs themselves, Muhammad's Companions,
had murmured against the 'adultery'. These misconceptions are
anachronistic. Some Arabs objected to marriage to a son's wife as
illegal, and the general law really promulgated was to deny
consanguinity in an adoptive relationship.[52] For Christians, on the
contrary, this episode would always remain the classic example of
false Revelation hypocritically made to serve an evil end.

From the same sūrah as treats of this question, another but
connected point arose. I cite the *reprobatio*:

. . . Muhammad said that God spoke to him and said: 'We allow thee thy
wives, to whom thou shouldst give dowries, and all thy slaves whom God
gave thee, and the daughters of thy paternal uncle and of thy paternal
aunt, and the daughters of thy maternal uncle and thy maternal aunt,
who have followed thee. And every believing woman, if she offers her
body or herself to the Prophet, and if the Prophet desires to lie with her,
let it be permitted, but only to thee and not to the other believers.' A few
words later (he goes on), 'Thou shalt give hope to whom thou pleasest,
that is, of those who offer themselves to thee, and thou shalt receive
whom thou pleasest, and, if thou desirest, one whom thou hast sent away;
and it is not a sin for thee.'

The implications of the text as this puts it are obvious. A careful
comparison with the Qur'anic original will show how, with a
minimum of inaccuracy, it gives an erroneous sense. Thus the
Prophet's being allowed more wives than the other believers
becomes promiscuous access to all women; a suggestive phrase
about their offering their bodies derives really from permission
for marriage without a dowry. The final verse refers to the
obligation of the Prophet to sleep with his wives in rotation;
instead of conferring promiscuous licence, it regulates marital
rights. It was to this Revelation that 'Ā'ishah referred when she

said that God hastened to satisfy Muhammad's desires; but the
reprobatio understood something much more shameful.

On account of this (revelation) many women offered themselves,
which is proved by the book of Bukhāri in the tractate of the exposition
of the Qur'ān, where 'Ā'ishah said: 'I was jealous of those women who
offered themselves to the Messenger of God . . . After God gave this
law, that Muhammad should give hope to whom he willed, and should
receive whom he willed, I said to Muhammad, "I see the Lord thy God
quickly fulfils thy desire." '

Even the Qur'anic title of the Prophet's wives, 'the Mothers of
the Believers', was given a nasty interpretation.[53] The favourite
Christian technique was to decide what a text must mean without
consultation of those most concerned, if these were Muslim
authorities; often, what a text must mean was what was nastiest.
Vitry and the Apology made out that Muhammad was notorious
among the Arabs for his adulteries, and that he reserved the right
to use the wives of other men 'in order to generate prophets and
sons of virtue'.[54] San Pedro, referring to Muhammad's 'special
privilege' in the case of Maymūna bint al-Hārith,[55] apostrophised
the Prophet in terms that seem rather to refer to the case of
Zaynab:

Indeed I say to thee, O Muhammad, that no prophet so relaxed the
controls and laws concerning the use of women as thou didst; but thou
didst never receive these laws from God, for how could a woman leave
her husband and her sons, and, against the will of her husband, go away
with another man, and that please God?

Ricoldo's climax of his version of the Zaynab story reduces the
argument to the absurd: 'God commanded me to commit this
adultery.' He did not see that this was absurd, since 'adultery'
could have no meaning here, except to a Christian. In real debate
with Muslims this sort of thing would have been ridiculed.[56]

Muhammad, always moved by religious considerations, shocked
Christians for this very reason, which made him always appear
hypocritical. It was less that wrong practices gave scandal, than
that their justification by religion did so. This is seen most clearly
when the Christian interpretation of events is furthest from the
truth. The revelation of sūrah 66 is a case in point; we may once
again cite the *reprobatio*:

. . . a certain Muqawqis presented to Muhammad a woman who was
called Marīyah the Copt, and he took her as concubine. It happened,
however, that he lay with her in the home of his wife, Hafṣah by name,
who was not present; but when she came she saw them having intercourse, and this made her very angry. She reproached him, saying, 'O

Prophet of God, was there none of your women lower than me? Why
did you lie with her in my home and on my bed?' Wanting to placate
her, he said to her, 'Would it please you if I abstained from her?' She
said, 'Yes.' He swore that he would not lie with Marīyah again, and
said to Ḥafṣah, 'Do not tell these things to anyone else.' Afterwards,
against this promise and oath, he lay with Marīyah again, and said in his
Qur'ān that *God appointed satisfaction of their oaths for the Muslims*, that
is, if they wished to make some oath, and if they wished to go against it,
that they could do so with expiation, without satisfaction.

The same triple reproach as was made over the Zaynab affair is
implicit here: Muhammad was promiscuous, and he justified himself by pretending to revelations, which he then erected into
general laws for the benefit of his followers.[57] Also, the same
author continued, 'To reveal his uncleanness he caused it to be
said in the Qur'ān in the tractate al-Fatḥ that God forgave him his
past and future sins.' There was some Arabic authority for
associating this verse with both the Marīyah and the Zaynab
affairs, and the Latin author may be presumed to have known this.
He discussed it again in relation to the question of oath-breaking,
and illustrated the general law of Islam by Muhammad's personal
behaviour on this occasion: expiation without satisfaction of the
oath.[58]

San Pedro's treatment of the Marīyah episode was fuller and
substituted 'Ā'ishah for Ḥafṣah, but was substantially the same.
He quoted the text of sūrah LXVI, to stress the Islamic justification
of oath-breaking: 'O Prophet, why dost thou prohibit what God
has allowed thee? God is righteous in sparing; God remits our
oaths for us and absolves us from them; our God is compassionate.'
The point was always the religious justification of sin. Ricoldo also
emphasised this story, which he told at length; he understood
simply that 'Ā'ishah and Ḥafṣah found the Prophet with Marīyah
and were jealous. The most probable explanation of the actual
incident is that it was a quarrel over the rotation of the Prophet's
visits to his women. Ricoldo quoted the sūrah at greater length
than other writers, and mistakenly associated with this text the
remark of 'Ā'ishah about God's revealing what suited the
Prophet. He too stressed the oath-breaking: '. . . thou art seeking
to please thy wives; now God has legislated for thee, to allow
thee to be free of thy oaths . . .'; this is his version of the Qur'anic
text. He went on to quote further:

(Muhammad) read to his wives all that followed in the chapter of the
Prohibition, and, as though in the person of God, he said: *Be penitent
before God, for your hearts have turned aside* – referring to the calumny
they had made against him, of impurity. There immediately follows: *If*

perhaps he repudiates you, God will give him better than you, Muslims, faithful, trusty, penitent, observant of ritual and prayer, hard-working and virgins. When they heard that, they said, *we are penitent.*

Ricoldo insisted that Muhammad's pretence to revelation, in order to justify himself, added blasphemy, the worst crime of all, to his other crimes.[59]

Much was made from little over the false accusation against 'Ā'ishah and her vindication by God; here too one Latin author adopted the attitude of Muhammad's contemporary enemies. San Pedro saw nothing worse in the episode than the manufacture of revelations, which was evidence of hypocrisy, or diabolical possession, or both; he also thought that Muhammad's fondness for 'Ā'ishah was unworthy of a prophet. This last was 'Alī's own argument at the time, which the Risālah quoted from Bukhārī. In the Latin translation of the Risālah, however, 'Ā'ishah was described as *libidini dedita*; beloved by Ṣafwān ibn al-Mu'aṭṭal as-Sulamī, *qui et consuetudinarium cum ea stuprum gerebat, ipso Mahumet sciente et consentiente.* The credit for this absurd, nasty and gratuitous invention (the final point in which would make nonsense of the entire story) must go to Peter of Toledo, in whose translation alone it occurs.[60]

Peter of Toledo may reflect the malice of Mozarab advisers, but the highly reliable *reprobatio* and San Pedro are at fault in another equally distasteful matter; conceivably they also were indebted to local Arabic-speaking Christian advice. According to the *reprobatio*, ' 'Ā'ishah said, "I and the Prophet washed ourselves from the same jar, and we were polluted, and he told me to cover myself with a cloth, et sic iacebat mecum seu contingebat me, et eram menstruata." ' It is clear from the immediate source, Bukhārī, that these words cannot bear the objectionable sense imputed to them; 'lie beside or touch' is meant literally, and not as a euphemism for sexual intercourse. San Pedro went further into detail, citing both 'Ā'ishah and Maymūna: 'ipsemet Mahometus, cum uxores eius impediebantur aegritudine qua femina laborant, iuxta earum naturam, coibat cum illis vase praepostero . . .' It is likely that both these authors were influenced by what Mālikite doctrine permitted, but there is no evidence that Muslim jurists ever adopted these unpleasant assertions about Muhammad's own practice, which strain the natural sense of known sources.[61]

It is not possible to consider in detail the lists of the Prophet's wives; their number alone gave sufficient scandal. San Pedro gave one list, and another derives from the Risālah. A different tradition that also gave scandal is best cited from San Pedro: 'Muhammad put on purple and used scented oils, that he might smell sweet, and coloured his lips and eyes, as the leaders of the Muslims (Moors) and many others, of both sexes, are accustomed to do nowadays.' Criticised by his own followers, the same author continues, Muhammad excused himself, saying, 'it is given to me to delight in three things, the first, unguents, the second, women, and the third, prayer'. It is obvious how scandalous the association of these three sounded in a Christian ear. Cruder versions omitted 'prayer'; the coarsest was Marino's 'scented things and coition'.[62]

Great attention was paid to all these aspects of Muhammad's life. Both as to facts and as to motives, the worst was always believed. The picture of the licentious hypocrite took shape inevitably. What clerical writers, always aware of the problems of moral and pastoral theology, most feared was the doctrinal justification of sexual acts which are already attractive to men who believe them to be wrong. This explains the virulence of educated Christian feeling about Muhammad, which always excluded charity and usually excluded the complete truth. The idea of Muhammad's hypocrisy was built up on the conviction that he was abnormally lubricious: Pedro de Alfonso's phrase, *valde feminas diligit*, was moderate. *Luxuriosus* was a common term; *libidinis ardore super omnes homines succensus* and *impudicus*, added Vitry; *prae cunctis hominibus in mulieres libidine insaniebat*, Ketton's annotator had already commented. *Immunditiae totius amator, vilissimus, in peccato luxuriae fetidissimus, carnalibus vitiis totus brutalis* and *impudicus adulter*: these are phrases taken almost at random.[63] It seemed very obvious to mediaeval Christians that Muhammad's behaviour with women alone made it quite impossible that he should have been a prophet. It is very interesting that the facts were so often invented, or else falsified, or just exaggerated; but, had they not been so, it is certain that the most sober relation of Muhammad's life would have caused Christians to say that no true prophet could conduct his personal life as Muhammad did his. In this matter there is little common ground between Christianity and Islam.

5. THE DEATH OF THE PROPHET

The deaths of the saints were thought specially significant by their biographers, and in mediaeval tradition the death of Muhammad, the antithesis of the saint, was considered a subject of theological importance. It was often shown as having been atrociously horrible, sometimes simply as just having been human, with no signs of God's special mercy. The methods of anti-hagiography necessarily varied according to how far the author was bound by knowledge of facts which Islamic sources established.

San Pedro exemplifies the best informed. He was unable to accept a fantastic version without also quoting an authentic Islamic one which he thought did not necessarily conflict with it. He told how Muhammad, when he was lying in his last illness, said that he was suffering from the poison that he and a companion had been given by a beautiful Jewess who belonged to tributary Jewish tribes; Muhammad went to dine with her, and she poisoned the shoulder of lamb which she knew he specially liked. The Prophet tasted a mouthful, detected the poison and spat it out; but his companion died on the spot. Muhammad asked her why she had done this, and she replied that he had enslaved the Jews. She reckoned that, if he died, the Jews would be restored to their former prosperity, but if he were really a prophet, he would recognise the poison, no harm would be done, and she herself would believe. All this fairly represents ibn Isḥāq, although, torn from its context, it leaves very vague the interval between this episode and the Prophet's death, which, in the original, occurred years later. The account of the same incident in the *reprobatio* is less full, but very similar, and more explicitly documented.[64]

There were also miraculous versions of the same story, also Islamic in origin. Vitry and the Syrian Apology cited very similar forms in which the shoulder of lamb spoke to the Prophet: 'I have poison in me, be careful not to eat me in the food', or 'See you do not eat me, for I am poisoned.' Why, asked Vitry, paraphrasing an argument that appeared in the Risālah, did Muhammad not recognise the poison that eighteen years later he died of; why, asked the original from which Paris and Viterbo derived, did he not save his companion who died? Acqui also described the miraculous warning uttered by the cooked lamb, and contrasted Muhammad's subsequent death by poison, unsaved by miracles. Some of the confusion here was due to the confusion of unorthodox Islamic sources. There were other less specific statements that Muhammad died by poison.[65]

Many of the stories relating to the death of Muhammad are not obviously discreditable; it was enough that what he did contrasted unfavourably with the sort of thing expected of a Christian saint on his death-bed. San Pedro recalled 'Ā'ishah's description of how great the Prophet's pain was, how he said that life displeased him. Particular points were to be noted: there were only twenty white hairs in the Prophet's beard, he died on a Monday in the home of 'Ā'ishah, and was buried there where he died, beneath the bed, in the middle of the night of the third day. Again according to 'Ā'ishah, he washed his face and poured water on it when he was at the point of death; and Christians were accustomed to say, added San Pedro, that he was trying to baptise himself, but the devils prevented him.[66] For the author of the *reprobatio*, Muhammad made a profane death. As he lay dying he abused the Christians and Jews for making oratories and churches at the tombs of their prophets; 'note', said the author sedately, 'that he sinned in the abuse; what he said following (i.e. as to the fact of the Christian and Jewish custom) was in no way untrue'. There was also a story that the Prophet was under a spell, so that he thought he had just known women, when in fact he had not. Again, during his last illness, Muhammad said, 'I will write a book, and ye shall not be in error after that book'; but the people round his bed wrangled about this, some arguing that the Qur'ān was enough, until Muhammad turned them out. The Christian author remarked that it is possible to argue from this that Muslims have been since Muhammad's death, and remain, in error. It was in 'Ā'ishah's house that Muhammad died, because it was then her day, which he was due to spend with her. When he died, his head was on her breast; his saliva and hers mingled, and so he died. There is nothing disreputable about this; it is even a little touching; but it is not the Christian picture of an edifying death-bed. The very fact that Muhammad was dead, and that Muslims agreed that this was so, whereas Christ had risen to Heaven, was felt to be important: 'he died, and he lies dead on earth . . . and this the Muslims affirm'.[67]

A mass of literature gave Muhammad a very much worse, and highly melodramatic death, one that now seems wholly ridiculous. A reader of mediaeval writings comes incidentally across references to the Prophet's shameful death. These take it for granted that he knows what this means – that Muhammad was eaten by dogs, or that he was eaten, or suffocated, by pigs. Thus Alan of Lille referred to Muhammad's monstrous life, more monstrous sect, most monstrous death; he believed him to have been devoured by dogs. Pigs were more popular; Guibert believed in them and so did some of the authors who reproduced the Corozan text. Gerald of Wales and Higden added that this happened when he was in a drunken stupor, and Gerald commented, 'since he taught uncleanness and shame, it was by pigs, which are considered unclean animals, that he was devoured'. Ludolf said that he was seized by an epileptic fit in the desert, and just that he was devoured by wild beasts. The 'aliud scriptum' copied by Matthew Paris supposed him suffocated in the course of an epileptic fit by a sow and her litter. In this genre the most remarkable version is undoubtedly that which Matthew Paris personally worked into the St Albans Chronicle, under the year 622. This allotted a triple death to Muhammad, combining all the less attractive alternatives that he had heard rumoured, simultaneously avenging the Prophet's

Trinitarian heresy. The margin of the manuscript, according to
its editor, shows this schematic device:

epilenticus	pecca-	In Patrem
venenatus	vit	in Filium
crapulatus	enim	in Spiritum Sanctum

He was handed over to be torn to pieces by pigs, by this threefold
agency, drunkenness, poison and epilepsy.[68]

San Pedro knew, and wanted to believe, a 'Christian' version of
the death of Muhammad which most ingeniously reconciles
several improbable stories. A cunning Jewess, whom Muhammad
desired, insisted that he should come to her bed alone, by night.
When he did so her relatives killed him, cut off his left foot, threw
the rest of his body to the pigs, who quickly devoured it. The
woman anointed and scented the foot, explaining to people who
came to fetch Muhammad that angels had come to carry him off
to Heaven. She had pulled him back by the foot, which, after a
tug-of-war with the celestial powers, was all of the Prophet that
remained. With its curious circumstantiality this story combines
the pig and Jew motifs, and also that of an angelic ascension into
Heaven, which the Prophet was often supposed to have expected
his body would experience.[69]

There was a large number of stories that related this supposed
announcement that his body would be carried to Heaven by angels.
San Pedro recounted the tale, and then apostrophised the Prophet:
'As to what thou didst say, that as thou hadst ascended living to
Heaven' – this refers to the 'night-journey', the miraculous mi'rāj
– 'so also the angels would descend and carry thy body to Heaven:
I say to thee, O Muhammad, that, as thou didst ascend living to
Heaven, so did the angels carry thy body to Heaven' – that is, not
at all. In the different versions of this supposed last prophetic
error, the purpose of all of which was to cast the greatest possible
discredit and unpleasantness on the memory of the Prophet, the
consequence was that the body stank and had to be buried hurriedly.
In some cases of writers who knew little about bodies in hot
climates, or did not think about what they knew, this happened
after twelve or even fifteen days. The story seemed valuable to
those who told it for its disproof of a hoped for miracle, but still
more for the contrasts, sometimes explicit, sometimes implicit,
between Muhammad and Christ.[70]

In Christian theories of the events after the death of Muhammad,
this myth of an expected ascension of the body which failed was
connected with the historical fact of confusion and disturbance in
Medina on the day he died. Also confused by them was the
'Apostasy of the Arabs', the rather grand name given to the

disaffection probably of only partly Islamised tribes at the death of one who, from their point of view, was only the architect of a Meccan alliance. San Pedro associated the Islamic myth of the washed heart with the quarrel of abū Bakr and 'Umar as to whether Muhammad was really dead, and the expectation that Muhammad's body would be carried to Heaven. Just as he had seen the authentic story of the Jewess who poisoned Muhammad as corroboration of the fabulous tale of the Jewess who cut off his foot while his body was thrown to the pigs, so he saw the burial in 'Ā'ishah's room as confirmation that the Muslims had expected an angelic ascension until it was so late that a hurried burial was necessary. He argued seriously that it was not true that there was any custom of burying prophets where they died; he instanced the known tombs of Abraham, Isaac, Moses, David and the Baptist. The quarrel between 'Umar and abū Bakr he thought confirmed by the genuine statement that 'Umar could not believe the Prophet dead, and that abū Bakr had to reassure the people; and the difference between them again seemed to confirm the idea that the Companions had expected, and been disappointed not to see, the body taken up into Heaven.[71]

Other authors made still more of the 'Apostasy of the Arabs', particularly those who depended on the Risālah, or on Pedro de Alfonso. Thus Vitry said that 'the more sensible among the Arabs realised the falseness of the seducer' after retention of the body for twelve days, and the ultimate burial in the earth unwashed. But the faith of the more simple was preserved, partly by blandishments and partly by fear, because the Prophet's relatives and companions received honour and profit from it. This accounted for the establishment of the Caliphate. William of Tyre, followed by Oliver of Paderborn, spoke only of the conflict among the Muslims after Muhammad's death, and he confused this with the later conflict between Sunni and Shī'ah.[72]

Also confused with the same events was the compilation of the Qur'ān, which in fact the death of the Prophet did make necessary. Thus, according to Paris' emendation of the St Albans Chronicle, it was at this stage that elements of the Old and New Testaments, and other additions, were inserted into the Qur'ān, in order to satisfy the demand of the people. This must represent his final conclusions, after hearing different versions which he included in his Chronicle. Tripoli's idea, that such Jews and Christians as had been forced into Islam were the authors of the Qur'ān, is similar, but does not seem to be related to the events that immediately followed the Prophet's death.[73]

As a good death marks the saint, so the Prophet was allotted an appropriate, and usually an appropriately horrible, one. This was

inevitably so, in order to seal his unsanctity. Where better information made it difficult to believe the death from swine, the
notion that he was poisoned was the best credible and authenti-
cated substitute; poison is not, among Christians, the hall-mark
of martyrdom, as it sometimes seems to be among Muslims. Such
stories as the Prophet's death in the arms of 'Ā'ishah were thought
valuable, because from the Christian point of view they were
unedifying, though only from the Christian point of view. The
contrast with Christ provoked the belief that hope of an angelic
ascension of the Prophet's body had been soon disappointed. The
renewal under the early Caliphs of the sequence of force and
promises, to retain the mistaken allegiance of the faithful, showed
continuity between the Prophet and his followers; arguments
against the one applied against the other.

6. CONCLUSION

Thus, partly with evidence imagined by themselves, and partly
with evidence authentically derived from Islamic sources, directly
and indirectly, Christians constructed one single picture of the life
of Muhammad. Details invented or taken over at widely different
periods were much alike in their character and drift. They varied
only in their approximation to reality; some might be absurdly
fabulous, others only a biased interpretation of what was authentic;
but the result was always the same. Some accounts of the state of
Arabia at the time of the Prophet's birth give an impression that
is not, in outline, misleading; others are wholly fantastic. Both
kinds make it clear that the Arabs who received Islam were incompetent to judge it, and this was greatly insisted on. The
different accounts of Muhammad's early life equally varied from
the accurate to the ridiculous; but again all agreed in thinking it
important to tell his early story in detail, and in making it clear
that it was a likely introduction to false prophecy, an unlikely one
to any true mission. The three marks of Muhammad's life were
thought to be the violence and force with which he imposed his
religion; the salacity and laxness with which he bribed followers
whom he did not compel; and finally his evident humanity, which
it was constantly believed to be necessary to prove, although no
Muslim denied, or even wished to deny, it; and although Christian
and Muslim concepts of holiness differ very greatly. It was on
these three points that the total fraud seemed to be based; fraud
was the sum of Muhammad's life. Violence, salacity and humanity
were what his pretence to receive Revelation was used to justify.
Muhammad was the great blasphemer, because he made religion
justify sin and weakness. It seems incredible now that so much of
what was said of Muhammad was believed in good faith; but not

only audiences, but authors, believed whatever tended to show
that Muhammad could not really have been the Messenger of God.
Muhammad's history and character were essential to mediaeval
polemic.

❧ IV ❧

The place of violence and power
in the attack on Islam

VIOLENCE had a double significance in the relations of Christendom and Islam: force was used by Islam and against it. The
theoretical defence of Crusading warfare is related to this problem.
The use of force was almost universally considered to be a major
and characteristic constituent of the Islamic religion, and an
evident sign of error. It was a part of the Christian approach to
take this view while embracing the necessity for Crusading.

1. ATTITUDE TO CRUSADE

Of the preaching of the Crusade in general, it is enough to recall
that it was seen as a Holy War primarily because it was intended
to recover land that rightly belonged to the Christians. The test
of true Christianity was coming to be thought of as loyalty to the
Apostolic See, so that, increasingly, Eastern Orthodoxy as well
as the Eastern heretical Churches began to seem more than
schismatical, something of an aberration; but in spite of this,
Christians were still thought to be, or at least to have been, a
single nation which in the rise of Islam had been robbed of a third
of its best provinces.[1] Authors with some knowledge of Islam and
chronicles taken from Byzantine sources would always trace the
stages of loss to the early Caliphs who followed Muhammad's
example of aggression. Their general approach was not different
here from that of writers who had no special knowledge of Islam
but who spoke of Crusading. Every Christian reference to lands
that had once been Christian, and particularly to the Holy Land,
must be understood to have been made on the assumption that
these were lost provinces belonging by right to the Latin Church.
St Bernard called upon the faithful to 'defend' their Lord in His
own land (*in terra sua*); he envisaged only the conversion or the
extermination of the Muslims living there. Vitry's *Historia* is
calculated precisely to show how Islam seduced the East from
Christendom; in the same way Roderick saw Muhammad as the
seducer of Spain. This was more than a general way of thinking.

109

It had juridical and liturgical expression; a region conquered from Islamic rule was *restored* to the Church in the language of the curia; and the Church of Jerusalem in the twelfth century celebrated the Feast of the *Recovery* of the city. There is some parallel to the Muslim doctrine of dār al-Islām and dār al-ḥarb.[2]

With this general attitude we must associate the very lively resentment that was felt for the loss of church buildings used as mosques, during the lifetimes of the writers who speak of it. Mark of Toledo connected the original loss of provinces with this theme: at the Arab Conquest of Spain, where 'formerly many priests offered the divine obsequy to God, now villainous men devoted supplications to the execrable Muhammad, and churches which had once been consecrated by the hands of bishops were now reduced to profane temples'. Humbert of Romans exemplifies the attitude to contemporary 'profanation', although his comments lead rather ludicrously up to an anticlimax. With his own eyes, he tells us, giving us to expect some horrible sacrilege committed in his presence, with his own eyes he has seen not, it turns out, the atrocity itself, but only the place where it was said to have been committed. 'These filthy Muslims', he said, 'polluted and profaned not only the Temple of the Lord, but even the Sepulchre of the Lord, and all the holy places in that region, and innumerable holy churches dedicated to the cult of the living God and of our Lord Jesus Christ. I myself with my own eyes saw the holy chapel, in which the Muslims who were on their way to the Lord Frederick (II) quartered themselves; and it was said as certain (pro certo) that they lay there at night with women before the crucifix . . .' This irresponsible reliance on gossip was both calculated war propaganda (it was intended for the eyes of the Fathers of the Council at Lyons) and the revelation of a state of mind.[3]

Profanation in the angry last stages of the Latin States produced strong feelings. The tendency was already sharp as early as the loss of the 'Temple of the Lord' in 1187. This building had never been anything but a mosque, the site having been ruinous when the Caliph 'Umar ibn al-Khaṭṭāb captured Jerusalem; nevertheless, it was the site of the Temple where Christ had taught, and it always held a peculiar place in the imagination of Crusaders, one of whose principal objects, as a popular song put it, was *templum Dei adquirere*. Its association with the Order of Chivalry named after it is well known, and its loss after the capture of the city by Ṣalāḥ ad-Dīn was bitterly resented.[4] The accounts of its restoration to Muslim worship and of the ceremonies of cleansing it by the Muslims, and also – rather less stressed – of the profanation of true Christian shrines in the city, suggest an angry desperation

on the part of Christians, which the thought of their past profanation of mosques was not enough to solace.[5]

Christians would always feel a pleasure if not a duty in the
desecration of mosques: 'synagogues of Satan', as one not especially immoderate commentator called them. The mere presence of
one, *idolum abominationis*, desecrated the holy mountain, Sinai.
There was nothing remarkable in referring in passing to the conversion of *fana Maumeti* into churches. A really noteworthy
episode is recorded by the *Gestes des Chiprois*, which asserts that
when the Prince of Antioch and the King of Armenia, in conjunction with Hūlāgū, took Damascus in 1258, Mass was sung
and bells were rung in the Ummayad mosque, which had originally
been a church 'of the Greeks', *pour despit des Sarazins et pour lor
honte*. In 'the other mosques of Muhammad, there where the
Muslims worshipped' the Prince had chargers and donkeys brought
in, the walls splashed with wine and anointed with fresh and
salted pork fat, and he also ordered his men to make heaps of
waste, and 'they made ten'.[6]

Muslim abuse of holy images was noted at every loss of
Christian territory; one work of propaganda for the third Crusade
made play with the throwing down of the golden cross of the
Dome of the Rock – the Temple – by attaching ropes, and of
other crosses in the city, 'to the shame of the Christians, with
great cries . . .'[7] Stories of a crucifix dragged through the streets
of Damietta at the end of a rope circulated in the West. With
increasing Christian losses, atrocities against churches and images
increased, whether because more territory was overrun or because
of increasing bitterness. Ricoldo gave many examples in his
lament for the fall of 'Akka.[8] A little earlier, at the fall of Tripoli,
the strength and nature of Islamic feeling appears rather more
clearly in the pages of Fidenzio's narrative. The Muslims put
holy pictures to an insulting use, subjected images to various
insults and dragged a crucifix through the streets at the tail of an
ass. These episodes may be exaggerated; but Fidenzio himself
followed the victorious army of the sultan as it retired to Damascus,
in the hope of helping the Christian prisoners, and some of the
Muslims, with the events of the capture of the Christian city fresh
in their minds, asked him why Christians adored pictures and
images. It was not, Fidenzio of course replied, the images, but
the saints in heaven whom they represented, that Christians
venerated. 'They were silent, not knowing what else to say.'
Mutual incomprehension made discussion of this sort sterile
indeed. Fidenzio was particularly sensitive to the Islamic contempt
for the veneration of images; the Christian children who were
captured, he reported, were made Muslim and taught to spit upon

the crucifixes.[9] Such episodes as these illustrate the feeling out of which sprang both the physical violence and the theoretic defence of Crusading.

To fight on the Crusade was itself a religious vocation, and the views of rigorous enthusiasts achieved a widespread popularity. For example, Caesarius tells us that it was St Bernard's advice to a man who had failed to make good his monastic vocation that he should end his days fighting the infidel. A century later Joinville tells us that the Bishop of Soissons wished to be with God rather than return to his native land, and so spurred against the enemy and was killed. Thus he joined the number of martyrs. These two examples are typical of this enduring sentiment.[10] The opportunity that the Crusade gave to acquire merit was, in fact, a justifying element in it, argued Humbert, in his day the protagonist of Crusading theory. His replies to criticism of the preaching of the Crusade and to resistance to it are contained in two works, one a brief intended for the Fathers at Lyons, the other a sermon series fortified by an anthology of passages relating to the Holy Land and to past wars against Islam. Here he preached the Crusade after the auspicious invocation of the Lord God of Hosts.

In the Crusade, he maintained, it was not the innocent who were attacked, as happened in the West, when poor farmers and hospitals and leper-colonies suffered; on the contrary, the Muslim nation was *summa culpabilis*. Also, there was sufficient cause, no mere injured pride, avarice or vainglory; the army of God fought for more even than material right: for the cause of faith. Finally, a war that was fought on inadequate authority was not just, but the Crusade was fought on *divine* authority. Thus it was the just war *par excellence, bellum justissimum*. The Church bore two swords, against heretics and against rebels; Muslims had the qualities of both of these, since they destroyed the body like the latter, and the soul like the former. Muslims already subject to Christendom were tolerated because they were not in a position to do harm, because they were useful and because they might be converted.[11] This attitude was not unlike that of Islam towards Christians under Islamic rule. Humbert's arguments for toleration were sensible, although reluctant; his justification of the war was enthusiastic and irrational. The *culpability* of Muslims was not argued, but stated as self-evident; so was the divine authority.

We can only conclude that the use of violence against Islam was seen as inherently or axiomatically just. This will appear more clearly from consideration of further arguments of Humbert's. When it was objected that on Crusade innocent Christians might suffer more than guilty Muslims, he replied that history showed more Muslims to have been killed than Christians, and he quoted

with nauseating relish that first capture of Jerusalem by the
Crusaders when the blood of the slaughtered prisoners 'came up
to the horses' knees'.[12] If objectors contrasted the shedding of
blood with the behaviour of Christ and His Apostles, the writer
contrasted conditions in his own day and in the early days of the
Church; then the powerless Christian people had proceeded by
humility, but now, having become powerful, quite otherwise, by
the power of the sword, and as possessing arms where it no longer
had miracles. In the last resort the appeal was pragmatic; who
was prepared, by not resisting, to see all Christians perish? All
this discussion, so much more emotional than ratiocinatory, was
set in an historical perspective of ancient examples, Charles the
Great, Turpinus, Godfrey of Bouillon.[13] Thus the enthusiasm of
the teacher stood out in contrast to the political realism of Europeans increasingly reluctant to Crusade at all, and, when they did
do so, rarely altruistic.

Humbert's attitude was shared by the intellectually unpretentious literature of the vernacular languages, with which it was
directly linked by its use of and appeal to the 'Turpinus' chronicles.
The chansons de geste contain many examples, but the chansons
that arose directly in Crusading context illustrate it best. The
state of mind was simple, straightforward, so unintellectual as to
be almost simple-minded. Fighting anonymously in a tournament,
King Richard at one point wore for crest a red hound, whose tail
hung down to the ground:

> That was synyfycacyoun
> The hethen folke to bringe downe,
> Them to slee for Goddes loue,
> And Cristen men to brynge aboue.

The essence of Crusading was to 'slay for God's love'. Occasional
comments of more serious writers reveal a similar attitude.
Fidenzio's whole purpose in writing was to encourage the Crusade,
but his mind is most revealed by a chance comment on the un-
mentionable *scelera carnalia* which Islam seemed to encourage:
'And if there were no other cause but this, it would be the duty of
Christians to fight against them, and to cleanse the earth . . .' The
Muslims, said Benedict of Alignan, were not worthy of disputing
with, 'but rather to be extirpated by fire and the sword'. As St
Bernard had written: 'a Christian glories in the death of a pagan
(i.e. Muslim) because Christ is glorified; the liberality of the
King is revealed in the death of the Christian, because he is led
out to his reward'. Innocent III genuinely deplored the blood he
believed must be shed; I know only one other text that seems from
the heart to regret those 'numberless men who have perished and

still perish on either side'; who, Christians and Muslims, destroyed each other, it well says, as if they were not all human creatures.[14]

2. TOLERATION AND CO-EXISTENCE

Toleration of Muslims who resided outside Christendom under their own government, even negotiation with them, was liable to be suspected as treasonable to the Western Church. A well-known example is the accusation of treachery against Raymund of Tripoli, for allowing al-Afḍal's party to cross his territory when war was impending; not only was there contemporary criticism, but Raymund and others of the opposition to the Lusignans passed into legend as traitors to Christendom.[15] Richard I was suspected because of his negotiations with al-'Ādil; in this connection even his friends reported that 'it was a common saying that a friendship with the Gentiles was a heinous offence'. Balian d'Ibelin feared to be described by the Imperial party as fonder of Muslims than of Christians. Among the crimes of Frederick II was his having had 'the name of Muhammad cried in the Temple'; that is, he had agreed that the Qubbat as-Ṣakhrah, built as a mosque and, except during the short period of Latin rule, used as one, should continue so to be used, at a time when he had no option, because there was no possibility at all of stopping Islamic possession of it. When the Templars were to be accused of horrifying crimes, secret agreements with the Muslims and a willingness to secede to Islam were included among them. From another side, the paintings of the Jerusalem and 'Akka scriptoria testify, as Buchthal has recently shown, to the isolation of the Latin Kingdom from its Islamic surroundings. With the Crusades, the world had moved far from Gregory VII's direct negotiations of 1078, his personal recommendation of protégés to a Muslim ruler.

The language which it seemed suitable to use of those who traded in war goods, despite the prohibitions of the Church Councils, with Islamic powers, was strong indeed: 'wicked sons (of the Church)', said William of Adam of Sulṭānīyah, 'that is, false Christians, professing the faith of the Roman Church by word, but denying it in their acts'. He was complaining about all kinds of dealing with 'oppressors' who 'destroyed the inheritance of the Lord'. The canons and papal bulls attempted to impose a strict blockade of war materials; trade in arms, iron, wood for shipbuilding and sea-going craft was forbidden at all times, and trade in food and other useful matter was forbidden in time of war. Shipping was immobilised when a Crusade was projected and Christians were forbidden to serve in Muslim ships. After the fall of 'Akka, all trade absolutely was prohibited, as though the war footing were permanent; and, from about the middle of the fourteenth century, the adoption of a system of special licences became an important source of revenue to the Holy See.[16]

The way in which the thirteenth-century system worked, by which friendly intercourse with Muslims was prohibited, is illuminated by a reply of San Ramón de Peñaforte to the Friars Preachers and Friars Minor in Morocco. His purpose was to define doubtful points in the practical exercise of the excommunication; this took effect automatically, and the missionaries had faculties to absolve only in certain cases. He began by recapitulating the essentials: the prohibition of trade in armaments at all times, and of trade in foods and other things only *in dispendium Terrae Sanctae*. The intention of the law was to avoid helping Muslims who were at war with Christians; this was interpreted to mean, *with any Christian*, which gave a wide meaning to what might be considered prejudicial to the Holy Land. If, in ignorance of the law, a man traded in the forbidden things, and if, when he was warned, he recovered the goods he had sold, he was still excommunicated, but the missionaries had authority to absolve him. Similarly a man who became involved, even indirectly, in the forbidden trade, in grave economic need: his case was more serious, but he might be treated leniently. In spite of so severe a law, both Latin and indigenous Christian communities flourished within Islam, and there were certain contacts with Muslims which were not commercial, or which at least did not come under the ban of the blockade, and so did not involve the automatic excommunication. Men who bound Christians to Muslim employers, as a result of which faith was endangered, were not excommunicated, but had committed mortal sin. The same was true of those who sold Christians as slaves, and even of those who sold Jewish and Muslim women, making them pretend, to the detriment of the Christian name, that they were Christians. There was only occasional licence for close association with Muslims. The relations, and particularly the parents, of renegades might still live with them, in order to reconvert them, or because they were dependent on them, or even, last resort, from charity towards them. In a marriage where one spouse became Muslim, they might remain together, *dummodo sine contumelia Creatoris sit*. It was clearly intended that a belligerent attitude should reduce fraternisation to a minimum. The writer earned the reputation of *zelator fidei propagandae inter Saracenos*.[17]

Within Christendom, we have seen already, subject Muslims were tolerated. The approach of canon law was sober and careful. The gloss on Gratian required that Jews and Muslims be recognised as *neighbours* in the evangelical sense. In practice this meant a very restricted freedom. A peaceful prince should not expel

Muslims from his lands without cause; nothing inhuman should be done to them; it might even be possible to form alliances with presumably non-subject Muslims, if this were for purposes of defence. These are licences of very limited effect. Christians were forbidden to take service in Muslim or Jewish households on any pretext whatever, and were excommunicated only for living in them (1179). Jews and Muslims might hold no position of public authority, and both must wear distinctive clothing, for fear of accidental *commixtio* of the sexes between them and Christians (1215). The *Clementinae* (1312) forbade the call to prayer and pilgrimages within the territory of Christian princes. Clement IV had a peculiar horror of the call to prayer; he called it *contumelia Creatoris* that among the worshippers of Christ the name of Muhammad should be publicly 'extolled' at certain hours of the day. He addressed a long and eloquent appeal to Jaime the Conqueror, I of Aragon, begging that prince to put down his Muslim and Jewish subjects, and pressing upon him that programme of expulsion which would in fact be effected only at the very end of the fifteenth century. Jaime's practice tolerated Islamic worship, enforced Islamic law, 'according to the sunna', for Muslims, and ensured the right of Muslims to teach their sons their religion, specifically, the Qur'ān and the ḥadīth; but we are concerned with the theory of the Church, not with the compromises of day-to-day politics. The position of Muslims in Christendom approximated temporarily to that of tributary Christians in Islam, except that the ultimate aim was their conversion. To-day none of the Islamic enclaves survives in Europe outside the old Ottoman Empire.[18]

San Ramón de Peñaforte, in his own canonical summa, insisted that Jews and Muslims must be converted, not by harshness, but by reason and kindness: *coacta servicia non placent Deo.* Christians might not eat with them (Jews 'attacked' Christianity by their rules of purity in food, and in this Muslims 'judaised'), or live with them, or invite them as guests; the only exception made was for missionaries outside the borders of Christendom. Muslims who became Christian and relapsed were pardonable only if they had been dragged bodily to what would then have been an invalid baptism; if they had only been forced by, for example, beating, the baptism was valid. Christians who left property by will to Muslims were pursued by posthumous anathemas; cases involving Christians had always to be tried in Christian courts, and there Christians were always to be preferred as witnesses to Jews and Muslims. These might not be provided with arms. It was, of course, one of Frederick II's offences to have employed mercenaries from Africa, but the Kings of Aragon expected normal military service from their *faithful* Muslim subjects. Muslim populations, like Jewish communities, were compelled to accept Christian missionaries, apparently in the mosques themselves.[19]

With this tradition, which assumed that force was a duty, and that even within the security of Christendom friendly relations were dangerous and evil, it was possible for a missionary spirit to co-exist. There was a certain unreality in the attitude of Peter the Venerable, which derived from the literary form of his choice, a refutation of Islam addressed to Muslims in Latin; he considered it suitable for translation, but apparently did not arrange for a translation to be made. An excess of rhetoric does not obscure a genuine apostolic fervour, tempered by smugness. 'I approach you, I say, not as our people often do, with arms, but with words, not by force, but by reason, not in hatred, but in love . . .' A similar approach was that of Oliver of Paderborn in his letter to the King of Babilon. The Christian Church, he pointed out, would prefer to send the 'sword of the Word', but, finding no other remedy than the material sword, allows it to be used against the Islamic power for the defence of Christendom *et iuris sui*. Oliver, like Peter before him, was conscious of his originality in using the pen (in Latin) instead of the sword. Adam Marsh felt some need to apologise for the use of the material sword, in a somewhat academic essay upon the taking of the Cross by Henry III of England: the Church had not only the right but the duty to wield both swords, but must maintain the spiritual sword as constantly as the material: *verbalis ad usum, ferreus ad nutum*. In other words, the work of the missions must supplement the labours of armies.[20]

This mood of missionary endeavour was related to that of St Francis, whose unarmed incursion into Islam, however unsuccessful, was at least made in person. In some accounts of his appearance before al-Kāmil it is his solicitude for the sultan's soul that moves the latter's heart and makes him protect the saint and try to pour gifts upon him. This episode is in some ways convincing; Muslims have always been liable to revere the sanctity of individual Christians. The Rule, moreover, encouraged suitable Brothers to go to Islamic lands. 'Spiritually they can behave among other people in two ways. One way is not to make disputes and controversies, but to be *subject to every human creature for God's sake*, and to witness that they are Christians. The other way is, when they see that God pleases, to preach the word of God . . .' They were to remember that they had given themselves and their bodies to Christ. If St Francis himself once chose the second of these two methods, the idea of silent witness, which is what the first amounts to, was even more revolutionary. These new themes, however, were added to, not substituted for, the old. At the battle of Damietta, we read in Bonaventura's *Life* how the saint 'forbids the battle, foretells disaster'; but this is only because he has prophetic knowledge of defeat; he does not oppose fighting. The story is curious because, uncharacteristically, he is at first reluctant to appear a fool by acting Cassandra. Presumably he did not trust his own prophetic insight, but there is also an obvious suggestion that both he and Bonaventura, as might be expected, disliked the worldliness which made the cause of God in the Latin Kingdom depend on material success. The actual passage to the East of so many friars created a new and important element in the Christian consciousness, but missionary thought did not replace the old Crusading ways of thinking.[21]

More strictly practical was the approach of some Spaniards. San Pedro wrote explicitly to save the faith of the Christians under Islamic rule who were in danger of despair and apostasy. Lull, ever eccentric, was in general more practical than his actions sometimes suggest. His *Life* tells the unattractive story of the Muslim slave who for many years had taught him Arabic, and whom, when he one day blasphemed the Holy Name, Lull beat on the face and head and body. After years of being a language master, explained Lull, the slave had become haughty; then he tried to kill Lull and was put in prison. Lull was then torn between fear of his release and reluctance that he should be executed. He attributed this reluctance, not to human affection for his old companion, but to respect for the means by which he had learned the language in which he proposed to evangelise the world. It is to our mind appalling that he felt relieved from his dilemma by the slave's suicide in prison. This unsympathetic story represents a general attitude; Islam could be tolerated only in silent subjection, the only final solution was its destruction. Lull, of course, took it for granted that a Muslim would be damned, irrespective of his suicide. Lull's personal taste was for disputation rather than for the use of force. His account of his personal invasion of Bujāyā was that he went to *defend* the Trinity, a theme that he introduced by publicly attacking Islam in the market-place. This sort of 'defence' seems parallel to treating military aggression in the Crusades as defensive. Lull's missionary fervour was genuine: 'sorrow have I and pity', he says, in Professor Peers' translation of *Blanquerna*, 'for the damnation of those innocent men'. At the same time he felt the obduracy of the Saracen; Muslims who disbelieved their own religion were still unwilling to receive the truth. It would seem practicable to secure reunion with the Greeks and the conversion of the Tartars by the 'necessary reasons' he put forward in dispute; but it would be more useful in the case of the Muslims to 'fight them and expel them from the land which is ours by right'. It would not be possible to convert them so long as they held power; it was only the conversion of subject Muslims that was practicable.[22]

In this connection there is an interesting justification of missionary work in Islamic territory which was sent, again by San Ramón de Peñaforte, to his Master-General. Its fruits in Africa and Spain were listed as, first, the care of the Christian knights, who thirsted for the Word of God; secondly, care of the indigenous Arabic-speaking Christians, who 'desired the friars with a great desire'; thirdly, the recovery of the renegades whose apostasy derived from excessive poverty or from 'the seduction of the Muslims' (this seems to imply motives of worldly advancement); fourthly, there was refutation of the calumny spread not only by Muslims but by some Christians duped by them, that Latins were idolators and image-worshippers; fifthly, came the instruction and consolation of Christian prisoners; lastly, there was the excellent impression that the religious made upon the Muslims, including the very highest; it even happened that there were conversions, particularly in Murcia.[23]

It is obvious how low in this list came communication of any sort with Muslims, and, even so, how small was the hope of their conversion, which might really be expected only where Christian arms were successful. Conversion was not despaired of; 'preaching' here means 'preaching to Muslims', and Alexander IV wished the Gospel to be preached without offence; but it was realistically relegated to a place of secondary importance. The treaty with the King of Tunis which was signed by Charles of Anjou on the death of Louis IX in 1270, and which was criticised by some Christians, allowed for churches and the cult to be maintained, and for Franciscans and Dominicans to preach and convert. Fr. Eleemosyna commented that the merchants and other Catholics resident in Tunis were able in consequence to receive the sacraments regularly, but that there was only very moderate fruit in conversion from Islam. Fifty years earlier Honorius had written to the 'Amīr al-Mu'minīn to ask for the freedom to make converts, surely a vain request, however difficulties might be glossed diplomatically over by Muslim rulers negotiating from weakness. A similar picture develops of serious missionary work in the East; thus in Cairo in 1303–4 the Franciscan Angelo da Spoleto and his companions took the sultan's permission to succour Christian prisoners first, and then devoted a season to spiritual and corporal works of mercy, distributing money and clothes, hearing confessions, giving absolution and Communion; even, secretly, reconciling Christians who had apostatised from fear.[24] The missions to Muslims in

Christian lands, of which we have already spoken, present so great a contrast. The famous Arabic studium founded by San Ramón claimed ten thousand conversions, and particularly the conversion of the educated. The admission of missionaries to Muslim populations in southern Italy was even the subject of successful negotation between the Pope and Frederick II. These efforts measure the failure of the missions overseas.[25]

Muslims, in their own countries, were thus rarely the objects of apostolic activity. We may recognise in the exemplary work among the needy and suffering Christian groups in Islamic cities, and also among the merchant communities, the silent witness recommended in St Francis' Rule. The alternative suggested in the Rule, 'preaching', raises more complex problems. Serious claims to have disputed with Muslims are rare, in any strict interpretation of the word. Ricoldo claimed to have disputed privately with Muslims in Baghdad, but his original contribution to Western knowledge is suspiciously small and he uses himself the adverb *aliquantulum* to describe his activities in this respect. His work is too literary in inspiration, his arguments too little suited to a Muslim public, for us to be able to suppose that he ever experienced more than a very limited interchange of ideas with Muslims in a rudimentary form of Arabic. Lull's work is so individual that it is usually impossible to distinguish recognisably Islamic terms in the language, and often in the thought, of the Muslims whose arguments he represents in some of his *disputationes*. These were imaginary conversations in which the Muslim participants were never very successful; in a public debate on neutral ground in real life, they might have done a great deal better. There is something of the same unreality about Lull's accounts of debates he took part in, as about Ricoldo's of his own experience; as we cannot conceive Ricoldo's successfully using the arguments he quotes to us, so Lull puts into his opponents' mouths words which sound more like that which Lull would have wished them to be, than like anything Muslims might be expected to have said.[26]

There is, however, another and a very different element in Lull's African incursions. Where acts of war were out of the question there often developed a strange desire to provoke violence instead. Some missionaries seem to have allowed or encouraged 'preaching' and 'disputation' to degenerate into provocation. Lull exemplified this when he 'defended' the Trinity by publicly abusing Islam; Ricoldo, more sympathetically, showed, amid considerable evidence of courage for religion's sake, no sign at all of zeal for the martyr's crown. We find Lull in Bujāyā in Tartary, in his old age rather like St Teresa in her childhood, the protagonist in a gratifying drama: 'in the midst of the market-place, forgetful of the peril of death, he began to cry in a loud voice, "the law of the Christians is holy and true, and the sect of the Moors is false and wrong . . ." ' This must have been the manner of his last provocation of the Tunis mob, if the tradition of his death is accurate; he had been three times expelled by Muslim governments before he was thus at last successful. Perhaps he despaired of his latest literary effort, the attempt to teach ordinary Christian traders means of Trinitarian apologetic, the dedication of more complex Trinitarian theology to the qādī; but his anxiety to provoke martyrdom was far from isolated.[27]

St Francis, before his own journey to Egypt, had already despatched a party to Africa who successfully forced a reluctant Muslim government to martyr them. Before they left Christian territory they announced that God had chosen them to be numbered in the glorious army, *Deus nos vult in numero suorum martyrum computare*. In Seville they tried to break into the Friday mosque, and, when they were driven away by the crowd, as 'ambassadors of the King of Kings' they went and abused Muhammad and Islam outside the royal palace instead. Arrested, they were moved from prison to prison in order to avoid publicity, but they continued to carry on in the same way, and were finally deported, at their own wish to Morocco. There they still behaved in the same way and were twice more deported, once by the local Christian community itself. When the goverment was finally stirred into action it put very heavy pressure upon them in the form of torture, and they were in due course executed, after refusing every offer of wealth, women and honour as reward for conversion to Islam.[28] This behaviour recalls very closely the Martyrs' Movement of the ninth century in Spain, but it served as exemplar to some friars for some time; perhaps St Teresa's childhood exploit was the last flicker of this ancient tradition. More than a century after St Francis, Fr. Pasquale de Vittoria, in central Asia, preached 'the deceits and falsities and blindnesses' of the Prophet for twenty-five days at the doors of the mosque, at the time of the 'Īd al-aḍhā'. In the unsettled conditions of Mongol rule, he escaped with insults and thrown stones; but again, this behaviour was a deliberate provocation to violence.

A particularly interesting case was that of Fr. Livin, martyred, or executed, in Cairo in 1345. Intellectually able, he had neglected theological study for prayer; his only ambition was martyrdom; there may be a psychological connection between his renunciation of intellectual exercise and his craving for death. At that time the rights of martyrdom were widely canvassed; the *quaestio* was disputed, *an sit licitum Christiano secundum Deum intrare Saracen-*

orum mesquitas ad praedicandum fidem catholicam et legem Macho-meticam impugnandum. It was accepted that it was not licit to induce certain death unnecessarily; Livin, subtly quibbling, and 'adducing the example of martyrs and saints' also pointed out that 'many of our brothers entered mosques from the zeal of faith, and preached, confessing the Christian faith', and still were not killed. Since his private intention was frankly to seek martyrdom this defence of provocation seems disingenuous; he also more openly argued that to tempt others to kill one was not suicide. In any case he followed his own recommendation, bursting into the Friday prayer in the presence of the sultan, and crying out in French against the *mortiferam sectam*: interpreters and renegades present alone understood what he said. It was explained to the sultan, and the rumour ran round the mosque that the intruder had 'presumed to vilify religion and the holy Prophet'; but still the sultan was reluctant to act, and he quietened the people by saying that the friar was obviously unbalanced by too much poverty and fasting. In the course of a few days' imprisonment the would-be martyr made himself so objectionable that the sultan was no longer able to resist the pressure put on him to secure to Livin the end he desired. In all these stories the reluctance of the Muslim rulers to execute is obvious and it is difficult not to impute the ultimate violence to those who provoked it. Theirs was a state of mind that could tolerate no relation between Christendom and Islam save that of violence exerted or undergone.[29]

Tripoli's attitude contrasts with those that we have so far considered and it is mysterious. Anxious to show Islam to be on the point of mass conversion, he has been said to have made, and obviously he did make, propaganda against the Crusade as being superfluous; and this was at a time immediately preceding the mamlūk triumph and the final collapse of the Latin States. His motives are obscure; perhaps he was no more than original. Prophecies of the fall of Islam had long circulated and the disappearance of the 'Abbāsid caliphate before Hūlāgū had made a great impression upon the Western, as upon the Eastern, world. 'They thus, by the simple word of God, without philosophical arguments or military arms, like simple sheep seek baptism of Christ and pass into the sheepfold of God. He who said and wrote thus, by the action of God, has now baptised more than a thousand.' However we should understand, and we must certainly have reservations about, the statistical claim, it is obvious that Tripoli's approach was the reverse of the usual one. His work was unknown to or ignored by all writers who had an advanced knowledge of Islam or a close interest in missionary or Crusading operations.[30] It is as the exception that he illustrates the rule.

3. ATTITUDE TO JIHĀD

It is evident that Christendom recognised a relationship which aimed primarily at the destruction of Islam, and in which missionary endeavour held a subordinate place. For various reasons, moreover, it was the wish of the Church to reduce communication with Muslims to a minimum. With this in mind we may consider the habitual condemnation of Islam for its inherent violence and for its refusal to allow rational disputation. Christians usually argued from the example and teaching given by Muhammad in his lifetime. His government of the community at Medina and his wars against the Quraysh and others had a more than episodic significance; from these, it was believed, derived essential parts of his religion, notably the justification and praise of force. 'They were ordered to rob, to make prisoner and to kill the adversaries of God and their prophet, and to persecute and destroy them in every way', said Pedro de Alfonso. Servitude, he said, was the best of the alternatives offered to the conquered Christians. Quotation from the Qur'ān even proved that Muhammad, as ever self-contradictory, had himself known this use of compulsion to be wrong. It was frequently emphasised that the rapid expansion of the Muslims under the early Caliphs had been a matter of armed strength.[31] A slightly more sophisticated view would distinguish between converts attracted by fear of the sword, others by the offer of rewards or by the promise of Paradise; these careful distinctions were inherited from the *Risālah* and the *Contrarietas*. With these more complex statements we may contrast Sigebert's brief assertion that Muhammad taught that he who killed or was killed by the enemy of Islam went to Paradise. This was part of that small body of information that reached even the less well-informed. What was least well understood was the position of Christians living under Islamic rule. The word *servitude* does not accurately describe the tributary situation of the Mozarabs and the Oriental Christians, although (in later authors) it can be understood fairly to define the state of individual Latin prisoners captured in fighting, or at the sack of towns, at either end of the Mediterranean.[32]

In sūrah LXXXVIII Ketton has 'Tu namque doctor es, non coactor.' To this the Annotator remarks, 'Why then dost thou teach that men are to be converted to thy religion by the sword? If thou art not a coercer, but a teacher, why dost thou subject men by power, like animals and brute beasts, and not by reasoning, like men? In fact, like the liar you are, you everywhere contradict yourself.' This early statement, while it emphasised the accusation of self-contradiction which many writers would bring forward, introduced also the assertion, equally popular, that Muhammad did not, and Islam would not, allow rational disputation. This theme was taken up at length by Peter the Venerable. He admonished his imaginary Islamic audience that the Qur'ān is alone in refusing to discuss religion; and, he thought, contrary therein to the custom of the Greeks and Romans, the Persians and Indians, who all sought ever after truth. Conversion of the world to Christianity had been peaceful; the conversion of the English was a case in point. His method was to enlarge rhetorically upon isolated Qur'anic verses:

For what is this? *If anyone wish to dispute with thee, say that thou hast turned thy face and the faces of thy followers to God.* O Muhammad . . . if . . . you make no other reply, except about turning your face and the faces of your followers to God, shall I believe what you say to be true? Shall I believe you to be a true prophet of God? Shall I believe the religion which you delivered to your people to have been delivered to you by God? I shall indeed be more than a donkey if I agree; I shall be more than cattle if I consent . . .

We may take another example briefly. '*Nolite, inquit, disputare cum legem habentibus, melior est enim caedes quam lis.* And who does not see that this is hellish counsel?' If Muhammad had confidence in his own religion, argued Peter, why did he forbid his people to dispute? If he was not confident, why did he write things that they could not defend? 'But he knew, or (what is said with apologies to you) Satan who spoke through him knew, that such was the strength of the Jewish and Christian religions . . .' Thus in his most humanistic style Peter the Venerable warned Islam that only falseness seeks the shadows. While he thus emphasised the supposed Islamic refusal to dispute, he did not neglect to speak also of Muslim violence: 'words fail . . . at such bestial cruelty'. Most of these are phrases without substance.[33]

The same themes, however, reappeared constantly. Godfrey of Viterbo and the Gregorian Report described the choice between conversion, death and tribute offered to the conquered, and the duty to wage war against the non-Muslims living beyond the dār al-Islām; enemies were to be killed and their women and children carried into slavery. These more precise and better informed accounts developed the theme that Muhammad claimed the power of arms in the place of that of miracles. Oliver of Paderborn said simply, like Sigebert, that to kill or be killed earned Paradise; he said too that Islam began by the sword, was maintained by the sword and by the sword would be ended[34]; it was upheld by 'worldly and human fear'; Muslims refused to accept Christian preachers in their territories. Vitry said that the use of force by Islam derived from Muhammad's practice; that, in his opinion, never from the infancy of the primitive Church till its old age was there or would there be a greater abomination of desolation; nor would the Church of God ever be oppressed by a greater flail. Matter from the Syrian Apology he quoted with less accuracy than Viterbo had done. Humbert of Romans, the apologist for the Crusade, found no difficulty in condemning Islam for aggression, or in criticising Muhammad for forcing men to follow him by the sword, where Christ had accepted only voluntary believers. The early Muslims forced Christians to become Muslim, and killed others, and Muslims have done the same ever since: 'they are so zealous for their religion that wherever they hold power they mercilessly behead every man who preaches against their religion.' (We have seen how fair a description of Islamic practice this really was.) In the long series of persecutors of the Church the Muslims were both the worst and the most persistent. It is interesting that Tripoli, whose purpose was the opposite of Humbert's, equally made clear the basis of compulsion on which he took Islam to stand. Part of his belief in its imminent collapse was that it would fall, as it had arisen, by the sword. Fidenzio stressed Muslim 'cruelty' as a practical issue. Varagine used an oddly non-committal phrase when he said that Muslims believed either spontaneously or from fear of the sword. On the whole there was very general agreement about this aspect of Islam, both in the substance of what was said, and in the way of saying it.[35]

The *reprobatio* proceeded always by the citation of texts from the Qur'ān and the Traditions, apparently seeking the Islamic authorities which would justify the traditional Christian accusations. Thus robbery, he said, was specifically permitted, on the authority of Bukhārī, by the *lex super rapinis*. Muhammad, similarly, said that it was 'given to him by God that he should attack or kill men until they witnessed that there was no other than God and that Muhammad was the messenger of God; and that they should give him tribute or rates'. He attributed the access of converts in the prophet's own time to genuine belief through *fatua simplicitas*, to family loyalty and to love of honour and riches. This diminishes the importance in the rise of Islam of force, usually included among the primary motives of conversion. In that section of the work that is most probably Ramón Martí's there appears the pun about Muhammad, 'nec fuit consolator, sed potius desolator', because he came with the sword to force men to accept his religion. In his *Capistrum Judaeorum*, Martí bracketed violence of arms with bestial attractions, and spoke of the Islamic substitution of military power for miracles. This last point, which several authors mentioned, contrasts strangely with Humbert's assertion that the Crusaders similarly used arms in default of the miracles of the primitive Church.[36]

What, asked San Pedro, had Muhammad commanded, but fornications and robberies? The Qur'ān inconsistently recommended both reason and war, and the ḥadīth confirmed this. Muslims were promised a heavenly reward for death in battle, that their wounds would be beautiful on the Day of Resurrection. He was confident that Islam would end, as it began, by the sword; he understood that Muhammad's teaching was that men who were not Muslims might be killed in jihād, their women dishonoured and taken prisoner with the children, their goods seized, their kingdoms occupied. This summary puts the position in extreme terms and omits the offer of tributary status (as alternative to jihād), but is otherwise not really inaccurate.[37]

Even more than San Pedro, Ricoldo summed up the arguments that so many others had used before him. His version of the prophesied fall of Islam was to the effect that Muhammad taught that 'that religion shall last as long as the victory of its sword shall last'. Islam was the religion of violence and murder: *lex violenta* and *lex occisionis et mortis*. The Qur'ān said that there was no compulsion in the religion of God, 'yet there is no greater compulsion than to compel by killing'. This was one of the contradictions characteristic of the Qur'ān; he took up Pedro de Alfonso's point, and said that the Qur'ān, which forbade bitter disputation with men of other religions, yet commanded the death of infidels; in reality God does not love forced service. Compulsion, together with a general approval of murder and robbery, was part of what was carried forward from Muhammad's personal practice into the future behaviour of Islam. In spite of his own claim to have disputed with Muslims, Ricoldo several times asserted what had now become a Christian dogma, the refusal of Muslims to dispute. He said that the wise among the Muslims did not believe, and refused to discuss the matter for that reason. The Qur'ān here was inferior to pagan philosophy, since it 'says practically nothing about the virtues, but (speaks of) wars and plunder'. Force was substituted for miracles. His analysis of the motives for which the first Muslims were converted resembles that in the *reprobatio*, but gives greater prominence to the violent element. With some reason he said that the failure to pay tribute is no just cause to kill; but this was no fair way to present the alternatives actually offered by Islam, war, tribute or conversion. The fifth part of the spoil of war of which the Prophet disposed he represented as Muhammad's personal profit from robbery, and added that Islam did not require restitution to be made. These were all more or less subtle restatements of Islamic doctrine, so devised as to make criticism easy.

Ricoldo recalled that the Gospel does not permit any violence at all: 'if one strike thee . . .' – 'him that taketh away from thee thy cloak . . .' He added the pertinent rider: 'Nor is it an objection if certain bad Christians do not observe these things.' In saying this he at least showed awareness of a problem that many Christians ignored. It was even possible to strengthen the contrast between the two religions by reversing the comment, when it was applied to practice; there was more fraternal love between the Muslims whose religion was the religion of killing, than between Christians, who followed the religion of love. In Ricoldo's case there was not the usual inconsistency of also making propaganda for the Crusade. He was alone in insisting that it was only the theories of the two religions that he compared; here he was fairer than his comtemporaries, and fairer than the sources available to him, which he usually followed uncritically.[38]

To all this Lull contributed very little, despite his life-long preoccupation with missionary aims; like so many, he contrasted the forceful seizure of the world by Islam with its peaceful conversion by the Apostles; more consistent than Humbert, and more aware of reality than Peter the Venerable, he was able to imagine a sultan sending to the Pope to complain that Christians used force when the Apostles had not done so.[39]

Most mediaevals assumed that Islamic refusal to dispute arose from a fear of reason. It is perhaps more likely that it came, on the part of Muslim governments, from a desire to avoid trouble, and on the part of Qur'anic scholars and jurisprudents from a contempt for Christianity. None of the Latins whose knowledge of Islam was extensive made an important point with which the relatively ignorant Acqui preceded a reference to the execution of those who publicly attacked Muhammad: whoever willed, whether Christians or Jews or people of any other faith, might live in the lands of the Muslims, so long as they did not speak against the Prophet. Mandeville, too, said, 'among the Saracens in divers places there dwell many Christian men under tribute'; but the Islamic toleration of tributaries was not a favourite theme.[40]

4. PROBLEMS OF PROVIDENCE

The seizure of power by Islam in the first place and the recapture of the Holy Land from the Latins as the energy of the Crusades was exhausted, the loss of so many provinces, of so many souls, constituted a theological problem which would greatly exercise contemporary Christian thought. The success of Islamic power in any form raised a deeply painful question to which there was no easy answer. A partial solution was sought in the comforting consideration that it had been prophesied.

Islam was foreshadowed in the fate of Ismael; to Tripoli, for example, the promise about the posterity of Agar was fulfilled in Muhammad, who was

. . . by nation an Arab of the seed of Ismael, of whom it is said in Genesis XVI.12: 'He shall be a wild man. His hand will be against all men, and all men's hands against him: and he shall pitch his tents against all his brethren.' The reader may understand whether this prophecy is fulfilled in Muhammad, since it seems that no other of his sons is found thus wild and powerful to pitch his tents against all men, as this one alone of whom we are speaking.

Another prophecy relating to the descendants of this *ferus homo* was said to have been fulfilled in the Holy Land: 'Servants have ruled over us . . .' The children of Agar, pointed out Humbert, are servants (bond-children). To William of Auvergne there was a special significance in the descent from Ismael. He said of Muhammad:

Know then first that he was of the seed of Abraham by Ismael, who was the founder of the Arab nation, as Josephus says, and it was from Ismael that the Arab nation received greatness, according to the promise of God, saying to Abraham: 'I will make the son also of the bondwoman a great nation.'

The prophecy of Methodius foretold that the Arabs, for the sins of the Christians, would leave the desert in such numbers and strength as to dominate the world until a king should arise to free the Christians and subdue the Ismaelites in their turn. This seemed to have been realised when merciful God scattered the Arabs by Charles the Great; if the prophecy were to be trusted, it could not happen again. In a similar but less closely argued passage, San Pedro cited the Epistle to the Galatians, not altogether relevantly. His Old Testament references were fuller, his citations of pseudo-Methodius less full, than those of William. Ismael was the savage or rustic ass; Muhammad descended from him through the idolator Nabajoth, progenitor of Moabites, Madianites and Idumaeans. The authentic Islamic genealogies of Muhammad had a mediaeval European public. Behind all this lay the conviction that the illegitimate progeny of Abraham must always war against the legitimate.[41]

All this was cold comfort for the prosperity of Islam, for that *numerositas Saracenorum* which, as a modern writer has put it, to mediaeval minds was a real torment.[42] 'Why these things should be permitted, only He knows to whom no one can say, why dost Thou do so? – and who said that, of many who are called, few are chosen.' This was essentially a mystery; one author spoke of God's 'just, *admittedly hidden*, judgement'. Behind the mental torment lay the fear that Muslim success did indeed show divine approval. There was only one answer, but this, though it was evangelical, was not emotionally satisfying: misfortunes, if they had anything to do with God's pleasure or displeasure must be taken as a sign of His love; the Devil often triumphed, and no one, Humbert suggested, would suppose that this was pleasing to God. In this matter Ricoldo's judgement was well-balanced and sensible. The Muslims could not claim that their success revealed the divine approval, because they would lay themselves open to attack on the same grounds; they themselves were most seriously castigated by the Tartars, who had no religion at all. Both the just and the un-just are castigated by God, but in different ways: Christians were chastised as just, and at the same time punished for their sins.[43]

The punishment of sin was the most frequent explanation of Christian misfortunes. Thus one comment attributed the original success of Islam to the heresy of Heraclius. When he 'deviated from the Catholic faith, therefore, by the divine judgement' the Agarenes arose under 'Umar ibn al-Khaṭṭāb. The failure of the Latin States was attributed to Latin sins: *tradidit nos Deus in manus barbarorum quia obliti sumus precepta Dei*. This explanation was generally accepted, so that it extended beyond writers primarily concerned with Crusading subjects. Caesarius, on the authority of a fellow-monk who in his youth had himself travelled to the East, attributed to the Muslims themselves the opinion that the Christians were punished for their sins by the success of Ṣalāḥ ad-Dīn. Later Lull made his fictional Muslims boast that Islam held Jerusalem because the Qur'ān is of God; the one proved the other. It seems that the idea that the success of Muslim arms marked the divine approval of Islam was held at least as a joke, and no doubt half-seriously, by the general public in the West. Salimbene describes how Dominicans and Franciscans preaching the Cross in France found people who would ostentatiously call a beggar over and give him money, saying, 'Take this in the name of Muhammad, who is more powerful than Christ.' This was the attitude that Humbert of Romans set out to combat, and this is how he became, a little superfluously, with that lack of proportion that was sometimes a weakness of the Schools, the apologist for the will of God. Augustine had said that evil was permitted only that good might come of it. Humbert was able to identify the three goods which came of the Islamic evil; the *manifestatio fidelium Christi*, a sort of public confession of loyalty; the *exercitio bonum*, in execution of God's wish that His people should not be unemployed; and *salutis facilitas*, in that many were willing to fight Saracens who would never consent to perform long or exacting penances.[44]

These are not very profound considerations. The problem of the
Islamic triumph presented itself most acutely in the form of the
sufferings of Christians and their subjection to Islamic rule, particularly when this was directly observed. The most serious and
sustained examination is Ricoldo's in his *Epistolae commentatoriae
de perditione Acconis.* Here what most shocked him was the death
of his own Dominican colleagues and the fate of the other Religious; this was natural enough; he had known them all, having in
fact set out from 'Akka on his own journey to the East. The
contrast of the disastrous collapse of the Latin States and the
wealth and beauty of the lands of Islam intensified his sense of
oppression and provided the opportunity for a dramatic opening
for his lament.

It happened that when I was in Baghdad 'in the midst of the captives
by the river Chobar' – the Tigris – in one respect the pleasantness of the
garden in which I was delighted me, because it was like Paradise, for
wealth of trees and fertility and variety of fruits; it had sprung up,
irrigated by the waters of Paradise, and golden houses were built about
it. In another respect, the massacre and capture of the Christian people
and their overthrow after the lamentable capture of 'Akka drove me to
sadness, when I saw the Muslims most joyful and flourishing, the
Christians really neglected and mentally dismayed . . . I began more
carefully than usual to reflect upon the judgements of God about the
government of the world, and specially about Muslims and Christians . . .

These letters may not less genuinely represent a sense of dereliction and the emotions of loneliness for their repetitiveness and
artificiality. The problem, moreover, really existed, and was at
least as much intellectual as emotional. 'From India to the regions
of the West, peacefully and without opposition (the Muslims) at
any rate possess the most choice and the most fertile kingdoms
and those that are full of earthly delights.' Theirs were '. . . mountains of salt, fountains of oil, manna of heaven, rivers of Paradise,
aromatic spices, precious stones, vines of balsam and the sweetest
fruits'.[45] The Muslims prospered in everything; even the Tartars,
who came to destroy them, were now nearly all turned Muslim.[46]
All this was permitted to Muhammad, *homini scelesto et sceleratis-
simo*; his people multiplied because he encouraged them to fornicate.[47] God had given the Muslims power to kill Religious and to
force Christians by torture to deny their faith. The Islamic
custom was not only to spare, but to reward apostates – with
women, wealth and honours; the martyred Religious rejected this
opportunity, but many of the *seculares* gave way, and people
generally preferred slavery to starvation.[48] Ricoldo was very
conscious of the carrying away of the women and children as

prisoners, of their selling dearly, of their being first triumphantly
paraded through the cities of Islam, of the despatch of some as
gifts to different kings; above all he thought of the fate of nuns,
used as concubines, who became the mothers, as he several times
insisted, of the worst Muslim tyrants.[49] Christian missions were
jeered at by the Muslims, who said that Jesus Christ could not
help them against Muhammad; also the Jews and Tartars jeered.
'Now among the peoples they openly say, Where is God, the God
of the Christians?' God was become the implementer of the Qur'ān:
factus executor Alcorani.[50]

The Latins had been unable to believe that God would allow
'Akka to fall. Women wept in vain before the crucifix for sons or
husbands killed or carried off into slavery. As the Muslims said
that Christ could not help, so 'the sophists' said that He could, but
would not; and while Ricoldo himself could not accept this, many
Christians were converted to Islam. If Christ went on as He had
begun, complained Ricoldo, it looked as though He were really
going to become a Muslim, as Islamic eschatology claimed He
would, at His return at the end of the world. It seemed as if the
age of miracles had returned, in favour of Islam, not of Christendom: 'Thou hast strengthened him by temporal power . . . and
what is worse, his power . . . begins to be confirmed by miracles.'
It was one of the 'absurdities' of the Qur'ān to speak of God's
'praying for' Muhammad; now it seemed as though just that were
really happening. If some of what Ricoldo said was a little ridiculous, it is obvious that he was genuinely unhappy and intellectually
disturbed.[51]

The interest in these eloquent epistles to the saints lies partly
in the seriousness with which the problem was felt, and partly in
the absence, so unscholastic, of a neat and easy solution. The
author was made more anxious because he received no reply from
God to his impetration, no special illumination; but this additional
worry was resolved by Gregory's *Moralia*; God speaks only once,
and does not repeat Himself or answer individual problems
individually. *Semel loquitur Deus et secundo ad ipsum non repetit . . .
Deus nobis ad omnia verba non respondit, id est, cogitationibus
singulorum . . .* In Scripture was God's sufficient revelation, and it
was there that Ricoldo was able to recognise the only answer to
his original problem, with which he would be content in his
Disputatio: some God punished as enemies, others, that they might
fear Him, as friends. Ricoldo's basic concern for Christianity in
the East remained unappeased, and he had to learn to accept his
anxiety.[52]

There is no work that can be compared to these *Epistolae* of
Ricoldo, although some aspects of it find an echo in other writers,

and sometimes a dissimilar reaction. Thus Vitry spoke of the way Christian wives were accepted by Muslim princes, and of the toleration that was generally extended to Christians by the off-spring of such marriages; even when allowance is made for the less savage age in which Vitry lived, his attitude seems more realistic than Ricoldo's somewhat fanciful view of persecutors sprung from the former nuns. Tripoli also was pleased rather than otherwise that the sultan should have a Christian wife.[53] The obduracy of Muslims, who throughout the ages have proved almost un-convertible, was several times stressed, and both theory and missionary practice recognised it. Such phrases as that Christ was crucified by Muslims and Jews in His members illustrated a sense of persecution which in modern eyes may seem sometimes exaggerated.[54]

Fidenzio gave considerable attention to the cruelties of the Muslims against the Latins, and, writing like Ricoldo of the later military campaigns of the mamlūks, he specified the same mis-fortunes, the killing and capturing, the reduction to slavery or beggary, the prostitution of women, the destruction of churches and their conversion into mosques. He said that women and children were beaten to make them become Muslim. Leaving aside terror, which prevailed only at the sack of cities, the practical reasons given for actual apostasies from Christianity were most commonly a matter of worldly pressure of various kinds; poverty in particular was often mentioned. Another reason is suggested by the statement that in certain uncanonical marriages the spouses were to be separated only if this could be done 'without scandal and fear of apostasy'; liberation from matrimonial tangles was no doubt often an element in attraction to Islam, and this might take the form either of seeking, or of avoiding, a divorce.[55] Once they had apostatised, these converts to Islam were sometimes over-anxious to convince their new co-religionists of their good faith, even though many professed Islam with the mouth and still worshipped Christ in their hearts.[56] It even happened that the missionaries themselves apostatised, as did a Franciscan and two Dominicans absolved by John XXII in 1334. William of Adam of Sultānīyah was, like Ricoldo, much preoccupied with the fate of prisoners, both women, and boys carried into Egypt and sold as catamites. This last scandal was the product of trade rather than of war.[57]

Ricoldo had sought in detail to justify the ways of God which puzzled many. There was compulsion under Islamic rule, if only the compulsion of worldliness, and when loss of faith accompanied loss of virtue the tragedy was most deeply felt. God's ways were very hard to understand in this.

5. CONCLUSION

It must be only too obvious that there was variation of only a few themes, and even phrases, whose repetition is a sign of how stereotyped the treatment of this subject of power and violence became. This indicates, not a lack of interest, but a deep and un-shakable conviction. There was little recognition that Christians were inconsistent to advocate the use of force against Islam, while condemning Islam for its theoretic approval of the use of force; and again, to cut themselves off from Islamic society, while despising Muslims for 'refusing to dispute'. In the condemnation of the Islamic attitude exaggeration had its usual place, but mostly it was a case of accepted attitudes which were never examined or questioned. Moreover, there was a lack of confidence that God's ways were indeed explicable, or even understandable. The absence of any real possibility of dispute, combined with this fear of failure as a Providential punishment, may explain the preference for a violence which allowed the relief of feelings without any necessity for ratiocination. It may explain why, when violence of a military nature and directed against the enemy was impossible, there was a movement which sought to provoke martyrdom, an extracting of violence out of the enemy's disposition.

The real interest of Christians was in their consciousness that the Providential dispensation accorded extremely ill with their own strong wish that worldly success should set a seal on religious truth. It was natural that they should bitterly resent that their failure should be attributed to their sins by anyone but the rightful occupant of a Christian pulpit. Ricoldo, usually so derivative, here thought originally; he spoke articulately for the unexpressed dis-appointment of many who were extremely reluctant to accept a situation in which Christians were *powerless*. Material success became too easily the criterion of divine justification, even for people whose religion is founded on the blood of martyrs. SEMEL LOQUITUR DEUS. The difficulty was to remember and to accept that Christianity was revealed once and for ever, and not as a religion of power. It was almost inevitable that the Christian attitude to Islam should here be inconsistent.

Plate 2

Bibliothèque Nationale, MS Latin 16274, f. 10v

Ymago Mahumeti: an ink drawing of Muhammad, from a late mediaeval manuscript, where it stands in isolation – it was apparently not intended to illustrate a text. The costume is conventionally oriental, but the treatment is dignified (contrast plate 5). Note the sword, *gladius Mahumeti pictus*, the Qur'ān, *lex et alcoranus*, and what seem to be talismans hanging from the collar.

❦ V ❧

The place of self-indulgence
in the attack on Islam

THE moral and social institutions of Islam were considered by
Western writers almost invariably with the closest attention,
often with a fascinated horror. Here we are concerned with social
intercourse and private morals, which were largely viewed as the
morals of sex. It was felt that this subject was as important for the
welfare of Christendom as it was inherently stimulating to the
imagination of individuals. The Christian criticism and exaggeration of the licence attributed to Muslims was often excessive;
there was great unanimity.

1. MARRIAGE LAW AND DIVORCE

The theology of the institution of marriage is the key to many
related questions. It needs to be kept in mind that Latin Christians
define the married relation as inherently indissoluble except by
death. The word *marriage* could not accurately, therefore, be used
of any other sexual relation; it could not, for example, be used of
many relations defined as marriages by the laws of modern
European States. This was not pedantry; mediaeval Europeans
simply understood only indissoluble monogamy by the word
'marriage'. On the other hand, it was well known that in Islam
there was polygamy. Latins always found it difficult to call any
polygynous relation marriage.

The staple of sound information about Islamic marriage law
was that stated by Pedro de Alfonso: he said that there might be
four wives, who might be divorced and replaced so long as the
number four was not exceeded at any one time; with a divorced
wife remarriage was allowed up to the third time, and relations
were permitted with any number of slaves, both such as were
bought, and such as were taken in war, with freedom to buy and
sell again, so long as there was no pregnancy. If this is as much as
most writers knew, Pedro was unrepresentative in being non-
committal in tone. Very many writers spoke of polygamy, of whom
some were less knowledgeable. Guibert, with no source of authentic

135

information, believed that polygamy was unlimited and unregu-
lated. Often odd pieces of authentic information were muddled up
in a shocked vagueness: there might be as many wives and concubines as a man could maintain, said Gerald of Wales; thus he was
wrong to suppose there was no limit to the wives allowed, but
quite right to specify the obligation upon the master of the household to provide adequately for those he accepted as dependents.

Some statements were less full than Pedro's, less vague than
Gerald's. The Patriarch's report to Innocent III, an account which
received some publicity during the first half of the thirteenth
century, in one version contained a passage which asserted that
seven wives were allowed; which said that by the marriage
contract each must have her separate household; and concluded by
adding that in practice many Muslims were religious enough to be
content with one. If the first of these statements is inaccurate, the
next two express a realistic knowledge that was for the most part
conspicuously absent. Vitry modified his source and said that
'many' wives were allowed, together with as many concubines
as could be maintained and kept in necessities; but that in his day
Muslims were mostly content with three or four wives. He was
apparently unaware that the injunction as to number was Qur'anic.
The same material, when utilised by Viterbo and Paris, was more
exact. Tripoli misconceived the Qur'ān, as it is generally understood, by adding together the numbers of wives it recommends as
alternatives: 'thou shalt have two wives and three and four and so
up to nine . . .' He may have been thinking of the number of
Muhammad's own wives. He went on, in what purported to be
the language of the Qur'ān still, to refer to concubines whose
number need only be limited by their cost. Fidenzio rendered the
Qur'ān better: 'Marry them that please you, a second, third and
fourth'; he also mentioned the concubines. It is curious that
Tripoli, capable of the most sustained accurate quotation from the
Qur'ān, should here have preferred a more inaccurate version.[1]

San Pedro appealed to the same text as abominable, but cited
it in what is really paraphrase. He was interested to understand
that different interpretations obtained among Muslims; some, he
claimed, thought that it meant nine wives and numberless concubines, others that it meant four wives, others again that no limit
was intended; this last, he said, agreed with al-Kindi, but everyone
was agreed that there was unrestricted permission for concubines.
These opinions are not Muslim opinions at all; both right and
wrong, they are a collection of Western beliefs about Muslims.
San Pedro included in his account of the Qur'anic instruction an
important element usually omitted by Western writers: the
requirement that wives must be treated equally.[2]

The *reprobatio* was the most accurate Latin version: marriage is contracted with the women that please you, and they may be two-fold and threefold and fourfold; if you fear that you cannot provide for all equally, marry one, and take (some) of the women that your right hand possesses; the author explains that this was interpreted to mean as many concubines as a man can afford to buy and keep.[3] He commented that such a rule meant four wives and ten concu-bines, or a hundred, or a thousand, or more. This was a lawyer's criticism; he meant that a moral theologian might understand the text to bear that meaning, not that that was what happened in practice. Among later writers there were a few new ideas, but no increase in accuracy. The most original statement was Verona's: he mentioned no limitation in the number of wives, and thought that polygamy was allowed in order to avoid the possibility of adultery. Any man who found that he coveted his neighbour's wife was bound to choose for himself a wife that was plump, fair, dark, small or large, so that she approximated to the wife he coveted. The source of this bizarre notion might be far to seek.[4]

What was common to all these accounts was the strong interest in the fact of polygyny in Islamic marriage. The greater freedom of Islamic law was responsible for some temporary apostasies, as well as for permanent conversions to Islam, among laymen and even Religious. It was usual to offer women, as well as riches and honours, as a reward for adopting Islam, in those cases where a Muslim government sought the conversion of a Christian; this may have been a defensive operation, since in the recorded cases the offer was made to active missionaries.[5] Apart from these practical reasons, the subject exercised a theoretical fascination for Christian writers, and one aspect in particular gave an almost disproportionate scandal, and was much exaggerated. This was the law of divorce, and particularly the law which forbids the fourth remarriage between the same spouses, unless the wife shall meantime have completed and dissolved a marriage with a third party; thus triple divorce was called 'definite'. The intention seems to have been to prevent irresponsible reiterated repudiation, but there has existed a practice, disapproved of in official Islamic jurisprudence, called *taḥlīl*, by which a false third-party marriage might be negotiated in order to nullify the effect of a triple divorce.[6] This *taḥlīl* became almost an obsession with the Christian West. No Christian was able to think of a divorced wife as no longer the wife of her original husband; a second marriage was therefore a legalised adultery, and the *taḥlīl* something a good deal worse than promiscuous prostitution because the husband became the procurer. Legalised adultery was worse than adultery forbidden though committed; but the *taḥlīl* seemed to Christians legally to compel adultery, in that it imposed it upon the wife whom they supposed continuously subject to her first husband. Logically, we might say that divorce establishes nothing more than consecutive polygamy, and this might be argued to be at least a shade better than the simultaneous form. Possibly the strength of the Christian objection really arose, though not specifically stated to have done so, from the fact that divorce with freedom to remarry implies polyandry (though not simultaneous polyandry), whereas ostensibly Islamic law only permits the lesser scandal, as it may have seemed to mediaevals, of polygynous marriage.

The earliest clear statement is in Viterbo:

If after dismissing his wife a man afterwards regretted it, and wished her to be restored to him, by no means would he be allowed to take her as his wife, nisi prius alii viri copulata fuerit et ipsa redeundi causa consenserit.

The author thought in terms of the causes for which divorce might take place, for example, because a wife displeased her husband or quarrelled with him. Really, a 'cause' is not essential to a Muslim divorce at all; San Pedro had some justification for saying *absque ulla causa*. In Viterbo's passage there is supposed to be a law that permits a man to take another man's repudiated wife; this pre-supposes, what is quite alien to Islam, that a repudiated wife is in some sense still a wife. Guido Terrena put the Christian attitude unambiguously, saying that a remarried repudiated wife remained the wife of her first husband while he lived. This view informed the Christian attitude as much when it was not consciously in the mind as when it was. Vitry thought the *taḥlīl* was supposed to cleanse a wife of the fault for which he wrongly assumed she must have been divorced. All these misconceptions derived from imagining not marriage but Christian marriage. Tripoli put words of Biblical flavour into the Qur'ān: 'and if thy wife be displeasing in thine eyes, hand her a bill of divorce and let her go.'[7]

Descriptions of the *taḥlīl* often betray the preoccupations of the authors. The *lex super repudio* was described by the *reprobatio* and the *explanatio simboli* as requiring that the fourth marriage of the same spouses shall take place after the wife is 'known' by another man, *uxor cognoscatur ab alio viro*. The choice of the verb here is tendentious; Fidenzio, not usually indulgent to Islam, more fairly said the fourth marriage could not take place until she had *married* another man, *donec cum alio viro nubat et contrahat*. San Pedro was also more careful, and was, indeed, exact: after she had married *and* lain with another man, he said, *nupserit et coiverit*. Ricoldo preferred to use the pejorative *cognosco*, to stress the sexual side at the expense of the legal. His account is interesting;

part is popular in source and robust in the telling, part, which derives from the *Contrarietas*, is legal but inaccurate. He deals with the consummation of the second or *taḥlīl* marriage in unpleasant detail.[8] It may be that part of this misconceives the injunction in Qur'ān XLV.1, but the whole is unnecessarily nasty, and there seems no point in bringing these matters up at all, except to demonstrate the squalor of Islamic law. That in itself is a squalid thing to do; and the process is also dangerous, since the details of casuistry could always be used to seem to discredit morals, but not without reflecting on all moral theology. To the modern reader, Ricoldo's choice of subject here must be a criticism of his methods, the more so that it was taken from another author. With better sense he then ridiculed the *taḥlīl* as an institution:

Men who want to bring about a reconciliation of this sort pay a fee to a blind man, or some other low person, in order that he should know the woman carnally, and afterwards testify publicly, and say that he wants to divorce her. If he does so, the first husband can reconcile her to himself. Sometimes, however, it happens that (the new spouses) suit each other, and say that they do not want to be separated; and then the first husband, with both his wife and his fee lost, is disappointed of his hopes.

It is clear that Ricoldo realised the second husband to have contracted some really effective form of marriage, although he carefully avoided actually referring to the *taḥlīl* as a marriage. That word was so far as possible preserved for the institution that Church and natural law prescribed.[9] This theme gave the imagination too free a rein; Lull said perfectly gratuitously that a man might not take his thrice repudiated wife again, nisi cum altero Saraceno habente rem cum ea, ipso sciente et existente in porta camerae.[10] This nasty imagination, which only invented unsavoury facts, must be sharply distinguished from the indignant interpretation of real facts in Christian terms; for example, 'if (the wife) observes chastity, (her first husband) cannot take her again; but if she acts the prostitute, then he can do so'.[11]

Other aspects of marital law were less well-known, although statements about them sometimes seem to be more authentic or to depend on more authentic sources. Mut'ah, the institution of temporary marriage (confined to the Shī'ah, and limited in its operation among them) may be referred to by Ricoldo in a passage which he derives, not from literary sources, but from his own experience.[12] The Qur'ān, he says, writes 'that fornication is forbidden . . . but a certain buying and selling is allowed; and also it is not forbidden that man should do as he pleases with his own property'. Thus even the 'more perfect' Muslims go to a brothel and say to the prostitute, 'I feel desire, but it is not allowed to fornicate. Sell thyself to me.' Then he is allowed to do as he likes with his own property, in his own alleged words, 'according to our (Muslim) religion'; and thus he 'lies with her untroubled'. This story seems to confuse temporary marriage with concubinage based on slavery; but the point of it is that Muslims who so act are hypocrites, and it seems to presuppose, as did Ricoldo's other story just quoted, that there is a background of moral law.[13] Fidenzio also may refer to mut'ah when he says that the Qur'ān permits fornication by the verse, *Do not prevent yourselves from satisfying desires with a woman, having paid her money.*[14] Most Christians would be bound to regard mut'ah as indistinguishable from prostitution.

Other examples of genuine citations of Islamic law, and of knowledge of other forms of divorce than the simple *talaq* of which we have been speaking, exist, but are not very clear and have little polemic significance. Mandeville referred to the condition in repudiation that the wife receive back her dowry (mahr), loosely described by him as 'a portion of her goods'. Mark quoted the formula of zihār, actually a form of divorce forbidden by the Qur'ān, a point that escaped him despite his own translation: 'May thy side be forbidden to me as the side of my mother.' Conceivably this was quoted as sounding barbaric.[15]

Summing up, we may say that the institution of concubinage, naturally enough, was misunderstood. There was widespread a belief in a Qur'anic text which allowed a man to do as he likes with his own; there was little realisation that it was regulated by law, and not a licensed promiscuity. Pedro de Alfonso mentioned the limitation on the sale of the mother of a son, umm al-walad; but the only limitation on concubinage frequently referred to was the capacity to maintain slaves; or more crudely, what was obviously not thought of as a limitation at all, the capacity to purchase them. Christians were naturally particularly sensitive to the acquisition of slaves in warfare, and were very concerned about the fate of their women when they were taken prisoner. Islamic law allowed these to be made concubines. Ricoldo was here a little confused, although his statements show some understanding; he noted that men had sexual rights over both their wives and prisoners of war (concubitum tam cum uxoribus quam cum illis quas in bello ceperunt); but he also complained that it was not enough that the Qur'ān should forbid women to be forced, without forbidding women freely to consent. With regard to the forcing of women, his statements conflict.[16]

Thus there was general interest in Islamic marriage law.

2. QUICUNQUE ACTUS VENEREUS

The accusation was, as it still is, very frequently made, that Islam either permits, or else that it encourages, unnatural intercourse between people of the same or of opposite sexes, and, indeed, any sexual act whatever, for its own sake.

Unnatural intercourse of spouses was the special subject of mediaeval attack, based on sūrah II.223, interpreted, according to the custom, in the sense desired by Christian criticism, not that usual in Islam. The source of the assertion must certainly be Spain, where Māliki law, which seems to have permitted what was forbidden elsewhere by the other Islamic schools of law (madhāhib), obtained. Peter of Poitiers made a special point of his when writing to his Abbot: 'Do not let the chapter that is there (i.e. in the headings sent to Peter the Venerable as material), *de uxoribus turpiter abutendis* scandalise you in any way, for it truly appears like this in the Qur'ān, and, as I heard for certain in Spain, both from Peter of Toledo, whose colleague I was in translating, and from Robert, now archdeacon of Pamplona, all the Muslims do this freely, as if by Muhammad's command.' We have to consider why there was such insistence on this matter, which even so unsqueamish an age might well have left alone, and Peter of Poitier's statement is significant for this. First, we should note how he stresses the Qur'anic source, although the locus classicus is ambiguous; indeed, Bibliander understood Ketton's text, the only one known to Peter, to exclude the very hypothesis that Peter pretended that it proved. It seems likely that Peter relied on hearsay for the positiveness of his assertion, and this is strengthened by the next point: he explicitly appeals to hearsay for evidence about a fact, the common marital practice of ordinary Muslims, which of its nature is unknowable. It seems clear that the assertion arises from common Christian malice; it is not difficult to imagine the venomous feelings towards Islam which may have prevailed among those whose background was Mozarab and who lived on the verge of dār al-Islām. It is not an attractive picture. The French monk would have been easily imposed upon, since he would see the sincerity of gossipers who believed their own exaggerated assertions.[17]

Before leaving this subject we must note that it was accepted in places widely distant. In particular a passage in Vitry piles one form of unnatural vice upon another, and includes this form, which can only have derived from the maghrib, where Māliki law obtained; it can never have had any relevance to Syria, where Vitry wrote; his source must, therefore, have been literary, perhaps spiced by oral malice. Both San Pedro and the *reprobatio* deal fully with this abuse, which they relate to the wife's menstrual periods.

San Pedro took the subject in more detail than any other author. The *reprobatio* cites Bukhārī, neglecting the obvious meaning, which is quite harmless, of the text cited, and prefers to follow a glossarius (*expositor Alcorani*), who must have been very obscure; the same work quotes him again for a most unusual and again unpleasant gloss. This work also attacks Islam rather more justifiably for permitting coitus interruptus or reservatus, but again in doing so erected a restricted permission into a general encouragement.[18]

There are other examples of the exaggeration of Muslim turpitude. Even in the process of translation something similar occurred; Ketton, certainly, was always liable to heighten or exaggerate a harmless text in order to give it a nasty or a licentious ring, or to prefer an improbable but unpleasant interpretation of the meaning to a likely but normal and decent one. There was too some unnecessary use of words that may be thought improper. In a verse that describes the attractions of this world, Ketton has *mulierum coitus et filiorum amplexus* where Sale renders, 'the love and eager desire of wives and children', where Mark of Toledo has (*suadetur hominibus*) *qui appetunt mulieres et proles* and Maracci says, *amor cupiditatum ex uxoribus ex filiis*. Ketton fairly obviously preferred to 'call a spade a bloody shovel'.[19] On one such occasion Sale was moved to protest. Where he has the wholly untendentious statement, 'when they saw him, they praised him greatly', Ketton put *quo viso, omnes menstruatae sunt*. 'The old Latin translators have strangely mistaken the sense of the original word', commented Sale, '. . . and then rebuke Mohammad for the indecency, crying out demurely in the margin, *O foedum et obscoenum prophetam! . . .*' Although the comment in the margin is actually Bibliander's, the rebuke is deserved, because it exactly delineates the weakest side of the Cluniac and Latin Christian attitude. Sale points out that, by itself, it would be possible to give the Arabic word (*akbara*) the meaning alleged; it is the absurdity of choosing it in the context that shocks us. Mark has *obstupuerunt*, which is closer to Rodwell ('amazed') than to Sale; Maracci, with *magnificaverunt eum*, agrees with Sale. The phrase thus quoted in different forms describes the reaction of the Egyptian ladies to their first glimpse of the beauty of the patriarch Joseph as a young man. Savary, with a humanistic axe to grind, has 'charmées de sa beauté . . .' for the same phrase. Just as Savary deformed the text to turn it into a prettier story, so Ketton deformed it to make it repulsive to decent readers.[20]

The *Contrarietas* was guilty of one complete fabrication. This was the interpolation into sūrah II.220 of the words, *nec etiam cognoscatis masculos participantes, donec credant*.[21] Although this is pure invention, and although it was not taken up by any other author, which allows us to consider it possible that it was creditably rejected as spurious, yet the crime referred to was considered characteristic of Islamic practice, and even of Islamic moral theory, in the Middle Ages, as it has been since. It was more reasonably supposed that sūrah IV.20 effectively legalised homosexual relations, since in the Islamic tradition this is in fact the subject of this revelation, which, however, is considered abrogated, by sūrah XXIV, prohibiting all kinds of illicit sexual intercourse. The abrogation governed Islamic law, but was not understood by Christians. The burden of their attack on sūrah IV.20 was that the prohibition there was so slight as to indicate that the crime was judged equally slight. San Pedro, after a fair paraphrase of the verse quoted the words, *Quoniam Deus est poenitentiae acceptor et misericors*, with which the verse ends, and commented that if God forgave so easily He tolerated the crime.[22]

Some writers actually asserted that Muhammad introduced sodomy into the 'garden of nature' in which his people lived[23]; others realised that in fact the Qur'ān forbids sodomy, without considering the prohibition so light as to amount to permission. In Ricoldo's *Disputatio* the Qur'anic treatment of unnatural vice figures among the contradictions of the Qur'ān: *concedit sodomiam tam in masculo quam in femina*, he said, quoting the Qur'ān very obscurely; yet in the same sūrah the sodomy of the contemporaries of Loth was condemned. Not only did Ricoldo realise that this condemnation existed in the Qur'ān; he also knew that Muslims denied that the crime was permitted by those verses that he (like so many others, always willing to tell Muslims what they believed) maintained gave it licence. Muhammad, he said, 'seems to have accepted sodomy committed both with a man and a woman, in the chapter of the Cow; although they (the Muslims) *cover it up with certain honourable explanations*'. By arguing that if Muhammad once allowed any sort of sexual licence, he could not confine it to the use of women, Ramón Martí in his *explanatio* implied that Muhammad had wished so to confine it, forbidding unnatural vice. William of Auvergne, and Benedict of Alignan following him, understood the opposite of the usual idea: *sodomiticam spurcitiam interdixit*, they said. William recognised the failure of the prohibition in practice, in spite of the multitude of wives who, he thought, might be expected to extinguish homosexual desires; but he accounted for this, realistically enough, as springing from irresistible desire, rather than from the encouragement or toleration of religion. Acqui thought that Islam caused men guilty of this crime to be burned; and that it was just because many women were permitted that there must be presumed to be less excuse.[25]

There is something abstract and theoretical about the works we have just been considering; but a similar indignation was provoked by Islamic practice, at least in certain countries at certain times. William of Adam, Bishop of Sulṭānīyah, was extreme by temperament, and in judgement political rather than philosophical:

> In the Muslim sect any sexual act at all is not only not forbidden, but allowed and praised. So, as well as the innumerable prostitutes that there are among them, there are many effeminate men who shave the beard, paint their own face, put on women's dress, wear bracelets on the arms and feet . . . The Muslims, therefore, forgetful of human dignity, are shamelessly attracted by those effeminates, and live together with them as with us husband and wife live together publicly.

He was rightly shocked that the market was supplied by Catholic traders, who sought and bought suitable victims, both Christian and pagan, for this unsavoury profession. He described how they deliberately prepared them for it by dressing them in silks, ornamenting them, washing them, feeding them 'that they should appear more plump and pink and voluptuous'. After this it seems excessive to describe the lewd Muslims, who, so he says, when they see these boys, are immediately on fire with lust, and rush on them like mad dogs, as 'the perverters of human nature', rather than the avaricious Catholics who coldly pander to other men's heats; but the fact remains that the market was considered to exist primarily in Islamic society.[26] There could be little sympathy with a society that did not count chastity among the public virtues.

At the same time we must not ourselves exaggerate the significance of this witness of Islamic depravity. An account by Verona which bears the marks of authenticity is explicitly directed against the Cairene mamlūk Court, and more general allegations are less obviously authentic.[27] It is worthy of note that Tripoli praises Baybars for his freedom from this vice, and that many writers with personal knowledge of life in Islamic societies made no allegations of personal knowledge of the commission of homosexual acts, although they subscribed to the general opinion that Islam did tolerate or encourage them. Among these are Ricoldo, who made a number of personal observations of matters he thought important, and would certainly not have considered this matter unimportant; Tripoli himself; San Pedro; Ramón Martí; and even Fidenzio, whose reference to unmentionable crimes, so many and so great that it would be shameful to speak of them, has all the hall-marks of hearsay.[28]

In general, sexual licentiousness, whether with women, or extended to various unnatural forms of vice, was particularly associated with Islam. A peculiarly absurd form of this occurs in the poems of Waltherius and du Pont, which must reflect the un-informed picture of Islamic society obtaining in the lay culture of the courts:

> Conjugium solves, corrumpes virginitatem,
> judicioque tuo castus adulter erat . . .

Fantastically, du Pont believed that Muhammad not only allowed every male Muslim ten wives, but every Muslim woman ten husbands.[29] The choice of Friday as the day of prayer was often associated with the worship of Venus, and there was a theory that Islam was the continuation of a pre-existing paganism which had been essentially Venus worship, and thus remained, as Roger Bacon put it, the *lex venerea*; the ḥajj, through the pagan Ka'bah, was thus also associated with this idea.[30]

In Abbot Joachim's prophecy, just as the heretics were opposed by the doctors of the Church, so Muhammad was opposed by the virgins. The special lubricity of Muslims was everywhere believed to be a fact, and this, of course sprang from the teaching and example of the Prophet, which the Qur'ān preserved. The annota-tions to Ketton include many such comments as 'Note his great enthusiasm for women'; but this is moderate compared with more popular assertions of how Muhammad established the Queen of vices in his own soul. 'No prophet', said San Pedro, 'so relaxed the controls and laws concerning the use of women as thou didst.'[31] The foulness of lust, claimed Fidenzio, among Muslims, can hardly be expressed in words; they were deep in this mud 'from the soles of the feet to the crown of the head'. Religion commended the sexual act itself: *accedite*, inquit, *ad uxores vestras*, a fact objection-able even in the context of marriage.[32] Muhammad had regarded continence as the inexpiable sin, according to a view taken as authoritative because it derived from Christians resident in the East.[33] Sexuality and violence were the characteristic marks of Islam: *fornicationes et furta*. This was indeed the sum of the impression of Islam that St Thomas Aquinas received.[34] Roger Bacon insisted on the opposition of Islam to holy virginity; Muslims 'are absorbed in the delights of lust on account of the multiplicity of wives', he points out. We may take two examples, one from the beginning one from the end, of the period with which we are dealing, to illustrate what the general, well-educated, clerical and scholastic public understood from what they read by authors who claimed direct knowledge of the subject. Guibert of Nogent said that Muhammad taught as revealed a 'new licence of promiscuous intercourse (*indifferenter coeundi nova licentia*)'; and Guido Terrena, beginning, 'they say every shame of carnal intercourse to be allowable', had no hesitation in specifying the crimes to which he referred, including bestiality and incest.[35]

3. THE CHRISTIAN POSITION DEFENDED

The real and still more the supposed sexual morals of Islam were combated by arguments which will be familiar to every reader of mediaeval theology. Reference to St Thomas Aquinas will show arguments of the type involved, particularly those establishing monogamy by the natural law, although authors were not always as discreet in judgement.[36] Pedro de Alfonso, justifying marriage by the hope of procreation, was at once Christian and Jewish in tradition; he thought of Muslims as seeking it for the sake of desire. The argument, at once rational and Scriptural, *una dicitur esse unius*, appears with Alan of Lille. Alan's arguments were idiosyncratic because of his mistaken assumption that Muslims argued from the Old Testament, in the text known to Christians. The patriarchs, he said, had been licensed, that the earth might be replenished, but now it was chastity that was needed, in order to replenish Heaven. The Gregorian Report used Scripture traditionally, but with some humour: 'according to Genesis, they shall be two in one flesh; it does not say, three or four'.[37]

A favourite argument was that what applied to men must equally apply to women; this was not always argued in a way likely to command Muslim acceptance. Martí said that marriage could not be ended for a light reason; a wife was a colleague, not a servant, *socia*, not *serva*. To send her away for illness would be contrary to compassion; if infirmity were a reason it would dissolve all marriages in old age; under such rules, women were deflowered and made pregnant and then sent away, and were thus dishonoured by all men; and so Islam was a Law of prostitution. Such an argument would not impress a Muslim, who knew that it did not correspond in any particular to what actually happened in Muslim society. Martí again argued that the *vis generativa* existed for the sake of offspring, not for pleasure; admittedly there was an incidental pleasure, but multiplicity of wives gave too much pleasure; pleasure intoxicates, softens, enervates and effeminates; it separates men from their spiritual ends. None of this would impress a Muslim; it is contrary to Islamic experience. Other writers suggested that polygamy was permitted to increase the sum of procreation, and sometimes felt bound to argue that this would not necessarily result. Martí also asserted that no decent man or woman would tolerate *taḥlīl*, when even birds and animals could be faithful to a single spouse. A Muslim who did not often happen against a case of *taḥlīl* and who could remark a good many examples in the animal world unsuited to Martí's argument, would again probably remain unmoved. All these arguments must have been intended primarily to fortify the faith of Christians, perhaps to discourage apostasy, which might happen for the sake of an easier marriage law.[38]

Ricoldo, while he asserted the irrationality of Islamic law in this matter, was content not to argue in detail, except in relation to the material Paradise. He liked to appeal to impartial tribunals in the abstract; to the Philosophers, even to the Muslims themselves: among all men, and even among Muslims, he for example asserted, it is thought more virtuous to abstain (from eating and copulating) than to indulge. 'The Muslims themselves have contemplatives and ascetics whom they especially praise.' San Pedro did not much argue discursively either. He stated Muhammad's answer to an objection to *coitus interruptus* that it impeded generation: no act of man's could impede a decision of God's to create a human soul. It is not obvious whether he thought this argument of the Prophet's foolish or wicked. Lull gave his personal touch to traditional arguments. He objected to polygyny that it caused women to sin mentally (by desire, because they must have less satisfaction individually) more than Christian women do. There is often a clownish element in Lull's notions, although in this case what at first sight seems whimsical may have a certain justification in the closed female societies of the magnates' harīms. Verona thought that polygamy was established to prevent adultery by removing temptation; Dubois said that Muslim wives would willingly turn Christian for monogamy's sake.[39]

We have already noted and stressed how much Islamic licence was seen as deriving from licence permitted to and by the Prophet in his lifetime. This might be thought accidental; or it might be argued that Islam was expressly calculated to suit the Arabs, the contemporaries whom Muhammad converted, by commending the vices to which they were already inclined. Seeking lust, given to gluttony, they would not otherwise have accepted his religion.[40] Alternatively, it was said that it was the Arabs who made Islam what they wished it to be. 'They only assert (polygamy)', said Alan of Lille, 'in order to satisfy lust: for the whole of their life is spent in the stench of lust.' Gerald of Wales maintained that Muhammad taught whatever he thought would best please, and especially lust, which was the particular temptation of orientals, who live in a climate of great natural heat. It was often said that there was something brutish as well as carnal in the Arabs, or in the religion which was suited to their tastes. Islam positively exploited universal human weakness: 'the religion that he established and the commandments that he gave were such as men are prone to even without commandments'. It encouraged those desires 'which fleshly men are not only prompt to obey, but from which they even can scarcely ever be much restrained by any fears or any punishments, or even by human shame, which for many people is harder than death'.[41]

Thus Islamic morals were attacked on Scriptural grounds and on grounds of the natural law; probably it was not fully understood that Muslims have no concept of natural, as opposed to revealed, law. Finally, they were attacked on 'modernist' or historical grounds, though not very systematically.

4. PARADISE

It was the Islamic Paradise which more than any other theme seemed to sum up the Christian idea of Islam. It proved the contention that this was no spiritual religion. Pedro de Alfonso's account became popular and may be called the standard mediaeval version of the Qur'ān's 'promised Paradise, that is, a garden of delights': the flowing waters, the mild air in which neither heat nor cold could afflict, the shady trees, the fruits, the many-coloured silken clothing and the palaces of precious stones and metals, the milk and wine served in gold and silver vessels by angels, saying, 'eat and drink in joy'; and beautiful virgins, 'untouched by men or demons'. 'Whatever (the blessed) desired would immediately be supplied.' This statement, which for the most part reflects the text of the Qur'ān closely, may be paralleled by many others. It must be said that it was usual for Christians to allow themselves a rather purple rendering of the gardens and precious metals of Paradise, though usually not of the virgins so beloved of later romanticism. There is a genuine latinisation here, that in one aspect recalls the lapidaries, and, in another, some of the background of romance, the legend of the Reine Sybille, a hint of the native pagan idyll. Other versions were very close indeed to the Qur'ān, notably that in the *reprobatio*, which simply quoted three well-chosen revelations shortly, and Ricoldo's, which yet shows some confusion. In spite of the enormous influence of the *Liber Scalae*, it must be said that the Qur'ān itself was the chief source of the picture of the Islamic Paradise familiar to so many mediaeval writers.[42]

With this garden of material delights it was usual to contrast the concept of a purely spiritual apprehension of God, the Beatific Vision of Christian tradition. It was not altogether realised that the religious and orthodox Muslim believes that he will see God with the eyes of the body. Lull took this belief in a crude form from the traditions (the 'proverbs of Muhammad'): men who are in Paradise will see God morning and evening; 'for by whatever place in the circuit they put their heads through the windows of the

palaces in which they are, God will appear to them . . .' This point
was usually missed. It was thought sufficient barely to contrast
an eternity of eating, drinking and copulating with the apprehension of beatitude by the intellect. 'He described a Paradise, not
of angelic society, nor of the divine vision, nor of that highest
good that *eye hath not seen* . . .' There was a clear note of contempt:
this, said Alan of Lille, was no sufficient reward for a martyr's
death. It was at once disgusting and ridiculous: 'to eat glutton-
ously, to wanton and to lie with women indefinitely'. Often the
use of strong epithets marked the degree of disapproval, *vanissimae
fantasiae, insaniae et deliramenta*.[43] Such remarks appealed to
intellectual snobbery, whether an actual consideration of philosophical reasons followed, or not. Learned Muslims, claimed
William of Auvergne, realised that through these ideas Muhammad 'was made ridiculous before the whole world'; later, Ramón
Martí would insist, with a wealth of illustrations, that even the
Muslim philosophers, ibn Sīna, al-Ghazālī and al-Fārābi, made
eternal beatitude consist in the knowledge and love of God. Roger
Bacon, without the same knowledge of Islam, made just the same
point, on the authority of ibn Sīna: Muhammad 'allowed only the
glory of bodies, not of souls, except in so far as the soul delights
with the body'; and ibn Sīna thus 'censures the giver of his
religion'. This was a widely shared attitude: the carnal Paradise
caused the Muslim doctors to despise Muhammad's doctrine and
to turn to that of Jesus, son of Mary; it is repugnant not only to
the words of Jesus Christ, but to reason and the sayings of the
philosophers and wise men of Christians, Gentiles and Jews;
Muslims might ignore Gospels and prophets but must listen to
philosophy.[44] The contrast, point by point, between the Christian
and Muslim Heavens was a recurring theme of the last book of
Lull's disputation with Hamar; it was always sufficient to cite the
two side by side. Lull shared the view that a carnal Paradise was
dialectically negligible; his fictional Tartar, innocent enquirer, is
represented as put off by, as well as rejecting, the idea. With these
attitudes of contempt was allied a sense of unreality sharply
expressed: 'what will Paradise be, but a tavern of unwearied
gorging and a brothel of perpetual turpitude?'[45]

Many of the arguments used against the Islamic position were
similar to, or identical with, those directed against Muslim ethics
of sex. Sometimes these were the simple practical arguments
directed *ad homines* which are not unlike modern rationalist arguments against all religion, as wish-fulfilment, or as formed by
geographical or economic circumstances.

Note that it is always this sort of Paradise he describes and promises; for the Muslims love such delights, that is, to be in gardens among trees and waters, to have beautiful women with them, to eat voluptuously, to lust and to lie with people indefinitely.

Pedro de Alfonso had already contrasted what wise men, and what rough, coarse Arabs, might be expected to believe. Lull said that Muslims expect to have women in the next world because of their great love of them in this. Thus Christians adopted the insensitive superiority which would often mark the nineteenth- or twentieth-century 'humanist': 'Because the Muslims thus set their hearts on the foulness of lust . . . they say that in the future they will have a paradise . . . in which they must have carnal delight.'[46] Muhammad's cunning was adapted to his dupes' folly. He preached a carnal enjoyment after the resurrection, because 'a carnal people, ignorant of spiritual things, is not easily moved, except by carnal things'. *Gentem illam brutalem seduxit.* An odd phrase would some-times reveal this trend of thought as much as a full argument: 'such things as men, however bestial, can grasp'.[47] Lull realised the importance of Muhammad's original preaching of the Resur-rection to the men othe Hifjāz, and estimated the attraction of sensual details an important element in this part of the Prophet's programme.[48] Another view was to see his teaching, less as calculated for its hearers, than as the inevitable product of his salacious mind: *homo totus lubricus,* he 'promised for beatitude what was predominant in his most carnal mind'. These views were not incompatible; he was an animal man himself, and he spoke to his like, *animalis, iste homo animalibus loquens.*[49]

Disproof of this corporal beatitude was taken very seriously. It was both the strength and the weakness of scholasticism to consider every objection seriously, whether plausible or im-plausible, and even irrespectively of its actually having been made by opponents. There was no seeking for the actual arguments of Muslims. Scholastics generally devoted long sections to their proofs. The author of the *reprobatio* was content to say that to make eternal beatitude consist in food, drink, coition and corporal delights is obviously false. If Martí was the author, he treated the same matter very much more fully in his *explanatio.* The two works are similar in approach and share some material; but the scholastic detail of the procedure of the *explanatio* is much more pronounced.[50]

The longest rational argument was that expounded with great thoroughness by William of Auvergne. He treated Islamic belief here under three heads, the foods served by angels to the blessed, the precious clothes and hangings, the embraces of women. His basic point was that eternal life thus conceived was no different from, in fact was inferior to, the life of this world. His method was scholastic; there is one appeal to Cicero in a long passage which otherwise has little in common with humanism. One quotation will not delineate the argument, which is complex, but it will just indicate the manner of approach:

Aut erunt fames et sitis in vita illa, aut non erunt. Si non erunt, aut erunt ibi evacuationes ventrium et consumptiones corporum . . . aut non. Si erunt ibi . . . duo inconvenientia manifeste sequuntur. Primum . . . Secundum . . . Si vero fames et sitis sunt ibi, magna pars presentis miseriae ibi est . . .

I cite this, not for the sense, but for the style. There were the constantly reiterated alternatives and the flashes of common sense interposed: 'if there are indeed hunger and thirst there, a great part of the wretchedness of this life is there'. This writer would constantly argue that if there were to be intensified worldly joys, the sorrows of this world would be correspondingly intensified. A limitation of his attitude lay in the rigid literalism which he carried as far as possible. 'Let us ask them whether there is digestion there . . .' 'Cum hominum digestiones et egestiones finem non habeant, non sufficit Paradisus illa etiam sole stercore egestionem capere.' This may seem to be a rather heavy ridicule, but arguments based on *egestiones* were popular.[51] Other passages seem less minute and suggest a less narrow sympathy. If there were spiritual delights, corporal delights would lose their savour; or else, if not, the greatest delights would be wanting. In Benedict's succint précis, *culpabiliter amabitur creatura, Creatore relicto*; the argument was really reducible to scholastic tags, despite the care William lavished on it. He concluded that the whole concept was a *somnialis felicitas*, dreamed by a crazy man. It was laughable; quis non rideat? he asked of the angels serving foods; but his ridicule never stopped short of detailed exposition.[52]

There were many similar arguments in the equivalent passages in Ricoldo; many of them bear a resemblance to those of St Thomas in his disproof of the Heavenly *usus ciborum et venereorum*; the tradition is one and the same, and was not confined to the direct contest against Islamic doctrine. Lull's arguments once again involve his peculiar philosophical concepts; if there were eating, drinking and women in Paradise, there would be 'a defect in Paradise, because there would be present, past and future time in it, by reason of generation and decay . . .' This is one phrase extracted from a subtle and complex discussion. It may be said of all scholastic thoughts in this matter that it rejected the idea that corporal pleasures could exist in Paradise (irrespective of whether they were supposed to constitute the whole, or the chief, pleasure there) on the ground that it made eternal life a mere continuation of life in this world, *sicut et nunc*. The idea was bestial; hence the citation of Cicero: *ut ait Tullius, voces istes pecudum videntur esse non hominum*.[53]

The enormous popularity of the kitāb al-miʿrāj, the *Liber Scalae*, the book of Muhammad's miraculous night ascent into Heaven, drew further attention to the Islamic Heaven, though less powerfully to the carnal delights than to what seemed the carnal misunderstanding of spiritual concepts and to the fabulous treatment of the Prophets and of Christ. In some accounts of the Islamic Paradise that we have been considering there occur references to implications of the *Liber Scalae*, to the vast but finite distances in Heaven, or to angels so big that there is a day's journey from one eye to the other. Some writers produced summaries of the *liber*; to judge from what these emphasised, its attraction lay in its absurdity, the constant fabulous element, and, in particular, the arrangement of the heavens, and of the prophets, and of their subordination to Muhammad. Interest in this theme in Spain antedates Abraham's translation of the whole work; but it is perhaps not necessary to consider this subject in great detail here; despite its great prominence for literary history and its popularity in the age that saw its translation, it is relatively unrevealing of ideological criticism of Islamic religion. Yet it is obvious how much the incidental detail appealed to the Christian reader who wished to feed his contempt for the gross and material things which he saw Islam as having substituted for the spiritual. 'I, Muhammad, and Gabriel, we found indeed the eighth Heaven named above, which was all one topaz . . . And its distance was a journey of five hundred years . . .'[54] The marvellous had its place in mediaeval Latin culture, but this place was not in speculative theology.

Christian commentators in all ages, and certainly not least in the Middle Ages, have seen that beatitude to which the Qur'ān invites believers as one of the most important disproofs of the Islamic religion. Because Christian thought is wholly bound up in the concept of eternal life, the irrationality of Islam *propter finem quam promittit* has seemed to Christians so clear a mark of its invalidity. Three distinct bodies of fact, the historical details of Muhammad's personal life, the requirements of Islamic sexual ethics and the elements in Paradise which the Qur'ān delineates were linked together to constitute one single theme. Islam was essentially built upon a foundation of sexual licence which was plainly contrary to the natural and the divine law. In one form or another, this opinion has always been part of the Christian attitude to Islam.

5. LATA ET SPATIOSA VIA

A few matters other than sexual ones were thought to exemplify the moral laxity of Islam.

Dress was thought to have been significant by a few, for example. Guido Terrena said that Muslims inappropriately wear a monastic habit; but suitably this lacked the hood, because they lacked a true head, 'and for head have the vile Muhammad'. The adoption of 'monastic' dress was sometimes attributed to Sergius; it was possibly thought to imply hypocrisy.[55] It is curious to find Acqui referring to the cosmetic use of oils without condemning it, and speaking of the cultivation of long and beautiful beards with sympathy and perhaps with admiration.[56]

There were also some points of real importance. It was argued that Muhammad, breaker of his own oath, taught also that oaths might always be broken.[57] The accusation that Muslims in general do not keep their oaths was surprisingly rare; it is an accusation common enough between enemies.[58] There were objections to the Islamic rules about witnesses, but not, strangely, to those that disqualified Christians from testifying in court cases that came before the qāḍī.[59] Discrepancy between the Qur'anic and Mosaic laws of witnesses mysteriously irritated Ricoldo, who pointed to it with that triumphant air characteristic of his work whenever he felt that he or his source had unearthed some particular conclusive and self-evident absurdity. What he thought so significant in this now escapes us. There might well have been more attack than there was upon the acceptance of magical practices in Muslim society.[60] Little polemic use was made of the Islamic seclusion of women.[61] The serious criticism of Islam that it made no provision for restitution in cases of injury was not raised widely.[62] None of these points loomed very large in the mediaeval tradition which was always dominated by the consideration of Islamic lubricity.

Yet, in its near-obsession with sordid detail, the West had not lost the capacity to generalise. The comprehensive contrast between the religion of indulgence and that of asceticism and sacrifice was crucial. It had wide application. Among Christians living under Muslim rule apostasy, both for fleshly and for worldly reasons, must have been a considerable temptation, and presumably contributed to the gradual Islamisation of Christian provinces. The criticism of it as a 'broad way' of perdition was bound to develop almost as soon as the Islamic state was first founded, and to have flourished wherever Islamic government obtained. In so far as this is not said inimically, Muslims may agree, may even claim, that their religion rejects some forms, at least, of asceticism: 'no monasticism in Islam'.[63] Pedro de Alfonso put it,

Without doubt, this religion is wide, keeping many commandments of the delights of this present life . . . If you seek the root of this religion, you will find it founded on a foundation [*sic*] of unshaken reason, namely, that God loves (men), and did not will to burden them with many commandments.

At the extreme of ignorance, remote from all authentic information, very much the same comment was made; the Pisan text represents Muhammad speaking to the people like this: '. . . you have established me as king that I may furnish you with an easier religion, by which you may both serve God and freely enjoy the delights of the world'. According to Waltherius, the Prophet taught a return from Christianity to the state of fallen nature:

> Utque loquar breviter, Adam veterem renovabis
> atque novas legés ad nichilum rediges.

This might also be conceived as a return to the spiritual aridity and legalistic thought of the Old Dispensation:

> Circoncisions de pensee
> Iert par toi desacoustumee
> Et cele de char revenra.[64]

Within this general theme a variety of different emphases is met. In this context sex has its place only as the chief among several symptoms of an underlying laxity. Peter the Venerable spoke of Islamic institutions as 'prudentes secundum carnem' – judicious in a fleshly way, we might almost say – as if to speak so were to make a significant concession to Islamic feeling. By comparison the *summula* was harsh to refer to loosening the restraints of gluttony and desire. Mark of Toledo described how Muhammad saw that the Arabs would not tolerate Christianity, because it was the religion of humility, and also of chastity and fasting.[65] To Muslims, said Vitry, the sweet yoke of Christ seemed severe and almost intolerable; it was the office of the Gospel to restrain desire from its carnal flow; but the fleshly and shameless Muslims believed that future beatitude was in no way hindered by temporal rewards and earthly desires and the delights of this present life. Indeed, they believed that it was meritorious to provoke filthy appetites. Muslims who were not taken up with the pleasures of the flesh sought baptism. Thus it was that especially in the hot regions of the East 'rough and lustful' men found the *straight way* and *narrow gate* intolerable; instead it was the fatal wide and broad way which they chose to follow. Paris, in the additions he made to Wendover, remarked that those early Muslims who (he asserted) borrowed from the Bible in order to revise the Qur'ān omitted the hard parts; and elsewhere he added the phrase, *in eo Epicurus*.

Vincent de Beauvais understood the sources which he marshalled in the same sense: Muhammad, he concluded, tempered the excessive rigidity and severity of the Jewish and Christian religions 'by the promulgation of gentler commandments'. Humbert actually argued that many Christians who could do so became Muslim in order to escape the austerity of their own religion; and doubtless this was sometimes the case.[66] In his description of Baghdad Ricoldo remarked that the Tartars had adopted Islam because it was the easy religion, as Christianity was the hard one.[67]

The *reprobatio* deplored this citation from Bukhārī: 'God forgives my people the passage of the sin of the heart, so long as it does not come to act or word'; he explained that this meant that no Muslim was punished for a sin of the heart, i.e. of intention.[68] He referred elsewhere to the ease of forgiveness in Islam. Fitzralph concluded from his own study of Ketton's Qur'anic text that the Qur'ān claims to be 'nothing but a completion and *a certain mitigation* of the Testaments'. One section of San Pedro's principal work on Islam treated turn by turn the *licentiae* which Islam permitted – *plurima pessima*. He made the very sensible comment that the Muslims ought rather to be blamed for what they believed than for doing the things that their beliefs allowed.[69]

This whole theme came gratefully to Ricoldo, who took it up with enthusiasm and expressed its general implications rather more clearly, as well as more fully, than most of his contemporaries. Citing the Gospel, *broad is the way, and many there are who go in*, he commented, 'it is obviously established that the religion of the Muslims is *broad, and many are* the Muslims *who go by it*'. The Qur'anic prohibitions, of robbery, as of oath-breaking and of sodomy, were feeble, and so stressed God's forgiveness that they were tantamount to permission, a theme that we have encountered in several connections:

Although the Qur'ān sometimes forbids robbery and perjury and some other evils, yet that prohibition is a kind of permission (est quaedam permissio). For it says, *do not do such and such evils, which are not pleasing to God; but if ye do them, He is compassionate and merciful and He will easily forgive you.*

It was an essential point that salvation in Islam came through simple repetition of the shahādah and that it was the reward of faith without works. Islam was the *lex salutis antonomasite*, in the sense that it was the law of *easy* salvation.[70]

Many were the Muslims who professed their faith for the sake of an easier life with a multitude of wives and other pleasant things; in the case of educated Muslims it was not so much that they were believers at all, as that 'the vehemence of delight carries away the judgement of reason'. Finally, there was the idea, a development of Mark's, that Islam accepted the Gospel as a divine revelation which proved too hard and was remitted in favour of the Qur'ān, which it was not beyond man's capacity to observe. Muslims claimed that '. . . . the Gospel contains such difficult and such perfect things that the world was not great enough to achieve them'. Who, for example, could love his neighbour, or pray for his persecutors? 'Because it was not a religion that could be commonly observed, God provided for the world – with a religion of salvation – and tempered the commandments; he gave the world the Qur'ān, which does not contain[71] these difficult things, but things that are easy for salvation.' Against this supposed Islamic position Ricoldo had no difficulty in arguing the impossibility of God's not having known what He was doing when He gave the Gospel to men; he was, after all, attacking a position that he attributed to his adversary, not one the adversary admitted. Unwilling to let well alone, he also argued that the Islamic religion, though so much easier than the Christians, could fairly have been made easier yet; imperfect in all things, it was even imperfectly easy.[72] This last point shows that the author, in spite of himself, did not really think Islam just a systematised licence at all. That it imposed a real, though alien, hierarchy of rules, we could hardly expect to find stressed, or even fully formulated, at this period.

Islam not only permitted sin; it reconciled religion with illicit fun; it encouraged people to think that they could be saved some easy way.

6. DETERMINIST MORALS

The fatalism of Islam in everyday mundane matters and misfortunes which later in Europe came to seem most typical of the East does not seem particularly to have impressed Western Christians of the Middle Ages. Perhaps they were themselves more habitually resigned to the will of God than men of the centuries that have followed the Renaissance have been. In so far as they could even less than we control their fate, they were certainly wise to submit to it. In travellers of the seventeenth century, for example, this fatalism was a mark of the difference between the two societies; Muslims would not, by taking precautions, struggle against the plague.[73] At the earlier period this sharp sense of difference was noticeably absent. That powerful moralist Jacques de Vitry noted exactly the sense of fatalism which would later be so greatly stressed; but he was the only mediaeval writer of the formative period to do so. 'For (Muhammad) said that death was not to be feared, since God has foreseen the last day and end of everyone, which no one can escape; nor can man in any way prevent or anticipate the end which God infallibly foresaw.'[74]

When the Islamic concept of the predestination of ordinary events was known, it was seen in purely theological terms as concerned with the mysteries of election. In this belief, said Lull, God was made the author of men's sins; the Judgement on the Last Day became false, and man was relieved of moral responsibility. A short Creed of unusual perspicacity gave as the second item of the belief of Islam, 'they believe all evil things, as well as good things, to be from God, the fault and the will'. The *reprobatio* quoted Bukhari.

. . . he said that God wrote over every man his share of lust and that he must by necessity follow his share. In this way, by these and many other things, he attributed it to God that He put men in error, so that they fornicate by necessity; and this is false and blasphemous . . . Against this same (opinion) a certain wise man of the Muslims said finely enough, *If God does not forbid me to sin, and requires me to do it, and damns me because of it, I am the first to say that he who does so is not God, but the Devil.*

This straightforward argument developed naturally, as a criticism of the mechanics of predestination of souls. San Pedro, who alone of mediaeval authors of this period gave much attention to the problem, said expressly that his interest sprang out of his actual controversial practice. This can hardly have been common experience, since it is not reflected comparably elsewhere. There is some resemblance between San Pedro's interests and Lull's; Lull had seen and rejected the Islamic attribution of the authorship of evil acts to God as part of a refusal to conceive any limitation to His power; San Pedro's arguments also centred round the qualities of God.[75]

It was the detraction from God's goodness, His mercy and the justice of His judgement implicit in predestinarian belief which was to San Pedro's mind the decisive condemnation of it. This could be seen in the notion that the good and evil that a man will experience in this life and the next are 'written' beforehand, and in the notion that God judges as He pleases, almost as the fancy takes Him.[76] If it were possible that God should just write a man down as saved, He failed in goodness if He did not write all down as saved; He could not in that case reward good actions or punish evil ones; He could not with mercy hear the penitence of the sinner. So argued San Pedro; a Christian, he said, asserted that the free will of men was proved by both Scripture and reason: God willed that Heaven should be earned, and men willed their own damnation. These are commonplaces of scholastic theology.

It seemed to the Christian disputant that experience of controversy
proved the usefulness of a logical quandary which might be set to
trap a Muslim: challenged to say whether Heaven was reward of
goodness, and pain the punishment of sin, he must either agree,
and contradict Muhammad, or else assert the doctrine of God's
writing the fate of the soul in advance. In that case he might be
refuted by Scripture, by arguments from natural reason ('which
anyone may find for himself') and by arguments from Muhammad's own contradictory sayings. The Prophet had said that
Paradise rewards fidelity to the Law, and that the damned suffer
for their disobedience to God; from these views belief in free will
must follow. Muslims believe that God governs the ordinary
affairs of the world and that He hears prayers, although this is
incompatible with a belief in a 'written' future. Finally, Muhammad, he complained, sometimes made it seem that the world is
ruled and disposed, not by the Providence of God, but by chance.
Essentially, this is a critique of the *Liber Scalae Machometi*.[77]

San Pedro was sufficiently perturbed by the problem itself to
examine the difficulties and objections to a belief in free will
which might arise in any Christian community. At the end of his
'disputation' he was anxious to point out that he wrote in order to
instruct Christians in their religion. Much of his thought in the
matter seems to escape altogether from the Islamic context. Predominantly he hoped to show the inconsistency of Islam with the
(Hebrew) prophets: the idea that no one can add to or decrease
his days conflicts with the commandment, honour thy father and
thy mother, that thou mayst be long-lived upon the land; again,
it seemed to him not enough to argue that Islamic doctrines here
detracted from goodness, mercy and justice in God, because it
needed also to be seen that the prophets had revealed that those
qualities were indeed God's. On the whole we cannot say that San
Pedro misrepresented the Islamic position about predestination,
although he certainly did not render the subtle detail of orthodox
Ash'arite opinion either; he did not improve upon his source. His
mistake was to understand the true proposition, that Islam takes
God to be the *Creator* of men's acts, to mean that Islam believes
Him to be their *author*. In fact, the Islamic position distinguishes
these two functions, so that any criticism which, like San Pedro's,
did not recognise this distinction, must be inadequate; but the
Liber Scalae is here itself defective.[78]

San Pedro was willing to admit the difficulties of the Christian
position about predestination. He had said that the goodness of
God could not be reconciled with the Muslim belief; he agreed
that it was equally hard to reconcile it with the creation of souls
whose damnation God foresees. His answers only partly satisfied

him; in the last resort he had to fall back upon pious agnosticism: God has given men as much understanding of things as it pleased Him to give, and all knowledge He has not given; Christ said we were not to know the times or moments; it is the universal experience that spiritual creatures can know only as much of the future as God has made manifest. This is a sensible attitude, but to be consistent he must imply that Muslims cannot adopt the same attitude, and this San Pedro did not attempt to show. San Pedro did hold it in mind that Islam claimed better than Christianity to defend the prerogatives of God. He concluded that Christians believe in the necessity for prevenient and consequent grace; that 'everyone must say and believe' that if he finds any good in himself, it comes from the mercy and grace of God. The point was to establish that Christian belief in free will did not belittle the dignity of God.[79]

The principal practical objection to the belief in predestination was, as it had always been and would be in Christian polemic, the conviction that it meant a determinist scheme of morals; in effect, the absence of a moral law. There were two allied perceptions. There was the sense of Islam as a body holding itself apart and promising exclusive salvation to its adherents; this point was often remarked, although Christianity did the same. There was also the accusation that the Judgement Day would be amoral, neglecting works, while rewarding faith. These questions were all closely related; thus San Pedro had first argued against predestination and in favour of free will, and from there in favour of works and against faith alone.[80] Authors who did not take up the abstract theology of the question, as San Pedro did, nevertheless condemned its consequences.

The salvation of Muslims by faith alone was known to be a matter of repeating the shahādah, *there is no God but God and Muhammad His messenger*; it was also known that there was an Islamic belief that Muhammad's people would be saved by his intercession for them at the Last Day. 'For those who do not believe in the true God or Muhammad . . . there will be endless pains of Hell.'[81] The first part of this formula is the direct reflection of the shahādah. Islam 'promised that at the prayers of Muhammad his own people would finally be saved'; or, as accounts deriving from Pedro de Alfonso put it, they would be spared, *Magumetho interveniente*. It was Ricoldo who insisted, and Peter de Pennis who repeated after him, that Islam was the *lex salutis* by antonomasia; they also said that the Muslims' name for themselves was *Muslim*, which, he maintained, meant *salvati*.[82]

Whatever dislike of the notion that Islam claimed to be a chosen people there might be, it was always the moral aspect that was most stressed. 'For them, nothing is necessary for salvation, except that they should say, there is no God but God and Muhammad is His messenger', said Ricoldo; 'as a body, the Muslims maintain that if a Muslim says only this he will be saved, even if he has committed all the sins in the world.' 'Even if he had accomplished any sin whatever, even the worst', said San Pedro; and Guido Terrena said, 'with whatever sins he was soiled'. This line of thought was carried further. Such doctrine was positive encouragement to sin. 'With this teaching he took away the fear of sinning from the people he deceived, and, inciting his people to all infamies and profanities, he rendered them secure in iniquities.' To this statement of Vitry's San Pedro would contribute the point that this was the reason why Muslims steal, rob and deceive 'for the increase of their religion', and commit sins of lust. In spite of this criticism, there was some recognition that good works at least bore upon salvation in Muslim belief; thus, in a summary of Islam, Mark said that there is resurrection and eternal life for those who believe *and do good* (bona faciunt); and Tripoli spoke of Paradise as reward for serving Muhammad's religion *well*, not just for serving it. Mandeville asserted that the good were to go to Paradise and the evil to Hell, and Acqui spoke of the pains of Hell, not only for those who do not believe in Muhammad, but also for those who do not 'serve his perfect law'.[83]

Thus Muslim fatalism made no peculiar impression on mediaeval thought; in Europe itself, the recognition of God's Providence in dangers and misfortunes was strongest then, when there was least opportunity to defy the fates. San Pedro's interest in predestination in individual souls was not generally shared; but, whenever the moral implications were perceived, they aroused the interest otherwise lacking.

7. CONCLUSION

If we review the Western approach to Islam over the whole field of morals, we shall be struck by the theoretical, and almost legalistic, character that it assumes. This draws attention to the inexactitude of the theoretical information so obstinately stated. In their assertions about Islamic jurisprudence, Christian writers were perhaps as often wrong as right, yet it was characteristic that they insisted on specifying minutely, for example, the numbers of wives and concubines permitted, and the regulations that governed marriage, divorce and remarriage. Of Muslim practice there can have been practically no information available. Thus it was the number of wives allowed that was the focus of interest, rather than the number Muslims mostly had; it was generally implied, rather naïvely, that they would always enjoy in practice as many as they could by law. It was the permission for divorce which was given attention, rather than its actual frequency; it was the very idea of a wife's legalised infidelity (as it appeared to be) in the *tahlīl*, or of *coitus interruptus*, or, in Spain, of unnatural relations between spouses, rather than any knowledge of the actual occurrence of these things, which gave scandal. If, on the other hand, condemnation of Islamic toleration of homosexual practice was based on observation, the accounts were both exaggerated, and generalised to apply to all ages and all places, till it was thought (quite falsely) to be permitted by law, and even encouraged by religion. Indignation was so often allowed to outstrip the facts.

Unlike the facts, which were missing, every point of abstract knowledge seemed to combine with the next to effect the homogeneous corpus of ideas about Islamic morals which to mediaevals was wholly convincing. The absence in Islam of natural law concepts weakened the force of prohibitions in matters of sex, and so produced that 'prohibition which is a kind of permission'. Laxity in one field was connected by critics with laxity in the next, and special laxity of sexual morals was connected with the hypocrisy of claiming revelation to justify sin by religion. The sensuality of the Paradise preached was related to the sensuality of this-worldly morals which it rewarded. Writers saw primarily the offence against the natural law whenever it occurred or was thought to occur; some saw also that determinist and arbitrary morals lay behind this; the Christian insistence upon free will fell short of Pelagianism, but only a few realised a need to combat the Islamic claim that Christian doctrine limited the omnipotence of God.

Plate 3

Edinburgh University Library, Arab. & Pers. MS 161 141v

A Muslim Annunciation

❧ VI ❧

The relation between Islam and Christianity: theory

IT was not possible simply to dismiss Islam as a concoction of errors; it was that, but truth which could not be ignored was mixed with the error. The difficulty was to assess the value of truths in such a context. It was from the discussion of this problem that the final assessment of the significance of Islam, and of its place in the history of the world, derived. There seemed always to be duality in Islam, of truth and untruth. The Qur'ān witnessed, as we have seen, to the truth of Scripture and to the existence of one God, as well as to certain other matters.[1] Falsely it asserted the prophethood of Muhammad, and so unintentionally revealed its own falsity; falsely also, it asserted the prophethood of Jesus, but in doing so asserted many truths. It was not wrong to call Christ a prophet; the error was to deny His divinity.

1. TRUTH AND ERROR

The Cluniacs distinguished a mixture of good and bad which resembled the fancy of the poet Horace, which joined a horse's neck and birds' feathers to a human head. The Prophet 'recommends the practice of alms and some other works of mercy, and praises prayers highly, in order not to be revealed as wholly shameful'. He persuaded the Arabs to leave idolatry and to worship the one God; they were inexperienced rustics to whom this would have seemed something new. 'Because this preaching was in agreement with their reason he was . . . believed by them to be the Prophet of God . . . Thus, mixing good things with bad, true things with false, he sowed the seeds of error . . .' This truthful element in Islam might be treated in different ways. Most often it was seen as a deliberate trick to deceive the innocent: 'smearing the mouth of the chalice with honey, and after with a deadly poison'. The annotator of the Qur'ān must have influenced many, many more readers than Peter the Venerable did, beginning with Peter himself; this is clear from the distribution of the manuscripts. These notes may have had a considerable impact: they

163

were not less forceful for being concisely written in margins.

In the first chapter (i.e. sūrah ii) he immediately praises prayers and alms, that is, in order that under the appearance of seeming good he may entice the unwary to believe in him. Notice throughout the whole book that, with marvellous cunning, when he is going to say something ungodly, or recalls having said it, he soon puts in something about fasting, or about prayer, or praising God . . .[2]

This idea frequently recurred. The misuse of truth had converted the 'uncertain hearts' of half-convinced Arabs; Muhammad 'mixed some worthy things with the shameful, that he might the more cunningly pass the poison mixed with honey'; the infancy miracles were introduced into the Qur'ān to attract innocent Christians by praising Christ; in a variation of the usual metaphor, Muhammad 'offered them a deadly poison in a sweet apple'. He preached the unity of God 'in order to hide the venom of his malice'; he 'cloaked evil things' under good; 'he began by certain good lessons, in order to lead men to act ill under hope of good'. An early scholastic view is particularly explicit:

In that religion there are both many truths inserted into the lies, and good things mixed with the bad, even with malice to deceive: namely, so that the false things should be believed because of the true, or else that the bad things should be received because of the good.[3]

It is important to realise that truths in the mouth of Muhammad, a 'corrupt witness' who put about a 'perversion of the sacred page', could never be trusted.[4] 'Thy sins', said San Pedro, 'so disordered thee, that wherever thou didst say something good, always thou didst mix in poison which corrupted it.'[5]

Sometimes, however, the presence of truth in Islam passed without comment. 'Mixing certain true things with the false', 'although it contains some sound things', 'he mixed certain false things with the true': these are neutral phrases.[6] Some authors used such, although elsewhere they stressed the intent to deceive. Vitry used the words, *vera quaedam falsis interserens*, and even the phrase 'in this they agree with the Christians', without further comment. William of Auvergne similarly remarked that 'some other worthy things he established, and some shameful things forbade'. The *reprobatio* did not say that truth was inserted to deceive, only remarking baldly that Muhammad was 'a liar, which is obvious from the words of the same, of which many were false, but some true'. Listing examples of both, the author did not maintain that the good was introduced to deceive.[7]

Most of these phrases about truths inserted into the Qur'ān referred to verses about God the Creator and about Jesus, son of

Mary, and His mother; more rarely they covered mention of the patriarchs, the Apostles, or even some aspect of morals. They were associated with the dependence of the Qur'ān upon Scripture; the 'sound things' of the Qur'ān were 'taken out of the Laws of Moses and Christ'. Truths were essentially borrowed; it would always seem fitting that a reference to them should begin, 'Although they agree with us in many things . . .'[8] Thus, in spite of the poison, the honey remained sweet. Peter the Venerable, for example, would always be deeply aware of those Qur'anic truths which were 'as if extracted' from Scripture: the patriarchs, Noe, Abraham and Lot, the Pharaoh, David and others; from the Gospel, 'Zacharias, Elizabeth, John, son of Zacharias, Jesus or Christ, son of Mary, Gabriel speaking to Zacharias or to Mary, the rise of John, the birth of Christ from the Virgin, and some other things'. It was agreeable to encounter *laudabilia de Deo* always – and even in the Qur'ān.[9] The presence of the sacred names in an Islamic context often caused irritation, but it very much reduced the sense of distance between faith and faith. Almost there was a transitory sense of solidarity with Islam. 'We Christians', said San Pedro, 'and the Jews and the aforementioned Muhammad, we are consistent and agreed in the need for praising the prophets, whose writings we accept and praise just as they are contained in the Scriptures.'[10] This was not correct, and yet it expressed at least the shadow of a real unity.

A very few authors in the Middle Ages could see a positive value in the truths shared by the two religions, and even a road by which Muslims might approach the Christian faith. Oliver's letter to the Ayyūbid sultan had a consciously missionary intent to exploit common truths and terms; and Tripoli's entire attitude was informed by a missionary experience and zeal that did everything conceivable in that age to ignore differences and enlarge the field of agreement. Of the Qur'ān he said that it

is really suitably likened to the crow that copied the feathers of different colours of the other birds, adorned with which it went into the meeting of the assembled birds, and was thought to be a heavenly bird, coming down from Heaven; but when it was realised that this was the crow adorned with the feathers of others, and when these were taken off, it provoked laughter. In this way the Book that we are talking about is black like the crow, having nothing of Muhammad, except blackness and deformity, and yet adorned with the beautiful authorities of the divine Scriptures inserted into it . . .[11]

It was Tripoli's fortunate faculty to dwell more upon the brightness of the borrowed plumage than upon the blackness of the crow that wore it; and Mandeville, with his wise choice of authorities, followed him. The classic reference was established by the *repro-*

batio, where it was attributed to St Augustine: *nulla falsa doctrina est quae aliquid veritatis non immisceat.*[12] Whatever motive might be attributed to Muhammad in his 'insertion of truths', the fact that Islam contains many truths was always there, and mediaeval writers did not close their eyes to it.

2. THE PRAISE OF CHRIST: 'ISA THE MESSIAS

The acceptance of Christ as a prophet and the denial of His Godhead seemed in the Middle Ages to be the most important aspect of the Qur'anic mixture of truth and untruth. The approach was generally an analytical one which attempted to formulate the Christological doctrine of the Qur'ān in terms readily intelligible to Christians. This subject was given much more attention, and was clearly considered much more significant, than the Islamic proclamation of the unity of God. The latter was barely considered a fit subject for prophecy at all; it was elementary, and it was attainable by reason. It was the approximation to the revealed truths of Christian faith that was of interest to Christians, and the Qur'anic references to Gospel stories were characteristically seen as the *praise of Christ*.

The *summula* summarises the story of Christ as the Qur'ān told it:

. . . a good prophet, most truthful, and immune from all lies and sin; son of Mary, born without a father, and never dead, because not worthy of death. On the contrary, when the Jews wanted to kill Him, He escaped from their hands and ascended to the heavens; and there He lives now in the flesh, in the presence of the Creator . . .

The Islamic doctrine of Christ, like the story of Him, was partly true: Muhammad preached Christ 'born of the Virgin, acknowledged Him messenger of God, Word of God, Spirit of God; he neither understood nor acknowledged Him messenger, Word or Spirit as we (do) . . .' This important warning about the use of terms was generally neglected.

The same annotator of the Cluniac Qur'ān who had very fully understood and apparently appreciated the Islamic Names of God was much less gracious about the Qur'anic story of Christ, which he despised as 'unheard of and monstrous', the 'absurdities of apocryphal writers'. He noted sūrah XIX for 'an impudent lie' that revealed total ignorance of Scripture. It was the doctrinal error that determined his attitude, and preoccupied him: 'Note that he everywhere says *Christ, son of Mary*, against the Christians – as if he said, *son of Mary, not Son of God*; which is the sum of all this devilish heresy.'[13] At the end of the same century the facts about the Islamic doctrine were known in the monastic schools of

France; Alan of Lille's information in this matter gives us a high
impression of their accuracy. He referred to Muslim belief in
Christ's birth of a Virgin who remained Virgin, and in His conception by the Holy Ghost. 'However, they do not understand the
Holy Ghost to be the Third Person of the Trinity, but rather a
natural breath . . .' He knew the belief that Christ was not crucified,
but misunderstood the reason to be that He was 'immortal and
impassible, because he was conceived of the blowing of God'. This
was guesswork, imagining reasons in the tradition of Christian
heresies; but Alan also referred to a genuinely Islamic reason,
saying that death at the hands of the Jews was thought unfitting.[14]

Mark of Toledo used language only slightly adapted from his
own version of the Qur'ān to express the Islamic Christ – the
Christ (Messias), the son of the Virgin Mary, the Word and
Spirit of God; 'nor did Christ disdain to be a servant to God, and
certainly the near angels did not disdain it, and God strengthened
Him with His holy Spirit'. This was close to the Islamic source,
but in so far as it expressed the humanisation of Christ, rather
than simply praise of Him, it was untypical of Christian writing.
Vitry felt more sympathy for the Qur'anic picture when he summed
it up, of Christ, as 'the greatest of the prophets before (Muhammad's) time' and, of Mary, as 'the most holy of all women'. He
understood very well the Qur'anic idea of Christ's persecution by
the Jews, and of the Ascension, and he attributed Muhammad's
disbelief in the crucifixion to his ignorance of the virtue of humility.
He rather disapproved the Qur'anic use of infancy miracles, such
as that 'when Christ was a boy he brought birds into existence
from the mud of the earth, and some other miracles which are not
contained in the Gospels or accepted by the Church'. Other Syrian
accounts of about the same time also show interest and knowledge.
The Damietta History shows a strong sense of the Islamic
Christ's life without sin and of His miracles, and includes a famous
passage about the Muslim 'ulamā' who went up to Jerusalem
during a truce and there venerated the Gospel manuscripts,
because of the cleanness of Christ's law, and 'especially because of
the Gospel of Luke, *Missus est angelus Gabriel*, which those of them
who could read (i.e. read Latin script) returned to, and picked up
again often'.[15]

There were variations in the versions of the Qur'anic Christ,
though most repeated the essential points of similarity and dis-
similarity in the Christian and Muslim beliefs. These are too
monotonous to read to be repeated here. The Syrian Apology
stressed the parallel of Adam and Christ; the version in the report
sent to Pope Gregory explained with curious circumstantiality
(the passage is absent in Viterbo) that darkness made possible

the substitution of another for Christ on the Cross. The rejection
of the crucifixion was violently attacked by Humbert of Romans:
'although they agree with us in matters to do with the praise of
Christ, yet, failing to understand the mystery of the Cross, but
abusing it like most vile swine, they think it a fatuity and a scandal
to the divine Majesty to confess that the Son of God was crucified . . .' Humbert knew that Muslims did not believe Christ to
be Son of God; his theme presumably carried him away, and he
must have had in mind I Cor. 1.23. Varagine, who had access to
some sound information, knew the infancy miracles as part of
Islamic belief, and, unlike Vitry, he thought them an acceptable
tribute.[16]

A closer approach to Islam in sympathy and a warmer appreciation of the words of the Qur'ān are met in the *Epistola Salutaris*
written by Oliver of Paderborn to the sultan al-Kāmil. The
intention is to persuade:

. . . in the conception, birth, Ascension (of Christ) and the Judgement to
come, you agree with us; you believe Christ the greatest of the Prophets,
and a most holy man who never sinned or could sin. The speech of God
and the spirit of God, as you put it, I call the Word of the Father; He
was conceived in the virginal womb by the breath of God, or, as I
profess, by the Holy Ghost; you call Him the power of God, and I do
too . . .

The Qur'ān 'bore lucid witness to the miracles and divine works
of Jesus Christ'. Muhammad 'himself extolled the Lord Christ,
son of Mary, above all men'. This idea was ever present; it
seemed to Christians like an admission on the part of their
opponents, and it seemed also to imply a contrast with Muhammad,
whom none but Muslims praised.

Martí certainly took very seriously the Islamic denial of the
Incarnation. The *reprobatio*, so closely associated with him,
illustrates the importance this theme was given. A list of the true
contents of the Qur'ān consisted of these verses: 'The Lord our
God is He who made the Heavens and the earth in six days'; 'God
fore-chose Mary above all the women of the ages'; 'Christ is the
Word of God which God placed in Mary, and a spirit from Him';
'God breathed on the Blessed Virgin by the Holy Ghost' – 'where',
the author commented, 'it gives him who understands aright to
understand that Christ was conceived of the Holy Ghost'; 'In the
Gospel is guidance and light and a sign to those who fear God';
'The Apostles themselves were the helpers of God.' The author
concluded curtly, 'these and some other things he said that were
true'. He had given equal attention to Christology and to all other
doctrines together.[17]

Quite the most remarkable of all Latin appreciations of the Qur'anic Jesus is that by William of Tripoli. His accurate use of the text of the Qur'ān is unique; he used it to tell how Muhammad praised Christ 'above all the sons of men, and Mary above all women', carefully rearranging most of the pertinent texts in a scheme which paragraphed long consecutive passages and associated isolated verses, to produce one continuous text. Tripoli introduced each of the sections of the resulting sequence with a short phrase which barely hinted at the argument, and left the rearranged text to make its own impact. This was an effective display of those borrowed plumes, 'beautiful and luminous', which concealed the dark deformity of the crow beneath; it amounted to an anthology in praise of Christ, His Mother and Apostles, to contrast with the absence of praise of Muhammad or Muslims.

The first sequence is the history of Mary and the prophecy of Christ's mission, taken from the third sūrah, how Mary was conceived, born, fed by God and instructed by the angels, and how God spoke with her:

They said to Mary: O Mary, thou knowest that God will send thee good tidings, the Word, from Himself: His name, Jesus Christ, the first-born son of Mary, glorious in this world and the world to come; and He will be of those that come near to God, and He will speak as a little child from the cradle, and He will be a man, and one of the saints and of the just . . . And Mary said thus: O God, will I have a son, when I have not been touched by a man? And God said thus: God shall create what He wills, and when He decrees what shall happen, and says 'Be', it is. And We shall teach Him the Book and wisdom and the Law and our Gospel; a messenger to the children of Israel. And He shall say: I have come to you a sign from God, for I will create the likeness of birds from the very mud, and I will breathe on them, and by the will of God they will be alive . . .

This sequence was naturally followed by the story of the conception and birth of Christ and the Child's consoling His mother; of her return with Him to her people, of the accusation against her chastity, and of the Child's defence of her from His cradle. There followed two isolated chapters that celebrate the chastity of Mary, who 'constituted her person like a castle, and We breathed in her with Our spirit, and We established her and her son for a spectacle and a sign for all men'. The section on the adult life of Christ began with the realisation of that angelic announcement which we have quoted and those miracles which were 'the authority which God gave to the son of Mary'.

The remaining passages did not follow so clear an order. They established the death and ascension of Christ: 'God said, O Jesus,

I am the sender of your death, and I will raise you to me'; and the sanctity of the Apostles and other Christians. Two passages 'praise Christ and His Gospel, in which is direction and light', but one of these misrepresents the actual Qur'anic attack on monasticism. Another shows how Christ 'excels all the envoys and messengers of God'. The section on 'the malice of the Jews and the ascension of Christ' raised not only the wicked slander against Mary but also the 'slander' of the crucifixion: the Jews 'lied a great lie about Mary and about Christ'. This was the only place where Tripoli thought he should elucidate the text, the idea that the Jews slandered Christ by claiming to have crucified Him. In order to do so he had recourse to Islamic sources, to the commentators of the Qur'ān 'on the false opinion of the death of Christ'. On this authority Tripoli explained that it was Islamic belief that Judas was crucified in place of Christ, whose likeness he had received. This careful distinction between the commentators and the Qur'ān is part of Tripoli's very rare respect for the text. Tripoli added that Muslims thought it would be contrary to God's justice that the innocent should suffer. Other passages concerned the infidelity of the Jews and the faith of the Apostles and the Christians; finally the section on the Table reveals 'the Sacrament of the Table, which is the altar'. This completed this most remarkable arrangement of Qur'anic texts.

Tripoli saw nothing sinister in the praise of Christ, or in other Christian themes, which he was prepared to take at their face value. These were things that 'Muslims believe with the heart to be true, and profess with the mouth, as words of God written in their Qur'ān'. There was no question with him of fearing the gifts of the Greeks: 'although these things are entangled with many lies and graced with fictions, yet already it appears clearly enough that (Muslims) are close to the Christian faith, and near to the way of salvation'. Tripoli believed that Islam was drawing to its end, and that the strayed sheep were at last returning to the fold, but it seems clear that the actual expression of truths by the Qur'ān gave him personal pleasure. It was the want of clear Christological formularies in Islam that seemed to him to make it possible to offer Muslims the Christian religion, as a more exact definition and a clearer interpretation of their own.[18]

It is interesting to compare some Franciscan writers who also knew Syria. Fra Fidenzio, Tripoli's (presumed) younger contemporary, used the same method as he, with a different bias; his chief interest was the Trinitarian controversy. He made use of the passage in sūrah III which Tripoli gave at greater length. His translation is accurate, but elliptical; his omissions do not pervert the true sense of the text. He used great concision. 'And Mary said, how will I have a son, and no man has touched me? And it was said to her, Thus does God create what he wills.' This may be compared with Tripoli's more literal version, quoted above. Fidenzio omitted the account of Christ's apocryphal miracles, but gave the orthodox ones correctly: 'I shall cure the born blind and the leprous and I shall raise the dead at the command of God.' He noted briefly a passage which Tripoli had omitted: 'The likeness of Jesus Christ before God is as the likeness of Adam.' He too realised that Muslims thought the idea that Christ suffered a shameful one. His was a well-prepared account of Christ in Islam which lacked Tripoli's zeal, but which the technique of using the Qur'ān itself enlivened.[19]

The Irish Franciscan pilgrim Simon Simeon blended a literary and studious approach with personal observation. He was interested in the Islamic Christ (pure prophet, born of the Virgin), in the denial of the crucifixion and the Trinity, in the malice of the Jews. He took the trouble to quote the Qur'anic authority for his assertions, using Ketton's translation. The note of direct experience, however, is unmistakable: although these fellows deny Christ's Godhead, he pointed out, they praise and revere Him above all the prophets; they revere Him *ineffabiliter* as the Messias, the son of Mary (*Messiach Ebyn Merian*, for *masīḥ ibn Mariam*) and never call Him *Ebyna Alla* (*ibn Allāhi*), that is, Son of God. Simon recognised (without comment) that the Muslim reason for denying that God could have a Son was that He lacked a wife or concubine and took no delight in such things.[20] The phrases of the Qur'ān echo, with differing emphases, in the writings of about that period.[21]

With most academic or intellectual writers, citation of the Qur'anic praise of Christ was for controversial ends, not for its own sake. San Pedro's account of the miracles of Christ in the Qur'ān suggests an appreciative sense of the marvellous: 'whatever Jesus Christ said, instantly it was so' – this 'Muhammad said, and has written in his Qur'ān'; but he strongly attacked the Christology of the Qur'ān as inconsistent. It made Jesus out to be a man, and yet not to die; made Him holy and sinless, yet supposed that He would allow another to die in His place; made out, in fact, that He was born by the power of God, only to deceive men by this false crucifixion, in a world already full of deceivers. San Pedro was oppressed by the thought of so many lies, of such great heresies in the Qur'ān and in the sayings of Muhammad which his followers had collected (ḥadīth); by the thought of the loss of souls of those who died Muslims. The latest recorded impression of the martyr's mind reflects simply the Islamic *praise* of Christ. On the whole, this was the dominant impression in the minds of ordinary educated people; Roger Bacon, for example, either knew, or spoke of, this aspect only.[21]

Ricoldo was charitable towards Islamic belief when it fell within his direct, as opposed to his literary, experience. 'And when they named Christ among us, they never did so except with fitting praise, such as, "Christ, may he be praised", or something of the sort.' He classed this as *affability* to strangers, rather than as religion. He felt no pleasure in the Qur'anic texts; the story which Tripoli had savoured, of the calling and the motherhood of Mary, provoked from Ricoldo a tirade against the supposed anachronism of identifying Mary, as daughter of 'Imrān, with the sister of Moses and Aaron. Blindly following the text of the *Contrarietas*, he would endow his opponents with a stupidity of his own imagining. His criticism that the Qur'anic story of Christ was as hard to believe as the Christian one was fair; but he would also use Qur'anic passages to make points of startling pedantry. For example, he pointed out that when the Qur'ān said that the Jews claimed to have killed the Messias, Jesus, it was quite in error, because the Jews did not believe that Jesus was the Messias. It was the heart of his argument that Muhammad did not understand the truths that he sometimes enunciated; he 'spoke the truth . . . but he did not understand'. Ricoldo made much of the comparison between Christ and Muhammad, which was traditional, and for which he was particularly indebted to the *Contrarietas*, because 'opposites placed side by side give greater light'. He summarised the 'praise of Christ' in the usual way – 'Christ was announced to His mother by the angel and sanctified by the Holy Spirit' and Mary was 'purified above all women'. 'But of Muhammad', he went on, 'it does not say any of these things, but that he was an orphan, and that when he strayed he was brought back by God . . .' To a mediaeval reader, the Qur'ān seemed bleak in what it said of its own Prophet, glorious in what it said of Jesus and Mary. The comparison was worked out fully and ungenerously. Ricoldo admitted that, since Jews deny that Christ was either God or good, 'as far as that goes, Christians agree more with Muslims'. He expressed an almost universal feeling in a phrase: 'We know that never is there such valid witness . . . as when he who is trying to offend speaks praise.'[22]

Certain aspects of this comparison were especially popular, as, for example, the Islamic Christ alive in Heaven while Muhammad lay admittedly buried in Arabia. The real comparison, perhaps, was between what Christians believed about Christ and what Muslims claimed for Muhammad. Peter de Pennis exemplifies this when he reproduces many of Ricoldo's passages dealing with the subject, summing them up or paraphrasing them in his own words; Ricoldo's influence was limited in many ways. Admitting that Muhammad 'in his Qur'ān wrote inadequately and falsely of our Lord Jesus Christ', Peter nevertheless made an anthology of true and admirable verses. In this way Christ was shown in Qur'anic shape, in a happy light, an achievement comparable to Tripoli's; but what is really remarkable is that Ricoldo, here de Pennis' sole source, had avoided doing just that, by using every agreeable quotation directly for some disagreeable controversial purpose. De Pennis, in fact, followed the plan of the *reprobatio*, although at much greater length, when he simply separated the true and false statements in the material he was reading, and treated the former quite uncontroversially as statements of fact. At the end of this group of statements he said, 'but Muhammad, after he said many true things of our Lord Jesus Christ, did not remain in truth'. The 'false' assertions of the Qur'ān follow at still greater length, especially the attack on the Trinity (with its rebuttal) and the denial of the Passion, Crucifixion and Resurrection of our Lord. De Pennis relied on a very few sources, mostly well-chosen. We may contrast Guido Terrena, another writer whose knowledge was wholly literary, but who was far more inaccurate. Either he was out of sympathy with, or, more probably, he was ignorant of, the Christian argument that Islam itself admitted Christ's greater sanctity, and he went to great length to prove that Scripture prophesies Christ rather than Muhammad.[23]

Lull used the traditional arguments that we have been considering, chiefly as they could be fitted into his favourite Trinitarian speculation. For example, the dishonour done to Christ's mother by robbing her Son of His divinity outweighed the possible value of direct praise of her. Muslims' praise of the humanity of Christ was vitiated in the same way: 'the Muslims love Your humanity, in that they believe and understand that it was conceived by the Holy Ghost, and in that they believe that Your humanity was in this world without sin; but, Lord, in another way they do not love Your humanity . . .' – that is, as united to the Godhead and as the means of salvation. He argued that, by rejection of the Incarnation, creation is honoured less, and, if creation, the Creator; this is an all but Chestertonian argument.

Richard Fitzralph was equally individual but very different in his approach. Working over Ketton's paraphrased Qur'ān with a scholarly care and scrupulous attention to the letter which he was unable to give to the Arabic, he formed an idea of the Islamic Christ as 'a pure and blessed one', and, together with this, some very odd notions indeed. This is the angelic greeting as he read it in Ketton:

O Mary, the joy of the highest news to you, with the Word of God, whose name is Christ Jesus, son of Mary, who is the likeness of all nations in this world and the next, suited to the old, and to the infants in their cradles, propitious, wise, the best man, who is sent by the Creator of the Universe.

On these words he commented:

This passage affirms not only that Christ is the best man, but that He is the likeness, which I think means exemplar, of all nations in this world and the next. Therefore any other is less than He, because exemplified by Him.

His text continued,

God shall teach your son, who will come with divine power, the book of the lawgivers and the knowledge of all government, and the Testament and the Gospel and the commission to the children of Israel.

To this he remarked, 'there he affirms that Christ, the transmitter of the evangelical law, had the knowledge of all government. This Muhammad did not have, as he himself admits.' Thus the polemic insistence that the Qur'ān seems to set Christ higher than Muhammad influenced Fitzralph also, although he was largely preoccupied by another theme and ignored much of the traditional arguments about Islam.

    In both cases quoted here, he selected, as significant, phrases which the translator of the Qur'ān had invented out of nothing. He did so by a fatality natural enough in the circumstances, and it is not surprising that they seemed not only to be polemically telling, but really to reveal important truths. Misled in matters of detail, he conceived the Qur'anic Christ along lines that were generally sound. His chief interest was in Qur'anic approval of the Old Law and of the Gospel; in commenting on 'the mandate to the children of Israel' he realised, not only that the Qur'ān approved it, but that it asserted that Christ confirmed it. This was perfectly sound; but his sole interest, in everything he wrote, was the corroboration of the Gospel.[24]

    This was only one attitude, and there was some variety of approach to this subject, despite the recurrence of particular themes. The use that the texts translated by Alfonso Buenhombre made of the Qur'anic material was quite different. The author tried to use the Qur'anic Christ to refute the Jewish faith, which, in its turn, he used to refute Islam. Thus it became particularly important that Islam recognises in Christ the Messias, the word of God, the son of the Virgin, and so on. These arguments belonged to that mediaeval tradition which saw the Jewish attitude as blasphemous, where that of Islam was not. Some Jewish books might need to be destroyed, where the Qur'ān did not; Talmudic

blasphemies against Christ constituted the reverse side of the
Qur'anic praise of Him.[25] In contrast to this we should remember
the monk who spoke of his sudden horror when he heard a darwish
at the door of the house in Constantinople utter the 'blasphemy'
that Christ was a pure man.[26]

There is nothing else in all the Qur'ān to parallel the warmth
with which Christ and His mother are spoken of. Christ is presented
as an unique being, but His mother's personality appears more
vividly. The Qur'ān inspires a devotion to Mary of which Muslims
might have made more, if they had not needed to differentiate
their attitude sharply from that of Catholics. Modernist Muslims
do not like the unambiguous proclamation of her perpetual
virginity. Protestants have sometimes liked to say that the
Catholic Church acquired the dogma of the Immaculate Conception from Islam.[27] The problem for Christians who meditate
upon Islam without prejudice is not at all an easy one. The Christ
of the Qur'ān is not the Christ in whom they believe, and yet there
is only one Christ, whose praise must always be grateful to
Christian ears. It cannot logically be less grateful when it is
uttered by those who have seriously erroneous ideas about Him;
but in matters that they feel to be important, people are not
logical. Even so, there are times when the traditions of ḥadīth
seem to come very close to the true Christ, the Qur'ān to the true
Mary. Mediaeval devotion to Christ and to His mother was too
powerful and personal to grudge an alien devotion that was
genuine. At the same time doctrinal orthodoxy was deeply
appreciated as the truest loyalty to Christ and Mary. The Christian
attitude to Muslims, who revered the sacred persons, but did so
in highly erroneous forms, was inevitably equivocal. Christians
were torn in a matter that affected them deeply.

3. TRINITARIAN DOCTRINE

Christology was the most important of all problems for the
mediaeval writer whose outlook was clerical. The Qur'anic representation of Christ had the power to fascinate; the Islamic denial
of the Trinity seemed to be the basic point of difference between
the religions. Guibert thought that it was the first thing popularly
attributed to Muhammad; and much later Fitzralph was to
characterise 'this pseudoprophet . . . whose attempt was always
and above all things to persuade (men) that there is no Trinity
of Persons in God, and that Christ was not God'. This was almost
the definition of Muhammad's teaching: 'Muhammad who said
to his people, There is no Trinity in God, nor is Christ God.' It
was Muhammad's characteristic error: 'in his religion he openly
and often denies the divine nature of the Lord Christ, and eternal

generation in God'. It was his primary service to the Devil:
'Nothing is so opposed to the enemy of the human race as faith in
the Incarnate God.' It was general to put the denial of the Trinity
at the beginning of any account of Islamic teaching. Paris had
supposed a triune death, by poison, epilepsy and drunkenness, to
punish a life given to blasphemy against the Trinity.[28]

The attitude of the Qur'ān was generally well-known, both
through literary knowledge – the *Contrarietas* and the Risālah –
and direct sources. The Annotator of Ketton spoke of the astonishing folly with which Muhammad thought that Christians worship
three gods. He understood the Islamic position perfectly: Muhammad 'called Christians *deviators* because he thought they adored
three gods as well as images'. He drew attention to sūrah ɪv.169,
which Ketton renders, 'Do not say that there are three gods, as
there is none but the one God, who is without a son'; and he
interpreted sūrah vɪ.55, in Ketton, 'that which you adore in place
of God', to refer either 'to idolators or to Christians'. Of verse
138 in the same sūrah, he said, 'he calls Christians partakers or
participators because they part God into three Persons'. Both
these verses in this sūrah refer really to pagans only, but the
annotations effectively drew attention to the Islamic view of the
Christian belief. The point must, indeed, have been clear to every
careful reader of Ketton's text. The *summula's* author, for example,
realised that the Sonship was denied because Muhammad, with
his own 'brutish' (vaccinus) intellect, judged 'the eternal birth of
the Son of God according to the likeness of human generation'.
Similarly, Fitzralph asserted that it was folly to deny the Sonship,
while accepting the authority of Gospel and Psalter; an argument
based on a false premise, but which made no mistake about the
doctrine of the Sonship. Mark of Toledo was, of course, still more
accurate, and Mark himself cited the words of the Qur'ān: 'Do
not say that there are three, but that God is one; nor did Christ
disdain to be the servant of God.' Other statements were quite
adequate, while showing less familiarity with actual Muslim
forms of speech. Vitry complained that Muslims 'laugh at us for
adoring three gods' and cannot accept the ineffable generation of
the Son, which they understand carnally, because (he added with
ecclesiastical wit) 'flesh and blood hath revealed it to them, and
not our Father who is in Heaven'.[29] Thus the real problem was
understood even when there was a complete lack of sympathy with
what prompted the Islamic attitude.

A falsely Augustinian cast of thought led some authors to
'prove' the Trinity by reason, and so to try to convict Islam of
being irrational. No mediaeval author could see any concept of
God that was not Trinitarian as other than wholly defective, and

there was only a narrow margin between rational explanations and rational 'proofs' of the Trinity. Thus Alan of Lille used explanations in his polemic against both Jews and Muslims; for example, unity begets itself, and between the begetting unity and the begotten unity there is a certain equality, so that there are three unities in one. Again, there is the vestige of the Trinity in the human soul which recollects, and loves, and understands, like candles burning with a single light. Alexander III's development of the theme is classic: the ineffable Trinity 'has so much more nicely the merit of faith that it is difficult to believe'. His approach was far removed from that which thought to 'prove'. His doctrine was illumined by *elegantes comparationes*: memory, intelligence and will are one mind; the ray and heat and splendour of the sun are all one; a light gives light to a new light, without being itself diminished. In Scripture, too, the Trinity is shown by the three-fold repetition in a single verse of the psalm, the trisagion, Holy, Holy, Holy.[30] San Pedro came to this problem with even greater humility. He feared to speak at all of an ineffable mystery; he did so only because he felt bound to reply to Jewish and Christian objections. His 'proofs' were Scriptural; his rational explanations only intended to be 'illustrations' – *enxemples*.[31]

Some polemists of the high scholastic period and later put these *comparationes* forward as logical proofs, ignoring the opinion of their greater contemporaries that the Mystery of the Trinity is not susceptible of rational proof, as distinct from rational illustration. The great scholastic theologians did not attempt 'proof'. 'Nullo modo trinitas personarum est cognoscibilis per creaturam rationabiliter ascendendo a creatura in Deum', said St Bonaventura. 'Impossibile est per rationem naturalem ad cognitionem Trinitatis divinarum personarum pervenire', said St Thomas; and he stressed the fact that the sole difference between the Persons is in their relationship: 'non possunt distingui nisi per relationem originis'.[32]

Martí seems to have thought that he could convince with argument. He based his case, first, upon Scriptural authorities; then, upon 'reasons', such as that good diffuses itself, or that power, wisdom and will are one in the human mind; and, finally, by 'likenesses', such as those we have met already under the name of 'comparationes': three candles burning with one light, and heat proceeding from both the light of the sun and the sun itself. His was a comprehensive exposition of the scholastic defence of the Trinity.[33] It was, however, Lull who more than any other man made this theme the spine of his whole missionary endeavour, as well as of his own, very personal, theological speculation. These questions obsessed him, till he came to think of the relation of

Christianity to Islam chiefly in these terms. He took rationalisation of the Trinity further than any other polemist and much further than contemporary schools of theology would allow.

The Trinity was the theme of his attempted martyrdom in the city square of Bujaya, and it was the favourite subject of his *Art*, or method of thought; of his egocentric sense of special illumination. '. . . the Christians prove that the Trinity of Persons is in the Divine Essence, the proof whereof by necessary reasons was, as I heard the other day, revealed to a certain hermit, who by Divine Inspiration received an *Art* which proves by reasoning how in the most simple Divine Essence there is Trinity of Persons . . .' The coyness with which he speaks of himself does not hide, on the contrary, it stresses and is meant to stress, the universal validity that he claimed for his argument. He seems without doubt to have believed that it was impossible that the instructed human reason should deny the Trinity.[34]

The actual arguments quoted in the Life are representative of many elaborated throughout his works in the terms of his idio-syncratic philosophy, which is beyond the scope of the present study. One characteristic argument asserts that to deny the Trinity is blasphemously to postulate otiosity of God. 'The divine unity has in itself infinite and eternal act' and God must be eternally diffusive, the Father generating the Son and both breathing the Holy Ghost. There is a Personal appropriation of all the divine qualities, *bonificativum*, *bonificabile* and *bonificare*, and so on, with all the other divine attributes.[35] The long debate with the Muslim 'ālim 'Hamar' conducted by Lull in his prison consists largely in the application of these principles to the seven 'conditions' and eleven 'qualities' of God which the Muslim attributed to Him. In the existing text the method is scholastic and must represent in written form Lull's later rationalisation of his re-collections. Under each of these eighteen heads he tried to show that the Christian doctrines of Trinity and Incarnation safeguarded the unity of God, and all the other qualities, better than the Islamic doctrine did. In so far as he was defending the Christian belief from the charge of being contrary to reason, he was, of course, in the full Christian tradition, but his main intention was to go much further, and to show that it alone fully honoured God, asserted His unity, proved His existence. The Muslim protagonist is represented only by what Lull chooses to make him say; pre-sumably, his arguments in this Latin text represent a translation into the terms of Lull's personal philosophical system, a change greater than from Arabic into Latin. Lull in another book admitted that he was interested, not in actual Muslim objections to the Christian dogma, but in those that he himself thought it might be reasonable for them to have. He had no patience with Islamic misapprehension of his own position.

. . . you Muslims, said the Latin, you think that we Christians believe many things about the Trinity and the Incarnation that we do not believe . . . If you object many opinions about these things which we do not believe, words will be multiplied between us from which no utility will follow.

By the real objections of Muslims, Lull was usually only irritated.[36]

His faith in Trinitarian ratiocination never shines forth more clearly than in his recommendations, made when he was a very old man and was again living in Muslim North Africa, to the Christian laity. Merchants, he said, who often did business in Islamic countries, were asked about the Christian religion by Muslims anxious for discussions; out of ignorance they often did not know how to answer and were 'in doubt about the religion of Muhammad'. Now Lull would dispel this difficulty. He would show them how to demonstrate that the Christian religion is better, greater and truer than any other, by a method, in fact, that was equally efficacious against the Jews. Of course, it was solely concerned with the Trinity. He did indeed make some concessions to the weakness of the laity; he omitted to use symbols for ideas in the course of this argument, which is by so much the easier to follow. The good Father's generation of the good Son, the procession of the good Spirit, all one in God who Himself is goodness – and is through goodness, because of it, in it, from it, with it – enabled the goodness of God to be better known, loved and contemplated than the otiose goodness of a God who is just good. So the argument continues with other qualities, God's greatness, power, wisdom, etc. A little doubtful whether the laity were really following, after all ('indeed the laity are not accustomed to subtleties like this'), he suggested a homely comparison based upon the King of Majorca, who rules there by and through justice, but through whom justice cannot be known if he does not make use of it. It is natural to suppose that there were merchants whom even this comparison would not greatly illuminate. In a very short work, perhaps two thousand words, Lull presents six forms of Trinitarian argument, including the argument that the qualities (goodness, unity, greatness, perfection, etc.) are themselves God, if God is the Trinity (the Father, *unicus, magnificans, bonificans, perficiens*, etc.; the Son, *unitum, magnificatum, bonificatum, completum*; the Holy Ghost proceeding from both, *unire, magnificare*, etc.); whereas, in a God of one Person, the divine qualities ('*dignitates*') would differ in essence and nature, which would be wholly destructive of the divine unity. Thus each of Lull's paragraphs is a variation upon a theme he had made familiar, without making plain. It is certainly difficult to imagine the merchant who could put all this over, using presumably a commercial vocabulary in a mixture of Latin, Catalan, Spanish and Arabic.[37]

In one work alone, also a late one, Lull showed himself aware of what was really being said by Muslims. He wished, in this work, to meet them half-way. If they maintained that God has no equal, and neither generates nor is generated, Christians might agree that, understood corporally, this was true. If they maintained that Christ was not God, it might be argued that in so far as He was man (though not, of course, in so far as He was God) this also was true. This syllogistic solution – and it is nothing more – is typical of one aspect of Lullism, and does nothing to solve the problems; at the same time, it reveals Lull's own personality at its most kindly and charitable, and points out a road of mutual understanding in discussion that both sides would always be very reluctant to follow. Lull's enthusiasm for rationalisation of the Trinity, unqualified by doubts, persisted to the end. Immediately before his death he was instructing the Qāḍī of Tunis in the 'necessary reasons' for the Trinity. The clarity of his own vision so impressed his mind that his expressions sometimes approached the paradoxical: Muslims fear to believe the Trinity for fear of doubting the unity of God, but Christians fear to doubt the Trinity for that very reason. By dishonouring the Incarnation, Muslims dishonour God just when they try to honour Him. Belief in the raising of human nature, by the Incarnation, so honours the creature as to honour the Creator more. To think the Incarnation against nature is to deny the creation of the world, the resurrection and Heaven and Hell, all of which are contrary to nature, and all of which, Lull of course realised, Muslims believe. By denying the Trinity, Muslims deny intrinsic infinite and eternal acts in God, and thus lessen their own fortitude to make acts to resist temptation. Much of this seems very tenuous to us, but Lull felt perpetually teased by the wilfulness or stupidity of Muslims who could not understand and would not accept what he had once explained to them.[38]

The authentic Qur'anic objection to the doctrine of the Trinity does not normally appear in these examples of false-Augustinian temper, but a number of writers did seek to use arguments from the Qur'ān which they felt Muslims would be bound to accept; this was done with more sympathy and with less, and both with, and without, the aid of the *comparationes*. It was held that the Qur'ān itself admitted the truth of the Trinity. Oliver of Paderborn sought ground common to the two religions in terms like 'breath of God'.

As God is simple in nature and there is nothing in God which is not God, and (Christ) was conceived by the breath of God, it is evident that He is God; and the breath of God is nothing but the Holy Ghost, and the speech of God nothing else but the Word of God.

Oliver shared the view that Muslims accepted the Christian canon of the Psalter, and that the Psalter was demonstrably Trinitarian.[39]

Fra Fidenzio, with his long experience of life in Syria, recalled that Muslims 'take it as very bad that the Christians speak of the Trinity'. He tried to analyse their objection and to oppose an attitude which might carry the conviction that it was not anthropomorphic:

... they do not understand the faith of the Christians: for they assert that the Christians say *Trinity* in a human manner, as though they said *three gods*, as one says *three men*. So Muslims even call Christians *partakers*, as though they gave a part to God; as if, that is, the Father had a part, and the Son a part and the Holy Ghost a part. And they say that God is without any beginning.

On the surface, he commented, they seemed to say well, but they had failed to follow the Christian distinction between essence and person; better and more subtle than the Muslim, was the Christian belief in one only God, unmultiplied, true, omnipotent, omnisapient, superbest, uncomposed, most simple, most pure, uncircumscribable and immense, in Trinity only of Persons, and unity of Godhead; there was not supposed to be trinity in the way that there might be a trinity of human persons, Socrates, Plato and Cicero. In all this there was a detached, academic element which made prudent conclusions possible: 'every comparison of a creature to God is called dissonant rather than suitable, as blessed Dionysius shows in the *Mystical Theology*; although affirmations are attributed to God, yet negations are more truly said of Him than affirmations'. The attitude of Muslims to the Sonship was similarly carnal, but should be met by a willingness to show how far Christians were from holding a carnal view.[40]

Tripoli, writing in the generation before Fidenzio's, expounded Christian doctrine in terms almost of poetic fire. Muslims, whose conversion in numbers he claimed, wonder at the mystery of the Trinity, unless it be expressed in language which makes it clear to them that it is what they already believe.

For when they hear that God, whom they worship, is, as they say, Creator of Heaven and earth and of all creatures, who created all things from nothing, His Word being co-eternal with Him, they joyfully concede that God has a Word, by which all things were created, and without which nothing was made. Again, when they hear that God, who is verbal, that is, having a Word, is living and the Life of lives, bestowing life on all living things, living in life, the Fountain of unfailing life, from whom every bodily and spiritual creature draws life, they concede God to have a Life or Spirit whom we call Holy.

To reject the Trinity would, therefore, make it seem that God was dumb, and even dead: *quod nefas est sentire de Deo*. If it was put to the Muslims, how the Word of God was the means of creation, prophecy, wisdom and knowledge of God, resurrection, judgement and retribution, 'they exclaimed, "Father, a great excellence of God is this Word", and they concluded, "he who does not know the Word of God, equally does not know God Himself" . . .' There is not room to illustrate further this attractive train of thought; without insisting that the Qur'ān implies the Trinity, Tripoli tried to find a terminology intelligible to Muslims. This passage, abridged and cut off from its context by Mandeville, reached a popular public which would have no idea of the situation in Syria that impelled Tripoli to write as he did.[41]

Despite the wide range of his knowledge and the vigour of his opinions, Ricoldo lacked the judgement of Fidenzio and the enthusiasm of Tripoli, the moderation of Martí and the single-mindedness of Lull. His arguments about the Trinity are of uneven quality and have diverse inspiration; he composed advice marked by good sense that he did not always follow. Muslims, he said, are peculiarly anxious to hear about the Incarnation and the Trinity, but, as these are above reason and intellect, they will not believe, and cannot understand, them; they laugh at them as contrary to the Qur'ān, which they believe to be the Word of God. It was better, he advised, not to begin immediately from divine principle, but to show them one Christian law, and to be brief in all things. It was easier to show Islam false, than Christianity true. What was necessary was only to defend the reasonableness of the faith, to accept the unity of God, and to insist also on His simplicity; to point out that it does not follow that the discretion of Persons is untrue because it is incomprehensible.

In practice, Ricoldo was fond of the counter-attack upon the Islamic interpretation; for example, he said that to assert that God has no Son because He has no wife is like saying that He is not living because He does not draw breath. He used the Trinitarian images to defend the reasonableness of Christian teaching: the light and heat of a fire can be communicated separately, yet are not separate from the fire itself. He also made an image for the Incarnation, in order to defend the Crucifixion: a king might send his words in a book, and the book be burned, but his words would not burn. He ridiculed the idea that God could only have a Son who was hostile to Him, presumptuous and disobedient.

Ricoldo also developed the argument that Trinitarian faith is implicit in the Qur'ān, which speaks of the *anima mundi*; which speaks with a plural pronoun for God, and which speaks of the Word and of the Spirit of God. He argued that if the latter terms were accidental there would not be, what the Qur'ān certainly intends, something special in their application to Christ. Here he flatly contradicted the actual Islamic attitude; to appeal beyond the Muslim interpretation to the actual text of the Qur'ān is not necessarily profitable. What else, he asked, could the Holy Spirit sent to Mary mean, if not the Third Person? Not, he suggested, an angel, which could not sanctify; and thus he dismissed the actual Islamic view with a phrase. From the text of the Qur'ān which he rendered, *Dedimus spiritum sanctum et insufflavimus de spiritu sancto nostro*, he derived a Giver who says, *we gave*, and the Spirit which is Given, necessarily distinguishable as Persons, but not in essence. Upon the Qur'anic warning, 'and ye shall not say three, because God is one', he more kindly than usual remarked, 'how near it approached to that which is most difficult in faith'. Some of this took the Islamic attitude into account, but much would have been instantly dismissed as irrelevant by any Muslim who heard it; and too much was repetitive.[42]

There is little evidence of the use of Trinitarian argument in debate; indeed, it is probable that much more ammunition was prepared than was ever discharged. Latins were not alone in favouring Trinitarian argument; Oriental literature had been familiar with it, since the work of St John of Damascus; and the Jacobite Yahya b. 'Adi, in the tenth century, had given the Holy Trinity a dialectical treatment pretentious in manner and almost as ambitious as Lull's.[43] Primarily such texts witness to literary, rather than to oral debate, however. Examples of actual debates in the mediaeval period are few. In an ugly episode, a party of Franciscans, challenged to show how there could be a Son of God, *cum Deus uxorem non habeat*, gave examples of divine generation, the rays of the sun, the trees and the seeds of the earth. These *comparationes* were harmless, and might be useful if they helped to show the enemies of the Christian faith that it was not opposed to reason; but they were useless as compelling reasons, and they did not help the Franciscans, as it turned out.[44] William of Rubruck, in Mongol territory, had to leave the defence of the Trinity to Nestorians who explained the doctrine 'by means of comparisons' – presumably they put the traditional case.[45] Pennis, presenting a selection of Ricoldo's arguments, said, 'as Blessed Thomas of Aquino says, *all objections* (rationes) *brought against the Catholic faith are soluble*'; and Lull fortified himself with the same thought.[46] It was equally true, however, that the Catholic case was spoiled by overstatement.

A Hebrew source relates a public debate, sponsored by San Ramón of Peñaforte, which is also documented from the Latin side. Even in the Hebrew version it can be seen that the Christian protagonist, a Dominican of Jewish birth and upbringing, argues ably against the Rabbi Nachman on Scriptural grounds, less convincingly from the Mishnah; but he and the other Christians who intervened (including King Jaime), when they put forward the rational exposition of the Trinity that was so popular, found that their arguments were easily demolished – at least, in any modern judgement that is so.[47] It is clear enough that the Trinity cannot be 'proved' in this way, and no theologian to-day would attempt to do so by philosophy; and it is equally clear that this method could never have succeeded against informed Muslim disputants, any more than against Jews of the same class. Yet, though so much was said that was useless, the Trinitarian literary debate did serve to make Christian readers realise the intimate relation between Christian faith, Islamic belief and the text of the Qur'ān.

4. ISLAM AND HERESY

From the Muslim point of view Christians are a privileged association of people who have become diverted from the right way; Muhammad 'called the Christians deviators because he thought they adored three gods as well as images'.[48] Reversing this Muslim attitude to themselves, Christians in their turn found a place for Islam as a deviation from the Church, that is, as a heresy. Heresy is in a familiar and identifiable relation to the whole truth which the Church represents; there is almost a family of Christian error in which Islam may be found a place. The great proportion of Christian truth contained in Islamic belief made this possible, although, as a heresy, Islam would always remain peculiarly formidable and, in fact, unique.

At times, the Cluniac position took the term *heresy* for granted: the denial of Christ's divinity was 'the sum of this diabolical heresy', as the annotator in Ketton put it. The *summula* claimed to sum up 'the heresy and diabolical fraud of the sect of the Saracens or Ismaelites', and Peter the Venerable echoed his secretary's phrases when he spoke of 'this error of errors, these dregs of all the heresies'. This imagery was not just poetic fancy, but had an exactly definable sense: 'regurgitating almost all the dregs of ancient heresies which, infected by the Devil, he had swallowed, with Sabellius he denied the Trinity, with his own Nestorius he rejected the divinity of Christ, with the Manicheans he disavowed the death of the Lord, although he did not deny His return to Heaven'. There was a special relationship with Arius, who had denied that Christ was Son of God, and to Antichrist, who would

deny, not only, like Muhammad, that Christ was God, but even
that He was a good man: 'the most impious Muhammad', half-way
between the two, represented a stage in the scheme of damnation.
These things which had been 'first sown by Arius, and then
advanced by this Satan, that is, Muhammad, would indeed be
wholly completed by Antichrist, according to the diabolical intention'. In the prologue to his principal polemic, Peter took one
by one the famous heresies, only some of which could be supposed
to have a relation to Islam; reasonably he saw Nestorianism – that
of Muhammad's 'own' Nestorius – as the most closely relevant.
The *summula* attributed the denial of the divinity of Christ to
Nestorian influences; the annotator of Ketton said, 'in this man the
Arian heresy lived again', *haeresis Arriana revixit*; again, of sūrah
v.76, which in Ketton's version read, 'certainly all who say that
Jesus Christ, son of Mary, is God will be found to be liars and
unbelievers', he commented, 'another impiety coming from
Nestorius'.[49]

The Devil's part in plotting Islam as the renewal of the heresies
was thought important by several writers. The Risālah had early
proposed a threefold distinction of dispensations; in Peter of
Toledo's wording, that of grace, which was divine; that of justice,
which was human, that is, the Mosaic Law; the third revelation
could only be diabolical. These schemes of the Devil's seemed to
many mediaeval thinkers to lie behind all the setbacks to the
Catholic religion throughout the centuries. Guibert had spoken of
heretical influence on Muhammad 'to the Devil's piping'. William
of Tyre characterised the Prophet as 'first-born of Satan' who
'seduced' the Orient with his 'pestilent' doctrine. In a series of
discussions of the Church's enemies, Gerald of Wales took
Muhammad after Arius, and saw in the supposed lasciviousness
of Islam the calculated cunning of the Devil's scheme for a hot
climate, in contrast to the avarice of the Patari, heretics of a
frigid zone, whom he considered next. For Vitry the strong words
thought suitable for the pulpit came tumbling out in a flow of
pejoration.

. . . like another Antichrist and the first-born son of Satan, transfigured
like Satan into an angel of light, Muhammad, upheld by God's great
anger and special displeasure, with the co-operation of the enemy of the
human race, perverted . . . more people than any other heretic before his
time.

His was the greatest abomination of desolation, and the greatest
scourge of the Church of God of times past or future. Ralph of
Coggeshall, using the words *heresy* and *heresiarch* emphatically,
cited the Abbot Joachim, in order to repeat the idea of Muhammad's

intermediate position in the diabolical plot: infidelity inexorably
extended from its first Arian flowering to its completion in Antichrist, whose precursors were the successful Ayyubid armies in
the contemporary scene. In Joachim's scheme of history, Muhammad and the Muslim 'persecution' had succeeded, fourth in line,
to those of the heretics, the pagans and the Jews, under Constantine,
Nero and Herod; the series was to culminate in Antichrist, whose
last predecessor was Ṣalāḥ ad-Dīn. One of the tribulations foreseen
by the chiliast John of Roquetaillade was a fresh Islamic invasion
of Christendom. Even in a more matter-of-fact view, it was the
Devil who introduced Muhammad to Christian heresy. These
instances illustrate the element attributed to the Devil in a stable
conception of Providence which changed little through those
centuries.[50]

Islam was reckoned the greatest enemy of the Christian Church.
Partly this was quantitative. Muhammad's was the last of seven
persecutions, said Humbert of Romans, and the only serious one
remaining. It was, of course, the worst of all: the longest, the
most continuous, the most widely extended, the most thorough-
going, the most obstinate, the most pernicious, the one with most
agents.[51] Ricoldo saw it as the sum of three former 'persecutions'
into which all the past sufferings of the Church might conveniently
be grouped. There had been the rabid *persecution* by pagan tyrants
up to the time of Constantine; directly after had arisen the *persecution* by heretics which the great doctors, Hilary, Augustine, Jerome
and Gregory had been raised to combat; directly after Gregory's
time had arisen the third plague, the danger of false brethren, men
of corrupt mind, hypocrites, a tribulation that would last until the
old age of the Church. Muhammad's *persecution* was above all
others. It was not confined to any one mode, but functioned in all
three. Sometimes it worked by tyranny, sometimes by deception
in religious doctrine (*per legem*), sometimes by subverting the
simple people by hypocrisy. This was a subtler statement and
nearer to historical fact than Humbert's. Ricoldo saw that Islam
partook of the genuine doctrinal fascination of heresy, and of that
apparent moral example which enables ostensibly exemplary men,
false brethren, to lead Christians into error.[52]

Although he wrote after the fall of 'Akka, he believed the
traditional apologetic to be still effective, and he worked out the
relation of Islam to the classic heresies with extreme thoroughness.
Thus Muhammad denied the Trinity with *Sabellius*, and agreed
with *Arius* and *Eunomius* that Christ was a creature excelling all
others; he taught with *Carpocrates* that God could have no son
save by the medium of a wife, and with *Cerdonius* and the *Jews*
that if God had a Son They would endanger the world with Their

dissension; and so he continues with the *Manichees, Donatists*, with *Origen*, the *Anthropomorphites, Macedonius, Cerinthus*, the *Ebionites* and the *Nicolaites*: the Anthropomorphites because in the mi'rāj, thought by all Latins to be authentically the work of Muhammad, it says that the Prophet touches God. Whether or not this listing of heretical elements was worth doing, Ricoldo did it effectively, echoing but improving Cluny. What the seducer could not accomplish in Arius he fulfilled in Muhammad and would yet confirm when Antichrist came to persuade the world to deny even the goodness of Christ. 'The filth of many ancient heretics which the Devil scattered here and there among the others he renewed all at once in Muhammad.' For Ricoldo this sequence of familiar, formally condemned heresies was apparently reassuring, perhaps in that it placed Islam as worse only in degree. He too stressed the part played by the Devil, that liar and father of lies at whose prompting Muhammad 'composed' his revelations; the Devil who saw that the plurality of gods could no longer be defended when Heraclius triumphed over Chosroes, and chose Muhammad as a new instrument.[53] The identification of Islam as a heresy and its place in the providential sequence of heresies and *persecutions* which the Devil excogitated were treated inseparably by all these writers.

Yet in spite of this widespread image of Islam as the culmination or summit of all heresy, it was not at all certain that technically it was a heresy at all. The clearest assertion that it was so was Oliver's; because of their Christological beliefs, he said, Muslims ought to be called *heretics* instead of *Saracens*, but 'the use of the wrong name has prevailed'. This flat statement is unique, but Peter the Venerable discussed the question fully. It was in the context of the catalogue of the heresies of the past that he came to the problem. 'I cannot clearly decide', he admitted, 'whether the Muhammadan error should be said to be a heresy, and whether its sectaries should be called heretics or heathens.' There were reasons to prefer the name of heretic. It might be correct to define as heretical nothing but what left the Church and acted against it, but ancient usage called any attack on some part of faith, even outside the Church, heresy, and Muslims, in the usual way of heretics, took what they liked from the sum of Christian doctrine, and rejected as much as they disliked. Yet they rejected baptism like pagans, disdained Christian sacrifice, and derided penance and the other sacraments of the Church.[54] Neither at Cluny nor elsewhere did polemists take the canonical position into account; a Muslim, unlike a heretic, had not been baptised and was not liable to penalties for leaving the Church.[55] Men would always remain conscious of the heresies, especially about Christ, that were con-

tained in Islam, and for Peter the question seemed otiose: on the
authority of Augustine, all error which was against Christian faith
should be combated, however it arose, in the Church or, like that
of Jews and pagans, outside it.[56]

Certainly the term *heresy* was used carelessly and casually in
this connection. It was treated as a common noun in referring to
Islam; for example, Mark of Toledo could speak of Muslims' en-
forcing 'their heresy'. Untechnically it meant no more than
'erroneous doctrine'; it was so used in the margins of Ketton's
text. Sigebert spoke of Muhammad's doctrines as his heresy, and
again, much later, San Pedro mentioned the heresies that Islam
contained.[57] This is not an exhaustive list of examples, and it is
hardly necessary to seek many. Islam was assimilated in practice
to heresy, both by its measure of agreement with some classic
heresies, and by the colloquial use of the word. Both these senses
related it to Christian doctrine. Just as Muslims believed that the
doctrines held by Christians were a corruption of those teachings
of Islam which God had revealed to them through Jesus, so
Christians could only see Islam as a corruption of Christian truth.
It was wholly and intimately connected with Christianity because
it was made up, partly of assertions, and partly of denials, of the
whole truth, and in either case stood in relation to truth.

5. THE RELIGIONS OF THE WORLD

Historically it was thought that Islam had been created, not
only by heretical Christian influences on Muhammad, but equally
by Jewish influences, either from the Old Testament or in Samaritan
or Talmudic form. The manner in which this was supposed to have
occurred was usually legendary, although there was more substance
in what was said of Jewish than in what was said of Christian
influence.[58] The classic statement is that of the Cluniac *summula*:
'in order that the plenitude of iniquity should come together in
Muhammad, and that nothing should be lacking for the perdition
of himself or others, to the heretic were added Jews'. Even when
this was put more calmly – *quaedam a Judaeis sumpsit et quaedam a
Christianis*, said Gerald of Wales; and Alan of Lille remarked
equally vaguely, *ad suum nutum ab utroque quaedam excipiant* – the
same general history was taken for granted.[59]

In any polemic work intended as a total defence of Christianity,
Islam found its natural place as one of the enemies of the faith.
Guibert dealt with Muhammad after the heresiarchs and before
the *Grecorum erronea doctrina*. Pedro de Alfonso, in his polemic
Dialogues against Judaism, gave one whole dialogue to the
Islamic alternative to either Judaism or Christianity. Peter the
Venerable himself wrote against the Jews and against the Petro-

brusians, these three works constituting the sum of his polemic. Islam often made a third with heresy and Judaism, and the word *perfidiae* covered them all; this expressive term was not as widespread as might have been expected.[60] A generation later than the Cluniac effort against Islam, Alan of Lille's *de fide catholica contra haereticos sui temporis*, as the printed text describes it, was conceived in the atmosphere of the Lateran Councils and their preoccupation with the intellectual defence of Christendom. The proportions of this work are significant: there was one book each against the Albigensians and the Waldensians, of seventy-six and twenty-five chapters respectively; the book against the Jews came third and contained twenty-one chapters, and in the fourth, against the Muslims, there were fourteen. What was said in earlier books that was relevant to the last, for example in defence of the Trinity, was not repeated in it; yet not only the relative space given to Islam, but the focus of attention on the better-known and geographically closer *perfidiae*, place anti-Muslim polemic as subsidiary. This final book was called *contra paganos seu Mahometanos* – 'quos communi vulgo vocabulo Saracenos vel paganos nuncupant'. Alan himself generally preferred to use the term *pagan*, but this does not imply that he meant *idolator* to be understood; in fact, it is clear from the body of the test that that is not the case. Credulous of unattractive and unconvincing legends of the life and death of the Prophet, his choice of terms may be a mere expression of dislike. Fitzralph, after his consideration of the Qur'ān, in his eighteenth book, went on to consider the damnation of the Jews during the Apostolic Age in the book following. Talmud and Qur'ān might be paired as sources of error; a manuscript of Peter de Pennis contains consecutively his treatise *contra Judaeos, nomine Thalamoth* and his *contra Alchoranum*.[61] Finally, the 'Rabbi Samuel' literature, translated by Alfonso de Buenhombre, conceived anti-Judaic and anti-Islamic polemic as essentially interwoven.[62]

The legal treatment *de Judaeis et Saracenis* associated these two religions throughout the thirteenth and fourteenth centuries; the two peoples were also associated in schemes for their conversion, and, in the popular mind, their destruction.[63] The collections of canons grouped them together; some individual canons treated them together, more treated them separately. In so far as Muslims did not 'judaise' that is, in so far as the Qur'ān condemned Jewish 'calumny' of Mary and of Christ, Islam was free of the *blasphemy* of which Jews were seen as guilty.[64] Jews and Muslims were thought to be different in that the former were Scriptural and were effectively harmless; in fact, toleration could be extended to Muslims when, as subject to Christian princes, they were placed like the Jews. The essential difference between them was that dār al-Islām existed, offering to error the security of a hostile society, whereas there was no Jewish state.

William of Auvergne reports two interesting comparisons of the three revealed religions that were current in his own day among people reputed *sapientes in mundo*. One of these views distinguished Fortune, Nature and Grace. The religion of the Hebrews was that of Fortune, which the Jews might be said to worship, since their reason for holding their religion was that it brought them temporal prosperity. Muslim religion was the religion of Nature, because it contained few requirements; nature here meant corrupt nature, and Muslims indulged carnal delights for which they thirsted. The Christian religion was that of Grace. William discarded this scheme as based on inadequate study of the religions concerned. Other people he quoted as saying that the Hebrew nation lived under Saturn, whose sign was their avarice, pertinacity and hardness, and whose appropriate day was Saturday, the day they kept holy. The Muslims lived under Venus, kept her day holy, and were much given to venery. The true religion, the Christian, belonged to the sun, symbol of spiritual things, observed Sunday, and obeyed the pope, who lived in the city of the sun. William was at pains to discredit a view which blamed the stars for diversity in religion; he would have no part in astrology. What interests us is the evidence for there having been this curious speculation, unchristian in its attitude to the Sabbath, and based on the comparison of the three 'laws'.[65]

It was common to speak of there being three revealed religions, three 'laws', in the world. Peter the Venerable went to some trouble to prove that only two religions were revealed before the time of Muhammad. The three religions were grouped by the Risālah. Three *laws*, Judaic, Christian and Islamic, had been given since the beginning of the world, said Humbert of Romans; his fellow-Dominican, Ramón Martí, with more care, said that 'those who have a law, *or who arrogate to themselves the name of a law*, are the Jews and the Christians and the Muslims.' This idea was general, and is reflected by the Emperor Frederick's famous blasphemy about the three impostors. It was the theme of part of Lull's instruction to his son.[66] For the Christian, Islam was the third of three religions and heretical in its relation to both the other two. Christianity has its special relation to the synagogue, so that Islam was doubly related to Christianity, directly, and, through the old Law, indirectly. This was illustrated by an argument of Oliver's, designed to show the relative status of Islam: in any assembly of a Christian, a Jew and a Muslim, the Christian and the Jew would alike regard Islam as the least of the three, the Muslim would put Christianity above Judaism.[67]

This simple pattern of heretics and Muslims, or of Jews, Christians and Muslims, would be modified and extended by time; heresy became for a while less menacing in the West and missionary opportunities in the East more prominent. Controversial literature reflected this, and wider groupings of religious bodies were envisaged. William of Auvergne already distinguished idolators and pagans from heretics and also from the *gens Machometi*. Humbert contrasted Muslims with certain heretics, who wished only to corrupt faith; with certain *Barbari*, who wished only to kill the bodies of the faithful; and with the Mongols, who were said to wish only to subjugate their lands; Muslims, of course, did all three. Martí distinguished those who had, from those who had not, revealed religions, saying that the latter were infinite. Fitzralph also thought in terms of wide national groupings: *Saraceni, Iudei, Tartari et Gentiles*. Ricoldo classified the populations of the East under four heads, in order of increasing remoteness from the truth: heretical Christians, Nestorian or Jacobite; Jews; Muslims; and Mongols or pagans. Heretics held the integral revelations, but were in error about the mode of Incarnation; Jews did not have the New Testament and were in error about the Old; Muslims had no revelation and no understanding, but had their Devil's law with some useful things; pagans had no law, understanding, worship or religion at all. Roger Bacon's is one of the most original and elaborate comparisons of *laws*, particularly of those of Moses, Christ and Muhammad; the aim of an important part of his *Moralis Philosophia* is to show the sole validity of the Christian. His were the most comprehensive catalogues of different *laws*; he distinguished pagans, who lacked a regular worship or priesthood; idolators, with priests, temples and sacrifices; Tartars, who adored Almighty God but also worshipped natural objects; Muslims; Jews; Christians; and lastly the followers of Antichrist to come. In another place he omitted Muslims from the list, apparently only because their religion was compounded of the pieces of others. Lull portrayed Christian, Jew and Muslim in competition for the soul of the pagan, in two works, and, in another, a dispute of a Latin with Greek, Nestorian, Jacobite and Muslim. This last work is entirely about the Trinity, over which each sect is in error; in the last resort this was to classify Greek Orthodox with Muslim, and to characterise both as heretics, although in the dialogue care was taken to set the Muslim apart from the others. In less theoretic vein, in works intended to persuade the authorities to effective action, he classed all who broke the unity of mankind, Muslims, Jews, schismatics, heretics, Tartars, together. He was thus equally liable to group all kinds of Christians competing for the Muslim or pagan soul, or all non-

Catholic bodies, Christian or otherwise, according to his purpose in writing.[68]

Sometimes, when the distinction between dissident Christian Churches and Islam was expressly drawn, this served only to suggest its contrary; such passages seem to reveal a natural tendency to think of every society that disowned Roman obedience in a single category. All the separated bodies called for reunion. William of Adam, the Bishop of Sultānīyah, expressly excluded Islam from the same class as the Greeks, whose greater feebleness (though equal malice), when compared with Muslims, derived from their having 'left the Roman Church'. Humbert also classed the *infidel* as outside even the riven unity of the Church; at the Council of Lyons the Western Church needed to reform its morals, the Eastern its faith, in order to unite against the external menace of Islam.[69] In these examples, William certainly thought of the different enemies of the Catholic Church together, and even with Humbert, the reunion with the Orthodox looks like the first stage in the reunion of the world. The distinction was also blurred in some cases by the opinion that Islam itself was primarily a schism, rather than a heresy. This is implicit in the idea of some sources that the Arabs had been converted to Christianity before they were 'perverted' to Islam, and it may owe much to the historical notion of the loss of the Christian provinces to Islam. The most influential champion of this view was Dante:

> seminator di scandalo e di scisma.

The aspect of *dottrina falsa* was not neglected by the early commentaries on Dante, and one explained the verses 'il tristo sacco / che merda fa di quel so trangugia' as meaning that 'all the doctrine which entered (Muhammad's) mind produced horrible error with which he soiled and infected nearly all the world'.[70] Such writers thought *schismatic* the best term because it included that of *heretic*.

Thus Islam was conceived in many contexts, not only as heresy, but as a schism belonging with the Eastern Churches, as part of a providential scheme of progressive error developing after the Christian revelation, as constituting the third *law*, that is, with Judaism and Christianity, the third of revealed religions, and as one in a wide sequence of all the religions of the world. These different approaches often mingled. Summing up, we can say that Islam was always seen to be in a definite relation to the Catholic Church; the mediaevals, though often querulously, looked ultimately to the reunion of all men.

6. CONCLUSION

Islam took its place rather dramatically, but inevitably, in the historical sequence as a prefiguration of Antichrist, for as long as political, economic and military requirements dominated European thought upon the subject. The more theoretical analysis of heresy and the more practical association of Islam with schism, with other *laws*, and with nations without *laws*, and the interrelation of all these concepts obviously reflect the conditions of political geography. Islam effectively dominated a large part of the world which it disputed with all kinds of religions. It was not only historically the great robber of the Christian provinces now lost to the Church; it was the greatest single obstacle to world unity. The dominant consideration was practical. The society which geographically separated the Roman Church from the new Mongol power was also that which seduced the souls of the same Mongols from a possible Roman allegiance. All schism is error and all error was thought of as in a sense schismatic. Every soul belongs to the Roman Church, from which it may be separated both formally and by erroneous tenets; the two go together.

All these considerations contributed to the assessment of Islam. Analytically, there was no clear-cut conclusion. Islam is not a mere negation of Christianity; it is not just a partial affirmation of it; but in practice it came to be seen in both these aspects. They were complementary; as soon as an error was identified, it drew attention to some connected truth; and when a truth was admitted, it was necessary to issue a warning of underlying error. In the Middle Ages, Islam was always related to the effective exposition and defence of the faith of Christ. There was little academic interest in a subject for its own sake; and the oecumenical urge to understand the doctrine and to love the persons of those in error was rare. This may be why the polemic purpose failed; no sustained effort was made to present argument in terms that Muslims could recognise as their own. The Christian faith was defended at too obvious a level, by men afraid of any divergence from orthodoxy, even in others; with greater confidence they might have deferred the repudiation of a few errors, in order to confront Islam more realistically on a limited number of selected issues. Their opposition was indiscriminate, we might almost say, promiscuous; and the choice of terms and subjects unintelligible to Muslims constituted a barrier to all communication between the two religions. When Islam was admitted to belong to the Christian family of error, it was stated in terms which would be as difficult for Muslims to understand as they were thus made easy for Christians.

Some conception of the strong character of the Qur'ān must have resulted from the reading of it, though it is not always obvious that it did so; apart from the criticism of its 'confusion', this appears chiefly in recognition of the truth and polemic utility of some of its contents. The greatest and the characteristic contribution of mediaeval thought to the study of Islam was the persistent sense of how that religion witnesses to Christ. This was often, as when the Qur'ān was said involuntarily to teach the Trinity, wholly unintelligible to Muslims; it came a little closer to Muslim interpretation when it developed the Qur'anic 'corroboration' of the Christians, and really close when it stressed God's election of Jesus and Mary. We shall see that in practice there was also some perception of Islamic works of religion and an appreciation of Islamic virtues. The theoretic assessment remains clear. Islam was a falling away from the truth which the Christian Church preserves; and in this way was paralleled the Islamic concept of Christianity as a falling short from the truth preserved in Islam. On both sides it was the extent of disagreement, not of shared beliefs, on which men concentrated their attention.

❧ VII ❧

The relation between Islam
and Christianity: religious practices

THE theoretic 'placing' of Islam, as a heresy, as one of the religions that struggled for the souls of men throughout the world, as a schism of the Catholic Church, as the greatest of the persecutions to which God's Kingdom was subject, as a prefiguration of the tribulation that will precede the Last Day, was always based on some general consideration, either the analysis of doctrine, or an estimate of history or of contemporary political circumstances. Thus to place Islam in theoretical fashion was satisfactory to those who did it, in so far as it served to support doctrinal orthodoxy. Doctrine, however, cannot, and is not intended to, exist abstracted from the actual events of the world. In practice there would have to be modification of theoretic opinions, as well as some confirmation of them, from experience of Muslim practice of religion and virtue in the world.

1. APPRECIATION OF PRACTICAL VIRTUE AMONG MUSLIMS

A strictly realistic view was rarely expressed. 'Muhammad taught his followers more and greater evil things, in example and speech, than they perform, when they try to imitate their master'; here San Pedro spoke sensibly and fairly, definitely admitting that there were limits to the evil he was prepared to believe Muslims actually committed.[1] Such an attitude was usually, however, less purely an estimate of fact, being modified by a satiric or an homiletic intent. There was sometimes more, sometimes less, eye to Islamic realities. 'Many educated Christians do not observe the Gospel religion which, however, they believe absolutely to be true and good. Rather do they imitate the way of the Qur'ān, which actually they believe to be false.'[2] This is the thought that underlies the theme. With it sometimes went an inclination to stress Christian delinquency by showing how Muslims practised Christian virtues. There was little interest in how they practised Islamic virtues.

It was apparently this satiric intention that governed Ricoldo

195

in his praise of various Muslim practices and institutions, as he personally found them in Baghdad. His is the best example of realistic satire, since what he praised are really Muslim virtues:

They received us indeed like angels of God, in their schools and colleges and monasteries, and in their churches or synagogues (i.e. in mosques), and their homes; and we diligently studied their religion and their works; and we were astounded how in so false a religion could be found works of such perfection. We refer here briefly to some of the works of perfection of the Muslims, rather to shame the Christians than to commend the Muslims. Who will not be astounded, if he carefully considers how great is the concern of these very Muslims for study, their devotion in prayer, their pity for the poor, their reverence for the name of God and the prophets and the Holy Places, their sobriety in manners, their hospitality to strangers, their harmony and love for each other?

Here observed fact is expressly made to serve the satiric purpose, 'to shame the Christians', but the facts are truly observed, and even generously interpreted. Most of the qualities praised are such as Arabs and Muslims have always been famous for, and the appreciation may be taken at its face value. Three of these qualities may be considered here. The first is *gravitas*: the absence, said Ricoldo, of raised heads or waving arms, even among small boys, and of recrimination in public. He claimed 'in many years' in Baghdad never to have heard a profane song instead of religious ones. All this sounds exaggerated, presumably by the satiric intention, although based in truth. Even in Islam the *gravitas* of serious and religious men, like that of well-brought-up children, does not extend throughout the city. There can have been no special purpose behind the account of Arab hospitality which the Christian Religious apparently refused so far as they could. What Ricoldo meant by *concordia Saracenorum* proves on examination to be the sense of brotherhood and solidarity within Islam. Thus the army of legitimate authority can say to the army of the rebel chief, 'Are we not all Muslims? It is not permissible to fight among ourselves. Let only he who rebelled against his lord be given up, and let us all be in peace.' To this Ricoldo remarked: 'Indeed, they so nourish harmony and love among themselves that they really do seem to be brothers; for talking among themselves, also, and especially to strangers, one says to another, *O son of my mother* . . .' Again, this was an exaggeration; he said that a Muslim might always travel with safety among Muslims; but the basic fact that he asserted was true. His purpose was constantly one of edification: 'they who have a religion of killing and death do not wish to kill each other, and wretched Christians, who have a religion of life and commandments of peace and love, kill each other without any mercy'. Ricoldo also repeated that he wrote in order to shame

Christians 'who do not wish to do for the law of life what the damned do for the law of death'. The lesson was too plain. 'See how much concord there is among the children of iniquity . . . so that the Muslims can say to Christians, *Be thou ashamed, O Sidon, the sea speaketh.*'[3]

Very much the same reaction was shown by St Bonaventura, who never visited an Islamic country himself, when he learned of Muslim charity to some Franciscans. Here we see the impact of facts, really representative of Islamic society, upon a man whose assumptions, however outstanding his intellect, were those of the general public. He described how two of the Brethren arrived in Islamic territory, and how a Muslim who saw that they were needy was moved to pity; he offered them money to buy food, which, in obedience to their Rule, they refused. He then understood that for the love of God they wished not to possess money, and offered to maintain them for as long as he had the means. 'What incalculable value poverty has', commented Bonaventura, 'when by its wonderful virtue the mind of barbarous savagery is changed into such sweet commiseration. Equally, it is a dreadful and abominable crime that a Christian should trample upon this noble pearl, which a Muslim exalts with so great a veneration.'[4]

Different in kind but similar in purpose is the story told by Caesarius of the benevolent Muslim noble in the port of 'Akka, after Ṣalāḥ ad-Dīn's advance in the summer of 1187. This is an earlier and more probable version of the story which provides Mandeville with the satire of his secret conversation with the Sultan. The purpose of both is once more to shame the Christians, but this time it is not so much the specifically Muslim virtues which are brought forward, as the worse observance by Christians of virtues which, implicitly in the story, are recognised by both religions; it is interesting that these virtues should include chastity. A Muslim noble, learning French *au pair* in Jerusalem in his youth, had observed the Christian way of life: *omnis vita Christianorum bene et optime nota est.* Now in 'Akka he asked the Western pilgrims how the Christians behaved in Europe, and those to whom he was talking, 'not wishing to tell the truth', replied, 'Well enough.' This did not tally with the Muslim's own experience as a youth in Jerusalem:

There was no citizen in Jerusalem so rich that he would not expose his sister, his daughter or, what was detestable, his wife, for money, to the lust of the pilgrims, whom in this way he cleared of the rewards of their labours. Thus everyone was given to gluttony and the enticements of the flesh; in no way were they different from the cattle.

Equally they were obsessed with vanity about their clothes.

Caesarius' informant, the monk William, who in his youth had been present at this conversation in the port of 'Akka, described how the Muslim continued:

Consider how loose and full are my clothes and shoes, how simply and humbly shaped. – As William described it to us, he had open, wide sleeves like a monk, and there was no multiplicity of pleats in his clothes, no fancy work, although the material itself of the clothes was precious enough.

These were the vices (said the Muslim) for which the Christians were expelled from the Holy Land. In Mandeville's story the mamlūk sultan was kept informed by an extensive system of spies about what went on in Europe; this was an extension of the criticism of what went on in the Latin States. There were priests who set no good example, people who drank at taverns when they should be at church, who drank and squabbled and fought, followed the constantly changing fashions in clothes, sold their womenfolk out of covetousness. Mandeville's story is less good than Caesarius', less probable in its setting, more generalised in its satire. Both castigate the sins of Christians, without praising Islam otherwise than by implication; Caesarius has verisimilitude.[5]

Rather different is the story of Joinville's where John the Armenian falls into argument with an old Muslim in the Damascus suq. John resents a suggestion that the sins of the Christians are more than the sins of the Muslims; then the old man asks if he has any children, and, finally, whether it would upset him more if his son hit him, or the Muslim speaker did so. God was more angry with the small sins of the Christians than with the great sins committed by the Muslims in ignorance.[6] It is not credible that any Muslim should speak like this, but there is something convincing in the detail of the earlier part of the narrative; perhaps it is an 'improved' version of an actual event. Its purpose is the same as that of the other tales we have recounted; it is less forceful, because it relies only upon the reproaches, and not on the better example, of the Muslims, in order to make its point, but it accords better with the traditional Christian attitude to Islamic morals. Joinville was conservative by temperament.

Another type of story is exemplified by that of two Cistercians taken before Ṣalāḥ ad-Dīn as prisoners of war. The Rule of St Benedict allows meat only in special cases, but wine in moderation always. When these two were served meat and water by two handsome girls, they resisted all temptation and stuck to prayer; but when they were served fish and wine, to help them forget their troubles, they became very gay, and fell upon the girls (irruerunt in foeminas illas). The next day Ṣalāḥ ad-Dīn criticised the Rule

in the light of his experiment, and dismissed the monks to expiate
their sins among their own people. This story may or may not be
intended in criticism of the Rule, but it at least assumes that all
parties shared the same view of fornication.[7]

What is common to all these stories, even Joinville's, is the
presumption that there exist standards in Islam by which Christians
could be judged, and judged justly; and in every case except
Joinville's a reader might acquire the idea that Christians and
Muslims behave in very much the same fashion in real life. This
is emphatically not the impression that a reader of the purely
polemical literature would derive from it.

There did also exist, but not commonly, an extreme of uncritical
appreciation of Islam which served the purpose of edifying
Christians, without much approximation to fact. The English
pilgrim said, 'They refrain from all harmful appetites of the world.'
If they had the true faith, he continued, and loved divine charity
as now they loved their own charity, with equity, its servant; and
if Christians were at one with them, and loved true charity as now
they loved iniquity, and vanity, its handmaid: there would then
be no lack of present grace, nor need to despair of future glory,
for either Christians or Muslims. The writer hoped that his
readers would not complain about this opinion of his; it was
justified by the example of the noble lion who was corrected by
means of the base dog; as well as by the words of St Paul, *I write
not these things to confound you* . . . Yet the writer so put it in this
passage, that the dog seems nobler than the lion. It is possible
that behind these words lies the author's surprise, when he
reached the Holy Land, to find the *Saracen* rather better than he
had been led to expect; if so, he was more percipient than most.[8]

A number of references to historical personages bear upon the
same question. The reputation of Ṣalāḥ ad-Dīn was so high, almost
from his first appearance, that it survived into modern times very
much in its original form.[9] In the Middle Ages there was an
absurd, and literary, legend of *Saladin* that was certainly satirical:
the legend of his travelling incognito in Europe, convinced at first
by Christian doctrine, but finally deterred by the behaviour of
clergy and pontiffs:

> . . . Spurcitiam, mores pravos, vitam(que) palustrem
> Luxuriam, fraudem, invidiam, scelus atque rapinam
> Et fraternum odium, cupidi quoque pectoris estum . . .

This is solely an attack upon Christian vices; Muslims might
possibly be exempted from *fraternum odium* but not from *luxuria*.
There is, too, Busone's anticipation of Boccaccio's more famous
Jew: such was the avarice of the Roman court, said 'Saladin', that

the Lord who suffered it to continue must be the mildest, most merciful, most just and wise, and His religion better than any other. Admittedly this fantastic Saladin was also the hero of purely romantic adventures; and there are examples of similar satire in which it is some non-Muslim infidel, or just any barbarian, who is scandalised. Yet it remains true that the satire, however common-place in itself, was in many instances specifically related to Islamic disapproval; the bare fact that it was supposed that Muslims must disapprove the wickedness of Christians is evidence of a sense of solidarity, perhaps even of community, with Islam, which persisted in spite of the theories about Muslim morals which then obtained. Moreover, there is at least sometimes the implication that Muslims exercised the virtues opposed to the Christian vices in question; and Busone's choice of epithets for Saladin to apply to God, *mild, merciful, just, wise*, is distantly suggestive of Qur'anic language.[11]

There was also the legend of the true Saladin of history. It would probably be true to say that this legend was known over a wider area for a longer period of time than that of any political figure of the mediaeval West, and almost as favourably. The famous Europeans, Frederick II, Louis IX, for example, had all in some ways a more provincial reputation than Saladin. Only such saints as Francis had comparable fame. We may attribute this partly to the exceptional character of Ṣalāḥ, and partly to his equitable or generous treatment of most Christians at his mercy. His military success was attributed to divine judgement on Christian sin; it might have been explained in less friendly fashion, for example by making him the precursor of Antichrist.[12] There is no altogether satisfactory explanation of why the legend developed exactly as it did, except that it was rooted in the actual facts. When it was forming there was certainly an element of satire in the sense of an exaggeration intended to serve a purpose of moral criticism by means of contrast.

It remained a practice to revere individual Muslim leaders. Al-'Ādil (*Safadin*) shared his brother's high standing: 'rare and praiseworthy virtue, although in an enemy' was said to be his. In the story from Caesarius quoted above, there is a passing reference to Nūr ad-Dīn, the son of Ṣalāḥ ad-Dīn, as *vir naturaliter pius et beneficus*. An outstanding example of satire occurs in Paris' account of English King John's embassy to Muhammad an-Nāṣir, in Marrakesh. In this story the Muslim monarch contemptuously rejected the proposition of his unworthy Christian fellow king, whose morals and social circumstances he assailed with all the indignation and enthusiasm of one of John's own subjects.[13]

The image of a Muslim, good, ripe for conversion, came easily

to Oliver of Paderborn's mind, although in his address to the
sultan al-Kāmil in Cairo there is doubtless an element of that
flattery with which it would be normal to approach the great: *tu,
quem Deus ingenio ditavit, patientia multaque urbanitate moribusque
laude dignis ornavit* . . . This sonorous rhetoric was not written
when Oliver was a client at the Ayyūbid court, and its flattery was
voluntary. Neither was it insincere or unreal; it was written out
of gratitude for the unusual generosity with which al-Kāmil had
treated his Frankish prisoners. They had not felt that he was a
tyrant, not even that he was their lord, but rather that he was their
father, helper and colleague, patient, even, before their acts of
insolence: rightly called al-Kāmil, *id est consummatus*, as above all
other princes. He was praised, in particular, as opposed to that
homosexuality which, said Oliver, publicly displayed, was the
characteristic vice of his people.[14]

An even more interesting example of the treatment of an
historical situation occurs in Tripoli's contemporary estimate of
the rule of the mamlūk aẓ-Ẓāhir Baybars, who more than any other
man worked for the final destruction of the Latin States.

He detests and hates wine and prostitutes, saying that these make
strong men silly, and effeminate them. For five years, therefore, in
virtue of his proclamation, no brothel with prostitutes has been found in
the land which is subject to him, and no one dares to drink wine, except
secretly. When he was told that his predecessors were accustomed to
employ five thousand mercenaries out of the rate, or farm, on wine and
prostitutes, he replied, 'I prefer to have a few chaste and sober soldiers,
rather than many who are baser than women, and who war for Venus,
rather than for Mars, the god of wars and battles.' He praises marriage
and has four wives, of whom the fourth is a young Christian girl from
Antioch, whom he always takes about with him. He disapproves of
having concubines, and condemns the sin against nature. He requires
his subjects to live justly and in peace, and protects the Christians who
are subject to him, and especially the monks who are on Mount Sinai;
and in the various parts of his dominion he appears to be favourable (to
Christians) and hears their causes immediately, decides them and
concludes their suits. His own monks, who are called fuqarā, he willingly
hears and honours . . .

This surprising and eirenic picture of an *anima naturaliter Christiana*
has probably a purpose primarily political; it tends to show that
Muslim rule was tolerable, and even favourable, to Christians.
Taken in its context in Tripoli's argument, it supported a theory
of the approaching conversion of Islam. Tripoli thought Muslims
good people, in that they realised their lack of faith and morals.
Ultimately, his aims remain obscure; but it is certain that he
surveyed Islamic society across the border with equanimity, and

in the light of a morality common to the two religions.[15] This and
the other examples I have given do not represent any serious
respect for Islamic moral behaviour on a considerable scale; what
there was seems mostly if not wholly to have been meant for a
goad for Christians. Nevertheless, it is important enough to need
to be taken into account whenever we try to assess the Christian
attitude. Praise and condemnation of Muslim morals have co-
existed within the Christian view since the Middle Ages and have
to that extent modified the theoretic estimate which was solely
condemnatory.

Serious estimates over the whole field of morals were rare; no
thorough one existed. Neither polemic treatment nor satiric reproof of Christians suits an academic and dispassionate examination.
There were only fragments. Mark put into the Prophet's mouth
a summary of the moral teaching of the Qur'ān which has no
tendentious purpose: 'Be humble, patient, chaste, except with your
wives; avoid adultery, murder, theft . . .' This largely corresponds
with the reality of Qur'anic doctrine, and reveals both resemblance
and divergence between Christian and Islamic morals, and does
so excellently, so far as it goes, which is not very far. Higden
praised the 'sobriety in food and drink' of Muslims, in plain
history as well as in fiction. Verona numbered praiseworthy things
that Muhammad taught, and among them, that 'men must beware
of sins, namely, anger, pride, hatred and ill-will'; it is difficult to
recall a verse of the Qur'ān which might have inspired this list.
Some Muslims, he added, were disgusted by the libidinousness of
their religion, 'as I have heard from many'.[16] The idea that the
moral scheme was shared by the two religions at all was accepted
only fitfully.

Every reader of the Qur'ān, whether in Ketton's translation or
in Mark's, or in major extracts quoted by other authors, must
have received a strong impression of piety and moral injunction,
and it was in fact just this that was so often denounced as a trap
for the unwary. A great deal of what was written about Islam
consisted in attacks upon the Qur'ān; it is possible to forget that
it was often not self-evident to the uninstructed reader that what
was attacked was objectionable. Even the passages in sūrah XXXIII
which refer to the story of Zayd and Zaynab and in sūrah LXVI
which deal with that of Marīyah would not seem so iniquitous if
there were no commentary to explain their contexts – from the
point of view of modern scholarship, to distort these. Muslim
commentators are accustomed to explain the occasions of different
revelations, and Christians would do so too, in order to discredit
them. Except where this could be done, the Qur'ān must have
seemed predominantly a work of piety, and after all not so unlike

the later prophecies of the Old Testament. It must have tended to give a good impression, which we may assume it was part of the purpose of the polemists to obliterate.

Even so we can say that there was in the West some knowledge that Islam was a system of positive requirements, and not only a series of relaxations. Praise of Muslim practice, to shame Christians, equally with attempts to describe Islamic morals, made it clear that to some extent Islam and Christianity drew upon a common stock of precepts. It cannot be said that there was as general a consensus to this effect as there was in condemnation of Islamic laxity, but yet it was important.

2. MUSLIM VENERATION FOR SACRED THINGS

Christian conceptions of Christianity's relation to Islam included legends about the veneration of Muslims for sacred things. Often there was confusion. For example, the Qubbat aṣ-Ṣakhrah, as we have seen, was thought as *Templum Domini* always to have been what during the period of Christian rule it did become, a Christian church. Vitry thought that Muslims held the Temple of the Lord to be sacred because they held Jesus so: 'also in many places they honour the churches of Blessed Mary the Virgin': it was the same with the site of the Burning Bush, but not, he did realise, with Calvary or the Holy Sepulchre.[17] Thus he related the Muslim treatment of churches to the Qur'anic treatment of Christian themes. This was also the spirit in which the Muslim divines who so lovingly handled the manuscript Gospels, *Missus est angelus. . .* , were described.[18] There were other stories of Muslims who honoured holy things and Christian places.

There is the story of the Damascene ruler who had fallen blind in his one remaining eye; he went to the shrine of a miraculous image and 'entered the oratory and, although he was a heathen, had faith in the Lord, that his health would be restored by the image of His mother'. Such behaviour is quite probable, although contrary to the letter and spirit of Muslim doctrine.[19] Falling down, 'he prayed prostrate a long time. When he rose up from prayer he saw the fire burning in the lamp which hung before the image of Mary the Mother of God . . .' Particularly interesting is the association in this episode of the enemy who is a good enemy because he seems to admit the Christian faith, with that language of orthodoxy (*genetrix Dei*) which is most alien, both objectionable and incomprehensible, to Muslims. On the whole, Latins were surprised by the presence of Muslims in their shrines. They were not familiar, as people are where it is customary to tolerate different religions, with the willingness of each sect to seek a miraculous cure or a magical protection at the shrines of all. We

notice that there seemed to a Western hagiographer to be something specially wonderful about two Muslim women cured of a
fever at the tomb of a holy Dominican.[20] There was a failure to
realise that a request for baptism might equally represent, not
faith, but magical beliefs. Vitry understood what was happening;
Muslims, he said, had their children baptised, not from faith, but
in superstitious hope of longer life or of cure from illness. Caesarius,
in contrast, tells the story of how the Bishop of Beauvais, in his
captivity after Damietta, baptised a young man, a sick Muslim,
who had dreamed that baptism would cure him. He was cured, and
the smiles of the Muslims standing around turned to wonder. The
author piously, and rather pathetically, hoped that the youth persevered in his new faith. The purely superstitious significance
which, without intending any sacrilege, a Muslim would see in
the ceremony can never have occurred to him.[21] Also alien to the
Latin conception was Islamic generosity to Christian churches.
Several writers of different periods remarked on the economic
support traditionally given by the Egyptian sultans to the Greek
monastery on Mount Sinai.[22]

Muslims might approach Christian holy places and sacred
ceremonies in a spirit of toleration or of superstition; this was of
course not true of the Christian use of images, at all times an
offence to the pious Muslim. Even when effective warfare had
subsided, the exhibition of images and holy medals to a Muslim
public might give rise to a threat of riot, as happened to Friar
Simon at the Alexandrian customs house. In consequence, this was
at all times felt to be a serious reproach that needed to be refuted.
Christian worship of images, according to Ketton's annotator, was
associated with worship of 'three gods' in the mind of Muhammad.
Usually Christians reacted more sharply than this to the Islamic
objection. Alan was the first to take the question at length. In his
usual delusion that the same arguments were acceptable to Jews
and Muslims as acknowledging the Old Testament, he imagined
that the presence of images of the cherubim in the Jewish Temple
would impress a Muslim audience. The classic argument against
the Islamic position was 'that men may be attracted through the
things they see to invisible things, that through the symbols they
may venerate what is symbolised; for, as written materials are the
letters of the clergy, so are pictures those of the laity'.[23] This
attitude, opposing rationalist to revealed religion, was defensive.

The worship of the saints was associated with that of the images;
Alan explained carefully the significance of *latria* and *dulia*. In all
this part of his argument he was followed by Oliver of Paderborn.
Ramón Martí added little to the Christian case, but it is interesting
that so discriminating and so learned a polemist should have

thought it advisable to contradict at length the accusation that
Christians worshipped Mary, the Cross and images of Mary and
the saints 'as God'. Similarly it was San Pedro's experience that
it was necessary to take the matter separately and treat it carefully. Peñaforte considered that the vindication of the practice of
the Latin church and the dispelling of misapprehension was an
important function of the Christian missionary. That learned
bishop and traveller, Giovanni de' Marignolli, explained almost
with sympathy how all the Orientals opposed the Latin belief: not
only Jews, Tartars and Muslims, but also Christians, who
venerated icons (*pictures*) but abominated carvings. Yet the un-
travelled Latin imagined that all Christendom adored the images
of Christ and the saints.[24]

I have referred above to the conversation between Fra Fidenzio
and the soldiers of the victorious Muslim army returning to
Damascus with so many Christian prisoners from the sack of
Tripoli. There was such mutual incomprehension as to reveal a
complete failure to relate Christian and Islamic doctrine, and it
was natural in conditions of warfare and mutual contempt, when
God seemed to smite the Christians in their failure, that there
should have been little room on either side for charitable, even for
academic, interest in the positive preferences of the worship of
opponents. The images found in the churches were subject to war
psychosis in a peculiar way. Yet the puzzlement of the Muslim
soldiers in Fidenzio's story, their curiosity and their interest to
discuss the matter, clearly implied those different ideas of prayer
from which the iconoclasm of the Qur'ān sprang. On the Latin side,
the defence of images, which were characteristic of the Latin rite,
helped to preclude any very clear conception of worship that lacked
both images and sacraments. There was 'no altar, no image, no
picture' in mosques, said Verona, and he was almost alone in
thinking it worth while to make even so slight a mention of
mosque furniture as this.[25]

3. MUSLIM REVERENCE

Lack of interest in Islamic religious practice marks the failure
to recognise any kind of spiritual life in Islam; but this does not
apply evenly to all aspects, and it is not that the authentic Islamic
accent in religion was wholly unfamiliar. It sometimes seemed,
indeed, as though the phraseology of an alien piety were relished,
but, if so, it was very mildly. The seriousness, and perhaps the
fervour, of Muslim devotion were known, but faintness of interest
defined the limits of knowledge very narrowly. There was some
sense of the religious formulas with which Muslims will speak of
God and of holy persons. These penetrated chiefly from literary

sources, the rare translations from Arabic. 'They reject', said
Pedro de Alfonso, 'whatever is not consecrated in the name of God.'
Those phrases which strike Western ears in all ages as exotic
occur in Mark's ibn Tūmart: '. . . It is said of 'Ā'Ishah (*may God
spare her*) that she said: The Prophet of God (*may God accept and
save him*) . . .' Ricoldo had been gratified at mention of the name
of Christ by the expression 'may He be praised'.[26]

The Arabic expressions are recognisable in Mark's Qur'anic
paraphrases, set in the mouth of the Prophet, whom he imagined
preaching to his people: 'Adore the living God who created the
Heavens and the Earth, angels and men and all that are in them;
do not adore gods who cannot do you good or harm you . . .' The
principle source of Qur'anic language was, of course, the Qur'ān
itself; Fitzralph, lacking all personal contact with Islam and using
Ketton's translation two centuries after it was written, noticed the
characteristic phrases without indicating that he found them in any
way outlandish: 'God, the Clement and Merciful, the Living and
the Most High, beside whom there is no other . . .' He seems to
savour them. The usual Mozarab translation of the basmala seems
to have been *in nomine Dei misericordis miseratoris*; Ketton's *in
nomine Domini Dei pii et misericordis* was a deliberate stylistic
'improvement'. Other translation also carried the authentic note
of Islamic piety: Ketton's annotator's notes on the Names of God,
and the widely known letter of Ṣalāḥ ad-Dīn to the Emperor, 'In
the name of God, the Merciful (*miserens*), by the grace of the One
God, the Powerful, the Victorious, the Conqueror, the Ever-
lasting . . . We beseech Him that He should pour His prayer over
His prophets and especially over our instructor, the Prophet
Muhammad . . .' Tripoli neatly expressed in a sentence the Islamic
summary of belief: the Creator, the Day of Judgement, God's
speaking through the Prophets. Sometimes, too, there was a use
of phrases that were Islamic or that struck their Western users as
Islamic, and that were self-consciously used to convey an exotic
atmosphere; James of Acqui repeatedly referred, in an Islamic
context exclusively, to 'the great God': *gratia Dei magni, amicus
Dei magni*; the weight of invisible inverted commas can be felt. A
similar phrase is 'the messenger of the high God' used by Tripoli;
and so is Verona's *Deus celi*.[27]

Ricoldo, followed by Peter de Pennis, was singularly ungenerous
in his abstract treatment of the Qur'ān, referring to 'one whole
sūrah in which he says nothing remarkable, except that God is
great, high, wise and lovely, and that His are all things which are
in Heaven and on Earth and between them; and that He judges
justly. At every phrase he repeats "may He be praised" . . .' Less
than temperate in his theoretic dealings with Islam, he rendered

to its practice that justice on which travellers in later ages would still more often insist.

The Muslims indeed have the greatest reverence for the name of God, and for prophets and saints and holy places. It is especially their practice to do or say or write nothing important without beginning in the name of the Lord. So in all written matter that they send to each other they reverently write the name of God first, and for this reason they diligently see to it that no written thing is torn up or thrown down on the ground. However, if they do find on the ground a piece of paper that has been written on, they reverently pick it up and put it high up in cracks in walls, lest the name of God be trampled on. Whenever they come across the name of God, either reading or speaking, they never dare to pronounce it alone, but always with some word of praise, such as, 'God, may He be praised' or some such.

Rather more grudgingly, Lull spoke of the great devotion of Muslim preachers and congregations.[28]

4. RITUAL AND OTHER WORSHIP

It was in this context of dimly apprehended and alien devotion that the public profession of Islamic faith was considered. The shahādah was widely known and was quoted in a variety of forms; the simplest was, with slight variations, the commonest: *Non est deus nisi Deus, Mahomad est nuncius Dei.*[29] This famous formula was also quoted in indirect speech and in paraphrase.[30] It was the form of words, remarked Tripoli, which was used to make a Muslim, as was the baptismal formula to make a Christian.[32] It was best known as part of the call to prayer, the *adhān*. The adhān seemed a highly significant and intolerable symbol. Roderick said that Muhammad instituted it after his conquest of Mecca, in order that a Muslim should proclaim it where (as he supposed to be the case) it had formerly been the custom for the bells to sound. He derived this statement from, if he had not imparted it to, his protégé Mark, who also, by stressing the substitution of mu'adhdhin for bells, implied the substitution of Islam for Christianity throughout Arabia.[33]

Within its own boundaries, on the other hand, Christendom would not tolerate the call to prayer. Clement IV held it in particular horror; and in the early fourteenth century a canon of the universal Church forbade the Christian princes to allow this public profession of faith on their territories. That the name of Muhammad should be used in the course of calling Muslims to prayer was said to be an offence against the Divine Name and a reproach to the Christian faith. In the Latin States the adhān was apparently thought of as a proclamation of the Law of Muhammad; Vitry used this phrase, and the *de expugnatione T. S. libellus* described the ceremonies by which the Qubbat aṣ-Ṣakhrah, Templum Domini, was returned to Islamic worship: 'calling the Law of Muhammad with horrible moanings and shouting *Allahu akbar, Allahu akbar'*. This sounds like the ordinary adhān rather than any special ceremony. Among fourteenth-century pilgrims, Verona only distinguished the repeated word 'Allah' (*quod idem est quod Deus*) and said that the call continued, 'I bear witness that Muhammad was a great prophet of God.' Here the phrase 'I bear witness' is an accurate detail not mentioned by earlier or by contemporary writers, although the other words are incorrect. Simon Simeon saw only the 'high tower', which he described as like a campanile, the exterior gallery round it, and 'priests . . . like look-outs' who 'at certain times' cried the praises of the Prophet and stimulated the people to praise him. There was an impression of sound – *clamoribus vocibus* – and this quite mistaken idea that adhan and prayer were in praise of Muhammad[34]; this is doubtless another reflection of the persistent delusion that Muslims treat Muhammad as Christians Christ.

The best account is in Giovanni d'Andrea's gloss on the Clementine canons; he had had his information from a Frenchman who had been a prisoner in Egypt.

. . . every mosque has . . . one minister who is called the *mu'adhdhin*, which means a *crier*, who supplies the want of bells . . . The office of this crier is this: at the times that I shall describe later he climbs the square tower of the mosque, which has a big window on each side, and at each one of these, blocking his ears with his fingers, so that his voice may carry more strongly, he cries aloud in his own language words which have this meaning: that there can be no other than God, and *Muhammad is His messenger; come to make the prayer for the revelation of your sins.* Then he adds, *Lā ilāha illa Allāhu,* which is to say, *There is no conqueror other than God*; these are the words that every soldier of the Muslims carries on his shield; and to this he adds, *God is almighty.*

Despite its mistakes, this is an intelligent description; the detail of the hands to the ears is misinterpreted but well observed. It is evident that the observer had some feeling for the Muslim ritual; living in isolation from Christian society he had a greater mental freedom to help him observe accurately.[35]

What is suggested by all these accounts is something that has been felt by travellers in many ages, that the public nature of the call to prayer makes it a great and solemn symbol of the unity of the Muslim community. It could not be distinguished from the prayer itself, and both together were the act of the whole quarter in which the mosque was situated. When that was in Christian territory it seemed to be a 'reproach to the Christian faith' and particularly intolerable where, as happened in Aragon, Muslims and Christians lived in the same quarter. Perhaps because it symbolised difference, there was some attempt to repeat the exact form of words, but even so, it often happened that inappropriate Christian terms were used, as by calling a mu'adhdhin a priest.

Another Islamic formula which penetrated Western literature through and beyond the translations of the Qur'ān was the fātiḥah, the opening verse of the whole Qur'ān, used as a prayer by Muslims on important occasions. Different mediaeval translations have attracted the attention of historians. The best version is certainly that cited by the annotator of Ketton's Qur'ān: 'In the name of God, the Compassionate, the Merciful. Thanks be to God, the Lord of the universe, the Compassionate, the Merciful, the Judge of the Day of Judgement. We pray to Thee, and we confide in Thee; put us on the right way, the way of those that Thou hast chosen, and not of those with whom Thou art angry, or of the unfaithful.' In contrast, Ketton's, as usual, was too much of a paraphrase, concerned chiefly with Latin style; but in one word he was more accurate than the alternative in the gloss, just quoted: he had 'erronei', those that are led astray, instead of 'infideles'. The annotator explained that those on whom God's anger came were the Jews, and those that were led astray, the Christians. This was the Islamic tradition of interpretation. It was the same writer who stressed the significance of the fātiḥah: 'this first chapter is called for short the Mother of the Book', for the reason that the whole Law draws its origin from it, as does our Law from the Lord's prayer; and it is the foundation, and the beginning and the height of all their prayers'. The versions of Lull, which he put into the mouth of a pious Muslim about to undertake an important work, and of Ludolf, are too free, and are incomplete. The great interest in Lull's version is its context; it was with prayer that the Muslim approached so serious a matter as the exposition of his faith, and these were the customary words of the prayer.[36] This brings us to the question of the ṣalāt, the ritual prayer proper, which is linked with the profession of faith by the adhān and the iqāmah, and of which the fātiḥah is part.

The preliminary ablutions apparently impinged more strongly on the mediaeval Latin mind than did the prayer itself, perhaps because of the suggestion of Christian parallels. The expectation that in Islam there would be little more than a parody of Christian practices, and some sort of false substitute for the sacraments, was not obviously fulfilled, and there was a predisposition to recognise the sacrament of baptism in ablutions whose true function was only dimly apprehended. Usually quite wild in his ideas, Hildebert was here typical of the Christian approach:

> Quare pollutis haec sit via prima salutis
>   Ut post peccata quisque lavetur aqua . . .

Also early, a matter-of-fact statement passed into Western tradition from Pedro de Alfonso. He described the parts of the body that Muslims wash before they pray 'that they may have perfect cleanness', and he subjoined the classic Christian criticism: 'the relevant thing for prayer is to be cleansed internally, not externally'. Pedro and most other writers after him confused *ghusl* with *wudū'*, and it was almost universally asserted that all the body must be washed before the prayer; it was much stressed that this included the private members. Really, where there had been no *effusio seminis* there would be minor impurity, and therefore no need for major ablution, which it is certainly not customary to perform at each prayer time. The annotator of Ketton, while sharing much of the common confusion, realised this point.[37]

It was often supposed that Muslims believe their ablutions to be for the remission of sin. It was unusual to mention the fact of washings as preliminary to prayer, as Mark did, without comment, or almost with admiration, as did Lull in his description of a Muslim praying, and Ricoldo in his *Itinerarium*.[38] These were spontaneous reactions to factual observations, instead of theoretical disquisitions. The *Liber Nicholay* supposed the Prophet to have taught just that men should pray for forgiveness (in the words of the psalm, *Miserere mei, Deus*, etc.) at the ablution. It was more usual to say that the washings were a false baptism, or imitation of baptism, and to administer the reproof that what was really required was penitence, or interior, not exterior, cleanliness; Muslims were even corrected for having thought that baptism (represented by this false washing) and not confession was for the remission of habitual sin.[39] In the light of so much interpretation in terms chiefly Christian, the curious stress upon the cleansing in the ablution of the sexual parts ought perhaps to be seen as reflecting the importance given to Islamic sexual sin in all mediaeval polemic. One statement reads like a straightforward reference to *ghusl* performed *post coitum*; Verona's circumstantial and absurd description – 'this they do in the presence of all' – is extraordinary in a pilgrim who must often have seen the prayer, but can never have personally observed *ghusl*.[40] The sermonising about interior cleanliness was probably inevitable, particularly as there is relatively little Christian ritual of impurity and cleansing to provide a standard of reference.[41] This subject reveals some familiar aspects of the Christian legend of Islam – interpretation in Christian terms, unwillingness to consider the actual intentions of Islam, and sometimes indignant, horrified scandalisation at a fiction of the Christians' own imagining.

The ritual worship itself interested some writers as another contrivance betwixt and between the Jewish and the Christian;

Pedro de Alfonso pointed out that prayer five times a day was the mean of the Jews' three and the Christians' seven. Acqui thought there were seven Muslim prayer times, but rightly specified the time of the mid-day prayer as *after the passage of noon*, where Verona mistakenly had *at noon*, evidently unaware how scrupulously Islam avoids the semblance of sun-worship.[42] Giovanni d'Andrea's informant was more detailed. He said that the first prayer at dawn was called ṣalāt as-subḥ, meaning morning prayer; the second was at terce, the third at vespers, the fourth at compline and the fifth at twilight 'which in their language is called *in darkness*'.[43] That the prayer begins with the fātiḥah the annotator had already pointed out – it was 'the beginning and the end of all their prayers'. Lull's description already referred to, of the Muslim who precedes an important operation with prayer, is in fact a rather loose description of a whole rak'ah:

After this, laying his head to the earth and in a kneeling posture kissing the earth, he three times rested his head upon it, and raising his heart and his eyes to Heaven, he said these words, In the name of the Most High, the merciful Creator . . .

The only words that he could actually quote were those of the fātiḥah; he had doubtless seen the ṣalāt often enough, but does not seem to have discussed it, despite his very many opportunities, with a Muslim; yet the ritual was less well observed by others.[44]

There were recurrent references, especially in Crusading chronicles, to Muhammad's being 'adored' in the mosques, and this means that the communal ṣalāt was thought to be some sort of liturgical worship of the Prophet, perhaps only comparable to Christian services beseeching the suffrages of saints. We have noted Friar Simon's speaking of the prayer as consisting in the 'praises of Muhammad'. Even Mark of Toledo repeated an assertion that in mosques that had once been churches now 'wicked men devote supplications to the execrable Muhammad'.[45]

Although the words, and often the intention, of the prayer were unknown, a few observers saw that it was a communal act when performed in the mosques. Vitry's account is muddled; he confused adhān with iqāmah and both with the prayer proper, and had no very clear idea of any of these; yet his idea of the ṣalāt was congregational, so that he perceived an important point which many Christians did not notice. He said that the mu'adhdhin proclaimed 'in the ears of all' that Muhammad's Law is holy and just, and that he is the highest prophet sent by God; 'all the others in response affirm it to be so; and this they believe to be enough for them for salvation'.[46] It seems that in the minds of Varagine and Benvenuto, as in Vitry's, was a close association of the profession of faith and the prayer: both began their accounts of the adhān, 'when they pray, they profess . . .' (*orantes profitentur*). Ricoldo understood better what happened in the mosque. 'When they assemble for preaching, and in order that the Law may be explained to them, the Khaṭīb, whose duty it is to hold forth, first bares the sword; and he holds it in the hand while he preaches, or else puts it in a prominent place, in order to frighten.'[47] The fault here is to dissociate the khutba ('preaching', etc.) from the prayer, although the sermon actually is integral to the Friday worship; nevertheless, the detail strongly suggests personal observation. The fact is that, although the prayer voiced and performed in unison in the mosque is characteristic of Islamic devotion, this was not understood by the Latins, who were never present, under normal conditions, in the mosque.

Even the fact that there is a special communal prayer, intended to bring together, not small groups, but the whole people – the Friday prayer when the entire Muslim community attended the same mosque – was barely known and rarely appreciated. That Muhammad had addressed the assembly of his own people was occasionally referred to, but not in this connection; it was not realised that this was the origin of the Friday prayer.[48] Only the superficial facts were understood, and more often they were misunderstood, and even elaborately embroidered. To the Latins the salient point about the Friday prayer was often that Friday was the day once sacred to Venus, and in this view the Muslims had once, before Muhammad, worshipped her, and still now treated her day as holy, or even still worshipped her on that day; or, more simply, it was said that it was appropriate that the religion which chiefly served venery should celebrate the day of Venus.[49] There were other less fantastic explanations. Lull and Verona both said that Friday was chosen because that was the day that Adam was created; also because it was the day of Abraham's sacrifice, said Verona; also because it was the day when man entered Paradise, said Lull; but he added that Christians reject it because it is the day of the first sin and the loss of Paradise, as well as of the Passion.[50] The way that Friday was observed was most often obscured.[51] It was customary to treat it as nothing more than, and in no way different from, the obvious parallel of the Christian *Lord's Day* and the Jewish *Sabbath*; but once more false parallels hid the actual differences. In some cases it was just said that Muslims 'celebrated' Friday.

San Pedro, however, said with greater truth that 'Muhammad established that the Muslims pray in a special way' on that day, and Lull criticised Muslims for the shortness of the time they allow for the prayer, only an hour on Friday. James of Acqui was quite wrong to say that Muslims do not work, but feast, on Friday; he took the Christian parallel for granted. James of Verona, however, had noted what actually happened, and with exceptional accuracy: '. . . they work every day of the week (*continuis diebus*), but they have a great devotion for the day of Venus . . . and on that day . . . they close their shops, and all go to their mosques to pray, and stay there for one or two hours, and afterwards return to their work'. Friar Simon remarked the extraordinary care with which the city of Alexandria was policed during the hour of prayer; he noted particularly the curfew imposed for that hour on Christians. He was scandalised because after the prayer some men hurried back to their businesses; others, however, went more properly to the cemeteries to pray for the dead. Others, again, never went to the prayer at all. Lull also disliked the return to work on a holy day, after prayer.[52] Only in a few passages, therefore, is there any distinct suggestion of the almost urban character of the Friday worship, of the absence of festivity, of the alternation of business and prayer, in short, of the functioning of a Muslim community and its expression of religion. Missionaries set on self-immolation frequently chose the Friday worship (or the 'īd worship at the Friday Mosque) as the most public occasion, and perhaps as the most religious occasion, in Islamic life, a time of solemn assembly of all citizens, in order to denounce Islam.[53]

Observation of Muslims praying seems something to have suggested a Christian parallel rather than a Christian contrast, and there was thought to be a connection between the ṣalāt and Christian monachism, just as there was between the ordinary dress of Muslims and the monastic habit. San Pedro said that under the secret influence of the monk, his adviser, 'Muhammad taught his people by what devout and ordered method they should pray, and should most often kneel; all which things the Muslims most punctiliously observe, as though they were monks; in other things, however, they observe monachism very badly indeed . . .' It has never come gratefully to Christian minds that in Islam incontinence, and even unchastity, can come together with prayer and devotion. The theme of false monachism was surprisingly widespread. 'In the likeness of monks, they pray exceedingly in a very ordered way', said Pennis, *multum ornate valde orant*, where the copyist, surely, mistook *ordinate*. Ludolf, too, spoke of their genuflections like those of monks; Higden said only that Muhammad taught them to pray with many genuflections; and the French prisoner quoted by Giovanni d'Andrea in the Clementine gloss remarked that 'at each of these hours (of prayer) the Muslims make certain genuflections, as we do at evening in praise of the Virgin'.[54]

It is probably already clear that not only the ritual acts but the interior devotion of Muslims at prayer willy-nilly impressed not the ingenuous pilgrim only, but the professional critic as well. The anonymous English traveller said: 'Wherever they are on the Earth, at certain hours of the day, with bended knee and prostrated to earth, they adore God devoutly.' This note of the ubiquity of the prayer in Muslim lands recurs; Mark said also that the prayer was to be 'in the mosque or at home'. San Pedro remarked contradictions in the ḥadīth relating to devotion; Muhammad had said that three things, a woman, an ass and a dog, interrupted prayer; and yet he also said that it was of such virtue that not even Satan could hinder it. This was not criticism of the observed devotion of Muslims. In Lull's romance, Blanquerna, the Pope's Arabic secretary told him that, being a man of 'heathen' (i.e. Muslim) birth, he was familiar with the way at their sermons Muslims weep, because they 'preach of devotion and of considerations upon the glory of Paradise and the pains of Hell . . .' One critic would somewhat meanly admit only the semblance of devotion in a dervish who was 'the most enthusiastic emulator of his ancestral traditions, adorned externally, indeed, and in a wonderful way, with the political virtues, very simple in appearance, very humbly dressed, modest in bearing, chary of speech; yet within he was empty'. This in the context may refer to the individual case; but more probably the vanity of all virtue outside the Church is implied. The most remarkable testimony springing from actual observation was once more Ricoldo's:

And what indeed shall I say of their prayer? So great is their scruple in prayer, and so great their devotion, that I was astonished when I saw it and proved it by experience. For three months and a half I travelled with and accompanied Muslim camel-men in the Arabian and Persian desert, nor once did the camel-men break up for any danger, without praying at the set hours both by day and by night, and especially morning and evening. They make the pretence of such devotion in prayer as to dismiss all other things entirely . . .

He described, too, the early training in reverent behaviour in mosques that the children were given, squatting back on their heels His was not the witness of a philarab.[55]

On a technical point, it was taken for granted that the Prophet had adopted the qiblah, the direction of the prayer, out of a contrary-minded attitude to the Christian and Jewish practices. Roderick, in a confused version of an Islamic tradition, mistakenly supposed that Muhammad taught the qiblah before he received his revelations or preached Islam; but almost universally those who mentioned the subject said that the qiblah was to the south. This was usually ascribed to an attempt to be different from the Jews (supposed to face west) and Christians (facing east), while copying both, on the general principle of choosing a point of the compass and directing worship in that particular direction. Higden said that the qiblah was chosen because 'there is plenitude of light' to the south, a remark that seems to be explained by Verona, who said that this was because God would judge in the south, and should be worshipped in the light of noon. This conflicts flatly with Islamic avoidance of apparent sun-worship at sunrise, noon and sunset; it is remarkable that there was general ignorance of this. The information that the qiblah is south is, of course, itself wholly mistaken; the qiblah is Mecca, and south, therefore, only in Syria.[56]

An unexpected omission was the reading aloud of the Qur'ān, which takes an important part in the life of a Muslim city, where the Qur'ān reader is an artist much in demand. It may have been of this that one Christian was thinking when he contrasted Christian psalmody with the *abhominabilis melodia* of Islam. Mark translated the word *Qur'ān* as *lectionarius* and Ketton started to number the earlier sūrahs according to the divisions used for reading; he was not consistent and his numbering became very muddled. San Pedro did refer to readings, but only in one relatively unimportant matter: the Muslims, he said, read the story of the rehabilitation of 'Ā'ishah in their Lent, as Christians do the story of Susannah in theirs. The reverence with which the Qur'ān was taught was favourably described both by San Pedro and by Ricoldo, authors who elsewhere insisted that it was in order to safeguard the Qur'ān that the teaching of philosophy had been excluded from Islam. In one of Lull's fictional debates, that favourite character of his imagining, a good and earnest pagan seeking truth, approached a learned Muslim:

The Tartar found the Muslim reading the Qur'ān to his students, and, saluting him and the students, he was going to tell them the cause of his coming, only the Muslim spoke to him first, and said: I ask you if you will not mind waiting until I have brought this reading to an end; and immediately the one fell silent, and the other in fact began again the interrupted reading.[57]

What was so much appreciated was a certain seemliness and dignity which have always marked the ancient places of study and of worship in Islam. This was true of the ordinary mosques. Lull would have liked to copy the segregation of sexes for the use of churches, and Giovanni d'Andrea, in his Clementine Gloss, remarked the same thing with favour, and also the way people entered a mosque with bare, washed feet, *et cum certa devotione*.

Friar Simon remarked how 'cleanly and really reverently' mosques were kept. The *Liber Nicholay* certainly expresses the local knowledge of Christians in places where Islam was practised, when – with surprise at something superfluous? – it describes how there is no spitting in mosques, so that of necessity people must go outside. It was generally understood that Christians defiled a mosque. Ricoldo also did justice to the ordinary reverent treatment of mosques, where men went barefoot and there was no spitting. Of the schools he spoke more elaborately, and named the two great Baghdad foundations, the Nizāmīyyah and the Mustanṣirīyyah. He admired the provision of board and lodging for provincial students, out of public funds, and he admired also the monastic spirit of these foundations, the austerity of a bread and water diet, and the students themselves, who, 'content with these things, in the greatest poverty pursue contemplation and study'. He was convinced that the Qur'ān was despised by those Muslims who followed philosophical studies which the caliphal government had, for that very reason, forbidden; and even that the learned Muslims derided secretly the Qur'ān in which they publicly professed their faith. In spite of this tendency to know better than the Muslims themselves what they thought and felt, he did justice to the atmosphere of learning:

But in their common schools, where the Qur'ān is expounded . . . they never enter, except barefoot. Therefore the master who expounds, as much as the pupils who listen, leave their shoes outside, and go into the schools barefoot; and there they read and dispute with the greatest gentleness and moderation.[58]

There was only very occasional perception of these Islamic virtues of propriety, moderation and learning; sometimes there was a more, sometimes a less, grudging admission of the popular strength of Muslim devotion, and some appreciation, in a dim form, of the details of Islamic ritual worship was commoner. Apart from this, the realities of Islamic worship were only distantly represented by these writers. The worship of individuals, which many Christians had had the daily opportunity to watch, was scarcely better known than the prayer at the mosque, which they could never have been allowed to attend. There was little curiosity on the Christian side, in spite of a general taste for the fantastic or the scandalous. Much that was known of the details was discoloured by the interpretation of Islam in the light of Christian practices. On subjects like the Friday prayer and the qiblah the real facts were not established, probably because it was taken for granted that there was no significant point by which they might be distinguished from Christian models. There was some invention

of 'facts', as in the details of the ablution, and the same subject
exemplifies forced misinterpretation, in this case, as pseudobaptism.
Christian comparisons, such as the equation of the hours of the
ṣalāt with those of the Christian Office, overshadowed every aspect,
and there was no reasoned contrast between Christian and Muslim
ritual over a large field. The entire subject brought no disgrace to
Islam, led, indeed, often to praise of it; and it may well have
seemed an unprofitable subject to pursue to mediaeval authors
concerned both to edify and to educate their public.

5. PILGRIMAGE TO MECCA: THE ḤAJJ

The pilgrimage to Mecca was early illuminated, and, it is
possible to say, at the same time obscured, by Pedro de Alfonso.
His interest was close both in the ḥajj itself and in the history of
the Ka'bah, the House of God which is the object of the pilgrims'
devotion. He knew something of the actual ceremonies, of the
iḥrām dress and the stoning (rajm), and he described the foundation of Bayt Allah, Domus Dei, by Adam, and its restoration by
Ismael and Abraham. To this Islamic pretence, he insisted, must
be opposed the truth that the Ka'bah had been a centre of the
worship of pagan idols until Muhammad purged it. He established
an anti-Islamic and pagan pedigree for the Ka'bah: two holy
stones, one white, one black, were named Chamos and Mercurius
respectively, by Amon and Moab, the sons of Lot. These were
worshipped by the Arabs, each at a separate solar festival, and
Muhammad, unable entirely to destroy the worship, had the
Saturn stone set backwards in the wall of the Ka'bah, and the Mars
stone, which was carved back and front, buried in the ground.
Miss d'Alverny has suggested that this account explains in part
the obscure and fanciful references with which Mark of Toledo
opens his Preface to his translation of the Qur'ān; and Grégoire
relates Pedro's information to mediaeval Jewish polemic against
both Islam and Christianity as idolatrous, and also to the 'idols'
alleged by the chansons de geste. There is even a possible mediaeval identification of Muhammad (Mahom or Malchom) with
Moloch; and, be that as it may, there was clearly thought to be
some polemic value in identifying the Muslims with the Ammon-
ites and Moabites condemned in the Old Testament by name.
Pedro's reasonably scientific account of the Islamic view was given
a widening publicity, exemplified by the Anonymous Minorita,
which omits his rationalised explanations and Christian criticism,
however, as do the Legenda Aurea and Peter de Pennis. Marino
Sanudo, explicitly citing Pedro as his authority, paraphrased both
of the relevant paragraphs of his source in one clear and consecutive passage. He 'improved' the source, suppressing Pedro's

unambiguous admission that Muhammad himself abolished the idol-worship that he found, so far as he was able; and he introduced the motif by which the lapidation became a deliberate form of Venereal worship.[59] For Pedro, the worship associated by Islam with the Ka'bah was invalidated by the pagan history of that shrine, which was true, as its Qur'anic pedigree was not; but this point of view was very moderate in comparison with Marino's, according to which Muhammad wished to preserve paganism. Of course, Marino knew better than that, and simply copied an account that he thought good propaganda, and that he could not be certain was not true.

The Risālah, in this matter faithfully represented both by Peter of Toledo and by Vincent of Beauvais, recognised in the practices of the ḥajj itself customs that were also known among pagan Indians: there was the circumambulation, lapidation and the howling of the crowd. The whole thing (in this version) was related equally to the paganism of the Old Testament and to that of the Hindus; and in both cases paganism meant the worship of Venus. In this the text appears to belong to the same general tradition as that to which Pedro subscribed, but the details which it contains most curiously do not seem to have attracted the attention of other writers. The Risālah in this was less than usually influential.

With all these writers we may contrast San Pedro Pascual's short paragraph which is not wholly accurate, yet reflects better than others the spirit of the ḥajj.

Muhammad also taught them that every year they should betake themselves to the House of God, which is in the city of Mecca, to pray and give thanks, and that they should make the circuit of it, wearing seamless garments; and should throw stones between their trouser-legs, to roll over the pavement of the House, so that as they say, the demon should be stoned by them.

Most of the features of this passage,[60] mistaken ones like the idea that there was a duty of annual pilgrimage upon Muslims, and the backwards act of lapidation; and true ones, such as the seamless garment, the circuit and the stoning of the demon, are common to San Pedro and his converted Jewish namesake and predecessor. Yet the terms of the two accounts are unlike. This, as well as the presence of new elements (such as the fictional stoning *over the pavement*) guarantees the independence of San Pedro's sources; we must suppose that he drew upon a living and oral tradition which Christians and Jews living in Islamic Spain may to some extent have shared. The changed tone of the passage contributes an original element, as it recognises a reasonable and even a religious intention: *they betake themselves to the House of God to pray and give thanks.*

Outside the influence of Pedro de Alfonso and the Risalāh, and whatever was San Pedro's source, the ḥajj was hardly comprehended at all.[61] There was some knowledge of the doctrine that Abraham founded the *Domus Dei,* and some evidence that the devotion of the pilgrims made an impression. Pilgrimages, like the adhān, were forbidden by the Council of Vienne, as a public reproach to Christendom, when performed by the subjects of Christian princes. Humbert had already noted that 'there is not thought to be one Muslim who does not pay a visit to the tomb of this fellow Muhammad'. The devotion of Islam receives a faint reflection in Mark's brief statement that Muslims were taught to 'go up to the temple of Mecca, *because of prayer'* and in James of Acqui's confused version 'once in two years they go to the House of God, which is in Mecca, *to pray'.*[62]

A few late writings showed more interest in the *'īd,* the feast with which Muslims everywhere celebrate the completion of the ḥajj, than in the ḥajj itself. Lull pointed out that Islamic sacrifice is quantitatively as well as qualitatively inferior to the Christian, since there is only the annual sacrifice of a single sheep, in honour of the sacrifice of Abraham. Incidental reference to the *'īd* as *pascha eorum* occurred in very different contexts. Verona gave his account a practical rather than a theological emphasis. He knew that a caravan crossed all Arabia, carrying its food supply with it; 'īd al aḍḥā' he dated eccentrically from the end of Ramaḍān. Throughout Islam

they make a great feast, in such a way that whoever is able to buys a live ram, and on that day he cuts off its head, and eats it, together with all his household and family; and he calls in all the poor men of the neighbourhood, and gives them to eat of the same ram; and thus on that day they make their Pasch in honour of Abraham.

This is well observed and implies intelligent questioning of Muslims; it brings out that social character which marks all the different aspects of Islamic religious practice, but which mediaeval writers were slow to recognise.[63]

In many accounts the influence of truth can only dimly be discerned. It was very generally believed that the Prophet's body was in Mecca; this cardinal error was found in a fine variety of forms which presuppose that the ḥajj was imagined as a Christian pilgrimage to the relics of a saint.[64] Roderick said that the Muslims made a mosque in Mecca of the house where Muhammad was born. Peter de Pennis reproduced Pedro de Alfonso's often quoted and relatively reliable passage, but inserted the phrase, *ubi jacet corpus Machometi*, as his personal contribution, at mention of the *Domus Dei* at Mecca. Guido Terrena seems more obviously to reveal a similar admixture of fact and fable. He knew that the *Domus Dei* was claimed to have been founded by Adam and to have been the place of prayer of Abraham and Ismael; in the same sentence he asserted that Muhammad was buried there. He knew about the stoning of the Devil, but he thought that the purpose of the pilgrimage was to 'adore Muhammad with shameful idolatry'. This suggests that he took the passage from Pedro de Alfonso in the form in which Pennis rendered it, then heightened the effect on his own account, and finally, like a Church Council, extracted propositions for condemnation. The mistake about Muhammad's tomb had extraordinary vitality. Lull appealed to the witness of converted Muslims to deny the legend of the tomb magnetically supported in the air, but twice he insisted that Muslims made Muhammad out to be buried in Mecca, which casts some doubt on his attitude to evidence; he would not appeal to the witness of unconverted Muslims, presumably because it would be inherently unreliable. Yet he made it clear that the object of Muslim devotion was the Meccan Temple which, as founded by Adam, Muhammad taught should be adored. The value even of muddled accounts such as some we have referred to stands out by contrast with a reference to the pilgrimage to Mecca, *ubi jacet corpus illius porci vilissimi*.[65]

6. THE FAST OF RAMAḌĀN

To this day, Christians and Muslims despise each others' methods of fasting. Mediaeval Europeans, like other Christians, believed in a long debilitating fast which would strengthen the spirit while it weakened the flesh, but which never required total abstention. Muslims intend, not bodily weakening, but intense discomfort for a series of limited periods; they take nothing, not even a drop of water, from sunrise to sunset, but the nights of their fast are festive occasions. Each side maintains that the other does not really fast at all.

Certainly the Latins never sought to know the intention of the Muslim fast. Pedro de Alfonso even complained that, far from debilitating the flesh, it strengthened it. Vitry said that Christians called the month of the Islamic fast the 'pagan (= Muslim) Lent': this was the comparison which would always sharpen Christian criticism. He exaggerated the festive night grossly, saying that it was taken to the point of drunkenness and vomiting. It is not surprising to find Guido Terrena expressing the same idea. San Pedro Pascual introduced his own interpretation when he said that Muslims failed to fast at night because they hoped in darkness to be able to deceive God; this was not even consistent with known facts, since he must have been familiar with the night-time illuminations. Elsewhere he showed himself aware of those readings from the Qur'ān which are typical of Ramaḍān, and once again he kept the Lenten comparison in mind. Lull compared Muslim and Christian fasting rather crudely as just the easy and the hard.[66]

That the sexual act, even performed conjugally, was permitted during the nights of Ramaḍān heightened the scandal given by the alternation of festival and fast by night and day; Viterbo and the Gregorian Report and Vitry all stressed it, and so did a wholly unrelated author, Friar Simon, who spoke, not of wives, but of women; Fidenzio, with restraint and accuracy, quoted the Qur'ān correctly: '(your wives) are your garments, and you are their garments'. Marino, using phrases from Pedro de Alfonso, reproduced his traditional argument with some force. Verona put the same case less strongly, but said that Ramaḍān was constituted in order to obliterate the thought of Lent from the hearts of Muslims.[67]

Sometimes facts, or supposed facts, were mentioned without critical comment. Roderick was not very interested in condemning Ramaḍān, and he mentioned Muḥarram as well. Mark was interested to explain that a rich man might redeem the fast he owed, if he had been prevented from fasting at the right time, by gift of alms; or a poor man might do the same by a voluntary fast. Viterbo and the Gregorian Report were partly accurate; they knew that the sick and travellers were excused in Ramaḍān the fast they must later make up; Varagine, the *Anonymus Minorita* and Pennis followed Pedro de Alfonso in his factual statement about Ramaḍān, and not in his comment; and by doing so they achieved what was at once the most accurate and the least committed statement. This is even more striking in Higden's summary, and in Mandeville's brief extract. Ricoldo counted both fast and prayer as burdens of religion in Islam that at least were not negligible. The contrast between the fasts of the two religions was often in mind even when it was not explicitly developed.[68]

Perhaps it is not surprising that the Muslim reason for the institution of the fast was lost sight of, or, more often, never known. Only the Cluniacs, Peter the Venerable, and the Annotator from whom he presumably gained his knowledge, mention that the fast marks the Night of Power, laylat al-qadar, on which the Qur'ān descended upon Muhammad; and even they did not know that the Night occurs (once) *during* the fast, but spoke of the descent of the Qur'ān, as occurring throughout the thirty nights of the month. The Annotator combined much that was typical of

Christian writers, as well as describing accurately the calculation of daybreak, for which Pedro de Alfonso was the only other source. He sneered graphically at the festivities of the nights: '... watching by their churches, which they call mosques, they chatter and dance and drink and rave; their fasting is of such a kind that they fast all day, and all night they really do not stop eating, drinking and copulating.'[69]

7. THE POOR-RATE: ZAKĀT

Ketton's annotator it was who also first drew attention to the Qur'anic stress on alms as an Islamic practice; the point was picked up and slightly elaborated in the *summula*: 'he commended zeal for alms and certain works of mercy'. Ketton's own translation was inexact, without minimising the charity of Islam generally.

> To pour out prayers to the east or the west by no means makes men faithful and true; but to believe in God and to bear faith in the coming of the next world, and in the angels and the Books, and the prophets; and to bestow their money in kindness on their relations, on orphans, on the poor and on beggars who ask in requital, and on prisoners; to pay debts to God, to have faith and constancy in words; in an unpleasant time to put up with evil and dispute: all these things, I say, make perfect those who fear and are faithful to God.

Especially in the latter part, this passage is one of Ketton's less happy translations, and it omits the phrase of the original that refers to payment of the poor-tax as distinct from voluntary alms. Thus the inheritance from the Cluniac corpus was true in its general effect, illustrating Islamic praise of alms and, up to a point, practical charity; but it was careless and vague in that the specific obligation of zakāt was ignored.[70]

This set the almost universal tone. Vitry's genuine interest in Islamic practice fell short of enquiry into the accuracy of his own material; thus he said that Muhammad 'much commended alms and prayers' and yet that Muslims 'do not pay tenths'. If he meant that alms were not specified or required legally, he was mistaken. *Liber Nicholay* speaks of specific payments as specific times, but gives no detail. Humbert spoke of the 'certain praiseworthy works of piety, of alms, prayers, fasts and suchlike' inserted into Islam. Acqui, later, was equally vague. Yet the impression left was strong, in spite of its imprecision: to a Franciscan living in the Holy Land, the example of the charity of the sultan who freed a slave at his servant's request came to mind quite naturally in an unpolemic context.[71]

Greater precision did exist. Mark of Toledo made only a passing reference: 'Yield the tenths and the first-fruits to God, to

the King, who among them discharges the office of priest, and to
his agent, and avoid sins'; he understood that there was a tax as
well as an act of virtue in question. Ricoldo alone, in that unique
group of passages in his *Itinerarium* which express his personal
observations, and on which I have drawn so largely in the present
chapter, did the subject that justice which the rest of his work
denied to Islam.

On the subject of pity for the poor, it ought to be known that Muslims
are most generous of alms. They have a strict command in the Qur'ān
to give a tenth; and they are required to give a fifth part of such things
as they acquire by force of arms. Yet beyond these things they make
great legacies, and put them in a treasury, and at an established time they
open them, and give them to a trustworthy Muslim, who goes off to the
different provinces and redeems prisoners, and Muslim slaves who are
held prisoner among Christian or other nations. Often they even buy
Christian slaves who are held prisoner among the Muslims themselves,
and take them to the cemetery and say, 'I redeem so much for the soul
of my father, and so much for the soul of my mother', and give them
letters of freedom and send them away. But for the poor, who cannot
redeem a slave, these Muslims carry wild birds in cages, and cry, 'Who
wants to buy these birds and free them for his father's soul?'

Equally astonishing to him were testamentary gifts to feed dogs
and river birds, and, finally, the existence of an agreeable hospital
with medical provision for the mentally deficient.[72] It is obvious
that Ricoldo was constrained to an awed and almost uncompre-
hending admiration; but it is curious that he should only barely
have mentioned gifts to religious trusts (awqāf) for purposes more
familiar in the West: not only the redemption of captives, but also
the endowment of mosques, hospitals and hostels. Similar accounts
would become commoner in later centuries when there was more
travelling and so more personal observation of Islam.

Yet prejudice could always overcome observation. Lull went so
far as to stress the benefactions habitually made by Christians to
churches, monasteries and hospitals for the poor, the sick and
travellers; and he added opprobriously: 'But I never heard that
the Muslims have more than two hospitals, one Tunisian and the
other in Alexandria.' Muslims have always been deservedly
famous for precisely the things for which he here praised Christians
exclusively.[73]

On this theme we cannot speak of any exact knowledge that was
widespread; only of a general impression that Muslims gave alms
freely, rather in the manner that Christians should do.

8. CHURCH AND CLERGY

The payment of tenths, and in particular Mark's reference to

the king who 'among them discharges the office of priest' draws
attention to the difference between the ecclesiastical establishments
which Christendom and Islam maintained. There is an interesting
contrast expressed by Humbert. He reproached the tepid Christian
clergy for grudging to God, that is, to the Crusade, those un-
earned tithes which the farming men paid, out of the greatest
labour and sweat, cultivating their lands. Thus in this Christian
picture the *decimae* were paid in Islam to the poor, but in Christendom, not just to clergy, but to clergy who would not employ it for
the work of God. For Lull, who, in his eccentric way, gave this
problem more thought than most other Christians did, the Muslim
failure to maintain a clerical establishment on a scale comparable
to the Christian was another inherent evidence of the inferiority
of Islam in the service of God. He combined a somewhat modern
perception which stressed the absence of sacraments in a priestless
religion with that intellectual clowning to which he was so prone.
The Christian Church, he said, had ten clerics for every Muslim
cleric, and for every prayer made by the Muslim cleric ten or more
were made by the Christian. This quantitative assessment of
prayer seems to ignore the orisons of the Christian laity as
statistically negligible, as well as those of ordinary Muslims.
Similarly he claimed that Christians honoured their Church because
they had Pope, Cardinals, Archbishops, Bishops and so on, whose
excommunications the rich, the powerful and the people all feared
alike. It was not so with the Muslims: 'their Bishops are poor
men, and so are their priests; and they have wives and children,
and really the greater proportion take part in trades . . .' What
this author here so clearly but not altogether intentionally reveals
is the popular character of Muslim worship, the organisation of
the religious duties which constitute it, communally rather than
clerically.[74]

The relation of the Muslim 'clergy' to their 'laity' was not
generally formulated although it was referred to remotely or
implicitly. Friar Simon assumed that the mu'adhdhin was a *priest*
or *cleric*. Thus, too, the informant of the commentator on the
Clementinae spoke of two kinds of Islamic 'clergy'; those who
served the mosques, he said, were *Foqua*, in the singular, *Foqui*
(for fuqahā' and faqīh); they were equivalent to the Christian
secular clergy, but were married and lived in the mosques. The
fuqahā' were better described by Ricoldo as 'great doctors and
expositors'. These are references to the Arabic word; there were
many references in Latin to the *sapientes Saracenorum*, that is,
fuqahā' or 'ulamā'; the phrase generally implies men learned in
the law or authoritative in defining it. From the Christian point
of view all these functionaries were men living in the ordinary

Islamic community, more like lawyers than like clergy. Christians also recognised what they called *Religious* (from Religious Orders – *fuqarā'*, *faqīr*), people either described in very vague terms, or said to be itinerant ascetics. The *fuqarā'*, said Verona, 'are held in great reverence among them; and they go about preaching and teaching the Law and the wonders of Muhammad'. Some of these Religious were bizarre in their activities; Ricoldo said that there were *religiosi* in Baghdad so desperate as to do away with themselves by walking in fire barefoot 'that men may admire'; and who ate scorpions and snakes, not only raw, but raw and living. These were the true miracles of Antichrist's precursors. Ludolf described men who constricted their naked bodies in iron rings and who beat themselves in expiation for not having had many wives; and others lived like beasts in the deserts, and would not look at the faces of women, although women were accustomed to consult them about the state of their loved ones' souls. After a night of watching and flagellation they would reply, according to the money they had received, in Heaven, or in Hell. This hodge-podge of travellers tales, or pilgrims' tales, possibly reflects the real eccentricities of darwishes; Ricoldo's account certainly looks authentic. It seems obvious that in each case the Christian writer is thinking of the Muslim holy man as a false Religious in the Christian sense.[75]

There was some attempt at an equation of Islamic and Christian dignitaries. It was widely said that the caliph was the 'heir or successor' of Muhammad, and, as was inevitable, he tended to be equated with the Pope; he was *sicut papa eorum*; the whole East venerated him in his city of Baghdad as the West venerated the Pope.[76] Superficially, the quasi-theocracy of the West approximated to the Islamic combination of the functions of government and of religion. The qāḍī was similarly identified with the bishop; sometimes the *cadini* were thought to form a caste of higher clergy. When Lull referred to a qāḍī as *magnus litteratus*, he realised that *sapientes* and *cadini* overlapped. *Liber Nicholay* equates *Archadi* with *cardinales*.[77]

It was certainly not widely understood that the Islamic attitude was consciously unpriestly, in spite of Mark's reference to the king's functioning for the priest. Ricoldo, duly followed by Pennis, referred with clarity to the Qur'anic condemnation of Christians for making their clergy 'lords'; he pointed out that there was a confusion of the Chaldean term suitably used of men, and the Arabic word used only of God. This was to rebut an objection that Christians might see, but not the objection actually levelled by Muslims to whom religious lordships of any kind, other than God's immediately, is alien. Verona in fact believed that the ordinary dress of Muslims was chosen in order to obliterate the distinction between clergy and laity.[78] The *Liber Nicholay* seems aware of unclerical and anti-Sacramental tendencies, but expresses them in terms of incorrect historical data: Muhammad abolished confession as subject to abuse, and commanded the sale of altar furniture to strengthen his army and feed his people with the proceeds.

Always, Islamic institutions were confused with Christian ones, and were criticised for not being identical with them. So often, the communal and unhierarchic aspects of Islam eluded Christian observers.

9. VARIOUS ISLAMIC PRACTICES

Of some aspects of Islamic religious practice more was made than their significance in Islam would justify. Circumcision and the prohibition of eating pig's flesh are the most important examples. Circumcision was occasionally represented as a false baptism, like the ablution; confirmation might have been a happier, though not a more useful, comparison, and it came to be more usual in the seventeenth-century period. Both of these aspects of Islamic Law were usually treated as examples of the derivative character of Islam, as compounded of Jewish as well as Christian elements.[79]

Only the *reprobatio* noticed the existence of rules that govern eating. Here exaggeration was used as a technique of ridicule. The Hanbali canon that black dogs cannot be eaten because they are jinn was referred directly to the authority of Muhammad; and the rule that the fingers must be licked before they are washed after eating was so stated as to lead to the conclusion, excessive by almost any standards but the most unfriendly, that this rule is 'unclean, bestial and ridiculous'. The prohibition of certain foods, particularly pig, and of wine, in certain writers gave rise to picturesque or curious legends to explain their origins. Here the interest of Christians only reflects the popular practice of Muslims; some food prohibitions, notably that of swine's flesh, have always been taken very seriously by Islam; and the customs of the populace have given circumcision an importance that Muhammad never did. Strictly, circumcision is related to ritual purity, and the rules governing food to questions of impurity; but these matters were never discussed in connection with ablutions, or in the course of any general discussion of religious impurity; no such impurity apart from actual sin was recognised by Christians.

10. CONCLUSION

Authors who were interested in Islamic religious practice were mostly those who, either directly or indirectly, had been in touch with Islam at some point in their lives. The same can be said almost as definitely for authors who showed an interest in the practice by Muslims of what Christians would recognise as virtues. The interest in either Islamic virtue or Islamic religious acts was a very moderate one. It thrived most on contrast: on the one hand, the virtuous actions of Muslims were only interesting in relation to the practice of Christians; on the other, ritual acts were supposed to be poor imitations of Christian models. A few writers drew attention to the absence of any sacramental system in Islam, but more were concerned to see Muslim practices as false-sacraments. In spite of the recognition of Islamic virtue, the idea was widespread that Islam was a religion of outward forms; particularly was this so in connection with the ablutions before the prayer. The French Franciscan Livin, seeking a short formula in which to denounce Islam in public, in the mosque before the sultan and the people, chose to say that the prayer there offered was vain.[80] The virtuous actions of Muslims were certainly thought of as vain; that was what made them so surprising, so impressive to Christians, for they could not avail to salvation.

In all these matters there was much ignorance, and many mistakes were made. Only a reader who was already well-informed would have been able to pick out the statements that were true. There was not even much interest. There was practically no systematic comparison of the interior life of the two religions. What interest did exist was genuine, but it was very limited. Christendom was relatively indifferent to what did not touch immediate Christian interests. This is not to say that there was no perception at all of the realities of Islamic spiritual practices; but these had little significance except as a contrast or a foil to the ways of Christians. Islam was always a reflection, often a muddied reflection, of what was familiar at home. In the consciousness of mediaeval writers, it was never inherently attractive or by its nature edifying. Even when Muslims were seen to obey the divine law in morals, it was usual to interpret Islam as a falling short of being Christian.

This brings out forcibly the contrast between what was observed and what was inferred; between what was accepted on evidence and what was believed even without an adequate authority. At the beginning of this chapter it was said that both modification and confirmation of theory were found in practice. What is really remarkable is that this did not happen more. The basic lines of theory were always stronger and more important than scientific observation. If they conflicted, observation usually proved the weaker; often it aroused no interest at all, but it was always subordinate.

Plate 4

Traditional Christian themes: the contrast between the two religions. (Top: the two Paradises; middle, purification, by baptism and by ablution; bottom, worship, the sun of Christ, and the crescent moon used to symbolise change.)

QVÆ SVNT SPIRITVS SAPIVNT.

QVÆ CARNIS SVNT SAPIVNT.

HÆC LAVAT.

INQVINAT ILLA.

IHS

HISTOIRE
GENERALE
DE LA RELIGION
DES TVRCS.

AVEC LA NAISSANCE,
la vie, et la mort, de leur
Prophete Mahomet, et
les actions des quatre
premiers Caliphes
qui l'ont suiui.
Celles du Prince Mahuuias.
Et les rauages des Sarra-
sins en Europe aux trois
premiers siecles
de leur loy.
Ensemble le tableau de toute
la Chrestienté a la venue
de Mahomet.
Par le Sr. MICHEL BAVDIER
de Languedoc.
A PARIS.

Auec approbation et Priuilege du Roy.

En la Boutique de L'Angelier.
Chez CLAVDE CRAMOISY
au premier Pillier de la grande
Salle du Palais. 1625.

SANCTA SALVTIS.

MVTANDA SEQVNTVR.

❧ VIII ❧

Polemic method
and the judgement of fact

IT is natural to ask how authors whom we can neither patronise
as foolish nor condemn as unscrupulous could consistently have
misrepresented facts, regularly crediting ridiculous fantasies. This
applies particularly to their treatment of the events of Muhammad's
life, but to some extent also to the whole of their attitude to
Islam. We cannot just excuse them as ignorant. Admittedly there
was less misrepresentation and less indulgence in fancy, generally
speaking, by authors whose lives brought them close to Muslim
sources. These were forced, by their contact with Muslims, or by
a study of Arabic material, or simply by a climate of opinion
formed by intercourse between Christians and Muslims, to discard
some absurd stories that remained popular among more remote
or less serious authors. In such circumstances there was no
alternative but to admit a greater degree of what we should now
recognise as truth, and to base polemic on data which Muslims
might accept, and would at any rate recognise. Even so, whenever
a choice between stories, or between interpretations of stories,
occurred, well-informed and ignorant authors alike often accepted
those which were quite untrue in the judgement of modern scholarship, and which, indeed, must have seemed to them highly improbable, had they been alleged of Christians in the world familiar
to themselves.

1. A GENERAL SURVEY OF THE ATTITUDE TO SOURCES

There are many indications of the deliberate editing of source
material in various ways. The greatest editorial achievement of
the twelfth century was unquestionably the Cluniac collection. In
this there appears to have been an exercise of choice on the side
of sobriety. The *summula* relied for facts about the Prophet upon
a sober Greek source.[1] It contains little that it would have been
altogether hopeless to maintain in public debate before a sympathetic or even neutral audience; clearly an editorial effort was
made which is remarkable at least for excluding wilder elements.

Treatment and substance in the *summula* are traditionally Christian, but it is characteristically Western in presentation; there is nothing that an Oriental Christian could have written.[2] Occasionally it seems to summarise, but more generally it ignores, the wealth of material to be found in the Risālah, which in Peter of Toledo's unabridged version belonged to the same corpus and normally the same manuscript.[3] It is not likely that the author of the *summula* did not know it; the presumption is that he felt that Latin and Greek sources were more reliable than Arabic ones, even Christian Arabic ones. This contrasts with San Pedro, who referred to the pseudonymous Christian author of the Risālah, 'Alquindus', as authoritative and knowledgeable, precisely because he wrote in Arabic; in practice, however, he ignored him as completely as the author of the *summula* did.[4]

Yet Peter of Toledo's translation of the Risālah was in fact the greatest Cluniac contribution to the biography of Muhammad and to the history of early Islam. Even so, we cannot attribute the enormous influence of the original work over all intelligent treatment of Muhammad's life solely to this Cluniac translation. William of Auvergne and Vincent de Beauvais, who referred to it expressly as the 'pamphlet of the disputation of a Christian and a Muslim', thought it important principally for its treatment of the textual history of the Qur'ān.[5] It seems likely that the portions of the Risālah that are about the life of the Prophet influenced many authors who may never have seen a complete or even a written text, either in Latin or in Arabic. Another Latin source of the information which the Risālah contributed to the subject of Muhammad's life is the Syrian *Apology*, i.e. the work represented by Viterbo, and later, in only slightly different form, by Paris' Gregorian Report. This does not claim to be identified with any part of the Risālah, but it must in fact be closely related. Vitry, who took over and adapted much of the *Apology* material, was in direct touch with possible sources in his episcopal city of 'Akka. Paris, who had no direct knowledge of Islam, personally accepted this *Apology* version; at least, the form *Nastoreus*, which seems to derive from it (this is the name *Nestor*, in other versions *Sosius*; in the Arabic original *Sergius* the *Nestorian*), Paris personally wrote into the St Albans Chronicle that he had inherited.[6]

The very great influence of the Risālah, in one form or another, is likely to have sprung, as San Pedro himself suggested, from its combination of authenticity with polemic utility. The authenticity of what derived from a Muslim country was generally recognised.[7] The Risālah material, however, had already been selected to illustrate its author's arguments and insinuations about Muhammad; it had not been assembled academically. This explains both

its appeal to mediaeval Europeans, and their general misunderstanding of the context to which the data referred to belong. One
of the greatest of collectors and editors was Vincent de Beauvais;
apart from material relating to geography and recent Crusading
and missionary history, he concentrated what he collected about
Muhammad and Islam in a single sequence of chapters. The
greater part of this is a series of extracts from Peter of Toledo's
Risālah, formed, by the simple omission of the passages of direct
polemic and of abstract theology, into a consecutive life of Muhammad and a short account of the history of the Qur'ān and of its
teaching. This omission of all the passages of argument, which the
quotation of factual matter was intended in the original to illustrate,
completed the process by which the historical facts were divorced
from their contexts. It implies without room for doubt that
Vincent sought facts rather than arguments, but facts useful for
polemic. Vincent preceded his extracts from the Risālah by, first,
the *Corozan* text, which is wholly removed from reality, and might
well be supposed so irreconcilable with the Risālah for it to be
pointless to publish the two together. Between them comes the
libellus in partibus transmarinis in which the false miracles (of
Oriental Christian origin) of the bull and the dove and the springs
of milk and honey are described. Finally, Vincent himself introduced his Risālah extracts as giving further, when he might better
have said conflicting, information. It seems probable that he
could not bring himself to give up the less likely and more gratifying for the sake of its reverse. He was probably impressed by the
quality of self-evident authenticity in the Risālah material, but he
could not be certain that the more legendary stories that he also
repeated were unreliable; he had no first-hand experience of Islam
and might quite reasonably suspect sobriety, rather than
picturesque fable, whereas the space in fact devoted to the former
shows that he esteemed it highly. We can only say that he collected
information about Islam which might be useful in attacking it,
without noticeable care for consistency, and that he ignored
theoretic disputation; his approach was scientific, in that he
sought interesting facts; if his intention was partly polemic, his
method was based upon historical assertions about events and not
upon abstract argument.[8]

The encyclopaedist in any case included all the material that
was available to him, without intending thereby positively to
signify assent to it, still less actively to assert its truth. Any
relevant matter was interesting and should be included without
further examination. To some extent most chroniclers, as well as
such writers as Gerald and Caesarius, edifying intellectual gossip-
writers, were encyclopaedic, but by making additions and altera-

tions to the stories they used, and by preferring one verse to another, they often exercised more editorial activity than the true encyclopaedist like Vincent. Humbert of Romans collected an anthology of literature about the Holy Land, the Crusades and the Spanish Reconquest, for the use of preachers; it was wholly uncritical and unselective. Vitry, in different parts of his history, repeated stories based on the imputation of idolatry to Muslims, which were quite inconsistent with his own substantially clear and accurate statements of Islamic belief. Both Varagine and Higden quoted stories that they explicitly realised were irreconcilable; for themselves, they preferred the better, but, as was the custom in such cases, they retained the discredited passages in their texts. As a general rule, there is a wide gap between the most sensible and the least sensible story in a single text.[9]

This phenomenon might be explained simply as a mixture of a poor judgement with an enquiring spirit. The same thing is at first sight suggested by the disparity of works associated in single manuscripts. A rare manuscript of the Latin original of Ricoldo's *Disputatio* is followed by a composite account of Islam which is interesting just because it is mixed in quality; part derives from Pedro de Alfonso, part represents a version of the Corozan text and perhaps the *libellus* of Vincent. The same mixed account occurs in the midst of an even more impressive collection in Cambridge, a short Muslim creed, the *reprobatio* and Tripoli and a number of excellent works of travel and history, Marco Polo and Haytun in particular. Another Cambridge manuscript perhaps omits this account deliberately, because it includes the *reprobatio* and Tripoli; however, the beginning of this manuscript is incomplete; it also includes Marco Polo as well as Odoric *de ritibus orientalium Regionum*, Peter of Russia *de ortu Tartarorum* and Tudebodus and Vitry. Ricoldo's *Itinerarium* occurs in a manuscript of oriental travels, not of theology. Peter de Pennis included fabulous stories about Muhammad in a work which was otherwise serious and derived from Ricoldo and Pedro de Alfonso.

There was an extraordinary variety of permutations and combinations of the items in the legend of Muhammad, and even in versions of Islamic religion, in many different books; this is in itself an indication of the amount of choosing and discarding of material that went on, but not of the reasons underlying this. Apparently the interest was often geographical and historical rather than theological; the marvellous – both strange and magical – had its special appeal; the authentic and the fabulous were about equally attractive, at least to an educated public; all reference to Muhammad and Islam was derogatory, and must be considered polemical.[10] One remarkable manuscript collection of the four-

teenth century noted by Miss d'Alverny contained, in addition to
the whole *Corpus Toletanum* (including Peter of Toledo), the
Qur'ān of Mark of Toledo, a *Prophetia* and the *Liber Nicholay*.
The last is itself an amalgam of rare information, accurate, or
nearly so, fabulous, and even ridiculous, and it is remarkable that
it and the Prophecy should have been included in this unique
collection of documents that is an entire library of authentic
information about Islam. They represent a tolerant and comprehensive attitude rather than a highly critical one.

It is curious that Peter the Venerable's own polemic was not
associated with the main corpus in the manuscripts, or, conse-
quently, by Bibliander; this may be the result of accident, but it
suggests, as did Vincent's treatment of Peter of Toledo's Risālah
text, that the European public was more interested in facts about
Muhammad and Islam than in argued polemic. It seems probable
that in some writers' eyes the great polemic lay in the selection,
arrangement and presentation of supposedly factual material,
rather than in such argumentation as Peter the Venerable, for
example, based upon it. Ratiocination might be superfluous, even
distracting, when a selection of facts – allegations – could be
relied on to induce the desired reaction in the mind of the reader.[11]

Although facts were sometimes more popular than argumentation, yet facts which stated a case had an attraction at the expense
of such as did not. The Cluniac Qur'ān might have been used as a
mine of information about the Prophet's life, but it does not seem
to have contributed either to Cluniac or to other biographies.
Verses of the Qur'ān which relate to historical events were not
polemically utilised until the thirteenth century in the West.
There was a very limited interest in some of the other Cluniac
translations, but, apart from the Risālah, the *de doctrina Machometi*
was a rich source of largely legendary, while authentically Islamic,
material about Muhammad. Both it and the *Liber Scalae Machometi*
were more popular sources of information about Muhammad than
the Qur'ān, because they could be more easily ridiculed. The same
attitude is implied by Mark's Preface to his Qur'ān. His own
faithful translation of the Qur'ān appears to be the sole source of
the paraphrase of Islamic doctrine in which he summarises the
teaching of the Prophet; but he gave equal prominence and credit
to a fictitious and very ordinary biography of Muhammad in this
same short preface.[12]

The ultimate editorial selection was made by the general
public. Some of the works on Islam which from a modern point
of view are most admirable had a very restricted circulation. We
have already seen how little Peter the Venerable's own work was
known, in spite of the wide distribution of the rest of the collection,

itself probably due, as Miss d'Alverny has said, to the weight of Peter's name. Mark of Toledo's translations had no popularity, although they were far more accurate than Ketton's work. The *reprobatio* is known in two forms, one wrongly attributed to Ricoldo and preserved in one manuscript, and the other known in two groups of closely associated pairs, of which one pair attribute the work to John of Wales, who cannot be its author. The *Contrarietas* itself is known only in one (sixteenth-century) manuscript. Even Ricoldo's own work was little known in the Middle Ages. The *Itinerarium* was printed in modern times from a single manuscript, and the *Disputatio* owes its great fame to the Renaissance retranslation of the fifteenth-century Greek version by Demetrius Cydones; only three manuscripts of the original Latin are known to the present writer. San Pedro's public was also very limited. Readers, even serious readers, were shy of the more serious works, and preferred to be amused as well as edified. Sources of sound information which did receive a wide circulation were Pedro de Alfonso, who was often quoted upon the subject of Islam, apart from the circulation of his *Dialogi* whole; the Risālah, in its different forms, and extracts from Tripoli; we may add the Cluniac translations and the *Liber Scalae*. Except for Pedro, whose work belonged primarily to anti-Judaic polemic literature, the popularity of a few works must have been due to their providing the easy reading matter about Islam that their public sought.[13]

A quick survey of the period suggests that writers often quite unconcernedly combined wholly inconsistent passages, even extremes of accuracy and inaccuracy; that there was a marked preference for what appeared to be facts (of polemic utility or otherwise) over argued polemic; and finally that, although material may often have been repeated because it was interesting, it almost always happened that it had polemic significance as well. Amusement, instruction and controversy were blended. It is worth while to make a closer analysis of the best-informed authors of the thirteenth century; they too failed to discriminate between reliable and unreliable sources, combined conflicting material, and sometimes preferred the poorest.

2. ANALYSIS OF INDIVIDUAL AUTHORS

In this connection, perhaps the most interesting and informative case is that of San Pedro Pascual, the writer most explicitly to contrast his Muslim and his Christian sources. Some of his comments provide a clue to the editorial activities of other writers. His Christian sources were among the most fabulous and fantastic, including versions of the disappointed Roman cleric, Maurus, who inspired Muhammad, and of the bull and dove pseudomiracles.

Yet in saying that these things were discovered by Christian writers, he admitted implicitly that they were formally denied by Islam. His Islamic sources were of the very best; he often apparently follows ibn Isḥāq. He was aware, too, that Arabic sources were valuable as such: 'Alquindus, who was from Arabia, and a Christian, extremely learned and skilled in the Arabic language'. He was not prepared definitely to discard the 'Christian' stories, however absurd, and was fairly convinced that aspects were true. Modern scholarship assumes that the Christian legend grew out of the Muslim one; San Pedro reckoned that the Muslim one went some way towards admitting, and unintentionally revealing, the Christian. He noted that Muslim (or, he added, Jewish) sources hinted at the truth of certain allegations about the Prophet:

Since, indeed, what is not found in authentic books no one ought to assert as certain, I neither affirm nor deny what I have written above about bulls and about Muhammad's death . . .

(This referred to the Christian legend that Jews murdered Muhammad and threw the body to swine; and to the Arabic story that Zaynab the Jewess of Khaybar poisoned him.)

. . . Yet the evidence that it is true that the Jews killed Muhammad is not lightly presumed; and it is made credible by what the Muslims themselves assert. From another angle it is certain that in their books is contained a certain Christian hermit, whose name, as they say themselves, was Baḥīrā – the one who said to Muhammad's uncle, who brought him up, that he should protect Muhammad from the Jews . . .

It seemed likely, not only that the Baḥīrā of Muslim legend was the same as the Christian apostate whom Muhammad, in Christian legend, customarily consulted, but also that Islamic sources betrayed the hidden truth when they spoke of Muhammad's retirement from the world just before the first revelation, in the hills around Mecca – this suggested that the time was really spent with the renegade, secretly preparing the details of the fraud. Similarly San Pedro identified the angel who was the vehicle of revelation in Islamic eyes with the dove, trained by Muhammad, of which Christian legend spoke; he identified the Muslim story of ox or bull that spoke miraculously for Muhammad with the Christian tale of a bull bearing the bogus book of the Law on his horns. Earlier in the same work he had written that all those things which were alleged by Christian, and seemed to be referred to by Muslim sources, represented 'a strong presumption, even certain proof' of the Christian assertions. This statement is too strong; it does not really represent his attitude. In practice he did not treat either series as certainly true; he treated them as being to an unknown extent mutually confirmatory.

His own summary of the stories he had selected from Muslim
sources to illustrate the life of the Prophet is instructive in this
connection. A consideration, he said, of what he had taken from
the Qur'ān and the other books of the Muslims would show that
Muhammad was demoniac, and that he admitted to the Meccans
that he was not sent to work miracles. It would show that the
Meccans reproached him for claiming as a revelation from God
what it was known 'a certain man' had taught him; that he killed
one Jew treacherously, as well as other Jews who accepted his
dominion; that he took as wife a beautiful Jewess, the 'lady' (i.e.
feudal lady) of the Jews, after killing the men and making the
women and children prisoners. Muhammad called himself messenger of God, yet seduced the wives of his own people, and in
God's name invented a law to justify his being allowed whatever
he desired. San Pedro also selected a separate, second list of what
were to his mind significant Muslim admissions: Muhammad's
having retired into solitude before he received the revelation from
Gabriel, the Meccan accusation that he had a secret teacher, the
story that his Jewish concubine poisoned him so that he sickened
and ultimately died, the warning of the hermit (Baḥīrā) that it
would be necessary to protect him from the Jews, 'Umar's inability to believe that he had died, his death with 'Ā'ishah as sole
witness, his burial under her bed. The second list contains only
stories that seemed to confirm Christian allegations, such as his
being instructed by the hermit, his death by poisoning, the claim
that he would ascend after death to Heaven. The first appears to
contain both stories of this kind and also incidents simply discreditable to the Prophet. It is not clear how far San Pedro recognised
'hidden truths'; in stressing the signs of demoniac possession in
Islamic accounts of the revelation made through Muhammad, he
may have been hinting at the Christian legends of Muhammad as
magus, but this is not certain. What is certain is that the two
series of historical assertions, Christian and Muslim, seemed to
him constantly and significantly to echo each other. This did not
mean that he was prepared to commit himself to the truth of any
single 'Christian' assertion. He could not deny himself the pleasure
of recounting any tale derogatory to the Prophet's honour, but
those that found no apparent Muslim confirmation he was content,
once told, to forget; and even where there was this 'confirmation'
he seems rather to have hoped, than to have been confident, that
the legends circulating in Christendom were true.

He was even willing at least to imagine the possibility that none
of them were true. The contents of the Muslims' books, he argued,
were enough, as they stood, to condemn Muhammad. 'Even if all
these (Christian sources) are left aside, still it is obviously

demonstrated that those things which he himself said are not from God . . .' Doctrine culled from Muslim sources, like information about Muhammad, was 'enough and more than enough for the shame and ruin of his religion; and many things of theirs also, which they (themselves) have written, they ignore, or openly deny, since those who hear them can only laugh'. This seems to refer to such works as the *Liber Scalae* which actually any orthodox Muslim might disown, but which Christians liked to insist was a work of Muhammad's, because it was so suitable for ridicule. San Pedro noted how Muslim sources admitted the Prophet's human weakness, as well as such supposed turpitude as his failure to arrest the practice of magic among the Arabs, among whom paganism thus survived. Christian and Muslim requirements in sanctity are so different that Muslim statements about Muhammad must always be rich soil for the Christian who seeks points of difference. To read San Pedro and Ibn Isḥāq side by side is to be given a striking lesson in the way the same material can be used in order to give totally different impressions. If San Pedro, who knew Islam, was unwilling to surrender any 'Christian' story, it is not surprising that less well-informed writers were more so.[14]

Other writers were less explicit, but it is interesting to see how far their approach resembles San Pedro's. William of Tripoli's work stands apart from that of other writers in many respects, and his presentation of facts was individual, even peculiar. Except for his version of the Baḥīrā legend, which comes direct from the Arabic form, there is no obvious literary source for his biography of Muhammad. He in turn was followed only by Mandeville, whose own editorial talent is illustrated by his reliance on Tripoli's book. Perhaps Tripoli used written or spoken material in Latin or Arabic that was available to him directly or through interpretation in the 'Akka convent. His biography of Muhammad is very patchy in its reflection of reality; his knowledge of the Qur'ān, equally individual but immeasurably superior, suggests that he knew and rejected better material about Muhammad's life than he actually used. Tripoli's historical polemic followed traditional lines, although he made use of stories authentically Islamic in origin.[15] His intentions are obscure. He may have hoped that his words would command the assent of Muslim hearers; his purpose in making his long quotations from the Qur'ān was to show Muslims that their beliefs were really, or nearly, Christian; I think that he may have wanted to convince them that the Bible is the source of the Qur'ān. He clearly excluded the life of Muhammad from this almost oecumenical approach. As long as his purposes remain obscure, it is difficult to assess the reasons for the uneven quality of his historical information about early Islam; but the

fact is that like every other writer he made use of very inferior
material, and particularly what related to Muhammad direct; and
that this is in marked contrast with other parts of his work.

Two writers who were as well informed as San Pedro and who
were equally in a position to make historical judgements were the
author of the *quadruplex reprobatio* and Ricoldo da Monte Croce.
Their methods constitute an interesting contrast. The conclusions
reached by the *reprobatio* often seem for polemic purposes slight:
a whole chapter of quotations from ḥadīth and other Muslim
sources goes to show only that Muhammad claimed to be a
prophet. It is not necessary to suppose that this material was
published out of a disinterested love of historical truth. The whole
work may have been intended to form a source-book for missionaries and controversialists and those who had the cure of souls *in
partibus infidelium*. It lists and classifies quotations from Muslim
books of high authority, al-Bukhārī and Muslim, for example,
relevant to polemic points customarily or popularly made against
Islam, for example, sexual laxity; and it seems likely that the
author's purpose was to make available suitable extracts that
would carry an authority really or arguably undeniable by Muslims,
in support of the theologians' favourite lines of dispute, so far as
that might be possible. There may have been an idea of correcting
less well-informed writings at the same time. The author thought
it important to be able to cite the very 'books of Muhammad'. In
this, and in other ways, the *reprobatio*, though more concise in
scope and method, has qualities in common with that of San Pedro.
Part is certainly devoted to proving the humanity of the Prophet;
the author will have known that Muslims claimed not otherwise,
but he may have felt it useful to insist, against popular Muslim
devotion, on Muhammad's very ordinary humanity. Of the death
in the arms of 'Ā'ishah he remarked: 'from this it is clear that the
death or end of Muhammad was vile, unclean and abominable, and
such a death by no means suits a Prophet or Messenger of God'.
The weakness of humanity, even when no sin was involved, was
a major offence in a recipient of a divine mission. Facts were used
polemically by this author, while first making sure that they were
facts indeed; it is curious that he made little or nothing of the
events between the call to the prophethood and the Prophet's
death. In spite of this, and perhaps because of its economy and
sobriety, his work remains more impressive polemically than
most Christian controversial writing; his copious use of extracts
from Islamic sources effortlessly effects his comparatively limited
ends. He achieved what others attempted, because he alone knew
the secret of self-discipline in the choice of material. His method
provides a further clue to what others did. He, like them, chose

only facts that he believed discreditable to Islam, and it was the
less discreet search for such facts that betrayed others into using
more and less authentic material mixed without distinction
together.[16]

Ricoldo's treatment was in some ways the reverse. He was
singularly indiscriminate in his choice of material; this may be
masked by his equally indiscriminate, and more obvious, use of
argument. In Ricoldo's *Disputatio* there is an overwhelming use
of arguments and statements taken from the *Contrarietas*. The
reprobatio and Tripoli's work were almost certainly known to him.[17]
There is very little sign of dependence on the former, and if the
latter was indeed known to Ricoldo, he deliberately rejected it.
He made no real effort to limit the strong element of almost personal malice in passages taken from the *Contrarietas*; there is a
startling contrast between his slavish attitude to his literary
sources and the freedom of his own observations. The borrowed
aspect of *spite* in his work nowhere finds a greater contrast than
in his own generous praise of Islamic virtues. The most sustained
passages of the latter are those in the *Itinerarium*, but these are
echoed in the *Disputatio* and elsewhere, and there is too close a
resemblance between the two principal works to allow doubt that
both represent Ricoldo's thoughts. If the encyclopaedists' inclusion
of a passage might only amount to a recommendation to read it,
Ricoldo on the contrary worked passages from the *Contrarietas*
too closely into the repetitive themes of the *Disputatio* for us to be
able to say that he did not wish to take full responsibility for all
that he asserted. What he intended to be a compendium for the use
of missionaries was a proliferation of arguments with unnecessary
repetitions, and with little discrimination between the serious and
the petty. He would even take over propaganda points without
reflection, for example, that Muhammad was epileptic; in this
case, even the *Contrarietas* was more prudent.[18] Another characteristic was the development of an argument based on data collected
from disparate sources. How, argued Ricoldo, could Muhammad
claim to have passed through the seven heavens, and yet to have
been unable to support a single angelic visitation upon earth? The
first 'fact' here derives from the mi'rāj, an Islamic legend, therefore, but at least not a Christian invention; the second belonged to
the Christian *epileptic* legend, in which the Prophet explained his
fits as the effect of converse with the angel. Thus he accused
Muslims of inconsistency on grounds derived from wholly different
sources, one the invention of Christians, and neither such as an
orthodox Muslim would be bound to accept. We must say of
Ricoldo that, although he had so wide a knowledge of Islam, and
although he was not one to repeat the more absurd fables, he yet

chose both facts and arguments for mention, and for emphasis, with very little discrimination indeed.

His preference for the authority of literary information over what he owed to his own observation finds some parallels in other travellers, none of whom in that age, however, combined as great practical experience with so much academic learning about Islamic questions. One example occurs in Verona's description of the ablutions before prayer, which he must derive from some second-hand source, since what he says is contrary to what happens, and he cannot have failed often to watch individual Muslims perform the *ṣalāt*. A considerable proportion of quite fabulous material was attributed in the West to Syrian and Crusading sources, and, if this were not to misrepresent them, people actually living in Palestine credited the tales of bogus miracles of bull and dove. Certainly in 1257 the Abbot and Fathers of St Albans were assured by a priest from 'Akka that Mecca, its temple and idol of Muhammad had just been destroyed by lightning and the Preceptor of the Temple told the Bishop of Arles that this had happened in an earthquake.[19] The human capacity to believe what one wishes of one's enemies is without bounds.

When in his turn Peter de Pennis came to edit Ricoldo's material, he made an effort to rearrange and simplify it. This was only partly successful, and, because he had no first-hand knowledge, could not be expected to show greater discrimination than his source. Such of Ricoldo's passages originating from the *Contrarietas* as he used he did not tone down; and on his own initiative he added fabulous material; moreover, in an account of the Islamic rules of marriage which he took partly from Ricoldo and partly from Pedro de Alfonso, he rendered his facts less correctly than either of his sources. Yet some of the material taken from Ricoldo he re-used in the arrangement characteristic of the *reprobatio* of 'true' and 'false' statements listed separately.[20] So positive an act of rearrangement implies a less polemic, more scientific, intention. This draws attention again to the way in which Ricoldo never left polemic effect to facts alone, but insisted on expounding the significance of every detail.

All writers tended – more or less – to cling to fantastic tales about Islam and its Prophet in a proprietary way, as belonging to the 'Christian' version. Polemists capable of highly informed argument inconsistently retained much that was quite untenable by our standards and that would have seemed ridiculous to Muslims. Those 'facts' which tended to show the falsity of Islam were preferred to all others. The same polemic outline is common to the more scholarly and the more popular works. There was a rough unity of purpose and a similar attitude to the use of data.

The difference lay only in degree. More that was incredible was excluded, more that was authentic admitted, in one case than in the next. The use of false evidence to attack Islam was all but universal.

3. THE CHRISTIAN CONSENSUS: FAULTS AND DEFORMITIES OF OPINION

It is useful to compare what was generally agreed about Islam in the Middle Ages with what is now considered an adequate statement. The absurdity in our eyes of some of the more fantastic legends about Muhammad must not make us forget that a great deal of true information was available and was believed, so long as it did not conflict with the interest of true religion. It cannot be said that the perception of the state of Muhammad's Arabia was altogether false. No doubt Western Europeans conceived what they read in terms of their own landed feudalism, and, only one degree less anachronistically, Spanish and Syrian Latins interpreted the jāhilīyah in terms of the Islamic society – often urban and scholastic – actually known to them. There is no evidence that the Islamic society of their own day struck Christians who knew it as fundamentally different from their own; and theirs was not an age of historical imagination. We can take it that they imagined Muhammad's Arabia to be like the society they lived in themselves. It is obvious that this favoured the belief in fabulous nonsense; the real Muhammad is inconceivable in mediaeval Europe, whereas the Muhammad of Christian legend was a villain of contemporary imagining. Yet the Scriptural picture of the wild men of the desert, sprung from Ismael, fitted neatly into the idea of a civilised Christendom overwhelmed, not by the Meccan merchants, but by the Medinan idolators, rough and simple-minded men, savages in fact. The Arabian scene was made to seem more likely, by supposing it accessible to the influence of heretical Christian and Jewish malice against the Church. This is not an unrecognisable caricature of pre-Islamic Arabia. In summary, the mediaeval consensus on this point is reasonable; on the other hand, many of the most widely believed details, such as those imputing a magical background to the Prophet, were quite fantastic.

More consistent deformation comes with the actual life of Muhammad. The development of the Baḥīrā legend is a case in point; the Muslim legend was wholly ignored, except, illogically, the bare assertion of a hermit who knew Muhammad, and whom the Christians give a new role. There was no reason why they should not create their own fantasies; what is significant is that they picked out of a series of Muslim statements just the one that suited them. The establishment of Islamic power by violence and fraud, by battle, banditry and assassination and by the authority of pretended visions; the intimate and often sordid details of the Prophet's personal relations with his family; in these cases also the picture was delineated by selecting just those facts that suited it, and ignoring all others. In war, unprotected by angels, Muhammad suffered the ordinary vicissitudes to which soldiers and highwaymen, but not prophets, are liable, and he paid the final debt of humanity more cheaply than he deserved. This is the verdict of the more moderate writers; unfair though it is, it is closer to reality than Muhammad, Cardinal or Mage, or Muhammad devoured by swine. At the worst there was the assertion of the fantastic, and its repetition without discrimination; at the best there was the selection of only those facts that served the purpose of controversy.

It is also important to remember how much was left out even of the most sober mediaeval account of Muhammad's life. Although the pagan state of Medina was asserted there was never recognition of Muhammad's social legislation for Arabian society; the victory at Badr which Muhammad believed to be specially providential was not simply discounted, but ignored; acts of the Prophet – for example, the appointment of the new qiblah – which had no polemic value, were very rarely mentioned; there was no reference to the alliances and other peaceful means used to unite the tribes; and the omission of all mention of Ḥudaybiyah, of the bloodless conquest of Mecca, of the final victories over paganism and the establishment of Islamic rule and religion leaves Muhammad's story ridiculously incomplete. Readers must often have been left with the idea of a countryside dominated by terror of a robber band, or of a town populace deceived by a confidence trickster. Mediaeval authors were concerned above all with Muhammad's personal qualities, and not with the sequence of events. Not everyone who repeated fables deliberately preferred them to sober truth or something like it; but so much was known that was accurate that there must very often have been a deliberate choice of the worst.[21]

Islamic institutions were treated as selectively as the life of Muhammad. Relatively little was suggested that was competely absurd, like the more fantastic legends about the Prophet; in this category might be classed the idea of sexual promiscuity (including ten husbands for every woman) but such absurdities as this were rare. Yet the more sober accounts of Islam resemble the more sober biographies of the Prophet in that actual facts were manipulated by selection and omission, by exaggeration and invention and misapplication. The Latin treatment of a subject tended again and again to be unreasonable, even when the general outline of what was said was not significantly false. Sexual questions provide the best example. The undue emphasis that they were given is perhaps the strongest evidence for this of all, but there are particular points to note.

It is curious that so much stress should have been put upon aspects of which the critics could have had no certain knowledge whatever. From the point of view of believers in a natural law, it was with reason that Christians complained of defects in Islamic moral law, but their assumptions about the actual commission of offences were gratuitous. Theory can never have been confirmed by direct access to educated Muslims, even in the rare case of writers who claimed to have taken part in active discussion, for example, Ricoldo and Lull; or where there was a close knowledge of written sources and some personal contact with Islamic society, for example, with the Cluniac translators, with Mark of Toledo, Ramón Martí or San Pedro. It is the same with those who lived among or near to Muslims, Vitry, Tripoli or Fidenzio; and, more obviously, with the pilgrims, who often, however, exercised a more lively curiosity than Latins resident in the East, with somewhat unreliable results. Vitry's acceptance of the Mālikite scandal about the abuse of wives, which could only have relevance in Mālikite Spain, although his own experience was confined to Syria and Egypt, is an example of the influence of literary, at the expense of direct, sources of knowledge; and in Spain itself it was surely the literary perpetuation of an oral Christian tradition that was the usual source of such unsavoury information. In any case, it was obviously impossible to observe much of Islamic sexual practice at first hand. Even Christian girls married to Muslims will have been largely cut off from their old friends; the life of the ḥarīm precluded any personal acquaintance with family life, and it is extremely difficult to imagine any reliable, serious and confidential discussion of such things between a pious Christian and a pious Muslim of the Middle Ages.[22]

The Christian canon of Muslim behaviour, that is, the received Christian opinion as to what Muslims actually did, was partly formed by the tendency of misconceptions to snowball, and to confirm as well as to add to one another. Mere repetition is enough to bring unshakable conviction; and once it had been asserted that Islamic teaching was sexually lax, every example of laxity would be noticed from that moment, and, once notified, attributed to the doctrine. If we suppose that there were an equal number of similar offences committed by Christians and by Muslims in any given time, in the former case they would be seen as having occurred in spite of doctrine, so that each individual case would be an exception, and in the latter it would be assumed that doctrine was the cause of whatever happened. Moreover, if it were not a matter of seeking examples to prove a thesis, each particular episode would be less likely to be noticed in the first place. When for some special reason it was convenient to show Islamic society and its morals in a favourable light, the attack on sexual morals was allowed to lapse. More often the polemic purpose guided the selection of facts, and there were few cases indeed where mistakes were made that showed Islam in a less disadvantageous light than was necessary.

Not only in treating the life of Muhammad and the sexual institutions of Islam, but in all aspects of that religion, facts were exaggerated, sometimes out of little or nothing, and were often distorted almost beyond recognition; sound information was regularly discarded for unsound. Only in matters apparently favourable to Christianity was a very high degree of accuracy achieved, as, for example, in treating the Qur'anic beliefs about Christ and His mother. This draws attention to the motives underlying inaccuracies on themes where there was conflict. Accuracy in the one case, inaccuracy in the other, were equally useful in support of Christian belief. The process of misrepresentation did not extend, with authors who were conceivably in a position to know better, so far as to make their picture of Islam unrecognisable, but it nevertheless needs explaining. We have no right to assume that intellectual dishonesty was involved, until every other explanation has been sought in vain.

4. THE MOTIVES OF MISREPRESENTATION

Misrepresentation was closely related to matters of Christian faith and morals, matters which aroused strong feelings among Christian writers, naturally enough. Information was extracted from the sources, whether Islamic or Christian, sometimes for amusement only, but more often to serve the high purposes of the Church. The polemic purpose was to attack the Islamic claim to be the true revelation of God, and to this end it was essential that the character of Muhammad be shown to be wholly and unquestionably incompatible with Revelation. Equally it was essential that Islamic institutions should appear incompatible with religion; but undoubtedly the greatest deformation of fact occurred in the lives of the Prophet. Thus what modern scholarship shows to be false was thought to be true, apparently because it was useful in a good cause.

It is difficult or impossible to see any alternative explanation. We might argue that mediaeval writers knew no better, only if there had been no effort to secure authentic information; but it is obvious, from what we have already said, that the Cluniacs, the *reprobatio*, San Pedro, Tripoli and Ricoldo, to mention only some of the most important, sought authentic information, in order to annihilate Islam. We might more plausibly argue that these writers lacked the power to discriminate between the truly authentic and the apparently so; but to say this is to beg the question. The real question is why they did not prefer Islamic authorities on Islamic subjects to Christian ones, whenever there was any conflict as to matters of fact; they all realised that it was desirable so far as possible to support allegations against Islam by Islamic testimony. Yet they were unable to bring themselves entirely to relinquish more damning testimony from Christian sources: testimony that would have been more damning had it been, in the modern sense, reliable; but which Muslims, like modern scholars, could never have considered other than a ridiculous travesty of fact. The most probable explanation of what happened must be that Christians thought that whatever tended to harm the enemies of truth was likely itself to be true.

We must next enquire whether there is any reason not to accept this explanation. If it implied dishonesty or hypocrisy on the part of Christian writers, there would be good reason to suspect it, but it is not necessary to assume that it does so. In this connection we have, first, to remember that for Latin writers Muhammad was the founder of a sect which had first thrived and still thrived enormously at the expense of Christendom; for them, the Crusades were a Muslim, not a Christian, aggression. A cause was naturally sought which would be commensurate with its effect: an honest or self-deluded founder of Islam was not easily conceived until the nineteenth century, when his followers were no longer felt to menace Western Europe, and his doctrines were no longer the only, or even the principal, threat to Christian orthodoxy. In the Middle Ages the evident harm caused by Islam – in mediaeval eyes – was too great and too effective to allow scope for generosity of attitude. Fine shades of character and subtleties of motive were a preoccupation of romantic verse, but did not affect ecclesiastical history writing, which tended to simplify. If an act were bad enough, it was beyond common sense to suppose that the agent could personally be good and sincere; and the act here in question was the creation of the most powerful instrument for the destruction of the Church, and for the loss of souls and provinces, then known. It would be almost as easy to believe that Judas was sincere; the suffering Church, and therefore Christ Himself, had been betrayed by Muhammad. He could not, then, have been a good man. Whether historical facts alleged were true was decided on theological grounds, and in a framework of exaggerated contrast; it was appropriate, and therefore true, that the enemy of Christ should be in every way and as much as possible unlike Him.

The treatment of Muhammad was a reversal of hagiography, from his unpropitious birth to his bad death at the last. When two societies are at war, or confidently expect to be at war, they must mutually be aware of whatever separates them, especially in belief, in the practices of daily life and in the events of past and contemporary history which they share. There is likely to be a tendency to exaggerate or invent differences. A society would have to be remarkably tolerant to recognise the virtues, and make allowance for the faults, of their enemies' leaders. It is surprising how often the Latin West did in fact admit the humane virtue, and even admire the chivalry or strength of government, of contemporary Muslim enemies; the legend of Saladin is the obvious case, and Tripoli's veneration for Baybars is another. On the other hand, there were few saints produced by the Reconquest and fewer by the Crusades; Godfrey of Bouillon's heroic aura acquired only in retrospect a sacred connotation. Worse was attributed to the long-dead Muhammad than to any living leader of Islam; partly because he was so distant in time, he could be made to impersonate all those things which seemed most abominable in his religion. The fraudulent demoniac or magician of Christian legend seems incredible to us, but the authentic Muhammad of Arab history would have seemed a good deal stranger to the mediaeval reader. This presentation of a wholly new version of the historical figure of Muhammad, one which no Arab could recognise, was facilitated by the ease with which it is possible to believe in some vast conspiracy to deceive; people have believed to an exaggerated extent in the conspiracies against society of Albigensians or Freemasons or Jesuits founded on esoteric knowledge. It is still easier to believe that a body of facts is suppressed by an openly hostile society. Thus a 'real truth' was substituted for an 'ostensible' one: for the Prophet of the Hijāz, the magician whom swine devoured.

Yet in seeking to know why one particular untruth was believed about Islam, rather than another, we may learn something from the heresies of a slightly later period. Largely, as we have seen, what was believed about Islam had been inherited from outside Latin Europe; but we ought as well to notice that the fictional *persona* of Muhammad which Christians invented (together with some of his supposed teaching) corresponds remarkably to the character of prophets of the 'Free Spirit' who did actually arise in Europe, and claim credence and collect followers. The chiliasts of the Middle Ages and of the Wars of Religion speak for God, or claim to be God, the prophecies of Christ are applied to them, and they are given the name of Messias; they initiate a new age; they receive Heavenly Letters; above all, sexual promiscuity, either licensed or encouraged by religion, and hatred of the Catholic clergy are characteristic of their doctrine; they are often apostate monks: thus the actual creations of the popular religious spirit resemble what was imagined about Muhammad and Islam by literate orthodoxy. The latter may have been a conscious or unconscious application of known facts about revolutionary proletarian movements at home to debatable data about the enemy of society abroad; this is chronologically possible, in that heresies of the 'Free Spirit' appear to have been established (though hardly widespread) already in the twelfth century. Yet they are much more characteristic of the later Middle Ages and cannot have inspired universal concern sooner than the fourteenth century. N. Cohn discusses the paranoiac character of much mediaeval and later millennialism; and it may be that there was a common source; that the same European imaginings, among the proletariat were translated into action, and among the educated remained in the imagination only, where they were projected upon the enemy of society. It seems possible that there was some relation – how important a relation is not clear – between the unresolved social conflicts within Christendom and the inconclusive conflict with the external enemy.[23]

The intelligent good faith which yet guided mediaeval opinion may be seen more clearly, if we reflect how little different are our attitudes to-day. The controversies which are now conducted by academic personalities and eminent men and women of outstanding culture are frequently based on the refusal to admit the same series of facts as a common basis for argument; moreover, people who have a particular dislike for some school of opinion or belief, or for a particular institution, or party, or sect, or church, or for all churches, or all parties, have their own versions of the beliefs they dislike, versions which the actual adherents of these doctrines are unable to accept or even to recognise as their own. Yet these are differences within a relatively small society; and the area of mutual understanding between antagonistic societies, and between societies with different histories and backgrounds, is to-day still extremely limited. Modern practice, outside a form of careful scholarship which flourished briefly and already begins to be considered old-fashioned, seems so similar to that of the Middle Ages, as to enable us better to understand and sympathise with what at first looked dishonest or foolish.

I sum up at the risk of seeming repetitive. Faced with a choice between alternative stories, more or less favourable to Muhammad or to Islamic institutions, the mediaeval historians of Muhammad and critics of his religion acted on the assumption that whatever seemed least creditable was most likely to be true. No improbability in the data was apparent to them; there was only a choice between data more and less consonant with the worldly welfare of doctrines known with certainty to be true. Theological standards did not supersede, but they helped to identify, the truth. Authors with didactic and moral intentions formed the belief that some 'facts' were true, because those 'facts' served the meritorious purpose of exposing error. Other authors whose intentions were a little less lofty, in histories and treatises composed to amuse and instruct, naturally took it that a more instructive and more amusing alternative was true, or at least was not certainly untrue; and the version that was more discreditable to Muhammad or to Islam was the more edifying, instructive and amusing; in fact, the more probably true. It would be anachronistic to say that such an attitude showed indifference to abstract truth; it was a question of finding the best means to recognise what was true. It seemed more reasonable to decide that what suited the author's purpose was true, provided his purpose was a sufficiently laudable one, than to decide according to the abstract reliability of his sources of information. The authenticity of the sources of knowledge was judged according to the apparent probability of what was said, and not according to the authority of the speaker to say it.

There is a subsidiary but also important consideration. Far from considering statements by Muslims to be reliable even about Islam, Christians thought all Islamic statements suspect. It was a general principle of law that a person of another religion was not a satisfactory witness,[24] and it was almost the same principle which mediaeval Christians in effect applied to historical statements about Muhammad or analyses of Islamic doctrine: Christian witness was presumed reliable, Islamic witness suspect. Where they conflicted it was natural to suppose the latter biased – biased in favour of untruth, as Christians were biased towards truth. Islamic sources were fit to be trusted only where they witnessed against Islam, where they were admissions of the 'real' truth; it was only with great reluctance that an author would use them to correct Christian testimony on any point at all. Their approximation to Christian belief, or at least their compatibility with it, was used as a measure; and was thought to be a more reliable criterion in dealing with Islamic sources than any evidence of the authority with which such sources spoke for Muslims. When Islamic testimony did seem likely to serve the purposes of Christian polemic, it was used to correct Christian fables, in order that the two might be combined, and the combination be irresistible. The authority of the Qur'ān itself, of Bukhārī and Muslim and ibn Isḥāq, of the *de doctrina Machometi* and the *liber Scalae Machometi*, depended on their utility to Christian polemic, more than on any other factor. They were quoted to discredit Islam, and not, even following scholastic method, as 'objections' to some Christian thesis.

The factors that open and close minds to one belief or another, and, in particular, that formulate opinion about what other people believe, are obscure and complex. Self-deception is so easy in private motive that it may be taken to be easier still in acts of communal loyalty. If it is sufficiently desirable that a thing should be true, it often seems to be so, especially in cases where the consuming good of a great society or a great ideal is thought to require it. A thing becomes true because it serves a higher end; men who would be horrified to assert that the end justifies the means, readily come to believe a means to be just in itself, if it leads to an end of sufficient moment, as they suppose, to the world. In this case, every demonstration of the villainous character of Muhammad and the pernicious nature of Islamic religion seemed to be of the highest value to the faith of Christ – and therefore seemed to be true. The self-congratulatory thought of how effective, as arguments, these histories of Muhammad must prove would alone have made them convincing to authors who would never have to put them to the test of debate with outsiders. Data were chosen because they were useful to an exalted end; writers did not think in terms of truth for its own sake, although they would have been sincerely horrified and understandably annoyed at any suggestion that their 'truths' were untrue; the whole good of true religion, of humanity, made a 'fact' seem probable, and probability is usually a ground of belief. The truth of the end made the data which seemed to demonstrate that end seem true. They seemed to prove the Christian faith, but what really happened in the mind of the polemist was that the Christian faith proved whatever supported it to be true.

Ultimately, Gresham's law would work in reverse in the circulation of statements about Islam, but it was a long time before the good drove out the bad, and until the end of the seventeenth century a general tendency to prefer false statements persisted. Credulity was all but universal, for as long as the good of the community seemed – however mistakenly – to require it.

Plate 5

Bibliothèque de l'Arsenal, MS Arsenal 1162, f. 11

A Spanish scribe's 'doodle': Muhammad (representing Islam) as a composite creature. Possibly the original Toledan manuscript of the Cluniac collection: a passage from the *de generatione*,

riam uiri altrologico testimonio ap-
pbasset. ecce sclo̅z̅ serie inipsis dieb'
suis. uiru̅ natu̅ audit inciuitate arabie
ieserab. om̅ia prudentie sue signacla
preferente. Gelebri demu̅ fama fre-
quentiq; testimonio motus homine̅
adit. que̅ undiq; uersum p̅spiciens.
omne̅q; modu̅ eius & conuersatione̅
obseruans. ita quide̅ ut ipsas etiam
corpis notas easdem quas presigna-
uerat repiret. ut in
fronte maclam. inter
scapulas huiusmodi
baracterem. hunc ipsum

(M)ahu-
meth

esse

✣ IX ✣

The establishment
of communal opinion

A BODY of firmly held opinions may be compatible with the capacity to imagine an attitude which is totally unlike them, and more or less contrary. Yet the association of the two is rare, not only among the ill-educated, as might be expected, but perhaps equally among the highly trained and academic. Historical discipline requires this imaginative capacity, but even among historians it is often confined within professional limits. Historical discipline of any kind is of comparatively recent growth; the imaginative reconstruction of strange and remote societies is even more so; and a sympathetic exploration of their beliefs, with 'suspension of unbelief', is still rarely met. It is even less frequent that societies which are contemporary achieve knowledge and understanding of each other. These points are relevant to the attitude of mediaeval Christendom towards Islam.

1. THE USE OF AUTHORITIES

If the opinions of individuals tend to exclude alien ideas, this applies even more to the body of opinion received by the societies to which an individual belongs. In this case the process of excluding dangerous thoughts, which in individuals may not be wholly conscious, is likely to be more deliberate. Both societies and individuals are reluctant to risk adopting such opinions as seem apt to cause major changes in their attitudes. Mediaeval society certainly did not desire any sudden disruption. It was always capable of absorbing new ideas, and in the period with which we have been dealing there was obvious development in the fields of metaphysics and natural science, and in political theory. There was an admirable willingness to admit new ideas from an outside society, but these were not the ideas upon which the beliefs of individuals were consciously based, or those that they most took for granted and would have feared to disturb. The ideas which Islamic religion stated or implied seemed on the contrary liable to destroy many of the theological and moral concepts which

251

Christendom most cherished. Mediaevals were almost excessively
rationalistic about the mysteries of religion, with an astonishing
faith in their provability, but certain groups of beliefs were never
disturbed by a realisation of what Islam, or any other opponent,
might question. These beliefs formed a circle which was never
broken by any imaginative exteriorisation. Questions of which
the importance was realised, for example, in the sphere of dogma
that of the mode of revelation, and in the sphere of morals the
value of abstinence and continence, were never conceived in the
terms Muslims conceived them, and Christians continued to view
their own beliefs from the inside.

Another important factor helped to make Christian views im-
penetrable by any open concept of Islam. This was the near
unanimity of opinion which almost enables us to speak of a communal attitude. It has been said of the Middle Ages that 'we may
doubt whether any but the finest spirits ever rose above a hazy
group consciousness'.[1] Perhaps we may take this further and
seriously doubt whether in any age a majority do this. Most
writers reveal minds filled with material heard and read – contemporary ideas generally expressed in clichés that are equally
contemporaneous. Even very original writers are only occasionally
exempt, and the individual no more than contributes to the thought
of his age and group. The Middle Ages were different only in so
far as they did not even seek or admire originality; thus whole
passages were copied into new contexts, old elements were
formed into new patterns. A thing once said well, the passage
was used continuously, like a tried and tested tool. There was a
very great deal of copying of statements and whole passages about
Islam, perhaps because of the general ignorance of the subject, or
because there was a special craving for unanimity. Whatever the
reasons, this nearly communal attitude existed. In the many cases
of writers' correcting one another, this was done to support
themes which, when the proofs had been discredited, must be
maintained with different evidence. Very largely, Christians drew
from a single kitty, to which they contributed again. The Christian
concept of Islam was integral and self-sufficient.

There was little that was fluid in a state of mind which was at
least partly congealed. Much of the mediaeval attitude was
destined to survive for many centuries, while other aspects were
peculiarly mediaeval. These are chiefly associated with scholastic
method, and here method had a share in determining substance.
What was most characteristic of the mediaeval attitude to Islam
was the strong dependence on Scripture, the determination to
defend Scripture from any attack, and the employment of the
Qur'ān to defend it. The use of Scriptural citations to prove

Scripture might seem astonishing only if we did not reflect how difficult it is to discard assumptions that we take most for granted. Scripture was the framework of all mediaeval thought; for no Latin writer was it ever possible to think himself into a position outside and independent of Scripture. If Moses or Solomon behaved differently in the Qur'ān and in Scripture, the account in the former constituted a legend too insubstantial to be believed by anyone. Christians often spoke of the Qur'anic claim to 'correct' Scripture, but they never really credited the idea that anyone could doubt Scripture or try to put it right on points of history or doctrine. It was inconceivable that the Qur'ān should be the sole source, or sole reliable source, of knowledge of the prophets, or that the prophecies should not have been concerned exclusively with the Kingdom of the Messias. The Old Testament would always seem to be the primary source of such knowledge, and therefore in practice the Old Testament was used to refute the Qur'ān.

The reason for what might appear absurd lies in the scholastic training which taught that both reason and authorities must be applied to problems. St Ramón of Peñaforte taught that Jews and Muslims ought to be 'stimulated to the Christian faith by authorities, by reasons and by kindnesses, and ought not to be forced'.[2] Martí and the *reprobatio*, belonging to the same Dominican milieu, explicitly defined the need for the same method in their anti-Islamic polemic.[3] The practice was universal. The question was what should be admitted as an authority in polemic of this kind. *Authority* might be the citation of philosophers or other secular writers, but more often it meant Scripture, and, second to Scripture, the Fathers. Authorities were conceived to function separately from reason based on first principles or observed phenomena. Quotations are necessarily made, in any age, less as a specially good expression of what the author wants to say, than for the validity which inheres in what has been said before and accepted by other men, and has entered into the general consensus of opinion. This quality was especially esteemed in the Middle Ages, and it is obvious that Scripture was in a class apart, as authority divinely inspired. Mediaeval authors could understand a refusal to accept the authority of Scripture, and there is no reason why they should not have expected to defend Scripture by reason. The point is rather that the whole scholastic method and training presupposed the use of *authorities*, and of Scripture above all others. It was in practice, not in theory, that it was impossible for a man to ignore the systematic discipline in which his mind had been trained. A scholastic without authorities was a craftsman robbed of half his tools; and few of his authorities were acceptable to Muslims.

It is this that explains some cases where Christians insisted that Muslims must mean something which in fact we know they did not mean, for example, that God 'prayed for' Muhammad.[3] The whole scheme of authorities was imperilled by Islamic culture, which recognised relatively few of them; a few, Aristotle for example, which it not only recognised but had actually imparted to the West, could be quoted against it. Here it was specifically Islamic religion which was in opposition and particularly the Qur'ān. Thus it was that the Qur'ān came to be used itself as an authority, in a Christian interpretation and from within the general consensus of Christian opinion. Authors, Christian and ancient, had been brought to fit into this consensus, and the Qur'ān was made to do so too. On the surface, mediaevals thought, it was wholly alien to them, and, on the most sanguine view, must always remain partly so. In so far as it did so, it was rejected. In so far as it could be used to forward the Christian case, it was admitted as an authority. This partly explains the apparently ridiculous interpretation of many of its texts according to arbitrary Christian requirements which no Muslim could recognise.

In effect, the Qur'ān was true when it was useful, and its polemic utility was partly to confirm Scripture, and partly to prove that Muhammad really taught the propositions which Christians felt most confident they could disprove, or show to be self-evidently false. Some writers also accepted as authorities some other books which were thought either to explain the hidden but authentic meaning of the Qur'ān (as was the case with Ricoldo and Lull and the commentators), or to be themselves 'written by Muhammad', like the *Liber Scalae*. The Qur'ān itself, of course, was thought to have been written by him, and not by God.[4]

The infinite respect for authority did not extend to the letter of the text. Provided that the words of the Qur'ān cited proved the untruth of Islam, they were correctly cited. Verbal accuracy was not sought at all. The Qur'ān would be quoted as rendering correctly some tenet of Islam (whether true or supposed) to which it was desired, for polemic reasons, to draw attention; for example, 'they were ordered to rob, to make prisoner and kill' or 'whatever (those in Paradise) desired would immediately be supplied'. These are not really Qur'anic phrases at all. The whole long paraphrase of the Qur'ān by Ketton is a case in point; and even Mark, with his literal translation, did not quote his own work with exactitude. Sometimes we can identify the use of Ketton's translation by other writers, as in the cases of Fitzralph and Simon Simeon; but most quotations from the Qur'ān were given in an author's private version or paraphrase. Thus the Qur'ān was used to support the Christian case, and this gave it authenticity; and any formula at all that met this need was believed to be an accurate quotation. Although a non-Christian authority was allowed to have meaning only in a Christian context and in Christian terms, the frequent citation of the Qur'ān, or of what purported to be the Qur'ān, and the translation of Islamic works of religion, testify to the felt need for such an authority.

The enormous popularity of the Risālah, in different forms, illustrates this point still more clearly. We have seen its importance as a source of authentic information, and of information already deployed in support of the Christian case against Islam. Either as an actual source or as representative of the common Christian tradition it almost sums up the Christian case. Yet even the Risālah contained information about Islam which was rarely or never quoted, presumably because its polemic value was no longer discerned.[5] If this is so of a work of polemic against Islam, it is not surprising that the wealth of material in the Qur'ān, and generally in works of Islamic origin, should have been ignored except in so far as it could be brought into service. Basically Islam itself lacked authority: that was Aquinas' chief point. It did not have *documenta veritatis* and the absence of miracles was the sign of this. If Islam had no authority, Muslim interpretations had none; the only authority of Islam could be against itself.

2. THE INTENTIONS OF THE POLEMISTS

We saw in the last chapter that a great deal of material which moderns must denominate legendary and false was preferred, or at least retained, more or less deliberately. Yet if authentic material was of interest to some authors as proving a case more convincingly, we have to ask why it seemed more convincing. Would not the fantastic, instead often of being studiously corrected by the learned, really have served the purpose better? Why was the need for Islamic authority ever felt? Much of the best writing claimed to be for use in disputations with Muslims; on the face, arguments against an Islamic position could have no other use. What was the whole polemic really intended to do?

Peter the Venerable insisted that the Latins – that is, the Cluniacs and their employees – could not be mistaken about the Qur'ān because of the excellence of their translators.[6] It would have been absurd to tell Muslims this, although ostensibly they were being addressed. Peter can only have been reassuring himself, and it is a sign of greatness in him that he ever realised that Muslims would make objections at all. Most mediaeval literature about Islam failed to conceive the possibility that Muslims might be unimpressed. It is difficult to think that the confident and positive and often smug assertions of the Latins hide even a hint of uncertainty. Those who felt doubts did not express them, or, if they did, their doubts have not survived. There was always a Muslim 'reader over the shoulder'; not a real one, of course, but one whom the Christian imagination created. He was unreal because he never objected to what was asserted against him. There was a remarkably wide use of the logical dilemma as a dialectical device, almost as a literary form, and there was more than a suggestion of the atmosphere of public challenge and debate. The mediaeval Latins seem always to be defending a public dissertation before favourable judges, judges whose approval has been assured in advance. It is a nightmare reversed: it is the opponent who cannot answer, except in words set in his mouth; it is a race in which the jockey on the rival horse is a dummy. Much of the literature about Islam seems to consist of debating points triumphantly enunciated and, of course, never answered, because the opponent is absent; and it is this which gives an air of unreality to so much of it.[7]

Admittedly, many writers wrote expressly for Christian consumption; but even where that is not so, it is very noticeable that nearly all the themes of Christian writings are far better suited to Christian consumption than to the sympathetic consideration of Muslims. The phrases of the Cluniacs reflect a real and an ostensible intention. Peter the Venerable apostrophised the Muslims constantly. Yet his use of Latin makes it impossible to suppose that he really intended his work to reach the Islamic world in integral form. His translators of Islamic sources claimed to have found their work profitable to them; if this was not said solely to flatter Peter's projects and decisions, it must mean that they thought the translation inherently interesting or polemically useful. It is most likely that they meant the latter; as Ketton put it, the Qur'ān was the witness to Christianity's sanctity and excellence (particularly, a cynical critic might think, as he translated it). Mark of Toledo, although his astonishing literalness in translation seems to condemn Ketton's work, introduced the Qur'ān in his own version to his readers, as sounding like the speech of a crazy man, and he must have believed this to be self-evident in the text. Both his and the Cluniac attitude would appeal only to Christians.

San Pedro claimed that his interest in predestination came from his experience of argument with Muslims, but the recorded examples of his discussions do not impress us as having been at a very serious level. He said that he had found a useful logical quandary with which to trap Muslims: they must either, contrary to Muhammad's teaching, accept eternal reward for good or evil actions, or else assert the doctrine of God's writing the fate of the soul from the beginning, which was contrary to reason, to Scripture and to the Prophet's own teaching. Even apart from the appeal to Scripture, this emphatically does not suggest discussion with any Muslim, except, perhaps, some simple soul who lacked theological perception or dialectical training, because the case is not argued in Islamic terms. For Muslim theologians, the problem is one of reconciling man's free will with God's power, and the argument as set out begs this question; first, by assuming that good and evil actions imply free will, and secondly, by asserting that the Prophet was inconsistent in speaking both of merit and of predestination. Another example that San Pedro gives is clearly set in illiterate surroundings. There is every indication that he had no serious discussions with educated Muslims.[8]

His work also claims to have been written in his Muslim prison, to fortify local Christians; and, although he must have taught in the presence of Muslims, sufficiently to annoy the 'ulamā' and earn his martyrdom, the idea that his primary purpose was to encourage Christians in Islamic territory accords exactly with the character of his arguments. His apostrophes of Muhammad are obviously a rhetorical device. What all his careful comparison of Islamic and Christian sources for Muhammad's biography amounts to is a reassurance that the traditional Christian views are sound at least in outline. Both he and the author of the *reprobatio*, as well as other writers, gave much attention to proving the average humanity of Muhammad. The absence of characteristics which for Christians were inseparable from a divine mission could never, for Christians, be emphasised enough. Almost equally they stressed the absence of divinity. That orthodox Muslims were wholly in agreement, that they did not wish, and by the very hub of their religion could not wish, to make Muhammad in any way more than ordinarily human was impossible for the Christian to credit, still less really to take to heart. If the intended public were Muslims, much energy was wasted on self-congratulatory comments on Islamic 'admissions' of points that told against the Prophet only in such Christian terms. San Pedro said that Muslims wrote in their books that Muhammad

. . . was affected by a great fear when there was thunder or lightning, or when it became gloomy or dark; and as they have written these things about him whom they are trying to praise as far as they can or know how, you can understand enough, without taking into account many things for which, if they were written down, Muhammad could be blamed.

There is so great a gap between the attitude of the Muslim ḥadīth and that of the Christian tradition of hagiography that this beating on air could continue indefinitely; nothing that Christians said would appeal greatly to anyone but a Christian. In the same class

falls all Christian indignation at *ad hoc* revelation, the Qur'anic
response to the circumstances of the moment: no Muslim would
see any reason to be scandalised, all Christians would and did. It
is particularly interesting to find Ramón Martí, possibly the
author of the *reprobatio*, using arguments, such as those in defence
of matrimony, which could not possibly appeal to Muslims; and
it is nearly certain that Martí knew very well what would, and
what would not, appeal.[9] In all these cases such authentic information was provided as would enable Christians to preserve their
already existing attitude to Islam. It may have been intended for
debate, but there is no evidence that it was intended for formal
debate, as distinct from arguments that might naturally arise in
mixed communities. It is far more likely that it was to give
Christians arguments that they might themselves believe, in
explanation of what they heard Muslims say.

Lull certainly claimed actually to have disputed more or less
formally both in public and in prison; but it also seems that he
regularly courted martyrdom, as some other missionaries did, by
public attacks on Muhammad which he combined with 'proofs' of
the Trinity; and he seems to have died in the course of what may
have been a provocation of the Tunis mob.[10] His constant insistence
upon Trinitarian argument indicates the very narrow limits of
debate within which he was prepared to argue, and is one of the
best examples of Christian unwillingness to venture away from
familiar ground. Christian arguments were sound enough defen-
sively thus they easily recognised Muhammad's objection that
the Sonship of God is anthropomorphic, and refuted the objection
as anthropomorphic itself. Offensively these 'proofs' were useless.
There is every sign that Christian accounts of Christian-Muslim
debate do not represent, in the Muslim half, replies actually made
by Muslims. Lull's rendering of his disputation with 'Hamar'
follows a dialectic pattern peculiar to and characteristic of his own
philosophico-theological writings, and does so much too closely
to represent the actual course of a discussion to which a living
Muslim really contributed seriously. It is not that Lull was
deceitful, but that the capacity for self-delusion is infinite. He and
all his predecessors who were addicted to the Trinitarian argument in its more rationalist forms show no suspicion that it was
inadequate for any but a Christian audience. It is easy to imagine
the replies that any unitarian believer would make; and in fact the
Jewish Rabbi Moses Nachman's own account of a formal debate
held before Jaime I of Aragon states just such replies as we
anticipate. The Latin announcement of the dispute which was
made by the Court after the event asserts that, on the contrary,
Nachman was unable to make any reply to this point. Apparently

it was then impossible to recognise what we to-day should call a devastatingly effective rejoinder. We must suppose these arguments to have been repeated often, just as if they were unanswerable, to Jews and Muslims who were wholly unimpressed.[11]

Ricoldo's express intention was to advise and inform missionaries, but his method, which consisted of collecting information and arguments without discrimination, makes it impossible that he should ever have used much of it effectively. We know that many arguments can never have been brought out before a Muslim audience, because a Muslim (if he had not been scandalised) would simply have laughed at the positions Ricoldo imputed to Islam; would have disowned, rather than bothered to argue about them: for example, the assertion that the Qur'ān says that God 'prays for' Muhammad. Alternatively, if such arguments were ever voiced, either they or the replies of the Muslims were not understood. Christians ludicrously asserted that Muslims believed what the Christians said they did; and such absurdity would have been, evidently was, proof against anything Muslims may have had to say. Ricoldo similarly asserted that the Qur'ān must imply the 'divided moon' miracle in the particular sense in which he was already prepared to ridicule it. He had adopted this from the *Contrarietas*, but we cannot be entirely positive that he did not use it in actual controversy. It is not easy to imagine those theological discussions which he speaks of, held in Baghdad of the second generation after the Mongol sack, in imperfect Arabic; yet, unless the *Itinerarium* cannot be trusted at all, they took place, in the house of some 'ālim, or in the cloisters of the Mustanṣirīyyah on the banks of the river. The Dominicans, suspicious even of the hospitality with which they had been received, were evidently fogged by discussion based solely on the Qur'ān and its commentaries; philosophical debates had been barred, but they hoped to find safe ground in simple arguments from reason. It seems impossible that in the flesh Muslims should have tolerated many of the arguments dear to Ricoldo; it is more likely that neither side understood clearly what the other was saying.[12]

Martí cited the argument that one should consult the farmer about agriculture and the doctor about medicine; it is ironic that the failure to find out what Muslims themselves asserted to be their beliefs should have been characteristic of Christian polemic. A brilliant Christian writer perceived what was far from obvious to his contemporaries: 'if Christians deny the histories of the Muslims and the Jews', said Bacon, who never, so far as we know, had the opportunity personally to speak to a Muslim, 'they, by the same right, will deny the histories of the Christians'.[13] The invariable tendency to neglect what the Qur'ān meant, or what

Muslims thought it meant, or what Muslims thought or did in any given circumstances, necessarily implies that Qur'anic and other Islamic doctrine was presented only in a form that would convince Christians; and more and more extravagant forms would stand a chance of acceptance as the distance of writers and public from the Islamic border increased. It was with very great reluctance that what Muslims said Muslims believed was accepted as what they did believe. There was a Christian picture in which the details (even under the pressure of facts) were abandoned as little as possible, and in which the general outline was never abandoned. There were shades of difference, but only within a common framework. All the corrections that were made in the interests of an increasing accuracy were only a defence of what had newly been realised to be vulnerable, a shoring up of a weakened structure. Christian opinion was an erection which could not be demolished, even to be rebuilt.

3. EQUIVOCAL ARGUMENTS

There were many cases in which Christians used arguments that could equally well be turned against them. One such was Ricoldo's violent criticism of the Qur'ān (again taken from the *Contrarietas*) for reasons which in a general sense could be used against the Bible.[14] In our own day it has been said that the facts related in St Matthew's Gospel were invented to make it *appear as though* Christ fulfilled the prophecies. This argument is of the same order as that which says that the Qur'ān was constructed deliberately to appeal to the existing expectations of the pagan Arabs and the Jews of Arabia. It is as difficult to believe that Christians used such rebounding arguments as that they used those of the 'God's prayer' type which were wholly erroneous. Could either type have been used in the schools of Baghdad with good effect, or even intelligibly put forward? Ricoldo's account of the schools reads like a first-hand one; but any suggestion that he there used the arguments that he later developed in his Latin writings is frankly incredible. It is more likely that, when he reached the tranquillity of his Florentine cloister, he liked to imagine having used these arguments to which he had indeed given much thought subsequently. He was fortunate never to have been brought back to earth by the replies he would really have received, had he succeeded in putting some of his attacks intelligibly before a Muslim audience.

Some similar arguments, equally unlikely to have been greatly used in real dispute, are of a type that could be directed against all religion. San Pedro's contempt for some Muslim authors, whose writings Muslims generally 'ignore or openly deny, since those who hear them can only laugh' is cognate to the derision which rationalists experience for the absurd beliefs credited by a few adherents of all religions.[15] The usual Christian argument that Muhammad taught what his, or the Arabs', natural desires disposed him to teach could have been applied to motives appropriate to Christians, or any other body of believers, as well as to the alleged Islamic propensity for violence and sexual laxity. 'Because you were profligate and you knew that the peoples whom you taught were inclined to profligacy, you gave such a religion of profligacy as pleased you and them.'[16] Yet if a lover of goodness gave a religion only because it was good, there would be no necessity to accept it as true. Arguments about the Islamic Paradise, as the sordid imagining of materialistic men, would be applicable, *mutatis mutandis*, to the more spiritual imaginings of which Christians boasted, or to any religious beliefs at all from which comfort can be extracted. At the present day there are arguments about the reduction of a revelation to pre-existing natural elements, arguments based on rationalistic interpretations of a sacred text and psychological interpretations of its supposed author's mind, arguments that people believe what they want to believe, and arguments based on a ground that perpetually shifts between an attack on the theory and an attack on the practice of religion. All these arguments are implied by much of what mediaeval Christians wrote about Islam, and all are essentially arguments that can be turned against any religion. The idea of the doctrine which was adapted to the circumstances of an age, or to the inherent tendencies of human nature, was not worked out systematically in the Middle Ages, but it belonged to the climate of opinion. The conviction that the loose morals of Islam were wholly exceptional – an opinion which modern experience makes untenable – provoked and encouraged this approach. It was not of course an approach that Muslims would be likely to share. In the last resort it was the fervour of utter conviction that secured Christian writers from any suspicion of the dangers of their stand.

Another group of arguments which it would have been impossible or extremely difficult actually to use to Muslims depended on applying judgements to Islam, while exempting Christianity from them. It is not now possible to see how Muslims could ever have accepted criticism of Islam as a religion of violence, so long as the Crusades were taught to be a meritorious work. It was not just that Christian practice was violent while its theory opposed violence. In matters of atrocities, as in all ages, one side might brand the other as cruel, indecent, and so on, while believing itself to commit no such atrocities, or to commit them only untypically. Fra Fidenzio's long treatment of the public vices of

Islam, and of cruelty in particular, is unconvincing for this reason. Yet much of his detail may be exact.[17] In so many cases the crimes of which Islam was accused were crimes of which Christians were equally guilty. The only excuse is that it was believed that Muslims justified these offences by doctrine; but Christians were inconsistent in not admitting, perhaps in not recognising, their own acts of violence. Islamic theory and practice were condemned by Christian theory, but not by Christian practice.

Another and distinct class of argument portrayed particular tenets of Islamic belief in terms of Christian doctrine. Islamic doctrines and religious acts were treated for the most part as approximations to some Christian equivalent, sometimes so as entirely to obscure the true meaning, but more often so only as to deform it this side of recognisability. A Muslim would inevitably have been struck by Christian misunderstanding of his religion, even at the best that Christians achieved; but unless he were very intimate with Christians, he would not necessarily realise how closely these misrepresentations corresponded to Christian practice, as with the cult duties, prayer, pilgrimage, fasting and the rest; these Islamic institutions were seen as failures to re-produce Christian institutions bearing the same names, and not as they should have been as a particular kind of prayer, a particular pilgrimage and fast, having only a few points in common with the generic Christian parallels. Such an attitude was generally en-couraged by the theoretic treatment of Islam as a heresy, as a concoction of errors intermixed with a partial truth. Islam came thus to be treated as a parody of bad Christianity, rather than as enjoying any independent existence of its own.

It was rather more reasonable to criticise Islamic morals as defective by standards of natural law, that is, by a law discoverable to reason unaided by revelation. Even in this field, when there was praise of Muslim morals, which occasionally there was, it is curious that it should largely have taken the form of satirical criticism of Christian practice; so that, when Islam in fact ex-emplified the working of the natural law, it was only used as a foil to exhort Christians. Christian polemic entirely ignored the question how far the natural law was actually observed by ordinary Muslims, and it did not seek for reasons that might minimise differences and enlarge understanding. Islamic morals were seen, either as denying, or else as reinforcing Christian morals, but never in themselves or distinct from Christianity.

4. THE TRUE PURPOSE OF THE POLEMIC

There is no great difficulty in identifying the public intended by anti-Islamic polemic of such kinds as we have just been summarising. Far and away the most probable explanation of its character is to suppose, not only that debates hardly ever happened, but that rarely was any particular debate planned to happen. This is not to imply that Christian polemists who thought in terms of debate with Muslims were hypocritical. Possibly they deceived themselves. They planned and imagined debates that might take place. This was entirely in the air; there was a general intention but no concrete actualisation. Thus mediaevals, radically anxious to speak on sound authority, and creditably so, signally failed to find what they claimed to have found: authorities that Muslims really would accept, or arguments that would stand up in debate before an outside witness. That is why Ricoldo disputed with learned Muslims only *aliquantulum*, and why his pages are filled by literary sources, and not by the fruit of personal contact. That is why missionaries gave their attention chiefly to Christians, Latin or Oriental, living under Islamic rule, rather than to the Muslims themselves; and those that turned to the Muslims sought, not the conversion of the infidel, but their own martyrdom. Practical men did not seek debate, and if they did it was unsuccessful. Where St Francis failed, no lesser man established common ground between the two religions. Tripoli was almost unique in encouraging Muslims to think that Islam and Christianity had much in common and that they themselves were in a fair way to becoming Christians; and it certainly cannot be said that even he wished to understand Islam in itself.

The overwhelming probability is that the public intended by the polemists was Christian. We may forget any suggestion that some real debate between the two religions was ever practicable. Nearly all the arguments that we have just reviewed were well calculated to be effective with such an audience, and only with such. They were admirably formulated to uphold faith. They would suitably horrify those who were at a distance from actual Muslims, but they would also fortify those who could not be guarded physically from Islamic realities. All alike would be confirmed in their suspicion and contempt. Within Christian territory Muslims might be isolated, and in the East Christian pilgrims and soldiers might be sheltered from articulate contact with Muslims. There still remained ordinary Christians under Islamic rule in Spain, and throughout Islam there were settled Christian communities, prisoners and merchants, as well as travelling merchants and missionaries; all these needed well-supported convictions to maintain their faith. The fiction of debate was retained because the writers were sincere and really believed that their arguments would have been effective, could they have been used; and they therefore felt justified in setting them against an imaginary background of disputation, which had its own very important function: it would convince the Christian public that these arguments would be effective over Muslims. Most authors valued very highly any opportunity of giving this impression, and would have justified their doing so, could they have been sufficiently candid with themselves, on the ground that what deserved to be effective would be so. This might occasionally be made nearly explicit. In the minds of some intellectual leaders the idea of showing forth the truth of Christianity was strong; thus, in the public dispute with the Jewish Rabbi Nachman, which did indeed take place, the communiqué asserted that there was no question of discussing the truth of the Christian faith, but only of making the truth of that faith manifest. This is no doubt why the Christian and Jewish accounts do not altogether agree.[18]

It was not only a question of fortifying the faith of Christians exposed to contact with Muslims. It was one of fortifying the faith of all Christians, however protected from the Islamic controversy by distance. Hostile communities can easily maintain opinions and arguments, which are available for the use of individuals at need, which are controversial in form, but which are not in fact shaped by actual controversy. This is as apparent in our own day as it was in the Middle Ages. The Middle Ages were like other ages in inventing and rearranging the facts of history and the beliefs of opponents in order to suit some noble purpose. It is important to realise that the facts and the Islamic doctrines thus rearranged were put into a form which primarily repelled, and must have been intended to repel, Christians; Islam was, in fact, not always described in terms necessarily repellent to Muslims. No doubt there was much that a Muslim would have had to resent; but the unpleasant image of Islam that the Christians drew was drawn to seem unpleasant to the Christian eye.

That is particularly exemplified by the stress on such points as the humanity of Muhammad, which were significant only from the Christian point of view. Those things were stressed that appealed to Christians as scandalous, not those that Muslims think important; and in this kind of picture-building exaggerations had an important part. Arguments which could not have impressed Muslims favourably, such as those that insisted that the Qur'ān must bear some special meaning dear to the polemist, become significant and pointed immediately we suppose that they were primarily intended for Christians to read. The dialectical trick of comparing Christian theory with Islamic practice, not Christian and Islamic practice, and the gratuitous assumption that Islamic practice must be as licentious as Islamic law was supposed to permit, without the least evidence derived from direct knowledge, were both well suited only to one end, the encouragement and comfort of Christians. That assumption must have been so easily believed only because it heightened the concept of a society hideously alien in what it permitted. In one way and another Islam was made to seem repellent, either as unlike or else as actually contrary to all the most important Christian teaching.

5. COMMUNAL HOSTILITY

There can be no doubt of the extent of Christian hatred and suspicion of Muslims. The occurrence of occasional favourable comparison between Christendom and Islam, generally with a satiric intent, must not suggest a general attitude. On the contrary, the general attitude among those who had no personal knowledge of Muslims, and often of those who had, was one of hatred; and we have seen in some detail the high degree of suspicion felt by those responsible for Christendom's relations with Muslims. Even passing references to Muhammad are often couched in superlatives such as *vilissimus*. One well-known example of how effective the general suspicion was may be cited, although there is little reason to choose one example more than another when there are so many. The account in Joinville of the deliberations of the Muslims, both the sultan Turān-Shah and the mamlūk 'amīrs, and of their treatment of their prisoners, is wholly pervaded by suspicion. No doubt the circumstances were extremely difficult, but it appears clearly that the French were at the mercy of interpreters' rumours, and that they felt their inability to judge soundly what was happening, while constantly crediting their expectation of the worst.

This suspicion was natural enough, in fact, inevitable, in the circumstances in which Christians lived. Since the authorities put so much pressure upon Muslims within Christendom to convert them, upon Christians within Islam to isolate them, and upon merchants and others to prevent any communication of intelligence at all, the two societies lived side by side as ignorantly of each other as possible. The way was nowhere open to an ordinary Christian to get to know Islam better, because he was prevented from knowing Muslims, from communicating freely and usefully with them. He was brought up to expect to be in a relationship of force and violence with them. It is difficult to erect learning upon a foundation of ignorance, to establish understanding in minds formed amid inherited prejudice and suspicion. Had more ordinary people been reasonably well-informed, the learned also would have achieved higher standards. In many ways they had a sound knowledge, which is remarkable enough; and occasionally they had more. Yet the missionaries, the only people really expected to link the two worlds, would have been better qualified to do so, if they had known a little more. No single one had a knowledge sound in all respects, or free from controversial bias in any. Ignorance was justified and fortified by the highest ideals: *liberatio humani generis*.[19] This freedom of the human race has a modern and an unconvincing ring to it.

The Christian case was not, of course, built out of nothing. There are real differences between the two religions of such a character as to exacerbate the irritated incomprehension each has for the other. In particular the extensive contrast between the religion of indulgence and the religion of asceticism has always been a key consideration in the Christian attitude. It may be conjectured that it arose spontaneously, both in the East and the West, and in the earliest times, among Christians living under Muslim rule; to such people apostasy was a real temptation, both for the sake of worldly success and for that of a more flexible code of private morals, to which many succumbed. The idea of this contrast has been almost universally adopted, and the contrast may not be unacceptable to Muslims themselves, when it is not tendentiously worded. For some modern Europeans the Islamic freedom from restrictions which they consider unnatural has seemed attractive.[20] Moreover, Christians were recommended, for example, to practise marital continence, where the reverse was encouraged by Islam. Certainly there is no question but that Islam does treat some vicious acts more tolerantly than Christianity in the past has ever done, and this difference, not in what is condemned, but in the degree of control exercised over condemned acts, constitutes a great difference in the moral practice of the two societies. We may almost say that what shocked the mediaeval was more the toleration than the commission of sins.

The clerical point of view (and our authorities were almost all clerical) is concerned with souls, that is to say, less with society as a whole or with general welfare, than with principles and with individuals. It is self-evident that in matters of principle the vital concession is toleration rather than encouragement; and those who have experience of souls generally associate loss of Christian faith with the coarsening of private morals and with self-indulgence generally. It is not possible to exaggerate the horror that the clergy felt for a doctrine which, without admitting that it was contrary to reason to do so, either permitted or encouraged things that men in any case would not give up, only too often, 'for any terrors or tortures or even for human shame, which for many is harder than death'.[21]

It is the fact that, in private morals, chiefly subjects connected with unchastity aroused strong interest in Western writers. Only the use of force in the public sphere received comparable attention. Within the field of sex most mistakes seem to have been made in the direction of greater salacity. If the most sordid and nastiest explanation was usually preferred, we cannot blame the Christians excessively, since they had neither the training nor the disposition to estimate degrees of abomination among forbidden things. To them the restraints imposed by the Qur'anic law were genuinely negligible; they could conceive no alternative to Christianity or unlimited licence. If we can do so to-day it is because events have shown it to us; we have to tolerate at home more than Islamic society has tolerated, except in its own more irreligious phases. Christian institutions then were seen as the norm from which everything else was a deviation. A divorced wife who had made another marriage was still her first husband's adulterous wife. Into a world where such institutions as matrimony were stable and fixed, an element that was both capricious and disturbing was interposed by every consideration of Islamic morals. Perhaps this was chiefly a danger to the imagination. Yet though the moralist sometimes exaggerated Muslim virtue to shame Christian vice, it was true that Christians often practised what they believed Muslims to preach. It is easy to see why these matters had the fascination both of attraction and of repulsion. In this situation was obliterated all possibility of detachment, and many brief glimmers of sympathy were extinguished. There was little sense of proportion.

This probably explains the constant preoccupation with Muhammad's 'hypocrisy'. Muhammad became essentially the *simulator sanctitatis*, although the things he had done were things that Islam, following him, did not believe to be sinful at all. Temptations of the world and the flesh were encouraged by the substitution of a fleshly Paradise for damnation. As Muhammad's life was understood, it was impossible to suppose that he acted contrary to Christian ethics without knowing what they are. He simply seemed by actions and doctrines alike to oppose Christianity. Enough was known about him for it to be clear that everything he did, he did for religious reasons and with religious motives. The only possible conclusion in those days was that he was a fraud who hid his wicked designs beneath a mask of religion; and the gravity of the matter made it inevitable that this view should always be stressed.

In our own time Pope Pius XII was reported to have described the Crusades as being only a quarrel between monotheists. The point of this is that the things that divide Christendom from atheists to-day are greater than those which Christendom and Islam quarrelled about in the Middle Ages. The attitude adopted

by a society in such a case is largely determined by the degree of
hostility it feels, rather than by any impartial assessment of the
importance of the quarrel. It is not suggested that hostile societies
to-day feel more antagonism than hostile societies felt during the
Crusades. In fact, the attribution of so many crimes to Islam, those
which most disgusted Christendom, was not just a means (even
sincerely and confidently brought forward) to discredit a rival
religion. It was also and more simply an expression of the hostility
that Christendom felt for the civilisation at its borders. It may be
that it is a human tendency for men to dislike other people's
thinking differently from themselves. This would explain why a
man often attributes to those who think differently from him a
version of their opinions that they themselves cannot recognise,
but which from his point of view is agreeably repulsive.

There is little doubt that, although some Christian polemic has
to-day learned to argue against rationalist and other opponents
on a common ground which they cannot but accept, most communal
hostilities in the modern world reflect the same attitude as did the
mediaeval ones. There are many controversies in which the
participants on each side argue against what they suppose their
opponents to mean, and not against what is actually meant and
said. There are many groups, especially national ones, that resent
and reject outside criticism, and that show more loyalty to causes,
the more it becomes irrational to do so. In many ways moderns
allow communal feeling to dominate opinion more than the
mediaevals did. It is possible to see in the modern division between
Parliamentary and People's Democracies a division similar to that
which divided Christendom and Islam in the Middle Ages. In such
a comparison it is possible that we should compare the mediaeval
Christians to modern Eastern Europe, the mediaeval Muslims to
the modern West, where survival is easier for communities which
are alien to the majority. Even within our national groups, our
different schools of opinion attack each other with no greater
respect for, or wish to understand, what their opponents are trying
to say, than is the case with mediaeval controversy. None of these
comparisons is important in itself. What is important is to say
that we cannot patronise the mediaevals about this. It is only about
the most ancient controversies that we begin to learn wisdom, and
then still only fitfully.

It may be that we can afford to be generous about controversy
that no longer excites us, only because we are no longer excited;
our vital interests are not now involved. It would be interesting,
but a very large subject, to consider how far Christian suspicion
of Islam implied an emotional basis in fear. A psychological
investigation, indeed, would take us too far, but there is an

historical question that may well be asked: had Christendom in fact any *reason* to fear Islam during this period? We need not argue exhaustively to prove that the Crusades were not a defence against military aggression, whether or no they were a defence of Christian rights, since they were fought on Islamic soil. When, later, under Ottoman leadership Islam did closely threaten European survival, the sense of Christian political solidarity had become relatively weak. There seems never to have been real fear of military invasion. The sole Christian fear was of Islamic doctrine, of the religion which endorsed pleasure, almost, perhaps, as a principle of religion. Yet it does not seem likely that Islam was feared because its antinomian heresy was believed seriously to threaten Christian doctrine. The tendency was ascetic in the most successful heresies of the day, Waldensian, Albigensian; it is true that the latter was believed to encourage extra-marital sexual relations, and, more particularly, unnatural vice, among its sympathisers, but there is no evidence that any of its tenets were associated with those of Islam in the minds of the Catholic authorities. If the clerical attitude to Islam was formed by fear, this was largely based upon 'paper' reasons, rather than upon the probabilities of everyday life; its doctrinal menace was theoretical, logical even, but unreal.

In all the circumstances, there is nothing remarkable about the mediaeval willingness always to believe the worst about Islam, or in the open and admitted hostility of the Muslim and Christian communities. Naturally, mediaevals never admitted that what was said about Islam was exaggerated or silly, still less that it was frequently untrue. What was admitted and stressed was that the religion of Islam was unlike, alien to and incompatible, in many ways, with a Christian tradition of which the truth, even in in-essentials, was not questioned. Even what was held in common sometimes only drew attention to this contrast. The difference was stressed partly with the conscious purpose of refuting the Islamic claim to fulfil the prophecies; but it was also an admission that the two cultures had distinct identities. The integrity of each required that the other should be rejected, and rejected whole. In religion, there was no compromise, or exchange of views or intermixture of ideas. It may well be that the internal consistency and integrity of the Christian concept of Islam was one reason for its long survival in the European consciousness.

At the same time, rejection did not cause the thing rejected to cease to exist: Islam was still at the frontier. For this reason it had to be admitted openly as an enemy, and presented in terms that did not make it necessary to change or adapt any single facet of Christian and European culture. This is why the data of an

inherited polemic were preferred to the fruits of personal observation; and why men living in Syria chose or consented to believe
fantastic nonsense about Islamic matters. This is why the Latin
West formed a more or less invariable canon of beliefs about
Islam; it decided for itself what Islam was, and formed a view
materially different from anything Muslims would recognise.
There was nothing original about the view thus formed. Every
main idea probably existed among Christians subject to Islamic
rule, and many also among the Greeks, from the earliest generations of Islam. The important thing was that it suited the West.
It corresponded to need; it made it possible to protect the minds
of Christians against apostasy and it gave Christendom self-respect
in dealing with a civilisation in many ways its superior. So much
did this canon suit the need that it survived many changes in the
relative positions of Islam and Christendom and in the interior
movements of Christian opinion. Within Christendom, the mediaevals preserved society, and the ideas to which society was
attached, by intolerance. Jews and Muslims subject to Christian
princes needed to be isolated, and heretics, as subject to the
Christian Church to be extirpated. The same preservation of
Christendom against the external enemy was ensured by the
development of the intellectual response to Islam; and it survived
longer than the internal unity of Christendom by many centuries.

The survival of mediaeval concepts

SUMMARISING the conclusions of the last two chapters, we can say that the Western view of Islam, which was formed during the period with which this book is primarily concerned, was based on a good deal of sound knowledge, but that it also accepted much that now seems nonsense, because what seemed useful to faith was thought likely to be true; that there developed and was established a communal mode of thought which had great internal coherence, and which represented the doctrinal unity of Christendom in its political opposition to Islamic society. The strength of this integral group, or series, of opinions, what we may call this established canon, proved to be so great as to survive the break-up of European ideological unity, both the division into Catholic and Protestant, and the growth of agnosticism and atheism. This process of survival I propose now very cursorily to trace.

1. THE SUBSTANCE OF THE MEDIAEVAL CANON

It may be convenient to begin by summarising the mediaeval idea of Islam.

During the period with which I have been concerned there was established in the minds of the Western reading public some fair idea of the claim of Islam to be the one religion of the prophets, and certainly of its claim to be the third and culminating prophetic revelation of a Book. The idea was sound, though not always formulated with precision. The Muslim belief that the Qur'ān was *sent down* was understood in a general way, though the details and the implications of the doctrine were not fully grasped; there was a marked failure to distinguish between the Qur'ān and other Islamic books thought to be equally authoritative. Much importance was attached to the defence of Scripture, both from the general charge of having been corrupted, and from the special charge that Christ's prophecy of *Aḥmad* had been suppressed. Although this Muslim accusation was widely known, it was also said that the Qur'ān confirmed the Scripture, which, quite unjustifiably, was taken to mean the existing Christian canonical Scripture. Arguments to defend Scripture were illogically based

271

upon Scripture, but the real disproof of the Qur'ān was seen to be its unlikeness to, or contradiction of, both Scripture and philosophy, and also in its being contrary to reason.

This outline of knowledge about Islamic belief in connection with Revelation was sound, although some popular ideas were wholly absurd. The educated view was so far set along the way to full and accurate information that it wanted only propitious circumstances (which eventually occurred, somewhat later in European history) for the more absurd elements to drop away and leave only the sound, at least where serious students were concerned. Two polemic lines in particular developed from this body of information about Revelation, of which one ceased to be important after the Middle Ages, and the other came almost to dominate Christian thought.

The first was the conviction that the Qur'ān was indeed a *corroboratio* of the Gospel. We have just seen that this led to a feeble logical position based on false premises, and yet we must allow it some force. The Qur'ān was sound only in this one respect, its confirmation of Scripture, or so it seemed to the mediaeval critic, but it seemed that it really was so; it might be loved and welcomed as a superfluous but valid witness to the truth of the Christian faith, perhaps more useful for being involuntary. This attitude can even be defended logically, provided it be not stated to a Muslim audience. The mediaevals saw much in the Qur'ān which could be understood in a Christian way and which seemed therefore to witness to the Christian truth. To tell a Muslim that the word and the spirit, referred to by the Qur'ān in connection with the conception of Jesus, were the Word and the Spirit as understood by Christians of the Persons of God, or to say that the plural pronoun in the Qur'ān implied the Trinity, was to ask for ridicule. In speaking to Christians, however, it was perfectly reasonable. To say that the Qur'ān is full of involuntary witness to Christ is something to delight a Christian, although it must annoy or be indifferent to any Muslim. We have seen that the intended audience was probably Christian all along; the only error, therefore, was to address these arguments ostensibly to Muslims, as though they had a polemic value, rather than one purely for edification. It might most reasonably edify a Christian to understand the great praise of Christ that there is in the Qur'ān; it would be unreasonable if he were not edified. Often this praise was quoted in words very close to the words of the Qur'ān, or in the very words themselves, and sometimes the spirit of it was successfully conveyed, because the subject was congenial.

It was not solely a question of the Person of Christ, however; the high and difficult doctrines of the Trinity and the Incarnation were almost an obsession to Christians, who argued both that the Qur'ān really implied the Trinity, and that the Trinity must any way be proved by the light of natural reason. It was agreed, with rare exceptions, that on the unity of God Islam was sound; but its purpose in speaking truth was only to ensnare. This at least was the scholastic view; in poetry the idea that Islam was idolatrous was expressed and implied often enough, but this seems to have been purely a literary convention. The general attitude of scholastics, however, resulted in Islam's being taken to be a heresy, and as the sum of all heresy it was often regarded. It was also regarded as one of the three great religions of the world which, historically related, still competed contemporaneously for the souls of the pagan Mongols; and again, it was regarded as a schism of Christian peoples. Indeed, it seemed to be a schism of the human race, which God had called, entire, to the Christian faith. What was least durable in all this was the preoccupation with the defence of the Scriptural text; but the relation of Christian and Islamic beliefs would never be examined much more closely or considered more fully; conclusions could hardly go further to-day.

The other point of great importance was the mediaeval objection to the Islamic teaching that revelation might come down to solve problems of a transient nature. When the implications of this objection are considered, it will be seen that the objection extends to any revelation related to the circumstances of a prophet at a time and place; it implies, in fact, all the detailed objections that were made to the character of Muhammad, and to his history, and that were thought definitively to preclude his claim to prophethood. Always contrasted with the true elements in the Qur'ān were the false ones; always associated with the Qur'anic picture of Christ was the Qur'anic picture of Muhammad – largely negatively, the absence of any 'praise' of Muhammad in the Qur'ān at all. His prophethood was seen as alien to all known prophethood; non-prophetic, untruthful in utterance, evil of life, unverified by miracles. This absence of miracles was considered one of the most damning weaknesses in the Muslim case; on the one hand, said the Christians, Muhammad denied the need, because he had not the gift; and, on the other, his followers, embarrassed by the lack and realising the need, attributed bogus miracles to him, in spite of his own denial. This attack on Muhammad's prophethood was worked out in great detail. The creation of a legend of his life was an important part of anti-Islamic polemic and of the Christian approach to Islam. The spectacle of what Muhammad did was proof enough that he was no prophet; San Pedro's remark that Muslims were to blame, not for doing what

Muhammad allowed, but for believing in him at all, represents the Christian attitude at its most logical.

The background of Muhammad's life, the Arabia into which he was born, his own early life, his call to the prophethood and the circumstances of his death were all presented as demonstrating that he was human, fallible and subject to every discreditable misfortune. Even to have lived in paganism till the age of forty was thought disgraceful. Heretical Christian and Jewish influences explained the content of his teaching; and the manner of revelation alleged of him, and his solution of his immediate, temporary and often personal problems were all thought so suspicious as to amount in themselves to a disproof of the prophetic claim. This was most true of revelations that allowed the Prophet marital privileges of one sort and another; many of these were invented by Christians, but such as were not were highly immoral in Christian eyes, especially when expressed in Christian terms. The two most important aspects of Muhammad's life, Christians believed, were his sexual licence and his use of force to establish his religion. In order to preserve this picture unblurred it was often necessary to prefer a false account to a true one (as we to-day see it); certainly as many false but desirable elements as could by any means be believed were usually accepted. Even so, there was a wide difference between what could be believed by those who lived in the heart of Christendom and what those who lived within or upon the borders of dār al-Islām could believe.

The salient elements in Muhammad's life, or in the Christian legend of his life, were reflected in the concept of Islam as a practical religion. Like its Prophet, it was said to be violent by nature and this was said despite the reflection on Crusading theory of the Islamic doctrine of the holy war. Christians were sincerely and seriously troubled because God permitted worldly success to Islam; this was an aspect of mediaeval thought that would prove impermanent. Except when they bore arms against Islam, Christians under Islamic rule enjoyed toleration in a tributary position. At the period with which we are concerned the position conceded to Muslims within Christendom approximated to this in general outline and in many details; but this proved at best a fluctuating tolerance which was always subject to propaganda, and which resulted in the expulsion or conversion, in time, of every Islamic enclave. Thus Muhammad's violence was essential, in the Christian opinion, to his religion, although Christians and Muslims alike practised holy war, and only Islam effectively tolerated other religions within itself, admittedly granting only second-class citizenship.

Equally important in the Christian concept was the moral

licence – and to an overwhelming extent this meant sexual licence
– attributed to Islamic doctrine and practice, as to the Prophet in
his lifetime; it is almost impossible to exaggerate how important
this was believed to be. At the same time there was a less prominent, but still persistent, tendency to hold Islam up as a good
example in practice, to a certain extent in certain matters only,
to the shaming of Christians. The more specifically religious
duties inculcated by Islam were also sometimes recognised as
setting a good example; but for the most part these were misconceived and misinterpreted as false copies of Christian exemplars.
One theme almost sums up every other theme: the Muslim
Paradise was achieved by determinist ethics and often by death in
the holy war; it was entirely sensual in its description; and it
typified the irrationality of the Qur'ān. For mediaevals it denied
two things that they regarded very highly, whether they served
them well or ill: chastity and reason.

Throughout the near fourteen centuries of Islam, Christians
have defended their faith in the Trinity and Incarnation from
Muslim attack; and they have in turn attacked Islam for accepting
the claim of Muhammad to be the vehicle of Revelation, chiefly
on the grounds that his character made it impossible reasonably
to do so. Finally they have had to decide upon the admixture of
truth and error: how to estimate its value, how to allow for the
error, how to balance judgement upon the significance of each,
and how to assess the final result. In respect of these points the
mediaeval concept proved extremely durable; this outline of it is
still a part of the cultural inheritance of the West to-day.

2. SURVIVAL OF THE MEDIAEVAL CANON: BARELY MODI-
   FIED NOTIONS OF ISLAM

Except for some shifts in emphasis, and for the increasing
neglect of certain arguments, notably those defending the integrity
of the text of the Scriptures, we may say that the views just
summarised outline the Western 'canon' of what constitutes
Islam. We are entitled to say that this canon was formed during
the twelfth and thirteenth centuries and the earlier part of the
fourteenth, by the absorption of Oriental, Byzantine and Mozarab
traditions and, to a lesser extent, of experience. By the middle of
the fourteenth century it was firmly established in Europe; and it
was to continue into the future so powerfully as to affect many
generations, even up to the present day. I have no space to
examine the centuries between 1350 and 1950 closely, as I have
the period immediately preceding them; and it would be monotonous to read mere variations on recognised themes, in which
new elements would be only slowly perceptible. I shall instead

illustrate the survival of the mediaeval canon with examples
chosen from different periods; I shall not attempt a complete
survey.

Of the points that I summarised, most had a long life. The
'fraudulent' or 'hypocritical' character of Muhammad's claim to
prophesy, while he was an ambitious schemer, a bandit and a
lecher; the emphasis on Islam as a falling short of Christianity, a
sum of heresy, particularly in connection with the Trinity; preoccupation with the Qur'anic teaching of Christ; the general lines,
if not all the details, of the most unflattering biography of Muhammad, and particularly the weight given to the influence of Sergius
and other guides upon him; the enormous importance given to
two moral questions, the public reliance on force and the supposed
private laxity in sexual matters; the ridicule and contempt of the
Qur'anic Paradise; the suspicion of determinist and predestinarian
ethics; the interest in Islamic religious practices, the admission of
some Islamic practice as a good example, but the treatment of the
cult in general as vain; all these, with some differences in emphasis,
but with great continuity in the attitude of intellectual contempt,
long dominated Christian and European thought.

In the later Middle Ages this is true equally of theoreticians
such as Nicholas of Cusa and Denys van Leeuwen, or the Spanish
ecclesiastics, John of Torquemada and Alfonso a Spina, and also
of experienced travellers like Francesco Suriano and Bernhard von
Breydenbach. At this period the Latins also gave back to the
Greeks a little of what they had borrowed from them.[1] I shall
take Nicholas of Cusa as representative of the period. His example
is of special interest on which it would be rewarding to spend longer.
His work contains some additional information, but very little.
Basically it is like Fitzralph's – the product of pondering the text
of Ketton's Qur'ān, although Cusa took other authors also into
account. It is in other ways unlike, in that Cusa's personality was
markedly individual; moreover, his was an intellect particularly
gifted for theological speculation; and this gives a new note to
some of his apologetic.

He would willingly (he said) cede to Muhammad or to anyone
else the right to announce a gospel of joy to those that fear God,
and of punishment for infidels; but 'in other things, how dare you
speak,' he asks Muhammad, 'when you have neither been enjoined
nor licensed to do so by God?' God had willed that some truths
should be inserted among the things which are abominable even
to learned Muslims. Muhammad, on the other hand, by including
the latter in the Qur'ān, had attributed change to the unchangeable
God. His handling of some themes is characteristic of his elevated
style of thought, which was not unscholarly. His comparison of

Christian and Islamic belief about God and Christ and Mary, of the field of heresy which is so important a part of the mediaeval canon, is carefully detailed and intellectually considerable. He addresses a Christian convert to Islam:

You do not think that you have denied Christ, but that you believe less about Him than you did before. You believed Him the true Son of God, now by the Islamic religion you do not. You have not denied faith in the one God, which you had, and hold still. You believed Mary the mother of Jesus Christ to be *theotokos*, that is, the mother of God; now you say that the Virgin Mary is mother of Christ, not of God. You believed Christ was crucified in Jerusalem by Pontius Pilate for our salvation, and you visited the place of the sepulchre . . . now you deny that He died, and add that He is living still. Often and devoutly you saw the place of the nativity near the manger, in Bethlehem; now you deny that this is true, saying that Christ was born in a solitary place, under a palm-tree.

This passage continued in a rather more polemic vein: if Mary were not the daughter of 'Imrān, the Qur'ān was false, and 'the Gospel Gabriel is true and the Qur'anic Gabriel a liar'.

Cusa's Trinitarian argument is polemically, and even speculatively, superior to anything that had gone before in the West, although he only re-used and refurbished arguments that he inherited. In chapters indebted for information to Ricoldo he takes a large view: he 'explains' the Trinity (*mens, scientia* and *voluntas*) but takes the trouble first to insist that there is both the *mystical* theology according to which God is ineffable, and which agrees directly with the Qur'ān; and the *affirmative* theology which he then elaborates. Even when he is demonstrating the Trinity, he remembers the special needs of readers of the Qur'ān; all creation, he says, creation which the Qur'ān insists is indeed God's creation, leads by affirmative theology to knowledge of the Trinity. Sometimes he is more firmly tied to traditional methods, for example in his attack upon the Qur'anic text, where he is less large-minded:

You (he is speaking to an imaginary Muslim interlocutor) you have to believe everything which (the Qur'ān) contains to be very true. Say, therefore, when you read in sūrah vi, *I indeed, to whom God has shown a right way and a straight one, that namely of Abraham, who was not an unbeliever; and directed me;* what do you understand by 'I'? If you say 'Muhammad', anyway those words are not God's, and they need not be believed. Muhammad proves nothing, therefore, when he bears witness to himself; and, as those words are written in the Qur'ān, you have premised that they are God's; and the two things cannot be at the same time.

Cusa's *Cribratio* is rambling and repetitive, like Ricoldo's

Disputatio. Here was a fresh mind working over old themes with varying success. The European response to the Turkish danger was more obviously reflected in his *de pace fidei*, reminiscent of Lull (whom his modern editors show to have been important among his sources) and in it he is heir to that tradition which united problems of Crusade, conversion and reunion in a single common approach. This legacy he shares – together with the ability to give a new turn to old arguments – with his correspondent, John of Segovia, whose conviction that force is profitless ('scarcely or never has the conversion of infidels been effected by fear of war'), his scholarly translation of the Qur'ān, and his relations with Cusa, Pius II and Jean Germain (a less original writer who depended on the Risālah) have been admirably studied by Cabanelas.[2]

In contrast, the work of Alfonso a Spina, written from the point of view of the Spanish Reconquest, sees the physical, and even the doctrinal, struggle of Islam as a gradual subjection to Christendom, bound finally to lead to extinction. The author, credulous of atrocities supposed to have been committed by Jews, is just a little less intolerant of Islam. He is in debt to Ricoldo. A well-written little book is the *Confusion* by Juan Andrés; a good deal of his material is new, his plan typically mediaeval. He might easily have written two centuries earlier; a 'converted Moor', his work strongly suggests traditional Christian influences; he might be the author of the *Contrarietas*, born again, perhaps with more discretion. The work of a third Spaniard, Torquemada, is not only traditional, but heavy and undistinguished; professedly hurried, it is abusive and undiscriminating, and it is overburdened by its use of Scripture. It attacks the Prophet in consecutive chapters for making God the author of sin, and for making out that the world is ruled by chance.

We must say something similar of Denys van Leeuwen (Dionysius Carthusianus). His work is solid, at times rhetorical, but in traditional terms. He rarely ventures beyond the arguments sanctioned by his predecessors, and never beyond the general scheme of such argument. His work, as Mademoiselle d'Alverny has pointed out, is dependent, like that of Cusa, on the Cluniac corpus. Like Fitzralph, van Leeuwen read his Ketton with care, and singled out one proposition after another for examination and dismissal. His *Dialogus* is realistic enough at the beginning, when the Muslim protagonist asks why Christians speak so ill of Muhammad, who speaks so well of Christ; and, throughout, the Muslim is allowed to make some good points against his opponent; but he is far too easily persuaded that the Qur'ān 'has been corrupted by evil men', and by the end he has been wholly, and most improbably, converted. All van Leeuwen's work is scholastic – Scriptural, theological and philosophical – and it exists in that rarefied atmosphere of unreality which we have already met in earlier mediaeval disputations, where all the parts are written by a Christian. I mention arguments that appealed to him. To Ketton's Qur'ān he objects, for example, that God cannot 'breathe part of His soul into man', because He has no soul, and man is not of his substance. He seems to have thought it important to correct the Qur'anic story of Joseph. He liked common-sense arguments that vary from such as critics make to-day (against sūrah xix he urged that the Book of Jeremias proves that the name 'John' was known before it was given to the Baptist) to such as moderns would consider quaint (against the same sūrah he argued that martyrs go straight to Heaven, as many miracles prove). He is not generous: all the almsgiving of the Muslims is but sin, since it is done in order to earn a carnal Heaven. Like his contemporaries, he was concerned at the Islamic danger, and associated together the needs for Reunion, Reform and Crusade, on which, indeed, he reckoned to have received special illuminations.[3]

When we come to the humanists we still meet no major change. Aeneas Sylvius was perhaps the last Pope to take the hope of Crusade seriously; but the Turks were in fact a real political menace. His letter to the Ottoman Muhammad II (the Conqueror) is a document that shows little originality, and of which the latinity is not as elegant as the author's reputation might make us expect. There is some agreeable apparatus of classical learning, and, although there are mistakes – the appeal, for example, to Old Testament prophetical books as though recognised by Muslims – this is a remarkable short, and useful, compendium of the anti-Islamic polemic of the past. Small familiar points are rephrased, with no improvement, as that Muhammad did not invent fasting, or the few other good things of his religion; Pius gave greater emphasis than his mediaeval predecessors to that over-simplified notion that Islam makes God to be explicitly the cause of sin. The graces of the Renaissance were displayed more freely by Juan Luis Vives half a century later, but his matter was wholly traditional, however tastefully brought forward. Lope Obregon's *Confutacion* (1555) is unoriginal and not greatly interesting, but it distantly reflects the new historical discipline in its manner of making the life of Muhammad the framework of the familiar but elaborate polemic.

I wish to take Polydore Vergil as typical of the high Renaissance and of new interests in the writing of history. It is particularly interesting to find his adept historical combination of disparate sources associated with a lack of knowledge or judgement. He was not able to recognise and reject legendary sources. What he has to say of Muhammad and Islam is some improvement on mediaeval legend-building at its worst, but his judgements are greatly inferior to the best of an earlier age. He tried to fit in much of the *Corozan* story, which he did with some ingenuity, thus helping to perpetuate the myth of Muhammad's epileptic-seeming fits. He thought him the son of a *cultor malorum daemonum* and himself a magician; he stressed the part played by *Sergius*, cited the usual catalogue of constituent heresies and included the standard mediaeval accounts of the institutions of Islam, culminating in the description of Paradise. In Renaissance style he refurbished a mediaeval libel, and referred to the celebration of Friday as sacred to the *Dea Veneris*; sexual indulgence and the use of arms in the spread of Islam he emphasised in the familiar way; he ends with the vain regret of all converts to Islam, upon rather a literary note: *Heu quam tunc infelices, sed sero stultitae poenitebit!*[4]

The Reformers do not seem to have conceived Islam any differently; in some ways Luther felt more strongly than his mediaeval predecessors, perhaps because of the Turkish military danger, which was still pressing. The Church of Rome might be thought the head, and Islam the body, of Antichrist, although, since 'out of God's Church there is no Antichrist', the Turk could not correspond closely to the description. On the other hand, certain prophecies, notably the Apocalypse, 'he shall make war against the Saints', applied strictly to the Turk, and not properly to the Pope at all; the latter warred, not by force, but by superstition. Melanchthon explicitly stated that the name of Antichrist was suitably applied to Muhammad, as *devastator* and *tyrant* of the Christian religion. In the mediaeval tradition, he pointed out that the unity of God needed no special revelation: 'this wisdom of theirs is nothing but a certain philosophy of the common human reason'. For Melanchthon the essential was the denial of the mediation and 'placation' worked by Christ, that He is 'born of the substance of the Eternal Father . . . (and) was the Victim of the human race'. Islam rejected the witness of the Apostles and of the Prophets equally; it even rejected the Mosaic Law itself, by breaking, for example, the rules of marriage. The Zwinglian Theodore Buchmann's own work as editor ('Bibliander') gave circulation to much important mediaeval and other work on Islam, which otherwise might well have been forgotten, so that for his readers he was a principal architect of anti-Islamic polemic. His introduction to his collection does not show him to be more, personally, than the summariser of what his own authors would say. He had a particularly vivid sense of the historical setting, and of the pressure of Islam upon Germany in his own day; a strong feeling for the identification of Muhammad as the head, of Islam as the body of Antichrist.[5]

A feature of the period of transition from mediaeval to more modern times was the retention of old material while new was added. Dedicated to Duke Federico of Urbino by Guglielmo of Moncata is a strange hodge-podge that contains the Cluniac *de doctrina Machumet*, together with a good translation of a long Qur'anic passage, a glossary of Arabic terms and names, and a long epitome, first of Qur'anic teaching, scholarly and completely untendentious, and then also of information and polemic of a traditional character. We may compare the Italian Qur'ān published by Arrivabene as late as 1547; it was taken from Ketton, and the *de doctrina, de generatione* and *chronica* of the Cluniac corpus were included as the first book of the actual Qur'ān. One of the most remarkable aspects of this question is the slowness of travellers with experience of their own to adopt new ideas of Islamic doctrine. Suriano, for instance, who visited Syria, Palestine, Arabia, Egypt and Abyssinia in the fifteenth century, and who reveals his own characteristic style, expressed only traditional material. He was perhaps particularly sensitive to Islamic veneration for Jesus Christ and for the Holy Places, and his is an early example of the appreciation that Religious, such as the Friars Minor or the Carmelites, felt for the respect often paid to them in Islam. Within an integral tradition that descends through centuries there are naturally differences of emphasis. In this period there was an increased interest in Muslim 'clergy', especially religious orders, and in religious practice generally. Among other travellers of the century, von Breydenbach treated the dogmatic differences between the two religions systematically, basing his work upon a wide reading of earlier European authors; Fabri, quite unsystematic, enjoyed using rhetorical phrases which reflect his knowledge of traditional works, of which he expressly cites a short list. Like Ricoldo, he admired in practice the disciplined tranquillity of pious Muslims, but even for that age he was extravagant in his theoretic dislike of Islam, and of its Prophet (such as he imagined him). In contrast, the devout Brascha, from the recollection of the prayers he had offered on pilgrimage, suitable to each occasion and place, spared the attention to speak gently of Islam, of its praise of Christ, and even of its own forms of worship. Piloti repeated the unislamic part of William of Tripoli's account of Baḥīra; he shared Tripoli's generous reaction to Muslim virtue, and Ricoldo's indignation at Christian feebleness in comparison. If Muslims were converted they would be so much the better Christians; already they extended justice and charity to all human creatures. Schiltberger and Vertomannus blended curiously their personal observations and their inherited suppositions, repeating the latter in guise of the former. There is an abrupt contrast with George of Hungary's percipient analysis of the temptation for Christian captives to change religion, and his uninhibited admiration for strict Turkish morals. Travellers always seem to show independent judgement most when they are speaking of actual encounters, and least when they discuss theory, dogma, or the life of Muhammad. They easily confused what they saw, what they were told, and what they had long ago read in books.[6] So it continued. Most travellers of the seventeenth century added practical observations of their own, but based their accounts of Islam as a religion, not on their own direct experience, but on tradition inherited from the mediaeval West.

On one subject a big increase of knowledge was brought home by travellers: this was the shī'ah faith, which most mediaevals had known only as the religion of obscure and eccentric sectaries, but which in the seventeenth century was the state religion of Persia, made most famous by Shah 'Abbās, whose renown in his day was unparalleled.[7] Naturally enough, the division between Shī'ah and Sunni was seen to have a Christian parallel – 'no lesse zealous and divided in their profession, than wee and the Papalins', said the Welsh Protestant, Thomas Herbert; its importance was inevitably political: 'whereby is sown such mortall hatred between these two potent Monarchs (the Turk and the Persian) that (to Europs good) they abominate each other with implacable hatred'. Apart from this we can say that what the travellers saw and heard they elected to fit into the theoretic scheme they had been brought up to.

Mahomet (whose name Arabically signifies Deceit, and many times *Conveniunt rebus nomina saepe suis*; affording also the number 666 the marke of Antichrist,) having accomplisht his desires, and runne his race, is summond to appeare before the Lord of all flesh, the God Omnipotent, Omniscient, and Judge of all mens actions; where (no doubt) he received a just judgement for his impiety.

It is a pity not to be able to quote at greater length this racy example of the lay culture of Europe, but one further example may illustrate the continuity of attitude:

Mahomets stomack grew weak, and one sort of meat begun to loath him; *Chodaige* (=Khadijah) was stale, and others fancied him: he therefore purpos'd in his Law (then in hatching) to allow all sorts of carnall liberty: and to incourage them by his example, solemnly . . . espoused *Aysce* (='Ā'ishah) the beloved child of his sonne in law *Abubocher* . . .

It is astonishing how even the details of their criticisms were repetitions passed down over centuries. The present writer many years ago prepared a statement of Islamic belief from the accounts of seventeenth-century travellers, and, although he did so in conditions which separated that work from the work on the Middle Ages with which this present book is concerned, the descriptions of the Christian attitudes of the two periods correspond so minutely as to astound the reader of both.

The relation of Islam to traditional heresies, for example, is often done in exactly the manner of Peter the Venerable and Ricoldo. There is the same stress on Islamic denial of the Trinity, the same appreciation of Qur'anic honour done to Jesus and (in the case of Catholics) to Mary. There is a wider realisation of the submission of Muslims to the eternal decrees of God in their daily lives, and a more general, but similar, defence of Christian doctrine of free will, against determinist ethics; there is a more general appreciation of Islamic reverence for God and for holy things, and of other such specifically Islamic virtues as are also Christian. Above all there is the same rationalist attack on the Qur'ān, as dictated to exploit the political hazards and to justify the personal indulgences of Muhammad's life and the desires and inclinations of the Arabs of his day. The idea that Islam was at first a schism of Christendom survived the divisions of Europe, and we find Herbert supposing that Muhammad preached against 'Pope Boniface's usurpation of the title of Universall Bishop'. Belief in the Sergius legend and in other mediaeval legends also still survived, even that of the dove that whispered in Muhammad's ear, trained to supply for the Holy Ghost; Febvre, the pseudonym of a rather aggressive but not ignorant Capuchin missionary, is a case in point; and George Sandys, whose voyage began in 1610, offers his readers much the same sort of anthology of mediaeval legends as Polydore Vergil's just a century earlier. Many travellers genuinely sought to correct misapprehensions; yet even when their approach was academic, as for example with Cotovicus, who allowed his personal experience to feed his theoretic knowledge, or highly individual, as in the case of La Boullaye le Gouz, the general outline of the image of Islam remained the same. Many of the best scholars found – and made good use of – the opportunity to travel in the East; but it long continued to be possible to maintain the ancient prejudice unmodified. Dr Humphrey Prideaux, no traveller but a scholar, at the end of the seventeenth century scarcely did more. Lastly, there was always the conviction that Islam is based upon force and violence.[8]

Although, as we shall shortly see, this was a period when Islamic scholarship was revolutionised, there survived an old-fashioned scholarship that we can hardly distinguish from the traditional polemic. Reineck's History (1602) is a conglomeration of mediaeval travellers and Crusading chroniclers. Sylburg thought it worth making an anthology of old Greek texts on Islam; it was based on Zigabenus and included the abjuration formula. Of the historians, Curio offers new information, and, without discrimination, much that is old and false as well; Drechsler's *Chronicon*, sound and bare and factual, seeks no original sources. Knolles' *Generall Historie* works a vast collection of historical matter and legend into a single masterpiece (1604), and the third book of *Purchas His Pilgrimage*, added in the edition of 1614, gathers solid information from older histories. Even Hottinger, who was prudently critical of the Cluniac corpus, and who used original sources judiciously in his *Historia Orientalis*, forced his work to serve a polemic end which is wholly traditional. Strukhusen, using material available by 1664, yet accepted traditional absurdities. Such authors as Pientini, whose aim was rather dogmatic than scientific, almost anthologised the old polemic writers; similarly Baudier, the pious layman, thorough, rather prim, covers almost all the old familiar ground. It is difficult to distinguish the polemist from the old-style *savant*.

The first vernacular translation of the Qur'ān was that of André du Ryer, in France, published in 1647; it must be classed as popular rather than academic, and was seen in a polemic aspect. The English version of Alexander Ross appeared in London two years later. This was the year of the king's execution, and the religious settlement of the country was more in doubt than ever. Ross thought it prudent to append a 'needfull Caveat or Admonition for them who desire to know what use may be made of, or if there be danger in reading the Alcoran'. How far it was traditional may be judged from his opening sentence: 'Good reader, the great *Arabian* Impostor now at last after a thousand years is by way of France arrived in England, and his Alcoran or gallimaufry of Errors, (a Brat as deformed as the Parent and as full of heresies, as his scald head was of scurffe) hath learned to speak English.' During the Commonwealth there also appeared a faithful and lively translation of Andrés' little book; Raue had found a sympathetic public, and Pocock at this time was gratified by the public interest in Arabic studies which waned at about the time of the Restoration.

Some reflections of European quarrels affected the traditional criticisms of Islam. On a superficial level we have already noted the parallel between Sunni and Shī'ah on one hand and Catholic and Protestant on the other. Deeper criticism occasionally occurred. A Catholic is probably thinking of the doctrines of the Reformed Church when he speaks of Muslims' 'false Religion, which makes them hope for the remission of all their sins, provided they believe in Mahomet'; he uses traditional polemic but has justification by faith in mind. Similarly a Lutheran so describes Islam that, although the comment is again traditional in type, it is made to sound papistical: when Muslims have commited a sin 'they go after their own invented devotion, to good works, alms, prayers, fasting, redeeming of captives, etc., to make satisfaction to God for their committed sins'. Here the writer tilts, surely, at works as a means of salvation. The Reformation controversies coloured, but added little to the substance of what was said.[9] However, a by-product was that Christians persecuted at home looked with longing at the system of toleration that obtained in Turkey, a recurring theme. The irenic vision of possible understanding was widened by men like Bodin and Postel, although the latter at least seems deeply indebted to mediaeval predecessors. There was a sensible diminution of bias, which showed in another way in Belon's strictly scientific enquiry into the phenomena of travel.

Any sample of seventeenth-century opinion shows polemic continuity. Herbert, the professional gentleman and dilettante of the English Court, contrasts personally with Père Nau, a French Jesuit with long experience in Syria, soundly theological, with some literary gift and a great deal of common sense; a serious clerical product of his age. He stated firmly the limits to which it was possible to blame the continued success of Islam upon its employment of force. 'There is almost no one', he said, 'but has the false conviction that it is forbidden to talk to the Turks about religion . . . By the grace of God, the Mahometans are not such ferocious wolves'; but, if dispute was always possible for such as 'deal with them with a humble air full of gentleness as the Gospel commands', yet Nau still saw the foundation of Islam upon force as fundamental to that faith. His treatment of the Qur'anic text is relatively sympathetic; his is the theme first enunciated by St John Damascene, that Christian truth lies implicit in the Qur'ān, waiting only to be drawn out of it; and he draws it, sometimes, with delicacy.

Did the Qur'ān say that those who hold God to be the Messias are infidels? It is right to do so; for this might mean, either that the three Persons all subsist in the Messias, or that the Godhead subsists only in the Son. The Gospel, of course, makes no such silly mistake as this reproves, and only maintains that the Messias is God. I think that it is clear that this is an advance in method, although none in matter, upon earlier polemic. Nau's Latin polemic is more formal than that which he wrote in French, and it cites the Qur'ān in Arabic script. The dialogue is intended to practise the precept of St Peter, to 'satisfy everyone that asketh you' *cum modestia et timore*, although some of it turns out to be fairly strongly expressed. It covers such familiar ground as the defence of the Scriptural text by the Qur'anic verse, 'we gave you the Gospel, in which is direction and light'. Nau was truly anxious to find persuasive reasons in the Qur'ān, despite language that sometimes seems offensive to Muslims – 'Hoc qui dicunt e vestris, reposuit Christianus, videntur garrire et fabulare gratuito.' He tried, for example, to penetrate to the reason lying behind the Qur'anic denial of the Crucifixion, quoted Philippians, 'obedient unto death, even to the death of the cross; for which cause, God also hath exalted him', to show that the Christian doctrine was the source of glory, not of shame: 'what you have repeated from the Qur'ān, if you intend the saying in that sense, agrees with the Gospel', he concludes. There is also a genuine attempt to predict the Islamic reaction to Christian argument. For example, discussing the verse, 'We gave proofs (Sale: evident miracles) to Christ the son of Mary and strengthened him with the Holy Spirit' the dialogue continued:

. . . 'You see what I said', added the Christian: 'in these words are professed three Persons in one God.' 'Not for the world!' said the Muslim, 'God spare me that! I do not say that there are three; I acknowledge (agnosco) one God. O, that He, to whom belong the things that Heaven and Earth contain, should (be said to) have a Son!'

Yet even in manner and method the contrast with the mediaeval can be exaggerated; Nau's Trinitarian argument is not basically new, and his demonstration of the Trinity as a triangle can never have been very effective; his attack upon Muhammad's personal life is very little improved on the older models. His Latin text is less tactful as well as less graceful than his French one, though entitled *Dialogus Pacificus*, less realistic, less likely to represent closely any real discussion.[10]

It is astonishing how late the prejudiced approach survived. Père Nau and many others were less prejudiced and fairer than, several generations later, Prideaux, the Dean of Norwich who acknowledged his debt to Ricoldo when he set out deliberately to establish the Prophet's *imposture*. His is the classic example of all that was least generous in the Christian attitude, and he was entirely indebted to the polemic lines of the mediaeval writers, though in balance of judgement inferior to the best of them. It may be that his real purpose was to defend revealed religion from the attacks of the Deists; but this cannot, by modern standards, excuse the use of false material. In particular, it is remarkable that he retained the *Sergius* material. Nau had attempted, as San Pedro Pascual had done, to reconcile Christian *Sergius* with Arabic *Baḥīra*; Prideaux was still taunting Islam with Sergius in the very last years of the seventeenth century; he died in 1724.[11]

The attitude of extreme prejudice survived without dilution long after it had become impossible that Orientalists should accept it. In a book published in 1785 we still find the dove that whispers in the Prophet's ear, the idea that he married his old master's widow, the complaint that the Qur'ān is disorderly and ill-expressed and that Muhammad was bred an idolator, the claim that he was epileptic, as well as accusations more generally accepted, as that he relied on force of arms. He is described in terms then fashionable as 'ignorant, rude and enthusiastic'. A *Life* published in 1799 would be distinguished in any period by the virulence of its hatred of Muhammad; its author conceived that Caligula, Nero and Domitian, and Judas Iscariot, would be 'ashamed to associate with him in the regions of the damned'; he considered that 'many millions of rational beings are degraded to the rank of brutes by the consummate artifice and wickedness of a single individual'. This sort of obsession seems incredible at so late a date; when this book appeared, Napoleon had already re-turned from Egypt, and the modern or 'imperialist' phase of European relations with the Arab world must be said to have begun. Yet even in 1859 Akehurst, in his *Imposture Instanced in the Life of Mahomet*, though free of many of the old inaccuracies, used traditional vituperation to make the traditional points.[11]

From the seventeenth century onwards, the original influence of Oriental Christianity had been reinfused into Western thought; from the time of Napoleon particularly, more and more Europeans travelled and resided in Islamic countries. Missionaries and others, both Catholic and Protestant, were largely dependent upon local Christians, among whom their work lay often almost ex-clusively. Oriental Christians revived in their visitors moribund prejudices which ultimately, if deviously, derived from the same sources as their own. Western religious circles at home were particularly vulnerable, and these ideas were reflected in the world of scholarship. Within our own lifetimes scholars have managed to maintain judgements that are not fundamentally different from the mediaeval judgements. Even with the facts that are now accepted, and which often they themselves established, such great men as D. S. Margoliouth, Sir William Muir and Père Lammens have maintained an attitude that is not fundamentally sympathetic to Muhammad or to Islam. Muir, the S.P.C.K. and the Turkish Mission Aid Society translated the Risālah with the same intention as Peter the Venerable. There are hints in these and other writers of sympathy with many ideas that have served Christian apologetic since the time of St John of Damascus; of criticism, for example, of Muhammad's personal standards, of his use of force and of diplomacy, even the suggestion of self-delusion that is only one stage removed from conscious fraud. So very balanced a judgement as that of Tor Andrae admits criticism of Muhammad under these heads. It may well be argued that such criticism is essential to a Christian position; certainly it is the same position as was taken up firmly by the mediaevals.

3. SURVIVAL OF THE MEDIAEVAL CANON: INFLUENCING NEW FORMS

We have seen how Prideaux' book was written against the Deists; he tried to show that Christianity is free from those marks of imposture that he believed he had successfully imputed to Islam. Another author used an attack on Islam in order to attack Unitarianism in a slightly different way; his *Historical and Critical Reflections upon Mahometanism and Socinianism* (1712) not only identifies the two doctrines (the differences are 'imperceptible') but postulates that the Socinians wanted an actual anti-Trinitarian confederacy with the Turks. There were two movements in the contrary direction. First, there was the common-sense reaction to Prideaux. *Mahomet No Impostor, or A Defence of Mahomet*, for example, was printed as the letter of a certain Abdulla Mahumed Omar, asking a friend in Europe 'as far as you dare' to remonstrate with Prideaux. This fiction made it possible to register points that might seem less innocent if put ostensibly by a Christian; what, for example, of the attack on Islamic polygamy, in view of the example of Jacob, or of David? To condemn Muhammad 'for a limited Polygamy, only because it was the Custom of a northerly People to have no more than one Wife, is a proceeding as whimsical as unjust'. There is satire that recalls the mediaeval attack on Christian practice: suppose, says 'Abdulla', that he should grant the moral superiority of the Gospel, 'I cannot see what Advantage that would be to any of the present Christians'. Only the humour is not mediaeval. The other contrary movement is more than a tease; the same device of Muslim authorship had already been used to attack Christian doctrine and the Churches.[12]

This is the background to the more famous writers of the eighteenth century, who liked to attack or to praise Islam only as a means to attack Christianity. Again the weapons of the mediaevals were used. Boulainvilliers and Savary, praising Islam as a natural religion, really extend the satiric attack on Christians from the field of morals where orthodox Latins kept it to the field of doctrine itself. Often mediaeval arguments against Islam which were capable of being applied against any religion were now used against Christianity.

I propose to consider most fully the case of Voltaire, but first to contrast his predecessor, Boulainvilliers, a more original historian, for whom the traditional sentiment about Islam, but not the traditional story, changes: for whom Muhammad retained the essentials of Christianity while purging the superfluous accretions; for whom Islam was not irrational, nor the Prophet an impostor; nevertheless, he rarely disagrees with the more discreet of his predecessors about what actually happened. He meant the same thing as they meant, only rejecting the word 'imposture' to describe it, a word which is indeed simply pejorative. The story that Muhammad constructed a religion in order to make himself world conqueror remained, only now the religion was reasonable, and the conqueror as admirable as Alexander or Caesar. And if the religion is now reasonable, that is because different things are thought to be reasonable, not because the religion is differently analysed. How refreshing this treatment is appears by contrast with the worthier, but vastly duller, traditionalist completion of the book attributed to Gagnier.

Voltaire's attitude in 1742 was different from that of the mediaeval Christian only in two respects. In his tragedy (*Fanatisme, ou Mahomet le prophète*) he frankly preferred to invent his own legends, rather than use those already circulating, which were apparently not scurrilous enough for his purpose; and his arguments against Islam are not only, like the mediaeval ones, such as might be used against all revealed religion: they are intended so to be used. The attack on Muhammad nevertheless made an excellent mask, and, although it was suspected of anti-royalism, the judicious Benedict XIV read it *con sommo piacere*. Yet Voltaire's neglect of accuracy, quite apart from his use of a fictional plot, suggests a man to whom accuracy is devoid of interest. 'Fanatic' Muhammad, begging his successor to hide from the people that wickedness in their Prophet which would destroy their faith, brings down the curtain with this couplet:

> Je dois régir en Dieu l'univers prévenu:
> Mon empire est détruit, si l'homme est reconnu.

The whole of this closing speech is a mine of malicious statement and invention. Hypocrisy is, of course, the gravamen of the attack:

> Dieu que j'ai fait servir au malheur des humains
> Adorable instrument de mes affreux desseins . . .

and religion itself was irrevocably committed to 'le fanatisme'. Voltaire's attitude at this time was compounded of the worst aspects of mediaeval obscurantism, even in small matters. The Middle Ages found their hierarchic sense of society shocked by Muhammad's rise to power from insignificance, and Voltaire shared a sentiment that in the *ancien régime* had degenerated into mere snobbery. 'M. le Comte de Boulainvilliers', he wrote (to Frederick of Prussia!), '. . . attempted to pass (Muhammad) off as a great man, chosen by Providence to punish the Christians'; Voltaire, however, required of Muhammad, if he were to be worthy of his respect, not only that he should have given peaceful laws, but that he should also have been born a legitimate prince, or at least properly elected by his people: 'But that a merchant of camels', he said,

should excite a revolt in his townlet; that, associated with some wretched Qurayshites, he should persuade them that he holds conversation with the angel Gabriel; that he should boast of being rapt to Heaven, and of having received there part of this unintelligible book, which affronts common sense at every page; that he should put his own country to fire and the sword, to make this book respected; that he should cut the fathers' throats and ravish the daughters; that he should give the vanquished the choice between his religion and death; this certainly is what no man can excuse . . .

The whole of this passage is a distillation of what was least pleasant in the mediaeval attitude, barely hidden under a polish of cultured enlightenment and such elegant references as 'Tartuffe armed'; it horrifies its modern reader by its disregard of the better information perfectly familiar to its author.

In another mood Voltaire was more willing after all to learn from Boulainvilliers and Sale, and complained self-righteously of other sources of knowledge, of 'what our historians, our rhetoricians and our prejudices tell us'. In the *essai sur les mœurs* he was content to analyse Islamic belief, in order to show that it was composed of pre-existing elements, while discounting the likelihood of Muhammad's having acquired his knowledge from 'Sergius' or Baḥīra; and to point out that, unlike Christianity, it tolerated other religions. He maintained his dislike of the Prophet himself, a 'terrible and powerful man' who 'established his dogmas by his courage and his arms', but whose religion afterwards became more indulgent of error than he would have liked. Voltaire contrasted the gentleness of Christ and the intolerance of Christians with this contrary state in Islam. He conceded, inconsistently with the position that he had earlier adopted, and even insisted, that Muhammad 'deceived himself in deceiving others'; nevertheless, he really remained unconverted on the issue of hypocrisy. Muhammad, according to him, saw from the ignorance, the credulity and the inclination to enthusiasm of his fellow-Arabs that he might successfully 'set himself up as a prophet'. He died, 'regarded as a great man even by those who knew he was an impostor, and revered as a prophet by all the rest'. We may say that Voltaire first thought an attack on Islam useful for the attack on religion generally; and later saw the advantages of treating the facts less passionately, in order to recommend natural religion at the expense of Christian belief. The dangerous nature of some of the arguments that had been used by mediaevals is illustrated by Voltaire's defence of polygyny: where they had quoted nature and the example of brute beasts, on the side of monogamy, Voltaire was able to do the same in the contrary sense. In fact, he moved round towards the position occupied by Boulainvilliers, discarding the more improbable detail of ancient legend. Even so, the more 'Enlightened' approach did not disturb the basic line established in the Middle Ages: Muhammad was seen as the inventor of a religion made up of bits and pieces acquired from round about; he was a deliberate deceiver, or at least a partly culpable deceiver, who established his religion by force. The framework of what Voltaire writes is the classic one of the Enlightenment; his assessment of Islam as a religion is, in its outline, nearly identical with the mediaeval one.

Something of the same is true also of our own Gibbon. Largely the architect of our modern historical perspectives, Gibbon derived his own from different sources, and his fiftieth chapter does not represent his most original thinking. We see displayed before us accurate and balanced statements, expressed with the familiar elegance, but not essentially new. The state of Arabia and the character of the Arabs, the contrivance, and the moral indulgence, of Muhammad: these are the old themes. 'From all sides the roving Arabs were allured by the standard of religion and plunder: the apostle sanctified the licence of embracing the female captives as their wives and concubines; and the enjoyment of wealth and beauty was a feeble type of the joys of paradise prepared for the valiant martyrs of the faith.' He omits nothing that the Middle Ages asserted of Muhammad's relations with women, and refuses to decide whether the Prophet should be described as *enthusiast* or *impostor*. He does realise that the problem is complex, Muhammad's character elusive.

Had I been intimately conversant with the son of Abdallah, the task would still be difficult and the success uncertain . . . could I truly delineate the portrait of an hour, the fleeting resemblance would not equally apply to the solitary of Mount Hera, to the preacher of Mecca, and to the conqueror of Arabia.

This, which in a way is true enough, anticipates and sets on its way the crude simplification by which in the nineteenth century two Muhammads were opposed, the reformer of Mecca and the politician of Medina. Yet it is clear that the reader of Gibbon finds nothing to shock, or even astonish; he is carried smoothly forward, assenting as he goes to tempered judgements in a customary sequence of themes. For Gibbon's first readers, also, the pages dealing with Islam must have been the least unexpected.

Savary presents a similar picture. We have already noted his tendency to 'humanise' in the translation of the Qur'ān. The same may be said of the Life of Muhammad which he took from Arabic authors to precede his translation; the story of Zayd and Zaynab, for example, is there told with all imaginable romantic trappings: the beauty of Zaynab's form, the politic *complaisance* of Zayd. Once again we read that Muhammad chose a basic tenet, simple and easy to grasp, the unity of God; pronounced his own prophethood, in order to guarantee the truth of the revelation; and then 'took from the ethics of Christianity and Judaism what seemed to him most suitable to peoples of warm climates'. For Savary Muhammad was a wise man and a subtle politician adapting doctrine as he went along. There is once more continuity with mediaevals who would have dissented only from Savary's approval of what he and they agreed to be the facts.[13]

Throughout the eighteenth century and the earlier part of the nineteenth there was a steady reappraisal of the character of the Prophet; this was partly the result of reaction against Christianity, but more of the exploration of authentic Muslim sources. The first thorough-going change of opinion that reached a large public in England came, as has been well and indisputably said, with Carlyle.[14] 'Sincerity', he said, 'in all senses seems to me the merit of the Koran.' The Romantic thus reversed almost every traditional view: 'The indulgences, criminal to us, which he permitted, were not of his appointment . . . His Religion is not an easy one'; and, in contradiction of the most popular opinion of all: 'We shall err widely if we consider this man as a common voluptuary.' Even the dogma of Islam's dependence on violence Carlyle shook: 'The sword indeed: but where will you get your sword! Every new opinion, at its starting, is precisely in a *minority of one*.' None of these views, taken in isolation and in germ, was new; but, expressed all together and very positively, they create a more powerful impression than Lamartine, who knew much more about Islam, was able to make in France. Perhaps Carlyle's strength is in his common sense which blasts tradition away.

So much may be accepted by every reasonable reader, whether Christian, anti-Christian or indifferent. Yet there is more to Carlyle than this, and the rest is less acceptable. For Carlyle there must be some deeper justification of the Hero, and this creates difficulty for those who do not share his assumption. He spoke of Muhammad's seeing through 'that rubbish of Arab idolatries, argumentative theologies, traditions, subtleties, rumours and hypotheses of Greeks and Jews', so as to penetrate 'into the kernel of the matter'. Muhammad thus substituted *fire* for *mere dead fuel*. This opinion has a splendid sound, but it is difficult to be sure what it really means; and it quite certainly implies that traditional view by which Muhammad sifted the Christian, Jewish and pagan religions in order to concoct his own. In this respect Carlyle's talk only masks the ancient view. Again, when defending Muhammad's sincerity, Carlyle does not doubt that he made up what he taught, although he thinks he made it up sincerely. He excuses him on the ground of wakeful nights: '*any* making up of his mind, so blessed, so indispensable for him there, would seem the inspiration of a Gabriel'. Carlyle does not think that even a vision of Gabriel came, and hardly suggests more than that Muhammad might reasonably persuade himself so; what he really thinks is that Muhammad's inspiration as Hero was its own justification, so that he might call it Gabriel, or anything else, without falsifying it. Yet this acceptance of some source of inspiration that does not come unambiguously from God is a Romantic, and not a Christian or an Islamic idea; mediaeval Christians would doubtless have seen inspiration originating other than in God as confirmation of their own theory of diabolical possession. Carlyle did much to purify the Western attitude to Muhammad, and even to Islam, but he failed to establish his appreciation on any sound theoretic basis. It is the practical part of his lecture, criticising the old views, which is most valuable.

It would be impossible to deal here with many modern attitudes to Islam that have developed, but all owe much to the attitudes of the Enlightenment and of the Romantic age, where they are no longer Christian. Voltaire's, Savary's and Carlyle's ideas are present in much that people are heard to say of Islam, as well as Christian ideas which survive explicitly and implicitly. One idea is so general, however, that it seems worth while to single it out. It was well put by Mr Muhammad Asad in a recent book. Mr Asad was born a Jew in Europe and he was converted to Islam. His attitude expresses the modern impatience with asceticism and finds in Islam the satisfaction of spiritual yearnings without necessity to renounce the satisfaction of those of this world. Islam, for him, is the religion of the body and the spirit in one; this is not just a matter of personal morals, but, for example, of social teaching also. He believes that Christianity is other-worldly and therefore lacks social teaching; in this respect he is at one with Lenin.[15] He also thinks that Islam is intellectual in conten̄, although requiring emotion in the subjective reaction of the believer, but that in Christianity the teaching itself is emotional, relying on a sense of 'numinous awe'. This brings up to date and to some

U

extent makes more practical the Enlightened view of Boulainvilliers and Savary; also it confirms the Christian rejection of
Islam for its lack of asceticism and its refusal to abstain from
pleasures of the world and the flesh. It is hard to be sure that
Islamic teaching lacks emotion substantially, or that it is ignorant
of numinous awe; but I think that there can be no doubt that a
mediaeval author who read Mr Asad's book would say immediately
that it exactly illustrated all that he had ever thought of Islam, as
calculated to indulge incontinence in the name of religion.

To analyse seriously the attitude of any age towards Islam
would not take less space than was required for the two centuries
and a half after 1100. Here it is only possible to say that later
thinkers of all schools of thought owed a great debt to the men of
Latin rite who first formed what we can call a European view.
Themes recur partly because of the nature of the subject; but both
in the choice and in the treatment of themes it seems clear that
writers have for centuries laboured in the shadow of their predecessors. What has been said already about Islam has so dominated the approach of all as to preclude original thought, in the
sense of thought that begins again from the beginning. Probably
even to-day emancipation from the traditions of the past is
possible only for minds wholly freed of old traditions, for men
born into an inheritance different from that of ordinary European
Christians. In the last section of this chapter I shall suggest that
there are useful possibilities of building upon, rather than escaping
from, these traditions.

4. THE DEVELOPMENT OF THE ACADEMIC APPROACH

From this brief survey of the changes and the continuity of
European attitudes, I have omitted to speak of the increasing
volume and improving quality of academic study. During the
seventeenth century much more authentic information became
available than had been made so since the thirteenth century.
The transition is marked by the career of such a man as Johann
Albrecht von Widmanstadt, born in the early years of the sixteenth. He studied Arabic in Spain and humanism in Turin. He
was a man of state under the Empire who as lawyer served
equally the Church; when the Jacobite Patriarch of Antioch
wanted to print a Syriac New Testament in Europe that would be
in line with the new scholarship, his agent was sent to Widmanstadt, whose enthusiasm and influence with the Emperor ensured
the achievement of this work. Yet this man with his Renaissance
scholarship, who in some ways looks forward to the linguistic
Orientalism of the coming age, thought it worth while to publish
the Cluniac *de doctrina* and an epitome of Ketton, with his own

adnotationes, which say very little that might not have been said centuries earlier.

Reland's *de religione mohammedica* (1705) is certainly the most important of several that helped to clear away legend and substitute fact, and only fact; it can be studied with profit to-day. Nonsense that had deceived the learned and indulged the ignorant for so long was not now just pushed temporarily aside by a few authors, but finally excluded from the canon acceptable to scholars. Prideaux's book (1697) was perhaps the last exception; between his and Reland's there is as great a chasm as there can be between contemporaries. 'If ever any Religion was perverted by Adversarys', said Reland, 'it was this Religion'; it was the custom to send a young man 'fir'd with a generous Ardor of understanding the Mahometan Religion' to study the old authorities, including Ketton, instead of advising him 'to learn the Arabick, to hear Mahomet speak in his own tongue'. Reland established the principle that the sole authority for facts about Islam must be Muslim but the point had been made, and effectively, by Edward Pocock the Elder more than half a century earlier. Others worked in the same way; it is obvious that the Oxford scholar, Thomas Hyde, of the Queen's College, in his notes on Bobovius' little book (1691) is solely concerned to clear up misconceptions. Jacob Ehrhart, in 1731, published a short but thorough and scholarly examination of the charges traditionally made against Islam and the Prophet; it is logically so devastating that we wonder how other views could ever have been maintained. It deserved to be better known than it was.

Historical information had already been very much improved, and original sources made available, in the course of the preceding century. The spring of this movement was linguistic. Rapheleng's *Lexicon Arabicum,* written before the turn of the century, was only published at Leyden in 1613. In the first quarter of the seventeenth century at Leyden Thomas d'Erpe (Erpenius) published grammars of several Oriental languages, as well as Arabic versions of Biblical books, but did not much extend the knowledge of Islamic religion or the life of the Prophet, except in an edition and Latin translation of sūrahs x and xi, and in his Latin translation of the History of Jirjīs al-Makīn ibn al-'Amid, which he printed with Roderick's *Historia Arabum.* The elder Pocock's Latin translations – with notes that were wise as well as erudite – of the historian Abu'l Faraj similarly provided material on the rise of Islam which was closer to the original sources than anything contemporary scholarship was accustomed to use.[16] The presence of the Maronites, Gabriel Sionita and Abraham Ecchelensis in Paris in the second quarter of the century, although their primary interests were

Biblical and Syriac, and although they were by no means friendly to Islam, undoubtedly favoured the influence of authentic scholarship in questions of religion, and Sionita sought his facts, about some aspects of Islam at least, in Muslim sources. His colleague preferred to stress Arabic philosophy (in a wide sense) rather than Islam; both felt pride in Arabic culture which they distinguished from a religion they detested. In the middle of the century Pierre Vattier, professor at the Collège de France, translated into French a motley of historical, medical, philosophical, oneirocritical and even poetic works, but, except for his French version of the Erpenius history (already adapted into English by Purchas in his fourth edition, 1626) he was uninterested in religious questions. The interest in religion, never dissociated from thoughts of missions, was better represented by the more academic scholar, such as Christian Raue, who combined an enthusiasm for Semitic languages with a sincere affection and respect for Muslim piety; he shared that subordination of orientalism to Biblical study which is so strong a feature of his age, and of the Western tradition since his day.[17]

The process of making available original sources, chiefly historical and philosophical, either in Latin or a vernacular, was also represented, in England by the younger Pocock, and in France, over three generations, by the dynasty of Pétis de la Croix, whose primary employment was as interpreters of State. The most influential translator of the day was Galland, whose *Mille et une Nuits* became a European classic and set the vogue for oriental tales. Sadi was translated from Latin into French. Such works affected the image of Muslims' religion, but more directly important was the publication of Gagnier's *Abu'l Feda de vita et rebus gestis Mohammedis* (1723). Meanwhile the Pococks' contemporary, Barthelemy d'Herbelot, had produced his *Bibliothèque Orientale* (published posthumously in 1697); this first serious encyclopaedia of Islam laid accurate notions of all aspects before the intelligent public, but it tended also to reinforce the prejudice against the Prophet. The weakness of all this literature, and especially of the long series of translations, if they be considered as an integral scheme (which they were not), is that, apart from the Qur'ān, it ignored the major sources for knowledge of Islam. Moreover, it tended, even when most just, to ignore the living spirituality of Islam. Père Richard Simon, the Biblical critic, was attacked for saying that 'when they ask God for something in prayer, they must abandon themselves entirely to his will . . . There is nothing they so much recommend as trust in God.'

The work of lesser scholars and even amateurs demonstrates the same clarification of fact and provision of new knowledge. An unpretentious translation of a treatise on the *Prophetick Light* 'written in Spanish and Arabick in the year MDCIII for the Instruction of the Moriscoes in Spain by Mahomet Rabadan, an Arragonian Moor', preceded by a prefatory letter addressed to Prideaux and a creed probably of the fifteenth century, appeared in London in 1723, with excellent engravings of the Ka'bah and of the prayer borrowed with the creed from Reland. There is sound information in Bobovius' *Turkish Liturgy* and in Wallich's *Turkische Religion*, with its interesting illustrations of prayer and of *dhikr*. L. Warner published a collection of texts to illustrate the Qur'anic attitude to Christ and the Christians; his approach was polemic, but not primarily so, and recalls that of William of Tripoli. One manuscript with no polemic purpose extracts all the histories from the Qur'ān, exactly like those 'Stories from the Bible' which we knew in childhood.[18] An excellent Latin account of Islam among the Lansdowne manuscripts gives the musical notation of the call to prayer (*testatio*) and an unusual translation which begins, *Deus maximus, Deus maximus, Fateor non esse Numen praeter Deum* . . . ; it concentrates information chosen mostly with discrimination; it is orderly and authentic. Henry Stubbe's work, circulated only in manuscript, has an astonishing feeling for Islam and almost anticipated Carlyle: 'that all mankind were to be enforced to the profession of his Religion; or that he compelled any thereunto is a falsehood'. The author took pleasure in citing Muslim attitudes, for example, the description of the Prophet: 'a grave Aspect, wherein the Awfullness of Majesty seemed to be tempered with an admirable sweetness . . . The Arabians compare him under their Accomplishments unto the purest Streams of some River, gently gliding along with delight to the use of every approaching traveller . . .'[19]

I have criticised Savary for his anxiety to prove a particular case at the expense of exactitude, and I should do him less than justice if I did not recognise that he helped greatly, by the presentation of much of the life of the Prophet in the terms used by Islamic historians, to present to the world a picture that would be more nearly recognisable to Muslims than so many Christian attempts had been. A similar appreciation should be made of Ockley (+1720), one of whose sentences, commenting on the Islamic description of Muhammad, almost sums up the whole tradition we are examining: 'he was a very subtle and crafty man, who put on the appearance only of those good qualities; while the principles of his soul were ambition and lust'; and yet Ockley made much sound and scholarly material available for the first time, and in English; his work, indeed, continued to be used by many generations.[20]

The mingling of polemic attitudes with genuine scholarship was common, even in circles at first glance wholly academic. The elder Pocock, for example, had been chaplain to the English Factory at Aleppo, was associated with Laud's orientalist schemes and translated into Arabic Grotius' great work of natural theology, *de veritate religionis Christianae* (1660). His friend, the Berliner, Christian Raue, bought manuscripts in the Levant for Archbishop Ussher, the metropolitan of Ireland, with whom he shared the interest in Biblical chronography, as well as in books. He taught in England and Holland, in Sweden and at Frankfurt on Oder, where the Elector finally recalled him. At Kiel he founded a College to train young men for the Oriental mission, and concerned himself about the conversion of the Jews. In the early decades of the next century two German scholars attempted to fit new techniques into old patterns, and to effect the traditional proof of the Qur'ān's dependence on Scripture by linguistic means. Ehrhart ridiculed this: scarcely three texts can reasonably be said to have been borrowed, he asserted, although all expressions of the love or praise of God must inevitably be much alike.[21]

The most remarkable case is that of Ludovici Maracci. He begins his introduction to his Qur'ān (1698) much as Peter the Venerable began his, detailing the heresies that Christian apologists had treated, while they neglected to attack Islam. In fact, Maracci, who was extremely well read in his polemic, harks back consciously to the mediaeval tradition to which he seeks to give new life. On the other hand, his linguistic scholarship is excellent; Mark of Toledo would have recognised in Maracci a similar spirit, and envied his living in an age better endowed by linguistic science; scholarly care, which had been rare in the Middle Ages, was now beginning to be generally admired, and was considered by informed public opinion to be necessary, in Maracci's day; it was increasingly indispensable even for polemic. Maracci personally reflects the new attitude, and apologises gracefully for faults in his scholarship: 'In the Arabic language, as also in others, there are certain peculiar colloquialisms, allusions, proverbs and apophthegms which none but Arabs born, and those the most learned and erudite, are able to explain; here in Rome it was not possible to find such.' In fact, the translation is good, and a source for Sale's own; and it is as agreeable stylistically as it is possible for a translation from Arabic into so different a language as Latin to be.

It is the more remarkable that the polemic aspects of Maracci's work are not at all new in spirit; this applies equally to the *Prodromus*, which precedes the translation, and to the *Refutatio*, which consists in detailed notes on the text. The *Prodromus* is divided into four parts, first, that which proves that Muhammad and Islam are unconfirmed by Scripture; secondly, that which proves that, unlike Christianity, Islam was unconfirmed by miracles; the third defends Christian dogma, the Trinity especially, and the impossibility that Christians can have corrupted the revelation left to them; it also refutes the attack on Christianity for being split into many sects by an account of the sects of Islam; the fourth compares Islamic religious practice with Christian, and attacks, of course, the supposed basis of Islam in sexual laxity and violence. The detailed *refutationes* miss nothing that it is conceivably possible to take up. Maracci presents, one might almost say, the sum of Christian polemic against Islam known before his day. The tone has not changed, and the author admits evidence on non-Arabic authority, on, for example, San Pedro's; but he has unequivocally recognised the need for textual accuracy. He supplies a great deal of authentic knowledge from Arabic sources, quite apart from the translation of the Qur'ān itself; what he lacks, and noticeably so, is personal acquaintance with his subject; he has not that combination of experience and judgement that makes Père Nau, for all his inferior scholarship, so formidable. Maracci provides a prefatory life of Muhammad, followed by an academic introduction to the Qur'ān, both in the modern manner. In his prefatory note, he explains that he utilises Muslim authors, not because he thinks them sincere, but because 'when we act against the enemies of religion, we attack them more happily with their own arms than with ours, and (thus) more happily overcome them'. In fact, Maracci's scholarship is not disinterested; his purpose is polemic, but he has mastered the new technique.

With Sale, whose translation was published in 1734, we reach scholarship at least equal to, though not perhaps so minute as, Maracci's; we also meet the first considerable attempt at an entirely academic judgement. Unlike so many of his contemporaries and predecessors, Sale seems to have no axe to grind; he wants to elucidate the facts. His is therefore one of the most interesting cases in the history of European treatment of Islam. What makes him invaluable, even to-day, is the width of his information, constituted simply by the presentation of Islamic sources, particularly in the notes which constantly cite a wide range of Muslim authors, and most frequently, perhaps, al-Baydāwī, az-Zamakhshari and Jalāl ad-Dīn, all of whom were Qur'anic commentators. People who to-day complain of his translation do not complain of its inaccuracy, but of its not being sufficiently lively in expression, or elevated in style. Where his translation has been superseded it is generally because there are new estimates of what Muhammad may have understood by a word or expression; but the reader who wishes to know what

Islam has traditionally understood can look nowhere better than to Sale. Naturally, his remarks belong to the context in which he wrote, and to the ideas that he and his contemporaries inherited. A Muslim who reads him is far from gratified by what appears to be prejudice against Islam; but such a reader does not realise the extent to which Sale reduced that same prejudice, and made Islamic sources of information available, even when he himself shared the traditional Christian view.

He did so share it. 'It is certainly one of the most convincing proofs that Mohammedism was no other than a human invention, that it owed its progress and establishment almost entirely to the sword', he said, and contrasted, as so many had done before him, the demonstration of the divine original of Christianity. Again, 'That Mohammad was, as the Arabs are by complexion, a great lover of women, we are assured by his own confessions.' Sale's judgements, however, are tempered. Muhammad's right to take up arms in self-defence 'may perhaps be allowed'; whether he should have used arms to establish his religion at all 'I will not here determine'; polygyny, he pointed out, already existed in pagan Arabia, and Jewish law permitted divorce. His description of Arabia in the 'Time of Ignorance' is calculated to show the predisposition of the Arabs to receive Islamic teaching, but it is an historical account drawn dispassionately from Arab sources, not an argument about the sins to which the Muslims-to-be were prone; it pays, indeed, little attention to vices, among which it includes only a tendency to robbery. On the main point of Muhammad's good intentions or hypocrisy, his views look forward to those that were to become established after his time: he disowns any intention to decide whether Muhammad proclaimed the unity of God as 'the effect of enthusiasm, or only a design to raise himself to the supreme government of the country'; he witnessed powerfully against Prideaux's view that Muhammad made the Arabs 'exchange their idolatry for another religion altogether as bad'. He did not doubt that Muhammad was 'fully satisfied in his conscience on the truth of his grand point, the unity of God . . . all his other doctrines and institutions being rather accidental and unavoidable, than premeditated and designed'.[22] This cannot look very friendly or respectful to the Muslim who, when he reads it, comes across the ancient Christian attitude for the first time, but, read in its context, it is singularly unprejudiced, represents the diminution of prejudice by scholarship; nor does it, like the works of Savary and Voltaire and others we have discussed, substitute some new prejudice for the old. Sale grinds no axes.

I cannot attempt to review the subsequent growth of the scientific treatment of Islam. I have only wished to indicate how this scientific attitude struggled out of the polemic frame in which nearly all Islamic studies had been enclosed. We should grossly simplify if we called this an emancipation from mediaeval modes of thought. In the Middle Ages, as we have seen, there was a serious attempt to establish sound knowledge that might, ostensibly at least, be undeniable by Muslims in the event of controversy. In this sense, it was not new to be academic. The point was rather that in the Middle Ages there were political, perhaps sociological, reasons why Islam should be suspect, and untrue things should seem more probable than true ones, and be believed. It is quite often apparent that in the Middle Ages there was no interest in Islam itself, but only in inducing some particular state of mind about it in Christians; or, in Lull's case, in proving some particular point to Muslims. As these reasons ceased to exist, a scientific attitude – that is, an attitude of pure science, interested in the thing in itself – was free to develop.

At the same time as this happened, academic and scholarly studies advanced greatly in many different fields. In our own day it is impossible not to notice that, in some fields at least, there is the beginning of a drift away from the academic; the educated public gives subjective scholarship an enthusiastic support which it combines with lip-service to research; and research has itself become discredited in certain contexts, by being too widely extended to inadequate and unimportant subjects. If our own day sometimes resembles more the Middle Ages, we must remember that about three hundred years ago Europe had just begun the ascent to the watershed we may be passing; and then was the moment when Islam ceased to be a danger to European society. It is natural that it began then to be studied disinterestedly; we may reasonably assume some causal relation, if we cannot precisely define it.

There is, of course, no reason why strong prejudice should not co-exist with accuracy; Maracci was a scholar as well as Sale, and equally a painstaking worker in detail. On the one hand, even the most virulent scholar was saturated in detailed work which he had personally executed; on the other, even when we read the most detached of scholars, we need to keep in mind how mediaeval Christendom argued, because it has always been and still is part of the make-up of every Western mind brought to bear upon this subject.

5. THE FUTURE EUROPEAN ATTITUDE TO ISLAM: SOME NOTES

If we consider the general situation in Europe to-day, it is difficult to foretell the future trends of studies, apart from such as have a practical value. One utilitarian trend is to study Islamic attitudes in order to be able to live in a Muslim country without causing offence. This sort of study is generally pursued at an elementary level; its purpose is to avoid trouble for some commercial or government undertaking with a quick turnover of employees in Muslim countries. Nevertheless, this has possibilities at a much less elementary level. There is almost endless scope for investigation of the reactions of Western and Eastern Christians and Muslims to each other. Here it is important to remember that 'Western Christian' means 'born in one of the Western countries traditionally considered Christian' and may include professed atheists and religious fanatics alike. At the same time we may expect, for a while at least, that abstract studies concerned to illuminate events in Islamic history, will continue; W. Montgomery Watt's two books[23] on Muhammad break new ground, and there is no reason why scholars should not continue to examine matters that have not been taken up before, particularly when it is a case of applying new academic disciplines to old subjects.

The character of research, and of new attitudes to research, depends obviously on the intentions of the researchers. The Russian Academician Mitin, in a speech at a conference on scientific-atheist propaganda, said, 'In demonstrating the anti-scientific character of Islam, we must at the same time take into consideration the part it is playing, under present-day conditions, when, under its banner, there are proceeding a number of movements of great progressive importance'; he added that 'in the Eastern countries there are still a great many people whose religious sentiments are fused with their nationalist sentiments'. A 'proper fight against Islam' requires 'great political insight, a profound grasp of contemporary social processes'.[24] It is obvious that the intention of the scientific-atheist propagandist is a special one which will affect his studies of Islam very much. Any approach to the subject from a special point of view, Marxist, 'humanist', Christian or Islamic, will affect, not only the opinions and the conclusions, but the actual choice of subjects to study and of methods of study.

From the Marxist-Leninist point of view, all religion is an invention with which we encourage ourselves to support dangers we cannot control, but the social utility of religious belief to groups in conflict will be clear to all. What we believe about the religion of our enemies as dangerous to our own religion might even be called *the hashish of the people*, since it arouses them to hatred and sustains them in conflict. At the slight cost of death or the danger of death, the conviction that a faith is worth fighting and dying for effects a socially invaluable condition of fearlessness; the Marxist, while he recognises its advantages, will consider that they explain the phenomenon. He can similarly explain the imperialism of the nineteenth century, which so often reflected the mediaeval attitude to Islam, as basing the exploitation of an inferior class – of 'native' – upon contempt for an inferior world-view or religion. How would he explain a change in our attitude now? Presumably it might be attributed to the weakening of the imperialist hold, now in the last stage before final failure; alternatively, to a new subtle technique of exploitation adapted to the mid-twentieth century; and it must be admitted that there is little that is subtle, or even twentieth-century, about much of the Western approach to Islam, even to-day. It is rare for the scholar to free himself of class or group thinking, but, though the Marxist will not admit this, it is possible. In the meantime, the Marxist-Leninist technique of working through not only nationalism but also Islam is fully developed and successfully practised; a Marxist-Titoist will presumably say that the Stalinist exploits or derides Islam, according to political expediency, in exactly the way of the imperialist. In actual fact, the orthodox Communist attitude resembles not only that of the modern imperialist but also that of the mediaeval 'feudalist'.

If we take this case of the Russian scientific-atheist in 1957, we immediately notice similarities with the mediaeval Christian approach. Academician Mitin is concerned to destroy Islam ideologically. This is a basic similarity; but there is a good deal less similarity in method. The Russian has to take into account the use to which he can put Islam temporarily, while it is 'fused' with nationalist sentiment which he expects to be able effectively to exploit. Mediaeval Christians did not take this sort of thing into account, even *mutatis mutandis*; but they did do this much, which is as much as the commercial companies do to-day: they tried to prepare missionaries for the ideological opposition they would actually encounter. Although what was written was in fact divorced from the realities of controversy, it contained a number of warnings about what Muslims say and do, so that actual encounter with them would have had its surprises, but would not have had only surprises. Where the atheist Russian and the Christian mediaeval points of view are most alike lies in the fact that they study Islam selectively, rather than in pursuit of an abstract and judicial assessment. The Russian has to have his 'profound grasp of contemporary social processes' in order to interpret Islam. That means that he has to consider Islam from a set point of view. He must be a Marxist-Leninist with a grasp of the current party-line, and he must not deviate into interest in

Islam in itself. He must be concerned only to illuminate means of extinguishing it. This is very close to the mediaeval Christian position. We have seen how academic standards developed rather late; that is, that standards of accuracy existed, but truth for its own sake was no explicit object till late. Accuracy was sought by those who saw the need for it, in order to improve propaganda. It was used, less for missions to Muslims, than among Christians living within Islamic territory. In the course of centuries, both the Catholic and later the Protestant, Churches had a considerable success among oriental Christians. The primary purpose was defensive. The same seems to be true of the Marxist-Leninist whose whole intention is presumably to safeguard the Revolution; while he destroys Islam within the U.S.S.R. he seeks allies in countries where 'nationalist' and 'religious' sentiments are 'fused', and Communist and non-Communist blocs thus both seek Muslim support, as once Christians and Muslims both sought to convert the Golden Horde.

The comparison between the Russian and the mediaeval approaches is made in order to emphasise the change that has occurred in Christian attitudes. In its matter, any Christian approach must tend always to be the same as any other. It must treat the same themes as mediaeval and other Christian writers on Islam have always treated. Revelation, prophethood, morals, violence, Trinitarian doctrine, these are necessarily the points at issue between Christians and Muslims, because they are the points of disagreement and divergence. In manner, however, the modern Christian, unlike the mediaevals and the Russians, may be as free as he pleases from any bias to polemics. He remains a Christian with belief in the sole truth of Christianity, but Islamic belief is no menace to him, Islamic society no menace to his civilisation. He has no need to stress differences, and when he does take up the points of divergence he is free to make the most of those aspects that are least different and least liable to arouse mutual irritation. He can take things calmly, and has no reason to seek anything but the truth, irrespective of utility, unless he positively prefers what may bring him closer in sympathy to Islam. If he does otherwise, he does so unnecessarily, because he is still governed, as many Christians undoubtedly still are, by the attitudes the mediaevals adopted. They themselves would, as likely as not, have responded to new conditions in new ways. The Christian, therefore, is, first, in the position of any 'pure' student who is uncommitted emotionally in relation to Islam.

Secondly, the Christian can find material, in the results of scholarship and in the sympathetic comprehension of Islamic attitudes, which he can apply to interests that are specifically his own. If we take the example of the work done by Montgomery Watt upon the social background of pre-Islamic Arabia, we shall find, among other things, that it seems to establish what the Qur'ān really required in its marriage law, by clarifying the existing institutions in relation to which the requirements were published. Definition of this kind enables the Christian to assess the true significance of Muhammad as the vehicle for religious precept in moral matters. Without it, he is incompetent to judge. He must, of course, like any student, be prepared constantly to revise his view; but as far as moral judgement is concerned, it is likely that each progressive discovery will necessitate, not a reversal of opinion, but a refinement of it. One particular way in which he can benefit from the new scholarship is in getting to see Islamic matters from the Islamic point of view. This is possible both by the means of modern scholarship and also by simply conversing frankly, if discreetly, with Muslims; but the power to be discreet and to exchange information reciprocally is one that we seem only to have acquired recently; previously converse was intended to lead to controversy, and not to mutual information.

With this new material the Christian can now approach again the problems that have been milled over by his co-religionists for so long. There is, first, the biography of Muhammad, and particularly his prophethood and the accidents of his life. It is essential for Christians to see Muhammad as a holy figure; to see him, that is, as Muslims see him. If they do not do so, they must cut themselves off from comprehension of Islam. This does not mean that they must assert that Muhammad was holy, or even, perhaps, think that he was so; it is possible not to accept as true the fact alleged by Muslims, that God spoke through Muhammad, but yet to judge the resulting situation as though it were true. If people believe it to be true, that will not make it true, but their actions will be the same as they would have been, if it had been true. Sympathy and understanding require that this should be understood. If there is this sympathetic approach it immediately becomes possible to pass into and share the state of mind of Muslims in many ages: the first Companions, the people of the golden age of the 'Abbāsids, the men of the Ottoman Empire, the Muslims of to-day. But if some such spiritual and mental borrowing does not take place, no further progress is possible.

The next field is the examination of points of theology which Christianity and Islam share – always shared – in many cases without being able to perceive it, or perceiving it, without being able to exploit it. This is the field in which most work has already been done by practising Christians. The first were those who interested themselves in mysticism, for example, L. Massignon in France, M. Asin Palacios in Spain and R. A. Nicholson in Britain. They have been followed by other scholars, who have greatly increased the field of sympathetic understanding, because it was found that Christian and Islamic mystics shared much theology. There were limits to the value of this work; mystics are rather suspect by orthodox Muslims, and they are not exactly representative of Christianity. Only if we include ritual and private prayer in our study is there common ground for the ordinary Christian and the ordinary Muslim. Professor Guillaume has made a stimulating comparison of Christian creed and Qur'anic doctrine in a popular series; and the study of Christian and Islamic theological development in relation to each other was the most important work set fully in train by L. Gardet and Père Anawati, whose research made it possible to compare the medi-aeval scholastic developments of the two religions. L. Gardet, moreover, has continued the work of Massignon on mysticism, and has carried still further his sympathetic approach to the whole range of activities of the Islamic community. Fr. R. McCarthy has undertaken the study of Muslim theologians, not because of their influence on Christian thought, but for their inherent interest. Of the relations between philosophers of the two societies I do not speak, because these lie outside my subject, but they are now being widely exploited.

One of the greatest Islamic scholars to-day, Sir Hamilton Gibb, writes of Islam explicitly as a Christian 'engaged in a common spiritual enterprise'. Something similar must be said of the great personal influence of Massignon. Meanwhile Père abd al-Jalil has gone further, with his studies of Islamic spiritual movements, and with his little book called *Marie et l'Islam*. The practical field has been well surveyed from an Episcopal point of view, and with a specifically missionary interest, by Canon K. Cragg, who, in his books and in the periodical *Operation Reach* (published by the Near East Christian Council Study Program in Islam), probes into the sources of both Islamic and Christian spirituality, and admirably combines study with a devotional approach. Perhaps the most interesting development has been the Maronite Fr. Y. Moubarac's deeply original work, *Abraham dans le Coran*; its treatment of the Qur'ān is revolutionary, in that it recognises, respects and uses critically the religious intention of the text; it also seeks in the figure of the Patriarch a common meeting-ground for Muslims and Christians.[25]

There are such possibilities for study of special interest to Christians of which one cannot now see the end. We may ask ourselves detail by detail what there is that is theologically acceptable to us in verse after verse of the Qur'ān, including those verses which are concerned with Christ and His mother. 'Acceptable' is not a generous word; we may ask ourselves better what is *illuminating* to us in these verses. We may equally examine, not only the works of mystics more or less distant from the main stream of Islamic thought, but also those theologians, such as al-Ash'ari, who are as representative of Islam as St Thomas Aquinas, or Calvin or Hooker, of different Christian Churches. These Qur'anic verses, these works of theology, if we continue seriously to examine them as friends of Islam, may sometimes give us actual light upon our own problems; more probably, may edify us; and most probably of all, may help us to find common ground where we can usefully agree with Muslims. It may even be possible to go back to one now long neglected train of mediaeval thought, the Qur'anic 'corroboration' of the Gospel, and see if it cannot be revived, not controversially to impose false dilemmas upon Muslim opponents, but to illuminate a real if limited community of thought.

Both Christianity and Islam suffer under the weight of worldly pressure, and the attack of scientific-atheists and their like. Both may reconsider the old controversies, not in any pointless expectation of ceasing to disagree, but in the hope of learning something new. There is also an opportunity of making sure that disagreement has not been exaggerated needlessly or wilfully. Christians may suddenly find that Islam is inherently attractive without there being need to surrender (still less, pretend to surrender) any of their own beliefs. What in the past was frozen has begun at last to thaw; what the mediaevals studied we may study again, making use of what they did; but we may do it for its own sake, and without thought of propaganda, and without hatred.

The imputation of idolatry to Islam

THERE is a widespread impression to-day that the general mediaeval belief was that Muslims were idolators. This is probably
because most people know the Middle Ages best in its literature,
and, although this was emphatically not the belief of educated men,
there was indeed a literary convention to that effect. The derivation of the English word 'mommet' is well known, and the poets
are full of the Saracens' worship of idols, Mahomet, Tervagan,
Apolin and Jupiter.[1] Chaucer most suitably chose the oath *by
Termagaunt* for the giant Olifaunt to use in Sir Topaz.[2] Still in the
fifteenth century, romances would speak seriously of these gods
and idols.[3] This seems most reasonably to be explained as the
requirement of a literary tradition; there is little that is similarly
absurd outside the poetic field.[4] At about the time of, and in
association with, the First Crusade, propaganda in the West
evoked statements about idols of Muhammad worshipped in
mosques, especially in the Qubbat aṣ-Ṣakhrah, *Templum Domini*.[5]
Whatever the origin of these ideas, there can be little doubt that
their literary impetus came from, or through, the chansons de
geste, together with such related prose as the Turpinus history,
all associated with Reconquest or Crusade. As such, they seem to
represent a form of war propaganda; but it remains true that both
in their first appearance and in their continuance they were mainly
literary.

Some serious works, and some authors who knew better,
repeated allegations of this sort. In Spain, accurate information
was never lacking, and, in Palestine, it was not lacking for long,
after the establishment of the Latin States; it began to circulate
increasingly freely in the course of the Spanish Reconquest and,
in Syria, after the beginnings of failure. In the extraordinarily unreliable report sent to Innocent III by the Latin Church of Jerusalem the fabulous element contrasted with others of great accuracy;
its reference to Baghdad 'where Muhammad is God and the caliph
is pope' may be thought to be one of the last fruits of an old-
fashioned school of propaganda.[6] Sober historians occasionally
admitted a false remark; Diceto followed Sigebert in the bare
assertion that Muslims offered Muhammad the worship of

Godhead. There was always some magpie exploitation of diverse material by authors who knew better. Godfrey of Viterbo, for example, repeated the vague statement often made, 'Machomet, quem hodie Saraceni colunt'; this does not of course assert that divine honours were paid to Muhammad, but it contrasts strangely with the excellent quality of the information from the Syrian Apology which he makes available elsewhere in his *Pantheon*. Vitry, with his own version of this same excellent material in a prominent position at the beginning of his History, later in the same book copied the assertion about secret worship of an *imago* of Muhammad in the Dome of the Rock; a modern study of his sources is badly needed. In these two cases neither assent to, nor rejection of, what is stated is implied; it is simply copied in. This sort of collecting and copying of all sorts of contradictory opinions probably nowhere denotes an author's convinced opinion. On the contrary, he is more likely to hold the views expressed in a long passage than those stated or implied in a brief reference; and still we cannot be sure that positively he assented to any of the ideas he republished by copying.[7] The unanimous opinion of well-educated people is described above, in Chapter I, Section 5.

Wherever it was possible to insinuate that those who reproached Christianity with a polytheist tendency were themselves inclined to the same crime, this was done. The very vague statement lent itself to this purpose. Acqui, for example, spoke of Muhammad's being received by the Arabs *quasi Deus*.[8] It is worth mentioning some obviously unintentional slips of the pen, as indicating, perhaps, what a copyist felt to be most natural: the climate of uninformed opinion. In a manuscript phrase of Pennis', *non est Deus nisi Machometus* is certainly not what the author intended; and similarly some manuscripts of Tripoli render the shahādah as *non est Deus et Machometus nuncius eius*.[9] Again, an author who knew the facts and respected them might feel that he could not pretend that an idol of Muhammad stood in the mosque; but he could still speak of 'the idol of abomination, that is, the mosque of Muhammad', thus avoiding any false statements while maintaining the traditional attitude.[10]

It is naturally among the illiterate that we find the crudest approach. The proletarian appeal of the *Conquête de Jérusalem* – a poem that combines the more fantastic tendencies of the chansons de geste with the cruel ethos of Crusading warfare – explains the only description known to me of the actual 'idol' of Muhammad and its adoration. It was conceived in vulgar splendour:

> Mahom fu aportés ens el tref l'Amiral.
> De l'or qui i reluist, des perres de cristal,
> Resclarcist tos li trés el paveillon roial.

In this popular fable, Peter the Hermit, taken prisoner of war, and required to 'adore' the 'idol', does so quite happily:

> Devant lui sont epris plus de mil estaval.
> Dans Perres l'inclina, mais il pensoit tot al.

To the poet this inglorious mental reservation is a smart trick which he much admires, and the Hermit figures henceforward as a Christian spy, with all the glamour of Reynard the Fox. We are very far here from the spirit of martyrdom or witnessing to Christ, and very far from the principles of moral theology. These ideas flourished only where literary imagination was worked on by war psychosis, in an atmosphere of illiteracy.[11]

It was also possible for a priest or a soldier to live in Palestine, in touch with Muslims surely to some extent at the least, and yet believe that there was an idol in Mecca.[12] This attitude was not shared, but may have been unintentionally encouraged, by well-informed writers. San Pedro was clearly pleased by the 'interpolated' and 'consolatory' verses of the Qur'ān; he does not make Muhammad himself reject the praise of the goddesses which Satan had set in his mouth as a false revelation: he makes his followers force the correction on the Prophet. The annotator of Ketton draws attention in the margin both to evidence of Arab idolatry and to Qur'anic condemnation; I see no polemic purpose here at all, but such remarks may have been misunderstood by careless readers.[13]

I have already noticed above the stress laid upon the supposed idol in the Qubbat as-Ṣakhrah. It is to be noted also that, although writers of the time of the First Crusade spoke of the idol in advance, none claimed to have found it when the Christians converted the Temple to their own use. The libel started to circulate again when the 'Temple' returned to Muslim use.[14] We must also bear in mind the stories of idols in the Ka'bah, and the association of ideas, in a nebulous or confused form, of the Ka'bah, of pagan worship of 'Aphrodite', of the ḥajj, of the choice of the *dies venerea* for worship and of the identification of Islam, by reason of its moral laxity, as *lex venerea*.[15]

There does seem to have been a genuine lingering suspicion in some quarters that Muslims were only incompletely de-paganised, despite their ostensible teaching, and even that they actually were crypto-polytheists. This point was made some ten years ago by Grégoire in his stimulating discussion of the problem. He concentrated on the idea that the cults of the Jāhilīyah were deliberately preserved in the Ka'bah. He suggested that this suspicion might have entered Christendom from Rabbinic writers known to Pedro de Alfonso. Pedro himself, of course, does not question the genuine monotheism of Islam; he is concerned only to establish the fetishistic origin of the Ka'bah, in opposition to the prophetic foundation of the House of God which the Qur'ān proclaims. Grégoire's theory is that the allegation of polytheism was deliberately invented as part of Crusade propaganda and out of *odium theologicum*, and also that the Jewish and other material out of which it was formed associated it with Solomon's whoring after strange gods. Muhammad, he thinks, in the forms *Mahom* and *Malcometto*, may even have been associated with Moloch. With this Grégoire connects the story of the idol in the Qubbat aṣ-Ṣakhrah, since the *Templum Dei* was supposed to be Solomon's Temple. This is not the place to discuss Grégoire's theories about the derivation of the names of the idols, Tervagan in particular, that adorn the chansons. He does, however, seem to me to have established that there is a probable connection between the Christian and Jewish suspicions of the Ka'bah, and also of the Qubbat aṣ-Ṣakhrah. It is also relevant to remember that the abjuration formula for converts from Islam which is thought to have its origin in the first years after the rise of Islam required the actual abjuration of the Ka'bah because of a carved stone of Aphrodite worshipped there; and St John of Damascus relates that there was such a stone, without asserting that Muhammad did not have it destroyed; the natural way to understand his text would be that pagan worship had ended.[16]

I have above dismissed the literary convention of Islamic idolatry as a convention that did not carry conviction with it, and in the absence of full, authoritative and explicit statements that Muslims worshipped these idols, it is necessary to take it that this was so. It is still interesting to consider Grégoire's suggestion that the libel was a deliberate invention, by a clerical writer concerned with propaganda for Crusade or Reconquest. We need not suppose hypocrisy, since the capacity for self-delusion is endless, and men are always prone to believe that they have discovered the esoteric truth that some conspiracy or other has kept hidden. If the attitude in the chansons was a deliberate lie, it was a successful one; and the fact that we can speak of the attitude of the chansons, as something well-marked and identifiable, distinct from other attitudes, is itself evidence that it was the achievement of a consistent liar. Its success was, however, limited; except for odd remarks casually repeated, it went no further than the chansons and other popular literature, and even in them, truth occasionally broke through.[17]

It remains to assess the significance of the crypto-polytheistic supposition; not, that is, the absurdity of the chansons, but the dark suspicion that seems to be hinted at by serious authors, and that may have inspired the inventor – if there was one – of the absurdities of the chansons. It should first be said that the idea of crypto-polytheism necessarily implies its corollary in ostensible monotheism. Secondly, and more importantly, we must stress that it is never explicitly affirmed. It rested entirely on ambiguous and confused statements and on short statements about the presence of idols in mosques, which may probably not have been believed even by those who repeated them. What is certain is that throughout this period every author with some pretensions to accuracy, that is, every writer who gave the matter more than a passing glance, thought that Islam stood as a third religion, as distinct from paganism as Christianity and Judaism are distinct from it, and that historically Muhammad called the Arabs away from idolatry.[18] Whether in the Latin Kingdom or in remoter Europe, a chivalric audience – nobles and their military retainers and their women – was naturally content with an unreal and romantic attitude which dehumanised an enemy, and which, while it ignored accuracy, by that means avoided those questions of theology which appealed to the scholastic. No serious writer doubted that Islam proclaims the one God.

It is possible that some ideas of the divinity of Muhammad derived from a misunderstanding of the relations of Jesus and Muhammad in Islamic belief; a vague notion that the two were regarded as being in the same class may have caused ill-informed people to suppose, not that Islam believes Christ to be not more than a man, but that it believes Muhammad to be divine. We must also remember that Crusaders had some contact with Nuṣairis and other Ismāʿīli sects, and certainly heard of the doctrine of nūr muḥammadī.

Finally, we should remember that 'idolatry' may always be correctly used to describe any mistaken idea of God that men may worship, but that it does not then mean the worship of physical idols.

The 'martyrdom' of Crusaders
who died in battle

THE history of the Crusades is full of descriptions of Christians who rashly provoked fighting in which they were killed; the classic example is Reginald of Chatillon's provocation of the Ḥaṭṭīn campaign.[1] If after the fighting a prisoner were offered his safety on condition of apostasy, and refused to apostatise, he must presumably be deemed a martyr, even although he had provoked the fighting originally; his behaviour would not, however, be set up as model behaviour, whereas a prisoner who had not brought trouble on himself would in such a case count without question as a martyr. The position was much the same as for those who called martyrdom upon themselves by grossly and publicly insulting Islam.

To call a man who was simply killed in the course of fighting the enemies of the Church a martyr was to adopt the Muslim doctrine of jihād. This was not the idea which prevailed at the opening of the Crusading period; Urban at Clermont recommended death, in the Christian tradition, primarily as an end to the exile of this life; he did not refer explicitly to the hope of martyrdom, but took it for granted that Crusaders who died would be saved.[2] Humbert, an enthusiast rather than otherwise, would later preach the Crusade, as a means of Salvation, indeed, but not as a road to martyrdom. Crusading was, of course, considered a meritorious act throughout its history.

Even when the term 'martyrdom' was applied to Crusading casualties, it may be doubted whether it was strictly martyrdom that was meant. Sir Steven Runciman, contrasting the Greek Church, has drawn attention to some ninth-century pontificates.[3] One of the most definite of the statements to which he refers us is the fragment from Leo IV, who asserts that those who die fighting Saracens will receive a Heavenly reward, since the Almighty knows that they die for the truth of the faith, for the safety of their country and the defence of Christians.[4] It is difficult to imagine the Greek Church (if the matter were raised) saying less, or failing to encourage the faithful to do as much, without greatly disturbing the Emperors. The Pope's language seems to fall short of that suitable to definitive theological pronouncement, and to express, rather, a pious hope.

Another positive passage is in a letter of John VIII to the Bishops of King Louis' dominions.[5] Here he is formally considering a query whether those who are killed in defence of the Church and of the Christian religion and State (*pro statu Christianae religionis et reipublicae*) may be absolved: *utrum . . . indulgentiam possint consequi delictorum.* He replies 'audaciously by the clemency of Christ' – *audenter Christi Dei nostri pietate* – that those who die fighting hard against the infidels will be received into eternal rest. He cites Scriptural examples of the remission of sin, including that of the penitent thief. He then pronounces an absolution, by Apostolic authority, *quantum fas est.* Again this seems to me to fall short of martyrdom strictly understood.

Much later, a passage in *Roland* is reminiscent of this; it shows Christian soldiers confessing and being absolved before battle, and being told for penance to strike the enemy. This is a little crude, but there is no note of martyrdom; there is, however, one line which asserts that those who die will die martyrs.[6] Even so, this seems to be rather a loose way of speaking than a firm theological assertion; and *Roland* is not, after all, a typical theological treatise.

The canonical position during the Crusades is not in doubt. Nothing was said of martyrdom, but for taking part a plenary indulgence was granted, on condition of a contrite heart and of oral confession. This positively excludes the idea of martyrdom.[7]

It may be safest to conclude that fighting against the Muslims was regarded as a holy exercise, a good work which would count very strongly on the side of salvation if one were killed in the process; but not, technically, as martyrdom. It did not make absolution superfluous. There was, however, no embarrassment in using the term 'martyr' emotionally and evocatively of those who died in battle. Runciman's main point is that in the West bellicosity was consecrated by Crusading in a way unknown to the Church before, but it may be argued with all respect that he slightly overstated it. We may certainly maintain that we are here concerned much more with a matter of sentiment than with theology proper.

Christ and the Last Day

THE pattern of eschatological events lacked popular appeal for Christians to whom Islamic belief in other fields was really interesting. When it was noticed, it was usually because the Islamic image of Christ was involved.

Although Muhammad's intervention at the Judgement, on behalf of his own people, was celebrated, the actual scene of the Judgement was generally ignored. The *summula* was unusually well-informed in the matter, but the author was interested only in the part attributed to Christ in the Last Things by Muslim doctrine.[1] Thus he said that in this belief Christ, who is now with the Creator, when Antichrist (i.e. ad-Dajjāl) comes, is to descend to earth and kill him; he is to convert the Jews and perfectly to teach his own followers, the Christians, who have now long lost the law he first taught them. At the sound of the trumpet of the Seraphim,[2] by whom the Muslims understand an archangel, all will die, and Christ with them; after, there will be the resurrection and the Judgement, at which Christ will be an assistant, but not the Judge; all the prophets will be intercessors for, and helpers of their peoples. This account is complete so far as Christ is concerned, but would be very misleading if it had to serve as a complete picture of the Last Things in Islamic belief. It is a contribution only to pseudo-Christology. The author went on to criticise the Islamic Paradise; of the Judgement itself he had nothing to say.

Simon Simeon, quoting the passage in the Qur'ān which describes how God took Christ to Himself because He would not permit the Jews to crucify Him, seemed to understand that Christ would speak for both Christians and Jews at the Last Day. Ketton's text, which he was using, is not clear: *eorum saeculo futuro testis adstabit ille* does not seem to imply an unfriendly witness, and Simon understood *viri legum* here to mean both Jews and Christians. This made the correct sense, by which Christ would witness against the Jews, impossible.[3] Fr. Antonio de' Reboldi understood the Muslim doctrine more clearly: he said that all the prophets at the judgement would admit that they had sinned, so that Muhammad would pray God to spare them. Christ would be accused by God of setting Himself to usurp the divine glory, and He would admit His fault; only Muhammad would be recognised as faithful, and Jesus would be spared for his sake.[4] This puts Christ in a less favourable position than Islam normally alleges of Him; it is usually said that He cannot pray to God for His people, because *they, his followers,* have set Him up to be God. The Syrian Apology said without comment that Christ is expected to reign for forty years at the end of the world. Ricoldo spoke bitterly of the idea that, although Christ was going to reign, He was going to do so as a Muslim.[5] Verona thought that Christ 'in the presence of God' would send Christians to Heaven and Muslims to Hell; Muhammad, appealed to by the Muslims to whom he had promised salvation, would secure a reversal of the situation, except that Christ and His mother would remain in Heaven. This is a very curious story suggestive of controversy at a petty level[6].

San Pedro made some comment here that is difficult to follow. He said that the worst heresy of all prevailing in Muhammad's day and adopted by him, the root of all evil, is the doctrine that souls shall die 'except the face of God'; and again, that all souls shall die, and again, in the description of the mi'rāj, that all angels shall die and nothing but God remain alive.[7] It is not easy to see why he thought this doctrine exceptionally pernicious. The attitude we should expect is that adopted by the annotator of Ketton – that the doctrine is silly.[8]

Two sources alone seemed to be interested in the whole sequence of Last Things, from the angels who visit the soul in its private grave to the final arrival in Paradise, by way of the death of all things and the mawqif, the waiting and the sweating before the Judgement. These two accounts are the remarkable creed in the Cambridge manuscript, which appears to render a Muslim creed without any polemical purpose whatever[9]; and the long account, with imaginary discussion, in Lull's *Liber de Gentile*. Lull made his Muslim philosopher defend these doctrines for typically Lullian reasons: if it be objected that angels cannot die, he replies that their doing so shows all the more the power of God, and, since they are purified like refined metal, His goodness also. This was to fit his controversy into a scheme pre-arranged by himself, but seems also to attempt to say the sort of thing a Muslim might say, if he were a Lullian philosopher.[10] Both these accounts stand out from the rest of mediaeval writing about Islamic eschatological belief, and for the same reason: they are not particularly interested in the subject from a Christological point of view. Few writers were interested in it at all, but all save these two saw it solely as Christology.

Shī'ah Islam

MEDIAEVAL Christians knew very little about Shī'ah Islam, because from the fall of the Fāṭimids in Egypt to the rise of the Ṣafawis in Persia there was no state professing Shī'ah beliefs to attract their attention.

Ḥasan, Ḥusayn and the drama of Karbalā' were unknown. Pedro de Alfonso had wild and confused ideas, natural in a Jew converted to Christianity in a country that never knew any but Sunni Islam. Latin writers who exploited Pedro's material all ignored what he said on this subject.

It has been pointed out[1] that it was in heterodox, Ismā'īli form that the Crusaders knew Shī'ism: the Assassins, who greatly intrigued them, and who have enjoyed a tremendous legend in Western literature[2]; and, less extreme, the Fāṭimids. Both were powers affecting policy in the Latin States. It is not possible here to consider the wide question of the relations of the Latins with the Ismā'īlis.

William of Tyre described the foundation of the Fāṭimid dynasty, quoting the descent of Ubaydullah correctly, except for large omissions[3]; and Vitry described its extinction.[4] Neither knew much about the religious character of Shī'ism. William thought that al-Mahdi (as Ubaydullah's title) meant *complanans*, the Leveller, 'he who directed all things to quiet, and without trouble made the ways level for the people'. William and those who followed him quoted the idea that 'Alī had been intended by God to receive the message which Gabriel by error gave to Muhammad; this is an extreme view which most Shī'ah of Ja'fari confession would repudiate to-day but which even in Ja'fari Shī'ism communicated itself to travellers in Persia of the seventeenth century.[5] Vitry was aware that religious differences between Sunni and Shī'ah existed, and he exaggerated them in a vague way: 'other rites and other institutions and another mode of praying' than Muhammad's characterised the followers of 'Alī.[6] Joinville, exceptionally confused, supposed 'Alī to have been Muhammad's uncle, who, despised by Muhammad, taught another religion.[7] Tripoli, although he was interested in the caliphate, treated it only as a political institution, so far as the simultaneous existence of rival caliphs was concerned: Ṣalāḥ ad-Dīn suppressed the Fāṭimid caliphate for reasons of state.[8]

Essentially, Shī'ism seems to have been thought of as a schism simply, even though one of implacable hatred; 'Alī was its anti-prophet, as Oliver of Paderborn's simplification of William of Tyre's statements brings out.[9] Shī'ah forms of religious expression were quite unknown. So was the moderate Ja'fari Shī'ah Islam, either as a temperate form of religious belief and practice, or as the religion of the oppressed that it has often become in the course of its history. This may just be hinted at by Ricoldo, who knew 'Iraq and passed through Sāmarra', where, of course, he was told that *quidam filius Ahali*, that is, the Mahdi (the twelfth Imam) would return, and where he heard of the wonderful mule, held ready harnessed on Fridays in expectation of the Mahdi's coming. He said, 'some Muslims follow Muhammad, and they are many; and some follow 'Alī, and are fewer and less evil, and say that Muhammad by tyrannical power usurped what was 'Alī's'.[10]

Res turpissima

THIS unpleasant matter was considered very important by medi-aeval Latin critics of Islam. It is therefore considered briefly here.

The chief Latin accusation is based by the earlier mediaevals on Q. II.223, which Sale translates, 'Your wives are your tillage; go in therefore unto your tillage in what manner soever ye will.' Maracci has, *Mulieres vestrae sunt ager vobis. Venite igitur ad agrum vestrum quomodocumque volueritis* (II.224). Ketton translated *Mulieres vobis subiectas penitus pro modo vestro, ubicunque volueritis, parate*, and Mark of Toledo, *Uxores enim vestrae sunt vobis tanquam vinea, excolite ergo eas qualitercunque libuerit.*[1] Fidenzio used Mark's version.[2] Ricoldo quoted this verse in the form, *mulieres sunt aratrum vestrum; arate eas ut vultis.* It seems possible that this verse contributes to the composite verse invented by him: *fatigate mulieres, fatigate, et non erit vobis peccatum, dummodo dederitis eis precium.* This last version we may here ignore.[3] The *reprobatio* has *mulieres vestrae sunt aratio vestra, ergo intrate arationem vestram quocunque modo volueritis*; San Pedro, *uxores vestrae terrae culturae adictae sunt, ideoque culturam vestram peragite quomodocunque vobis placuerit.*[4] Vitry has a paraphrase: *si uxores vel ancillas habetis, ipsas pro modo vestro ad voluntatem vestram parate.*[5] This must be the verse most often translated in the whole Middle Ages.

This was universally considered in the Middle Ages to have the meaning alleged by Peter of Poitiers and quoted above in chapter V. Sale, however, says that it refers to postures and gives his authorities for so saying; they comment that 'preposterous venery' is forbidden by the preceding verse, by the words, 'as God has commanded you'; it is interesting that this is just what Bibliander understood, commenting marginally on the words following 'parate', that is, 'Deum timentes', to this effect: *Violentius hic locus a nostris tortus est quasi nefaria permittat, quum adjiciat, Deum timentes, etc.*[6] Maracci in his notes cites Jalāl ad-Dīn's commentary which supports Sale's opinion, but in his *refutatio*, while realising that there is a doubt, prefers the 'Christian' view, and quotes San Pedro. The *reprobatio* also supports this interpretation; after citing II.223 it continues: 'Ubi dicit glossarius Sarracenorum, expositor Alcorani, super istud verbum: *"Quocunque modo*, id est, ante et retro." Hanc autem detestabilem turpitudinem . . . .' There is no reason for us to reject Sale's interpretation of the *glossarius*. For Muslims, the 'tillage' has always meant the vagina, in which alone the seed is deposited (cf. Baydāwī on this verse). This is not the sense assumed by the Spaniards. San Pedro believed that verse II.223 was given in reply to a man who asked the Prophet *utrum liceret eis cum uxoribus coire quomodocunque placuerit, relicta concipiendi seu pariendi natura.* There is some mistake here; San Pedro is not likely to have invented it, but neither can this be a genuine tradition as quoted.

Muhammad is also represented as teaching a man during his wife's menstruation: *comprime femoralia eius super naturam, et quod reliquum est, scias te uti posse.* In support of this, the *reprobatio* misinterprets a tradition of Bukhārī's, but the traditions on which San Pedro relies in this case are not invented. The Qur'ān unequivocally forbade all marital relations during menstruation, but a few doubtful traditions do seem to permit marital access to parts of the body unaffected by this (cf. Zamakhsharī on this verse).[7]

To sum up: the Latins thought this matter very important. In their principal contention about verse II.223 they were perversely wrong. In their minor contention they had some justification, although there is no evidence that what they so stressed was ever encouraged, let alone generally taught, or that it was even accepted at all widely. On none of these points can they have had any reliable knowledge of actual practice.

This is the place to note another point arising out of the *reprobatio* here. 'Whoredom' (Sale) in Q. IV.19 is taken by the author to mean *facinus inter se*, for which there appears to be no Islamic authority, although the author claims the authority of the *glossarius*. He took the following verse to refer to male homosexuality, and was there on surer ground, since that is traditional; he commented that the punishment was inadequate. The verse is considered abrogated, however, and this crime in Islam is punishable as *zinā'*, or any other illicit sexual crime. So is *al-fāḥishah*, the crime of women referred to above, which Sale considers in the context to mean fornication or adultery.[8]

The right to kill

DR SMALLEY, in her *English Friars and Antiquity*, draws attention to an interesting discussion of the right to kill Muslims.[1]
Robert Holcot, a Dominican scholastic who died in 1349, an
associate of Richard de Bury, literary, a bibliophil, a professional
moralist, represents humane literate opinion in a great provincial
university. It is interesting that his liberal approach to antiquity
did not extend to Islam.

Holcot distinguishes between infidels (pagans, Jews, Muslims,
idolators, heretics). Those that submit to the Church may be
tolerated like the Gabaonites (AV: Gibeon), as hewers of wood
and drawers of water, provided there be no *contumelia Creatoris*,
and in the hope of their conversion. Muslims who do not submit
qualify as rebels and persecutors, heretics par excellence. It is
lawful and sometimes meritorious to attack them with the prior
authority of the Church – 'to despoil them and kill them and devote
their goods to the faithful'. Some Jews must be left unkilled to
fulfil the prophecy of the final conversion of a remnant, but this
does not apply to Muslims who have unjustly occupied the land
promised to Abraham and his seed, and other Christian lands, by
force, and who kill missionaries who attack Islam. He gives other
justifications: thus, all goods rightly belong to the just, who may
forcibly take whatever the unjust hold, and kill them if they
refuse to be converted; again, a putrid member may be cut off
from the natural body, and so may it from the mystical body of
Christ, which is the redeemed human race; again, it is lawful to
induce a right attitude by fear; and the community must be protected from dangerous elements.[2]

The doctrines of Crusade and jihād here approximate, first, in
the willingness to tolerate people of an alien religion only as
subjects (though their status within Christendom in theory and
practice was less safe than in Islam); in the direction of holy war
against all kinds of rebels and dissenters; and in the insistence on
duly constituted authority for waging war.[3]

Notes

For abbreviations, see p. 393.

Introduction

1. See Montet for the formula and Cumont for his comment, in bibliography.

2. For idolatry in Islam, see also appendix A.

3. Migne, PG, 94, col. 761ff. The *Dialexis* is ibid., col. 1585 (very fragmentary form), and MPG 96, col. 1335.

4. See below, chapter III, note 51 and text.

5. See Perier in bibliography. For Lull, see below, chapter VI, notes 34-38 and text. For Arabic Christian literature generally see Graf's *Geschichte*.

6. Ibn Isḥāq (tr. Guillaume), p. 79ff.

7. See also below, chapter III, notes 19, 20, 21, p. 343.

8. See A. Abel, also Bignani-Odier, in bibliography.

9. *Anatrope*, capp. III-XVIII and XXVIII cited.

10. *Panoplia*, titulus XXVIII. Cf. Cedrenus, whose ideas do not seem to have passed into the Western tradition. Nearly all Christian writers share with him his indignation at the 'sensual Paradise' of the Qur'ān, as they understood it, and some share his anger that God should be made the 'cause' of evil; again, many share the notion that Islam serves the pagan goddess Venus, and a few, even, the idea that in some unexplained way it consciously worships her. (For these points in the Western tradition, see chapter V, sections 4 and 6, passim; chapter VI, section 4, p. 212, and appendix A, p. 312.) But if his idea that the call to prayer explicitly designated Venus as God had been known in the West, it would almost certainly have been given some credit and would quite certainly have been repeated. (MPG 121, coll. 811-15.)

11. This account also contains the gratuitous assertion that the body was eaten by dogs, which also recurs among credulous later writers. These, however, are the only ways in which Eulogius seems to be a source of later statements. See bibliography for Eulogius, and see also Alvarus.

12. Ed. Tien; see also Muir's *Apology*. As well as Graf, see d'Alverny, *Deux Traductions*, for the translations and for identification and dating.

13. See d'Alverny in bibliography; also under *Cluny*, Mark of Toledo and *Contrarietas*.

14. Translated as *Liber Scalae Machometi* by Abraham 'al-faquin' and Bonaventura of Siena. See also Asin, Cerulli and Munoz; and also below, section 3 of this introduction.

15. For a discussion of Tafurs and Pastoureaux, see N. Cohn, *Pursuit of the Millennium*.

Chapter I. *Revelation: Christian understanding of Islamic belief*

1. Q. iii.60. The prophets are listed in Q. vi.83-86 and iv.161; of these only some were apostles, who included Mūsā (Moses) and 'Īsā (Jesus) as well as Muhammad. For Muslims, the Qur'ān is the only source of true information about the Prophets; the Old and New Testaments are not sound sources (see chapter II, section 1, p. 47 below) and may more or less misrepresent the one message of all the prophets ('Islam'). ('Prophet' is *nabī*; 'apostle' or 'messenger' is *rasūl*.)

2. CSS. ii.3.

3. Q. iv.168. Ketton, Az. xii, Bibl. p. 37, line 32. Cf. 'For (God) is almighty, and the wise Ruler, maintaining power and strength over His people. There is no testimony greater than His; may He be witness to judge between you and me, Who sent down this Qur'ān to me, for your correction and admonition.' Q. vi.17-19. Ketton, Az. xiv, Bibl. p. 45, lines 10-13.

4. Cap. vi, MS f. 38v.

5. *Quad. reprobatio*, i and passim; Simon Simeon. The *Lib. Scalae* uses the phrase *propheta et nuncius* (e.g. cap. lii).

6. Will. Tyr. i.1.

7. De leg., xviii/18.q. William of Tyre used the phrase *legis lator* of Gabriel, who bore the Law to the Prophet (xix.xx). It might be used in the modern sense of legislator, or, more nearly to the modern idiom, 'Founder of a religion'; Bacon used it for Moses, Christ and Muhammad equally. (Mor. Phil. iv.2a.iv.1ff, and passim.)

8. SSM i.viii.75; Op. Trip. i.vi; Arm 21(22).

9. SSM i.vi.14-16; ibn Isḥāq, 1012. For how Muhammad was 'killed' see chapter III below.

10. Mor. Phil. iv.2a.iii.24.

11. All versions of the Corozan text: Hugh of Fleury, Gerald of Wales, St Albans Chronicle (Roger of Wendover, Matthew Paris and 'Matthew of Westminster'), Vincent de Beauvais (23.39, 40), Andrea Dandolo, Marino Sanudo, M. Polonus, Continuatio Chron. B. Isidori. Also in Legenda Aurea, Higdens and Cronica de Espana. (See bibliography individually.) The phrase *legis lator*, in a sense that is far from clear, was echoed by some of these texts, Hugh, Gerald, St Albans and Vincent. The word *propheta* is used by the pseudo-Isidore. Dandalo and Marino stress the magical side, and also Muhammad's supposed claim (a mistake confined to them, except for some confusion in the *Epistola Abitalib Saraceni ad Samuelem Judaeum*) to be Messias. Acqui used the word *consiliarius*, which may suggest augury and a magical interpretation of the divine will. The two Venetians blended the Corozan account with that of the *libellus* given by Vincent; this uses the word *propheta*.

12. Mancini; see bibliography.

13. M. T. d'Alverny, *Deux Traductions* . . . (see bibliography).

14. Q. iv.161. Ketton, Az. xi, Bibl. p. 37, line 21 ff.

15. Q. ii.130. Cf. Mark of Toledo's more accurate version: 'We have indeed revealed to thee as we have revealed to Noe and the prophets after him . . .' and 'Say (ye): We have believed in God and in what was directed to us and to Abraham and Ismael and Isaac and Jacob and the

tribes, and in what was given to Moses and to Jesus, and in what was transmitted to the Prophets by their Creator; I do not distinguish between them; and we are offered to Him' (cap. ii, MS f. 8r). Ketton's reference is Az. ii, Bibl. p. 13, line 30 ff. Cf. also Q. ix.112 which in Ketton reads 'certainly nobody must doubt a thing that God has promised, which is confirmed by the Testament, the Evangel and Alfurcan (= Qur'ān) for (Sale) 'the promise for the same is assuredly due by the Law, the Gospel and the Qur'ān' (the Arabic has Qur'ān, *not* furqan). Mark has 'the pledges of God made in the Decalogue (=Tawrāt), the Gospel and the Qur'ān'. (Cap. xi, MS f. 73v; the Ketton reference is Az. xviii, Bibl. xix, p. 67, line 21ff.) As a general rule it is true that a literal translation of the Qur'ān, without a commentary, and without the words which need to be supplied in any translation from a Semitic language (cf. our Bibles), would be very difficult to follow; and this is the case with Mark, whose accuracy must therefore be balanced against the obscurity resulting from it. (In the passage quoted, Ketton was definitely misleading; 'Old Testament' is wrong; *Tawrāt* should be rendered *Law* or *Pentateuch* for which Mark's *Decalogue* may have been intended to stand.)

16. The *de doctrina Machumet*, the *de generatione Machumet* and the *Chronica Mendosa* (Bibl. p. 201ff; for the MSS, see M. T. d'Alverny, loc. cit.).

17. The Law, the Gospel, the Psalter, the prophetical books, the Qur'ān. Actually, the Qur'ān does not recognise the prophetical books, or the prophets concerned, in any way at all. See also below, chapter II, section 1, p. 47 ff, and notes 25-27, pp. 325-6. The appropriations of functions to the (Islamic) prophets are correct, except that Moses should have been shown as spoken *to* by God, not as speaking to Him.

18. *Reprobatio* xi. Arm. 10/11. San Pedro, SSM i.iii.4.

19. Lib. de Tart., de T. et S., 8; Lib. de Gent. viii. See also ibid. iv.iv.

20. Vitry, op. cit., i.v, cf. vi: 'Christ the greatest prophet before Muhammad'; Fidenzio, op. cit., xiv.

21. Anon. Fior. Cf. Higden, op. cit., loc. cit., 'Summum Dei prophetam'.

22. Disp. viii. This theme is discussed below, chapter II.

23. Capitula, iii.vi; cf. *de generatione Machumet*, Bibl. p. 201. See Massignon in SEI under nūr muhammadī and Nuṣairī'.

24. Joinville, xc. The report omits Muhammad from the series, which thus runs from Abraham only so far as St Peter. In Nuṣairī' doctrine Shim'ūn (Simon) is the 'silent imam' superior to the 'articulate prophetic voice' of 'Īsā (Jesus), as 'Alī is the 'silent imam' to Muhammad ('the voice'). Naturally enough, King Louis' emissary understood very little of this; but it does seem clear that he and all the Franks realised that this was not orthodox Islam.

25. The best example is in Thomas of Pavia (op. cit.). The idea seems implicit whenever the prophets are confined to the three 'lawgivers' as in Vitry, i.v and *summula*, also Leg. Aur., loc. cit., Humbert, de pred. S.C. xii; cf. chapter VI below for the idea of three 'laws' or three world religions: the Qur'ānic idea of successive revelations was

perhaps assimilated into, or possibly itself helped to create, this. Burcard said Muhammad was sent only to the Arabs (loc. cit.).

26. Paris, aliud scr. Cf. Ludolf: as Jesus put the Law of Moses in the shade, so was Muhammad sent to correct His; and Lull, lib. de Gent., IV.iii, where the Muslim divine speaks of the validity of each Law till superseded by the next. Cf. also the English pilgrim ('quidam anglicus' in bibliography) who thought Muslims place Christ at the left hand, Muhammad at the right hand, of God.

27. Tripoli, XXVII. Higden also quoted Tripoli's statement about the 'five books' which descended from Heaven, as he supposed Muslims to believe; but the bulk of his account (refer bibliography) is made up of the material 'temporibus Bonifacii'.

28. Q. V.48-52. Ketton, Az. XII, Bibl. p. 24, line 8ff. Mark, cap. VII, MS f. 42v, 43r.

29. Salāḥ ad-Dīn: St Albans Chronicle, yr. 1188; de expug. T.S. and Itin. Regis Richardi. Also see Vitry, I.V.

30. Humbert, de pred. S.C., XII and Op. Trip. I.iv; Ricoldo, Disp. XVIII, cf. III and also cf. Tripoli, as cited note 27 above.

31. Q. II.38; Arm. 10(11); Ket. Az. II, Bibl. p. 10, lines 5-9. Cf. Q. II.77, Ket. II, Bibl. p. 15, lines 4-11; Arm., loc. cit., Arm. 10(11), Q. III.1-2, Ket. Az. V, Bibl. p. 21, line 26ff, Arm. 13(14), Q. XXIII. 46-53, Ket. Az. XXXII, Bibl. XXXIII, p. 110, line 29ff; and Q. XLI.43, Ket. Az. L, Bibl. LI, p. 149, lines 20-21. Arm. 13(14), where he omits the words nunc docemus from Ket. Az. LI, Bibl. LII, p. 150, lines 11-12; Q. XLIII.11: cf. Arm., passim 10-15 (11-16). Fitzralph also took particular care to record the supposed Qur'ānic endorsement of the Psalter. Cf. Q. IX.112, Arm. 12(13); Ket. Az. XVIII, Bibl. XIX, p. 67, lines 21-22.

32. See chapter II below.

33. 'Arabico tantum semoto velamine' says Ketton of his own translation; this unhappily was one of the cases where the sense of the original completely disappeared, under treatment, with the velamen. Because it was the source of errors, Reland had no patience with this – 'pessima versio Alcorani', he says (de relig. II.viii); whatever may be said in its favour, and that is not much, it is at the opposite pole from Reland's scholarly common sense and his passion for accuracy. See chapter X, section 4, p. 295.

34. This became the text for long passages of Peter the Venerable's contra sectam; see below, chapter IV, note 33.

35. Q. II.122-30; Ket. Az. II, Bibl. p. 13, lines 12-13, 18-19, 21-22, 30-34; cf. Arm. 10(11). Q. III.18; Ket. Az. V, Bibl. p. 22, line 10ff. Q. III.58-60; Ket. Az. V, Bibl. p. 24, line 8ff. Q. XXXIII.35; Ket. Az. XLII, Bibl. XLIII, p. 132, line 28ff. Cf. passages in Ketton, quoted both in this chapter and also by Fitzralph, which illustrate the use of Muslim, and related words in the Qur'ān: Q. II.130, Ket. Az. II, Bibl. p. 13, lines 21-22 Arm. 10(11); Q. III.17-19, Ket. Az. V, Bibl. p. 22, line 10ff; Arm. 16(17); Q. III.58-60, Ket. Az. V, Bibl. p. 24, line 8ff; Arm. 11(12), 16(17); cf. also Q. VI.82-89. Ket. Az. XV, Bibl. p. 47, line 45ff, and the comments in Fitzralph, quoted by me.

36. Cap. I (ff. 7v, 8r); cf. note 35. Cap. IV (MS ff. 19v, 20r and 22r).

The phrase 'die not' etc. in the manuscript available to me contains a straightforward error, whether translator's or copyist's: 'nolite *timere priusquam sitis oblati* . . .' (This does not affect the point here at issue; the mistake must derive from ignorance; it cannot be a case of prejudice or axe-grinding.) *Lux*, however, must surely be a copyist's mistake for *lex*, so that Mark's text ought to read, 'there is no *religion* with God . . .' Cf. Maracci's choice of words to Mark's. He has *addictus* and *Moslemus* where Mark has *oblatus* and *Ismaelitus*: cf. Q. II.122ff, Maracci, refutationes in suram II.129ff (pp. 50ff): *et nos sumus addicti* (137); Q. III.45ff, Maracci, refut. in suram III.51ff (pp. 129ff); or cf. Q. LXVI.5 (Q. and Maracci): . . . *uxores meliores vobis, Moslemas, Fideles* . . . Mistakes in Mark's translation cited are *Gospels* for *Gospel* (which might imply the mistaken idea that Muslims accept our four Gospel texts as opposed to one unique 'Gospel' revelation not represented by any known text); and he gives no rendering for ḥanīf in the description of Abraham. In the final example of the use of *Muslim* of which I have quoted Ketton's translation (note 35 above) Mark had *Saraceni*, which seems to preclude the idea which must naturally occur to Mark's reader that by translating *Muslim* as *Ismaelitus* he implied a semantic relation between *Ismael* and *Muslim*.

37. M. T. d'Alverny has pointed out that it had the weight of the Cluniac recommendation behind it (loc. cit.) and it was also more readable; also as I have said, Mark unglossed is obscure, because without explanation the meaning of the Qur'ān is obscure.

38. Bibl. p. 224. MS margin at foot left (CCCD 184). See also treatment of Christ at the Last Day, appendix C.

39. de leg., loc. cit.

40. Viterbo, *renuisse* (Cerulli), must be *tenuisse,* as in Paris. Cf. B.M. MS Royal 14.C.XI.

41. SSM I.i.20; ibn Isḥāq, 159. San Pedro's knowledge of Muhammad's life seems to be based on the *sīrat rasūl Allāh*, as will appear more particularly in chapter III.

42. Reprob. v; cf. Q. LXI.14 and III.45. Ricoldo, Disp. IX; cf. Ep. III; (Bart. Pic. has 'Muslims, imitators and apostles of Muhammad').

43. Ricoldo: Disp. VI; cf. ibid. IX and Epp. III, IX; Q.III.58-60. Gregory: lib. III, ep. xxi, to Nāsir b. 'Alnas. Cf. the work of Y. Moubarac in our own day.

44. Op. cit. v.i. For an account of the manner of Revelation as Muslims understood it, see Watt's *Muhammad at Mecca*. Other Islamic accounts are cited in Muir's less sympathetic *Life of Muhammed*. See also ibn Isḥāq (translation by Guillaume).

45. From Vincent 23.39; cf. other Corozan sources and Paris, al. scr. and Vitry I.v.

46. Guibert, Waltherius, du Pont; Vitry I.v.

47. Sigebert; Ricoldo, Dispp. XIII, XIV; Ottimo Commento; Ludolf, VIII.

48. Disp. XIV which derives from *Contrarietas* IV (MS f. 242v ff). This is fuller, but less cocksure about epilepsy; Ricoldo for once suffered in accuracy and judgement by not following more closely. *Cont.* says M.

imitated, or perhaps suffered from epilepsy; Ric. that because he suffered from it (*quia epilenticus erat*) he had to explain away his fits as angelic visitations – thus he adopted the Corozan version, always colourful and absurd.

49. Pref. Q.; M. T. d'Alverny draws attention (*Marc de Tolède*) to Mark's stress on medical details.

50. Loc. cit.

51. Cap. III. *Muslim*: the name of this authority appears unrecognisably in the 'Galensis' printed text as *Moium* (and Berlin MSS have *noyum* but the B. nat. MS has *Muzlim* clearly. Some texts have *God* for *Lord thy God*. See Q. XCVI.1-5; Muslim, 1.252-8; cf. az-Zuhri, quoted by Watt, *Mecca*, p. 40. Bukhārī appears as 'Bohari'. The only vestige of an equally authentic account in Ricoldo's work is a passing reference to Muhammad's having said that revelation seemed like bells, which Ricoldo, whether recognising the supposed medical significance, or accidentally, associated with the alleged epilepsy (Disp. XIII). The account in the *Contrarietas* is similar to that in the *reprobatio* but less close to Bukhārī's text (this refers to that part of my quotation only); it quotes the isnād but calls 'Ā'ishah *daughter* of Muhammad.

52 ·Chapter IX.

53. SSM I.i.13-16; ibn Isḥāq, 150ff, 154. Ibid. 17-19; 24-32. Ibid. ii.2, 22 and vii.9. Cf. also passing references, e.g. i.32. In one episode where the Quraysh spoke to Muhammad they took it for granted (in the story as San Pedro told it) that his 'familiar' was either an angel or a demon (I.i.23ff). Cont. Chr. Isid. states that it was reported as true that the Devil appeared to Muhammad in the form of an angel of light, and foretold future events.

54. Mor. Phil. IV.2a.iii.24. Pisan text in Mancini (q.v. in bibliography) which is related to San Pedro's work. 'Going to speak to God in Heaven' is likely to refer to the mi'rāj, here confused with ordinary revelations. (For relation this text and San Pedro, see Mancini.)

55. Pedro de Alfonso, Dialogi, V; *Contrarietas*, VII; Risālah, Toletanus MS p. 299, col. 1; Vincent 23.44; Muir, p. 50. Chapter V below.

56. Reprob. VI; Bu. LXV.xxxi.7; Disp. VIII derived from Cont. VII direct; San Pedro, SSM I.ii.7.

57. San Pedro varies in his suppositions; he implies at one time that a single book was sent from Heaven; at another he makes it clear that revelations occurred over a period of twenty-three years, but does not make it clear when he thought they were collected and written down, whether this was done during the Prophet's lifetime or after his death. This picture is not altogether integrated with that of demoniac possession. It would be a mistake to look for consistency. Reference – SSM I.i.43.

58. CSS 1.16, information probably deriving from annotator to Ketton's Qur'ān; see note 81 below.

59. Rod., Hist. Arab. II; cf. ibid. V. VI.

60. Pedro de Alfonso; Sigebert; Guibert; Fleury; Gerald; Peter the Venerable (*summula* and CSS I.16 and II.3, 5); St Albans; Waltherius; du Pont; Mark, Pref. Q.; William of Tyre, XIX.xx; Rod., Hist. Arab. II, V, VI, and Cron. de Esp., CVI/478, CXXI/493; Vincent 23.39; Oliver,

Hist Dam., Hist. Reg., and Ep. Sal.; Will. Alv. de leg. xviii/18.p;
Vita Mahometi Benedict; Fidenzio, xiv; Paris, al. scr.; Leg. Aur.,
reprobatio, loc. cit.; Tripoli xxv; Ricoldo, Disp. xiii; San Pedro SSM
I.i.13ff; i.i.68, i.ii.22 etc.; Lull, D.P., *5,* 6 and Hamar sig. 9 etc.; Higden;
Acqui; Pennis i; Martinus Polonus; Cont. Chr. Isid.; Marino iii.ii;
Ludolf, viii; Anon. Fior.; Ottimo Comm.; Benvenuto. This does not
claim to be an exhaustive list.

61. Vincent 23.40 and MS version *Bonifacii temporibus quinti*; Leg.
Aur., loc. cit.; San Pedro, i.viii.27ff and 59ff (SSM); Marino, Higden
and Ludolf, loc. cit. Thomas of Pavia has a very remarkable version:
Muhammad's evil counsellor and guide, having taught him his tricks to
fool the people, for a final trick stood in a dry well where, being hidden,
he could simulate the voice of God. After he had spoken, Muhammad
called on everyone to throw a stone into the well, ostensibly to mark the
sacred occasion, practically to kill the inconvenient witness whose advice
he now no longer needed. This version was not popular during the
Middle Ages, but is still alive to-day in Oriental circles of little discrimination that are hostile to Islam. Cf. the variant in *Vita Mahometi.*

62. Chapter III below.

63. *Summula*; Arm. 10(11); Ricoldo, Disp. prologue, in the form
collectaneum preceptorum. Cf. the Spanish Renaissance phrase: 'Alcoran
quiere dezir congregacion de capitulos o psalmos y versos' (Juan Andrés,
refer bibliography). (Maracci explains qara'a as *legere* but says this
is to be understood as *legere* and as *colligere*: as a book of *readings* and as
a *collection* of twenty-three years of revelations, alternatively, a collection
of Saracen statutes. Prodromus, de Alcorano, cap. i: de nomine Alcorani,
p. 33.) Mark very correctly defined Q. as 'lectionarius' (Ref. Q.).
Cf. the seventeenth-century MS *Epitome Fidei*: 'Alcoran (i. Legenda)'.
Tripoli used also masāḥif and ḥarām (Vat. MS 'haracenorum', is an
obvious copyist's confusion). (Capp. xxv and xxvi.)

64. For 'the People of the Book' Ketton (cf. *summula*) has *viri legis,*
and Vitry has *homines legis*; Mark (e.g. Alcor. vi, MS f. 37v) has *qui
librum acceperunt.*

65. Lib. de Gent. iv.xii. To speak of the Qur'ān as a revelation that
contains the law would correspond very well with the reality of the
Islamic claim. At the same time, the two concepts are very close, and
sharī'ah, which originally meant 'revelation', is now the ordinary word
for the divine law, one might almost say, 'divine jurisprudence'; and
even so it is roughly equivalent to the English 'Divinity' or 'theology'
used to designate the subject of study.

66. Bibl. p. 224; MS p. 50 right-hand margin and f. 33r margin at
foot left; Bibl. 224 and MSS p. 50 top left margin and f. 33r top middle
right margin; also ad Az. 58.

67. Although a 'collectio praeceptorum' sounds as much like an
anthology of proverbs or maxims as like a Book of Revelation, the
meaning must obviously depend entirely on the meaning attached to the
word *praeceptum.*

The word was used by Pedro de Alfonso to describe a thing deriving
directly from God: 'haec universa praecepta idcirco sunt a Deo proposita'

(Dial. v, cit.). The word apparently had for Ketton the association of the inherently divine; for example, he used it to translate *ayat* in sūrah XIX: 'cum divinae virtutes praeceptaque legebantur . . .' (Q. XIX.59; Ketton, Az. XXVIII, Bibl. XXIX, p. 100, line 4). The explicit of his Qur'ān refers to it as 'Collection of chapters or of *praecepta*'. This seems to equate *praeceptum* with *sūrah* (or 'chapter') and certainly implies that *revelation* is a near synonym. (The word *sūrah* itself was well-known, usually as *azoara*. Ketton's annotator, as well as explaining that it was a revelation, said that it might be translated *chapter* – Bibl. p. 224, MSS p. 50 top left margin and f. 33r upper middle right margin.)

Some Spanish authors of the thirteenth century used the term *praeceptum*. Mark of Toledo spoke of Muhammad's making excerpts of *praecepta* from the Old and New Testaments (in composing the Qur'ān) (Pref. Q.). Archbishop Roderick described a sūrah as made up of *praecepta*; in the Spanish version of the same text this appeared as *leys*. In another place *zohara* (= (lat.) *azoara* = sūrah) was explained as meaning *mandamiento*; and in another, as meaning *laws of God*. (Hist. Arab. VI; Cron. de Esp. CXXI/493, cf. CVI/478.) Fitzralph naturally followed Ketton on his use of words of Arabic origin.

Similar use of language occurred in Syria (apart from Ricoldo's use, taken from a Spanish source). The letter of the Church of Jerusalem to Innocent III mentioned 'a written law . . . called Alcoran, the *command-ments* (praecepta) of which . . .' (Pseudo-Vitriacus; Vincent, 31.59ff, St Albans Chronicle, yr. 1193.) Tripoli spoke of convincing Muslims that the Christian faith was the only *praeceptum* given to believers; this implies its contrary and that Islam claimed that the revelation given to Muhammad was such a *praeceptum* (cap. LIII). The word was also used to express a divine command to execute a particular enterprise (or, in the mediaeval view, a claim to revelation, in order to justify a shady enterprise), e.g. a *praeceptum* from God to wage war under pretext of spreading religion. (Higden, loc. cit.)

The exact connotation of *praeceptum* in this period is obscure, but it seems (specially in Spain) definitely to have carried some idea of a specifically revealed, or divine, commandment; and this is so, in spite of the Vulgate use, mandatum novum do vobis, etc. (John XIII.34).

68. Will. Alv. de leg. XVIII/18.s; Vincent 23.40. Vincent's chapter headings, which he introduced into his abridged text of Peter of Toledo's Risālah, show point by point how he understood the text. For example: *Qualiter Alchorani liber connexus sit. Qualiter eiusdem scriptura dilacerata sit. De iterata collectione illius, et dissipatione. Qualiter recollecta et dissipata sit. De vilitate stili eius et materiae.* (23, 51-56). See Paris's emendations to Wendover in Rolls Series Paris (yr. 622). Tripoli, XXV. San Pedro, SSM I.i.43, 68.

69. Disp. XIII; Cont. VI (MS ff. 244v-245r).

70. CSS I.23, II.13.

71. MSS: CCCD p. 50 and Sed. f. 33r.

72. San Pedro, SSM I.iii.7 for example; Fitzralph, Arm. 11(12), 12(13) etc.; Lull, D.P. 6, 7.

73. Oliver, Ep. Sal.; Peter, CSS II.13; also refers to works other than

Q. as less authoritative, CSS I.16; of the other Cluniac translations, the *explicit* of the *de doctrina*, by Hermann Dalmata, describes it as 'of great authority' which is very much the way Ketton refers to the Qur'ān.

74. Pedro de Alfonso; loc. cit.; Viterbo and Greg. Rep. also speak of *scriptura* in a context that probably refers to ḥadīth. The belief that the name of Muhammad was written in Heaven from the creation, which is not Qur'anic, is their subject; on the other hand nūr muḥammadī has been given Qur'anic authority, but this is not likely to be meant here, unless there is Ismā'īli or Fāṭimid influence. Latins liked this theme because it seemed to them absurd; it reached them through the Risālah (cf. Muir, *Apology*, p. 88).

75. Mark, Pref. 'Aqīdah. *Reprob.* passim; *Lib. Scalae*, cap. LXXXV (the end of the work) reads: 'Transactis autem supradictis, prout *ego Machometus, Dei propheta et nuncius, dixi* vobis . . .' and 'Nos autem supradicti Halbubeker (=abū Bakr) et Habnez (=ibn 'Abbās) testificamus corde vero et conscientia pura quod omnia que *Machometus in precedentibus enarravit* vera sunt . . .' (Refer Munoz and Cerulli.) With such emphatic language it is no wonder that this book was taken seriously. The translator in his prologue stressed this again: . . . *fecit Machometus et imposuit ei hoc nomen.* San Pedro, SSM I.iv, title reads: 'de las contrariedades que se fallan en los dichos de Mahomad, en el libro que los moros dizen Alhadiz (=ḥadīth)' and ff; I.viii.63; and treatment of the mi'rāj generally and especially at CFM v and SSM I.viii.76ff. Ricoldo, Itin. XXXIII, Disp. IV. In Itin. Ricoldo treated the *expositio* as though it were part of the text of the Qur'ān; in Disp. he more openly argued, insisted in fact, that the text can only be understood in terms of the 'exposition', but admitting thereby that they are not identical. His source was *Contrarietas.* He also repeated (not as a quotation, but as his own) the Cluniac reference to the *de doctrina* as 'of great authority' among Muslims (Disp. VIII). Refer also Disp. IX. Lull, see Lib. . de Gent., vii, xii.

76. Peter, CSS I.24 and II.15; WillAlv., de leg. XVIII/18.T.

77. Q. VI.146, Ket. XVI, Bibl. p. 50, line 38 (Bibl. *nisi* for *mihi*); Q. II.38, Ket. II, Bibl. p. 10, line 7; Q. V.70, Ket. XII, Bibl. p. 41, lines 38-39. *Destinare* was used by Mark for *anzala*. In the first quotation from Ketton in the text, however, the Q. has *ūḥīya*, and Mark translates *revelatum est.* In the other two examples he has *id quod destinavi* and *quod destinatum est eis a Creatore suo.* (Alcor. Mach. cap. VII, MS f. 54v, and cap. I, MS f. 3r, and cap. VII, MS f. 43v.)

78. The same three quotations appear in Arm. 12(13), 10(11) and 11(12) respectively. Ketton used *divinitus* and *celitus* generally to refer to revelation; there are many examples where these words refer directly to the Qur'ān. Q. II.115, Ket. II, Bibl. p. 13, lines 3-6; verse 130, Bibl. line 32; Q. IV.28, Ket. IX, opening, Bibl. p. 31, line 6; Q. VII.1, Ket. XVII, Bibl. p. 51, line 38.

79. Arm. 13(14); Q. XLI.42; Ket. L, Bibl. LI, p. 149, line 19.

80. e.g. Oliver, Ep. Sal., Tripoli, XXVIII; Benvenuto, op. cit. Divinitus likewise occurs, used by William of Tyre for Gabriel's mission (XIX.xx); by the *libellus transmar.* Vincent 23.40 and by Marino (op. cit. III.iii): 'Ā'ishah's innocence was *divinitus revelatum.*

81. Ad Az. 58 and introductory material in margins, Bibl. p. 224, MS CCCD p. 50 mid left margin; Seld. right margin, low middle. Cf. also description in margin ad Az. 2, CCCD p. 60, Seld. f. 38v (uses *celitus*); also ad Az. 17 and 18 (pp. 113, 122).

82. Bibl. pp. 223-4; MS CCCD p. 50 lower margin left and at bottom and p. 51 bottom margin right, Seld. ff. 33r bottom margin right and 32v bottom margin.

83. *Lib. Scalae*, cap. LXIX.

84. Tripoli, XXV, XXVI, XXVII, XXVIII, XLVII. Tripoli fails to establish the idea that the Qur'ān was verbally guaranteed in any way that the previous revelations were not.

85. SSM I.i.68; cf. also I.i.43 and similar vague comments.

86. Itin, XXXIII, XXXV; Ep. I; Disp. II; Disp. XIII (*Custodientes*, for keeper, to agree with the first person plural of the verb, of which the subject is God – 'we'). Cf. reprob. (this passage is discussed in more detail in chapter II). Itin. XXXIV, Disp. IV, VIII, IX etc. Ricoldo also said that Muslims believe only God can explain Q. (this actually is said of certain verses only) (Itin. XXXII); and that Muslims agree that the first author of Q. was the Devil (Disp. XIII); it would be interesting to know what sort of agreement he had evidence of.

87. XI, MS f. 37v.

88. *Summula* and Humbert, de pred. S.C.

89. Cf. Wendover, Paris and 'Matthew of Westminster'.

90. Sowdone of Babilone, lines 2761-2 and 2271-2. It is remarkable that there were not more comparisons of Bible and Qur'ān. Occasionally they were treated as equivalent (cf. Paris, al. scr. and Tripoli XXVI). For the attitude of chansons de geste on 'idols' see appendix A. Chaucer is reasonably accurate: 'The hooly lawes of oure Alkaron,/Yeven by Goddes message Makomete.' (Man of Lawe's Tale, 332-3.)

91. Higden. Cf. Guibert; Thomas of Pavia; Varagine, leg. Aur.; Vincent, 23.40; San Pedro, SSM I.viii.27, 28, 59; Marino III.ii; Dandalo Ludolf VIII; Clementinarum lib. v, gloss cited; cf. also Hildebert and see Ziolecki and d'Ancona (refer bibliography).

92. See appendix A.

93. Bibl. p. 223; MS CCCD p. 52 (whole margin of col. 1) Seld. f. 33v, margins of upper part of page. For *misericors* and *pius* Mark has *Misericors, miserator*. The seventeenth-century critic who corrected the manuscript wished to reverse this, but Mark is at least arguably right. This critic could make mistakes: he began badly by correcting the first verse of sūrah II from *in isto libro non est dubitandum* to *non est erratum* (Maracci: *non est dubium in eo*); but in the case of the divine epithets he was following the majority opinion of his age. Cf. Rapheleng (*misericors* for 'rahīm', p. 550; he does not render 'rahmān', though a manuscript annotation in the British Museum copy gives *miserator*, p. 173), Erpenius, Nissel, the elder Pocock and Maracci; Raue, however, and the younger Pocock preferred Mark's order. (See Qur'anic and other translations listed under these authors in bibliography, list B.) The thirteenth-century papal translator cited by Paris used Mark's order (*Cron. Maj.* vol. IV, p. 566) but Gol., commenting on this, gives the usual translation

of the papal Chancery at this time as *miserans et misericors*. (Vol. II, p. 328.)

94. Paris (who has *multi Saraceni* for *Muslims*; *multi* interlined and not in all manuscripts, says the editor. This implies a copyist who could not believe that this would be true of all Muslims). (See also appendix A, note 9.) Will. Alv. de leg., XVIII/18.R.

95. Mor. Phil. IV.2a.i.18. (First Cause, Unending, Necessary Being, Infinite Power, Wisdom, Goodness, Creator and Ruler of all things.)

96. The account, *temporibus Bonifacii papae*, in Cambridge MS Dd.1. 17 f. 79.R, in B.M. Royal 13.E.Ix f. 93; in Higden, etc. Cf. Spanish *Vita*.

97. De expug.; Itin. Regis Ric. I.xviii; St Albans Chr., yr. 1188. Paris, yr. 1213. Serrano's *Vita* spoke of belief in the Creator 'nullum alium habens participem', a clear Qur'anic echo.

98. 'Unio gloriosi laudabilis': murshidah I; Pref. Q.; Q. xxv.3, 4; cf. Pref. 'Aqīdah.

99. Alan IV.i; Vitry I.vi. Scaleless fish: cf. al-Bayḍāwī, quoted Sale, on Q. III.44. Fidenzio, xv. San Pedro, SSM I.viii.62, I.vi.16, I.i.44, 60; Q. LIII.19. Tripoli, xxv; cf. XLVIII.

100. CSS II.23; cf. also I.11: 'We are not unaware that you believe that you have a full knowledge of the Deity . . .' For Lull, see chapter VI below.

101. Abjuration formula, see Montet in bibliography, and cf. Cumont. In a short (not necessarily complete) account of a Latin reception of a convert, the latter only repeats the Creed and Our Father and is then baptised (MOFPH as cited below, chapter VI, note 26, p. 364).

102. Op. Trip. I.xiv. But if Humbert refers to 'crypto-polytheism', see appendix A for this subject.

103. Quid. Anglicus, loc. cit. The account I have just given omits one curious point in the Patriarchal statement to Pope Innocent III: 'they believe in God the Saviour' (see bibliography for references); does this mean 'the saving power of God'? 'Current distinction': see Aquinas, S.T., 2a, 2ae, qu. II, Art. II. *Credere Deum*: God as 'materiale obiectum fidei'. *Credere Deo*: God as 'formale obiectum fidei'. *Credere in Deum*: God as 'obiectum fidei secundum quod intellectus est motus a voluntate'. In these terms, Peter the Venerable and the Byzantines seem to imply that God is not even the material object of Muslim faith. Lull's point here would be supported by most modern Trinitarians, however. Gregory: Lib. III, Ep. xxi. The other reference is to *Liber Nicholay*, concluding phrase.

104. Disp. xv; Itin. xxx; Disp. VIII, cf. IV; Itin. xxvi. Arabic uses an article that is missing in Latin: 'there is no god but *the* (one) God'; thus the parallel assertion would be, 'there is no dog but the one dog', which is obvious nonsense. Ricoldo has no excuse for this; the language barely masks the error. Cf. Mark's criticism of the Qur'ān (above) for not expressing its doctrine of God in scholastic form.

105. Lib. de Gent. IV.iii; D.P. 7; Hamar, II.ii.1; treatment of the first two articles of belief in Lib. de Gent. IV.

106. Cambridge MS Dd.1.17, *credunt Saraceni*. For other Spanish creeds cf. Morgan (see bibliography under *Rabadan*), *Mahometism Explained*.

107. Dawson (see bibliography) pp. 190-4. (The translation is from Dawson's book.) This was the account to which Bacon was indebted for most of the information on which he based his ideas about comparative religion.

CHAPTER II. *Revelation: the Christian attack upon 'Pseudoprophecy'*

1. Poitiers, capitula, i. ii-vi. Peter the Venerable, CSS i.15-28. For the donkey, see Q. LXII.5.

2. This is the series of passages common to the *quadruplex reprobatio* (capp. x-xv) and the *explanatio simboli* (introductory section). Nabuchodonosar: Vulgate IV Kings (A.V. II Kings). 'A single work of grammar': kitāb of Sībawayhi? Scriptural warnings: Deut. xiv; Prov. xxx; Apoc. xxii.

3. Itin. xxxiv. Disp. iii, cf. Pennis xii. Mecca: Ricoldo did not claim to have visited Mecca in person, naturally.

4. Arm. 16(17)-20(21), esp. 17(18) and also 16(17) and 20(21). For the divisio apostolorum, cf. Roger Bacon, Mor. Phil. iv.2a.viii.10.

5. Vitry i.vi. Some Islamic polemists, e.g. ibn Khaldūn and al-Ghazzalī in his Radd al-Jamīl, came to realise the uselessness of taḥrīf argument in convincing Christians. Cf. Chidiac (see bibliography) p. 30 and Buhl, taḥrīf, in SEI.

6. Praefatio Roberti translatoris.

7. Quad. reprob. xi. The Qur'anic citations are v.50, v.72 and v.52 respectively; for the commentators on the latter, see Sale's quotation from al-Baydāwī; Q. ii.130 and xv.9. On the latter text ('we have caused a reminder . . .') the MSS of *reprob*. vary. (Cambridge MS f. 73v col. 2 and G and C f. 8r-v, Berlin Qu. 85 f. 247v Fol. 425, f. 128r, col. 1; Bib. nat. MS f. 155v, col. 2); the translation is therefore composite, but the sense is not seriously affected. Both the argument based on this Qur'anic text and also that based on the appeal of the Jews to the Prophet appear in the *Contrarietas*, but the *reprobatio* does not seem to be directly indebted in the way that Ricoldo is. Its words are its own, even in Qur'anic quotation. Thus *rep*. has *Nos (dimisimus vel) fecimus descendere memoriale et sumus eius custodes*; compare with *Descendere fecimus recordationem Dei, et nos eandem custodiemus* (*Cont.* MS f. 241r). The sense of the two arguments is however just the same. It may be that the author of *reprob*. is refurbishing the argument of the *Cont.*, but it seems more likely that they depend separately from a living Spanish tradition of polemic. 'There is no alteration': Q. xlviii.15? The *rep*. also quotes in one chapter near the end (Q. vi.155) 'We gave the Book to Moses, a completion for him who does right, a discernment in everything, and direction and mercy.' He concluded that a corrupt law does not *correct*, but causes to err; therefore the Law of Moses is not corrupt.

8. Disp. iii. Ricoldo repeated the mistake about the *reminder*. He reproduced the form of the argument in the *Contrarietas* (with the word *recordatio*, against the *reprob.'s memoriale*. Pennis followed Ric. (xii, f. 39v). This historical emphasis recalls the Cluniac approach.

9. SSM i.viii.240-4 (as an example of the contradiction of the Qur'ān

by the Gospel, that Christ forbade divorce in this world and said there
would be no marrying in the next; ibid., I.iii.3-5, Q. II.59; the quotation
should read 'those who believe' (i.e. the Muslims); 'the wise' ought to
read 'the Sabaeans'. CFM III.2.

10. Arm. 8(9).

11. Ibid. 12(13); 10(11), 15(16), 11(12).

12. Ibid. 15(16). Q. refs. are all, of course, to Ketton's numbering.

13. Ibid. 16(17). (Oliver of Paderborn had anticipated this argument;
if Christ, he maintained, had lived an innocent, holy and just life, his
religion must be blameless, respectable and wholesome. Ep. doct.) Arm.
18(19) and 19(20).

14. Fitzralph's only known contact with the East was his meeting
with Armenians of the Romanising party at Avignon (December 1333),
see Gwynne, Studies.

15. Arm. 20(21).

16. Ibid. 11(12).

17. Benedict (in Cerulli) who derives it from Will. Alv. who derives
it from the Cluniac corpus. Bacon: Mor. Phil. IV.2a.viii.3, cites Al-Fārābi,
see Catal. cienc. (Not in Alonso, de scientiis.) Aquinas: contra Gentiles
I.vi.

18. Q. LXI.6. The classic explanation by some Muslims of this foretelling of Muhammad by Jesus is that Aḥmad = Perikleitos = Parakletos
(and Aḥmad, of course, is said to equal Muhammad).

19. Viterbo, Paris (Report). Vitry may be referring to this when he
speaks of Muslims who expound some things from the (Christian)
Scriptures perversely. Annot. ad Az. 17, p. 113 in CCCD.

20. Capp. XI, XIII, XV and Martí, explan., introductory.

21. San P. SSM I.i.51. This story may derive from acceptance of the
rare mistake that Muslims suppose Muhammad the Messias (see chapter
I, note 11). Lull, Hamar, sig. 3.

22. Disp. III, Itin. XXXIV, Ep. III. Cf. Pennis XII (f. 39r).

23. Epistolae or Disputatio Abutalib Saraceni . . . etc. and Tractatus
Rabbi Samuelis . . . etc. 'Their translator': the Scriptures are not cited
in the Vulgate, so that it is not likely that Buenhombre is the real author,
and we may accept his claim to be only translator. For a discussion of
origin and authorship (still undetermined) see van den Oudenryn.

24. CSS I.16. Peter asserted that there is nothing about this prophecy
in the Q., and nothing in those other books of the Muslims which have
less authority. It is stupid, he added, to believe things on doubtful
authority, and senseless to believe them on none – remarks that in the
circumstances have an unintentional irony. The authorities he meant
(and named) were the liber Abdiae (=doctrina Mach.) and the de
genealogia Mach. (not the chronica mendosa). Ketton, Az. II, Bibl. p. 11,
line 16ff, Q. II.70. The sentence three verses later, 'woe to them who
transcribe corruptly the Book . . .' is not, it must be admitted, intelligibly
translated by Ketton. See also annotator ad Az. XXXI (MS CCCD p. 31).
On the Islamic side the protagonist of the literal interpretation of taḥrīf,
i.e. that Christians had literally forged the Gospel, Abū Muḥammad
'Ali ibn Ḥazm (d. 1064), was a Spaniard, so that it is not surprising to

find that Spanish Christians (followed by Ricoldo), argued against literal forgery, superfluously, as it may seem to us.

25. Poitiers, capitula i.vi; CSS i.14, ii.28; i.24, 29; ii.29. Aquinas (contra Gentiles i.1) argued that, as the Scriptures are unacceptable to Muslims, it is necessary to have recourse to natural reason. Because of this very fact, he can scarcely be counted among writers on the religion of Islam. His rational scheme was constructed with little (if any) reference to it.

26. Alan, for example, assuming that Muslims defend polygamous marriage on Old Testament grounds (the example set by the Patriarchs), iv.vii. Alexander: in Petrus. Bles., MPL 207 and Paris, yr. 1169 (personal insertion in the old chronicle). Guido: 15, citing Isa. LXVIII.5. (Parallel to the assumption by Christian polemists that Muslims will accept the text of the canonical Old Testament, is that Jews will accept the (Catholic) deuterocanonical or (Protestant) apocryphal books of the Old Testament. This happens even in the Rabbi Samuel correspondence. (See bibliography.)

27. Verona xi; Oliver, Ep. Doct.; Vitry, i.vi; Tripoli xxvii and cf. Higden, loc. cit.; Martí, loc. cit.; Ricoldo, Disp. ii; Pennis iii; San Pedro, SSM i.viii.292 and CFM iii.2; Peñaforte, summa canonum i.iv para. 1. Contrast, however, Annotator to Ketton, who commented that, though the Qur'ān mentioned the Psalter, he personally doubted if Muhammad had heard it, as distinct from just hear someone speak of it. Ad Az. 64, Bibl. p. 227. San Pedro, e.g. xv.15, 16, 18, made use of Wisdom, against both Jews and Muslims, when it was acceptable to neither.

28. Ricoldo, Disp. i and viii and Pennis viii; Disp. xvii and iii; Itin. xxxiv, citing Q. x.94. Reprob. xiii and introd. to exp. simb. Ricoldo seems to combine Martí's argument with those of the Contrarietas (cap. ii); as usual, it is to the latter that he was principally indebted. Thus he argued, as Martí had done, that the Gospel was incorrupt in Muhammad's time, and also that Christians and Jews were permanent guarantors of the text of Scripture. But the actual arguments employed are inferior; they are repetitive, arguments of the aut-aut type, seeking to impose a generally unreal logical dilemma on the opponent; finally, they sometimes treat unlikely alternatives as seriously important ones.

29. Disp. iii, Q. v.72. Here Ricoldo was apparently indebted to the reprobatio and not to the Contrarietas; yet from the same Qur'ānic citation the reprob. drew a single conclusion: that in Muhammad's time the Law and the Gospel were incorrupt. Ricoldo, however, (on the same datum) went on to claim that the Qur'ān shows in many places that Muhammad meant the Muslims by the people of the Book; for example, 'in the chapter al-nisa' . . . about the end' (Q. iv.169); the same thing is 'shown explicitly in the chapter lem at the end of the book' (unidentified – Q. xx.122-3? Q. LXVI.12?). Ricoldo twice returned to this theme in arguments elsewhere; his work is very repetitive, and it was his temperament to insist on anything he had taken up. (Bart. Pic. has 'tulem' for 'lem'.)

30. Annot. ad Az. ii, Bibl. p. 224, MS CCCD p. 50 bottom margin

right; Seld. f. 33r bottom margin left. Ricoldo: Disp. VIII, IV; the passages making the accusation of obscenity are omitted from the manuscripts of the Latin text and occur only in the Greek original of Demetrius Cydones and the Latin retranslation. It is on the whole easier to believe the Latin copiers prudish than the Greek prurient.

31. Praefatio Rob. Translatoris. Peter the Venerable's opinion of the style of the Qur'ān was probably formed on that of Ketton whom he trusted, along with Hermann Dalmata, as *utriusque linguae peritus*. (See ep. de trans. sua.) Mark, Pref. Q., Pref. 'Aqīdah. Miss d'Alverny has drawn attention to the difference between Mark's style as a translator and as a writer in his own right (*Marc de Tolède*).

32. Martí, Cap. Jud. (in Cerulli's extract); Lull, Lib. de Tart. de T. et S., 10 and 11. The dictum about the virtue of words is essentially scholastic. The difficult text in which the Q. says that it would have been less acceptable had it not been revealed in Arabic is obscure in Ketton's version (Qui si Latine notaretur, fieret quaestio, cur Latinis – for 'ajami – et Arabicis litteris non distingueretur?) and Fitzralph, citing it, had nothing whatever to say about it. Mark also translated 'ajami by *latinus*. Q. XLI.44; Ket. Az. L, Bibl. LI, p. 149, lines 21-22; Fitzralph, Arm. 13(14); cf. Q. XVI.105, Ket. Az. XXV, Bibl. XXVI, p. 90, line 12ff. Mark: cap. XLIII f. 170v.

33. Q. XVII.90; Ricoldo, Disp. IX, Itin. XXXV, Ep. III. The jinn having no European equivalent, Latins happily assumed them to be devils. (Cf. Ket. Az. XXVI, Bibl. XXVII p. 93, line 38ff. Mark cap. XIX f. 111v.) Ric. Disp. IV and Pennis II, a passage that blends two of Ricoldo's. Q. XXI.5.

34. Vincent 23.40.

35. Disp. XI, Q. V.98, *Cont.* IX (here the source of text and comment); Disp., ibid., Q. CIX; *Cont.* VIII (here the source of the text, but the argument apparently Ricoldo's own); Itin. XXXI. Latin forms of Arabic words: *elmeide* for *al-maydah* and *elharam* for *al-ḥaram*.

36. De leg. XVIII/18.R and Lull, Lib. de Gent. IV.xii, Ricoldo, Itin. XXXIII. The creed *credunt Saraceni* (Camb. Dd.1.17) makes it clear that it is heretical in Islam to interpret the delights of Paradise spiritually.

37. Annot. ad Az. 24, 50, 65 and passim.

38. Annot. ad. 17; Poitiers: capitula IV.v; Peter Ven., CSS II.4ff. This argument was not new when the Cluniacs used it; the *Contrarietas* had spoken of fables interwoven into base things in Q. (VIII); Pedro de Alfonso had stressed the difference between O.T. and Q. versions of the same stories (op. cit.). Much of the Cluniac material was really fabulous; Poitiers tells us he found the 'nūr muhammadī' laughable (III.iv) and Paris says that the company laughed at the story of Noe and the prohibition of swine's flesh (al. acr.). If what was laughed at was the de doctrina and the *de generatione* (Bibl. p. 197ff and p. 201ff) rather than Q. itself, this reminds us how important was the failure to distinguish carefully between more and less authoritative Islamic religious literature.

39. Mark, Pref. Q. Alforcan for al-Fūrqan.

40. SSM I.vii.12, I.v; cf. I.ii.25; I.i.66 and CFM v.4; SSM I.viii.148, 203.

41. Pennis VI; Ricoldo, Disp. IV (for Hārūt and Mārūt, Q. II.96, cf.

IW Z

Will. of Auvergne (de universo ii.xxxvii) who notes but does not exploit the legend); Disp. v and xv.

42. Pennis xi and cf. viii and the citation probably following Ricoldo of *de doctrina* by name; this translation was the source of much attack on the fabulous. See also Peter the Ven.'s own attack on Islam for its 'ridiculosa' CSS i.5.

43. Ad Az. 25 (p. 152), Q. xvi.81.

44. Bacon, Mor. Phil. iv.2a.vi.1.

45. Disp. viii, v; Itin. xxxv. It is interesting that al-Ghazālī accuses the Christians of excessive philosophising (cf. Chidiac).

46. Annot. ad Az. 38, ad Az. 97.

47. SSM i.ii.25 and iii passim; i.iv.26; cf. CFM v.4ff.

48. Arm. 11(12). Christians were not apparently aware of the doctrine of abrogations in the Qur'ān but it is unlikely that they would have been favourably impressed by it, or that it would have stopped their attacking the 'inconsistencies'.

49. A close comparison between the working out of the same theme by Ricoldo, by San Pedro, and by *Contrarietas* (cap. ix) shows much variety despite dependence.

50. Disp. vi and cf. ix and xii; Itin. xxxii; elnesa = al-nisā' (or an-nisā'). 'God did not create the world in play': but cf. Vulgate, Prov. viii.30-31, which have 'ludens' where A.V. has 'rejoicing'. Ricoldo made very merry on the subject of God's 'praying' which he had already raised, Ep. iii, cf. 1. The reference to Q. is xxxiii.56, cf. 43. The idea of God's praying derives from the Arabic use in this context ('God's blessing upon Muhammad' or 'may God bless him') of the same word as is used for the ritual worship or prayer: in the Qur'anic verse cited by Ricoldo it is 'yuṣalūna', *God and the angels bless Muhammad.* Clearly it is ridiculous to insist that the word must mean 'pray' on the grounds that it means 'pray' (or something like it) in other contexts; this is an extreme example of the Latin custom of accusing Muslims of something that Muslims would themselves be bound wholly to disown; of claiming to know better than they what they themselves do or do not do, and then waxing as rhetorical about it as if it were a crime they openly admitted. If the phrase *yuṣallūna 'ala* were really taken literally it would mean, not 'pray for' but 'say the ritual prayer on top of', so that even the pedantry was inaccurate. Ricoldo can hardly have mentioned this idea to a Muslim in the flesh. See also Reland, *de relig.*, ii.viii.

Mark's usage in this connection is discussed by d'Alverny and Vajda (*Marc de Tolède*). Mark uses *oretur pro* for *ṣalawāt 'ala* but *quem Deus acceptet* for *ṣallā allāhu 'ala.* Need we assume that Mark intended to distinguish so drastically between these two Arabic phrases, to both of which the same arguments seem to apply? It might be that *oretur pro* represented a compromise between common sense and the apparent meaning, if he did not know the real meaning. *Quem Deus acceptet* would then represent a subsequent discovery of the real meaning, and *oretur pro* just an error left uncorrected.

For the 'discrepancies' see Q. iv.84; Ric. Disp. vi and Pennis xiv.

51. Mark: Pref. 'Aqīdah. (I am not sure that this cannot be under-

stood as 'a philosopher and disciple of al-Ghazālī' but Miss d'Alverny amends to read *philosophi*. Mark's attribution to ibn Tūmart was not very apt.) Vitry I.vi. Will. Alv. de leg. XIX.19.R (cf. XVIII/18.o) and Benedict. Also XVIII/18.R., S.

52. Bacon, Mor. Phil. IV.2a.vii.12; IV.2a.vi.4; IV.1a.vi.4; IV.2a.iii.13; IV.2a.iv.3; Op. Maj. (of which foregoing Mor. Phil.=septima pars) Math. in Div. utilitas.

53. Tripoli, L. Ricoldo, Itin. XXXIV, Disp. XIII and IX. Lull, D.P., 10, 11; Lib. de Gent. IV.xii; Lib. de V sap., prol.; Blanquerna, 144.3. In another place Lull said that Muslims disbelieve the Q. because of Muhammad's ill life (obras rimadas, *Desconort*, xxviii) (cf. HLF XXIX p. 28). Buenhombre: appendix to ep. Rabbi Samuel quoted by Meersseman, *Chronologie*. In Islamic belief the Qur'ān can only exist in Arabic; it is the Arabic that was revealed, and a translation is not the Qur'ān itself. This is why translation was long discouraged. It is impossible that Ricoldo should have had the knowledge necessary to discuss the Qur'ān on anything like equal terms with Muslim theological teachers or students. Mediaeval contempt for the Islamic world as unphilosophical contrasts strangely with our modern concept of the mediaeval Latin West as wholly indebted for its philosophy to the Islamic East. Even if the modern view is correct, we need not assume mediaeval hypocrisy, but just a lack of historical perspective.

54. Cf. also chapter X below.

55. CSS II.3.

56. Ibid.

57. Capitula, libb. II and III.

58. Cf. S. Gregory super Ezech. Homil. 1 cited by Aquinas, S.T., 2a, 2ae qu. 171 art. 3. CSS II.4-11. Cf. Vincent 23, 45; Muir p. 53. For denial of assertion that Muhammad foretold his immediate successors, see ibid. II. 12, 13 and *Chron. mendosa*, Bibl. p. 218. A similar view of prophecy in the Rabbi Samuel's letter to Rabbi Isaac: 'Mahometus, qui dixit se prophetam, nec ventura praedixit' (conclusion, MPL 149 col. 367). Peter the Venerable cannot have seen a Latin version but the ideas of the original Arabic may have been directly or indirectly available; probably all these works represent ideas that were widely repeated.

59. Missale Romanum: this is even clearer in the old liturgy superseded in 1956 than in the new ceremonies of Easter Eve.

60. Cf. I Cor. x.1ff. May the Islamic concept derive from the Christian here?

61. Cf. Aquinas, S.T., 2a, 2ae qu. 174 art. 4 (conc.)

62. Ibid.

63. Ibid. 172 art. 5 and 6 ad 1, ad 2; cf. contra Gentiles III.154. In principle, St Thomas conceded that a 'prophet of demons' might speak truth, not only with intent to deceive, or incidentally to his purpose, 'by the action of the demon', but even *ex inspiratione divina* (he instances Baalam).

64. e.g. Prophetia filii Achab, in Roehricht; pseudo-Methodius, in Will. Alv. de leg. XVIII/18.Nff; Prophetia in Bib. nat. MS lat. 14503. Cf. also *Vita Mahometi*.

65. Mor. Phil. iv.2a.viii.5ff.

66. CSS ii.17-21; cf. 22-26, 28, 29.

67. Matthew vii.15, 16. This survives in Ricoldo's Disp. iii (MS f. 162 col. 2) as a passing reference: there is no mention of Muhammad in the Gospel, he says, 'except for what he says about bewaring of false prophets'.

68. Deut. xviii.22.

69. Ps. c (A.V. ci) 6.

70. Cap. i. 'Whoever did not have the four signs was a false prophet. Muhammad not only did not have them, but had the opposite.' Printed text has *non solum habuit* for *non solum non habuit*, but MSS are correct.

71. The working out of these points is fully exemplified in the course of the present book.

72. De pred. S.C. xii; cf. Op. Trip. i.vi.

73. Disp. viii; cf. xiii and Itin. xxxv. Jerome: misquotation for Origen, Homil. 6 in Num. Aristotle: it was Maimonides who actually said this (*Director dubitantium*, ii.xli f. lxvi (v); Friedländer text, vol. ii, cap. xl, p. 192), citing Aristotle's authority for the assertion that, of all the senses, touch, especially as used in the sexual act, is the most animal; naturally, Aristotle says nothing about prophets. (*Ethics*, iii.x.8, 9, 11; in the *antiqua translatio*, lib. iii, lectio xx: 'talibus utique gaudere et maxime diligere bestiale', which St Thomas, in his commentary, by a slight change makes more emphatic: 'delectari autem in talibus . . . videtur esse maxime brutale' – *Commentarii in decem libros Ethicorum Aristotelis*.) St Thomas repeats Maimonides' points in similar emphatic terms in the *qu. de veritate*, xii. It was the prophet's sexual life which made him, in Ricoldo's view, *hypocrite*, and to be classified as such as well as a *tyrant* and *heretic*. (Disp., prol.) Pennis omits the sentences I have quoted, though he reproduces an intervening passage: cap. iv.

74. iii.iv.

75. S.T. 2a, 2ae, qu. 171-8; contra Gentiles iii.154; de veritate xii.

76. Lull, Lib. Tart., loc. cit. (6); San Pedro, SSM i.vii.12; Quid. Anglicus; Guido, 14 (G. thought Muhammad claimed to be Messias).

77. cf. S.T. 2a, 2ae qu. 178 art. 1; cf. 171 art. 1. 'Tertio ad prophetiam pertinet operatio miraculorum quasi confirmatio quaedam propheticae annuntiationis.' Moreover, it was by the absence of miracles that, in the last resort, the absence of authority was manifested. (Contra Gentiles i.vi.)

78. The Q. is full of accounts of miracles worked by Moses and by Jesus (cf. Q. vii.160, x.92, xl.24, xliii.45 for Moses and iii.43 for Christ) but for Muhammad it disowns miracles. When the Quraysh demanded certain wonders, Muhammad declared by revelation that 'though a Qur'ān were revealed by which mountains should be removed or the earth cleaved in sunder or the dead be caused to speak, it would be vain' (Q. xiii.30; cf. viii.23). The Q. was its own witness: see Q. xvii.90. Most of this sort of mediaeval argument seems rather pointless except where it is concerned to insist that a prophet must work miracles. So far as I know, no mediaeval author accused Q. of plagiarising Luke xvi.31 in this connection.

79. Loc. cit. This seems to refer to Q. x.40.

80. Poitiers, ii.vi; iii.iii; iv.vii; CSS ii.14, 15.

81. Other examples are in Vitry (i.v), Oliver of Paderborn (Ep. Sal.) Benedict of Alignan (Cerulli), Humbert, de pred. S.C. xii.

82. Viterbo and Paris (Report). This is the fullest list. Pedro de Alfonso missed the wolf. The Risālah lacked the 'divided moon' (Tolet. MS p. 302 col. 2ff; Vincent 23.46; Muir, p. 58); on the other hand it distinguished more variants among single or related stories. The *Contrarietas* was exclusively interested in the 'divided moon' (cap. ix). In quite a different category are those false miracles, which no Muslim ever claimed, but which entered early into Christian legend about Islam: the dove that whispered in the Prophet's ear, the bull that bore the Law in its horns, and so on. To Vincent they suggested the 'model of Moses' but really they are pagan, non-Arabic and non-Islamic in origin; see Ziolecki. The Spanish *Vita* relates alleged miracles of both categories: some from Islamic sources (including the divided moon) and also a remarkable group of bogus miracles alleged by Christian sources to have been projected by the Prophet.

83. iv.14.

84. Capistrum Jud. in Cerulli; cf. Viterbo and Paris for Apology.

85. Mor. Phil. iv.2a.viii.14ff.

86. Paris, *aliud scriptum*.

87. Ketton: cf. note 78 above. For Q. xiii.30 Ketton has: '. . . many remained unbelievers, which is what would happen, even if this Qur'ān flattened mountains, cut apart the earth and made the dead to speak . . .' and for xvii.90, 'if all men and devils came in order to compose one such book, and helped each other, by no means could they do it . . .' (Ket. xxii, Bibl. xxiii, p. 82 lines 23-25; and xxvi, Bibl xxvii, p. 93 line 37ff.

88. SSM i.vii.9. Encounter with Quraysh, ibid. i.i.24ff and see ibn Isḥāq 188ff. Cf. SSM i.viii.24 for the reaction of the Quraysh to the announcement of the mi'rāj (and see *Liber Scalae* lxxxiiff); for the Quraysh and the revelation of the Cave, see SSM i.i.27ff and ibn Isḥāq 192ff.

89. *Reprob.* vii who cites Bukhārī here 'in tractatu fidei' (= ii) but the passage is not there. Cf. Bu. cxvi.1; but also Muslim, i.239. Q. cited: xvii.94 and 95. Ibn Isḥāq cited by name for the encounter with Quraysh (188, 189).

90. Disp. vii and viii. Ricoldo said Christians had never ceased to work miracles (unlike Humbert who spoke of them as no longer an effective instrument of the Church). For the divided moon arguments, see Ricoldo, Itin. xxxiii and Disp. iv; *reprob.* vii; *Cont.* ix; Q. liv.1.

91. Arm. 21(22); Q. ii.110-3; Ket. Az. 2, Bibl. p. 12, line 40ff. Arm 23(24) and 22(23).

92. De fide, iii; Q. iii.43.

CHAPTER III. *The life of Muhammad: polemic biography*

1. Corozan story: see all main version. The general sense in Sigebert, Viterbo (xvi yr. 612, not Apology), Vitry i.v; Alv. de leg. xviii/18.m; *reprob.* ii, Paris; *Vita Mah.*; Rod. Cron. de Esp. xciv; Higden; Verona

xi, Ludolf viii, Tripoli xxv, xxvii; Humbert, Op. Trip. i.vii; Guido, opening para. in Cerulli; Chiose s. Dante; anon. Fior.

2. Paris; Chron, de Esp. xciv; not in Viterbo; cf. *de gen. Machumet* and *chron. mendosa* in Bibliander. Excellent example in B.M. Cotton, Nero, C. 11 f. 123.

3. Cf. Vitry i.v; Paris, loc. cit.; Anon. Fior.; Higden; Verona x, xi.

4. Peter, CSS ii.27; Will. de leg. xviii/18.m citing Gen. xxi.13; Tripoli ii citing Gen. xvi.12.

5. Op. cit. i.v.

6. SSM i.i.38 and viii.2-8.

7. In the popular Corozan legend Jews and Arabs flocked to Muhammad as the Messias expected by the Jews.

8. This appears from the accounts of Muhammad's childhood and youth, when he is often shown as travelling with the merchants; see below.

9. The Latin of Theophanes' *Chronographica* by Anastasius Biblio-thecarius is responsible for much of the accurate dating of Muhammad in the pattern of world events. Hugh of Fleury said of Anastasius in this connection, 'pauca quidem locutus est, sed quibus temporibus fuerit lucide designavit'. The most extraordinary anachronism was that of Hildebert of Mans, who placed Muhammad in the fourth century (in the course of an account at no point more accurate than this).

10. Pedro de Alfonso, loc. cit. and Anon. Minorita 16; Viterbo in xvi yr. 612; Mark, Pref. Q. (San Pedro had another version of this pun: Mecca means adulteress in Latin, 'a deviation from the right law, and so Muhammad fulfilled the signification of the city': SSM i.i.1); Rod. Hist. Arab. i, Cron. de Esp. xcv/467 and cxxi/493.

11. Hist. Arab. iii, Cron. de Esp. cxi; cf. ibn Isḥāq 122-5. The Spanish text is further from authentic sources. The Black Stone is described as magnetic, which recalls the legend of the magnetised tomb suspended in mid-air. The Spanish *Vita* tells us that the Meccans expelled Muhammad, of whom, as a merchant, they were jealous; also, that he belonged to the Quraysh, who were a tribe of merchants; but what were supposed to be the status, character and motives of the Meccans this leaves still obscure.

12. *Reprob.* ii c(f. ibn Isḥāq 119). Also vii. San Pedro, SSM i.i.23, 34 (cf. ibn Isḥāq 188); San Pedro's account of the Jewish challenge over the three questions suits ibn Isḥaq's account more nearly than Baydāwī's (quoted by Sale) (ibn Isḥāq ref. 192-7). The Jews said the true prophet would not be able to answer all three questions, so that the 'obscurity' of the last reply was really part of his triumph in the original story, and not a new failure as San Pedro takes it to be. SSM i.i.27ff, i.viii.220-1; cf. vii.10 and ibn Isḥāq, 264-5.

13. Vitry i.vi; Viterbo and Paris; the quotation in Paris only.

14. Will., de leg. xviii/18.r (Benedict in his précis omits); Fidenzio xiv; Pp. Trip. vi.6; Ludolf viii. Aquinas (contra Gentiles): 'brutish men dwelling in deserts'; his sources were close to Humbert's.

15. Yathrib: (Catalan) 'Tripe'; D.P. 71.3 and 8. Cf. Lib. de Gent. iv.iii. Acqui.

16. Acqui, loc. cit. Anonimo Fiorentino, loc. cit.

17. *Summula*, loc. cit. Pedro de Alfonso, loc. cit., cf. Higden, Benvenuto, but Varagine, Leg. Aur., is best. Q. xciii.6-8. A different translation of the same text by Peter of Toledo (MS p. 295.1; Vincent, 23.41). Mark of Toledo, Pref. Q. and Fidenzio, xiv. 'Habedileth' represents 'Abdullat' = 'abd al-Lāt. The author may have had the 'Satanic verses' in mind; only San Pedro seems to refer to these explicitly. But cf. de generatione Machumet, Bibl. p. 206. Cf. M. T. d'Alverny, *Marc de Tolède. Reprob.* ii; cf. Tripoli ii. For Bukhārī see 64.85: I cannot trace the reference as cited by *reprob.* here. For San Pedro see SSM i.i.19-21 and i.iv.3, 4. Ricoldo, Disp. vi, xiii; Pennis, xiv; cf. Vitry, Anon. Fior. and Marino; lists of relations who died heathens, in *reprob.* ii and SSM i.i. ibn Ishāq, 121. Lull, lib. de Gent. iv. viii and Hamar, sig. 32. Trevisa's translation of Higden in Rolls Series.

18. Rod. Hist. Arab. i; the same work describes the wish of the Quraysh to be left in peace to their idolatry. It was realised that Abū Ṭālib protected Muhammad while remaining a pagan himself, although the sequence of events was not clear. Cf. also *Summula*, Mark Pref. Q. and Fidenzio, loc. cit.

19. It is not possible here to trace the full story of these legends; see however d'Ancona and Ziolecki; also Mancini, d'Alverny and the *Liber Nicholay*. See also *Summula*, loc. cit., Mark, loc. cit. and Rod. Hist. Arab. iii and iv; San Pedro's *Maurus* story, SSM i.viii, 2ff and Buenhombre, *Disp. Abutalib*. The phrase quoted is from Cont. Chron. Isid.

20. Waltherius: see also du Pont. San Pedro had some doubts about the Maurus legend but felt sure that episodes told by ibn Ishāq (the delay in revelation over the Seven Sleepers of Ephesus and the accusation by the Quraysh that Muhammad had a foreign teacher) implied the substantial truth of the main point of it. SSM i.vii.14; cf. i.i.26. Auvergne (de leg. xviii/18.p) here confuses the Councils of Ephesus (Oec. iii.431) and Constantinople iii (Oec. vi?.680?). Cf. also Benedict. Cf. here also Apology. This version was accepted by Paris personally, and he wrote *Nastoreus* over the text of the Flores. Cf. Leg. Aur., loc. cit. and Lull, D.P. 4 for other versions. *Reprob.* also quotes the complaint by the Quraysh that Muhammad had a foreign helper: cap. vii. It refers to 'a certain man of Armenia called Rahman', i.e. 'a man from Yamāmah named Raḥmān' = Musaylimah (ibn Ishāq, 200). The printed text has *Rahinet* and *Armenia*; B.n. MS has *Ramen* and *Armenia*; the Berlin MSS have both *Rahymen* and *Rahynet*, the name of the country being difficult to read; the Cambridge MSS have *Yamema* and *Rahmet*, the former transliteration being very good indeed. (B.n. f. 193v col. 2; Berlin MSS f. 244v and f. 125v; Cambridge, f. 72v, from foot of col. 1 to top of col. 2; Q. xvi.105.) Cf. also Benvenuto.

21. Pedro de Alfonso, loc. cit., Annotator ad Az. 2 (Bibl. p. 224 and MS CCCD p. 50 foot col. 2). In connection with the Cluniac attitude (see esp. Poitiers, capitula, iv.v) d'Ancona says that the Cluniac inclination to blame the Jews should be related to a contemporary outbreak of anti-Semitism, rather than to their perception of historical reality. Yet many modern scholars have thought they could identify Talmudic and other

influences upon Islam and it seems more reasonable to allow the Cluniacs the same liberty of speculation. Peter the Venerable (CSS I.12) was proud of the Christian toleration of Jews. The Spanish *Vita* has a complex tale of a group of Christian and Jewish teachers. For Jewish influences, cf. also Vitry (I.vi), Oliver, Ep. Sal. and Hist. Dam.; Fidenzio, XIV; Mark, Pref. Q. Ricoldo on this subject is more lengthy than *Cont.* and may owe material to Pedro de Alfonso. e.g. in speaking of a *Jacobite* influence. The latter is a natural mistake for Pedro, who can never have known a real Jacobite or a real Nestorian, but was inexcusable on Ricoldo's part. Ricoldo identifies two Jews, Salon the Persian and Abdallah son of Sela (cf. Q. XVI.105 cit.). Salman the Persian, to whom one of these must refer, was not of course, a Jew; the other is Abdallah ibn Salam, who was a Jew (cf. *Cont.*). Ric. also speaks of Baheyyin, for Baḥīrā; this may represent a debt to Tripoli, of which there are usually no signs, although it is thought that Ric. must have read his work. (Cf. Monneret de Villard, *Ricoldo*, and my chapter VIII Note 17, below.) *Cont.* cap. v; Ric., Itin. XXXV, Disp. XIII, VI. Cf. also *de doctrina*. For conflicting stories cf. Varagine (Leg. Aur.) who positively prefers a less unreasonable to a more unreasonable Sergius story, and Pennis, who gives more and less fantastic versions without expressing any preference. For Pedro's interesting idea that an *heretical* Jew may have influenced Muhammad, cf. the theory of the modern Jewish scholar, Chaim Rabin, who thinks that the Medinan Jews who acceded to the party of the Prophet may have been a remnant of the Qumran community, who were expecting a Messiah to come very shortly.

22. Sigebert: loc. cit. See note 17 above for Q reference and for Pedro de Alfonso and authors copying him.

23. See Oliver, Ep. Sal., Guibert, loc. cit., *summula*, loc. cit., Pavia, Marino III.ii. Dandalo, loc. cit., Anon. Fior., Benvenuto, Legenda Aurea, Ludolf, all loc. cit.

24. Mark, Pref. Q.; *Reprob.* II, ibn Ishāq, 120; in the latter Khadījah refers to 'our relationship' which becomes in *reprob.* 'genus tuum nobile' (B.n. MS omits). *Reprob.* cites ibn Ishāq as *Ciar* (=sīrah); San Pedro, though he often follows very closely, never cites Ishāq by name. Ricoldo, Disp. XIII ('fortuna pauperem . . . de genere et opinione vilis'; *de genere* missing in MS and supplied from Bart. Pic.). Tripoli II.

25. See du Pont's poem passim.

26. San Pedro, SSM I.viii.1ff and Hildebert, op. cit., Guibert, op. cit.; the two extreme views: Clementinae and Acqui, loc. cit.

27. All loc. cit. but Ricoldo, Disp. XIII, itin. XXXV. San Pedro, SSM I.i.29, I.viii.237, 246 and cf. I.vii.14. Mark: Pref. Q: and Q. VII. Mark uses the double expression: 'non novi litteras: maternus enim sum'. This translates *ummi* twice; 'illiterate' is traditional; 'motherly' would be possible in the right context. In Q. 'ydiota'.

28. In principal Corozan writers e.g. Fleury, Gerald of Wales and St Albans; retained in Martin the Pole's precis. Cron. de Esp., CVI/478. Waltherius, du Meril p. 379.

29. *Reprob.* II (ibn Ishāq, 103) (B.n. version abbreviated). San Pedro, SSM I.i.3, 4; I.vii.7, from ibn Ishāq 103-15. 'Saw a devil possessed him'

- more accurately, 'feared a devil possessed him' (ibn Ishāq). Hist. Arab. I = ibn Ishāq 106. Another version in de generatione (Bibl. p. 211).
30. San Pedro and *reprob.* – loc. cit. Hist. Arab. II, cf. Cron. de Esp. xcv/467, xcvii/469. Tripoli, I, II. Cf. among others, Paris, Fidenzio and Lull, D.P. 71-74.
31. Loc. cit. In the Muslim versions of the Baḥīrā legend Muhammad generally meets Baḥīrā at Busra; Tripoli has a visit to Egypt in mind and supposes him to travel north and east rather than north and west.
32. The text adds to 'Syrian, Arab and Egyptian' 'Christiani et Saraceni', a very odd use of the latter word, which cannot mean *Muslim* in a pre-Islamic context, or *Arab*, since that has already been specified. It really here means 'those people who would shortly become Muslims'.
33. Murdered out of jealousy; Tripoli has the legend that wine was forbidden by Muhammad because he was intoxicated when his companions murdered Baḥīrā and told him later that he had done it himself.
34. SSM I.i.3-7, ibn Ishāq, 115, 116. Perhaps the strangest story of Muhammad's travels comes from the Cont. Chron. Isid. and the Cron. de Esp., where the Prophet travels personally to Spain, teaches heresy at Cordova, and is summoned to appear before St Isidore, to give an account of himself.
35. *Reprob.* II, ibn Ishāq 119ff. Vitry, Viterbo and Paris, loc. cit. Lull, Hamar, sig. 32. Cf. Tripoli and Anon. Fior. It is at this point that San Pedro and *reprob.* come closest together.
36. Mark, Pref. Q.
37. Viterbo, Paris and Vitry I.v. Cf. Hist. Arab. III, Ricoldo, Disp. xiii, Anon. Fior., Hist. Arab. iv, v. Lull, Hamar, sig. 11 and cf. D.P. cap. 71 passim. Cf. *Vita.*
38. 'Fiction' and 'oppression': Fidenzio, xiv; cf. Mark. Pref. Q. Risālah summary: cf. Viterbo, Paris and Vitry at loc. cit.
39. That the author (whether Peter the Venerable himself or not) had read the Cluniac translations seems clear from internal evidence although it is in some ways surprising that he does not take greater advantage of all the material available. When Peter of Poitiers speaks of Muhammad in these terms: *proditor fuerit, incautos et dormientes saepe jugulans*, he conveys the natural but rather humourless impression of one who has read the Risālah knowing nothing whatever of the background.
40. Vitry I.v; Fidenzio, xiv; Tripoli, III; Ricoldo, Disp. xiii.
41. All authors cited at the places already cited.
42. Cf. Hist. Arab. III. Cron. de Esp. cxiv and the same, vi and cxxi/493. Lull, Hamar, sig. 10.
43. *Reprob.* iv (Matth. xv.14).
44. Above, p. 81. San Pedro did not distinguish between the three tribes of Medinan Jews, but called them all the 'aliama (an unexplained word), id est, synagoga Beneccoraydae', thus naming them all from one tribe.
45. Above, p. 42.
46. Rukāna al-Muṭṭalibi: SSM I.i.45, ibn Ishāq 258.
47. 'Frightened them with the threat of Hell' etc. Cf. the account by Lull, D.P., loc. cit., of the Prophet's Meccan teaching.

48. Recognised as prophet; never in San Pedro as Messiah. The Jew here referred to is the unfortunate testator Mukhayrik, but he was not killed at Uḥud. The sabbatarian reason or excuse was supposed to have been used really by the banū Qurayẓa, at the Battle of the Ditch, because they had not supported Muhammad against the attack of the Quraysh. This incident seems to have been grafted onto two real aspects of Uḥud – the refusal of Muhammad to allow the Jewish clients of 'Abdallāh ibn Ubayy to fight on the Muslim side, and the part played by 'Abdallāh himself, the patron of the banu Qaynuqā'.

49. SSM I.i.23-58 covers both Meccan and Medinan periods.

50. In the form generally cited this tradition is Bukhārī 6.xii; *reprob.* was mistaken (cap. vi) in the reference (3 for 6 and the title *locutionis* for *lotionis*) and in the phrase 'in una hora noctis vel diei': cf. Houdas/ Marçais: 'dans le seul espace de temps d'un jour et d'une nuit'. Cf. San Pedro, SSM I.ii.14 and statements specifying eleven and nine wives in different authors (there are Bukhārī references justifying the alternative *nine*). See Risālah (Tolet. p. 298 and Vincent 23.44: cf. Muir: 'an objectionable passage . . . based on a weak tradition', p. 50); Pedro de Alfonso, loc. cit.; see Ricoldo, Itin. xxxv and Disp. viii; Marino (iii.iii) shows evidence of having read both Pedro de Alfonso and Risālah in one form or another, probably Vincent's; for an emphatic statement, see Humbert, de pred. S.C. xii; and Simon.

51. This episode may be said to have been by far the best-known actual incident of Muhammad's life, though always seen, of course, out of context, and thoroughly misunderstood from every point of view. It was first (so far as I know) stated by St John of Damascus (cf. Introduction). In our period it is stated by all major sources, esp. Pedro de Alfonso (loc. cit.) and *Contrarietas* (vii, MS f. 246v-247r). Cf. also Vitry (i.v) and Viterbo and Paris.

52. See Q. xxxiii.37 Cf. Legenda Aurea for Christian comment. San Pedro, SSM I.ii.5 and Fidenzio, loc. cit.; both the latter are rather colourful and romantic accounts, and so, in some ways, is Lull's in Hamar (sig. 9). Ricoldo (Disp. viii and references in xii) adds nothing to Contrarietas. The general laws supposed to have been imposed in consequence of this episode are sometimes amazingly confused; for example, in Anonimo Fiorentino, that a man can always take another man's repudiated wife, if repudiated on an unproven charge of adultery; Acqui's that the sultan is entitled to repudiated wives who are not pregnant as his concubines.

53. *Reprob.* vi; Q. xxxiii.49, 51; cf. commentaries quoted by Sale on these verses; also Bu. 65.33.7. The second passage cited here is Q. xxxiii.37.

54. Vitry, Viterbo and Paris, loc. cit. Cf. Humbert, de pred. S.C. loc. cit. and *summula*; also annotator of Ketton ad Az. 43 (Bibl. numbering): *multorum aliorum uxores ex responso divino adulterans* etc. and Poitiers ii.v *adulteria perpetrare sibi a Deo concessum in Alcorano suo dicens.*

55. SSM I.ii.7, 11, 12.

56. Loc. cit. This is another argument we cannot imagine Ricoldo's ever having tried on a live Muslim, or he would never have recommended

it (in effect) to future missionaries. His more sober view was that what mattered was less the 'adultery' than its justification in the name of God. This derives from *Cont.* (Disp. xii); cf. Lull, Hamar, sig. 9.

57. *Reprob.*, loc. cit. Q. lxvi passim (verse 2 verbatim). (Forms of proper names corrected.)

58. Q. xlviii.1; cf. authorities quoted by Sale. *Reprob.* ix.

59. SSM i.iv.11 citing Q lxvi, 1 and 2. Ric. loc. cit. The better explanation, that Marīyah took, not Ḥafṣah's bed, but Ḥafṣah's or 'Ā'ishah's day in the rota was never mentioned; in fact the mediaevals do not at all seem to have grasped the Prophet's rotation system for wives; they may not have believed that his disordered passions (as they conceived them) could be so orderly (but see note 67).

60. SSM i.ii.1ff; Q. xxiv.11ff. Cf. ibn Isḥāq, 731ff; Bu. 65.24.6. Tolet. MS p. 299; Vincent 23.44; and see summary in Marino iii.iv.

61. *Reprob.* vi; Bu. 6.5, cf. 6.4, 21, 22 and Q. ii. 222; Bukhari's heading incorrectly cited. Cf. San Pedro, SSM i.iv.18, 19, even more indelicate; see Bu. 6.5 and Wensinck, Handbook, under 'menstruation', and see appendix E, below, p. 320.

62. Lists of wives in Apology and SSM i.ii.9, 10. Cosmetics, etc., SSM i.ii.16-18 cf. viii.12 and Wensinck, Handbook, under 'Muhammad'.

63. The epithets not identified in the text are in order from Waltherius, Humbert, loc. cit., Fidenzio, Marino and Benvenuto.

64. SSM i.vi.2, 3; cf. vii.14 and ibn Isḥāq 764, 765. Leg. Aur., though in every other way less inaccurate, was correct to assert the lapse of years between the poisoning and the death of the Prophet (loc. cit.). *Reprob.* ix.

65. Loc. cit.

66. SSM loc. cit. cf. ibn Isḥāq, 1005ff, 1018ff and Wensinck loc. cit.

67. *Reprob.* ix. Muslim (cited) 5, 19-23; cf. Bu. 8.55, 23.96. Bu. (cited) 76.49. 'Ibanabez' for ibn 'Abbas (incorrectly attributed). *Vita* cited – ibn Sa'd? (ii/ii, 36ff, etc.) cf. Abū'l Fidā', cap. lxi, Bu. 3.39. Muhammad was not in 'Ā'ishah's house because it was her day but because when he fell ill the other wives agreed he should stay with 'Ā'ishah. It still is not clear to me whether the author of *reprob.*, unlike all his contemporaries, understood the rotation of wives. The final quotation is from Lull, Hamar, sig. 32.

68. Authors mentioned at places previously cited. Cf. Hidebert of Mans and also the fate of the 'idol' of Muhammad in *Roland*, lines 2590-1.

69. SSM i.viii.225ff. For a variant of this foot story, see *Lib. Nic.*

70. SSM i.vi.8, 12. Cf. Pedro de Alfonso, Viterbo, Vitry, Paris, Fidenzio xiv, Anon, Fior. The foretold ascension of Muhammad's body occurs in Risālah (Tolet. p. 304, Vincent 23.47, Muir p. 62). The contrast with Christ is the reason for the special attraction of this idea for Christians.

71. SSM i.vi.6; ibn Isḥāq 1019-20; SSM i.vi.14-16 and ibn Isḥāq 1012. *Reprob.* did not discuss this and no other author knows of the episode of the quarrel.

72. Will. Tyr. xx.xix; Oliver, Hist. Reg., 56.

73. Cap. iv.

CHAPTER IV. *The place of violence and power in the attack on Islam*
1. Cf. Urban's Clermont sermon, Malmesbury, yr. 1095. The note
of 'defence' was clear to all Urban's hearers: cf. Fulcher (iii), Robert (i
and ii), Baudry (i.iv) and Guibert (Gesta, ii.iv). Cf. also Dana Munro
Speech of Urban II. There is a great sameness in all accounts of the rise
of Islam. Cf. Guibert; Peter the Venerable, CSS prol. 12; *summula*;
Gerald; St Albans Chr.; Will. Alv. de leg. xviii/18.N; Paris, al. scr.;
Vitry i.iv; Humbert, de pred. S.C., ii; Tripoli ivff; Leg. Aur.; Rod. Hist.
Arab., viiff; Lull, D.P. and Hamar, sig. 10; Higden; Marino, iii.v; Anon.
Fior. For a discussion of the concept of Christendom, with further bibliographical references, see D. Hay, *Europe.*
2. Dār al-Islām means the part of the world in which Islam obtains;
dār al-ḥarb means the part which is subject to war, i.e. where Islam does
not obtain, and where it ought to be made to obtain, by the classic offer
of the alternatives of conversion, subjection and battle. The collect of
the Feast of the Recovery began: Omnipotens sempiterne Deus, qui
virtute tua mirabili Jerusalem, civitatem tuam, de manu paganorum
eruisti et christianis *reddidisti* . . . (descriptio T. S. Johan. Wirziburgen-
sis). For papal bulls cf. one of Urban II's which speaks of the *restitution*
of the Church of Sicily (1093, ed. Taurinensis); Gregory IX's references
to the *restoration* of the Kingdom of Majorca to the Christian cult
(MOFPH vol. iv, 2, Raymundiana xxxviii). Cf. also a bull of Alexander
IV which actually speaks of Muslims' *returning* to the obedience of the
Apostolic See (Coll, *Escuelas* . . . – re Tunis missions). Cf. also *illa
nostra Hierusalem*, Hist. Dip. Fred. Secundi (Huillard-Bréholles) vol.
5 p. 249. Innocent III wrote to al-'Adil, 'non ad terrorem', to warn him
that Christians would be compelled to fight, if he would not 'restore'
Jerusalem (*Soldanus obsecratur*, Acta, p. 444); cf. Holcot (Appendix F).
St Bernard: Ep. 458; cf. 457 and *de laude* iii. Vitry: one MS (Paris, B. nat.,
lat. 6244A) presents the biography of Muhammad specifically in juxta-
position to the Islamic aggression and the Christian defence, i.e. Crusade:
'Vita Machometi, qualiter seduxit terram sanctam, sive ecclesiam
orientalem'. There was, as for all Christians always, a special mystique
of Jerusalem: 'umbilicus est terrarum, quasi alter Paradisus deliciarum'
(Robert, loc. cit.) is representative. For a general discussion of the
Jerusalem image in the Western imagination, see Cohn, op. cit.
3. Mark: Pref. Q. Humbert, Op. Trip. i.vii.
4. Du Meril, *poésies pop. lat. ant. au XIIe siècle*; cf. Fulcher, ROL,
vol. 8, Ch. Kohler, *Un Sermon*, etc. At the first preaching of the Crusade
the Temple was less prominent than the Sepulchre (but see Baudry of
Dol, i.iv); but its importance grew. (Cf. also Bernard, *de laude*, cap. v.)
For the *Templum Dei* see also chapter VII note 17.
5. For example, in *de expug. T.S. libellus*; cf. Fidenzio, xvii and
Ricoldo, Epistolae v, passim.
6. *Gestes des Chiprois* in AOL, vol. v; yr. 1258. 'Synagogues of
Satan': Simon Simeon; Mount Sinai: Antonio de' Reboldi, Itin. ad
montem Sinai, Gol. vol. iii; fana Maumeti: Walter of Coventry, RS
p. 333.
7. *De expug.*, loc. cit., cf. St Albans Chr.

8. Caesarius, op. cit., xx.xxvii; Ricoldo, Epistolae, passim.
9. Op. cit., xv.
10. Caesarius, op. cit. i.vi; Joinville LXXVII. Cf. Cron. Père Marsili XXI. For the general question of 'martyrdom' in battle, see appendix B.
11. Op. Trip. i.xii ff; de pred. S.C. ii, viii.
12. Op. Trip. i.xii; Gesta Francorum, p. 202. The massacre so complacently described by the Gesta was in fact the worst mediaeval 'profanation' of the Holy Land known to us. It is the same occasion which the Conquête, expressing the popular attitude, unblushingly describes – the looting and raping and the indiscriminate massacre:

> De Turs et de paiens font grant carpenterie
> Tex ia sa seror, ou sa fille, ou sa mie,
> Que por peor de mort l'a en l'estor laissie.
> Moult fu la sainte vile icel estormie,
> Sarrasin et paien morent a grant haschie.
> . . .
> Encontre Portes orrés, que Dex a benéie,
> Ont consevi les Turs, nes espargnerent mie;
> Del sanc as mescreans est la terre soillie;
> Les Sarrasines plorent, chascune brait et crie,
> Et maldient la terre, ou tex gent fu norie . . .
> Li ribaut les saisirent, mainte en ont efforcie;
> Chascuns en fait son bon, apres l'a despoillie
> Ne mais fors la chemise ne li a pas laissie. (v.xii.4474ff)

It is an agreeable irony to read the Christian justification of the First Crusade; Robert the Monk speaks of the destruction and murder of Christians and concludes the passage, 'quid dicam de nefanda mulierum constupratione, de qua loqui deterius est quam silere?' (Cap. i.)
13. Op. Trip. i.xi; de pred. S.C. xvi, xxix-xliii. St Bernard's defence of the use of violence, stripped of its rhetoric, is similarly pragmatic. (*De laude*, iii.)
14. *Lib. Nic.*, conclusion; Innocent, St Bernard, Benedict, loc. cit.; Fidenzio, op. cit., xvi; the verse is from Richard Loewenherz, lines 339-42. Cf. chansons de Roland and d'Antioche and Conquête de Jérusalem and Godefroid de Bouillon, passim, and Holcot, Appendix F.
15. Cf. G. Paris, Légende de Saladin.
16. Itin. Reg. Ricardi, iv.31; Philippe de Novare for Balian, p. 14; for Frederick II, see Salimbene, yr. 1250 and Huillard-Breholles, vol. 6, p. 325: 'conjunctus amicicia detestabili Sarracenis'; 'Machometi nomen in templo Domini diebus et noctibus publice proclamari permisit'; cf. ibid., p. 427; see also Paris. Templars: cf. Oursel, *Procés*; Lizerand, *Dossier*. Buchthal: *Miniature Painting*. Gregory: lib. iii, ep. xxi. The Church Councils: Conc. Lat. iii, 1179, Mansi xxii, col. 230; Conc. Lat. iv, 1215, ibid., col. 1066; Conc. Lugdun. i, 1245, xxiii, col. 631. Héfélé-Leclercq, 11th General (3rd Lateran) and 13th General (1st Lyons). There was a slight increase of precision as the years passed. (Cf. also edit. bullarum Taurin., Gregory X, anno 1272, ii.) See Heyd, vol. i, p. 386ff. William of Adam: de modo, i. Bulla Bonifacii Pp. VIII, anno

1299, xiii. Not only to trade, but even to travel as a pilgrim to the Holy Land long required a licence (cf. Ludolf, ed. Deycks). For the licensing system, see Heyd, vol. ii, p. 33ff, esp. p. 44ff.

17. Peñaforte's reply has the express authority of the Holy See. The word 'heresy' used in this must refer to Islam. Text in MOFPH vol. iv.2, Raymundiana, xviii; the description of Raymund is in MOFPH vol. i, Cron. Ord. Cf. Monneret de Villard, *Lo studio*. A provincial council held in Spain some time after 1215 illustrates the further working of the canons (or their failure to work). (Conc. Incerti Loci, Mansi, xxii, 1090ff, cap. xx.) Every Sunday priests were to denounce all those who had incurred the automatic excommunications for trafficking with Saracens. Heyd has pointed out that the prohibitions were always to some extent a dead letter. Here however we are more concerned with the intention than with the actual achievement.

18. It is strange to reflect that Peter the Venerable recommended Muslims to introduce the admirable toleration of which Christendom provided the model – they allowed a multitude of Jews to live among them and to speak against the Christian faith; and were not moved to anger, *sed audiunt patienter, respondent sapienter*. (CSS i.12.) For the Canons, see Grat. decretum, de Jud. et Sarac., col. 1722; Durandus, Spec. jur. de Jud. et Sarac.; Clementinarum lib v, de Jud. et Sarac., Tit. ii, cap. unicum. Conc. Lat. iii; Lat. iv and Vienn., Héfélé-Leclercq. For Spanish practice, see Janer and Bofarull. Ultimately Inquisitors were given authority over Muslims (to examine cases where Muslims were alleged to have led Christians into error (Gregory XI, viii anno 1372, Edit. Taurin. bullarum). (Cf. also Greg. IX, xxxvi anno 1233, ibid.) See also *Clemens IV Iacobum reg. Arag. monet* etc., Denifle, Quellen (see bibliography).

19. Sancti Raymundi summa sacrorum canonum, Lib. i, tit. iv. 'Coacta servicia': the Dominicans at Constantinople, during the brief period of Latin Empire, argued with a dervish who 'blasphemed' Christ that logically he must either be beheaded or agree that Islam is unjust, because in Islam a Christian who 'blasphemed' Muhammad would be beheaded. This was hardly to compare like with like, in that blaspheming Christ here meant denying His divinity (with reverence), whereas blaspheming Muhammad meant calling him by many bad names. The dervish was put in prison, where he refused food for two days, but had a vision and was converted. It does not seem that the Christians felt conscious that they were coercing him. (For references, see chapter VI, section 2, p. 175 and note 26.) Bzovius, Annal, xiii, 1238; . . . Bofarull, vol. vi, num. 57 (p. 196), Janer, xiii. There are many instructions to princes to ensure the acceptance of missionaries, e.g. in Huillard-Bréholles, vol. 4 (1), 1233, Gregory IX to Frederick II. Preaching to Muslims was indulgenced (Clement III, 1190, see Decret. v.vi.x).

20. Peter the Venerable, CSS i prol. 16, i.1; Oliver, Epistola Salutaris; Adam Marsh, RS, ep. to Pp, follows letter ccxlvi; capp. ix, x, but see also capp. v, viii, etc. 'King of Babilon' – the Ayyūbid sultan, al-Kāmil Muhammad.

21. St Francis: note in Bonaventura's Life (XI.3) the phrase *vir Dei*,

non armis, sed fide munitus. Sources cited by Gol., vol. 1. The Rule: Reg. ia, cap. xvi; cf. sus, iii. The friars themselves were capable of reinforcing the old crusading attitude, although the general effect of their work was contrary. The rule for Tertiaries (approved by Nicholas IV in 1221) forbade them to carry arms, *except* in defence of the Roman Church, the Christian faith or their lands. Humbert himself is an outstanding example of the double approach. The great apologist of the Crusade, he was not only Master-General of the Dominicans but in an encyclical letter enjoined the study of languages in order to evangelise 'schismatics, Jews and barbarous nations'. (Monneret de Villard discusses this and also refers to Adam Marsh. For the more general aspects see Roncaglia, *I Francescani in Oriente* and C. Dawson, *The Mongol Mission.*) It was customary for the Crusade to be preached by Franciscans and Dominicans in Europe and both were active during the last years of the Latin States. Franciscan influence increased in the fourteenth century with the confirmation of the custody of the Holy Places to the Minors.

Since this was written I have read the recent study by Fr. Basetti-Sani, who sees a more profound significance in the encounter between Francis and al-Kāmil than many will be willing to concede. The analysis of the actual encounter in this stimulating book is very interesting (refer bibliography, list C).

22. I do not wish to assert that the Eastern missionaries were wholly impractical. Ricoldo's scheme in the *libellus ad nationes orientales* (cf. Itin. and Disp. passim) was very sensible about the approach to oriental Christians and interesting on that to Tartars. San Pedro, SSM, prol. Lull: Vita, cap. vi; cf. cap. iv; Blanquerna, xliii and xliv; de recuperatione T. S. in Atiya. For discussions, see Monneret de Villard, Atiya, also Peers and Zwemer. (Refer bibliography.)

23. MOFPH vol. i, appendix.

24. *De fratribus . . . visitantibus captivos* and Eleemosyna both in Gol. iii; Alexander IV cit.; Honorius, in Bzovius, xiii, 1220. Latin communities were organised in *fondacos*, equivalent to the national *factories* of a later age; the word is from funduq, a khan or public hostel. Each trading nation, Venetian, Pisan and so on, had its own; wandering Franks, such as pilgrims, if they had no national *fondaco* of their own, would be the guests of whichever seemed most suitable. There was no question of individuals living independently in Muslim parts of the town. Renegades will have been largely cut off from their former co-religionists, although, as we have seen, the dependants of the bread-winner might continue to live with him. Segregation, through Church discipline, natural disapproval of Islam and pre-occupation with trade, is likely to have been effective. Gol. vol. xiii for treaty of 1270 (pp. 298ff).

25. MOFPH vol. vi pp. 31-32 for Peñaforte's studium; for Frederick, Hist. Dipl., vol. iv anno 1233 (cit.) pp. 452, 457-8; Bzovius, anno 1233 col. 430.

26. Ricoldo, Itin. xxi, cf. xxviii. Lull: Vita; Hamar, prologue, end of pars. ia and opening iia and iiia; but in *liber de gentile* the Muslim is not definitely defeated, and he is allowed arguments more credibly Islamic.

Cf. however Muslim participants in other Lullian dialogues (see bibliography). It is true that Lull sometimes allows the Muslim protagonist in a debate actually to defend what Lull knows to be an Islamic theological position (e.g. on the qualities of God), but the reasons he puts into the Muslim's mouth always fit only his own private philosophical terminology and methods (e.g. Hamar, passim). The chief reason why it is hard to believe that Ricoldo ever used the arguments in spoken debates is that they are inherently unlikely to impress; had he used them he would have been compelled to revise them; but as it is they represent literary sources unmodified. Monneret de Villard's assertion 'egli lavorò sempre direttamente sul testo arabo' (of the Qur'ān) antedates Miss d'Alverny's discovery that he took all these quotations over from the *Contrarietas*. One small point – when Ricoldo and his companions (Itin. xxviii) refused to eat when food was prepared for them in the houses of Muslims in which they were guests, it is implied, not only that the Latins rejected overtures of friendship, but that their talk with Muslims was never acrimonious enough to cause bad feeling, as it certainly would have, if a fraction of the *Disputatio* had been repeated. The group of missionaries with Angelo da Spoleto (note 24 above) 'discussed several matters of Scripture with the Caliph of the Muslims, who seemed to agree with the brethren in many things'. The Christians did not claim that this was a dispute. As far as the Muslims were concerned, the friars were working, with permission, for charitable objects. It is likely to have been an occasion when both sides wished to avoid controversy, and spoke of things they expected to agree about.

27. Lull, Vita vi. For Lull's chronology see Peers, *Ramon Lull*; and *Hist lit. de France* (see bibliography). The three missions to Africa were spaced between his sixtieth and eighty-third years. There is no evidence of any change in his approach to Islam during his final residence in Tunis; the phrase, *dixit Raymundus Alcadi episcopo Tunisii*, etc. in his *de maiori fine intellectus* only indicates at most that he was still trying to persuade Muslims into Trinitarian controversy (Munich MS 10517, f. 74v). Professor Peers, a sincere admirer of Lull, says of the unlikelihood of his ever being canonised, 'The little that is known of his death makes it impossible for a Postulator to show that he was killed *in odium fidei*; and, since there is presumptive evidence that his vigorous methods of attack and the boldness of his character may themselves have antagonised the Mohammedans and caused the final attack on him, the burden of proof lies with the Postulator' (op. cit., p. 393; pp. 370-1). At most it is only asserted that he was killed by stones thrown by an angry crowd that he had provoked.

28. Cron. xxiv Generalium. A rather similar case is that recounted with approval by the Minister Vicar General for the East ('qualiter tres nostre vicarie . . .', Gol. ii, p. 66ff), in which the friars go to the Friday prayer and, while insisting that Christ is God, also denounce Muhammad, whom not Scriptures, miracles nor a good life, they say, attest. Thus they reflected the polemic arguments we have been discussing in previous chapters.

29. Arnold's description of the original Spanish Martyrs' Movement

seems to apply only too well to these ill-advised missionaries: 'a party
. . . set itself openly and unprovokedly to insult the religion of the
Muslims and blaspheme their Prophet, with the deliberate intention of
incurring the penalty of death' (*Preaching of Islam*, p. 141). Cf. Basetti-
Sani's account of St Francis' appearance before al-Kāmil; also Runciman's
(Hist. Crus., vol. III). For Pasquale and Livin, see Gol. iv. Livin, from
Chron. xxiv Gen. Pasquale also finally achieved martyrdom; Gol. ii,
p. 273; cf. p. 543. A case only superficially different is that of Fr. Nicolas
of Montecorvino (Gol. v, p. 73) who superfluously required a penitent
Hungarian noble renegade to proclaim publicly his return to Christ, a
penance which resulted in the foreseen and intended martyrdom of both
priest and penitent. Cf. also a group of friars who did not set out to
achieve martyrdom, but did so by their intransigence before the qāḍī:
Gol. ii, p. 70; and another similar case, ibid., p. 446. Of course, there is
plenty of evidence for unprovoked martyrdoms, but these are not
relevant to my point here. Such occurred chiefly in the course of war
(examples in Gol. i, p. 264 and p. 350), when, by Islamic law, Christians
had already by hypothesis refused willing and tolerated subjection within
Islam. The other occasion of martyrdoms not deliberately provoked was
the rare occurrence of a Muslim ruler whose extreme opinions led him
to seek out and oppress Christians, against his own law. For the most
part the governments were amazingly patient.

30. Tractatus, xxiii, xxiv, liii. Only Mandeville followed Tripoli. It
is very difficult to assess Tripoli's claim to have baptised so many converts. Adults may have sought a magical protection for themselves or
their children; there may have been baptisms of dissident Christians
under some misapprehension; neither of these is a very convincing
explanation, and yet the fact asserted is nearly as impossible to believe
as the idea that Tripoli might be a liar.

31. Cf. *summula* and references in note 1 to this chapter. The relevant
verses in the Qur'ān are in fact not consistent; there is a shift of emphasis;
cf. Bell, *Origin of Islam*. Pedro de Alfonso: loc. cit.

32. Risālah, Toletanus, MS p. 112; Vincent, 23.56; Muir p. 85ff;
Contrarietas, capp. II and IV. Sigebert: cf. *Vita*.

33. CSS I.5, 6; Q. III.18; Ketton, Az. v, Bibl. p. 22, line 10ff. Sūrah
lxxxviii: verses 21, 22; Ketton, Az. 97, Bibl. Az. 98, p. 185, line 1. For
Annotator see ad loc. (Bibl. p. 227); note also his statements that he who
attacked the Qur'ān was immediately killed (Bibl. p. 224; MS CCCD
184 p. 51, margin at foot right; note also marginal comment on wars
passim).

34. Monneret de Villard drew attention (loc. cit.) to the popularity
of this phrase, which may be associated with the anticipation of the total
collapse of Islam. Oliver, Hist. Dam. and Ep. Sal.

35. See Humbert, Op. Trip. i.iv.v and de pred. S.C. ii, ix, viii, xii;
Ricoldo, Disp., prol.; prophecy of Joachim, in Salimbene; Viterbo and
Paris, loc. cit., Vitry, i.iv; Tripoli, xxiii, xxiv; Fidenzio, xvii; Verona, xi.

36. *Reprobatio*, vi and viii (referring Bu. lvii.viii.6); iv; and xv, cf.
explanatio, prologue.

37. SSM i.iii.3-5; i.i.62; i.vi.18; i.vii.11.

38. Itin., xxix and xxxv; Disp., i, v, vii, viii, ix, x, xii, xiv, xvi. The four classes of Muslim believers were, first, those who were forced by the sword to believe; secondly genuine believers, *decepti a diabolo*; thirdly, those who were loyal to the beliefs of their ancestors; and finally those who sought a lax morality. This derives direct from *Contrarietas* (ii) and was adopted by Pennis (x). There were three signs of Islamic violence, said Ricoldo, the prophecy that it would last as long as the victory of its arms and the maintenance of its temporal power being the first of these; the other two were the sword bared by the khaṭīb when he enters the minbar and the (false) derivation of the name *Ismā'īli* (for Assassin) from Ismael, so that the violent Assassins were named Ismaelites (=Muslims) par excellence. (Disp. x; cf. Pennis, x.) A small point is of interest: if a passage contained in Bart. Pic.'s version but omitted in the B.N. and B.M. MSS is authentic, Ricoldo objected to Muhammad's having encouraged bellicosity in his people by condemning desertion on the battlefield; but what sin, asked Ricoldo with engaging frankness, would it be for a man to run away, if his life were in danger? (Disp. viii, Bibl. col. 147.)

39. D.P. 11, 12; Blanquerna, lxxx.

40. Acqui, loc. cit.; Mandeville, xiii; contained but not explained in Viterbo, Paris and Vitry.

41. Tripoli, cap. ii; Humbert, Op. Trip., i.vii; William of Auvergne, de leg. xviii/18.mff; Genesis xxi.13; Josephus, Antiquities, i.x; for pseudo-Methodius, see Magna Bibliotheca Veterum Patrum, iii, p. 363ff; San Pedro, i.viii.4-17; Galatians, iv.22-31; genealogies of Muhammad, e.g. a fine MS B.M., Cotton, Nero C. ii f. 123, where there are three parallel columns, titled respectively *De machometo, quod machometus qui cepit anno domini dcxxij habuit vi uxores*; *arbor generationis machometi qui descendit de stirpe hysmaelis*; and *de machometo, de inicio regni machometi et duratione*. The descent from Ismael, without further detail, was very generally asserted.

42. *Prima epistola Abutaleb ad Samuelem*; van den Oudenryn, *de opusculis arabicis* . . . (see bibliography).

43. Vitry, i.iv; Humbert, de pred. S.C. xv; cf. Fidenzio, v-xii, who analysed the reason for Christian failure much more minutely and with practical intent; Ricoldo, Disp. ix.

44. Vincent, 23.39; Prophetia, MS B.N. 14503; Caesarius, viii.27; Lull, lib. de Gent., iv.iv; lib. de Tart., de T. et S., 8; yr. 1251, in MGH, p. 445; Humbert, loc. cit.

45. Prefatio; Ezechiel, i.1; Ep.i.

46. Ep. iii.

47. Epp. i, iii. It was quite often alleged that this was the purpose of the polygamous institutions of Islam, the extent of which was exaggerated. (Cf. Guibert, loc. cit., St Albans Chr., note to illustration in margin, yr. 622; Paris, al. scr.; Lull, D.P. 8; Anon. Fior.)

48. Ep. iv. ep. iii.

49. Epp. i, iii. E.g. '. . . circumducuntur per mundum et impregnantur a Sarracenis et ex eis generantur tyranni et satrapes Sarraceni, qui contra Christianos in hostilitate alios Sarracenos excedunt' (iii).

50. Ep. i; cf. also ep. ii and in ep. iii the failure of the angels to protect churches and dedicated virgins.

51. Epp. i, ii, iii, iv.

52. Ep. v. Ricoldo seems to have discovered this text with the sense of a special revelation made to him personally after a period of excessive religious anxiety; on the other hand, we also get the impression that he expected a revelation, and preferably one more sensational than this. Basically the one he received, or persuaded himself that he had received, is a credit to his good sense.

53. Vitry, i.vi; Tripoli, xxi.

54. Cf. Caesarius, viii, xxvii.

55. Fidenzio, xvii, xxi; MOFPH, vol. iv.2, loc. cit.; cf. MOFPH vol. i, appendix, 'fructus qui fit . . .' and memoria T.S., ROL, vol. 10.

56. Simon Simeon.

57. Gol. iv, p. 234; cf. chapter V note 26.

CHAPTER V. *The place of self-indulgence in the attack on Islam*

1. Pedro de Alfonso, op. cit.; Guibert, Gerald, Viterbo and Paris (greg. Report), loc. cit.; Oliver, Ep. Sal.; Martí, explanatio simboli X; Lull, Hamar, sig. 6; pseudo-Vitriacus (in Bongars) but omitted from Vincent 31.54ff; Vitry i.vi, apparently tries to improve on his source (cf. with Viterbo and Paris texts); Tripoli, xlix, refers Q. iv.3, misquoting *possess* as *buy*, which makes a great difference; San Pedro, 'by buying, or any other way' SSM i.iv.16; Fidenzio, xvi. Wild notions in *Lib. Nic.*

2. SSM, loc. cit. This does less than justice to the Risālah ('al-Kindi'); cf. Muir p. 107, Vincent 23.63 and Tolet. *Vita*: a thousand concubines.

3. The verse of the Qur'ān is itself not clear and needs to be understood in the light of traditional interpretation (so far as Islamic jurisprudence is concerned). Sale has 'marry one only or the slaves which ye shall have acquired'. *Reprobatio*, viii.

4. Verona applied this doctrine particularly to journeys, so that what he says recalls mut'ah, the temporary marriage practised on journeys in Shī'ah Islam; but there is no mention of the price paid in such marriages.

5. Lull, Hamar; see above, chapter IV, p. 121.

6. Consult SEI, esp. under *Talak* and *Nikah*.

7. Viterbo, loc. cit.; San Pedro, SSM i.iv.21, cf. *reprobatio*, viii; Guido, op. cit., 22; Vitry, Viterbo and Paris are more divergent here than is usual; Tripoli, xlix. 'Absque ulla causa' – i.e. no *legal* cause: in Islam, divorce without a reason is reprehensible but valid. *Vita Mahometi* betrays an interest in the use of a legal formula as the means of divorce, and shares the usual obsession with *tahlīl*.

8. Quod si calcaret eam menstruosam, oportet quod cognoscat eam sine menstruis. Quod si etiam cognovit veretro non bene erecto, oportet ulterius quod cognoscat eam bene rigato membro.

9. *Rep.* viii; exp. sym. X; Fidenzio, xvi; San Pedro, SSM i.viii.73; Ricoldo, Itin. xxxiv and Disp. viii; *Contrarietas* vii.

10. Hamar, sig. 6.

11. Op. cit., xi.

12. His own experience in the sense that he is more likely to have heard this in the East than read it in the West; at least, I have not traced a literary source. Naturally, it will not derive from first-hand experience, and must therefore represent hearsay, perhaps Oriental Christian in origin.

13. Itin. xxxii. 'It is also not forbidden that . . .' . . . licitum et non prohibitum et quod . . . I assume a copying error, and that the second *et* should be *etiam*, or else omitted altogether. Ricoldo say that the Qur'ān 'seems to mean the same thing' by the phrase, *Fatigate mulieres et non erit aliquod peccatum, dummodo dederitis precium quod promistisis*. This quotation seems to hint both at Q. iv.28 and at ii.223 and appears in much the same form in the Epistolae. It is good evidence of the limits of Ricoldo's knowledge of the Qur'ān, and is one more reason to doubt his having any direct acquaintance with the Arabic text.

14. Fidenzio, xvi. Q. – paraphrasing iv.28?

15. Pref. Q. See. Q. lviii.1ff.

16. Oliver and Ricoldo, quoted above; Tripoli, xlix; Pedro de Alfonso and all those who copied him; Viterbo, Paris, Vitry, all asserted mistakenly that wives must be chosen from among free women. Cf. also Patriarch Haymar's report to Pope Innocent (Paris yr. 1193 and Vincent and pseudo-Vitriacus). Ricoldo, Disp. v and Q. xxiv.33 for the position of slaves in relation to the sexual rights of their masters. Ricoldo has *perhibetur quod non compellant eas perdere castitatem*, which seems to imply a more general sense than Sale's 'compel not your maid-servants to prostitute themselves, if they be willing to live chastely' and this may be taken to be the traditional sense of the verse. Maracci has *ne cogatis ancillas vestras ad meretricium, si voluerint pudice vivere*, which agrees exactly with Sale; his comment is concerned purely to explain the historical circumstance of the revelation following Jalāl ad-Dīn. (xxiv.34 with corresponding notes.) The mediaeval comment was muddled. The account here given of the mediaeval treatment of marriage law and concubinage in Islam is very incomplete; for references to related points and for a fuller treatment of the points here considered, see the author's thesis, *The Concept of Islam*, pp. 476-91.

17. This sort of malice is likely to have been felt by 'second-class citizens' towards the master-race, especially when it was felt as having a religious justification; it would also only have been natural that they should wish to impress their orthodoxy and enthusiasm on the advancing and sometimes aggressive victors from Latin Christendom; they had every reason to wish to communicate hatred of and contempt for Islam (though not, of course, the remotest justification for doing so). The reference is to Peter of Poitiers' *Capitula*; the heading itself reads, *quod insuper rem Sodomicam atque turpissimam docuerit, praecipiens in Alchorano suo, et velut ex persona Dei, sic loquens: 'O viri . . .'* Various versions of this verse of the Qur'ān (ii.223) and the point of jurisprudence arising are discussed briefly in appendix E.

18. Vitry i.v; cf. Paris, al. scr.; Op. Trip. i.vi, with a possible reference in de pred. S.C., xii; note, however, that Fidenzio cites Q. ii.223 as evidence of sexual licentiousness in general rather than of homosexual

practice in particular. He refers to sodomy later in the same passage, but where it is divorced from the usual text. *Reprobatio* VIII. San Pedro, SSM I.iv.18, 19. See appendix E.

19. Q. III.12; Ket. Az. v, Bibl. p. 21, line 46; Mark, cap. III (MS f. 19v); Maracci, Ref. in suram III Alcorani, 14.

20. Q. XII.31; Ket. Az. XXI, Bibl. XXII, p. 77, line 43; Mark, cap. XIV, f. 94v; Maracci, Ref. in suram XII Alcor., 32.

21. Cap. X.

22. SSM I.iv.22, 25 etc. Cf. references in note 18 above.

23. Pisan text in Mancini; cf. *Liber Nicholay*.

24. Disp. VI; Bart. Pic. is more confused than the MSS. The citation of Qur'ān seems to be intended for sūrah II or IV, but the condemnations of the men of Sodom come in sūrahs VII, XXVII and XXIX.

25. Martí, *explanatio* art. X; Benedict, loc. cit., William Alv. de leg. XVIII/18.R and XX/19.X; Acqui, loc. cit.; cf. Verona, X, XI.

26. De modo exterpandi Sarac. I.

27. Verona IX, cf. X. The sultan commits this crime 'execrabile et publice'. Verona describes 'amalucos parvos juvenes qui sibi venduntur ad Kayram'; there were over five hundred from Tartary, Greece, Italy and all parts of the world; 'et quum magni sunt effecti, facit eos armigeros suos, et sic ipse soldanus et admirati sui et comiter omnes Saraceni hoc horribile facinus sine omni Dei timore committunt . . .' Cf. Ludolf's rather eccentric comment, 'viri sunt debiles et libidinosi, abutentes masculis'.

28. Tripoli, XLVIII; Oliver, Ep. Sal.; Fidenzio and others quoted above. Although the Templars were accused both of sodomy and of favouring Muslims, the Muslims do not seem to have been held responsible for Templar morals. Indeed, the authority of Salāḥ ad-Dīn (on somewhat flimsy evidence) was cited for his contempt for the Order, because of their sodomitical practices. (Asserted by Guillaume de Nogaret; interrogation of 28 Nov. 1309.) The accusations against the Order under this head seem to be those usually made when it is wished to discredit any group of men, and especially religious orders. On the other hand, the accusations of obscene initiation ceremonies, whether true or untrue, were the invention of somebody's prurient schoolboy mentality, but these too have no parallel in the more adult and practical accusations made against Islam. (Cf. Oursel, *Procés*, and Lizerand, *Dossier*.)

29. Waltherius, loc. cit. (lines unnumbered) p. 381; cf. du Pont: Abateras saint mariage / . . . Tu dampneras virginite / Li chastes par t'iniquite / Sera avoutres et par toi / La gens sera fole et sans foi. Cf. Pisan text. In the chanson, 'Godefroid de Bouillon', the Caliph, hearing that the First Crusade threatens Islam, commands every Muslim to bring the number of his wives up to six (in order that there shall be more children to fill the armies). Ed. Hippeau, p. 88. The idea recurs from time to time, either, as here, that Muslims have many women, in order to have children who will fight against Christendom; or, more reasonably, that Muhammad married many wives in order to have sons.

30. Bacon, Mor. Phil., 4.1.111.5 et alibi; I.VI; Will. Alv. de leg.

xx/19.U; San Pedro, SSM I.viii.65; Varagine; Higden; Marino III.iv; Pisan text; Ludolf VIII; for the ḥajj, see also chapter VII below, and for worship of idols of Venus in Ka'bah appendix A.

31. San Pedro, SSM I.ii.12; Joachim in Salimbène cit.; annotator in Ketton ad Az. 3 (MS p. 63 col. 1); Pisan text. This is also a theme of the Man of Lawe's Tale: for Muslims to adopt Christianity would mean 'thraldom to oure bodies and penance' (338).

32. Fidenzio, XVI.

33. Introductory phrases to aliud scriptum in Paris.

34. San Pedro, SSM I.i.48. Similar statements were Oliver's that Islam is based on *terror mundanus* and *voluptas carnalis* (Hist. Dam.); Martí's that some Muslims were forced, others attracted by the licence of desire (Capistr. Jud.); Fidenzio's phrases about Muhammad as *humani sanguinis effusor pessimus* and *in peccato luxurie fetidissimus* (XIV); Ricoldo's 'murder, robbery and concupiscence' (Disp. v); and a casual description of Damietta as *catena captivorum et scortus et domus Sodomorun* (in obsid. Dam., from Quinti Belli Sacri ss. Minores). These examples are almost at random to illustrate the habitual way in which Islam was thought of as bearing this double implication. Aquinas, contra Gentiles I.vi, where the phrases reflect the opinion of educated people.

35. Bacon, Mor. Phil. IV.ii, VIII.19; Guibert, loc. cit.; Guido, err. 8. Other aspects of sexuality in *Concept of Islam* p. 504n.

36. e.g., contra Gentiles III.124, cf. 123-4; IV.78.

37. Alan, IV.viii; the Gregorian report joke is not in Viterbo; other authors, loc. cit.

38. *Explanatio symboli*, art. x. Note how Aquinas (loc. cit.) uses the example of animals more carefully and accurately.

39. Ricoldo, Disp. v cf. VIII on law of divorce; San Pedro, SSM I.iv.24; Lull, Hamar, sigg. VI, XII; Verona XI; Dubois, de recuperatione T.S. 43/69.

40. Pedro de Alfonso, loc. cit.; examples of association of this theme with the personal licence allowed Muhammad, see Ketton's annotator (talk of chastity intended to cover lechery, ad Az. 42, Bibl. 43, p. 226, col. 1; Q. XXXIII.30ff). see Vitry, I.vi; Fid. XVI; Higden; Benvenuto; cf. San Pedro, SSM I.iv.18 (cit.) ff. Cf. all accounts of Zayd and Marīyah episodes.

41. Alan, IV.vii; Gerald, loc. cit., cf. Urban's Clermont sermon; the two quotations are respectively from Ricoldo, Disp. VII, Pennis IX and Martí, Cap. Jud., loc. cit.; cf. also Mark, Pref. Q.; Paris, additions to St Albans text for yr. 622; Will. Alv. XVIII/18.R; Verona, XI; Humbert, Op. Trip. I.vi (re Paradise); Anon. Fior.

42. Q. LII.19ff and LV.74; Pedro de Alfonso, loc. cit.; An. Min. 13; San Pedro, SSM I.viii.74; Marino III.iv; Varagine; Higden; Simon Simeon; *reprobatio*, v; Ricoldo, Disp. VIII and Itin. XXXIV ('the pupil of one eye black like ink and of the other like an ostrich egg' for Q. XXXVII. 47; this last refers to the virgins of Paradise, a subject variously reported. The daily restoration of their virginity appears in Tripoli (L) and therefore in Mandeville; for a more elaborate version, see Vitry I.vi; three authors, Sigebert (loc. cit.), Alan (IV.v) and Guido (err. 4), speak of

the material Paradise, food included, without mentioning women. The Spanish *Vita* has a full account.

43. Lull, lib. de Gent., art. XII; *summula*, quoting I Cor. II.9 and Isa. LXIV.4, cf. Oliver in Ep. Sal.; Alan, IV.vi; Fidenzio XVI; Will. Alv. de leg. XVIII/18.M: cf. Benedict and annotator, passim 'insanissima deliramenta' etc. The last three are all related within the Cluniac group. See esp. Annot. ad Az. 65. It is interesting to note that the *urbs beata Jerusalem*, which is roughly contemporary with Muhammad, expresses spiritual delights of Heaven in a material language which Christians, of course, understood only in a spiritual sense. If the idiom of Qur'ān and this hymn are similar they have certainly been very differently understood.

44. Will. Alv., de leg. XIX/19.R; Martí, exp. sym. XII; Bacon, Mor. Phil. IV.2a.iii.6; IV.2a.v.4; cf. IV.2a.iii.14; Tripoli, L; San Pedro, SSM I.viii.244; Ric. Disp. VIII; Pennis VIII.

45. Benedict of Alignan, loc. cit. (Cerulli), copying William of Auvergne's 'quid est paradisus iste' which it seems slightly to improve (de leg. XIX/19.F); Lull, Hamar, signa 18-21, 26, 27, 34, 40; Lib. Tart., de T. et S.

46. Fidenzio, XVI; Lull, Contemp. D. 240.12; Annotator ad Az. 65 (Ketton 66).

47. Humbert, Op. Trip. I.vi; cf. Verona XI and Martí's citation of al-Ghazālī to show that he characterised the Arabs as 'omnibus hominibus . . . bestiis propiores' (Cap. Jud.); Will. Alv., loc. cit.; Vitry, I.vi; Fidenzio XVI.

48. Doctrina Pueril, 7.

49. Ricoldo, Itin. XXXIV; Will. Alv. de leg., loc. cit.

50. *Reprobatio*, v and *explanatio*, loc. cit.

51. They were brought to the attention of the scholarly public by the de doctrina Machometi, one of the group of Cluniac translations.

52. De legibus, XIX/18.Z-19.F and Q. Benedict, loc. cit.

53. Ricoldo, Disp. VIII, Pennis, VIII; St Thomas, contra Gentiles, IV.83; Cerulli has drawn attention to and discusses the treatment, by Thomas of York, Roger Bacon and Richard of Middleton of beatitude in Arabic philosophers, especially al-Ghazālī, ibn Sīna and ibn Rushd, cf. his comments p. 431: only Bacon has been cited by me here; Lull, Lib. de Gent., IV.xii; Contemp. D., 243, 311, cf. San Pedro, SSM I.viii.244; *sicut et nunc*: Aquinas, loc. cit.; *ut ait Tullius* . . . Will. Alv. loc. cit. (XIX/18.U, 19.R).

54. *Liber Scalae*, XIX; cf. Asin Palacios, Munoz Sendino and Cerulli for general questions of the kitab al-mi'rāj (see bibliography); cf. Varagine; Tripoli, L; *Contrarietas* XII; Rod., Hist. Arab. v and Cron. de Esp. CXVII/489; Ric., Itin. XXXV and Disp. I, VI, VII, IX and esp. XIV; Pennis XIII; San Pedro, CFM passim and SSM I.viii.76ff; Vita Mahometi.

55. There are several references to the 'monk-like' habit, described as like the Benedictine (Caesarius IV.xv; San Pedro SSM I.viii.68) the Franciscan (Acqui) or in summer the Canons Regular's (San Pedro, ibid.); its adoption was attributed to the spoiled monk, Sergius (Varagine, Acqui); this monastic dress was most often spoken of without elucidation (Varagine, Quidam Anglicus, Ludolf, VIII, Acqui); San Pedro spoke of

the tonsure in Cistercian style put to superstitious use (SSM ɪ.viii.94);
Verona said that Muslims consider it a sin to go uncovered (xɪ) and
added that this was an anti-clerical and anti-Roman act. These comments
vary in tone between simple interest and obscure disapproval, but there
seems to have been a suggestion of hypocrisy in many of these examples.
    56. Op. cit.
    57. *Reprobatio* vɪɪɪ; Ricoldo, Disp. xɪɪ; SSM ɪ.iv.6.
    58. Vitry (ɪ.v) said that Muhammad taught that Muslims need not
keep faith with their enemies, and San Pedro warned that Muslims
would not observe oaths *nisi ibi propriam utilitatem videant*; 'an accusation
common among enemies': e.g. used against each other by Catholics and
Protestants. Most later travellers had something to say on the trust-
worthiness of Muslims (see bibliography).
    59. Ricoldo, Disp. v; cf. Guido, err. 21; cf. Viterbo and Paris.
    60. San Pedro alone showed considerable interest in this theme: e.g.
SSM ɪ.viii.11. cf. reference in Ricoldo, Disp. vɪ.
    61. Associated vaguely with Muhammad's 'lechery' by Ketton's
annotator (ad Az. 42, Q. xxxɪɪɪ, Bibl. Az. 43) and remarked by Vitry
ɪ.vi.
    62. Ricoldo, Disp. xɪɪ; Lull, Hamar, signa 8, 25. San Pedro spoke of
stealing and robbing in the name of religion (SSM ɪ.viii.249) and
Guido thought theft was permitted (err. 7). The Qur'anic punishment
for theft was stressed by Pedro de Alfonso (loc. cit.) and those who
followed him (e.g. An. Min.).
    63. The earliest anti-Islamic polemic stresses this attitude. In the
East it was made by the Risālah (Vincent 23.63; Tolet.; Muir p. 110)
and in the West by Alvaro of Cordova, in the *Indiculus Luminosus*:
'Christus . . . naturalem motum . . . constrinxit . . .' etc., paragraph 33.
The germ is of course in the attack on Muhammad's life and in the
moral institutions of Islam, and this begins with the abjuration formula
and St John of Damascus (*de haeresibus*, not *disputatio*) (see bibliography).
    64. Pedro de Alfonso, loc. cit.; Pisan text, Mancini, op. cit.; Wal-
therius, p. 381; du Pont, op. cit.
    65. Peter the Venerable, CSS ɪ.10; *summula* (loc. cit.): 'gulae ac
libidini frena laxavit'; Mark, Pref. Q.
    66. Humbert, Op. Trip. ɪ.vi; Vitry ɪ.vi; St Albans Chr., loc. cit.;
Vincent 23.40.
    67. Ricoldo, Itin. xɪɪɪ, de Baldaco.
    68. *Reprobatio* vɪɪɪ, following MSS which do not entirely agree with
printed text. For Bukhārī see Wensinck in SEI under Khaṭī'a.
    69. San Pedro, SSM ɪ.iv passim, and 76; Fitzralph, Arm. 15(16).
    70. Disp. v, xɪɪ (cf. Itin. xxxɪ and Ep. ɪ). *Antonomasite* because
Muslim was thought to mean *saved*.
    71. The word *not* absent in Bib. nat. MS but present (as sense re-
quires) in B.M. Royal 13.E.IX; and also supplied by Bart. Pic. in his translation, Bibl. col. 182. Disp. xvɪɪ; refer also to cap. x and *Contrarietas* ɪɪ.
    72. This alludes to Islamic laws of fasting, prayer etc. They were
easier than the Christian, but might be easier yet; Ric. added that they
were not observed anyway. This was for the sake of the argument; his

true opinion, derived from personal observation, was much more favourable to Islam. See chapter VII, section 4, p. 214 below.

73. e.g., Père Nau, *état* (see bibliography); this is discussed a little more fully in chapter X, section 2, below.

74. Vitry I.vi.

75. Lull, Hamar, sig. 2; cf. Disputatio Fidelis et Infidelis, 8. MS Cambridge Dd.1.17, p. 451; *reprobatio*, v (refers Bu. LX.1? – see Wensinck, Handbook, under 'Decrees', for other possible references); San Pedro, CFM I.1.

76. Of those things that Islamic tradition has taken to be predestined, some relate to physical occurrences which are morally indifferent, some to moral actions and the eternal destiny of souls. It was the latter that interested San Pedro. See Montgomery Watt, *Free Will*, pp. 17-19, for the traditions.

77. San Pedro's criticism was unsound in that it depended on the assumption that Muhammad was not only the author of the Qur'ān but also of the traditions and of the kitāb al-miʿrāj; a single author would indeed be inconsistent. See CFM v.1-4, 8-11, 13-29; cf. SSM I.viii.93. For the relation of San Pedro's work to the *Liber Scalae*, see Cerulli and Munoz (bibliography).

78. In the *seta* San Pedro summed the position up thus: Muhammad had rightly said that we should attribute the good in us to God alone, and quite wrongly that good and evil alike 'proceed from God' (I.ii.9; cf. CFM VIII.2). See CFM, part VII passim; part VIII for the whole subject. Inconsistency with O.T.: see CFM III.2ff and Exod. xx.12 and cf. Watt, loc. cit. The *seta* (I.viii.94) describes one brush with Muslims that actually did take place; it does not, however, deal with the central issue and involved superstitious and unlearned Muslims, as is apparent from all the internal evidence. He says there were popular ceremonies intended to influence the angelic fates who visited every child on its seventh night, in order to establish his or her future life. This was a wrong opinion (*heregia*), silly, and something to be ashamed of. San Pedro had challenged the more learned and the elders about this, asking if these fates had ever been seen, or had ever left signs of their coming behind them; and how it was known what fate had been accorded to the child. His interlocutors could not answer and he told them that they knew nothing about it because there was nothing to know about. It is not clear whether the more learned elders thus confounded were 'ulamā' or just the better educated men of the village or quarter where the ceremonies (or some particular ceremony noted by San Pedro) took place. San Pedro pointed out to them that this belief contradicted the idea of the angel of death who wrote the eternal destiny of each man to Heaven or Hell from the beginning. This further illustrates the weakness of his method, since he here asserts a contradiction between a generally accepted doctrine and a local superstition; on the other hand, we should remember that he may not have had the means to distinguish the authority of the one from that of the other. He must have known, however, that there was no written authority for the one, even of such doubtful validity (from the modern point of view) as the *Liber Scalae*.

79. CFM viii.1.2. (Refers Acts i.7.)

80. SSM i.viii.248.

81. Pedro de Alfonso, loc. cit.; An. Min., cf. Higden, Varagine, Acqui and Verona (xi); also Viterbo, Paris, report. For explicit statements bringing in the shahādah, see Ric. Disp. i and vii and Itin. xxx; Pennis viii, ix; San Pedro, SSM i.viii.75, 198, 248. Belief in 'God and Muhammad' probably reflects this form of words (e.g. Guido 23).

82. Vitry, i.vi; Humbert, Op. Trip. i.vi; for the translation *salvati* see Ric. Disp. vii and xvii and Pennis ix and x. MSS give such variations as *melsamanini* and *messelamin* and Bart. Pic. has *meselamini* (Bibl. ii. col. 142); Pennis, *messlani*. Cf. also Ric. Ep. i. The translation of *Muslim* as *saved* survived for a long time.

83. Ric. Itin. xxx; San Pedro, SSM i.viii.75; Guido err. 23. There may be some influence of *Contrarietas* iv. Vitry, i.vi. San Pedro, ibid., 249; Mark, Pref. Q. followed by Fidenzio, xvi, 'qui crediderunt et operati sunt bene'; Tripoli xlix.

CHAPTER VI.   *The relation between Islam and Christianity: theory*

1. Chapter 1.

2. Ad Az. 2 (Bibl. p. 224 for annotation; MSS do not show from position of annotation the exact point of reference. 'In hoc *primo* capitulo' may perfectly well refer to sūrah ii which may be described as i or ii. The opening sūrah has been treated as supernumerary in Islamic history, and Mark in his translation, nearly contemporary with Ketton, counted sūrah ii as i. The earlier quotations are from *summula*.

3. Will. Alv. de leg. xviii/18.t, this obviously derives from *summula*, and Benedict of Alignan (loc. cit.) derives in turn from William. Other references: Guibert, loc. cit.; Gregorian report (not in Viterbo); Vitry, i.vi; Rod. Hist. Arab. v, Cron. de Esp. cxxi/493; Humbert, Op. Trip. i.vi; Verona, xi. This point relates to doctrine; it is extremely rare for even apparently good actions to be admitted of Muhammad's life. The individualistic *Liber Nicholay* is an exception, and speaks of his 'rejoicing with those who rejoiced, weeping with those who wept, giving all he possessed to the poor, devoting his time by day and night to prayer, and fasting daily'; but this again was all a trick to gain acceptance as a prophet.

4. Continuatio Chron. Isid.

5. San Pedro, SSM i.i.72; cf. also i.viii.48: deceits, lies and contradictions were 'inserted' into Mosaic and Gospel truths.

6. Leg. Aur.; Humbert, de pred. S.C. xii; Higden, loc. cit.

7. Vitry, i.vi; cf. Alan iv.i; Will. Alv. de leg., xviii/18.r; *reprobatio* v; cf. Pennis v. Aquinas is also unemphatic on this point (Contra Gentiles i.vi).

8. Humbert, loc. cit and iv.

9. Peter Venerable, CSS i.14, refers sūrah iii.31ff; Pennis, loc. cit.

10. San Pedro, CFM iii.2.

11. Tripoli, xxv.

12. *Reprobatio*, loc. cit. The quotation is not Augustine, but Bede, Comment. in Luc., lib. 5, cap. 17, v. 12.

13. *Summula,* loc. cit.; Annotator, ad Az. xxviii (=Ketton xxix = Q. xix); ad Az. v (MS pp. 68, 69, 70, not in Bibliander); but cf. ad Az. iv.

14. Alan, iv.i, iii, xiv. The doctrine of the living Ascension of Christ is not unambiguous in Q. but is certainly so understood by many (see Q. iv.155-7). It was usual to approve at least the Qur'anic condemnation of the Jews, but Pedro de Alfonso, doubtless a converted Jew, stressed the unity of Christians and Jews, who at least agreed that Christ really suffered (loc. cit.).

15. Mark, Pref. Q; Vitry i.vi; Oliver, Hist. Dam., loc. cit. This last passage appeared widely: cf. second part of pseudo-Vitriacus; St Albans Chronicle; Paris, aliud scriptum; see also Testimonia Minora de Quinto Bello Sacro.

16. Syrian Apology: Viterbo, loc. cit. Paris, report; Humbert, de pred. S.C. iv; Varagine, loc. cit. Among other accounts of Christ in Islam note the rather dull account in the Patriarch's statement to Innocent (pseudo-Vitriacus, Vincent 31.54ff, etc); *Vita*; *Lib. Nic.*; see also the creed 'credunt Saraceni' (Cambridge MS Dd.1.17, p. 71) and in Buenhombre's translation, Epistola Rabbi Samuelis, a good statement that was translated rather late to influence writers to whom equally impressive statements had long been available.

17. Ep. Salutaris – loc. cit.; cf. also ep. doctoribus. *Reprobatio,* v. The Q. verses cited are in order: lvii.4 (the name of the sūrah should read Iron, but was debased in copying); iii.57 (summarised rendering): *tractatus ambularii* ought to be Family of Imran; iv.169; lxvi.127; v.50 cited as *messie,* debased from *mense* for *mensae*: printed text has *duratio* for (correct) MS *directio*; the last quotation seems to represent lxi.14 since it can hardly be meant for iii.45; the name of the sūrah is given as 'of the apostles'. In the Bib. nat. MS the list of 'vera' is altogether omitted and only a statement that true things were said in the Qur'ān survives.

18. A new edition is needed, but the general sequence of the Qur'anic story of Christ and Mary as seen by Tripoli is clear enough. One curious omission is of some of Christ's miracles, for no apparent reason, since Tripoli's aim was to emphasise the Christian orthodoxy of the Qur'ān in this matter. It was highly inconsistent to omit authentic Gospel miracles while including apocryphal ones; but the point is not important. Tripoli xxv-xlvi. Q. iii.31, 32, 40-44; xix.16-34; xxi.91 and lxvi.12; iii.48; v.50 and lvii.27; ii.254; iv.154-6; xliii.57; lxi.14; v.112-5. Tripoli was certainly putting before Christian readers the view that Islam inclined to Christianity; whether he was also trying to put the same view before Muslims is arguable, since he wrote in Latin, but he undoubtedly wanted Christians to understand that this was his aim. Cf. the impression gained by Mandeville whose account is dependent on, among other sources, this of Tripoli's.

19. Fid. xiv; Q. iii.37, 40-43, part 44, 52.

20. Loc. cit. The verses of Q. quoted are iv.155-6 and 169-70. Ketton xi, Bibl. p. 37 lines 7ff and 34ff. For other late examples cf. Verona xi; Ludolf viii; Higden; Mandeville; Acqui.

21. San Pedro, SSM ɪ.viii.63, 240, 265, CFM ɪɪɪ.1, 2; Bacon, Mor.
Phil. ɪv.2a.iii.5, iv.1, viii.4, 17, 18.

22. Itin. xxvɪɪɪ, xxxɪv; Disp., ɪɪɪ, ɪx, xv, xvɪ, xvɪɪ; Ep. ɪ, ɪɪɪ; for the
anachronism argument, which has often been brought forward by
Christian anti-Qur'anic polemics, see Itin. xxxɪɪɪ; Disp. ɪx; Ep. ɪɪ. Cf.
San Pedro, SSM ɪ.iii.11 and *Contrarietas* (Ricoldo's source) ɪx. The
point was ignored by Ketton's annotator and Ketton himself either
thought he should correct (or just mistranslated) *Family of 'Imrān* as
Family of Joachim.

23. Pennis, v; cf. also Tripoli xʟ.

24. Fitzralph, Arm. 12(13) referring Ketton, Az. xɪɪɪ, Bibl. p. 43,
line 48ff, Q. v.110 22(23); referring Ketton, Az. v, Bibl. p. 23, lines
10ff, 16ff, who here omits parts of Qur'ān wholly as well as making
additions: Q. ɪɪɪ.40, 41, 43; 11(12), commenting on Ketton, Az. v,
Bibl. p. 23, line 14ff, Q. ɪɪɪ.42-44. Bibliander thought the passage ɪɪɪ.40ff
important also, commenting in the margin of his edition of Ketton, 'Hold
this, good Saracen men, and we shall easily restore agreement.' For Lull,
quoted earlier, see Contemp. D., 34.25; 287.10ff, 278.7 (cf. 326.25) and
186.7; Hamar, sig. 32; Lib. de Gent. ɪv.iii.

25. Buenhombre, works, see bibliography; for Jewish *blasphemies* see
Documentos Ineditos . . . de la Corona de Aragon (Bofarull), no. 41
(p. 164) and Peter the Venerable, epistola xxxvɪ ('longeque Saracenis
deteriores Judaei . . .' etc.) (lib. ɪv).

26. MOFPH vol. 1, p. 218; Bzovius, Ann. Eccles. 1263 – xxi; col.
724ff; Gol. ii, p. 302. 'Pure man': it is not always clear whether 'purus
homo' means 'only a man' or 'a man pure in heart', since both meanings,
in this context, are bound always to apply. The account that I have given
here of the mediaeval view of the Islamic Christ omits the special question
of the place of Christ on the Last Day, treated in appendix C.

27. Gibbon (ch. ʟ) asserts what Sale (on whose authority he expressly relies) suggests (note on Q. ɪɪɪ.31) and what Maracci (to whom
equally he refers the reader) naturally does not even suggest; who does,
however, cite authorities that would entitle Gibbon to say that the
Qur'ān witnessed to, but hardly that it lent the Latin Church, the dogma
of the Immaculate Conception.

28. Guibert, loc. cit.; Fitzralph, Arm. 11(12); Lull, Hamar, prol.;
Will. Alv. de leg. xvɪɪɪ/18.ᴘ; *summula*; Paris cit. (ch. ɪɪɪ).

29. *Contrarietas* (x) and *Risālah* (cf. Muir pp. 41 and 110) both
deriving, of course, from the oldest Christian traditions; cf. St John of
Damascus (de haer. and Disp.) and *abjuration*. See also Introduction,
above. Annotator ad Az. ɪɪɪ: *credere* as MS not *colere* as Bibl. p. 224;
Ketton, Az. xɪ, Bibl. p. 37, line 38, Annot. ad Az. xɪ (not in MS, Bibl.
p. 225); Az. xv, Bibl. p. 46, line 34, annot. not in Bibl; Az. xvɪ, Bibl. p.
50, line 13, annot. not in Bibl.; *summula*, loc. cit.; Fitzralph, Arm.
15(16); Mark, Pref. Q., quoting Q. ɪv.169-70; Vitry ɪ.vi (cf. Matt.
xvɪ.17); cf. Viterbo and Paris whose statement is much thinner than
Vitry's here.

30. Alan, op. cit., ɪv.i; cf. ɪɪɪ.iv, v; Alexander, epistola ad soldanum
Iconii in Paris, under yr. 1169 and in Pet. Bles.; Isa. vɪ.3.

31. San Pedro, SSM xv.45, 47; cf. 49; see xv.1-5 for his general approach; 6-54 for the polemic care; 55-83 for a thorough statement of the Christian position.

32. St Thomas, contra Gentiles, iv.xxvi; S.T. ia pars, qu. xxxii art. 1; St Bonaventura, comm. in Sent. lib. i Dist. iii qu. iv, conclusio.

33. Exp. sym. art. primus.

34. *Vita* ('Contemporary Life' ed. Peers); if this life was not actually written by Lull it was inspired by him direct; it is most characteristic of his style.

35. Hamar, ii.ii.1 and Vita, etc. iv and vi. cf. de maj. fine, MS f. 72v ff; and *de confirmatione* quoted below, note 37.

36. Hamar, pars i and ii.ia; de V. sap., dist. i. Lull regretted that Muslims should think Catholics capable of believing that God could suffer hunger and thirst and die: Contemp. D. 65.12, 54; cf. 346.17.

37. Liber de confirmatione legis Christianae etc. ('per quem poterit').

38. De particip., MS f. 205v-206v; de maj. fine, MS f. 72v, 74v; Contemp. D. 72.23; cf. 255.16, 17; 283.23; 186.7; Hamar, ii.iia; signum xx.

39. Ep. Sal. The reference to the Psalter's Trinitarian doctrine is to the threefold mention of the name of God in Ps. lxvi.7-8 (A.V. lxvii. 6-7); this argument is the same as that based on the trisagion by Alexander III.

40. De recuperatione T. S., xv.

41. Tractatus, li, lii; Mandeville, loc. cit.

42. Ricoldo, here much indebted to *Contrarietas* and Risālah (above, n. 29): Disp. ix, cf. Ep. i, ii and iii; Disp. ii, cf. xv; for Q. see ii.81, 254; iv.169; v.109; xix.17 and xxi.91. The Qur'anic references are not always clear; the passage beginning *Dedimus spiritum* appears to be composite (Q. ii.81 or 254 with xxi.91?).

43. Ibn 'Adi: see A. Perier in bibliography. One reason why Buenhombre's 'Abutalib' correspondence cannot be exactly what it purports to be is (as Fr. van den Oudenryn points out) that in it a Muslim uses Trinitarian argument.

44. Gol.

45. Dawson, pp. 193-4.

46. Pennis, op. cit., cap. iii; and Lull, de confirmatione.

47. Rankin, *Polemic* and Denifle, *Quellen*.

48. Annotator, ad Az. i; MS (CCCD 184, right margin, high) and Bibl. p. 224.

49. *Summula*; annotator ad Az. iii; Bibl. p. 224; he also spoke of belief in a carnal Paradise as reviving ancient heresy (*haeresis* may mean *erroneous opinion* in general as well as technically *heresy*); Peter the Venerable, CSS prol. 2-9, referring in some detail to the Manichees, Arians, Macedonians, Sabellians, Donatists, Pelagians, Nestorians and Eutychians, to Jovinian, Helvidius and Vigilantius. His point was to justify himself for writing against Islam by the precedent of earlier writers against other heresies. Guibert (loc. cit.) had already complained of the absence of anti-Islamic polemic.

50. Toletanus, MS p. 306, col. 2ff; Vincent 23.50; Muir, p. 66. The

reference to Old Testament revelation as *human* is curious; Muir has *natural*; the Arabic was *tabi'i*. Guibert, loc. cit. Will. of Tyre, Hist. rerum . . . I.i; Gerald, de princ. instr., loc. cit.; Vitry, I.iv; Coggeshall, Chron. Angl., de abbate Joachim, anno 1195; Salimbene, yr. 1249, MGH vol. 32, p. 440. As Alphandery has pointed out (see bibliog.) the Middle Ages were not free with the name of Antichrist; not, at any rate, to the same extent as the Reformation period. Roquetaillade: *Vade mecum*. Final reference is to Anon. Fior., loc. cit.

51. Humbert, Op. Trip. I.vi passim. *Persecution* in this context means *attack* upon the Church.

52. Ricoldo, Disp., prol. The association of the heretics with the Doctors of the Church was natural and traditional; Peter the Venerable used it and it has a key place in Abbot Joachim's scheme.

53. Ricoldo, ibid., prol., I and XIII.

54. Oliver, Hist. Dam., loc. cit., Peter, CSS prol. 13.

55. Orthodox Catholic doctrine to-day is that a *persona* in the Church of Christ (one who can plead in Church courts) is constituted by baptism. A heretic is a *persona* and an unbaptised person is not; therefore a heretic is baptised. Codex Iuris Canonici, canon 87.

56. CSS, loc. cit. with para. 14; annotator, ad Az. XXVIII (Bibl. XXIX = Q. XIX).

57. Mark, Pref. Q.; annotator, passim; Peñaforte, cited above, chapter IV; Sigebert, loc. cit.; San Pedro, SSM I.vii.12; I.viii.63, 94, 187.

58. A modern Jewish scholar of great distinction, Mr Chaim Rabin, has suggested that the Qumran community survived in an attenuated form in Arabia and that those Medinan Jews who accepted Muhammad were the remnant (or a remnant) of the Qumran sectaries who were in fact expecting a Messiah, as Latin authors say they were. He does not, of course, suggest that the bulk of the Jews, with whom the Prophet quarrelled in Medina, were anything but orthodox. If this view came to be accepted, the learned world would in this respect be returning to something very like the opinion of the Latin Middle Ages.

59. *Summula* and Gerald, loc. cit., Alan, op. cit. IV.i. Other examples: annotator, ad Az. II (Bibl. p. 224); Mark, Pref. Q.; Fidenzio, XIV; Rod., Hist. Arab. III; Paris's additions to St Albans Chr.; Pedro de Alfonso alleged that the Christian influence on Muhammad was Jacobite (by which he probably meant Nestorian; he clearly had no comprehension of the meaning of Jacobite) and the Jewish equally heretical: Samaritan, in fact; this suggests loyalty to his former co-religionists. Varagine, following him, noted that both Jacobite and Nestorian had been suggested (op. cit.). Guido Terrena, loc. cit., 2, 6, for Islamic 'judaising'.

60. Other examples of this use of *perfidia*: see Will. Alv., *de fide*, praefatio; Rod. Hist. Arab. I; Sermon attributed to Fulcher in Ch. Kohler (see bibliog.); in Ric., Disp. XIII, we find *perfidia antichristi*; another word used in the same sense, of a false religion, is *credulitas*: cf. *Liber Nicholay*.

61. Alan, op. cit. *Paganus* was used thoughtlessly, just as *hereticus* was, by authors not actually needing to distinguish at the moment of writing; in such cases it really means 'neither a Christian nor a Jew'.

Alan's thought may be clarified by his final prayer that the heretics should leave their deformed dogmas and opinions, the Jews their carnal observances, the 'pagans' their superstitious opinions; this seems to place Islam mid-way, with the faults of each, both superstitious and erroneous. St Bernard regularly said 'paganus'. For Fitzralph and Pennis, see bibliography.

62. The pseudonymous epistles of the Rabbi Samuel, translated by Alfonso Buenhombre: see bibliography.

63. See chapter IV above, references at note 18. See also Cohn, *Millennium*. For iconographical association, see Bulard, *Scorpion*.

64. See note 25, this chapter, above, also section 2.

65. Will. Alv. de leg., xx/19.s, т, uff.

66. Peter the Venerable, CSS 1.8; Humbert, de pred. S.C., xii; Martí, Pugio Fidei, i.iii; Lull, Doctrina Pueril 'de les III ligs'. The three chapters in this work which precede that on Islam are on the *Ley de natura*, the *Ley vella* and the *Ley nova*; it is followed by that on pagans, *de gentils*. (Capp. 68-72.) Thus there are actually three Laws, Jewish, Christian, Islamic, but the context is widened by two factors: there was a Law of innocence which is lost, and there are unfortunates living without a law at all. For the 'three impostors' theme (this legend has many forms) see M. T. d'Alverny, *Deux Traductions* . . . For the three-fold grouping see also G. Paris, *Légende* . . .

67. Ep. Sal.

68. Will. Alv., *de fide*, iii; Humbert, Op. Trip. i.vi; cf. the same author's earlier classification into rebels (who hear but do not obey the Church and who kill the body), heretics (who neither hear nor obey and kill the soul) and Muslims (who neither hear nor obey, but kill body and soul): de pred. S.C. viii; Martí, Pugio Fidei, loc. cit.; Fitzralph, Arm. 8(9); Ricoldo, libellus ad nationes orient., the order of remoteness from the truth was also the reverse order of convertibility, which surely exaggerates the ease of converting Muslims; Bacon, Mor. Phil. iv.2a.v and iv.1a.ii; Lull: Lib. de gent. esp. prologue and conclusion; Lib. Tart., passim; cf. D.P. and Lib. de V. sapient., prol. In the lib. de S. S., Latin and Greek compete for the soul of a Muslim self-converted to the Christian faith; cf. also Disp. Fidelis et Infidelis. For Lull's oecumenical and political thought see e.g. de recup. T.S. (in Atiya) and HLF (refer bibliography). Islam was rarely related to the errors of the ancients. Paris remarked on its 'laxity' in the words *in eo Epicurus*; Martí, classifying Islam with the other Laws explicitly distinguished it from the 'lawless' Epicureans, Naturals and Philosophers (*lawless*: i.e. without revelation); this is more representative; mediaevals certainly always thought of Islam with the revelations. Cf. also Holcot (Appendix F).

69. Will. of Adam: de modo, iv; Humbert, Op. Trip, i.ii.

70. Inferno, xxviii, line 35; Benvenuto's commentary.

CHAPTER VII. *The relation between Islam and Christianity: Religious practices*

1. SSM i.iv.26; cf. CFM v.4ff.

2. Ricoldo, Disp. x.

3. Itin., xxi, xxii, xxvii, xxix. Perhaps Ricoldo's most sober estimate of the virtues of Islam is that found in his *libellus ad nationes orientales*, where he said that Islamic religion contains *multa utilia*. Elsewhere he said that the Jews have a Law but no understanding and no works; the Muslims have works, but no Law or understanding; Christians have a Law and understanding, but no works (Ep. ii). In another mood he imputed to Muslims the hypocrisy of pretended virtue calculated to deceive the unwary. (Disp., prol.) He was never so generous as in the *Itinerarium* and was always least generous when most literary. For his comments on the Islamic scholarly world, cf. Tritton, *Materials*.
The Biblical reference is Isaias xxiii.4. The *Liber Nicholay* says that the Prophet required the Muslims to be literate, in order to read and understand their law. Whether the author (whose presuppositions are obscure) finds this admirable or otherwise, I cannot say; there is no indication of satiric intent.

4. Vita, iv.7.

5. Dial. iv.xv. 'Consider how loose . . .' The word I have translated *loose* is *rotundus*. I think that the point is to contrast a loose robe with the waisted garment of the Christians who *stringerent et cultellarent*. Mandeville, op. cit. A slightly different story of Muslim reproof of Christians is that of thirty Dominicans before the sultan in Cairo. Vitodurani, Gol. ii, p. 145.

6. lxxxviii. Cf. the comparison of Italy and Syria in the Vita S. Francisci versificata, Gol. i, p. 23.

7. Higden (loc. cit.) who commented with propriety in defence of the Rule, which was his own.

8. Quid. Angl.; I Cor. iv.14.

9. Gaston Paris published and discussed a highly unfavourable legend of Saladin that began to develop, and was reversed after the fall of Jerusalem and its conqueror's generous treatment of the Christian population; they had no right to expect any fate other than that of the Muslim citizens of 1099, or that which the Christians would later have at Acre (in 1291) and elsewhere. (See bibliography under Paris.)

10. Gilles de Corbeil, *Ierapigra ad purgandos prelatos*, quoted by Paris.

11. Busone (ed. Nott, p. 352). The resemblance is not exceedingly close, but it is perhaps rather closer to Ketton's Qur'ān than to the original revelation. The epithets quoted read in the Italian text, *piu umile e piu misericordioso e piu giusto . . . e piu saggio*. *Umile*, in conjunction with *misericordioso*, may just conceivably represent *ar-Raḥmān*, in the basmala. The phrases would be even more curious if they were not to be explained as a distant echo of Qur'anic language. The general problem is discussed by Paris, op. cit.

12. Cf. the prophecy of Joachim, which almost does this (Salimbene, yr. 1249).

13. Yr. 1213. As told, the episode would follow the Muslim defeat at Las Navas de Tolosa, and just precede an-Nāṣir's death.

14. *Consummatus* is a good translation. (Ep. Sal.) Cf. the French lawyer's story that Ṣalāḥ ad-Dīn had publicly expressed his contempt for

the Templars, as given to sodomy, and as bad Christians. (Ref. chapter V, note 28.)

15. XLVIII. The phraseology of classical Rome is the only unconvincing part of this passage. For mamlūk favour to the monks of Mount Sinai, see n. 204 below. 'He protects'; *mandat ad sibi subiectos christianos* – ? (Pruetz and the Vatican and Cambridge manuscripts agree.)

16. Verona, op. cit., IX; Higden, loc. cit.; Mark, Pref. Q. A possible example of the distant penetration of the fame of real Muslim virtues is the hospitality offered by the Sowdan of Surrye in the Man of Law's Tale.

17. Op. cit., I.vi. The actual facts about the Qubbat as-Ṣakhra were known to some writers, but ignored, at least, by most. William of Tyre gave an admirably clear statement of the erection of the Dome of the Rock, the designation of funds and the convocation of craftsmen, and also of the ornamentation and the inscription in mosaic which dated it to the early days of Islam (op. cit. I.ii). Sigebert spoke with some legendary detail of the building by (as he supposed) 'Umar (ibn al-Khaṭṭāb). (See under yr. 644; cf. Marino, op. cit., III.i.) It was in spite of this knowledge that Christians persisted in regarding the Dome of the Rock as a Christian shrine. More ignorant writers believed a story that there was an idol of Muhammad in the shrine, and that it was for this reason that Christians were excluded from it; this exclusion was a cause of bitterness (cf. Oliver, Ep. Sal.); and we have seen above that it was one of Frederick II's crimes to have agreed that Muslims who were in full control of it might have the use of it. For the idol, see appendix A.

18. Hist. Dam.

19. St Albans Chr., yr. 1204. In our own day superstitious Muslims are alleged to resort to the shrine of St Teresa of Lisieux in Cairo; and also the tomb of the Maronite Sharbel, at Anaya in Lebanon. Actions that would be normal for a Christian in this connection must be superstitious for a Muslim. Cf. Hasluck, ch. VI and Lane, Manners, ch. X (Everyman ed., p. 241): see bibliography.

20. MOFPH, vol. i, p. 296.

21. Caesarius, x.xliii; Vitry, I.vi.

22. Tripoli, XXI; Ludolf, loc. cit.; Angelo da Spoleto, Gol. iii.

23. Annotator, on Ketton, ad Az. 1, in Bibl. p. 224, col. 2; MS. CCCD 184, p. 50, high on right margin; SEL. Sup. 31, foot of margin at left, f. Alan, IV.12. Simon Sim., loc. cit.

24. Alan, loc. cit.; Oliver, Ep. Sal.; Martí, Exp. Sym., primus art.; SSM I.xiv (titulo de las imagines); Peñaforte, MOFPH, vol. I, app.; Marignolli in Gol. iv, p. 291 (Lull also had a certain sympathy for suspicion of images, cf. Blanquerna, LXXXIV); Galvano de Levanto, de recup. T. S., ROL, vol. vi, 1898.

25. For Fidenzio, see above, p. 111; Verona, op. cit., XI.

26. Pedro de Alfonso, Dial., loc. cit. (It is not clear in the context whether the author is referring to foods only or to all objects generally. In either case he is speaking of the basmala.) Mark of Toledo: '*Aqīdah* (For the phrase, (*Deus*) *oretur pro Mafometo* and Ricoldo's *Deus oret*, see above, p. 338 n50. Ricoldo, Itin. XXVI.)

27. Mark, Pref. Q.; RF, de Arm. 18:10/11; Ket., Az. v, Bibl. p. 21 lines 26-27; Q. iii.1 (for *vivus* the printed text of Fitzralph has *unus*, which, though mistaken, suggests that the copyist or printer had a sound idea of Islamic theology; 'clement' =*pius*); the fātiḥah is Q. i, and there were Mozarab alternatives to Ketton's version, cf. Mark's Q. and alternatives in Ketton's MS, below, n. 36; cf. also d'Alverny, *Deux Traductions*; for Ṣalāḥ ad-Dīn's letter see for instance St Albans Chr., yr. 1188; Tripoli, op. cit. viii; Acqui, op. cit.; Verona, op. cit., xi. For the basmala, see chapter I above, note 93.

28. Ricoldo, Itin. xxvi; Lull, Blanquerna, 88.

29. San Pedro, SSM, i.viii.198; cf. Ricoldo, Itin. xxx, Disp., VIII, IX, XII, Tripoli, VIII.

30. Direct speech: *Non est alius Deus nisi solus Deus et Mahometus servus et eiusdem propheta; Non est Deus praeter unum* (paraphrases); indirect: *Deum esse tantummodo . . .; Deum qui nullum aequalem vel similem habeat . . .; unum Deum sine compari . . .; nil aliud posse nisi Deus . . .* (all paraphrases). (*Vita*, San Pedro, SSM i.viii.75; Pedro de Alfonso, loc. cit.; Leg. Aur., loc. cit.; Benevenuto and FR de Arm., loc. cit., respectively.)

31. [Note deleted in proof.]

32. Mandeville, in a passage distinct from those that he took from Tripoli, spoke of the use of the Shahādah to receive a convert into Islam (loc. cit.).

33. Roderick, Hist. Arab., iii; Mark, Pref. Q. The bare contrast between adhān and bells has been a commonplace of travellers' reportage, but was rare in the Middle Ages. The anonymous English pilgrim said that 'five or six fellows' (*ribaldi*) made the call 'to the three corners of the world, leaving out the east'; this was 'in place of bells'. The adhān actually is made facing the Qiblah, that is, in the direction of Mecca, the mu'adhdhin turning left and right at the phrase 'come to prayer'. The east would be omitted, therefore, only at a point east of Mecca. It is impossible that this author could have observed the adhān at such a point. (Quid. Ang., loc. cit.)

34. Clemens IV Iacobum reg. Arag. monet . . . in Denifle, Quellen (see bibliography); Clementinarum lib. v, de judaeis et Saracenis, in Con. Vienn.; Vitry, op. cit. i.vi (he said he heard the adhān 'everywhere at night'); Verona xi. The phrase in the *de expugnatione libellus* reads in the text *Halla haucaber, Halla haucaber*. The sound of this transliteration is remarkably effective, not for the Arabic pronounced normally, but for the impression of the phrase called out in the adhān, upon a Christian ear, particularly the lengthening and stressing of the first syllable of akbar. 'Moanings' (mugitus) doubtless expresses mere dislike, based on theological reasons, conjoined with the difficulty of distinguishing the remaining words. Another version of the return of the Qubbat as-Ṣakhrah to Islamic worship said that the 'superstitions of (Muḥammad's) error were proclaimed from the four corners of the Temple with a great cry' (St Albans Chr., yr. 1187). See also above, chapter IV, note 18.

35. Gloss at the place cited. In the text, for mu'adhdhin is *Muetdem*. 'The revelation of your sins' for al-falāh is wrong, but this phrase is not

easily translated, as many different versions attest. In the text *legalip ille Halla* (for *lā ilāha illa Allāhu*) is better than at first sight appears; if *g* and *p* are copyists' errors, it is not far out. 'Victor' is a fiction of the author's; *omnipotens* for *akbar* is not impossible. The final phrases have become transposed, presumably in the memory of the observer.

36. M. T. d'Alverny (loc. cit.) prints the textual and marginal versions of the fātiḥah from the Cluniac corpus, together with Mark's. Bibliander prints the two Cluniac translations (see also the MSS). Peers translates, and refers to, Lull's translation (*Ramon Lull*, p. 91). Ludolf's translation does not seem to have attracted attention (loc. cit.); its beginning and end recall Mark's strongly, but the inaccurate middle is certainly his own. See Bibliander, p. 8, line 34ff. In MS CCCD 184, p. 50, left margin; Seld. Sup. 31, f. 33r (right margin). For the annotations, see Bibl. p. 224, col. 1 (ad Az. 1) and MS CCCD 184 p. 50, top margin and Seld. sup. 31, f. 33r, right margin. These MSS do not have the phrase 'as does our Law from the Lord's prayer'. Lull, lib. de Gent., iv.iv.

37. 'Ghusl is the so-called "major" ritual ablution, which the law ordains for . . . a man who is in a state of major ritual impurity . . . (It) consists in washing the whole body' (*Shorter Encyclopaedia of Islam*). 'The formulation . . . of the intention is indispensable for this and the believer has to be careful that not only is every impurity removed from his body but also that the water moistens every part of his body and his hair' (ibid.) Wuḍū' is the minor ritual ablution which involves washing only certain parts; Shi'is perform it always before ṣalāt, and Sunnis most often, because ritual minor impurities are so easily incurred. It is strange that Pedro, a Jew by upbringing, should have argued that ritual washings are an effeminacy properly belonging to the worship of Venus and therefore appropriately prescribed by Muhammad. His statement was followed by the Legenda Aurea (loc. cit.) and constituted the opening passage of the extracts edited by the Anon. Min., who was much interested in ritual and law. The annotator's words are: et praecepta quadam stulta, sicut post coitum et egestionem antequam orent lavent culum et cetera verenda (ad Az. 9, Bibl. pp. 224-5).

38. Mark, Pref. Q.; Sim. and *Lib. Nic.* stated (erroneously) that purity was required to enter a mosque; they should have said, for ritual worship. Lull's description of washing is correct for wuḍū', except for his vague reference to 'other members of the body'; it suggests slightly confused personal observation, rather than a paper acquaintance with the requirements of Islamic law. Ricoldo said that the *Hanefa* had to wash in fifteen hundred *rotuli* of water, because they were more perfect than other Muslims. It is not clear what he means by *Hanefa*: this is not Hanafite doctrine; *ḥunafā'* is apparently not relevant, and neither does the fact that *ḥanīfī* was the original name of the Muslims seem to be relevant. He expounded in some detail: 'digitum in anum infigit, et si sentit aliquid fetoris, non est aptus ut oret', etc. *Rotulus* may here represent the Arabic *ratl*, which is not however a liquid, but a solid measure. The whole passage must represent a misunderstanding.

39. Alan of Lille, op. cit., iv.9, 10. He thought it necessary to show

that there can be no remission of sin in water except by invocation of the Trinity, which is essential to the form of baptism; also that such remission could never be repeated (an argument used by others after him); that the baptism of John, which was not Christian baptism, was not for the remission of sins, and so on. None of this has any real relevance to Islamic religious requirements. See Paris, aliud scriptum; Joinville, LXXXVIII; San Pedro, SSM I.viii.70; Marino, II.iv; Higden, loc. cit.; Acqui, loc. cit. Lull alone spoke of wuḍū' as intended by Islam to *symbolise* the cleansing of the heart from original sin, and though this avoids the assertion that Muslims thought it cleansed from actual sin, its terminology is purely Christian (loc. cit.). In a story of Joinville's, Muslims expect to be absolved by water on their death-beds (loc. cit.). The general theme of Christian authors is well put by Higden (loc. cit.); he specifies the copying of the Christian sacraments.

40. Verona, op. cit., XI. '. . . wherever they are, whether in the mosque, or the field, or on a journey, before the prayer they observe this most shameful instruction which he gave them: for first they wash the hands, then the feet, then the face, and after, virilia sua et membrum genitale, and this they do in the presence of all, and in no other way will they pray, without first performing this enormous washing, which is abominable in nature and every law . . .' Cf. Acqui (loc. cit.) 'lavent genitalia sua, et homines et mulieres'; cf. Pedro de Alfonso, An. Min., Leg. Aur., et al. cited in notes 37 and 39.

41. On the other hand, the *lavabo* of the Roman and Dominican rites (which many of our authors will have used) must have been familiar to all writers. Ricoldo in the *Disputatio* was unoriginal; it was unreasonable to wash the body rather than the heart; his details were correct, except for repetition of the genitalia element.

42. Pedro, loc. cit., Acqui and Verona, loc. cit.; Marino also. *Vita*: five prayers daily.

43. In the text, *Zalarazobh*. The comment in the Clementinae reads 'sacerdotes eorum Zabazala vulgariter nuncupati . . . nomen Mahometi . . . alta voce invocant'. *In darkness* = ṣalāt al-'isha', at nightfall. The fourth prayer, counting Christian fashion, is the first, Muslim fashion, or sunset prayer = *in completorio* – 'quae resonet in coenam'.

44. 'Kissing': the forehead, not the mouth, touches the earth. The raising of hands and eyes to Heaven is a purely Christian interpretation given to the ritual by the Christian observer; it is not Islamic. For the number of the times of prayer, see also the kitāb al-mi'rāj, Muhammad's bargaining with God to reduce the number to five; this theme was popular with Spanish authors. Cerulli, *Liber Scalae*, cap. L (pp. 265, 302); cf. Rod., Hist. Arab., v; San Pedro, SSM I.viii.76ff and CFM I.2, 3 and v.1ff. Annotator, Ketton, Bibliander p. 224 and MSS, cited; also 'in orationibus discumbendum est', ad Az. 26 (=Bibl. 27, p. 225).

45. Pref. Q.

46. Op. cit. I.vi. The *khutba* is the address or sermon which is given during the Friday prayer. The *adhān* is the call to prayer made from the minaret. The *iqāmah* is the repetition of the call made within the mosque at the beginning of the prayer. Vitry's reference to congregational

responses suggests the responses made during the khuṭba, but it is not likely to spring from personal observation in any case.

47. Disp. x; cf. Pennis, ix. For *khatīb*: *magister Saracenorum*. Varagine and Benvenuto (loc. cit.) are not likely themselves to have heard the adhān.

48. The opportunity to quote a set speech invented by the author was often taken; this applied to such a writer as Mark (pref. Q.) and also to the romancers (e.g. Waltherius); it may not really denote the idea of actual Muslim assembly, if it is only a literary fiction. Cf. Acqui; and San Pedro, SSM ɪ.i.27 and viii.219.

49. Will. Alv. de leg., xx/19.x; Leg. Aur., San Pedro SSM ɪ.viii.65; Higden (an important passage); Ludolf; Pennis, ɪ; cf. Vitry, loc. cit, Lull, Hamar, sig. 2. Pisan text (Mancini).

50. These arguments are Islamic in origin. For Lull, see Cont. D., 257, and Hamar, sig. 2; for Verona, see x and xɪ.

51. Cf. Vitry, op. cit. ɪ.vi; Leg. Aur., Ludolf, Higden Acqui, and Pennis, loc. cit.

52. San Pedro, SSM ɪ.viii.65; Lull, Hamar, loc. cit., Verona, loc. cit. '. . . velut canes ad vomitum ad opera servilia . . .'

53. See above, chapter IV, section 2, pp. 121-2, and note 28.

54. San Pedro, SSM ɪ.viii.69; Pennis, ɪ; other authors loc. cit.

55. Quid. Ang., loc. cit.; Mark, Pref. Q.; San Pedro, SSM ɪ.iv.1; Lull, Blanquerna, xcɪɪɪ, cf. ʟxxxvɪɪɪ; the dervish: refer chapter VI, note 26 (I follow MOFPH, not Bzovius, where they diverge); Ricoldo, Itin. xxɪv and xxvɪ.

56. Rod., Hist. Arab. ɪɪ and Cron. de Esp. cxɪ was right in associating Kaʿbah and qiblah though mistaken in other points. For statements about the qiblah see Viterbo, Paris (Gregorian Report), Higden; Quid. Ang.; Acqui; Verona, x, xɪ; Benvenuto; San Pedro SSM ɪ.viii.69; Pennis, ɪ; Leg. Aur., Vitry ɪ.vi; except where otherwise stated, all in places cited. Cerulli bases an argument that Viterbo's source was Syrian on his reference to the qiblah as south; but there was too much copying for this to be a sound argument; moreover, it was customary to say south in Egypt, not very accurately (cf. Lane, *Manners*). San Pedro, in Spain, also said south, which obviously springs not from observation but from copying a literary source. For the Jewish comparison see Vitry, Leg. Aur., San Pedro and Benvenuto, in places cited. Strictly the places where a Muslim (who faces Mecca) faces south and at the same time a Jew (who faces Jerusalem) faces west, are few; the fief of Oultrejourdain would logically be the only such place ever in Latin Christian possession.

57. Galvano de Levanto, de recup. T.S., ROL, vol. vi, 1898. Mark, Pref. Q.; Ketton, for sūrah divisions, Bibl. pp. 13-49 (azoara xvɪ = sūrah vɪ). The MSS diverge at azoara xvɪɪ; MSS xvɪɪ = Bibl. xvɪɪ + xvɪɪɪ; xvɪɪɪ = xɪx, etc. Mark divided the second sūrah (but only this one sūrah) in the same way. Thus, Ketton, Az. ɪɪɪ = Mark, cap. ɪɪ (Mark does not, Ketton does, count the fātiḥah) = Q. ɪɪ.199. San Pedro, SSM ɪ.ii.2 and Lull, Lib. Tart. de T. et S.

58. Blanquerna, LXXI; Simon, loc. cit. and cf. *Lib. Nic.*; Ricoldo, Itin. xxɪɪɪ; cf. Disp. xɪɪɪ; Pennis, ɪɪ.

59. The Islamic precept is not, as Pedro thought, to make the ḥajj annually, but once in a lifetime; the confusion arose because the ḥajj occurs annually. For the foundation of the Ka'bah see SEI; Abraham is sometimes the founder, not the restorer. There is an Islamic belief that the Stone was originally white, but turned black because of sin committed during the pagan period. See Pedro de Alfonso, loc. cit., An. Min., Higden (a corrupt form of the same version), Pennis, xi, Leg. Aur. (pointing out that Pedro, as 'Judaeus conversus', would be an authority on the children of Lot), Marino, ii.iv. Pedro's interests seem to run parallel to those of modern critics who have speculated about the solar festival from which they suppose the ḥajj to derive. It might be profitable to compare in some detail the forms taken by rationalism in the mediaeval and modern periods. The questions of the Black Stone and of stories of an idol in the Ka'bah are discussed by M. T. d'Alverny in *Marc* and by Grégoire (see bibliography for these important references).

60. San Pedro, SSM i.viii.72; Risālah, Tolet. MS p. 316, col. 1ff; Vincent, 23.60; cf. Muir, p. 92ff.

61. The account in the *Contrarietas* (cap. xi) claims to be an eye-witness one. It is not at all clear and does not sound authentic. It had little influence and was ignored by Ricoldo. The general failure to realise that the Muslim year is lunar, and, being shorter, moves back through the solar year, made all confusion worse.

62. Annotator on Ketton, ad Az. 32, Bibl. p. 225; ad Az. 25; Clementinae lib. v, loc. cit.; Humbert, de pred. S.C. xiv; Mark, loc. cit. Acqui (loc. cit.) said that 'this House was made by God for love of Muhammad'; this suggests a sympathetic, but is not an Islamic, interpretation.

63. Lull, Hamar, sig. 14; 'Incidental reference': e.g. Janer xv and Fr. Pasquale in Gol. iv. Verona (x) calculated *forty* days from the end of the *fast*, so that he seems to confuse 'Īd al adhhā' with 'Id al-Fiṭr; the latter ends the Ramaḍān fast, and the former follows two months and ten days later; but possibly the muddle arises out of the date of Muḥarram – 10th Muḥarram falling thirty days after 10th Dhu al-Hijjah. The *Vita* distinguishes the two feasts, quite normally, as major and minor. The *Liber Nicholay* speaks of a thirty-day fast, and a feast when the March moon wanes. Either this confuses the lunar and solar calendars, in accordance with a particular year noted by the author of the statement, when Ramaḍān fell in March; or it derives from some popular solar festival of the Spring equinox, confused with 'Īd al-Fiṭr (observed in a year when they coincided), such as the Persian Nawrūz. The *Liber* contains a long account with several obscure features.

64. Vitry was more interested in Islamic pilgrimage to the 'Temple of the Lord' than to Mecca; he thought the Prophet's tomb to be there and to be the object of pilgrimage (i.vi). Inn. missum: report from the patriarch Haymar, in Paris, loc. cit. In the same work is a reference to the Prophet's bones in Mecca, which was often copied; see AOL, Testimonia Minora . . .

65. Roderick, Hist. Arab., iii; Pennis, xi; Guido Terrena, 16, 17, 18. 'Mahomet's tomb' could be used as late as the nineteenth century as a atural literary metaphor. Cf. Ziolecki, op. cit. (see bibliography).

Simon, Ludolf, Verona, loc. cit. The *Liber Nicholay* which, despite its absurd historical framework, contains authentic information about practices, confuses Baghdad, which it recognises as the seat of the Caliphate, with Mecca, and Mecca, of course, with Medina.

66. Vitry, ɪ.vi; Guido Terrena, 15; San Pedro, SSM ɪ.viii.71 and ɪ.ii.2; Lull, Hamar, sig. 36.

67. Viterbo and Paris, i.e. their common original, says that coition was taken to be meritorious in Ramaḍān; but actually marital coition follows exactly the same rules as eating (forbidden during the fast but permitted after sunset). The *Contrarietas* has a perversion of the Qur'anic text here. For 'it is *lawful* for you . . . to go unto your *wives*' it has 'estote *soliciti* ut impregnetis *mulieres*' (Q. ɪɪ.183; *Cont.* ɪx). Fidenzio, xvɪ; Marino, ɪɪɪ.iv; Verona, x, xɪ (he thought Ramaḍān a solar date like Easter).

68. Hist. Arab., ɪɪɪ; Cron. de Esp. cxɪv: Mark, op. cit., Varagine, An. Min., Pedro De Alfonso, Pennis, xɪ: information from Pedro was exceptionally accurate and included the fact that day-time was recognised from the moment when a black and a white thread could be distinguished; the same information in Annotator, Ketton, references in note 69; Ricoldo, Disp. xvɪɪ. Acqui, not quoted here, spoke of Muslims' 'many Lents'; he may refer to voluntary fasts, but it is difficult to see what caused this error.

69. Peter the Venerable, CSS ɪ. 16 Annotator, ad Az. ɪɪ (p. 60, f. 38v) and ad Az. xvɪ (p. 104) (not in Bibliander).

70. Annot. ad Az. ɪɪ; Bibl. p. 224; MSS p. 51 (margin at foot, left) and f. 33r, right margin at top. Q. ɪɪ.172; Ketton ɪɪ, Bibl. p. 15, lines 4-11. Fitzralph, as so often, bridges the beginning and end of my period, because his knowledge was confined to the Cluniac text. He cites the whole Ketton passage quoted by me but comments only on the phrase 'and the prophets', his sole interest in it being the 'endorsement' of Scripture.

71. Vitry, loc. cit.; Humbert, Op. Trip. ɪ.vi; Acqui: Muhammad taught Muslims to make 'many and great alms, for the love of God and of His friend Muhammad'. The sultan and the slave: MOFPH, vol. II, Fasc. 1, Cron. O.P., 112.28, p. 77.

72. Mark, loc. cit., Ricoldo, Itin. xxv.

73. Hamar, sig. 35.

74. Op. Trip. ɪ.xviii; Lull, Hamar, sigg. 33, 34; sig. 3; cf. 15, 38.

75. *Fuqahā'*, singular, *faqīh*; Clementinae, loc. cit.; See Ricoldo, Disp. xɪɪɪ, cf. Pennis, ɪɪ (MS *el fochaha*). 'Men learned in the law', cf. Oliver, Hist. Dam., loc. cit., St Albans Chr., yr. 1118; Will. Alv. de leg. xvɪɪɪ/18ʀ; Viterbo (Cerulli, p. 424); Paris, loc. cit.; Ricoldo, Itin. xxxɪv; Disp. x; San Pedro, SSM ɪ.viii.242; Lull, Hamar, prol.; de V. sapientibus, prol.; lib. Tart., 1.2; vita, 4.6; Pennis xɪ. This is not an exhaustive list of authors who used the phrase, or of examples of its use in single authors. *Fuqarā'*, *faqīr*. In Verona, *Facher*, pl. *facheri*; in Tripoli *focara* (Vat. MS) or *fecora* (Cambridge MS) or *focora* (Prutz) (cap. xxɪ). *Contrarietas* defined *El foquera* as *perfecti* (vɪɪɪ). Ricoldo used *religiosi* to cover a variety of different functions. He used it of *sapientes* teaching in the schools, whom he much admired, and of eccentrics described in this

text (Itin. xxi). It was to *Focarii* that he owed the sad relic of a pierced and bloodstained Dominican habit brought from 'Akka. Cf. Itin. xxxvi. The phenomena may be associated in some turuq with the dhikr. Possibly here Rifā'īyah? Ludolf, op. cit. The account in Giovanni d'Andrea's commentary on the Clementine constitutions contrasted 'secular' *foqui* with 'religious' *alhages*. The latter are, obviously, ḥajjis – isti semel accedunt ad sepulchrum Machometi – but the author was mistaken in thinking them to be unmarried, and to have relinquished the world in the same sense as Christian monks have done; just as he was about the purpose of the pilgrimage.

76. Oliver, Hist. Reg.; Bacon (Bridges edition of Opus Major, vol. i, p. 266, Pars 4ta, Mathematicae in Divinis utilitas); Paris, Lib. Additamentorum, vi, p. 348; *Liber Nicholay*; cf. all the literature chronicling the early days of Islam, passim, esp. Haymar's report to Innocent III.

77. e.g., Lull, in vita, 6: Pasquale, Gol., loc. cit. and Gol. ii, p. 66 and p. 70. Chron. xxiv Gen. cf. Gol. iv, Passio fr. Livini Gallici. Lull, Hamar, prol. The *Liber Nicholay* is clear about the different functions of caliph and sultan.

78. Q. ix.31; Ricoldo, Disp. ix; Pennis, vii; Verona, xi.

79. On circumcision see Guibert, loc. cit.; Peter the Venerable, CSS 2.27; Itinerarium Regis Ricardi, i.iii; Vitry, i.vi; Paris, aliud scriptum; Leg. Aur.; Ricoldo, Disp. xvii; Lull, Hamar, sig. 11; Pennis, vii; Higden, Acqui, Ludolf, loc. cit. On rules of eating, see *reprobatio*, v and viii (refers Bu. 52.53; cf. also re fly in food, *reprobatio*, loc. cit. and Bu. 76.58); see also Wensinck, Handbook, under 'Eating'. For prohibitions of pig flesh and wine drinking, see Pedro de Alfonso, loc. cit., Vitry, loc. cit.: Mark, cit.; Will. Alv. de universo, ii.xxxvii; Leg. Aur.; An. Min.; Ricoldo Disp. xvii; Marino ii.iv, Verona xi; Acqui; Higden; Ludolf; Lull, Hamar, sig. 26. This is not an exhaustive list. For Tripoli's story to explain the prohibition of drinking wine, see his cap. iii. For the legend of Noe and the prohibition of swine's flesh, see the *de doctrina Machometi* (Bibl. p. 197); Paris, al. scr.; Ricoldo, Disp. ix; Pennis xi. For another explanation, see Gerald, loc. cit, who relates it to Muhammad's supposed death by swine.

80. Chron. xxiv Gen., loc. cit. For the point about sacraments, see *summula*; CSS prol.; Lull, Hamar, sigg. 11-17; Ricoldo, Disp. i; Pennis v. Ricoldo connected the absence of sacraments with the denial of the Crucifixion whence the sacraments derive their efficacy. (Bart. Pic's translation has *mysteria* for Latin original *sacramenta ecclesiae*.) See also *Lib. Nic.*, reference above, p. 210. The sentence, 'tantummodo invocetur nomen tuum super nos, aufer opprobrium nostrum' may imply the idea of a vain sacrament.

CHAPTER VIII. *Polemic method and the judgement of fact*

1. Anastasius Bibliothecarius Romanus, translating the account in Theophanes' Chronographica.

2. Monneret de Villard asserted oriental authorship (in *Lo studio*) and was correct by M. T. d'Alverny (*Deux traductions*). This statement,

as she points out, arises in a misunderstanding of Mandonnet's; but Mandonnet did not know what to expect and what not to expect of an oriental Christian author, and we must assume that Monneret de Villard did not pay attention to the issue. He has now been followed in his error by Sweetman.

3. See M. T. d'Alverny, loc. cit.

4. SSM ɪ.ii.13; cf. also ɪ.iii.15, where he stresses that 'al-Kindi' was learned in Christian as well as in Muslim sources.

5. Will. Alv. de leg., xvɪɪɪ/18.ʀ/s; Vincent 23.40.

6. The common source of Vitry with Viterbo and the report to Gregory in Paris is obvious even on a casual reading; the variations between Viterbo and Paris are almost insignificant. Paris explains that the text was sent as a report, and it must therefore derive from a manuscript held in the East; therefore, probably, Viterbo's source is some closely related form, deriving from the Latin states. The 'divided moon' miracle does not appear in the Risālah, but does in Viterbo, Paris and Vitry; the relation between the original of these three and the Risālah is obscure, but it is interesting to note that the author of the *reprobatio* quotes the authority of al-Kindi for the story, and he may therefore have been attributing the source of the three accounts (equating this with the Risālah) to the authorship of Kindi. His reference is another link between these related sources. (Vitry: ɪ.vii.) For the 'divided moon' miracle, see chapter IX, note 12. For Sergius, see Muir's *Kindy*, p. 70.

7. Cf. Paris introducing his *aliud scriptum*, and Vincent's remarks loc. cit.

8. It has also to be remembered that what Vincent says of Islam takes its relatively insignificant place in a vast compilation, the purpose of which was primarily didactic.

9. Varagine and Higden, loc. cit.; Humbert, de pred. S.C., capp. 29-43; for Vitry, see also appendix A. The author of the *Vita* set out explicitly to correct error about Muhammad. If by modern standards he showed no discrimination in judging his authorities, he may well have sought what he thought authentic sources.

10. The composite account here referred to is closely related to the account in the Legenda Aurea; a study of MSS is needed to determine this relation. B.M. Royal 13.E.IX and Cambridge Dd.1.17; Gonville and Caius 162/83. Itinerarium of Ricoldo in Laurent (see bibliography); Pennis, loc. cit. In a later period the parts of Ricoldo's Itinerarium which relate to Islam in general were extracted to form a tractate of purely theological interest, and this was used (together with his Disputatio, incomplete, and with part of the Cluniac corpus) in a manuscript collection inspired by the fall of Constantinople. (Paris, Bib. nat. lat. 6225, ff. 154-61.)

11. See M. T. d'Alverny, *Deux traductions*, for a full discussion of the manuscripts and their history.

12. See also the same author's *Marc de Tolède*, together with the works of Cerulli and Munoz (see bibliography).

13. Again consult d'Alverny. See also MSS used (bibliography below).

14. SSM I.i.29; I.ii passim, esp. 1, 13, 20ff, 23, 25; I.iv.4; I.vi.4; I.vii.9-14; I.viii.235-7, 239. The Islamic sources are ibn Hishām's version (presumably) of ibn Isḥāq and the *Liber Scalae*. San Pedro's second list contains one episode which is not in the first and is of special interest, that is 'Ā'ishah's statement that she and the other wives poured water over the Prophet in his last illness; this 'supported' the Christian story that he sought baptism on his death-bed. Baḥīrā appears as *Bayra*.

15. Tractatus I-III; cf. for events after death of Muhammad, ibid., cap. XXV.

16. 'Very books of Muhammad' – *libri istius*. The death of Muhammad – cap. IX. The giving of detailed references to Muslim authors does suggest an intention to quote *to Muslims*.

17. The MS of Tripoli, Gonville and Caius, referred to above, attributes it to Ricoldo; the adapted version of the *reprobatio* in the Bib. nat. attributes that to Ricoldo also. In the latter case the manuscript also contains the rare Latin original of the Disputatio, which really is Ricoldo's. Ricoldo knew the Dominican House at 'Akka, and although the date of Tripoli's death is unknown, he must have been either alive or remembered, and in the latter case, remembered well; and it is not likely that there was no copy of his work in the Library or that Ricoldo did not read it. See M. T. d'Alverny again. She also suggests that the attribution of the *reprobatio* to Ricoldo may indicate that this was his copy. See also Monneret de Villard, *Ricoldo*, for the relation with Tripoli. It is also quite possible that, since Ricoldo knew the *Contrarietas*, he also knew other translations of Mark's; if so, he ignored these also.

18. For examples of Ricoldo's preference for poor information in certain cases, see my chapter I, and also chapter II for the attack on the Qur'ān itself, above.

19. See appendix A, note 12; Verona: see chapter VII, under ṣalāt; Paris Additamenta, No. 183 (A.D. 1257) for the St Albans story; Preceptor: Guy de Basainville. Another example of the tyranny of a literary source is the persistence of the statement that the qiblah is south (see chapter VII, note 56).

20. Pennis, cap. I for the poor life of Muhammad; v for the arrangement of 'true things'. Pennis was interested in the Near East as well as specifically in Islam but there is no reason to think that he had personal knowledge of either. Cf. Kohler, 'Le libellus' etc.

21. Cf. chapter III, passim.

22. Cf. chapter V, sections 2, 5 and 7.

23. The evidence relating to chiliasm is assembled and discussed by N. Cohn, *Pursuit*.

24. S. Raymundi summa sac. canonum, lib. I, tit. IV para. II. Christian witnesses were always to be preferred to Jews and Muslims. Similarly, in Islam, Christians might not witness before the *qāḍī*, i.e. he could not witness in a case involving a Muslim.

CHAPTER IX.　*The establishment of communal opinion*

1. Galbraith, *Roger Wendover and Matthew Paris*.

2. Summa . . . sac. canonum, I.iv (cited chapter IV, note 19 above).

3. The passage 'v' that is common to the *reprobatio* and Martí's *explanatio* set out to establish the authority of Scripture, in order that from thenceforward a Muslim reader would have to accept arguments based on Scripture. In the *reprobatio* there is a further but implicit acceptance of Islamic authorities as necessary in discussion of Islam.

4. The material discussed in these paragraphs was discussed from other points of view in chapters I and II above.

On the general question it is worth noting that in the field of natural science reliance on authorities was criticised explicitly (for example, by Adelard of Bath, *de quaestionibus naturalibus*) and also implicitly by the adoption of experimental methods (cf. Crombie, *Robert Grosseteste*); it may also be said that critical methods were applied to theology and philosophy; but they were never applied to history or to sciences of which the existence was not recognised, such as sociology or comparative religion.

5. Aquinas: contra Gentiles, I.vi; the other points he makes are more obviously dependent on the information he had been given. Risālah: information never quoted, e.g., about the ḥajj, and the parallel made with Hinduism. (See p. 218 above.)

6. CSS I.16; cf. prol. 15ff.

7. The point is well taken by Reland, who in 1705 compared Christian apologetic to Caligula's battle against the sea: 'After the same manner', he said, 'these Writers seem to me to have employ'd their Wit and Parts, not against true Enemys, but fictitious ones, where they were sure of the Victory, since no body was to defend them; and were certain of carrying away . . . the Applause of all those, who are no wiser than themselves, and Rejoice to see the Truth of the Christian Religion so bravely defended against the Turks.

>   Non in tali auxilio, nec defensoribus istis,
>   Tempus egit.

Let us act candidly, lest we become a Jest to our Adversarys.' (*De relig. moham.*, praefatio, IX; I cite the English version of 1712.)

8. It must be admitted that my opinion here does not exactly co-incide with San Pedro's own statements, and at the same time I should be wrong to suggest that he was a liar or anything like it. See the account described in chapter V, note 78, however; a reference to a discussion with learned Muslims never shows unequivocally (*a*) that these were really learned men; and (*b*) that there was real communication and serious discussion. There are many reasons why Christians may have been unable to distinguish under (*a*) or have been deluded under (*b*). As far as the latter is concerned there seems often to have been the aim on the Muslim side to avoid controversy which would be bound to lead to trouble for the Christian concerned, and silence that was really due to kindness may have been mistaken for inability to reply. The proof of this is that we cannot assume that any Muslim would have been silenced by any argument to which there is a fairly obvious answer from a Muslim point of view.

9. Examples in chapter V above; it must also be admitted that not

every use of a sound Islamic authority by the *reprobatio* would have seemed reasonable to a Muslim.

10. See chapter IV, section 2, and VI, section 3, above.

11. Rabbi Moses Nachman debate: chapter VI above; references at note 47. For Lull, see also comments in HLF p. 23ff. Lull at one time thought only a knowledge of Arabic was necessary in order to convert Islam, and that that was easily acquired (*obras rimadas*).

12. This applies particularly to arguments taken by Ricoldo from the *Contrarietas*. An example of the sort of argument from reason that Ricoldo maintained was, or would be, successful is that based on the 'divided moon' supposed miracle of Muhammad. How could the moon be divided, argued Ricoldo; is it a heavy body, that it should fall? And if it fell, how is it that it did not take up a great part of the earth? Or the sea and the waters not become troubled? How could so great a miracle be hid from the world? The *reprobatio* argued similarly; as the moon is greater than the earth, how could it fall on a part of the earth, much less hide in the Prophet's sleeve? And the event could not have happened at all without the whole world seeing, or succeeding generations passing the story down, as happened in the case of the Flood (Itin. XXXIII, *reprob.* VII). It is not usually fair to mock at the outmoded science of a past age; but in the present case it must be said that if some of these arguments now seem particularly ridiculous, their authors were to blame for using 'reason' so lightly and almost irresponsibly. They should have known that reason is no basis to attack faith, and that ridicule is dangerous. There does not, however, seem to be the slightest sign that Muslims heard and understood such arguments as these; if they had Ricoldo would have been bound to mention the sort of reaction they provoked. The *Vita's* reference to the 'divided moon' is interesting.

13. Bacon, Mor. Phil. IV.2a.viii.1; Martí, exp. sym. prol., also *reprob.* XIII. Cf. Aquinas, contra Gentiles, I.i.

14. See chapter II, section 2, above.

15. SSM I.viii.239.

16. Ibid., 148.

17. Op. cit., chapters XV-XXI.

18. Note 11 above. The case of William of Rubruck showed that debates controlled by pagans were feasible. The implications of Tripoli's assertions in the course of his book are difficult to assess. He tells us about ways of explaining Christian doctrine to Muslims that he has found to satisfy them, which implies that he discussed doctrine widely. Moreover (as I have noted above) he claims a large number of converts; so large, that it is difficult for us to accept his claim as it stands. Had the Latin States been victorious we might imagine a number of converts from Islam climbing on to the band-waggon; but exactly the contrary was the case. It is safer to conclude nothing from Tripoli's statements until his background and intentions have been elucidated by future research. With regard to Lull's arguments prepared for the use of the laity (chapter VI above), as we have seen, the laity cannot have found them easy to reproduce and there is no reason to think that anyone ever used them at all. There is no convincing evidence of debates against

Muslims within Islam under anything resembling normal conditions. No doubt Muslims and Christians, when they did live side by side, normally refrained from discussing religion, as happens now; and, as happens now, each side may have retained a number of false ideas of the other in consequence.

19. Adam Marsh, op. cit. IX.
20. Muhammad Asád; see bibliography and chapter X below.
21. Martí, Capistr. Jud., cited by Cerulli, loc. cit., and quoted above, chapter V.

CHAPTER X. *The survival of mediaeval concepts*

1. Demetrius Cydones translated Ricoldo's *Disputatio* into Greek, and it was the Renaissance retranslation into Latin by Bartolomeo Piceno de Montearduo that was printed by Bibliander and reprinted by Migne. The *contra Mahometicam fidem* of the Emperor John Canta-cuzenos acknowledges indebtedness to Ricoldo (oratio prima, Bibliander II, col. 311).

2. Nicholas quotes Ricoldo and gives the translation of *Muslim* as *salvati* (Cribratio III.iii); in another place (I.ii) he gives as translation of the same word *sanae fidei*. In his prologue he acknowledges his sources: he has read the Cluniac corpus (including the Risālah), but he has seen the Arabic Qur'ān at Pera, where the Friars Minor explained to him what they understood by certain points; he cites Ricoldo, and, among the Greek Fathers, St John Damascene, and the rest are con-temporaries. On Cusa's sources see also Klibansky and Bascour, p. xxxiv. References to the *Cribratio Alcorani*: III.18; III.17; II.1-11; II.19, citing Q. VI.162 (=Ketton, Az. XVI, Bibl. p. 51, line 26ff); I.7. The argument based on the attribution of change to the unchanging God recalls Nicetas of Byzantium, although the tone is gentler; cf. above, Introduction, note 9. *De pace fidei*: ed. Klibansky and Bascour. Segovia: texts in Cabanelas.

3. Andrés and Torquemada: see bibliography. Spina: lib. IV, *de bello saracenico*; III, *judaico*. Van Leeuwen: specific reference to *contra perfidiam*, lib. II, cap. viii and xxxiii; *dialogus*, art. VI, XI, XIII, XIX; *de particulari judicio*, art. VII; *epistola paraenetica*. The creation of man: 'When I shall have completely formed him and shall have breathed my spirit into him . . .' (Q. XV.28-29). Ketton has 'eidem animae meae portionem insufflaturum . . .' (cap. 24, Bibl. 25, p. 85, l. 34). The objection, there-fore, was only to what Ketton rendered. The passage about the Baptist is Q. XIX.8 (Ketton 28, Bibl. 29, p. 98, l. 22); the idea that all who go to heaven pass by Hell is from Q. XIX.72 – van Leeuwen understood that they pass *through* Hell; Ketton has 'ad ignem' (28, Bibl. 29, p. 100, l. 20). A remarkable author of the period, whom, as untypical, I have not discussed, I ought however to mention: Pedro de la Cavalleria, whose manuscript, written in 1450, was published by M. A. Vivaldo in 1592. Cavalleria claims to be expert in Arabic, Hebrew and Chaldean (i.e. Syriac) and he certainly quotes the Qur'ān in an accurate form otherwise unknown to me. He supposes that no one before him has written against Islam, and it is very hard to believe that he had never read any of his

predecessors in this field. He was at least familiar with many old Christian arguments, from oral if not from written sources, but it is true that his work has an individual character. His line is Scriptural, but he tries to show the truth of Christ by insisting upon the general scheme and economy of redemption rather than allow himself to become bogged down in much of the traditional detail.

4. *Pius episcopus*, in bibliography. Vergil: *de inventoribus*, vii.viii.

5. An interesting anthology of Luther's *dicta* upon the Pope, 'the Turk' and the Emperor (as inadequately defending Germany) is 'The Prophecyes of the incomparable and famous Dr Martin Luther . . .' taken from his *Tischreden*, the bulk from the two colloquia 'de Turca' and 'de Antichristo'. This concentration on a few closely related subjects may give an unrepresentative picture, but the Reformers were disturbed by Islamic progress. Melanchthon: *Comm. in Danielem*. Bibliander: *apologia in editione Alcorani*. It was in this context that Luther used Turkish morality to argue Catholic immorality: *ad pium lectorem*; and see note 9.

6. *Traductio Alchorani Maumethis*: in Bib. nat. (lat. 3671); this MS was kindly drawn to my attention by Miss d'Alverny, who is working on Moncata. Arrivabene was a printer (and publisher) like a later Caxton, rather than a scholar or a publisher of the new type of which the Elzevirs were the greatest. He fell, indeed, short of his own claim for himself, but in a later generation Rapheleng did in fact study Arabic in order to prepare his Lexicon. Of the travellers of the later Middle Ages, Varthema, von Harff, Sanseverino, La Brocquière and Thenaud are examples of practical writers little interested in abstract aspects of Islam. Von Breydenbach: *Peregrinatio*, in 2am partem prime partis principalis; Fabri: e.g. see *Evagatorium* 225A, 266B, 72a, 104a ff and 108b (references to MS as printed in Stuttgart edition); cf. Güglingen, who was naturally credulous of scandals about Islam, but within limits; '*Some say*', he remarked, saving his own judgement, 'that at night [the muadhdhins] call out, "Increase and multiply and fill the earth", inciting the heathen to the sexual act' (p. 156). Brascha, f. 15r and v; Piloti: *Passage*, p. 334ff, 393; Schiltberger, *Bondage*, cap. 46-56; Vertomannus: 'They saye that their Doues are of the progenie of the Doue that spake in the eare of Mahomet, in lykenesse of the Holye Ghost' (*Navigation*, cap. 18) – a thing quite impossible for any Muslim to have said. Suriano: *Trattado di Terra Santa*.

7. Most travellers of this period who went to Persia contributed to the new knowledge of Shī'ism, but incomparably the most interesting was Jean Chardin (1643-1713) whose *Description de la Perse* is both carefully scholarly and intelligently discerning. Cf. Krusinski for Persian society in a somewhat later period.

8. The corresponding notion of Crusade was very much alive, at least among writers, and as long as the Ottoman expansion threatened; accounts of the Turkish wars and Islamic chronologies flourished throughout the sixteenth century, and the Crusading ideal, though moribund, long survived; cf. for example, Sturmius (1598) and even Febvre (1682). Similarities also occur in descriptions of Islamic practices, for example of Ramaḍān. For lists of heresies, cf. Baudier and Fryer. For authors cited, see bibliography by name.

9. The quotations about justification are Rauwolff, III.6, and Febvre, 12.1. Luther constantly named the Pope and the Turk together, though rather arbitrarily, since he did not usually insist on specific points of resemblance: *Turca et Papa in forma religionis nihil differunt aut variant, nisi in ceremoniis.* The one corrupted the ritual of the Old, the other that of the New Testament. Luther seems to have feared a coalition of his enemies, 'an alliance of the Papists with the Turk . . . for unbelievable is the malice of Satan'. (Colloquia, 1863, vol. I, p. 406, and see note 5, above.) Specific comparisons between Catholics and Protestants occurred inevitably. Reland ridiculed the parallel drawn between Islam and Lutheranism by Vivaldo, and certainly many of the points are incredibly thin, e.g. that Muslims reduce Lent to a month, and Lutherans (by which he seems to designate all Protestants indiscriminately) abolish it altogether. Another author, published under one cover with the English translation of Reland, pointed out that the marks of the true Church claimed by Catholics 'do exactly quadrate to the impious imposture of *Mahomet*' (he meant by these marks the success of a religion in the world and the 'habitual Practice of certain moral Virtues void of charity'). Prideaux argued that the Bishop of Rome first claimed to be Pope about the time that Muhammad claimed to be Prophet: 'so that Antichrist seems at this time to have set both his Feet upon Christendom together, the one in the East, the other in the West', a notion that apparently originated with Luther himself. The most detailed comparison between Pope and Muhammad known to me is Wallich's, which, like Vivaldo's on the other side, is often far-fetched, except in comparing the show of force by Church and Turk. Incidentally, he recognises the number of the Beast from the Greek figures for the letters making up each of the two words, *Moametis* and *Lateinos*. There is a more modern comparison by Forster; the most effective point again is that of the resemblance of jihād and Crusade. (Reland, loc. cit.; Vivaldo, to Cavalleria's para. 847, p. 130, but pagination is faulty; the *Life and Actions*, but cf. Hottinger, *Historia*, lib. II, cap. v; Prideaux, cap. 1, plagiarised in the anonymous Falkirk *Life*; Lutheri Colloquia (1863) vol. II, p. 113, and see also note 5 above; Wallich, *Comparation*; Forster, *Mahometanism*, vol. II, section x.)

The mediaeval way of refuting miscellaneous opponents in a single summa was reflected in the *Les Trois Veritez contre les Athées, Idolâtres, Iuifs, Mahumétans, Hérétiques et Schismatiques* (1593), by the humanist and friend of Montaigne, P. Charron (himself accused of atheism when, in another work, he anthologised other men's opinions). By defending the existence of God and the need for religion separately from the truth of Christianity, and from the truth of the Catholic Church, he implicitly distinguishes different classes of opponents, rather than seeks resemblances. This applies in differing degree to a number of works. Vivaldo, by publishing in 1592 Cavalleria's manuscript of 1450, linked two ages. In the former, Spina had attacked Jews and Muslims in turn, and Torquemada in his *Defensorium* maintained the integrity of Catholic doctrine against all kinds of infidel, just as Cavalleria defended the integrity of Scriptural redemption against Jews, Muslims and other unbelievers. Vives in his turn envisaged the same group of opponents. In a later period we find Protestant authors engaged in a very similar process. The greatest of all was Grotius, whose general plan is very like that of Vives, although his style is incomparably more academic; he depended heavily upon the Cluniac corpus and quoted the Qur'ān from Ketton. The most thorough was the Dutch Reformed Hoornbeeck, who (1653) itemised separately and point by point the heresies of every sect, including Muslims, Papists, Lutherans, Brownists, Jews, Greeks and Pagans. A late example of this genre, on the Catholic side, is Alamín's *Impugnacion* (1727).

In the sixteenth century, Turkish pressure naturally called forth a considerable literature; this was unlike that which I have been discussing; a feature of it was that, unlike what went before and after, it was practical rather than dogmatic. It recorded wars and exhorted to war. It was neither Protestant nor Catholic, but European. (See bibliography in list B.)

Authors specially utilised in these pages but not otherwise mentioned by name (for works see bibliography): Alberti; Beauvais; Carré; Chinon; Dandini; Della Valle; Gemelli; Godinho; Manrique; Pacifique; Philippe de la Trinité; Pires; Pitts; Savary de Brèves; Tavernier; Teixeira; Thevenot.

10. Nau, *L'état présent* and *Religio Christiana*. I Peter III.15, 16. Philippians II.8, 9. Q. II.81, 254; IV.156, 157; V.19, 50.

11. The 1799 *Life* expresses horror at the thought that Muslims 'go about their religious farrago as if they worshipped God in the best possible manner, resulting from a well-informed judgement and an explicit, indubitable revelation of his mind and will' – this author apparently cannot bear that Muslims should believe this to be exactly the case; he seems scarcely sane on the subject. He naturally gives the Sergius legend full credit; but among serious writers it disappeared after Prideaux with remarkable, if overdue, rapidity; Sale thought its debunking worth only a footnote. The earlier references are to *A Comprehensive View*: although its author was so credulous, what he says is not always wrong or unkind; he is capable of quaint assertions, as when he says that 'A'ishah (actually, all the Prophet's wives) could not remarry after his death – 'a great affliction in that sultry region'. Another late survival of virulence is the Falkirk *Life*, a cheap little book, but with pretensions; it repeats the ancient mistake that 'Muslim' means 'saved'. For a case of unexpected survival of prejudice based on inadequate evidence, see Burckhardt, *Judgements on History, etc.*, London, 1959, p. 65. (Where no specific references are given in this chapter, refer direct to bibliography.) Prideaux, himself one of the worst disseminators of the absurd, pointed out that 'the Christians, who abhorred [Muhammad's] wickedness, are apt to say too much. . . . To snatch at every story which would disparage the Religion they were against . . .' (2nd edition, pp. 38-39).

12. The works referred to as attacking Christian doctrine are *Mohammedica sive Dissertatio Epistolaris* and *Lettre d'un Médecin Arabe*. This was the technique of that interesting medley, the *Turkish Spy*, and inspired Montesquieu and his imitators. For comparable technique, intended to correct inaccuracies, cf. the 'Hadgi Mehemmed' letters by the

youngest Pétis de la Croix. Another satiric use of Islamic themes was political; cf. the Dialogue between Muhammad and Colbert in Hell. For the defence of Christian revelation it is interesting to compare Paley's selection of familiar arguments in his *Evidences* with Prideaux', of which they seem a dim reflection, though much fairer to Islam. The publication of Sale's Qur'ān promoted the criticism of Prideaux; for example, the sensible and well-written 'Reflections . . . occasioned by a late learned Translation', which may be warmly recommended to a reader; this little book says with force and moderation much the same as *Mahomet no Impostor*, but may seem less suspect, as being unsatirical.

13. Savary's 'humanising'; chapter V, section 2, above, p. 142. A rather more pedestrian English writer may be compared to Savary for his general outlook: Nathan Alcock in his *Rise of Mahomet accounted for on Natural and Civil Principles* argues 'from the nature of the climate, the character of the Arabians and neighbouring nations resulting from the climate, the particular circumstances of the times and the political institutions of the founder adapted to the climate and the times'. The romanticising aspect of Savary's work is reflected in form of caricature by Lancelin's *Histoire sécrette du Prophète des Turcs*, purporting to be translated from a manuscript in the possession of the Sharīf of Mecca: it is an account of his 'aventures galantes et merveilleuses'.

14. Cf. Watt, *Carlyle on Muhammad* and cf. also his *Medina*, and Tor Andrae, *Mohammad*. Reappraisal: e.g. Perronet Thompson.

15. For another modern Islamic opinion with the same tendency, see M. M. Atta: 'Islam is for this world and for the next world' (*The Islamic Call*, p. 202).

16. Hottinger, writing contemporarily with Pocock, was at much pains to justify the use of Arabic sources, but for Biblical or universal history, rather than for the study of Islam. See especially his *Smegma Orientalis*. Reland: quoted in the English translation made from the first edition. Pocock: Reland (2nd edition, cap. xxxix) refers to Pocock's account, in his notes on Abu'l Faraj, first edition, p. 186, of an interview with Grotius. Pocock, despite his enormous respect for the latter's Occidental learning, taxed him with having referred to the supposed dove who spoke to Muhammad, although he had found it in no Islamic source. Grotius did not remove the offending phrase in the next edition (the interview took place in the winter of 1640-41 and the third edition of *de veritate* was in 1650). See also note 21. The preparation of lexicons and grammars was characteristic of the earlier seventeenth century; so was the translation of Biblical books into Arabic; cf. the career of William Bedwell, one of the translators of the Authorised Version; he published the Epistles of St John in English and Arabic at Leyden, as well as translations of mathematical treatises. He also translated an anti-Islamic dialogue (from Arabic) ostensibly between Muslims. At first he felt that the author must be Christian, but reflected that 'whatsoever is here alledged and layd down, though never so good and Christianlike; or contrariwise absurd and monstrous; is nevertheless found and read in that their law'; moreover, he knew for a fact that Muslims compose 'the like morall sayings and zealous exhortations unto vertue, and holinesse

IW2 C

of life'. So he changed his mind; in other words, he thought that if they could be moral, they could be anti-Islamic. (I note in passing that the early Arabic vocabularies and grammars were associated with Christian Scripture and ritual (for references, see Dannenfeldt, bibliography, list C); this is true even of Kirsten, whose primary affection was for Avicenna.) Al-Makīn and Abu'l Faraj: both Christian Arab writers, moderate and usually reliable.

17. Gabriel Sionita: see his *tractatus brevis*, passim. D'Herbelot: the title page runs: 'Bibliothèque Orientale ou Dictionaire Universel, contenant generalement tout ce qui regarde la connoissance des peuples de l'Orient, leurs histoires et traditions . . . leurs religions, sectes et politique . . . leurs sciences, et leurs arts, les vies et actions remarquables de tous leurs saints . . . des jugements critiques et des extraits de tous leurs ouvrages . . .'. Raue cites Muslim prayers in his edition of Qur'anic extracts. For the rapid absorption of new knowledge by a discriminating public, compare the article *Mahomet* in Bayle's first edition (1697) with that of the revised third edition (1720). The latter refers to the contemporary criticism of Père Simon, for whose views see chapter xv of his *Histoire critique*.

18. *Historiae ex Alcorano depromptae*: Miss d'Alverny kindly drew my attention to this manuscript (Paris, nouv. acq. lat. 130). This series of extracted histories may be compared with short extracts – including single histories of the Patriarchs – Abraham, Joseph – published for their religious and linguistic interest. Erpenius and Nissel printed Ketton's text as well as their own literal translations; the latter printed also du Ryer's, then recently published, but whether he printed either version in approval or disapproval of a measure of literary paraphrase, I do not know. Raue demonstrated an interesting system of transliteration; for the beginning of the fātihah: bsm œllh œlrHmn œlrHim œlHmd llh rb œlaœlmin. Cf. also Hackspan (closely textual but polemic) and, later, Beck (interested to elucidate the meaning in the historical context, but otherwise not greatly original) and Starcke (who printed the Mary sūrah). For interest shown during this period in Mark's translations, see d'Alverny, *Marc*. Another feature of this type of literature was the popularity of Muhammad's 'Testamentum' or treaty with the Christians; there were editions by J. G. Nissel, Gabriel Sionita, Nagy de Harsany and J. Fabricius. It was associated with practical ideas of friendship with Muslims, v. Pacifique. Spanish creed: v. L. P. Harvey.

19. *Epitome Fidei*, in B.M. Lansdowne 722 (f. 106r ff). Stubbe: *Rise and Progress of Mahometanism*, Harleian 6189, pp. 2-3. There is unwilling admission of Muhammad's personal charm in the anonymous *Life and Actions* and in Akehurst's *Imposture*. An earlier description of the same type occurs in Curio (q.v.).

20. Both Savary and Ockley published collections of Muslim religious aphorisms, apparently recommended oecumenically and in good faith to a serious public: Ockley, his *Sentences of Ali*; and Savary, a 'recueil des plus pures maximes du Coran', assuring his readers that he includes only such as are 'fitted to elevate the soul, and to recall to man his duties towards the Divinity, towards himself and towards his fellows'

(*Morale de Mahomet*). Another book of a similar character, based on the theme that truth is universal, is *The Morality of the East, extracted from the Koran of Mohammed* (1766).

21. Pocock's career spans almost all the aspects of seventeenth-century scholarship. As a young man he edited some of the New Testament Epistles in Syriac which were needed to complete the Syriac New Testament which Widmanstadt had successfully published despite omissions so long before. His voyages in the Levant and his European contacts are typical of an age when scholarship was primarily European rather than national. His Arabic studies continued under Charles I and the Commonwealth, but at the Restoration he found that 'the love of *Arabick* learning was now waxed cold'; this was not so in England only, but it was 'beginning to decline in *Holland* also'; fortunately, this was only a temporary ebb, and in any case his latter years were given to an immense work of Biblical criticism. His Hebrew interests extended beyond the ancient Jews and he was always interested in Maimonides. He was representative of the age also in his extensive purchase in the East of manuscripts. He held Grotius in great reverence and in his translation of the *de veritate* he had the author's permission to add to and omit from the section on Islam as much as he pleased. Two German scholars: J. C. Schwartz and M. G. Schroeder. Ehrhart: cap. VII.

22. References to Preliminary Discourse. It is interesting to note that the earliest German Qur'āns were translations of translations – in 1623 Arrivabene's (itself a paraphrased translation of a paraphrased translation); in 1688 du Ryer's; and Sale's in 1746.

23. *Muhammad at Mecca* and *Muhammad at Medina*. A shorter Life of Muhammad is to be published.

24. Article by E. Crankshaw in *Observer*, 1st December 1957.

25. For all references, see authors by name in bibliography. The quotation from Gibb is from the Preface to *Modern Trends*. The Guillaume reference is to his *Islam*.

This is not an exhaustive account of the modern Christian approach. In the first place, I have not attempted to trace its origins, and have omitted any comprehensive discussion of nineteenth-century trends. The beginnings of a new approach came earlier than we sometimes think. For example, C. Forster in 1829 was writing, 'To be unjust to the fair claims of any other system is, in fact, to be guilty of gross injustice to the unrivalled merits of the Gospel.' He realised that 'the Christian has no reasonable grounds of doubt or fear to withhold him from doing the fullest justice to the phenomena of Mahometanism'. He saw a 'twofold instrumentality, acting co-ordinately'; where Christianity operates directly to make the Lord known, Islam 'shapes the course of things indirectly' to the same end. It is a preparation for the full truth, *ordained* in the twofold promise to Abraham: 'by the convergement, in the fulness of time, of Ishmael to Isaac, of Mahometanism to Christianity, the whole world shall one day be poured into the fold of the true shepherd, our only Lord and Saviour Jesus Christ'. We are sharply reminded of William of Tripoli (above, chapter IV, section 2, page 122); but it is by no means missionary experience that Islam prepares the individual soul for conversion, and Forster may be thinking rather of the world as a whole. In any case he raises questions that still await an answer.

In the second place, I have even omitted much from the history of the present century. I have not discussed the work of various study groups and conferences that have met in recent years, both Catholic and Protestant. I have not discussed the very sound, if conservative, work done by Protestant missionary groups before the first war (see Zwemer, Hooper and Speer) or the associated (and still continuing) work of the American publication, the *Muslim World*. Of this tradition Canon Cragg and his group, whom I have only mentioned, are the heirs. I have equally omitted to discuss authors on the Catholic side, at the two extremes of opinion. There have been virulently anti-Muslim books published pseudonymously (see al-Ghalwiry and Zakarias); there has also been an attempt to establish the theory of a separate economy of salvation for Islam, in substitution for Israel (see Ledit); this goes further than orthodox opinion is ever likely to go.

Since I wrote these words several important books have appeared; the Maronite Fr. Michel Hayek's study of the Qur'anic Christ, in which two further studies are announced (*L'Islam face à la Trinité et à l'Incarnation* and *Le Mystère d'Ismael*); and Fr. Basetti-Sani's comparative study of Muhammad and St Francis (recalling Forster). A little book by Père Jomier, rather conservative, usefully defines the minimum appreciation of Islam which every Christian should have. A series of articles in a Greek Catholic publication over the signature P. Khoury deals with the traditional Christian attitude exemplified by St John Damascene, in a spirit that is at once calm, sensible, scholarly and understanding. Kraemer's *World Cultures and World Religions* sets Islam in the modern 'dialogue'. Cragg's translation of Hussein's *City of Wrong* (a philosophical Muslim fiction of the Passion) and Constance Padwick's *Muslim Devotions* illustrate the spirit of Islamic piety. Zaehner's works on mysticism are important.

APPENDICES

Appendix A

1. Cf. Richard Loewenherz, Godefroid de Bouillon, Chanson d'Antioche, Conquête de Jérusalem, Chanson d'Aspremont and Chanson de Roland, passim, also Busone da Gubbio and, in less degree, Aliscans, for 'Cette singulière confusion du mahométisme avec le paganisme qui règne dans toutes nos chansons de geste', as Gaston Paris put it (*Légende de Saladin*). But cf. the ideas of H. Grégoire. The great exception is Eschenbach's *Parzival* with its image of the noble enemy.

2. *Canterbury Tales*, ed. Robinson, p. 199, line 810/2000. Robinson in his notes points out (p. 844) that there are five cases of this oath in *Guy of Warwick*. Some commentators have shown less sense than Chaucer. The note on this oath by Tyrwhitt (1775) reads, 'a Saracen deity'.

3. English Charlemagne Romances: *Sowdone of Babilone*. Cf. Greban's *Mystère de la Passion*, where *Mahomet* is apparently an ancient Egyptian god. Cf. Lovelich's *Grail*, taken from *Lestoire*, early 13th C.

4. The pseudo-Turpinus, though prose, belongs to the same literature.

5. See for example Baudry of Dol or William of Malmesbury ón the First Crusade.

6. This account refers to the caliph's being 'adored' as is the Roman Pontiff by Christians. Words to do with worship may often not imply divine honours at all, as obviously in the title of address, 'your worship', etc. *Adorare* was used of the Christian worship of images, although ecclesiastical writers were very conscious that these were not to be given the kind of worship to which only God is entitled. Other examples of words used in a sense which may not be as strong as it looks at first sight to be are 'turba deorum' in the versified Life of St Francis (Gol. vol. i) and the Muslims who at the siege of Damietta are imagined as threatening Muhammad that they will cease to worship him (*colere* and *adorare*). (Quinti Belli Sacri SS. Minores, in obsidione Damiettae; p. 163.)

7. Diceto, yr. 633, which specifies *exhibere cultum Deitatis*. Viterbo: cf. Pantheon, yr. 612, with the extract published by Cerulli and in MS (Syrian Apology). Vitry: i.vi and lxii (mis-numbered in Bongars). Vitry also has the story of the camel seized by the Prophet and buried at Mecca ('camel of God' and Ka'bah confused?) where 'to-day it is adored by the unrighteous and deluded people' (loc. cit., vi). Humbert of Romans approves of 'stoning' the 'image' of Muhammad with dung; is this in metaphor? He speaks also of the 'idol' of Muhammad as worse than the idol of Baal. (De pred. S.C., xi and xii.) It is far from clear that in either case he means an idol literally. It is always possible, moreover, for a man to hold mutually exclusive views simultaneously; or consecutively; or, as we have seen above, to repeat mutually exclusive views without giving both – or either – credence.

8. Loc. cit. For resentment at the Islamic accusation that Latins are idolatrous, see Peñaforte, MOFPH vol. i, appendix; and above, chapter VII, p. 204.

9. Pennis, MS cit., f. 34r; Tripoli, Cambridge MS Dd. 1.17 f. 75v and Gonville and Caius 162/83 f. 14v.

10. Fr. Antonio de' Reboldi: 'ydolum abhominationis id est moscheta Machometi' (*Itin. ad montem Sinai*, in Gol. iii).

11. Conquête: vii.xiii.6462-6.

12. The letter brought from 'Akka by the priest of St Thomas's and delivered to the Abbot of St Albans (entered by Matthew Paris in 1257) is something of a mystery. The Chronicler claims only to have extracted an interesting passage, so that the assertion that the idol of Muhammad at Mecca had come to grief belongs to a context that we do not know ('de cujus certa relatione accepimus quod . . .') and we cannot assess the implications of the statement. It appears to mean that the 'priest of Acre' believed there to be an idol, and perhaps that he drew attention to the story. Guy de Basainville, Preceptor of the Temple, believed it (Du Chesne, vol. 5); again the background is obscure. In the fifteenth century fire damage at Mecca again gave rise to a crop of similar rumours, but the association of the themes of the 'idol' and of destruction remains mysterious.

13. Q. LIII.19, 20; XXII.51. San Pedro, SSM I.i.44, 60. Annotator ad Az. 9, 15, 62.

14. See chapter VII, note 17. Cf. Will. Malmesbury and Baudry of Dol, loc. cit., and also Vitry, loc. cit.

15. See chapter VII and also chapter V; for actual stories about idols see especially Pedro de Alfonso, Roderick and Mark of Toledo, and the Risālah.

16. For H. Grégoire, see bibliography. For the abjuration formula, see Montet, and for St John, see 'de haeresibus', opening paragraph of section on Islam, MPG 94 coll. 764-5; also above, Introduction. Cf. also Cedrenus' belief that 'akbar' ('greatest') means 'Venus', e.g. in the adhan.

17. Cf. M. Jones (refer bibliography).

18. See chapters I and III.

Appendix B

1. Other examples in text, chapter IV above, p. 112.

2. See Malmesbury; cf. Baudry: 'Pulchrum sit vobis mori in illa civitate pro Christo in qua Christus pro vobis mortuus est' (i.iv). Humbert: opening pages of *de pred.* S.C.

3. Hist. Crus., vol. I, p. 84.

4. Mansi, XIV, col. 888.

5. MPL 126; ep. CLXXXVI.

6. LXXXIX.

7. We do not know the exact terms of the indulgence offered by Urban himself. Dana Munro drew attention to the confusion among Urban's hearers on this point, from which it seems certain that they did not think it important, and probable that he did not do so himself. The evidence of William of Tyre (I.xv), although he was remote from the Council of Clermont, must represent the tradition of the Latin Kingdom, where the indulgences were earned in the first place. He says that Urban promised his hearers that if they died in true penitence they need not fear to receive their eternal reward. If this sounds truistic, it agrees well enough with the precise terms of indulgences that were actually made available in the course of time. St Bernard, though protagonist of the sanctity of Crusading, and while he dangled the *lucrum mori* as a bait, rendered clearly the terms of the indulgence, as given to those who confessed themselves with contrite heart. (Ep. CDLVIII.) The Councils offered a plenary indulgence both to those who crusaded in person and to those who paid the expenses of others; the exact details of the bene-ficiaries varied slightly from time to time. (Cf. Innocent III, *expeditio pro recuperanda Terra Sancta*, Conc. Lat. IV; Conc. Lugdun. I, can. 17; both in Héfélé.) An indulgence is a Catholic technicality, remitting the 'temporal pains' of sin, either fully or partly, on stated conditions, which would include not being in a state of sin, even if that were not specified (see Denzinger, *Enchiridion Symbolorum*); in other words, it remits the 'temporal pains' (or 'penalties') of sins of which the guilt has already and independently been remitted. Thus Crusaders were remitted all (or

in certain cases some of) the penalties incurred through the commission of their sins, subject to confession and absolution; and this was done for going on, or aiding, the Crusade, not for dying in battle. True martyrdom on the other hand occurs only in case of death and gives immediate remission of the guilt of all sins (and not only their penalties) irrespective of confession and absolution.

Appendix C

1. Loc. cit. The source is the *de doctrina* . . . Bibliander p. 199ff.
2. That is, Asrafil, thought to derive from Seraphim (see SEI under *Isrāfīl*); the creed 'Credunt Saraceni' has the same phrase. The *de doctrina* has the Arabic variant Sarafil ('Seraphiel').
3. Simon, loc. cit.; Q. iv.157, Ket., Az. xi, Bibl. p. 37, lines 13-14.
4. Itin. ad montem Sinai, Gol. iii.
5. Viterbo and Paris, loc. cit.; Ricoldo, Ep. ii.
6. Loc. cit.
7. SSM i.i.7 (referring to *Liber Scalae*).
8. Annotator ad Az. 88: *prosequitur suam fatuitatem de angelis, quos de igne creatos asserit, et mortuos, et tandem resurrecturos.*
9. Dd.1.17, f. 71r, col. 1.
10. Lib. de Gent., Artt. vi-xi; Hamar, sig. 8.

Appendix D

1. Donaldson, *The Shī'ite Religion*.
2. Cf. Scott's *Talisman* for this, as much as for the Saladin legend, in its modern Romantic revival.
3. 'Abdalla, Mehemet' (then follows a big lacuna: doubtful ancestors omitted but also the important Ismā'īl, which suggests failure to understand the main issue) 'Japhar, Mehemet, Hali, Hussen, Hali major'; Will. Tyr., xix.xx; cf. i.iv.
4. Vitry, i.viii.
5. 'Al-Mahdi' should be, *the guided one*. Will. Tyr., loc. cit. Cf. Oliver, Hist. Reg.
6. Loc. cit.
7. xc.
8. Cap. xiv. Cf. xi (only the Baghdad caliphate is mentioned).
9. Hist. Reg. 56.
10. Itin. xviii; Disp. xiii; Pennis ii.

Appendix E

1. Ketton, iii, Bibl. p. 17, line 25ff. Mark, cap. ii (MS f. 13r).
2. Op. cit., xvi.
3. Disp. vi; Ep. iii; Itin. xxxii.
4. *Reprobatio*, viii; San Pedro, SSM i.iv.18.
5. Op. cit. i.vi.

6. Loc. cit. (Bibl. p. 17, line 26); 'Deum timentes' is asterisked.
7. VIII, cf. Bukhārī 65.39.2; and VI, cf. Bukhārī 6.5 (also 6.4, 21, 22); Bukhārī's heading is cited incorrectly by the author. San Pedro, I.iv.18, 18. These traditions have been associated with the Māliki madhhab which obtained in Spain. Perron's translation of the modern Māliki jurisprudent, Khalīl ibn Isḥāq, however, reads, 'Il est defendu . . . d'approcher maritalement de la femme en menstrues, de se permettre de la toucher (même pardessus les vêtements) à partir de la ceinture jusqu'aux genoux (mais il est permis de toucher à partir d'en haut de la ceinture vers la tête . . .).' Précis de Jurisprudence, I.83. Cf. Wensinck, Handbook, under menstruation.
8. See Zina' in SEI and Wensinck, Handbook.

Appendix F

1. p. 150.
2. Among arguments rejected by Holcot are that God desires not the death of the sinner but his conversion; that God is as merciful now as in the Passion when He prayed for the Jews and bade Peter put up his sword; that Aristotle warned Alexander to shed no blood because when creature kills creature the heavenly powers are moved to vengeance; again, vengeance is mine, saith the Lord; pagans ignorant of Christian law deserve better than bad Christians; pagans cannot believe till God takes away the veil from their hearts. Against these points he argues that the death that God does not desire is that of the soul, not that of the body; Christ rebuked Peter because he chose the wrong time to draw the sword; what Aristotle reproved was taking pleasure in cruelty, and the Christian must not delight when he sheds blood; the Lord may take His vengeance through His servants; we daily see bad Christians, thieves, traitors, heretics and many others killed by proper authority; God will remove the veil from the heart of whoever desires it. Thus the right to kill remains intact. (Holcot: opus in librum Sapientie, cap, v, lect. lxv. The Scriptural references are Josue ix.23; Ezechiel xxxiii.11 (not verbatim; cf. xviii, 23, 32 and Sarum Compline absolution); Matthew xxvi.51, 52, John xviii.10, 11; Hebrews x.30, Deuteronomy xxxii.35, 36. Aristotle: (from Smalley) pseudo-Aristotle, secretum secretorum, ed. Steele, Opera hactenus inedita Rogeri Baconi 5, Oxford, 1920.)
3. Cf. Daniel, Holy War.

Bibliography: references and abbreviations

A FEW authors are quoted only in one work, or only in one passage of a single work, and the detailed reference is not then given each time; e.g. for *Acqui*, understand *Chronicon Imaginis Mundi*, at the year 619. The title will be made clear by the bibliography. The following supplementary information will be needed: for *Fleury*, understand, from p. 149 of the edition cited; for *Gerald* of Wales, understand, work cited, i.xvii; for *Dandalo* understand vi.vii.5; for *Giovanni de Andrea*, de Judaeis et Saracenis; for *Guibert*, i.iv; for *Higden*, v.xiv; for *Hugh of St Victor*, i.ix.ix; for *Mandeville*, chapter xv (Egerton text); for *Martinus Polonus*, p. 273ff; for *Sigebert*, under yr. 630; for *Varagine*, CLXXXI (176); for *Wendover* and *'Westminster'* under yr. 622. For short works without internal division, no reference beyond the name of the work is given. The edition used is always that stated in the bibliography.

Certain works are quoted by chapter numbers, even though the actual text used is a MS without the numbering; in such cases the passage quoted is identified according to the best-known *printed* text (even if the order in the MS is different). Ricoldo's *Disputatio* is cited by the chapter numbers in the Migne/Bibliander Latin retranslation from Greek, although only the Latin original (from MS) is used; for the *reprobatio* Drechsler's text chapter numbers are used; and for Tripoli Prutz's numbering. 'St Albans Chronicle' means the text common to Wendover, Matthew Paris and 'Matthew of Westminster' (what is not common is not so designated). 'Syrian Apology' means the common ancestor of the Gregorian Report and Viterbo, and 'Gregorian Report' means the version quoted by Paris as sent to Pope Gregory. References to the Cronica de España are given jointly with those to Alfonso X's version. Auvergne is cited jointly by the two editions given in bibliography (Venice and Paris identical); Fitzralph is quoted jointly by the printed text first and then the manuscript (there is a constant difference of one). References to ibn Isḥāq (unless stated otherwise) are those of the Arabic text marked marginally in Guillaume's translation. All references are to editions mentioned in the bibliography; e.g. Bibliander page references to the 1550 edition.

Other difficulties should be solved by the bibliography, and most abbreviations will be immediately obvious. A few that may need to be stated are:

Alv.: Alvernatus (Auvergne)
Arm.: de quest. Armenorum
AOL: see SOL
Bu.: Bukhari
CFM: contra los fatalistas mahometanos

CSS: contra sectam Saracenorum
Gol.: Golubovich (see list A (i))
HLF: Histoire littéraire de France
MGH: Monumenta German. Hist.
MOFPH: Monumenta Ordinis Fr. Praedicatorum Historica

393

MPL: Migne, Patrologia latina
MPG: Migne, Pat. graeco-latina
Q.: Qur'ān
Recueil: des historiens des croisades
RS: Rolls Series
ROL see SOL

SEI: Shorter Encyclopaedia Islam
SOL: Société de l'Orient Latin
   (ROL, Revue; and AOL, Arch-
   ives)
SSM: sobre el seta mahometana
ST: Summa Theologica

Bibliography A: Direct Sources (to 1350)

(This list includes works belonging to the periods before and after 1100 that I have made use of in the Introduction and chapters I to IX. For Western authors during the period 1100-1350 it is as complete as I have been able to make it. There is no attempt to cover the fields of scientific and philosophic translations, except for a few cases related to my text.)

(i) *Collections*

Acta Sanctorum quotquot toto orbe colentur. (ed.) J. Bollandus. Venice, Antwerp, Paris, Brussels etc., 1734-.

Analecta Franciscana. Quaracchi, 1885-1912 (5 vols.).

BIBLIANDER. *Machumetis Saracenorum principis, eiusque successorum vitae, doctrina ac ipse Alcoran . . . Haec omnia . . . redacta sunt opera et studio Theodori Bibliandri.* Bâle, 1550 (2nd edition).

BOFARULL. *Coleccion de Documentos Ineditos del Archivo General de la Corona de Aragon.* (ed.) D. Prospero de Bofarull y Mascaró Vols. 1-7, Barcelona, 1847-51.

BONGARS. *Gesta Dei per Francos, sive orientalium expeditionum et regni Francorum Hierosolymitani historia . . . a Jacobo Bongersio.* Hanover, 1611.

BROWN, E. *Fasciculus Rerum Expetendarum et Fugiendarum* (with *Appendix sive tomus secundus*). London, 1690.

Bullarum . . . editio Taurinensis (vols. 1-4).

BZOVIUS, A. *Annalium Ecclesiasticorum tomus XIII.* Cologne, 1616.

Clementinarum materia, etc. Paris, 1513. (See also Sextus.)

Decretum Gratiani. Una cum glossis. Lyons, 1584.

DU CHESNE, F. and A. *Historiae Francorum Scriptores.* 5 vols., Paris, 1636-49.

DU MÉRIL, M. E. *Poésies populaires latines antérieures au douzième siècle.* Paris, 1843. (See also in bibliography C.)

GOLUBOVICH, P. GIROLAMO. *Biblioteca Bio-bibliografica della Terra Santa e dell' oriente Francescano.* Vols. 1-5, Quaracchi, 1905-; vol. 13, 1920.

HÉFÉLÉ. *Histoire des Conciles d'après les documents originaux.* Ed. C.-J. Héfélé and H. Leclercq. 10 vols., Paris, 1907-38.

HUILLARD-BREHOLLES, J.-L.-A. *Historia Diplomatica Frederici Secundi.* Paris, 1853ff.

JANER, P. *Collecion Diplomática,* in *Condicion Social* (see list C).

LAURENT, J. C. M. *Peregrinatores medii aevi quatuor.* Leipzig, 1864.

LIZERAND, G. *Le Dossier de l'Affaire des Templiers.* Paris, 1923.

MANSI, J. D. *Sacrorum Conciliorum Amplissima Collectio.* Florence and Venice 1759-98. (Facsimile edition.)

MICHAUD, *Bibliothèque des Croisades*. Paris, 1829.
MIGNE, *Patrologia Graeco-Latina*.
MIGNE, *Patrologia Latina*.
Monumenta Germaniae Historica. Hanover, 1826-.
Monumenta Ordinis Fratrum Praedicatorum Historica. Louvain, Rome and Stuttgart, 1896ff.
MURATORI, L. A. *Rerum Italicarum Scriptores*. Milan, 1723-51.
QUADRADO, D. J. M. *Historia de la Conquista de Mallorca: Cronicas Ineditas*. Palma, 1850.
Recueil des historiens des croisades. Paris. Historiens occidentaux, 5 vols., 1844-95; documents arméniens, 2 vols., 1869-1906; historiens orientaux, 5 vols., 1872-1906; historiens grecs, 2 vols., 1875-81. Rolls Series.
RUBIO Y LIUCH, A. *Documents per l'Historia de la Cultura Catalane*. Barcelona, 1908.
Sextus decretalium liber, with *Clementiae seu Clementi V Pont. Max. constitutiones* . . . Antwerp, 1573.
Société de l'Orient latin:
   Archives de l'Orient latin, vols. I and II. Paris, 1881, 1884.
   Quinti Belli Sacri Scriptores Minores. (ed.) E. Roehricht. Geneva, 1879.
   Testimonia Minora de Quinto Bello Sacro. (ed.) E. Roehricht. Geneva, 1882.
   Itinéraires à Jérusalem. (ed.) H. V. Michelant and G. Raynaud. Geneva, 1882.
   Itinera Hierosolymitana. (ed.) T. Tobler. Geneva, 1877-85.

(ii)   *Anonymous works*

Abjuration formula: see Montet in list C.
Aliscans, chanson de geste. Ed. F. Guessard and A. de Montaiglon. Paris, 1870.
Aliud scriptum in Paris, Chron. maj., yr. 1236.
Anonimus Minorita (-?-) *de Saracenis et ritu ipsorum*, etc. (see also *mores*). In Golubovich, vol. 1, p. 399.
Antioche, chanson de. See Richard, list A (iii).
Aspremont, chanson d' – d'après un poème du XIIIe siècle. (ed.) L. Bréhier. Paris, 1919-20.
Chiose anonime alla prima cantica della Divina Commedia di un contemporaneo del poeta. (ed.) F. Selmi. Turin, 1865.
Chiose sopra Dante testo inedito . . . Florence, 1846.
Chronica XXIV Generalium, in *Analecta Franciscana III*.
Chronica Ordinis Pr. in MOFPH (see list A (i)).
Cid, Poema del. (ed. and tr.) A. Reyes. Buenos Aires, 1938.
Commento alla Divina Commedia d'Anonimo Fiorentino del seculo XIV. (ed.) P. Fanfani. Bologna, 1866.
Conquête de Jérusalem. See Richard, list A (iii).
Continuatio Chronicorum B. Isidori S. Hildefonso falso adscripta. In MPL 96 and in *SS. PP. Toletanorum quotquot extant opera*. Madrid, 1786.
Contrarietas elfolica. See Mark of Toledo in list A (iii).

Credunt Saraceni . . . See note on MSS (Cambridge).

De expugnatione T. S. per Saladinum libellus. In R.S., 66.

De fratribus minoribus visitantibus captivos in Babilonia. In Gol., 3, pp. 68-72.

De Machomete. Arbor generationis Machometi. See note on MSS (London).

Gesta Francorum: Histoire anonyme de la première Croisade. (ed.) L. Bréhier. Paris, 1924.

Gestes des Chiprois, Les. In *Recueil de chroniques françaises éditées en orient.* In AOL.

Godefroid de Bouillon, chanson de. Ed. C. Hippeau. Paris, 1877.

Gregorian Report: scriptum domino Pp. Gregorio nono missum. In Matthew Paris, Chron. maj. yr. 1236.

Horn. King Horn. Text in W. H. French, *Essays on King Horn*, Ithaca, N.Y., and London, 1940.

Itinerarium peregrinorum et gesta regis Ricardi (attributed to Richard, canon of Holy Trinity). (ed.) W. Stubbs. R.S. 38.

Lestoire del Saint Graal. (ed.) H. O. Sommer. Washington, 1909.

Libellus in partibus transmarinis de Macumeti fallaciis (scriptus). In Vincent (q.v.) 23.40.

Memoria Terre Sancte. In Kohler, *Deux projets* . . . (see list C).

Ménestrel de Reims, Récits d'un. (ed.) N. de Wailly, Paris, 1876.

Miracle de saint Ignace, in *Miracles de Nostre Dame par personnages.* Ed. G. Paris and U. Robert, vol. 4. Paris, 1879.

Mores Saracenorum . . . See note on MSS (London). Equivalent to An. Min. (see above).

Nicholay Liber. See note on MSS (see note, s.v. Paris). Edition by M. T. d'Alverny in *Cahiers de civilisation mediévale* of the University of Poitiers, expected, but not seen by me.

Ottimo Commento della Divina Commedia, testo inedito d'un contemporaneo di Dante. Pisa, 1827.

Pisan text. In Mancini. See list C.

Prophetiae:
    Sciendum autem est . . . In MS (Paris). See note.
    La prophétie de Hannan. In SOL, *Quinti Belli S. ss. min.*
    Prophetia filii Agap. Ibid.
    Expositio libri filii Achab. In MS (London). See note.

Quidam Anglicus: Itinerarium cuiusdam Anglici Terram Sanctam et alia loca sancta visitantis. In Gol. iv (appendix).

Reprobatio: quadruplex reprobatio. In MSS (see note) in Berlin, Paris and Cambridge. Attributed in Berlin MSS to Galensis and in Paris MS to Ricoldo. Printed as *Ioannis Galensis Angli de origine et progressu et fine Machometis et quadruplici reprobatione prophetiae ejus liber.* In *de Saracenis et Turcis chronicon,* ed. W. Drechsler. Strasburg, 1550. (MSS other than Paris correspond roughly with printed text.)

Richard Loewenherz: Versroman ueber R.L. (ed.) K. Brunner, Vienna and Leipzig, 1913.

Roland, Chanson de. (ed.) J. Bedier. Paris, 1937.

Scripta domino Pp. Innocentio (III) ab ecclesia Hierosolymitana missa. In Wendover and Paris (yr. 1193) and pseudo-Vitriacus (i.e. third book of Vitry's Hist. Hieros. in Bongars).

Sowdone of Babylone. The English Charlemagne Romances, part V: The Romance of the S. of B. (ed.) E. Hausknecht, London, 1861. (Listed for convenience here, but later than 1350.)

Temporibus Bonifacii papae . . . See note on MSS (Cambridge). Also contained in Higden, etc.

Thomae, S., Acconensis, epistola ab ecclesia. Summary in Paris, *Lib. Addit.* and under 1257 in Chron. Maj.

Turpinus, pseudo-: Historia Turpini. In C. Meredith Jones, *Historia Caroli Magni et Rotholani ou Chronique du pseudo-Turpin.* Paris, 1936. Also in *Pseudo-Turpinus*, edited etc. by H. M. Smyser. Cambridge, Mass., 1937.

Vita Mahometi. Ed. Serrano y Sanz (see list C).

(iii)   *Alphabetical list of attributed works, by authors*

ABRAHAM AL-FAQUIN and BONAVENTURA of SIENA (tr.). *Liber Scalae Machometi.* In Cerulli and in Munoz (list C).

ACQUI, JAMES OF. *Chronicon Imaginis Mundi fr. Iacobi ab Acquis.* in *Monumenta Historiae Patriae Scriptorum,* III. Turin, 1848.

ADAM, WILLIAM OF (b. of Sultaniyah). *Guillelmi Adae . . . de modo Saracenis extirpandi.* In *Recueil,* Documents Arméniens, tome 2. 1906.

ADELARD OF BATH. *Die Quaestiones naturales des Adelardus von Bath.* Beiträge zur Geschichte der Philosophie und Theologie des Mittelalters, band XXXI.2. Münster, 1934.

A AN OF LILLE. *Alani de Insulis de fide catholica contra hereticos sui temporis libri quatuor.* In MPL 210.

ALEXANDER III. *Alexandri Pp III epistola ad soldanum Yconii.* In Peter of Blois, MPL 107 and Matthew Paris, Chr. Maj., yr. 1169.

ALEXANDER IV. Bull on the Tunis missions. In Coll (see list C).

ALFONSO X EL SABIO. *Cronica de España.* (ed.) A. G. Solalinde. B.A., 1940. (See also Roderick.)

ALVARO OF CORDOVA:
  (1) *Indiculus Luminosus.*
  (2) *Alvarus Cordubensis de vita vel passione Eulogii . . .*
  (3) *Epistolae.* All in MPL 115.

ALIGNAN, BENEDICT OF. *Tractatus fidei contra diversos errores.* Part relating to Islam in Cerulli, p. 412ff. (See list C.)

ANASTASIUS BIBLIOTHECARIUS. *Anastasii Historia Ecclesiastica.* In *Corpus Scriptorum Historiae Byzantinae,* vol. 2: Theophanis Chronographica, ex rec. Ioannis Classeni.

AQUINAS, ST THOMAS:
  (1) *Summa Theologia.* Editio Leonina. Rome (*opera omnia* 1882ff).
  (2) *Summa contra Gentiles.* Editio Leonina manualis. Rome.
  (3) *Commentarii in decem libros Ethicorum Aristotelis.* Paris, 1644.
  (4) *Quaestiones disputatae de veritate.* Lyons, 1557.

ARISTOTLE. *Decem libri Ethicorum* (antiqua translatio). See Aquinas (3).

AUVERGNE, WILLIAM OF:
  (1) *Guillelmi Alverni . . . tractatus de fide et de legibus.*
  (2) *De universo.*

(3) *De virtutibus*. All in *Opera Omnia*, editions at Nuremberg, 1497, Venice, 1591, and Paris, 1674.

BACON, ROGER:
(1) *The 'Opus Majus' of Roger Bacon*. (ed.) J. H. Bridges, Oxford, 1897.
(2) *Baconis Operis Majoris Pars Septima seu Moralis Philosophia*. Post F. Delorme OFM + critice instruxit et edidit E. Massa. Zuerich, 1953.

BASAINVILLE, GUY DE. *Epistola de rumoribus partium transmarinarum*. In Du Chesne, vol. 5.

BAUDRY OF DOL. *Historia Jerosolimitana*. In *Recueil*, vol. 4, and Bongars.

BEAUVAIS, VINCENT OF. *Speculum Historiale*. In *Bibliotheca Mundi*, v. Bellovacensis speculum quadruplex. Douai, 1629.

BENVENUTO DE RAMBALDIS DE IMOLA. *Comentum super Dantis Aldigherij comaediam*. Florence, 1887.

BERNARD, SAINT, OF CLAIRVAUX:
(1) *Epistolae*.
(2) *De laude Novae Militiae ad Milites Templi liber*. Both in *Opera Omnia*, ed. D. J. Mabillon, MPL 182.

BONAVENTURA, SAINT:
(1) *Commentaria in IV libros Sententiarum Mag. P. Lombardi*. Quaracchi, 1882.
(2) *Sancti Patris Francisci Vita* In *B. Fr. Ass. Opera*, see Francis.

BONAVENTURA OF SIENA. See Abraham al-faquin.

BUENHOMBRE, ALFONSO DE (tr.):
(1) *Tractatus Rabbi Samuelis ad Rabbi Isaac de adventu Messiae*. In van den Oudenryn (see list C) and MPL 149.
(2) *Disputatio Abutalib Saraceni et Samuelis Iudaei, quae fides praecellat* . . . (See note on MSS, London.)

BURCARD. *Burchardi de mont Sion Descriptio Terrae Sanctas*. In Laurent (list A (i)).

BUSONE DA GUBBIO. *L'Avventuroso Ciciliano*. (ed.) G. F. Nott. Florence, 1832.

CAESARIUS HEISTERBACENSIS . . . *Dialogus Miraculorum*. (ed.) J. Strange. Cologne, 1851.

CATALANI, JOURDAIN C. DE SEVERAC. *Les Merveilles de l'Asie*. In H. Cordier, *Les Merveilles*, etc. Paris, 1925.

CEDRENUS. *Georgiou tou Kedrenou Synopsis Historion. Historiarum Compendium*. MPG 121-2.

CLEMENS PP. IV. *Iacobum regem Aragonum monet* . . . In Denifle, list C.

CLUNY. The Toletano-Cluniac corpus; all writings in this group are listed here together. For bibliographical study, v. d'Alverny.
(1) ROBERT OF KETTON (tr.). *Liber legis Saracenorum quem Alcoran vocant*. Ketton is sometimes called 'of Chester' by modern writers and 'Retenensis' by old ones. For his identity, refer d'Alverny.
(2) KETTON also tr. *Chronica mendosa*.
(3) KETTON wrote a brief *Praefatio translatoris*.
(4) Annotator on Ketton's Qur'ān (in margins). It has been suggested that this annotator may be Peter of Poitiers (see d'Alverny

and Kritzeck) but I do not feel convinced. Miss d'Alverny suggests that the material would be supplied, but I personally suspect that the author is himself a Mozarab – on internal evidence. I therefore list him as separate, while stressing the uncertainty.

(5) HERMANN OF DALMATA tr. *De doctrina Machumet,* and also
(6) *De generatione Machumet.*
(7) PETER OF TOLEDO tr. *Epistola Saraceni* with *Rescriptum Christiani.* This is the translation of the Risālah. I have not seen the edition by Munoz.
(8) PETER OF POITIERS. *Capitula ad domnum Petrum abbatem.*
(9) PETER THE VENERABLE. *Liber contra sectam sive haeresim Saracenorum.*
(10) Also, *Summula quaedam brevis.* (It is assumed that this good short compilation is by Peter; but it might have been prepared for his use by any Latin, probably by a Frenchman rather than a Spaniard, his name and his own remarks being added at the end.)
(11) Also, *Epistola de translatione sua,* two versions; and finally,
(12) *Epistola Ludovico reg. Francorum.*

Of these, 1, 2, 3, 4, 5, 6, 10 and 11 are in Bibliander; 3, 8, 9, 10, 11 (in two forms) and 12 are in MPL; I have taken 7 from MS (see note, Oxford) which source also supplements 4, very inadequately represented by Bibliander.

COGGESHALL, RADULPHI DE. *Chronicon Anglicanum.* (ed.) J. Stevenson, in R.S. 66. London, 1875.

CORBEIL, GILLES DE. *Ierapigra ad purgandos prelatos.* Fragment given by Gaston Paris, *Légende* (see list C).

CREMONA, GERARD OF. *Liber Alfarabii de Scientiis.* In Palencia (see list C).

CREMONA. See also Reboldi, Antonio de', of Cremona.

DANDALO. *Andreae Danduli Venetorum Ducis Chronicon Venetum.* In Muratori (list A (i)).

DANTE. *Inferno.* (Temple Classics edition, London, 1900).

DICETO, RALPH OF. *Radulphi de D. Abbreviationes Chronicorum.* In *Opera Historica* (ed.) W. Stubbs. R.S. 68, London, 1876.

DOUAI, GRAINDOR DE. See Richard le Pélerin.

DUBOIS, PIERRE. *De recuperatione Terrae Sanctae . . .* (ed.) ch. v, Langlois. Paris, 1891.

DU PONT, ALEXANDRE. *Roman de Mahomet.* See Reinaud in list C.

ELEEMOSINA, FR. JOANNIS. *Liber historiarum* and *Chronicon.* Extracts in Gol. ii, p. 103ff, and xiii.

ERNOUL. *Chronique d'E. et de Bernard le Trésorier.* (ed.) M. L. de Mas Latrie. Paris, 1871.

ESCHENBACH, WOLFRAM VON. *Parzival.* Tr. by Jessie L. Weston. London, 1894.

EULOGIUS:
(1) *S. Eulogii Memoriale Sanctorum.*
(2) *Liber Apologeticus Martyrum.* Both in MPL 115.

EUTHEMIUS ZIGABENUS. *Panoplia Dogmatike.* In MPG 130.

FIDENZIO OF PADUA. *Fidentii . . . liber de recuperatione Terrae Sanctae.* In Gol. ii, p. 9ff.

FITZRALPH, RICHARD. *Summa Domini Armacani in Questionibus Armenorum.* Printed 1512; also in MS (see note, Oxford).

FLEURY, HUGH OF. *Hugonis Floriacensus Chronica.* Munster, 1588.

FRANCIS, ST. *Beati Francisci Assisiatis opera omnia.* (ed.) von der Burh, J. J. Cologne and Brussels, 1849.

FULCHER OF CHARTRES. *Historia Iherosolymitana.* In *Recueil,* vol. 3, and Bongars.

GERALD OF WALES. *Geraldus Cambrensis de principis instructione liber.* R.S. 21. London, 1891.

GIOVANNI D'ANDREA. Gloss in *Clementinarum lib.* v (see list (i)).

GRÉBAN, A. *Le Mystère de la Passion.* Ed. G. Paris and G. Reynaud. Paris, 1878.

GUIBERT OF NOGENT:
(1) *Ven. Guiberti abbatis S. Mariae de Novigento historia quae dicitur Gesta Dei per Frances.* MPL 161, *Recueil,* vol. 4, and Bongars.
(2) *De vita sua.* MPL 161.

GUNDISALVO, DOMINGO. *De Scientiis.* (Compilacion a base principalmente de al-Farabi. ed. Alonso, P.M.A. Madrid-Granada, 1954.) Also in Palencia (see list C).

HAITONI ARMENI *Historia Orientalis.* In Reineck (see list B) cf. *Recueil,* Docs. arms. (See also MSS note, Camb., below.)

HAYMAR. See scripta . . . ab ecclesia Hierosolymitana . . . (list (ii)).

HILDEBERT OF MANS. *Historia de Mahumete.* MPL 171.

HIGDEN, RANULPHI. *Polychronicaon.* R.S. London, 1865-86.

HOLCOT, ROBERT. *Opus . . . in librum Sapientie.* Paris, 1511.

HUGH OF SAINT VICTOR. *Excerptionum Allegoricarum libri XXIV.* MPL 177.

HUMBERT OF ROMANS:
(1) *Tractatus Solemnis fr. H. de predicatione Sanctae Crucis.* Nuremburg (?), 1490.
(2) *Opusculum Tripartitum.* In *appendix ad Fasciculum Rerum Expetendarum et Fugiendarum sive tomus secundus.* (ed.) Edward Brown. London, 1690. Summary in Mansi (*in Conc. Lugdun.* II) by Mabillon.

JAIME, I. *Historia del Rey de Aragon Don Jaime I. El Conquistador,* tr. M. Flotats and A. de Bofarull. Madrid, 1848. *Gestas del Rey Don Jayme de Aragon.* Madrid, 1909.

INNOCENT III. *Acta Innocenti Pp. III,* in Haluscynskyj, P. Th., Pontificia Commisio ad Redigendum codicem iuris canonis orientalis, Fontes, series III, vol. II; see also MPL 214-7 and Héfélé/Leclercq.

JOHN, SAINT, OF DAMASCUS:
(1) *De Haeresibus liber.* MPG 94.
(2) *Dialexis Sarrakenou kai Christianou.* MPG 94, 96.

JOHN VIII. *Johannis Pp. VIII epistolae.* MPL 126.

JOHN OF WALES. See *reprobatio* in list (ii).

JOINVILLE, JEAN DE. *Histoire de Saint Louis.* (ed.) N. de Wailly. Paris, 1906.

KETTON, ROBERT OF. See Cluny.

LEO IV. *Leonis Pp IV fragmenta epistolarum.* Mansi 14.

402   ISLAM AND THE WEST

LEVANTO, GALVANO DE. *Liber sancti passagii Christicolarum contra Sarracenos . . .* In Kohler (list C).

LOVELICH, H. *History of the Holy Grail.* Ed. F. J. Furnivall, E.E.T.S. Extra series xx. London, 1874.

LUCCA, BARTHOLOMEW OF. See Ptolomaeus.

LUDOLF DE SUDHEIM (Suchem). *De itinere Terrae Sanctae.* (ed.) G. A. Neumann in AOL tome II. Paris, 1884. Also (ed.) F. Deycks. Stuttgart, 1851. (I refer to Neumann.)

LULL, RAMON:
(1) *Vita Beati Raymundi Lulli.*
(2) *Vida Coetania* (in English tr.).
(3) *Liber Contemplationis in Deum*; alias *Libre de Contemplacio en Deu.*
(4) *Disputatio Raymundi Christiani et Hamar Saraceni.*
(5) *Liber de Quinque Sapientibus.*
(6) *Liber super psalmum Quicunque Vult seu Liber de Tartari et Christiani.*
(7) *Disputatio Fidelis et Infidelis.*
(8) *Liber de Sancto Spiritu.*
(9) *Liber de Gentili et Tribus Sapientibus.*
(10) *Liber de confirmatione legis Christianae . . .*
(11) *Liber de majori fine intellectus, amoris et honoris.*
(12) *Liber de Deo et Mundo.*
(13) *Liber de participatione christianorum et saracenorum.*
(14) *Pro recuperatione Terrae Sanctae petitio.*
(15) *Libre de Doctrina Pueril.*
(16) *Blanquerna: A Thirteenth-Century Romance.*
(17) *Obras rimadas.*

1 and 2 are in Peers, A., *A Life of Ramon Lull.* London, 1927. 16 translated by E. A. Peers. London, 1925.

3, 4, 5, 6, 7, 8 and 9 are all in *Beati Raymundi Lulli Opera Omnia.* (ed.) I. Salzinger. Mayence 1721- ff.

3 in Catalan, (ed.) M. Obrador y Bennassar. Palma de Mallorca, 1906.
15 (ed.) M. Obrador y Bennassar. Barcelona, 1907.
10, 11, 12 and 13 in MS (see note on MSS, Munich).
14 in Atiya (see list C).
9 also as 'quaestio quae claruit' in MS (Munich) and fourth book in French version in Reinaud and Michel (see list C).
4. also as 'Disputatio de fide catholica' in MS (Munich).
17 (ed.) Gerónimo Rosselló. Palma, 1859.

MAIMONIDES. *Director dubitantium,* etc. Ed. R. P. Augustin Justinian, O.P., Paris, 1520. (Modern English version by M. Friedländer, 3 vols., London, 1881-5.)

MALMESBURY, WILLIAM OF. *De gestis regum Anglorum.* (ed.) T. Duffus Hardy, 2 vols. London, 1840.

MANDEVILLE. *Travels.* (ed.) M. Letts. London, 1953. (I have cited Egerton text.)

MANUEL, DON JUAN. *El Conde Lucanor.* (ed.) F. J. Sanchez Canton. Madrid, 1920.

MARCO POLO, *Travels*. ed. and tr. A. C. Maule and P. Pelliòt. London, 1938. See also note on MSS (Cambridge).

MARIGNOLLI, GIOVANNI DE'. *Chronicon* (Itinerarium). Extracts in Gol. v, p. 271ff. See also Yule vol. iii (list C).

MARINO SANUDO. *Liber Secretorum Fidelium Crucis super Terrae Sanctae recuperatione et conservatione*. In Bongars.

MARK OF TOLEDO:
(1) Preface to his translation of the Qur'ān.
(2) (tr.) *Alcorani Machometi Liber*.
(3) Preface to the translation of ibn Tumart.
(4) (tr.) *Tractatus Habentometi de unione Dei*, with murshidah: I. unio gloriosi laudabilis; and II. vinculum; Laudatio dei gloriosi; and Laus secunda.
(5) (tr.) *Contrarietas elfolica*.
1, 3 and 4 are published by d'Alverny and Vajda (see list C).
2 in MS, see note, Vienna. (For other MSS see d'Alverny.)
5 only known in one MS, see note, Paris.

MARSH, ADAM. *Epistolae* in Monumenta Franciscana. (ed.) J. S. Brown, London, 1858-82.

MARSILI, PERE. *Cronica*. In Quadrado (see list (1)).

MARTÍ, RAMÓN:
(1) *Explanatio simboli*, in March, *en Ramon Marti*, see list C.
(2) *Pugio Fidei*. Leipzig, 1687.
(3) *Capistrum Judaeorum*. Extract in Cerulli (list C).
(See also *reprobatio* in list (ii)).

MARTINUS POLONUS. *Chronica*. Antwerp, 1574.

METHODIUS, PSEUDO-. *Methodii Patarensis Ep. et Mart. Revelationes*. In *Magna Bibliotheca Veterum Patrum*. Cologne, 1618.

NICETAS OF BYZANTIUM:
(1) *Refutatio Mohamedis*. (Anatrope tes para tou Arabos . . .)
(2) *Expositio demonstrativa*, etc. (Elthesis . . .)
Both in MPG 105.

NACHMAN, RABBI MOSES:
(1) *Disputatio*: Latin version in Denifle (list C).
(2) English translation of Hebrew version in Rankin (list C).

NICOLA DE CASOLA. *Li pavillon de Forest*. Extracts in Ziolecki (C).

NOVARE, PHILIPPE DE. *Mémoires*, 1218-1243. (ed.) Ch. Kohler. Paris, 1913.

OLDENBURG. *Wildebrandi de Oldenburg Peregrinatio*. In Laurnet (i).

Oxford, school of. For philosophical discussions of Paradise, see also extracts in Cerulli.

PABLOS CHRISTIANI: as Nachman:
(1) *Disputatio* in Denifle.
(2) Version of Hebrew version in Rankin. See list C.

PADERBORN, OLIVER OF (Scolasticus):
(1) *Historia Damiatina*.
(2) *Historia Regum Terrae Sanctae*.
(3) *Epistola Salutaris regi Babilonis* . . .

(4) *Epistola doctoribus Egipti transmissa* . . .
All in *Die Schriften des Koelner Domscholasters, Spaeteren Bischofs von Paderborn . . . Oliverus.* (ed.) Hoogeweg, Tuebingen, 1894. *Hist. Dam.* also found in pseudo-Vitriacus (Bongars, Vitriac. lib. III); *Gesta Crucigerorum Rhenanorum* (*Q. Belli S. ss. Min.*, in SOL); and Wendover, yr. 1218; and doubtless elsewhere.

PARIS, MATTHEW:
(1) *Chronica Majora.* (ed.) Luard, R.S. 57. London, 1872-83.
(2) *Historia Anglorum.* R.S. 44. London, 1866-9.
(3) *Liber Additamentorum.* R.S. 57 (vi).

PAUL THE DEACON. *Historia Miscella.* In MPL 95.

PAVIA, THOMAS OF. *Gesta imperatorum et pontificum.* Extract (complete section) in MGH (ss) 22; and cf. Gol. i, p. 309ff.

PEDRO DE ALFONSO (Petrus Alphunsi). Dialogus v from *Dialogi in quibus impiae Judaeorum confutantur.* MPL 157.

PEDRO, SAN, PASCUAL (Petrus Paschasius):
(1) *Sobre el seta mahometana.*
(2) *Contra los fatalistas mahometanos.*
Both in *Obras,* ed. P. Armengol Valenzuela. Rome, 1905-8.

PEÑAFORTE, RAMÓN DE:
(1) *Summa sacrorum canonum.* Verona, 1744.
(2) Fragments in Raymundiana (MOFPH IV.2).

PENNIS, PETER DE:
(1) *Tractatus contra alchoranum.* In MS only (see note, Paris).
(2) *De locis ultramarinis.* In Kohler (see list C).

PETER THE VENERABLE. See Cluny.

PETER OF POITIERS. See Cluny.

PETER OF TOLEDO. See Cluny.

PLANO CARPINI, JOHN DE. *Libellus Historicus,* etc. In *The Texts and Versions of J. de P. C.,* etc. (ed.) C. R. Beazley. London, 1903 (Hakluyt version). Modern tr. in Dawson (see list C).

PORDENONE, ODORIC OF. *Travels.* English tr. with Latin and Italian texts. In Yule, vol. ii (see list C).

PTOLOMAEUS OF LUCCA. *Historia Ecclesiastica* in Muratori, vol. XI.

REBOLDI, ANTONIO DE', OF CREMONA. *Itinerarium ad montem Sinai.* In Gol. iii, p. 338.

RICHARD:
(1) *Le chanson d'Antioche composé par le pèlerin R.* (ed.) P. Paris.
(2) *La Conquête de Jérusalem.* Ed. C. Hippeau. Paris, 1868.

RICHARD THE CANON OF HOLY TRINITY. See Itinerarium in A (ii).

RICOLDO DA MONTE CROCE:
(1) *Disputatio contra Saracenos et Alchoranum.* Title given by Paris MS; British Museum Royal MS gives *Antialcoran Machometi.* I use Disputatio to distinguish this Latin original (unpublished; for MSS see note, Paris and London; and see d'Alverny, *Marc.*). The old titles Confutatio or Improbatio alchorani were used for the Latin version of the Greek by Demetrius Cydones. The latter is in MPG 104; and the retranslation, under the dedication, Bartholomaeus

Picenus de Montearduo Ferdinando regi Aragoniae, etc., appears in MPG 104 and also in Bibliander.
(2) *Itinerarium.* In Laurent (list A (i)).
(3) *Epistolae V de commentatoriae de perditione Acconis* 1291. In AOL II; see A (i) and Roehricht in list C).
(4) *Libellus ad nationes orientales.* In MS; see note, Oxford.
(5) *Christianae fidei confessio facta saracenis*; doubtfully attributed. In MPG 104 and Bibliander.
ROBERT THE MONK. *Historia Iherosolimitana.* In *Recueil*, vol. 3, and Bongars.
RODERICK. Don Rodrigo Jiménez de Rada, Archbishop of Toledo:
(1) *Historia Arabum.* In *PP. Toletanorum quotquot extant opera.* Madrid, 1793.
(2) *Cronica de Espana del arzobispo Don Rodrigo* etc. *tradujola i in castellano.* In *Coleccion de documentos ineditos para la historia de Espana.* Tomo cv. Madrid, 1893.
(3) *Estorio de los godos.* Same collection, LXXXVIII. Madrid, 1887.
ROQUETAILLADE, JOHN OF. *Johannis de Rupescissa vade mecum in tribulatione.* In Brown (Appendix).
RUBRUCK. WILLIAM OF. *Journey*:
In Hakluyt's version in Beazley (see Plano Carpini, above);
In new tr. from Quaracchi text, in Dawson (see list C).
RUTEBEUF. *Onze poèmes de R. concernant la Croisade.* (ed.) J. Bastin and E. Faral. Paris, 1946.
SAINT-PATHUS, GUILLAUME DE. *Vie de Saint Louis.* (ed.) H.-F. Delaborde. Paris, 1899.
SALIMBENE DE ADAM. *Cronica.* In MGH (ss.) 32.
SIGEBERT OF GEMBLOUX. *Gemblacensis Chronica.* MPL 160.
SIMON SIMEON. *Itinerarium ad Terram Sanctam fr. Symon Simeonis et Hugonis Illuminatoris.* In Gol. iii, p. 246ff.
TERRENA, GUIDO. *De haeresibus ad dominum Gaucelinum . . . incipiunt errores Sarracenorum.* In Cerulli p. 491ff (see list C).
THEOPHANES. *Chronographica.* See Anastasius.
TRIPOLI, WILLIAM OF. *Tractatus de statu Saracenorum,* etc.:
In Prutz (see list C).
MSS include Vatican (discussed Monneret de Villard in his *Ricoldo* and giving purer forms of Arabic words) and Cambridge. See note.
TUDEBODUS. *Historia de Hierosolymitano itinere.* In *Recueil*, vol. 3, and Bongars.
TYRE, WILLIAM OF. *Historia rerum in partibus transmarinis gestarum.* In MPL 201, in *Recueil*, 1, etc., and in Bongars.
UBERTI, FAZIO DEGLI. *Opera . . . chiamato Ditta Mundi.* Venice, 1501.
VARAGINE, JACOBUS A. *Legenda Aurea.* (ed.) Th. Graesse. Dresden and Leipzig, 1846.
VERONA, JACOPO DA. *Liber peregrinationis*:
In *Le Pèlerinage*, by Roehricht, see list C.
In *L. P. di J. da V. a cura di Ugo Monneret de Villard.* Rome, 1950.
VITERBO, GODFREY OF. *Pantheon sive Memoria Sanctorum,* in Muratori 8.
Passage previously unpublished in Cerulli, p. 417ff (see list C).
See also MS (in note under London).

VITODURANI, JOHN. *Chronica*. In Gol. ii, p. 143ff.
VITRY, JACQUES DE. *Historia Hierosolimitana Abbreviata*. In Bongars. See also MSS note, Cambridge.
WALTHERIUS. *Poema de Machomete*. In du Meril, *Poésies populaires*. See list C.
WENDOVER, ROGER OF. *Flores Historiarum*. R.S. 84. London, 1886-9.
'WESTMINSTER, MATTHEW OF'. *Flores Hist*. R.S. 95. London, 1890.
WURZBURG, JOHN OF. *Descriptio Terrae Sanctae Johannis W*. In *Descriptiones T. S.* (ed.) T. Tobler. Leipzig, 1874.

ADDENDA
EMBRICON. *Vita Mahumeti* ed. M. G. Cambier as *Embricon de Mayence, La vie de Mahomet*. Brussels, 1961.
WALTER OF COMPIÈGNE. *Otia de Machomete* ed. R. B. C. Huygens in *Sacris erudiri* 8, 1956.

NOTE ON MANUSCRIPTS USED (LISTS A AND B)
Berlin (Tuebingen)
MS theol. lat. Qu. 85.
MS theol. lat. Fol. 425.
Both contain *reprobatio* (see A (ii)).

Cambridge
Dd.1.17
1. Lib. Dom. Marci Pauli de conditionibus et consuetudinibus orientalium regionum. See A (iii).
2. Flos Ystoriarum Terrae Orientis quem compilavit fr. Haytonis. A (iii).
3. Credunt Saraceni . . . See A (ii).
4. Ad ostendendum quod Machometus . . . (=*reprobatio*). See A (ii).
5. Gesta Machometi (=Tripoli, de statu . . .). See A (iii).
6. Temporibus Bonifacii papae . . . See A (ii).
Gonville and Caius 162/83
1. Tractatus de ortu, processu et actibus Machometi (=*reprobatio*; part only). See A (ii).
2. Marci Pauli Veneti historia. See A (iii).
3. Jac. de Vitriaco Historia Hierosol. See A (iii).
4. De statu Saracenorum (Tripoli). See A (iii).

London (British Museum)
Royal 2.D.VI
Expositio libri filii Achab. See A (ii) (under Prophetiae).
Royal 6.E.III
Disputatio Abitalib et Samuel Iudei . . .. See A (iii) (Buenhombre).
Royal 13.E.IX
Antialcoran Machomet (=*Disputatio*). See A (iii) (Ricoldo).
Royal 14.C.XI
Sarraceni se putant esse de sarra . . . (part of Pantheon contained in this MS). See A (iii), Viterbo.
Cotton, Nero C.II
De machometo. Arbor generationis Machometi. See A (ii).

Cotton, Faustina A.VII
  Mores Saracenorum. See A (ii).
Lansdowne 722
  Epitome Fidei et Religionis Turcicae . . . See list B.
Lansdowne 775
  A relation of the Turkish Empire, etc. See list B, Harborne.
Harleian 6188
  History of the Turks.
Harleian 6189
  The Rise and Progress of Mahometanism. Stubbe, list B.
Stowe 462
  Richards' Diary, list B.
Additional 19894
  Liber murat beg interpretis.
Additional 22914
  Of the Religion, etc., list B.

Munich (Bayerischen Staatsbibliothek)
10517
  Liber de majori fine intellectus, amoris et honoris.
  Liber de Deo et mundo.
10564
  Quaestio quae claruit . . .
10495
  Liber de participatione.
10497
  Disputatio de fide catholica.
10655
  Liber de confirmatione legis Christianae.
  For all these see Lull in A (iii).

Oxford (Bodleian Library)
Can. Pat. Lat. 142
  Libellus ad nationes. See A (iii) (Ricoldo).
New College 90
  Summa de questionibus Armenorum. See A (iii) (Fitzralph).
C.C.C. d 184
Selden Supra 31
  Both contain Ketton's Qur'ān and the first contains Peter of Toledo's
    Risālah. See A (iii) under Cluny.
  The best manuscript for the Cluniac corpus is Arsenal 1162 (Paris),
    but the Oxford MSS are satisfactory, and were more easily available
    to me. Refer d'Alverny, *Deux traductions*, p. 108ff.
Marsh 179 (Murad), *Smith* 88 (Smith), *Selden Supra* 33 (Libro de
  Lustre) and *Eng. misc. f.* 17 (Turkish Faith): list B.

Paris (Bibliothèque nationale)
Lat. 3394.
  Contrarietas elfolica. See A (iii) under Mark.

Paris, continued

Lat. 3646
   Contra alchoranum. See A (iii) under Pennis.
Lat. 3671
   Traductio Alchorani Maumethis. See B, under Moncata.
Lat. 4230
   Reprobatio (A (ii)) and Disputatio (A (iii), under Ricoldo).
Lat. 14503
   Prophetia and Liber Nicholay (A (ii)).
Lat. nouv. acq. 130
   Historiae ex Alcorano depromptae. See B.

Vienna (Oesterr. Nationalbibliothek)
Cod. 4297
   Alcorani Machometi Liber. See A (iii) under Mark.

Vatican City (Biblioteca Apostolica Vaticana)
Lat. 314
   Tripoli de statu – see A (iii).
Lat. 971
   Sancius de Arevalo, list B.

Bibliography B:
Writers on Islam of the period 1350-1850

(This is not an exhaustive list; it is a list of the books on which sections 2, 3 and 4 of chapter X are based. Travellers later than 1700, and historical, philosophical, poetic, or linguistic works of all dates, with a few exceptions, are excluded.)

'ABD AL-LAṬĪF ibn Yūsuf ibn Muḥammad ibn 'Alī al-Baghdādī. See Pocock.

'ABDULLA MAHUMED OMAR'. See *Mahomet no Impostor*.

ABRAHAM ECCHELLENSIS (Ibrāhīm al-Ḥaqalāni). *Chronicon Orientale nunc primum Latinitate donatum*. Paris, 1651, and Beirut, Paris and Leipzig, 1903.

—— *Semita Sapientiae sive ad scientias comparandas methodus nunc primum Latini iuris facta*. Paris, 1646.

—— *Synopsis Propositorum Sapientiae Arabum Philosophorum nunc primum ex Arabico sermone Latini iuris facta*. Paris, 1641.

ABŪ BAKR MUHAMMAD ibn Ṭufail al-Qaisī. See Pocock.

ABU'L FIDĀ'. See Gagnier.

'ACHMET BENABDULLA ERUDITUM MAURUM'. *Mohammedica sive Dissertatio Epistolaris*. Altorf, 1700.

ADISON, L. *The First State of Mahumedism*. London, 1679.

—— *West Barbary, or a short Narrative of the Revolutions*. Oxford, 1671.

AHMAD ibn Muhammad ibn Abdallah. See Vattier (Tamerlan).

ALAMÍN, F. DE. *Impugnacion contra el Talmud de los judios, Alcoran de Mahoma y contra los Hereges, y segunda de la Religion Christiana*, etc. Madrid, 1727.

'ALI-GIER-BER'. See Cloots.

ALBERTI, TOMMASO. *Viaggio a Constantinopoli 1609-1621*. Ed. A. Bacchi-della Lega. Bologna, 1889.

ALBUQUERQUE. *The Commentaries of the Great Afonso Dalboquerque*. Tr. and ed. W. de Gray Birch. 3 vols., London (Hakluyt Society), 1875-84.

ALCMARIANUS. See P. Nanning.

ALCOCK, NATHAN. *The Rise of Mahomet accounted for on Natural and Civil Principles*. London, 1796.

Alcoran Mahometicus, Das ist Der Turcken Alcoran, Religion und Aberglauben. Nuremberg, 1623.

AL-HASAN ibn Muhammad Al-Wazzān az-Zaiyātī. See Leo Africanus.

'ALI BEY. See Bobovius.

AL-MAKĪN ibn al-'Amīd, Jirjīs. See Erpenius and Vattier.

Alphabeta. *Alphabetum Arabicum*, by J. Christman. Neustadt an der

Hardt, 1582. *Alphabetum Arabicum.* Cum licentia . . . Rome, 1592. *Specimen characterum Arabicorum,* by F. Rapheleng. Leyden, 1595.

ANDRÉS, JUAN. *Confusion de la secta mahomatica y del alcoran compuesta por mossen juan andres . . . quondam Alfaqui dexatina agora por la divina bondad cristiano y sacerdote.* Valencia, 1515.

—— *The Confusion of Muhamed's Sect, or a Confutation of the Turkish Alcoran Being a Discovery of many secret Policies and practices of that Religion, not till now revealed.* London, 1652. (Tr. J. Notstock.)

Antiquity of Reformation, or an Observation proving the Great Turk a Triangle and the rest of the World Roundheads. London, 1647.

D'ARANDA, E. *Relation de la Captivité.* Brussels, 1662.

ARRIVABENE, ANDREA. *L'Alcorano di Macometto.* Venice, 1598.

BARBERINO, ANDREA DA. *L'Aspramonte.* Bologna, 1951.

—— *I Reali di Francia.* Bari, 1959.

BAR ʿEBHRĀYĀ, ibn al-ʿIbrī (Gregorius Abu'l Faraj). See Pocock, E.

BARBOSA. *The Book of Duarte Barbosa.* Ed. M. L. Dames, 2 vols., London (Hakluyt Society), 1918-21.

BAUDIER, M. *Histoire Genérale de la Religion de Turcs.* Paris, 1625.

BAUER, J. C. V. *Conspectum Theologiae Turcarum Mochammedicae.* Iena, 1720.

BAYLE, PIERRE. *Dictionaire Historique et Critique,* s.v. *Mahomet.* Rotterdam, 1697. Troisième edition, revue, corrigée et augmentée. Rotterdam, 1720.

BEAUVAIS. *Relation iournalière du Voyage du Levant faict et descrit par haut et puissant seigneur Henry de Beauvais, Baron,* etc. Nancy, 1619.

BECK, M. F. *Specimen Arabicum, hoc est bina capitula Alcorani XXX de Roma et XLIIX de Victoria.* Augsburg, 1688.

BEDWELL, WILLIAM. *Mohammedis Imposturae, that is, a Discovery of the Manifold Forgeries* etc. *Written long since in Arabicke and now done into English* by W. B. London, 1615.

BELFOUR, F. C. *The Life of Sheikh Mohammed Ali Hazin.* London, 1830.

BELLARMINE. *Roberti Bellarmini Disputatio de notis Ecclesiae,* in *Disputationes.* Ingolstadt, 1590.

—— *Doctrina Christiana D.D. Roberti S.R.E. Card. Bellarmini nunc primum ex Italico idiomate in Arabicum, iussu S.D.N. Pauli V Pont. Max. translata,* per Victorium Scialac Accurensem et Gabrielem Sionitam Edeniensem, Maronitas . . . Rome, 1613.

BELON, PIERRE. *Les Observations de Plusieurs Singularitez.* Paris, 1553.

BIBLIANDER (Theodore Buchmann). *Th. Bibliandri Apologia in editione Alcorani.* In *Machumetis Saracenorum principis . . .* etc. (see list A (i)). See also Fabricius, M. J.

BIONDI, FLAVIO. *Historiarum . . . decades III.* Basle, 1559.

—— *De expeditione in Turchos,* etc., in Nogara (list C).

BOBOVIUS, A. (ʿAli Bey). *Tractatus de Turcarum Liturgia, Peregrinatione Meccana,* etc. *Nonnullas annotatiunculas . . . passim adjecit Thomas Hyde, S.T.D., e Coll. Reginae, Oxon.* In *Syntagma Dissertationum.* Oxford, 1767 (1st edition, 1691).

—— *A treatise concerning the Turkish Liturgy, with notes by Thomas Hyde STD of Queen's College, Oxford.* London, 1712.

Bobrowski, A. ('Ali Bey). See Bobovius.

Bodin, J. *Colloquium heptaplomeres de rerum sublimium arcanis abditis.*
Schwerin, 1857.

―― *Les Secrets Cachez des Choses Sublimes.* Livres iv-vi. In Chauviré
(list C).

―― *De republica.* Paris, 1591. (English version, *Booke of a Common-weale,* London, 1616.)

Boulainvilliers, Henri Comte de. *Vie de Mahomed.* Londres, 1730.

―― *The Life of Mahomet translated from the French Original by the
Count of Boulainvilliers.* London, 1731.

Boullaye, see La Boullaye le Gouz.

Bradshaw, W. See Marana.

Brascha, Santo. *L'itinerario de giorno in giorno . . . particularmente tute
le deuotione: indulgentie: e oratione* etc. Milan, 1481.

Breydenbach, Bernhard von. *Opus transmarine peregrinationis ad
venerandum et gloriosum sepulcrum Dominicum in Jherusalem.* Mayence,
1486.

Brerewood, E. *Enquiries touching the Diversity of Languages and Religions
throughout the cheife parts of the world.* London, 1614.

Brocquiere, see La Brocquiere, Bertrandon de.

Brunfels, Otto. *Ad Christianos Principes ut Rhodiorum . . . afflictionibus
succuratur Oratio.* In Sadoleti.

Bry, Io. Theodores & Io. Israel de Bry fratres. *Acta Mechometi Sara-cenorum principis.* Frankfurt, 1597.

Bullinger, H. *Daniel sapientissimus Dei propheta . . . expositus.* Zürich,
1565.

Burhān ad-Dīn az-Zarnūjī. See Abraham Ecchellensis (Semita).

Burke, Edmund. *Speeches in the Impeachment of Warren Hastings, Esq.*
in *Works,* London, 1852.

Butrus ibn Muhaddib. See Abraham Ecchellensis (Chronicon).

Busbecq, Seigneur de. *Gislenii Busbequii Omnia Quae Extant.* Leyden
1633.

Carlyle, T. *On Heroes. (The Hero as Prophet.)* London (1st edition
1841).

Carré de Chambon, Abbé Barthélemy. *Voyages des Indes Orientales.*
Paris, 1699.

―― *Travels in India and the Near East 1672-1674.* Tr. from MS by
Lady Fawcett. London (Hakluyt Society), 1947.

Carruthers. *The Desert Route to India, being the journals of four travellers,
1745-1751.* Ed. D. Carruthers. London (Hakluyt Society), 1929.

Castel de Saint Pierre, C. I. *Discours contre le Mahométisme* in *Ouvrajes
de Politique,* tome Ve, Rotterdam, 1733.

Casola, *Canon Pietro's Pilgrimage to Jerusalem in the year 1494.* Tr.
M. M. Newett. Manchester, 1907.

Cavalleria, Petro de la, see La Cavalleria.

Chalcondylas. *Laonici Chalcondylae Atheniensis de origine et rebus gestis
Turcorum libri decem nuper a Graeco in Latinum conversi,* C. Clausero
interprete. Basle, 1615.

Chardin, J. *Description de la Perse.* Ed. L. Langlès. Paris, 1811.

CHARRON, P. *Les Trois Veritez*, etc. Bordeaux, 1593.

CHATEAUBRIAND, F.-R. VICOMTE DE. *Note sur la Grèce*, 3rd edition, in *Itinéraire*. Paris, 1829.

CHEMIN, J.-B. *Code religieux et moral des Théophilantropes*. Paris, an VI (1797-8).

CHENIER, L. DE. *Récherches historiques sur les Maures*. Paris, 1787.

—— *Révolutions de l'Empire Ottoman*. Paris, 1789.

CHINON, LE P. GABRIEL DE. *Relations nouvelles du Levant ou Traités de la Religion*, etc. Lyons, 1671.

CHRISTMAN, J. See Alphabeta.

Chronicle of Events. See Gollancz.

CLAVIJO, RUY GONZALEZ DE. *Life and Acts of the Great Tamerlane*, etc., 1403. Ed. C. R. Markham. London (Hakluyt Society), 1859.

CLODIUS, J. C. *Theoria et praxis Linguae Arabicae*. Leipzig, 1729.

CLOOTS, J. B. BARON DE ('Anacharsis Cloots', 'Ali-Gier-Ber, Alfaki'). *La Certitude des Preuves du Mahométisme*. London, 1780.

Comprehensive View of the Various Controversies, etc. Edinburgh, 1785.

COTOVICUS, J. *Itinerarium hierosolymitanum et syriacum in quo variarum gentium mores et instituta delucide recensentur*. Antwerp, 1619.

COVEL, DR JOHN. *Extracts from the Diaries*. In *Early Voyages and Travels in the Levant*. London (Hakluyt Society), 1893.

CURIO, C. A. *Sarracenicae Historiae libri III*. Basle, 1567. Eng. tr., *A Notable Historie of the Saracens*, etc., by Thomas Newton. London, 1575.

DALLAM, MASTER THOMAS. *Diary*, in *Early Voyages in the Levant*. Ed. J. T. Bent. London (Hakluyt Society), 1893.

DAN, PIERRE. *Histoire de Barbarie*. Paris, 1637.

DANDINI, G. *Missione apostolica al Patriarcha*, etc. Cesena, 1656.

DANIEL, WILLIAM. *A Journal or Account* (London, 1702) in *The Red Sea and Adjacent Countries* (ed. Sir W. Forster). London (Hakluyt Society), 1949.

DAPPER, O. *Africa, being an accurate description* (adapted by John Ogilby from the *Naukeurige Leschrijvinge der Afrikaensche gewesten van Egypten*). London, 1670.

Description of the Turks Prayers and Fasts; Relation of the Procession, Fasting and Penance enjoyned by MAHOMET-SOLYMAN (Edinburgh, 1686); and similar pamphlets.

De thurcie destructione. Trèves, 1498.

Dialogo che fanno nell' inferno Maometto et il signor di Colbert Ministro di Francia sopra gl'affari de Tempi correnti. Cologne, 1683. (French original not seen by me.)

DIONYSIUS CARTHUSIANUS. See Leeuwen, Denys van.

DRESCHLER, WOLFGANG. *De Saracenis et Turcis Chronicon*, with Curio, *Sarrac. Hist.*, and with *quad. rep.* (list A (ii)). Strasburg, 1550.

DU RYER, ANDRÉ. *L'alcoran de Mahomet translaté d'arabe en françois*. Paris, 1647.

—— *The Alcoran of Mahomet translated out of Arabique into French . . . and newly Englished*, with *The Life and Death of Mahomet*, and *A Needfull Caveat*, by Alexander Ross. London, 1649.

EHRHART, JACOB. *De illustrium ac obscurum scriptorum erroribus praecipuis in Historia Mahometi eorumque causis dissertatio.* Memmingen, 1731.

Encyclopédie ou Dictionnaire Raisonné des Sciences, des Arts et des Métiers. s.v. *Alcoran, Dervis, Mahométisme, Muphti,* etc. Paris, 1751ff.

Epitome Fidei et Religionis Turcicae. In MS (see note to list A, London).

ERPENIUS, T. *Historia Josephi Patriarchae, ex Alcorano.* Leyden, 1617.

—— *Historia Saracenica qua res gestae Muslimorum inde a Muhammede Arabe . . . Arabice olim exarata a Georgio Elmacino,* etc. *et Latine reddita op. et st. Thomae Erpenii.* Leyden, 1625.

—— *The Saracenical Historie* in Purchas, 4th edition.

FABRI, F. *Fr. Felicis Fabri Evagatorium in Terrae Sanctae Arabiae et Egypti Peregrinationem,* ed. C. D. Hassler, 3 vols. Stuttgart, 1843-9.

FABRI, J. *Oratio de origine potentia ac tyrrannide Turcarum . . . ad Henricum . . . ejus nomine VIII . . .* In Brown (vol. 1).

FABRICIUS, J. *Muhammedis Testamentum sive Pacta cum Christianis inita* (with Bibliander's Apologia), Rostock, 1638.

FEBVRE, M. *Théâtre de la Turquie.* Paris, 1682. (Also, *Teatro de la Turchia.* Bologna, 1683.)

FONTANI, I. *de Rhodi expugnatione epistola.* In Sadoleti.

FORSTER, C. *Mahometanism Unveiled.* 2 vols., London, 1829.

—— *A Vindication of the Theory of Mahometanism Unveiled.* London, 1830 (not published).

FOSS, J. *A Journal of the Captivity and Sufferings.* Newburyport, 1798.

FRYER, J. *A new Account of East India and Persia,* ed. W. Crooke. 3 vols., London (Hakluyt Society), 1909-15.

GAGNIER, J. *Abu'l Feda de vita et rebus gestis Mohammedis.* Oxford, 1723.

—— *Vie de Mahomet.* 2 vols. Amsterdam, 1732.

GALLAND, A. *Les Mille et Une Nuits.* (ed. G. Picard), Paris, 1960.

—— *The Remarkable Sayings, Apothegms and Maxims.* Translated out of the French. London, 1695.

GAUDIN, JACQUES. *Le Jardin des Roses. Traduction du Gulistan de Sady; suivi d'un essai historique.* Paris, 1789.

GEMELLI-CARERI, G. F. *Giro del mondo.* Nuova edizione, Venice, 1728.

GENTIUS. *Rosarium Politicum sive Amoenum Sortis Humanae Theatrum in Latinum versum . . . a Georgio Gentio.* Amsterdam, 1610.

GEORGIEUIZ, BARTHOLOMAEO. *De Turcarum moribus epitome; de afflictione captivorum, disputationis narratio, exhortatio contra Turcas,* etc. Lyons, 1558.

—— *Profetia de Maomettani in Lingua Turchescha.* In Sansovino.

GEORGIUS DE HUNGARIA. See Septemcastrensis.

GERMAIN, JEAN. *Le discours du voyage d'oultremer prononcé en 1452.* See Schefer, list C.

—— *Le Débat du Crestien et du Sarrazin.* Paris, Bib. nat., MS franc. 6745; not seen by me.

GIBBON, E. *Decline and Fall of the Roman Empire.* London, 1776-88.

GIFFORD, W. See Rainolds.

GODINHO, M. *Overland Return from India.* Extracts tr. in *Portuguese Voyages,* ed. C. D. Ley. London, 1947.

GOLLANCZ, SIR H. (Ed.) *Chronicle of Events relating to the Settlement of the Carmelites in Mesopotamia.* London, 1927.

GROOT, H. DE. Grotius *de veritate religionis Christianae.* Paris, 1627. Editio nova, Paris, 1640; editio novissima, Paris, 1650.

GUADAGNOLI, P. *Considerationes ad Mahometanos cum Responsione ad Objectiones Ahmed Filii Zin Alahedin* (with Arabic translation). Rome, 1649.

GUERINO IL MESCHINO. *Ystoria breve de re Karlo.* Padua, 1473.

GÜGLINGEN. *Fr. Pauli Waltheri Guglingensis Itinerarium.* Ed. M. Sollweck. Tübingen, 1892. (With *tractatus, 'stante me per Dei gratiam . . . quiete . . .'*)

HACKSPAN, TH. *Fides et Leges Mohammaedis exhibitae ex Alcorani manuscripto duplici.* Altorf, 1646.

'HADGI MEHEMMED EFFENDI'. See Pétis de la Croix.

HAKLUYT, RICHARD. *The Principal Navigations, Voiages, Traffiques and Discoveries of the English Nation.* The second volume, London, 1599.

HARBORNE, W. *A relation of the Turkish Empire gathered in Anno 1580, with the Originall of Mahomett and the howse of the Ottomans.* In MS (see note to list A s.v. London).

HARDT, H. VON DER. *Sura prima,* etc., in *Arabia Graeca.* Helmstedt, 1714.

HARFF, ARNOLD VON. *The pilgrimage . . . 1496 to 1499.* Tr. and ed. M. Letts. London (Hakluyt Society), 1946.

D'HERBELOT, BARTHÉLEMY. *Bibliothèque Orientale ou dictionaire universel.* Paris, 1697.

HERBERT, SIR THOMAS, BART. *Travels begun anno 1626.* London, 1634.

Here after foloweth a lytell treatise agaynst Mahumet. London, 1530.

HIGGINS, G. *Mohamed, or the Illustrious.* London, 1829.

Historical and Critical Reflections upon Mahometanism and Socinianism. London, 1712.

History of Mahomet, the Great Impostor. Falkirk, 1821.

Historiae ex Alcorano depromptae. In MS (see note to list A).

HORNBEECK, J. *Summa Controversiarum Religionis cum Infidelibus, Haereticis, Schismaticis,* etc. Utrecht, 1653.

HOTMANUS, D. F. See Sionita.

HOTTINGER, J. H. *Historia Orientalis.* Zürich, 1651.

―― *Smegma Orientalis.* Heidelberg, 1658.

HUSAIN ibn 'Ali aṭ-Ṭughrā'i. See Pocock, Carmen Tograi.

HUSAIN ibn Mu'in ad-Dīn al-Maybudī. See Abraham Ecchellensis (Synopsis).

HYDE, T. See Bobovius.

IBN ṬUFAYL. See Pocock, Ockley.

IRVING, W. *Lives of Mahomet and his successors.* London, 1850.

ISMA'IL ibn 'Ali imād ad-Dīn Abu'l Fidā. See Gagnier, Abu'l Feda.

JONES, SIR W. *On the Mystical Poetry of the Persians and Hindus* and other lectures in *Works,* London, 1799.

JOYE, GEORGE. *The Exposicion of Daniel the Prophete gathered,* etc. Geneva, 1545.

KINGLAKE, A. W. *Eothen.*

KIRSTEN, P. *Epistola Dedicatoria,* in *Grammatices Arabicae.* Breslaw, 1608.

KNIGHT, F. *Relation of Seven Yeares Slaverie.* London, 1640.
KNOLLES, RICHARD. *The Generall Historie of the Turkes* (3rd edition). London, 1621.
KRUSINSKI, J. T. *Hoc est Chronicon Peregrinationis,* etc. Leipzig, 1731.
LA BOULLAYE LE GOUZ, FRANÇOIS DE. *Voyages et Observations.* Paris, 1653.
LA BROCQUIÈRE, BERTRANDON DE. *Voyage d'outremer et retour de Jerusalem en France* . . . pub. Legrand d'Aussy; in Hakluyt, a new edition with additions, vol. IV, supplement. London, 1811.
LA CAVALLERIA, PETRO DE. *Tractatus Zelus Christi contra Iudaeos, Sarracenos, et infideles.* Venice, 1592.
LAMARTINE, M. L. A. DE. *Histoire de la Turquie.* Paris, 1854.
—— *Voyage en Orient* (ed. L. Fam). Paris, 1960.
—— *La question d'Orient.* Brussels, 1841.
LANCELIN DE LAVAL. *Histoire secrette du Prophète des Turcs.* 'Constantinople' (Paris), 1754.
LAS CASES, EMMANUEL COMTE DE. *Mémorial de Sainte-Hélène.* London, 1823.
LAUGIER DE TASSY. *Histoire du Royaume d'Alger.* Amsterdam, 1725. (English version by Morgan, London, 1750.)
LEEUWEN, DENYS VAN, or OF RICKEL. *Contra perfidiam Mahometi, libri quatuor.*
—— *Dialogus Disputationis inter Christianum et Sarracenum de lege Christi* etc.
Both in *Opera Omnia* vol. 36 (opera minora IV) Tournai, 1908.
—— *De particulari judicio,* same edition, vol. 41 (min. IX).
—— *D. Dionysii Carthusiani Epistola Paraenetica qua per Scripturas et tres revelationes sibi divinitus factas* . . . *ad generale celebrandum Concilium et bellum adversus Turcam suscipiendum hortatur.* Cologne, 1533.
LEIBNIZ, G. W. BARON VON. Theodicée. Paris, 1839.
—— Textes inédits. Ed. G. Grua. Paris, 1948.
LEO AFRICANUS. (Al-Ḥasan ibn Muhammad al-Wazzān az-Zaiyāti). *History and Description of Africa.* Tr. J. Pory (1600). Ed. R. Brown, London (Hakluyt Society), 3 vols. 1896.
—— *De viris quibusdam illustribus apud Arabes libellus.* In J. A. Fabricii Bibliothecae Graecae, vol. XIII. Hamburg, 1726.
LEONARDUS CHIENSIS. See Rotting.
Lettre d'un Médecin Arabe. Paris, 1713.
Libro de Lustre de la Lampise. (In MS, see note, s.v. Oxford.)
Life and Actions of Mahomet. London, 1712.
Life of Mahomet or the History of that Imposture. London, 1799.
LITHGOW, W. *The totall discourse* . . . London, 1632.
LUTHER, MARTIN. *Doctoris Martini Lutheri Colloquia Mensalia,* etc. Collected by A. Lauterbach and disposed . . . by John Aurifaber. Tr. out of the high Germane by Capt. Henrie Bell. London, 1652.
—— *Colloquia oder Tisch-Reden D. Martin Luther.* Leipzig, 1700.
—— *D. Martini Lutheri Colloquia* etc. ed. H. E. Bindeil. 3 vols. Lemgo and Detmold. 1863-6.
—— *Analecta Lutherana et Melanthoniana – Tischreden Luthers und*

Aussprüche Melanthons. J. Mathesius and G. Loesche Gotha, 1892.
—— *Catechismus minor arabice.* Halle, 1729. (Not seen by me.)
—— *Epistola ad pium lectorem.* In Bibliander (see A (i)).
—— *In . . . (Danielem) prophetam commentarius.* 1546.
—— *The Prophecyes of the incomparable and famous Dr Martin Luther.* London, 1664.
MAENAVINO, J. A., OF GENOA, tr. P. Lonicerus. *De Mahometanis Turcorum Legibus, religione* etc. In *Chronicorum Turcicorum tomus primus.* Frankfurt on Main, 1578.
MAFFEI, R., VOLATERRANUS. *De Mahumeto eiusque legibus,* etc. In Bibliander.
Mahomet no Impostor (A Defence of Mahomet), in *Miscellanea Aurea or the Golden Medley.* London, 1720.
MANRIQUE, S. *Travels, 1629-43.* Tr. C. E. Luard and H. Hosten. (Hakluyt Society) Oxford, 1927.
MARACCI, L. *Alcorani Textus Universus . . . His omnibus praemissus est Prodromus.* Together with *Refutatio Alcorani.* Padua, 1698.
MARANA, G. P. *Letters written by a Turkish Spy.* 23rd English edition (tr. W. Bradshaw?), London, 1730.
MARTONI, N. DE. *Relation du Pèlerinage, 1394-1395.* Ed. L. Le Grand ROL, 1895.
MELANCHTHON, P. *Commentarius in Danielem.* In *Opera omnia,* ed. C. G. Bretschneider, *Corpus Reformatorum;* Halle, 1834ff.
—— *Praemonitio ad lectorem.* In Bibliander (A (i)).
MELANCHTHON P. *Enerrationes:* in evang. Ioh. xv; ep. prior. ad Tim. IV; in Ps. CXVIV; and sermo, dom. xxv post Trin.
—— *Loci Communes Theologici.* Basle, 1561. French version: *La Somme de Théologie ou Lieux Communs reveuz & augmentés de nouveau.* Geneva, 1551.
—— See also Luther, *Analecta.*
MEYER, P. *Mahometi Arabis Pseudoprophetae vita versibus expressa.* Arras, 1594.
MILLER, G. *Lectures on the Philosophy of Modern History.* Dublin, 1816-28.
Miroir de l'Empire Ottoman. Paris, 1678-88.
MOHAMMED ALI HAZIN. See Belfour.
MONCATA, WILLIAM OF. *Traductio Alcorani Maumethi. Guiglemi Ramundi de Moncata,* etc. In MS. (See note to list A.)
MONTAGU, LADY MARY WORTLEY. *Letters of the Right Hon. Lady M—y W—y M—e.* London, 1763.
MONTESQUIEU, C. DE SECONDAT, BARON DE. *Lettres persanes.* (Ed. P. Vernière) Paris, 1960.
Morality of the East, extracted from the Koran of Mohammed. London, 1766.
MORGAN, J. *A Complete History of Algiers.* London, 1728. See also Laugier, Rabadan.
MURAD BEG. *Codex supra tres linguas.* (In MS, see note, s.v. Oxford.)
—— *Liber murat beg interpretis* (in MS., see note, s.v. London).
NAGY DE HARSANY, J. *Colloquia Familiaria . . . subnexum est testamentum seu foedus Mahomedis cum Xanis initum.* Brandenburg, 1672.
NANNING, P., OF ALKMAR. *P. Nanni in eos qui negant bellum Turcae inferendum.* (In Sadoleti.)

Nau, M. *Religio Christiana contra Alcoranum pacifice defensa et probata.* Paris, 1680.

—— *L'Etat présent de la Religion Mahometane.* Paris, 1684.

Newman, J. H. *Lectures on the History of the Turks.* Dublin, 1854.

Nicolas of Cusa. *Cribrationis Alcoran libri III.* In Bibliander (A (i)).

—— *De pace fidei; cum epistula ad Ioannem deSegovia.* (See Klibansky, list C.)

Nissel, J. G. *Historia de Abrahamo et de Gomorro-Sodomitica Eversione ex Alcorano.* Leyden, 1655.

—— *Testamentum inter Muhamedem et Christianae Religionis populos initum.* Leyden, 1655.

Notstock, Joshua. See Andrés.

Obregón, Lope. *Confutacion del Alcoran y secta Mahometana facada de sus proprios libros: y de la vida del mesmo Mahoma.* Granada, 1555.

Ockley, S. *History of the Saracens.* London, 1708-18, in *The Conquest of Syria*, etc., 2 vols. 2nd edition, 2 vols., 1718.

—— *Sentences of Ali.* London, 1717.

—— (tr.) *The Improvement of Human Reason Exhibited . . . by Abu Jaafer Ebn Tophail.* London, 1708.

—— *Introductio ad Linguas Orientales.* Cambridge, 1706.

Oelsner, M. *Des effets de la Religion de Mohammed.* Paris, 1810.

Of the Religion of the Turks. Preceded by various notes and a *Narrative of Transilvania*, and followed by *Epistola missa ad Urbem Romanam.* (In MS. See note s.v. London.)

Ogilby, John. See Dapper.

Ogier VIII, seigneur d'Anglure. *Le saint voyage de Jherusalem* ed. F. Bonnardot and A. Longnon. Paris, 1878.

Pacifique de Provins, Père, OFM Cap. *Relation du Voyage . . . ensemble le bon traitement que le roy du Perse fit au R.P.P. avec le Testament de Mahomet.* Paris, 1631.

Paley, W. *Evidences of Christianity*, in *Works*, London, 1838.

Pasor, M. *Oratio pro Linguae Arabicae professione.* Oxford, 1627.

Pastoret, C. E. J. P. de. *Zoroastre, Confucius et Mahomet.* Paris, 1787.

Pereira, João José. *Historia da Vida, Conquistas e Religião de Mafoma.* Lisbon, 1791.

Pétis de la Croix, F. (Père). *Histoire du Grand Genghizcan.* Paris, 1710. English version by P. Aubin, London, 1722.

Pétis de la Croix, F. (Fils). *Extrait du Journal.* Paris, 1810.

—— *Histoire de Timur-Bec.* Paris, 1722. English version, London, 1723.

Pétis de la Croix, A. L. M. *Lettres critiques de Hadgi Mehemmed Effendi.* Paris, 1735.

Philippe de la Trés-Sainte Trinité. *Voyage d'Orient.* Lyons, 1652.

Pientini. R. P. F. Angelo Pientini da Corsignano, O.P. *Alcorano riprivato nel quale si mostra le falsita della setta Macomettana.* Florence, 1603.

Piloti. *Traité d'Emmanuel Piloti sur le Passage dans la Terre Sainte.* 1420 tr. (into French) 1441. In *Monuments pour servir à l'Histoire des provinces de Namur, de Hainaut et de Luxembourg.* Ed. le Baron de Reiffenberg. Tome iv, Brussels, 1846.

PIRES, TOMÉ. *Suma Oriental.* 2 vols., London (Hakluyt Society), 1944.

PITTS, J. *A true and faithful account of the religion and manners of the Mohammetans.* Exeter, 1704.

PIUS II. *Pius episcopus servus servorum Dei illustri Mahumeti principi turcorum Timorem divini nominis et amorem* . . . (1470?) printed by Bibliander as *Epistola Pii Papae II ad Morbisanum Turcarum principem* (with epistola Morbisani magni Turcae ad Pium Papam II).

—— *Aeneae Sylvii Pii II Pontif. Max. de Constantinopolitana Clade et bello contra Turcas congregando Oratio,* in Reusner.

POCOCK, E. (the elder). *Specimen historiae Arabum sive Gregorii Abu'l Fargii* . . . *de origine et moribus Arabum* . . . *narratio.* Oxford, 1650.

—— *Historia compendiosa dynastiarum.* Oxford, 1663.

—— *Lamiato l Ajam, Carmen Tograi poetae Arabis Doctissimi, una cum versione latina et notis* . . . Oxford, 1661.

See also Twells, 6.

POCOCK, E. (the younger). *Philosophus autodidactus sive epistola Jaafar ebn Tophail de Hai ebn Yakdhan, in qua ostenditur quomodo ex inferiorem notitiam ratio humana ascendere possit.* Oxford, 1671 (English translation, 1674 as *An Account of the Oriental Philosophy*).

—— *Abdollatiphi historiae Egypti compendium.* 1681(?).

PONCET, CHARLES JACQUES. *A Voyage to Aethoipia* (London, 1709) in *The Red Sea and Adjacent Countries* (ed. Sir W. Foster). London (Hakluyt Society), 1949.

PORTER, SIR J. *Observations on the Religion.* London, 1768.

—— *Turkey, its History and Progress.* London, 1854.

PORY, J. *A summarie discourse of the manifold religions professed in Africa.* In Leo Africanus, q.v.

POSTEL, GUILLAUME. *De orbis terrae concordia.* Basle, 1544.

—— *De la république des Turcs.* Poitiers, 1560.

—— *Des histoires Orientales,* Paris, 1575.

—— *Alcorani et Evangelistarum Concordiae liber.* Paris, 1543.

—— *Descriptio Alcahirae.* Venice, 1549.

PRIDEAUX, HUMPHREY. *The True Nature of Imposture Fully Display'd in the Life of Mahomet, with a Discourse annexed for the Vindicating of Christianity.* London, 1697.

Purchas His Pilgrimage or Relations of the Worlds and the Religions. Second edition, London, 1614. Fourth edition, London, 1626.

RABADAN, MAHOMET. *Mahometism Explained.* (Tr.) J. Morgan. London, 1723.

RABBATH, A. *Documents inédits pour servir à l'Histoire du Christianisme en Orient.* Paris, Leipzig and London, 1905-10.

RAINOLDS, W. *Calvino-Turcismus, id est, Calvinisticae Perfidiae* (ed. by W. Gifford) Antwerp, 1597.

RAPHELENG. (François Ravlenghien.) *Lexicon Arabicum.* Leyden, 1613.

—— See also Alphabeta.

RAUE, CHRISTIAN. *A Discourse concerning the Easterne Tongues* in *A Generall Grammer,* etc. by Christian Ravis. London, 1649.

—— *Prima tredecim partium Alcorani Arabico-Latini.* Amsterdam(?), 1646(?).

RAUWOLFF, L. *Travels into the Eastern Countries.* In Ray's *Curious Travels.* London, 1783.

Reflections on Mohammedism and the conduct of Mohammed, occasioned by a late learned Translation and Exposition of the Koran or Al Koran. London, 1735.

REINECK. *Historia Orientalis polyhistoris clarissimi Reineccii Reineri.* Helmstedt, 1602.

RELAND, A. *Adriani Relandi de religione Mohammedica.* Utrecht, 1705.

—— *De religione Mohammedica.* Editio altera auctior. Utrecht, 1717.

—— *Reland on the Mahometan Religion.* London, 1712. (From the first edition.)

—— *La Religion des Mahométans, exposée par leurs propres Docteurs,* etc. The Hague, 1721. (From the second edition.)

REUSNER, N. *De bello Turcico selectissimarum orationum et consultationum variorum et diversorum auctorum volumen primum.* Leipzig, 1595.

RICHARDS, JOHN. *Diary.* (In MS, see note s.v. London.)

RICHER, CHR. *De rebus Turcarum ad Franciscum Gallorum Regem Christianissimum libri quinque.* Paris, 1540.

ROBERTS, A. *The Adventures of Mr. T. S., an English merchant.* London, 1670.

ROBERTSON, W. *An Historical Disquisition.* London, 1791.

ROE, SIR T. *The Embassy.* Ed. W. Foster (Hakluyt Society). London, 1899.

—— *The Negotiations.* Ed. S. Richardson. London, 1740.

ROSS, A. See du Ryer.

ROTTING, M. *Historia Captae a Turca Constantinopolis Descripta a Leonardo Chiensi* etc. *M.R. in eandem Praefatio.* Nurembourg, 1544.

RYCAUT, P. *Histoire de l'état présent de l'empire ottoman.* Amsterdam, 1670.

SA'DĪ. See Gaudin, Gentius.

SADOLETI, I. *De bello Turcis inferendo Oratio.* Basle, 1538.

SALE, G. *The Koran . . . to which is prefixed a Preliminary Discourse.* London, 1734.

SANCIUS DE AREVALO, RODERICUS. *Liber de sceleribus et infelicitate perfidi Turchi.* (In MS, see note s.v. Vatican.)

—— *Epistola lugubris.* Cologne, 1475.

SANDYS, G. *A Relation of a Journey.* London, 1627.

SANSEVERINO, ROBERTO DA. *Viaggio in Terra Santa.* Ed. G. Maruffi, Bologna, 1888.

SANSOVINO. *Della Historia Turchesca nella quale si contengono la vita, le legge et li costumi di quella natione.* Venice, 1573.

SARMIENTO, M. *Meco-Moro-Agudo.* Madrid, 1789.

SAVARY DE BRÈVES. *Relation des Voyages,* with *Un Traicté faict entre le Roy Henry le Grand et l'Empereur des Turcs;* and *Trois Discours du dit Sieur.* Paris, 1628.

SAVARY, M. *Le Coran, traduit de l'arabe, accompagné de notes, et précédé d'un abrégé de la vie de Mahomet.* Paris, 1783.

—— *Morale de Mahomet ou Recueil des plus pures maximes du Coran.* Paris, 1784.

SAVONAROLA. *Mahumetanorum sectam omni ratione carere Commenta-tiuncula, Hieronymo Sauonarola auctore* in Bibliander.

SCHILTBERGER, JOHANNES. *The bondage and travels, 1396-1427.* ed. K. F. Neumann, J. B. Telfer and P. Brunn. London (Hakluyt Society), 1879.

SCHROEDER, MATTH. GEORG. *Muhammad testis veritatis contra seipsum.* Leipzig, 1719.

SCHWARTZ, JO. CONRAD. *De Mohammedi Furto Sententiarum Scripturae Sacrae Liber unus.* Leipzig, 1711.

SCIALAC, VICTORIUS. (Naṣr Allāh Shalaq). See Bellarmine.

SEGOVIA, JOHN OF. *Epistolae; Praefatio in translationem libri Alchorani; de mittendo gladio* (summary); texts printed by Cabanelas (list C).

SEPTEMCASTRENSIS. *Tractatus de moribus, conditionibus et nequitia Tur-corum.* In Bibliander (A (i)).

SEPULVEDA. *Genesii Sepuluedae ut . . . bellum suscipiat in Turcas ad Carolum V exhortatio.* Bonn, 1529.

SIME, W. *History of Mohammed and his Successors.* Edinburgh, 1837.

SIONITA, GABRIEL EHDENENSIS (Jabrā'īl as-Sahiūnī al-Ahdani). *De nonnullis orientalium urbibus nec non Indigenarum Religione ac moribus tractatus brevis.* Amsterdam, 1633.

SIONITA, GABRIEL EHDENENSIS. *Testamentum et Pactiones initae inter Mohammedem et Christianae fidei cultores.* Paris, 1630. (With D. F. Hotman; see also Pacifique.)

—— See also Bellarmine.

SIMON, LE P. RICHARD, as 'Le Sr. De Moni'. *Histoire critique de la créance et des coûtumes des nations du Levant.* Frankfurt, 1684.

SMITH, THOS. *Remarks upon the Religion, Manners and Government of the Turks.* London, 1678.

—— *Praelectio de origine nominis Saracenorum* (in MS, see note, s.v. Oxford).

SPINA, ALPHONSUS A. *Fortalitium fidei contra iudeos saracenos aliosque christianae fidei inimicos.* Lyons, 1525.

STARCKE, S. G. *Specimen Versionis Coranicae adornatum in Caput XIX quod inscribitur Caput Mariae.* Kölln in Brandenburg, 1698.

STRUKHUSEN, J. *Syntagma Historiae Sarraceno-Turcicae.* Helmstedt, 1664.

STUBBE, H. *The Rise and Progress of Mahometanism.* For MSS, see the modern impression, London, 1911, and note above, s.v. London.

STURMIUS, J. *De Bello adversus Turcos perpetuo administrando.* Iena, 1598.

SURIANO. *Il trattato di Terra Santa e dell'Oriente di frate Francesco Suriano.* Milan, 1900 (ed. G. Golubovich).

SUTCLIFF, M. *De Turcopapismo adversus Giffordi Calvinoturcismum.* London, 1599.

SUTTON, SIR R. *The despatches.* (Camden Society, 3rd series, vol. 78.) London, 1953.

SYLBURG, F. *Saracenica sive Moamethica.* Heidelberg, 1595.

TAFUR, PERO. *Travels and Adventures, 1435-1439.* Tr. and ed. M. Letts. London, 1926.

TAVERNIER, J.-B. *Les Six Voyages.* Paris, 1712-13.
—— *Nouvelle Relation de l'intérieur du Sérrail.* Paris, 1713.
TEMPLE, SIR W., BART. *On Heroick Virtue,* in *Works.* London, 1720.
TEXEIRA, PEDRO. *Travels.* Ed. W. F. Sinclair (tr.) and D. Ferguson. London (Hakluyt Society), 1902.
THENAUD, FRÈRE JEHAN. *Le Voyage d'Outremer.* Ed. Ch. Schefer. Paris, 1884.
THEVENOT, JEAN DE. *Voyage du Levant.* Amsterdam, 1727.
THOMPSON, T. PERRONET. 'Arabs and Persians' in the *Westminster Review,* vol. v, January, 1826.
TIMUR. *Institutes Political and Military.* Tr. by Major Davy, etc. Oxford, 1783. (See also Pétis.)
TORQUEMADA, JOHN OF (Turrecremata). *Defensorium fidei contra Iudaeos, hereticos et Saracenos.* 1473(?).
—— *Tractatus contra principales errores perfidi Machometi et Turchorum sive Saracenorum festinanter copulatus per reverendissimum Ioh. de T.* Paris, 1510.
Tratado de los articulos que tudo buen Muslim esta obligado a creer, etc. Tr. as *Mahometan Confession of Faith.* In Rabadan.
TREVISAN, DOMENICO. *La Relation de l'Ambassade auprès du Soudan d'Egypte,* 1512. ed. Ch. Schefer. Paris, 1884.
Turkish Faith and Religion preached by Mahomet. (In MS, see note, s.v. Oxford.) English version of Epitome Fidei, q.v.
TWELLS, L. *Life of Dr Pocock.* In *Theological Works of the Learned Dr Pocock.* London, 1740.
TYPOEST, J. *Iac. Typotij Orationes III ut Christiani se mutuo in Turcarum Tyrannum arma convertant.* Frankfurt, 1595.
URI, J. 'On the Christianity of the Mohammedans' in *Oriental Collections,* No. 1. London, 1797.
URQUHART, D. *Turkey and its Resources.* London, 1833.
—— *The Spirit of the East.* London, 1838.
VARTHEMA, LUDOVICO DI. *Travels, 1503-1508.* Ed. J. W. Jones (tr.) and G. P. Badger. London (Hakluyt Society), 1863.
VATTIER, PIERRE. *L'Histoire du Grand Tamerlan nouvellement traduite en François de l'Arabe.* Paris, 1658.
—— *L'Histoire Mahometane ou les Quarante-Neuf Chalifes du Macine. Nouvellement traduite de l'Arabe en François. Le tout par Mre. Pierre Vattier.* Paris, 1657. (Apparently from Erpenius, q.v.)
VERGIL. *Polydori Vergilii de rerum inventoribus libri VIII.* Amsterdam, 1671.
VERTOMANNUS. *The Navigation and Voyages of Lewes Vertomannus, Gentleman of the Citie of Rome . . . in the Yeere of our Lorde 1503.* Tr. Richard Eden. 1576. In Hakluyt's Collection, etc., a new edition with additions, vol. IV, supplement. London, 1811.
VIVALDO, M. A. *Glossa* on La Cavalleria, q.v.
VIVES, JUAN LUIS. *De conditione vitae Christianorum sub Turca.* In Bibliander (A (i)).
—— *De veritate Fidei christianae libri quinque.* Basle, 1543.
VOLATERRANUS. See Maffei.

VOLTAIRE, F. M. A. *Le fanatisme, ou Mahomet le prophète* (with *Lettre au roi de Prusse; lettre au Pape; réponse du souverain pontife*).
—— *Questions sur l'Encyclopédie,* s.v. *Alcoran, Arot et Marot, Femme,* etc. 1770-2, n.p.
—— *Histoire des Croisades* (London, 1752).
—— *Essai sur les mœurs et l'esprit des nations.*
WALLICH, J. U. *Religio Turcica: Mahometis Vita et Orientalis cum Occidentalis Antichristi Comparatio. Kurtzer Vegriff und Inhalt Turkischer Religion und Glaubens,* etc. *Vita Mahometis, Das ist: Geburt | Urhsprung | Leben | Wandel und Todt . . . Comparation oder Veigleichung der benden Orientalischen und Occidentalischer Antichristen des Turcken und Papstes zu Rom.* Stade, 1659.
WARNER, LEVINUS. *Compendium Historicum eorum qui Muhammedani de Christo et praecipuis aliquot religionis Christianae capitibus tradiderunt.* Leyden, 1643.
WHITE, JOSEPH. *Sermons containing a View of Christianity and Mahometanism. The second edition, to which now is added a Sermon . . . on the Duty of attempting the Propagation of the Gospel.* London, 1785.
WIDMANSTADT, JOHANN ALBRECHT VON. *Ioannis Alberti Vuidmestadij Notationes* etc. Vienna(?), 1543.

Bibliography C: Modern Works

(Including a few modern translations from, and editions in, Arabic. As far as books that do not bear directly on the subject are concerned, I have simply included those of which I have made use.)

ABD-EL-JALIL, J.-M. *L'Islam et Nous*. Paris, 1947.
—— *Aspects intérieurs de l'Islam*. Paris, 1949.
—— *Marie et l'Islam*. Paris, 1950.
—— 'L'Islam et la Civilisation moderne', in *Echanges*, No. 41, Paris, 1959.
ABEL, A. 'La Portée Apologétique de la "Vie" de St Théodore d'Edesse'. In *Byzantinoslavica*. Prague, 1949 (vol. x).
—— 'L'Apocalypse de Bahirâ et la notion islamique du Mahdî'. In *Annuaire de l'Institut de Philologie et d'Histoire Orientales* (III). 1955.
—— Le Livre pour la Refutation des Trois Sectes Chrétiennes de Abû 'Îsa Muhammad ibn Hârûn al Warrâq, sa date, son importance, sa place dans la littérature polémique arabe. Brussels, 1949.
ADDISON, J. T. *The Christian Approach to the Moslem*. N.Y. 1942.
AKEHURST, G. *Imposture Instanced in the Life of Mahomet*. London, 1859.
AL-ASH'ARĪ. ed. and tr. R. J. McCarthy, *The Theology of Al-Ash'arī*. Beirut, 1953.
AL-BAYDAWI. *Chrestomathie Baidawiana*. D. S. Margoliouth, London, 1894.
AL-BUKHARI. *Les traditions islamiques*. Tr. par O. Houdas and W. Marcais. 4 vols. Paris, 1903-14.
AL-GHALWIRY, A. M. *Les Miracles de Mahomet*. Harissa (Lebanon), 1937.
AL-KINDI Abd al-Masīḥ ibn Isḥāq (pseudo-al-Kindi). *Risālah*. ed. Tien. London, 1880.
ALONSO, P. M. A. See bibliography A (iii) under Gundisalvo.
ALPHANDERY, P. 'Mahomet-Antéchrist dans le Moyen Age Latin'. In *Mélanges Martwig Derenbourg*. Paris, 1909.
—— *La Chrétienté et l'idée de Croisade*. Paris, 1954.
ALTANER, B. 'Die Dominikanermission des 13. Jahrhunderts'. In *Breslauer Studien zur historischen Theologie*, Bd. III.
—— 'Zur Geschichte der anti-Islamischen Polemik waehrend des 13. und 14. Jahrhunderts'. In *Historische Jahrbuch*, 56 Band. 1936.
D'ALVERNY, M. T. 'Deux traductions latines du Coran au Moyen Age'. In *Archives d'histoire doctrinale et littéraire du Moyen Age*, années 1946-8. Paris, 1948.
D'ALVERNY, M. T. and VAJDA, G. 'Marc de Tolède, Traducteur d'ibn Tumart'. In *Al-Andalus*, vol. XVI, fasc. 1 and 2, vol. XVII, fasc. 1, 1951-2.

AMES, R. M. 'The Source and Significance of "The Jew and the Pagan" ';
in *Mediaeval Studies* XIX, Toronto, 1957.

ANAWATI, M. *Lo svolgimento storico* on *Mistica Islamica*, Turin, 1960;
and see Gardet, L.

D'ANCONA, ALESSANDRO. *La Leggenda di Maometto in Occidente*, seconda
edizione. Bologna, 1912.

ARBERRY, A. J. *Revelation and Reason in Islam*. London, 1957.

—— *Oriental Essays*. London, 1960.

ARNOLD, E. *Pearls of the Faith*. London, 1896.

ARNALDEZ, R. *Grammaire et théologie chez ibn Hazm de Cordoue*. Paris,
1956.

ARNOLD, T. W. *The Preaching of Islam*. London, 1929.

ASIN Y PALACIOS, M. 'El lulismo exagerado'. In *Cultura Española*,
Madrid, May 1906.

—— 'Logia et agrapha Dni. J. apud Moslemorum scripta usitata'. In
Patrologia Orientalis. Paris, 1919.

—— *Escatología musulmana en la Divina Comedia*. Second edition,
Madrid-Granada.

—— *El Islam Cristianizado*. Madrid, 1931.

—— *Abenhazem de Cordoba y su Historia critica de las ideas religiosas*.
Madrid, 1927-32.

—— *Huellas del Islam*. Madrid, 1941.

ATIYA, A. S. *The Crusade in the Later Middle Ages*. London, 1938.

ATKINSON, A. *Les Nouveaux Horizons de la Renaissance française*. Paris,
1935.

ATTA, M. M. *The Islamic Call*. Cairo, n.d.

BALDWIN, M. W. History of the Crusades. vol. i. The First Hundred
Years. Philadelphia, 1955.

BASCOUR, H. See Klibansky.

BASETTI-SANI, G. *Mohammed et Saint François*. Ottawa, 1959.

BASSET, R. 'Hercule et Mahomet'. In *Journal des Savants*. Paris, July
1903.

BEDIER, J. *Les Légendes Epiques*, third edition. Paris, 1927.

BELL, R. *The Origin of Islam in its Christian Environment*. London, 1913.

—— *Introduction to the Qur'ān*. Edinburgh, 1954.

BERTHIER, A. 'Un Maître Orientaliste du XIIe siècle, Raymund Martin,
O.P.' In *Archivum F. P.* vol. vi, 1906.

BIGNANI-ODIER, J. and DELLA VIDA, M.-G. LÉVI. 'Une version latine de
l'Apocalypse Syro-Arabe de Serge-Bahira'. In *Mélanges d'Archéologie
et d'Histoire* (École. fr. de Rome), tome LXII, Paris, 1950.

BLACHÈRE, R. *Le Problème de Mahomet*. Paris, 1952.

—— *Le Coran*. Paris, 1949-51.

BLACKBURN, C. A. *Mahomet et le Koran comparés au Christ et à l'Evangile*.
Mauritius, 1895.

BUCHTAL, H. *Miniature Painting in the Latin Kingdom of Jerusalem*.
Oxford, 1957.

BULARD, M. *Le Scorpion, symbole du peuple juif*. Paris, 1935.

CABANELAS, DARÍO RODRÍGUEZ. *Juan de Segovia y el Problema Islámico*.
Madrid, 1952.

CAHEN, C. 'L'Islam et les minorités confessionelles au cours de l'histoire', in *La Table Ronde*, No. 126, Paris, June 1958.

CARRERAS Y ARTAN, T. and J. *Historia de la Filosofia Española*. Madrid, 1939.

CERULLI, E. *Il 'Libro della Scala' e la questione delle fonte arabo-spagnole della Divina Commedia*. Vatican, 1949.

CHAUVIRÉ, R. *Colloque de Jean Bodin*. Paris, 1914.

CHEW, S. C. *The Crescent and the Rose*. New York, 1937.

CHIDIAC, R. *Al Ghazali, Réfutation excellente de la Divinité de Jésus-Christ*. Paris, 1939.

COHN, N. *The Pursuit of the Millennium*. London, 1957.

COLL, J. M. 'Escuelas de lenguas orientales en los siglos XIII y XIV (Periodo Raymundiano)'. In *Analecta Sacra Tarraconensia*, Barcelona, 1946.

CORDIER, H. See bibliography A (iii) under Catalani.

CRAGG, K. *The Call of the Minaret*. New York, 1956.

—— *Operation Reach*. Beirut, in progress (1957-).

—— *Sandals at the Mosque*. London, 1960.

See also Hussein.

CROMBIE, A. C. *Robert Grosseteste and the Origins of Experimental Science*. Oxford, 1953.

CUMONT, F. 'L'origine de la formule grècque d'abjuration imposée aux musulmans'. In *Revue d'Histoire des Religions*, tome 64, Paris, 1911.

DANNENFELDT, KARL H. *The Renaissance Humanists and the Knowledge of Arabic*, in *Studies in the Renaissance*, vol. ii. New York, 1955.

DANIEL, N. A. 'The Development of the Christian Attitude to Islam', in *Dublin Review*, Winter 1957/8.

—— 'Holy War in Islam and Christendom', in *Blackfriars*, September 1958.

DARBISHIRE, R. S. 'Islam in the "Chanson d'Antioche"'. In *Moslem World*, XXVIII.

DAWSON, C. *The Mongol Mission*. London, 1955.

DELLA VIDA, M.-G. LÉVI. See Bignani-Odier.

DENIFLE, H. *Quellen zur Disputation Pablos Christiani mit Mose Nachman zu Barcelon 1263*.

DEN OUDENRYN, M. A. VAN. 'De opusculis Arabicis quae latine vertit fr. Alphonsus Buenhombre O.P.' In *Analecta S.O.F.P.*, 1920.

DONALDSON, D. M. *The Shi'ite Religion*. London, 1933.

DONDAINE, A. *Le dominicain français Jean de Mailly et la Légende Dorée*. Paris, 1946.

DU MÉRIL, M. E. *Poésies populaires latines du moyen âge*. Paris, 1847.

ERDMANN, C. *Die Entstehung des Kreuzzugsgedankens*. Stuttgart, 1935.

FIELD, C. H. A. 'Christ in Mohammedan Tradition', in *Church Missionary Review*, July 1910, reprinted in *The Moslem World*, 1911.

FISHER, SIR G. *Barbary Legend*. Oxford, 1959.

FUECK, J. *Die Arabischen Studien in Europa vom 12. bis in dem Anfang des 19. Jahrhunderts*. Leipzig, 1944.

GALBRAITH, V. H. *Roger of Wendover and Matthew Paris*. Glasgow, 1944.

GARDET, L. 'Al-Asmā' al-Husnā', in NEI.
—— 'Allah', in NEI.
—— *La cité Musulmane*. Paris, 1954.
—— *Connaître L'Islam*. Paris, 1958.
—— 'Données Juives et Pensée Religieuse Musulmane', in *Cahiers Sioniens*, No. 2, Paris, 1955.
—— *Expériences mystiques en terres non-chrétiennes*. Paris, 1953.
—— 'L'Islam – "Remise à Dieu" ', in *Revue de l'Aucam*, Louvain, April 1959.
—— 'Le Monde de l'Islam face à la Civilisation Technique', in *Bulletin du Cercle Saint Jean Baptiste*, Paris, March 1959.
—— 'Le prophète', in *La Table Ronde*, No. 126 (juin 1958).
GARDET, L. and ANAWATI, M. *Introduction à la théologie musulmane*. Paris, 1948.
—— *Mistica Islamica*. Turin, 1960.
GAVIGAN, J. J. *The Capture of Damietta*. Philadelphia and London, 1948.
GIBB, H. A. R. *Modern Trends in Islam*. Chicago, 1947.
—— 'The Achievement of Saladin', in *Bulletin of the John Rylands Library*, vol. 35. Manchester, 1952.
—— 'The Influence of Islamic Culture on Mediaeval Europe', in *Bulletin of the John Rylands Library*, vol. 38. Manchester, 1955.
—— *Whither Islam?* London, 1932.
GILSON, E. *Les Métamorphoses de la cité de Dieu*.
GOTTRON, A. *Ramon Lulls Kreuzzuegsideen*. Berlin and Leipzig, 1912.
GOYAU, G. *Un Précurseur: François Picquet*. Paris, 1942.
GRAF, G. *Geschichte der Christlichen Arabischen Literatur*. Vatican, 1944.
GRÉGOIRE, H. 'Des Dieux Cahu, Baraton, Tervagant . . .' In *Annuaire de l'Institut de Philologie et d'Histoire Orientales et Slaves*, Tome VII (1939-44). New York.
—— 'L'Etymologie de Tervagant (Trivigant)'. In *Mélanges offerts à Gustave Cohen*. Paris, 1950.
GROUSSET, R. *Histoire des Croisades*. Paris, 1934-6.
GUILLAUME, A. *Islam*. London, 1954 (Penguin Books).
—— See ibn Ishaq.
GWYNNE, A. 'Richard Fitzralph'. Series of articles in *Studies*, 1933-7, especially December 1933.
HARVEY, L. P. *Un Manuscrito Aljamiado en la Biblioteca de la Universidad de Cambridge*, in *Al-Andalus*, vol. xxiii. Fasc. 1, 1958.
HASKINS, C. H. *Studies in the History of Mediaeval Science*. Cambridge, Mass., 1927.
HASLUCK, F. W. and M. M. *Christianity and Islam under the Sultans*. Oxford, 1929.
HATEM, A. *Les poèmes épiques des Croisades*.
HAURÉAU, B. See Littré, M.-P.-E.
HAY, D. *Europe, the Emergence of an Idea*. Edinburgh, 1957.
—— *Flavio Biondo and the Middle Ages* in *Proceedings of the British Academy*, vol. xlv. London (1959).
HAYEK, M. *Le Christ de l'Islam*. Paris, 1959.
—— 'Le Christ de l'Islam', in *Revue de l'Aucam*, Louvain, April 1959,

and in *Echanges*, No. 41, Paris, 1959. (Variations between texts.)

HEYD, W. *Histoire du Commerce du Levant au moyen âge*. Leipzig, 1885.

HODGSON, M. G. S. *The Order of Assassins*. 's-Gravenhage, 1955.

HOLT, P. M. 'Arabic Historians in Seventeenth Century England' in *Bulletin of the School of Oriental and African Studies*, xix/3. London, 1957.

—— 'The Treatment of Arab History by Prideaux, Ockley and Sale', to be published in *Historians of the Near and Middle East*, announced, London, 1962.

HOOPER, W. and WILSON, S. G. 'Presentation of Christian Doctrine', in *Methods of Mission Work among Moslems* (ed. E. M. Wherry), New York etc., 1906.

HUSSEIN, M. K. *City of Wrong, a Friday in Jerusalem*. (Tr. K. Cragg). London, 1959.

IBN ISḤĀQ: *The Life of Muhammad, a translation of Isḥāq's sīrat rasūl Allāh*, with introduction and notes, by A. Guillaume.

JANER, F. *Condicion social de los moriscos de España*. Madrid, 1857.

JEFFERY, A. *Material of the History of the Text of the Qur'ān*. Leiden, 1937.

JOMIER, J. *Bible et Coran*. Paris, 1959.

—— 'Chrétiens et musulmans', in *Echanges*, No. 41, Paris, 1959.

JONES, C. MEREDITH. 'The Conventional Saracen of the Songs of Geste'. *Speculum*, XVII.2, April 1942.

JONES, L. B. *The People of the Mosque*. London, 1932.

KATSH, A. I. *Judaism in Islam*. New York, 1954.

KEICHER, P. O. *Raymundus Lullus und Seine Stellung zur Arabischen Philosophie*. Munster, 1909.

KERN, A. *Der 'Libellus de Notitia Orbis' Iohannes' III*.

KHADDURI, MAJID. *War and Peace in the Law of Islam*. Baltimore, 1955.

KHALĪL IBN ISḤĀQ: *Précis de Jurisprudence civile et religieuse selon le rite Malékite par Khalîl-ibn-Ishâk, traduit . . . par M. Perron*. 1844.

KHOURY, P. 'Jean Damascène et l'Islam', in *Proche Orient Chrétien*, VII.i and VIII.iv, Jerusalem, 1957 and 1958.

KLIBANSKY, R. and BASCOUR, H. *Nicolas de Cusa de pace fidei*. London, 1956.

KOHLER, CH. 'Traité du Recouvrement de la Terre Sainte . . . par Galvano de Levanto'. ROL. Paris, 1898.

—— 'Un Sermon Commémoratif de la Prise de Jérusalem par les Croisés'. ROL. 1900-1.

—— 'Le libellus de locis transmarinis de Pierre "de Pennis" '. ROL. 1902.

—— 'Documents relatifs à Guillaume d'Adam'. ROL. 1903-4.

—— 'Deux projets de Croisade en Terre Sainte'. Ibid.

—— Introduction to *Receuil des Historiens des Croisades, Documents latins relatifs à l'Arménie*. Paris, 1906.

KRAEMER, H. *World Cultures and World Religions*. London, 1960.

KRITZECK, J. 'Robert of Ketton's Translation of the Qur'ān'. In *Islamic Quarterly*, II.4, 1955.

—— 'Peter the Venerable and the Toledan Collection', in *Petrus Venerabilis*, ed. G. Constable and J. Kritzeck, Rome, 1956.

—— 'Jews, Christians and Moslems' in *The Bridge*, ed. J. M. Oesterreicher, New York, 1958-9.

LACAZE, J. *Un représentant de la polémique antimusalmane au XVe siècle. Jean Germain.* Thèses soutenues par les élèves de l'Ecole des Chartes, 1958.

LAGE, G. R. DE. *Alain de Lille.* Paris, 1951.

LANE, E. W. *Manners and Customs of the Modern Egyptians.* Fifth edition 1860.

LANE-POOLE, S. *The Mohammedan Dynasties.* London, 1894.

LAMMENS, H. *Mahomet, fut-il sincère?* 1911.

LATOURETTE, K. SCOTT. *A History of the Expansion of Christianity;* volume II: The Thousand Years of Uncertainty. London, 1940.

LECLER, J. *Histoire de la tolérance au siècle de la réforme. Paris, 1955.* (Eng. tr., London, 1960, as *Toleration and the Reformation.*)

LECLERCQ, J. *Pierre le Vénérable.* Saint-Wandrille, 1946.

LEDIT, C.-J. *Mahomet, Israël et le Christ.* Paris, 1956.

LEE, S. *Controversial Tracts,* Cambridge, 1824.

LE STRANGE, G. *Palestine under the Moslems.* London, 1890.

—— *Baghdad under the Abbasid Caliphate.* Oxford, 1900.

—— *Lands of the Eastern Caliphate.* Cambridge, 1930.

LETTS, M. *Sir John Mandeville, the Man and his Book.* London, 1949. See also list A(iii) (Mandeville) and list B (von Harff, Tafur).

LEVENQ, G. *La Première Mission de la Compagnie de Jésus en Syrie.* Beirut, 1925.

LÉVI-PROVENÇALE. *Séville Musulmane au début du 12e siècle – le traité d'ibn Abdun.* Paris, 1948.

—— *La Péninsule Ibérique au Moyen âge d'après le Kitab el Rawd el Mi'tar* . . . Leyden, 1948-51.

LITTRÉ, M.-P.-E. and HAURÉAU, B. 'Raimond Lulle'. In *Histoire Littéraire de France,* tome XXIX. Paris, 1885.

LIZERAND, G. 'Les dépositions du grand maître Jacques de Molay', in *Le Moyen Age,* 2e série, t. XVII.

—— *Le Dossier de l'Affaire des Templiers.* Paris, 1923.

LOENERTZ, P. R. 'Les Missions Dominicaines en Orient au quatorzième siècle et la société des frères pérégrinants pour le Christ'. In *Archivum F. P.*, 1932.

MALVEZZI, A. *L'Islamismo e la Cultura Europea.* Florence, 1956.

MANCINI, A. 'Per lo studio della legende di Maometto in Occidente'. In *Rendiconti della R. Ac. Naz. dei Lincei, Cl. di Sc. Morali, Storiche e Filologiche,* vol. X, series sesta. Rome, 1934.

MANDONNET, P. F. 'Fra Ricoldo de Monte Croce'. In *Revue Biblique,* 1893.

—— 'Pierre le Vénérable et son activité littéraire contre l'Islam'. *Revue Thomiste,* 1893.

MARCH, J. M. 'En Ramon Marti y la Seva "Explanatio simboli apostolorum" '. In *Anuari MCMVIII*, Barcelona, Institut d'estudis Catalans.

MARGOLIOUTH, D. S. *Mohammad and the Rise of Islam.* London, 1923.

MASSIGNON, L. *Al-Hallaj, martyr mystique de l'Islam.* Paris, 1922.

—— *Essai sur les origines du lexique technique de la mystique musulmane.* New edition, Paris, 1954.

—— 'Le Christ dans l'Evangile selon al-Ghazâlî'. R.E.I. 1932, cahier IV.

MASSIGNON, L. 'L'Islam et le témoignage du croyant', in *Esprit*, September, 1953.
—— 'Les Sept Dormants de l'Eglise en Islam et en Chrétienté'. R.E.I. 1934 (t. xxii).
—— *Situation de l'Islam*. Paris, 1939.
—— 'Textes Musulmanes pouvant concerner la nuit de l'esprit'. *Etudes Carmélitaines*, 23e année, vol. ii, October 1958.
—— See also Moubarac.
MASSON, D. *Le Coran et la Révélation Judéo-Chrétienne*. 2 vols., Paris, 1958.
MENENDEZ PIDAL, R. *Estudios Literarios* (reprinted, B.A., 1938).
MENENDEZ Y PILAYO, M. *Historia de los Heterodoxos Españoles*. (Reprinted B.A.)
MEERSSEMAN, G. 'La chronologie des voyages et des œuvres du frère Alphonse Buenhombre O.P.' In *Archivum O.F.P.*, x, 1940.
MICHEL, F. See Reinaud.
MONCHANIN, P. J. 'Islam et christianisme', in *Bulletin des Missions*, xvii, Bruges, 1938.
MONNERET DE VILLARD, U. *Lo Studio dell' Islam in Europa nel XII e nel XIII secolo*. Vatican, 1944.
—— *Il libro della Peregrinazione nelle parti d'Oriente di frate Ricoldo da Montecroce*. Rome, 1948.
—— See bibliography A (iii), Verona.
MONTET. 'Un rituel de l'Abjuration des Musulmans dans l'Eglise grécque'. *Revue de l'Histoire des Religions*, 53. Paris, 1906.
MOUBARAC, Y. *Abraham dans le Coran*. Paris, 1958.
—— 'Bibliographie L. Massignon', in *Mélanges Louis Massignon*, Damascus, 1957.
MUHAMMAD ASAD. *The Road to Mecca*. London, 1954.
MUHAMMAD ALI MAULVI. *The Holy Qur-an with English translation and commentary*. Woking, 1917.
MUIR, W. *The Apology of Al Kindy*. London, 1887.
—— *The Mohammedan Controversy*, Edinburgh, 1897.
—— *The Life of Mohammed*. Edinburgh, 1923.
—— *The Corân. Its composition and teaching and the Testimony it bears to the Holy Scripture*. (Incorporates *The Testimony of the Coran* of which it is a new and revised edition.) London, 1878.
MUÑOZ, SENDINO, J. *La Escala de Mahoma*. Madrid, 1949.
MUNRO, D. C. 'The Speech of Pope Urban II at Clermont, 1095'. *American Historical Review*, xi, 1906.
MUNRO, D. C. 'The Western Attitude towards Islam during the Crusades'. *Speculum*, vi. 1931.
NICHOLSON, R. A. *The Mystics of Islam*. London, 1914.
—— *Studies in Islamic Mysticism*. Cambridge, 1921.
—— *A Literary History of the Arabs*. Cambridge, 1930.
NOGARA, B. *Scritti inediti e rari di Biondo Flavio*. Vatican, 1927.
NYKL, A. R. *A Book Containing the Risala known as the Dove's Neck Ring*. Paris, 1931.
OLIGER, L. 'La caduta di S. Giovanni d'Acri'. *Miscellanea Pio Paschini*. Rome, 1948.

OURSEL, R. *Le Procès des Templiers.* Paris, 1955.

PADWICK, C. *Muslim Devotions.* London, 1961.

PALENCIA, A. GONZALEZ. (Alfarabi). *Catálogo de las Ciencias.* Madrid, 1932.

PALMER, J. A. B. *Fr. Georgius de Hungaria, O.P.,* in *Bulletin of the John Rylands Library,* vol. 34, No. 1, Sept. 1951. (Manchester, reprinted 1951.)

PARIS, G. 'Un poème latin contemporain sur Saladin'. ROL. 1893.

—— 'La légende de Saladin'. In *Journal des Savants,* May, June, July, August, 1893.

—— *De Pseudo-Turpino.* Paris, 1865.

PARKES, J. *The Jew in the Mediaeval Community.* London, 1938.

PARRY. J. J. *The Art of Courtly Love,* introduction. New York, 1941.

PASQUAL, A.-R. *Vindicae Lullianae.* Avignon, 1778.

PEERS, E. A. *Ramon Lull, a Biography.* London, 1929.

—— See bibliography A (iii), Lull.

PÉRÈS, H. *La Poésie andalouse en arabe au XIe siècle.* Paris, 1937.

PERIER, A. *Yahya ben 'Adi – un philosophe chrétien du Xe siècle.* Paris, 1920.

PERROQUET, M. *La Vie et le Martyre du Docteur Illuminé Raymond Lulle.* Vendôme, 1667.

PONSOYE, P. *L'Islam et le Graal.* Paris, 1957.

POWICKE, F. M. *The Compilation of the Chronica Majora of Matthew Paris.* London, 1945 (second edition).

PRESCOTT, H. F. M. *Jerusalem Journey.* London, 1954.

—— *Once to Sinai.* London, 1957.

PRUTZ, H. *Kulturgeschichte der Kreuzzuege.* Berlin, 1883.

RABIN, C. *Qumran Studies.* Oxford, 1957.

RAHMAN, F. *Prophecy in Islam.* London, 1958.

RANKIN, O. S. *Jewish Religious Polemic.* Edinburgh, 1956.

REINAUD and MICHEL, F. *Roman de Mahomet,* etc. Paris, 1831.

RIANT, P. E. D. *De Haymaro Monacho Disquisitionem Criticam Facultati litterarum Parisiensi proponebat P.E.D. Riant.* Paris, 1865.

ROBSON, J. *Christ in Islam.* London, 1929.

ROEHRICHT, R. 'Lettres de Ricoldo de Monte Croce'. AOL II. Paris, 1884.

—— 'Le Pélerinage du moine Augustin Jacques de Verone'. ROL. 1895.

RONCAGLIA, M. 'I Francescani in Oriente durante le Crociate'. In *Biblioteca bio-bibliografica,* serie quarta, studi, 1954.

ROUILLARD, C. D. *The Turk in French History.* Paris, 1939.

RUNCIMAN, S. *A History of the Crusades.* 3 vols. Cambridge, 1951-5.

—— *The Eastern Schism,* Oxford, 1955.

—— *The Mediaeval Manichee,* Cambridge, 1955.

—— *The Sicilian Vespers,* Cambridge, 1958.

RUPP, J. *L'idée de chrétienté dans la pensée pontificale dès origines à Innocent III.* Paris, 1939.

SAGE, C. M. *Paul Albar of Cordoba.*

SALAH KHALIS. 'La vie littéraire à Seville au XIème siècle.' Thèse de doctorat, Paris, 1953.

SAUNDERS, J. J. 'Mohammed in Europe – a note on Western interpretations of the life of the Prophet'. In *History*, 1954.

SAYOUS, E. *Jésus-Christ d'après Mahomet.* Paris and Leipzig, 1880.

SCHACHT, J. *The Origins of Muhammadan Jurisprudence.* Oxford, 1950.

SCHEFER, CH. 'Jean Germain, Evêque de Chalon', ROL, 1895.

—— *Le Voyage d'outremer, etc.* Paris, 1884.

SERRANO Y SANZ, M. 'Vida del Mahoma', in *Erudicion Iberoultramarina* II, 1932.

SMALLEY, B. *The Study of the Bible in the Middle Ages.* 2nd edition, Oxford, 1952.

—— *The English Friars and Antiquity.* Oxford, 1960.

SMITH, BYRON P. *Islam in English Literature.* Beirut, 1939.

SOUTHERN, R. W. *Western Views of Islam in the Middle Ages.* Cambridge, Mass., 1962.

SPEER, R. E. 'The Attitude of the Evangelist towards the Muslim and his Religion', in *Lucknow*, 1911 (ed. E. M. Wherry, C. G. Mylrea, S. M. Zwemer). Madras, 1911.

STEINSCHNEIDER, M. *Polemische und apologetische Literatur in Arabischer Sprache zwischen Muslimen, Christen und Juden.* Leipzig, 1877.

—— *Die Europaeischen uebersetzungen aus dem Arabischen bis Mitte des 17. Jahrhunderts.* Vienna, 1904.

SWEETMAN, J. W. *Islam and Christian Theology*, Part Two, Volume One. London, 1955.

THÉRY, G. *Tolède, Grande Ville de la Renaissance Médiévale. Point de jonction entre les cultures musulmane et chrétienne.* Oran, 1944.

TOR ANDRAE. *Mohammed, sein Leben und Glaube.* Goettingen, 1932.

DE TOURTOULON, CH. *Don Jaime I El Conquistador.* Valencia 1874.

THROOP, P. A. *Criticism of the Crusade, a study of public opinion.* Amsterdam, 1940.

TRIMINGHAM, J. S. *The Christian Approach to Islam in the Sudan.* London, 1948.

—— *The Christian Church and Islam in West Africa.* London, 1956.

TRITTON, A. S. *Muslim Theology.* London, 1947.

—— *Materials on Muslim Education in the Middle Ages.* London, 1957.

ULLMAN, W. *Growth of Papal Government in the Middle Ages.* London, 1955.

VAJDA, G. *Introduction à la pensée juive du moyen âge.* Paris, 1947.

—— See also d'Alverny.

VANDEWALLE, CH. B. *Roger Bacon dans l'Histoire de la Philologie.* Paris, 1929.

WAAS, A. *Geschichte der Kreuzzüge.* 2 vols. Freiburg, 1955.

WATT, W. MONTGOMERY. *Free Will and Predestination in Early Islam.* London, 1948.

—— 'Islamic Theology and the Christian Theologian'. In *Hibbert Journal*, 1950-1.

—— *Muhammad at Mecca.* Oxford, 1953.

—— 'Carlyle on Muhammad'. In *Hibbert Journal*, 1954-5.

—— *Muhammad at Medina.* Oxford, 1956.

WATT, W. MONTGOMERY. *Muhammad, Prophet and Statesman*. London, 1961.
—— *Islam and the Integration of Society*. London, 1961.
—— Islamic Philosophy and Theology: Islamic Surveys I. Edinburgh, 1962. General Editor W. Montgomery Watt.
WENSINCK, A. J. *A Handbook of Early Muhammadan Tradition*. Leiden, 1927.
—— *The Muslim Creed*. Cambridge, 1932.
WILLIAMS, A. LUKYN. *Adversus Judaeos; a Bird's-eye view of Christian Apologiae until the Renaissance*. Cambridge, 1935.
WILSON, S. G. See Hooper.
YULE, H. *Cathay and the Way Thither*. London, 1915-.
ZAEHNER, R. C. *At Sundry Times*. London, 1958.
—— *Hindu and Muslim Mysticism*. London, 1960.
ZAKARIAS, H. *L'Islam, entreprise juive: de Moïse à Mohammed*. Cahors, 1955.
ZIOLECKI, B. *Alexandre du Pont's Roman de Mahomet, ein altfranzoesische Gedicht des XIII. Jahrhunderts, neu herausgegeben*; translated by Ch. Pellat and reprinted in *En Terre d'Islam* (3e trimestre 1943) as 'La Légende de Mahomet au moyen âge'.
ZWEMER, S. M. *Raymund Lull, First Missionary to the Muslims*. New York and London, 1902.
—— *The Jesus Christ of the Koran*. Bombay, 1893.
—— *The Moslem Christ*. Edinburgh and London, 1912.
—— *The Moslem Doctrine of God*. Edinburgh and London, 1905.
—— (ed.) *The Vital Forces of Christianity and Islam*. London, 1915.

ADDENDA

ABEL, A. 'L'influence de la polémique islamo-chrétienne dans les débuts de la pensée islamique' in *Actes du Colloque d'histoire des religions*. Strasburg, 1959.
—— 'Réflexions comparatives sur la sensibilité médiévale autour de la Mediterranée aux XIIIe et XIVe siècles' in *Studia islamica*, XIII, 1960.
—— *L'apologie d'al-Kindi et sa place dans la polémique islamo-chrétienne*. Rome, 1964.
d'ALVERNY, M. T. 'La Connaissance de l'Islam en Occident du IXe au milieu du XIIe siècle' in *Settimane di studio del Centro italiano di studi sull 'alto medioevo* XII. Spoleto, 1965.
CUTLER, A. Who was the "Monk of France" and when did he write?' in *Al-Andalus*, vol. XXVIII, Fasc. 2, 1963.
DUNLOP, D. M. 'A Christian Mission to Muslim Spain in the 11th Century' in *Al-Andalus*, vol. XVII, Fasc. 2, 1952.
KRITZECK, J. *Peter the Venerable and Islam*. Princeton, 1964.

Index

Except in the case of modern authors, only critical references to authors cited are included. There is no table of references as such, and the only complete lists of the authorities cited are those in the bibliography. Where there is inconsistency in the transliteration in the text, it is not necessarily reflected in the index. The article *al-* is ignored in the index, but not in the bibliography.